CW01550009

The Oxford Illustrated Literary Guide to Canada

Stephen Leacock's study in his summer home in Orillia, Ontario

The Oxford Illustrated Literary Guide to Canada

Albert & Theresa Moritz

TORONTO OXFORD NEW YORK
Oxford University Press
1987

To A.G. Bailey

Canadian Cataloguing in Publication Data
Moritz, A.F.
The Oxford illustrated literary guide to Canada
Includes index.
ISBN 0-19-540596-X
1. Literary landmarks—Canada—Dictionaries.
2. Authors, Canadian—Homes and haunts—
Dictionaries. 3. Canada—Description and travel—
1981- —Guide-books. I. Moritz, Theresa.
II. Title
PS8087.M67 1987 917.1'046470248 C87-094927-6
PR9187.M67 1987

---

1 2 3 4 - 0 9 8 7
Printed in Canada by John Deyell Company

Contents

Acknowledgements

Some of the people who helped us during our work on the *Literary Guide* died before the project's completion. We wish to acknowledge our gratitude to Michel Beaulieu, Lovat Dickson, Marian Engel, and Paul Hiebert.

Many authors have been very generous with information and photographs. Our thanks to Margaret Atwood, A.G. Bailey, Earle Birney, Fred Bodsworth, George Bowering, Max Braithwaite, Elizabeth Brewster, Roch Carrier, Fred Cogswell, Matt Cohen, Robertson Davies, James Deahl, Mary di Michele, Kildare Dobbs, Robert Finch, Timothy Findley, R.A.D. Ford, David French, Greg Gatenby, Gratien Gélinas, Phyllis Gotlieb, Ralph Gustafson, Ray Guy, David Helwig, John Herbert, Hugh Hood, Harold Horwood, D.G. Jones, Joy Kogawa, Robert Kroetsch, Irving Layton, Dennis Lee, Roger Lemelin, Norman Levine, Dorothy Livesay, Fred Louder, Gwendolyn MacEwen, Jay Macpherson, Tom Marshall, Sid Marty, Farley Mowat, John Newlove, bp Nichol, Eric Nicol, Patrick O'Flaherty, Michael Ondaatje, P.K. Page, Gordon Pinsent, Al Purdy, James Reaney, Mordecai Richler, Jane Rule, Josef Skvorecky, Francis Sparshott, Miriam Waddington, Sheila Watson, and George Woodcock.

We also have been kindly assisted by Georgina Barker, King Gordon, Leonard Grove, Ann Haig-Brown, Janine Zend, and members of the family of Milton Acorn.

We owe a great deal to the help and encouragement of artist and photographer Kim Herbener, whose photographs appear in the eastern provinces.

There is not space to acknowledge all the libraries, archivists, local historians, public servants, and others who provided us with valuable pieces of information. Among those whose aid was particularly important are *V Magazine*; Vancouver East Cultural Centre; Pat Cooper, Penguin Books Canada Ltd; André Carron, Energy Mines and Resources Canada; Jennifer Shepherd, McClelland and Stewart Ltd; Gilbert Russel, Parks Canada—Atlantic Region; E.J. Pratt Library, Victoria University in the University of Toronto; Lynette Walton, Glenbow Alberta Institute; Luba Hussel, Thomas Fisher Rare Book Library, University of Toronto; Marjory Whitelaw; Brian Cuthbertson, Heritage Unit, Nova Scotia Department of Culture, Recreation and Fitness; Marcel Ouellette, Éditions d'Acadie; Marion Helen Cobb, Queen's University Archives; Julie Scriver, Fiddlehead Poetry Books/Goose Lane Editions; Marilyn Bell, Prince Edward Island Provincial Archives; Paul Wyczynski and Lucie Pagé, Centre de recherche en civilisation canadienne-française, Université d'Ottawa; the pastor of the Presbytère de Clermont; Margaret Northam, Rapid City Public Library; Archibald Museum, La Rivière; Nancy Grenville, Centre for Newfoundland Studies; Breakwater Books; Steve Payne; Stanstead Collegiate; Linda Hoad, National Library of Canada; Sheila Latham; Jay Cody, Stephen Leacock Memorial Home; staff of the Baldwin Room, Metropolitan Toronto Library; Scott Robson, Nova Scotia Museum; Bruce Meyer; Andrew Armitage, Owen Sound Public Library; Frances Therrien, Sundridge-Strong Union Public Library; Frits Pannekoek, Alberta Historic Sites Services; Henri Têtu, Parks Canada, National Historic Parks & Sites Branch; Peter G. Menzies and Kathy Kosuta, Dawson City Museum and Historical Society; Vrenia Ivonofski, Ontario Heritage Foundation; Mrs F.W. Melvanin, East Durham Historical Society; Mona Cram, Newfoundland Public Library Services; Robin S. Harris, historian of the University of Toronto; Corner Brook Pulp & Paper Co.; Emily Carr Art Gallery; Michael O. Nowlan; Paul Thériault, New Brunswick Historical and Cultural Resources; Estelle Morin, Chapleau Public Library; Norma Martin; Donna Dul, Manitoba Department of Cultural Affairs and Historical Resources; Laura Desjarlais, Northwest Territories Archives; E. Frank Korvemaker, Saskatchewan Culture and Recreation; Michelle Quealey, Huronia Historical Resource Centre; A. Michel Clouthier, Ministère des Affaires culturelles du Québec; William M. Curran, archives of the Royal Bank of Canada; James Anderson, Stratford-Perth Archives; and Wynne Morgan. We have drawn facts from innumerable printed sources, but a few publications were particularly helpful: Thomas Vincent, 'A Brief Literary History of Frontenac County'; Mary Pacey (editor), *Walking Tours of Fredericton, The Colonial Capital*; John Robert Colombo, *Canadian Literary Landmarks*; Rodolphe Fournier, *Lieux et monuments historiques de l'Île de Montreal*; Alan Twigg, *Vancouver and Its Writers*; and pamphlets on Frederick Philip Grove, Nellie McClung, and Ernest Thompson Seton produced by the Manitoba Department of Cultural Affairs and Historical Resources.

The Canada Council provided us with a project grant that greatly aided us in visiting archives and gathering facts and photographs. We thank A.G. Bailey, Miriam Waddington, and Brian Stock for supporting our grant proposal.

One of our greatest debts, of course, is to the staff of Oxford University Press Canada: Richard Teleky, Pat Sillers, and Phyllis Wilson of the editorial staff, and especially editorial director William Toye, whose contribution to the content and spirit of the book is evident on every page.

We depart from the time-honoured custom of authors who thank their spouses for long-suffering support and instead acknowledge the invaluable help of our son, Albert, who participated in the long process of developing the *Guide* as research assistant, index compiler, photographer, and answering service.

Photographs

JAMES ALLEN PHOTOGRAPHICS: 100b. JOHN AYNIS: 175b. VICTOR AZIZ: 113c. NIR BAREKET: 85b. BIRGIT: 88a. BRIDGENS LIMITED: 164b (bottom). CANADA WIDE FEATURE SERVICE LTD: 80a, 84a. JACK CLAYTON: 71a. GREGORY COOK: 45b. TEE A. CORINNE: 215c (bottom). THE CORNWALL PRESS, INC.: 2a. WILLIAM DENDY: 161bc, 166b (top). JOHN DE VISSER: 12bc, 26c, 234c. FRANCINE DICK PHOTOGRAPHY: 174b (bottom). LUTZ DILLE: 170b. GUY DUBOIS: 40b. EDITIONS FIDES: 81b. HORST EHRICHT: 225a. ENVIRONMENT CANADA-PARKS: 18bc, 28ab. DAVID EYRE: Frontispiece. BETTY FAIRBANK: 219b. ELIZABETH FERYN: 171a. OWEN FITZBERALD: 26ab. EDWINA FRANKFORT: 209b. GRAEME GIBSON: 169b. GLENBOW ARCHIVES, CALGARY: 193b, NA-4887-6; 208a, NA-273-3; 235c, ND-1-1293d. SHELDON GRIMSON: 70b, 168b, 177b. A.L. GROVE: 147b, 147c, 185a, 188a (top), 188a (bottom). MRS RODERICK HAIG-BROWN: 212bc. DON HALL: 203a. BEN HANSEN: 13b. KIM HERBENER: 41bc, 42c (bottom), 44b (top), 60a (bottom), 93a, 93c, 109bc, 118b (bottom), 125c (top), 126bc (bottom), 127a, 143c. ANDRÉ LAROSE: 82c. PAUL LINDELL: 59c. LONDON FREE PRESS: 129a. MCCLELLAND AND STEWART LIMITED: 83b, 98b, 126c (top), 199a. METROPOLITAN TORONTO LIBRARY BOARD: 47a; 84c; 96bc; 97c; 118ab (top), T13438; 152a, T11506; 152c, T13789; 153ab (top), T30716; 154ab (top), T11180; 162bc (top), T13060; 172a, S1-219A; 191a; 206a; 239ab (bottom), T13563. BRUCE MEYER: 89ab (bottom). BARBARA MITCHELL: 209c, 217c. MONTREAL STAR-CANADA WIDE: 60c, 72b. A.M. MORITZ: 111a (top), 111b, 114b, 119bc, 130bc, 149b. THERESA MORITZ: 113a, 130a, 131b (top), 133b, 137a (bottom), 140c, 151a, 151b, 154a (bottom), 156c, 158a. BRUCE MURPHY: 225c. NATIONAL ARCHIVES OF CANADA: 6bc, C-76107; 7bc, C-27567; 8bc (top), C-7746; 8bc (bottom), PA-45309; 11a, PA-128024; 17a (bottom), PA-111555; 19ab, A-626; 21b, C-22002; 27a, C-23228; 36c, PA-127394; 42a, C-345; 42c (top), C-2554; 43c (bottom), C-25816; 44ab (bottom), C-25554, 46ab, PA-45740; 52b, C-22015; 53c, C-1477; 54a, C-28198; 54c, C-16657; 58c, PA-36907; 60a (top), PA-33744; 61b, PA-23362; 63bc, PA-C-65438; 65b, C-68846; 66a, C-19919; 66c, C-33106; 68b, C-64035; 68c, PA-127569; 70a (bottom), PA-149284; 72a, PA-128686; 74b (top), PA-123942; 74bc (bottom), PA-123943; 75a, C-1532; 76a, C-88566; 77c, C-88563; 78a, C-19197; 79a, C-79595; 82b, C-6722; 90bc (bottom), C-88571; 92ab, PA-23967; 94bc, C-5938; 99ab, PA-36914; 102ab, PA-36853; 106c, PA-36754; 108a, C-68845; 111a (bottom), PA-127297; 119a, PA-66923; 123a, C-37819; 125bc (bottom), PA-117831; 126a, C-67346; 128ab, PA-135690; 134b, C-31968; 134c, C-53537; 135ab, C-23067; 136b, C-53485; 137a (top), C-68850; 191bc, C-25612; 185b, C-36086; 186bc, C-27674; 189a, C-18087; 192bc, PA-12854; 194b, McLuhan Papers; 201bc (top), C-43147; 201bc (bottom), C-43151; 202bc, C-1879; 205bc, PA-120219; 207a, C-89580; 210a, C-23316; 213bc, C-6803; 223c, C-31950; 228bc, C-20364; 229ab, C-20368; 236b, PA-102415; 237bc, 81024; 238ab, C-10944; 239b (top), C-5479. THE NEW BRUNSWICK MUSEUM: 50c, 3395. NOVA SCOTIA ARCHIVES: 20b, 22a. NOVA SCOTIA MUSEUM: 24ab, N-8032; 25ab, N-1642; 27ab, N-3856; 30ab (top), N-9300; 30ab (bottom), N-974. OBERON PRESS: 231b. MICHAEL ONDAATJE: 108c, 123bc, 209a, 218bc. ONTARIO ARCHIVES: 109a, 13281-144; 230a, S17323. EDITH OWEN: 70a (top). S. PAYNE: 10c, 12a. PUBLIC ARCHIVES OF PEI, CHARLOTTETOWN CAMERA CLUB: 38bc, 2320/2-13. QUEEN'S ARCHIVES: 5a, 25a, 43bc (top), 49ab, 49c, 95b, 110c, 121c, 122a, 129c, 134a, 143b, 145b, 153b (bottom), 155c, 157ab, 173b, 180a, 181b, 216c, 229c. DAVID ROBINSON: 215c (top). MARY RUBIO: 37c (top), 37bc (bottom), 39bc. LINDA SPALDING: 174b (top). DAVID STREET: 224a. THOMAS FISHER RARE BOOK LIBRARY, UNIVERSITY OF TORONTO:

Birney Collection: 179a (top), 214bc; Deacon Collection: 51b, 71a, 90b, 105ab, 112c, 117b, 122b, 124a, 156a, 162c (bottom), 164ab (top), 171b, 176c, 178a (bottom), 179c, 189b, 195a, 206c, 210c, 222b (top), 222b (bottom), 232c. Mazo de la Roche Collection: 131b (bottom), 177c; D.C. Scott Collection: 132a, 181a. TORONTO STAR SYNDICATE: 70c. TORONTO SUN SYNDICATE: 178a (top). WILLIAM TOYE: 56c, 57c, 88bc, 165a, 217a, 217b, 230c. UNIVERSITÉ D'OTTAWA, CENTRES DE RECHERCHE EN CIVILISATION CANADIENNE-FRANÇAISE: 55bc, Ph42-8,8B; 64c, Ph43-24; 75c, Ph6-4; 76b, Ph29-7; 76c, Ph29-8; 77b, Ph151-5; 78c, Ph6-1; 138b, Ph63-3. UNIVERSITY OF GUELPH LIBRARY, ARCHIVAL AND SPECIAL COLLECTIONS: 21a, 33b, 33c, 34ab (top), 34a (bottom), 34c, 36a, 127bc, 175a. VANCOUVER SUN: 226a. VICTORIA COLLEGE LIBRARY, TORONTO: 11b. JAN WALTER: 216b. MARJORY WHITELAW: 16b, 17a (top) 20c, 22b, 22c, 23c, 24c, 28c, 29c, 31a, 32a, 32bc.

Preface

The Oxford Illustrated Literary Guide to Canada surveys the literary past and present of the country from the standpoint of regions and places. Beginning in Newfoundland and ending in the northern territories, more than 500 entries detail the literary associations of cities, towns, villages, hamlets, and even rivers and islands. We have attempted to describe and to provide anecdotes about the careers and residences, and moves from place to place, not only of our best-known writers but also of early writers who made their own slight contribution to a barely existing literature, or whose life in letters had some poignancy or heroism, or who gave memorable expression to the character of their environment. The entries on cities constitute perhaps the first historical sketch of their literature. The long entries on Montreal (where the discussion of English literary associations is followed by the French) and Toronto have been divided chronologically into numbered sections.

In this treatment a richly layered—though necessarily brief—history appears, along with many curiosities and coincidences. In Montreal there is an elementary school that graduated both Émile Nelligan and Hubert Aquin, and a mental hospital in which Nelligan spent much of his adult life and where Jacques Ferron was a doctor. Max Braithwaite spent part of his childhood in a house in Saskatoon, of which he has written warmly, that was later occupied by Edward McCourt. Marjorie Pickthall sought vainly to recover her health in the same Victoria nursing home where Charles Mair died a few years later. Our research for this *Guide* enabled us to observe the nation's writers successively residing in the same places, walking the same streets, and appearing to be engaged with one another even though separated by time. A few of the places described have been made into shrines or marked with plaques. Canadian writers present a challenge to those who would remember them in this way—or who would attempt to document their perigrinations as we have tried to do. Moving about a good deal, sometimes in search of cheaper lodgings, with no idea that they might be special in any way, or would be remembered or valued, writers often left a difficult trail to follow. Their various places of residence sometimes had to be searched out in old directories, the files of periodicals and organizations, records in local libraries and archives, letter collections, and other such sources. Many of their dwellings have disappeared. Sometimes forgotten or vanished houses had an important place in a writer's career. Leacock's summer home in Orillia, one of the country's best-kept literary sites, was no less important to him than his house in Montreal, which was demolished long ago to make way for a hospital expansion. Lucy Maud Montgomery is famous for her imaginative identification with, and portrayal of, her native Prince Edward Island, where there are several shrines to her memory. But she wrote most of her novels far from her early home, in church manses in Leaskdale and Norval, Ontario—houses that still stand and one of which bears a plaque. Where the literary associations of places have been obscured, only a collective memory offers signposts and markers to commemorate the lives of our writers. In this book they have been documented and their significance has been revealed.

The illustration possibilities for this *Guide* were manifold—though considerations of space, placement, and availability exerted limitations. In choosing more than 300 illustrations we opted for photographs of many of the authors (occasionally of two or more together)—of long-deceased authors in unfamiliar portraits and of modern authors not always as they appear today but more often as we think of them—along with photographs of their homes or of the landscape they lived in or responded to. We hope that this combination of text and pictures will cast new and interesting light on our literary history and bring readers closer to the works and lives of the creators of our literature.

Newfoundland and Labrador

ARNOLD'S COVE

This is the home town of **Ray Guy**, essayist and humorist, whose book *That Far Greater Bay* (1976) won a Stephen Leacock Medal for humour. Born in 1939 at the hospital in nearby Come-By-Chance, Guy spent his childhood at this tiny outport on the neck of land that joins the Avalon Peninsula to the rest of Newfoundland. In this area Newfoundland's oral storytelling flourishes and Guy's writing, rich in the idiom of the pre-Confederation outports, reflects the values he draws from his childhood. *That Far Greater Bay* and Guy's first book, *You May Know Them as Sea Urchins, Ma'am* (1975), are compilations of his columns in the ST JOHN'S *Evening Telegram*, which he joined in 1963 after education at Memorial University and Ryerson Polytechnical Institute, Toronto. Many of the essays collected in these books are idyllic memoirs of an outport boyhood; sometimes—as in 'Landwash', from Guy's first collection—Arnold's Cove is mentioned by name.

Ray Guy

BAY ROBERTS

From 1843 until the winter of 1846–7 **Robert Traill Spence Lowell**, older brother of the prominent American poet James Russell Lowell, was a missionary minister of St Matthew's Anglican Church in this thriving fishing community on Conception Bay. Lowell's stay here provided the material for his novel *The New Priest in Conception Bay* (1858), in which Bay Roberts is called Peterport. Though marred by its melodramatic anti-Catholic plot, it contains much of the best available portraiture of nineteenth-century Newfoundland outport life and speech. Lowell is one of the few writers, especially of fiction, ever to depict both the coastal seascape and the terrain inland from the fishing villages. After leaving Newfoundland Lowell became a professor and poet in the United States. His novel was well received there by critics, but was not a popular success. It was reprinted in the New Canadian Library in 1974. Other works by Lowell that draw on his Newfoundland experience are the poems in his books *Fresh Hearts That Failed Three Thousand Years Ago* (1860) and *Poems* (1864), and a story of adventure in the sealing trade, 'A Raft That No Man Made', which appeared in the *Atlantic Monthly* in 1862.

The family of **E.J. Pratt** lived here in 1898–1900 while his father, John Pratt, was Methodist minister of Bay Roberts; at this time the future poet was living mainly in ST JOHN'S to be educated there. (See ST JOHN'S, WESTERN BAY.)

> BAY ROBERTS
>
> *'Yes, our rough country has its beauties,' said Mr Wellon. 'We've as good an ocean as anybody, and I think we could make a pretty good show of rocks.'*
>
> —Robert Traill Spence Lowell, *The New Priest in Conception Bay* (1858)

BEACHY COVE

Harold Horwood moved to this village after retiring from the ST JOHN'S *Evening Telegram* in 1958. He used his observations of the surrounding district in *The Foxes of Beachy Cove* (1969), a non-fiction work in which he writes as a naturalist; his talent as a nature writer had already emerged in his first novel, *Tomorrow Will Be Sunday*, published the preceding year. Other books written by Horwood during his years at Beachy Cove include his second novel, *The White Eskimo* (1972), and a collection of non-fiction pieces, *Newfoundland* (1969). In the late 1970s he moved with his wife and two children to the family's present home in UPPER CLEMENTS, N.S. During his residence at Beachy Cove, Horwood lived in two houses, which he extensively rebuilt: both are still in use. The first of them especially—a small white cottage with a brass fox knocker on the front door—became a centre for Newfoundland writing. The Newfoundland poet **Des Walsh** wrote much of his early verse in this house, and **Farley Mowat** wrote *The Black Joke* (1974) there; Harry Boyle, Glenn Gould, Margaret Laurence, and many other Canadian artists visited Horwood there, and met Newfoundland writers. Nearby are the places named and described in *The Foxes of Beachy Cove*, all accessible to visitors: Beachy Cove Mountain, the Beaver Pond, the Long Marsh, Witch Hazel Ridge, the Cliff Path, and others.

BELL ISLAND

Bell Island was the second parish served by **E.J. Pratt** during his three-year period (1904–7) of probationary preaching for the Methodist ministry. Every second Sunday he crossed a three-mile channel to preach at the mainland village of Portugal Cove. Pratt based many of the lyrics in his first book of poetry, *Newfoundland Verse* (1923), on his experiences among the people of these two communities. At Bell Island, Pratt was a frequent visitor in the home of Willis Pike, 'Uncle Billy', and often ate with the Pike family; a feast at the Pike home is memorialized in Pratt's 'The Pursuit' from *Many Moods* (1932). It was from Bell Island, after a summer spent raising money by selling patent medicine, that he left Newfoundland to begin studies at Victoria College, University of Toronto. The move was a decisive one: Pratt, who eventually became a professor of English literature at Victoria, remained in Toronto until his death in 1964. (See also ST JOHN'S, WESTERN BAY.)

About 1910 some balladeers on this island in Conception Bay gave birth to an important group of songs that capture the experience of the Bell Island miners in an idiom derived from the traditions of the Newfoundland folksong and broadside ballad. Peter Neary collected examples here in November 1972 and February 1973, recording 'Wabana You're a Corker' and other songs from the renditions of **John Fred Squires**, who began working as a miner on the island in 1910. Among the earliest examples of Newfoundland's indigenous folk culture dealing with modern developments, these songs express the early reactions of Newfoundlanders to this kind of work: 'Down in those dark and weary deeps, / Where the drills do hum and the rats do squeak,

/ Day after day, week after week.' Dominion Wabana Ore Limited, which began large-scale iron ore mining operations on Bell Island in 1895, closed the last of the mines in 1966.

'Hawthorne Cottage', the house of Bob Bartlett

BRIGUS

In the winter of 1913–14 the American artist and writer **Rockwell Kent** (1882–1971) acquired and repaired a small house at this village on the southwest shore of Conception Bay. Kent added a room to use as a studio and lived here with his wife Kathleen and their children for nearly two years; his fourth child was born here. In mid-July 1915 he was expelled from Newfoundland by order of the then British colony's Inspector General on suspicion of being a German spy—a suspicion based apparently on nothing more than Kent's profession of 'picture painter', an unusual one in those days and in that place. In February 1915, when this allegation had already been voiced, Kent wrote to the St John's *Daily News* that 'perhaps suspicion takes root too readily in this land. Four years ago on a visit to this country, I stopped a day or two at Burin on the Avalon Peninsula South Shore and walked about the hill tops. I was at once reported as a notorious bank defaulter who happened to be then at large.'

This forgotten incident was unearthed by Premier Joseph Smallwood (see GAMBO, ST JOHN'S) fifty-two years later in a review of government papers. At Smallwood's invitation Kent returned to Newfoundland in July 1968 and visited Brigus, where his house still stands. In a limited-edition booklet later published in Mount Vernon, New York, Kent retold the story and stated that, before he was deported, he had intended to make Newfoundland his permanent home. Smallwood reprinted Kent's text in *The Book of Newfoundland* (Vol. V, 1975). In addition, Rockwell Kent wrote of his life and experiences in Newfoundland in his autobiography, *It's Me, O Lord* (1955).

Rockwell Kent and his Newfoundland sojourn provided some basis for a character in **Margaret Duley**'s novel *The Eyes of the Gull* (1936): the artist Peter Keen, who comes from the outside world to a Newfoundland outport and there loves and leaves the novel's heroine Isobel Pike. Duley was a nineteen-year-old St John's debutante at the time Kent was deported.

'Brigus' by Rockwell Kent—chapter heading from his *N by E* (1936)

Brigus was the birthplace and home of the famous explorer and adventurer, Captain **Bob** [Robert Abram] **Bartlett** (1875–1946), who wrote of his exploits in a well-known autobiography, *The Log of Bob Bartlett: The True Story of Forty Years of Seafaring and Exploration* (1928). His house here, Hawthorne Cottage, was designated a historic site in 1982; it stands not far from the churchyard where he is buried and where there is a monument to him. Bartlett accompanied R.E. Peary on polar expeditions three times, commanding Peary's *Roosevelt* on the 1905–6 expedition and sledging part way to the pole on the 1908–9 expedition. On Vilhjalmur Stefansson's 1913–18 Arctic expedition, Bartlett was commanding Stefansson's flagship *Karluk* when it was caught in ice and drifted to the Siberian Sea, where it was crushed and sank; Bartlett managed to save many of his crew. This story, as told by Bartlett to Ralph Hale, appears in *The Last Voyage of the Karluk* (1916; reprinted as *Northward Ho! The Last Voyage of the Karluk*, 1919). After 1925, Bartlett spent much time cruising in his own schooner, *Effie M. Morrisey*; he describes these voyages in *Sails Over Ice* (1934). The Newfoundland author Harold Horwood has written a biography, *Bartlett: The Great Canadian Explorer* (1977).

The poet **E.J. Pratt** spent part of his childhood here. Pratt's father was Methodist minister of Brigus in 1891–2. (See WESTERN BAY.)

BURGEO

Farley Mowat lived in Newfoundland from 1962–7, primarily in this southwestern outport, although he also lived briefly in other Newfoundland fishing villages, including Muddy Hole and Burin. He caused an international controversy when he unsuccessfully attempted to save an 80-ton female finback whale that had become trapped in Aldridge's Pond, a saltwater pool near Burgeo (pronounced burr-gee-oh). Mowat heard of the whale's plight after the animal had already been injured by townspeople idly shooting at it with rifles. Despite promises of help from Premier Joseph Smallwood, who named Mowat to protect the whale, the writer was unable to obtain medicines, professional care, or effective defenders in time to save its life. This incident occurred between 20 Jan. 1967, when the whale was beached, and 7 Feb., when it died. Mowat's house here still stands 'out to Messers Cove way'; there are no addresses in Burgeo, but local residents can point it out.

Finding that this incident and the publicity surrounding it had damaged his relations with the town, Mowat left Newfoundland and established a home in Port Hope, Ontario, where he still lives. Four years after his departure, he published *A Whale for the Killing* (1972), which combines a plea for whale conservation with the affecting story of his futile effort to save the fin whale of Burgeo. Of its cry, he wrote, 'It was a deep vibration, low pitched and throbbing moaning beneath the wail of the wind in the cliffs of Richards Head. It was the most desolate cry I have ever heard.'

Burgeo also features in *This Rock Within the Sea: A Heritage Lost* (1968), Mowat's attack on the course of Newfoundland's modern economic development. In *The Boat Who Wouldn't Float* (1969), winner of the 1970 Stephen Leacock Medal for humour, the town is portrayed in a more light-hearted vein as the jumping-off point for Mowat's trip by sail up the St Lawrence River to Expo '67. Mowat's wife, Claire Mowat, is the author of a portrait of outport life in Newfoundland, *The Outport People* (1983), in which Burgeo appears as 'Baleen'. (See also RIVER BOURGEOIS, N.S.; BELLEVILLE, PALGRAVE, Ont.; MAGDALEN ISLANDS, MONTREAL: 6, Que.; REGINA, Sask.; KEEWATIN BARRENS, N.W.T.)

Burgeo was the birthplace in 1937 of **Clyde Rose**, founder, publisher, and editor of Breakwater Books and one of Newfoundland's most prominent literary figures (see PORTUGAL COVE).

CAPE RACE

In some of his most famous narrative poems **E.J. Pratt** drew on the tragic and herioc real-life dramas of the sea played out on the stormy waters around Cape Race, the southeastern tip of the Avalon Peninsula. Pratt's poems associated with the Cape include the lyric 'The Way of Cape Race' and the epic *The Titanic* (1935), his story of the 'unsinkable' ocean liner that struck an iceberg shortly before midnight on 14 April 1912. It was also off Cape Race, though much nearer to land, that the celebrated rescue of the crew of the British freighter *Antinoë* by the American ship *Roosevelt* occurred during a storm in 1926. Pratt travelled to New York to see the *Roosevelt* and meet her crew, while gathering detailed information on the rescue that he incorporated into his long poem *The Roosevelt and the Antinoë* (1930). (See also ST JOHN'S, WESTERN BAY.)

CAPE RACE

And out there in the starlight, with no trace
Upon it of its dead but the last wave
From the Titanic *fretting at its base,*
Silent, composed, ringed by its icy broods,
The grey shape with the paleolithic face
Was still the master of the longitudes.

—E.J. Pratt, *The Titanic*

CARBONEAR

On the west coast of Conception Bay, Carbonear is one of Newfoundland's largest communities, with a population of about 5,000. It was the birthplace in January 1814 of **Philip Tocque**, probably the first writer of note to be born in Newfoundland. He taught school in various parts of his native island and wrote *Wandering Thoughts; or Solitary Hours* (1846), a collection of brief essays. After studying for the Episcopal ministry in Connecticut, he assumed charges in Canada and the United States. He died in Toronto in 1899. Tocque's works include an important collection of historical essays, *Newfoundland, as it was and as it is in 1877* (1878).

HIS LAST VISIT TO CARBONEAR

In the grey-haired, wrinkled, old ladies, I found the once blooming and handsome belles of the place—the companions of my youth.

—Philip Tocque, *Kaleidoscope Echoes* (1895)

Harold Horwood, a ST JOHN'S native, has said that he acquired his knowledge of and opinions about outport life at Carbonear, where he stayed with an aunt during frequent boyhood visits; he is descended from a prominent Carbonear merchant family. His novel *Tomorrow Will Be Sunday* (1966) gives a generalized portrait of the outports. (The caplin, a variety of smelt used for both food and bait, is very important to Newfoundland outports and has given its name to several places in the province.) Horwood has commented: 'People who grew up in every part of Newfoundland firmly believed that I had the particular little town they grew up in in mind when I wrote about Caplin Bight.' (See also BEACHY COVE.)

CARTWRIGHT, LABRADOR

This village at the mouth of Sandwich Bay owes its origin and name to **George Cartwright**, author of *A Journal of Transactions and Events, during a Residence of Nearly Sixteen Years on the Coast of Labrador* (1792), the earliest published account of a European's prolonged experience of Labrador. About 1778 Cartwright permanently shifted the centre of his hunting and trapping activities from the site he had first occupied, CHARLES HARBOUR, to Sandwich Bay, where he established several posts (see also PARADISE RIVER). The village of Cartwright, which the author called Cartwright Harbour, was one of the explorer-diarists's early Sandwich Bay settlements, dating from about 1775.

CARTWRIGHT

In the lower part of the pool were several island-rocks, from one to two yards over; with salmon innumerable, continually leaping into the air, which had attracted a great concourse of bears. Some of them were diving after the fish: and I often observed them to get upon a rock, from whence they would take a high leap, fall head foremost into the water, dive to the bottom, and come up again at seventy or eighty yards distance. Others again were walking along shore; some were going into the woods, and others coming out.

—George Cartwright, *A Journal of Transactions and Events . . . on the Coast of Labrador* (1792)

CHANGE ISLANDS

Arthur Reginald Scammell, writer of Newfoundland folk songs, was born at Change Islands on 12 Feb. 1913 and was educated through his junior matriculation at St Margaret's Anglican School here. After attending Memorial University in St John's and St Francis Xavier University in Antigonish, N.S., he taught school at various places in Newfoundland, finally moving to Montreal. His best-loved ballad is 'The Squid-Jiggin' Ground'. Scammell has said that he composed his famous song as a high-school assignment when he was only fifteen. A collection of his writings, *My Newfoundland* (1966), gives an idealized picture of outport life in earlier days. (See also WOODY POINT; MONTREAL: 6, Que.)

CHARLES HARBOUR, LABRADOR

Situated near present-day Cape Charles, Charles Harbour was the initial settlement

Squid jigging at dawn

'Captain Cartwright visiting his Fox-traps'

of the first important writer of Labrador, **George Cartwright**. Cartwright's works concerning his 'loved Labrador' consist chiefly of the massive *A Journal of Transactions and Events, during a Residence of Nearly Sixteen Years on the Coast of Labrador* (1792), a great success in Britain in the years immediately following its publication; it was one of the books of travels that influenced Coleridge when he wrote 'The Rime of the Ancient Mariner'. Cartwright's long poem, 'Labrador, a Poetical Epistle' (1785), was included in the third volume of his *Journal*.

Charles Harbour was only the first of many posts Cartwright and his employees occupied on the Labrador coast. On 30 July 1770 he took possession of quarters abandoned three years earlier by the English trader Nicholas Darby after a skirmish with Eskimos that left three white men dead. There Cartwright began a yearly round of hunting, trapping, and fishing for survival and profit, which he recorded in meticulous detail until his departure from the coast in 1786. After several years he moved his headquarters to a more favourable site farther north on Sandwich Bay (see also PARADISE RIVER, CARTWRIGHT), even though three of his men sent to winter there in 1774 had frozen to death. The scope of Cartwright's hunting and trapping operations can be gleaned from his *Journal*: for instance, when the Boston privateer *Minerva* plundered his fishing station on Great Island, Blackguard Bay, in August 1778, 36 of 73 employees, and goods worth £14,000, were carried off.

In August 1768, two years before Cartwright took up residence in Charles Harbour, he had joined his brother John in a brief and unsuccessful expedition up the Exploits River in Newfoundland in an attempt to contact the Beothuck Indians, then known by the British government to be in danger of extinction. After returning to England in 1786, he maintained his interests in Labrador hunting and trapping activities, apparently deriving good profits from them in later life.

CLARKE'S BEACH

E.J. Pratt came to Clarke's Beach, on the west shore of Conception Bay, in 1904, after a year of teaching primary school at MORETON'S HARBOUR. Here he began three years of probationary preaching in preparation for the Methodist ministry. A schedule of Sunday services that required him to cover 15 miles in order to preach three times and conduct two school classes, in addition to his weekday routine, damaged his health and forced him to leave the post. After recovering, he was assigned to BELL ISLAND, where he completed his student preaching in 1907. (See also ST JOHN'S, WESTERN BAY.)

COLEY'S POINT

Too small to appear on most maps, this fishing village on Conception Bay is the birthplace of two of Newfoundland's best-known twentieth-century authors. **Ted** [Edward] **Russell** was born here in 1904 and received his early education in Coley's Point schools before moving to ST JOHN'S to complete high school and attend Memorial University College. Russell, who died in 1977, was known and loved primarily for his affectionate but penetrating sketches of outport life, delivered in the voice of 'Uncle Mose', a character he first developed for the more than 800 'Uncle Mose' radio stories that he broadcast over Newfoundland CBC from 1954 to 1960. Some of them were later collected in *The Chronicles of Uncle Mose* (1975) and *Tales from Pigeon Inlet* (1977; see also PASS ISLAND). Russell is also important in Newfoundland drama for his radio plays, particularly *The Holdin' Ground* (1972). Russell published his memoirs in the St John's *Evening Telegram* in October and November 1966. His daughter, Elizabeth Russell Miller, has written a biography of him, *The Life and Times of Ted Russell* (1981).

The dramatist **David French** was also born at Coley's Point, though in 1945, at the age of six, he moved to TORONTO (2) with his family. His plays *Leaving Home* (1972) and *Of the Fields, Lately* (1975) chronicle the disintegration of a Newfoundland family that has followed the same course of emigration. A later play, *Salt-water Moon* (1985), is set in Coley's Point.

CORNER BROOK

Newfoundland's second-largest city, Corner Brook is on the scenic Bay of Islands at the mouth of the Humber River on the west coast; the heart of the local economy is the huge mill of the Corner Brook Pulp & Paper Co., whose production capacity is 362,000 metric tonnes of newsprint annually. Corner Brook is the 'Milltown' of **Percy Janes**' novel *House of Hate* (1970), the story of a family's misery after moving to this industrial town in an attempt to escape both the poverty of outport life and the lack of opportunity in St John's. Janes was born in the Newfoundland capital in 1922 but in 1929 was brought to Corner Brook, where he lived until he returned to St John's to attend Memorial College (now University). Throughout *House of Hate* Janes vividly evokes 'all this beauty—harbour, river and town' and the 'immensely sprawling paper factory', with its never-ceasing 'hiss of steam and belch of smoke and hum of power.'

> CORNER BROOK
>
> *Our home was a one-storey frame house of matchless ugliness, built on land so steep that in our basement there was head clearance of ten feet on the lower side, while on the upper there was hardly room to push a shovel between the sill and the ground. This gave the building a towering, up-ended look and made one feel, as do so many of the terribly exposed houses throughout Newfoundland, that a good stiff offshore breeze would tumble the whole place right down into the salt water.*
>
> —Percy Janes, *House of Hate* (1970)

A 1920s view of the Newfoundland Power and Paper Company, Corner Brook (now the Corner Brook Pulp & Paper Co.)

Norman Duncan

EXPLOITS ISLAND

Beset by seasickness on a journey to Labrador in the summer of 1900 to interview Dr Wilfred Grenfell for *McClure's Magazine*, **Norman Duncan** decided to stop here. The decision formed his career as a writer. When Duncan—who was born in NORWICH, Ont., and spent most of his professional life in the U.S. or travelling to remote parts of the world—came to Newfoundland he had written only one book. Eleven of the nineteen volumes he completed after that concerned the lives of Newfoundlanders in their struggle with the sea. Here on Exploits Island the incapacitated Duncan lodged with the family of Jabez Manuel, a local merchant. He developed close relations with the Manuels and made prolonged visits to the family each summer from 1901 to 1906, and again in the summer of 1910. On these occasions Duncan gathered his intimate knowledge of the people and seascapes of Newfoundland's northwest coast, from Cape Bauld on the Great Northern Peninsula to Notre Dame Bay, where Exploits Island is located. He quickly gained a deep understanding of and admiration for Newfoundland fishermen, best reflected in his volume of stories *The Way of the Sea* (1903).

Duncan—who spent part of one summer cruising the Labrador coast on Grenfell's hospital ship, although it is not known when—produced a volume of essays on Grenfell's work and on Newfoundland life, *Dr Grenfell's Parish: the Deep Sea Fishermen* (1905), and Grenfell was the model for the chief character in Duncan's *Doctor Luke of the Labrador* (1904). Among other books by Duncan drawing on his Newfoundland and Labrador experience are *The Cruise of the Shining Light* (1907), *Harbour Tales Down North* (1918), and the Billy Topsail adventures, a series of stories for children.

> EXPLOITS ISLAND
>
> *. . . inevitably, from generation to generation, the people of that barren match their strength against the might of tempestuous waters, fighting with their bare hands—great, knotty, sore, grimy hands; match, also, their spirit against the invisible terrors which the sea's space harbours, in sunshine and mist, by all the superstition of her children. He had been brought forth and nurtured into hardy childhood—into brown, lithe, quick strength—no more for love than for the labour of his hands. Obviously, then, he was committed to the toil of the sea.*
>
> —Norman Duncan,
> *The Way of the Sea* (1903)

GAMBO

The Honourable **Joseph ('Joey') Smallwood**, premier of Newfoundland (1949–71) and a prolific author, was born on 24 Dec. 1900 in Gambo, a tiny outport (its population was then 107) in Bonavista Bay. Unlike most such villages, which are dependent on fishing, Gambo was a lumbering town, and Smallwood's family established the first sawmill here. Smallwood spent only the first year of his life in Gambo, but he wrote of the town and of its importance to his family in the first chapter of his autobiography, *I Chose Canada* (1973). See also ST JOHN'S.

GRAND FALLS

This important pulp-and-paper industry town was the birthplace, on 12 July 1930, of the novelist, screenwriter, and actor **Gordon Pinsent**, who was the youngest of six children of a paper-maker. The family's house (gone) stood at 9 Fourth Ave (now 64 Circular Rd). Since graduating from the Grand Falls Academy in 1948, Pinsent has lived outside Newfoundland, mainly in Toronto. His two novels, *The Rowdyman* (1973) and *John and the Missus* (1974), are both set in Newfoundland, primarily its mill towns, and portray the impact of post-Second-World-War industrialization and economic growth. *The Rowdyman*, based on Grand Falls and its people, was developed from a film of the same name (screenplay written by Pinsent in 1971) that was shot in Corner Brook. Pinsent is also the co-author, with Grahame Woods, of the novel *A Gift to Last* (1978), based on his CBC-TV series; he is a member of the Order of Canada and holds an honorary doctorate from the University of Prince Edward Island.

HARBOUR GRACE

Founded in 1550, this historic town on Conception Bay, on the east coast of Newfoundland, is the oldest in the province. About 1618 **Robert Hayman** (1575?–1629) became governor of the plantation maintained here by Bristol merchants; at the time the colony was called Bristol's Hope. Hayman's first visit lasted fifteen months, and he returned in successive summers until 1628. He wrote poems and epigrams in support of the Harbour Grace colony and the advantages of settlement in Newfoundland, which he collected in his book *Quodlibets* (1628). This is the first book of English poetry to be written in North America; on its title page Hayman states that all the verses were composed at Harbour Grace. During years spent at Lincoln's Inn before 1618, Hayman had already become known as a poet and been acquainted with Ben Jonson, George Withers, Michael Drayton, and others.

Exploits, *c.*1900

Every year in the first week of July, Harbour Grace holds the Conception Bay Folk Festival, an event that features Newfoundland ballads and songs, folk poetry, monologues, and traditional songs of both indigenous or British and Irish origin.

NEWFOUNDLAND

The Aire in Newfound-land is wholesome, good;
The Fire, as sweet as any made of wood;
The Waters, very rich, both salt and fresh;
The Earth more rich, you know it is no lesse.
Where all are good, Fire, Water, Earth, and Aire,
What man made of these foure would not live there?

—Robert Hayman, *Quodlibets* (1628)

KELLIGREWS

This village on Conception Bay was celebrated by the most famous of the St John's balladeers, **Johnny Burke** (1851–1930). In 1904 Burke composed what is often considered the best of his many topical and humorous songs, 'The Kelligrews' Soirée', whose rollicking rhythms and slapstick language depict a local jamboree. An annual July festival held at Kelligrews is called—inevitably—the Kelligrews' Soirée. (See also ST JOHN'S.)

FROM 'THE KELLIGREWS' SOIRÉE'

There was birch rind, tar wine,
Cherry wine and turpentine,
Jowls and calavances,
Ginger beer and tea;
Pig's feet and cat's teeth,
Dumplin's boiled up in a sheet,
Dandelion and crackie's meat,
At the Kelligrews' Soiree.

—Johnny Burke

Johnny Burke

Moreton's Harbour, *c.*1919

L'ANSE AUX MEADOWS

Situated at the northern tip of the Great Northern Peninsula of Newfoundland, L'Anse aux Meadows is the site of the excavated ruins of eight Norse buildings dating from about the year 1000. The Norwegian archaeologist Helge Ingstad discovered the remains of these buildings, which include an eighty-foot longhouse, and such artifacts as a bronze pin, a stone lamp, and a spindle whorl, in 1961–8. The earliest-known location in the New World of European landing, settlement, and iron working, L'Anse aux Meadows is one of several places in the Atlantic provinces that have been associated with the Vinland celebrated in Norse literature. It has been placed on the UNESCO World Heritage List of cultural and natural sites of universal importance. First mentioned in *The Book of the Icelanders* (1122–3) by Avi Thorgilsson, Vinland also figures in the later *Saga of the Greenlanders* (translated by the Canadian poet George Johnston in 1976) and the *Saga of Eric the Red.*

In *Westviking* (1965) **Farley Mowat** reconstructs the drama of Norse exploration into Newfoundland from the saga accounts of the journeys of Eric the Red, Bjarni Herjolfsson, and others. Mowat—for whom the sagas place Vinland not at L'Anse aux Meadows but at Tickle Cove on the south shore of Trinity Bay—identifies L'Anse aux Meadows instead with a temporary Norse settlement made in about 1004 by Thornfinn Karlsefni and Thorvald Eriksson in their futile search for Eric the Red's lost, and by then already legendary, Vinland. (See also BURGEO.)

L'Anse aux Meadows National Historic Park is open daily except for weekends and holidays in the winter season (mid-Oct. to mid-June). The nearest sizeable town, 30 miles south, is ST ANTHONY, famous as the base of the Labrador medical missions of the physician and writer **Wilfred Grenfell**.

MILTON

The tiny community of Milton contains a national historic plaque to **William Epps Cormack** in commemoration of his trek across Newfoundland in 1822. Starting from nearby SMITH SOUND, an inlet of Trinity Bay, Cormack and his Micmac guide Joseph Sylvester crossed the island between 5 Sept. and 2 Nov. Cormack gave an account of the journey in his *Narrative of a Journey Across the Island of Newfoundland in 1822*, published in Scotland in 1824 and in St John's in 1856. Milton is near Clarenville, which is on Highway 1. (See also ST JOHN'S.)

MORETON'S HARBOUR

After graduating from Methodist College, St John's, the poet **E.J. Pratt** took a $200-a-year job teaching primary school at Moreton's Harbour. In this small community on New World Island in Notre Dame Bay, Pratt taught in a two-room frame school that had once been a church. Here he sought to emulate his revered professor, R.E. Holloway, by supplementing normal classroom teaching with nature walks and stargazing excursions, but he found that his class obtained disappointingly low marks in its term examinations. The following year, 1904, Pratt began his term of probationary preaching, in preparation for the Methodist ministry, with a post at CLARKE'S BEACH. (See also ST JOHN'S, WESTERN BAY.)

NAIN, LABRADOR

This village on the Labrador coast near Paul Island is the setting for **Harold Horwood**'s novel *The White Eskimo* (1972). The title character is Horwood's imaginative embodiment of Esau Gillingham, a legendary hunter who appears in stories told by the Inuit living around Nain. Gillingham becomes for Horwood a champion of the Inuit way of life against the forces of civilization, especially the church, in Nain. With his adopted (and fictional) Inuit brother, Abel Shiwak, Gillingham for a time finds peace and prosperity at Okak Bay, about 80 miles farther north; but in the tragic aftermath of Abel's violent death, Gillingham is tried for his murder. (See also BEACHY COVE, CARBONEAR, ST JOHN'S.)

The church, as depicted by Horwood, is represented primarily by the Moravian missionaries. A Moravian mission was sent to Labrador in 1752 but was lost. In 1771 two missionaries arrived at Nain and established a permanent mission; in the late eighteenth century the Moravians at Labrador produced Inuit-language Scriptures in the Roman alphabet (rather than in the syllabic alphabet now used, which is a much later development). The famous medical missionary to Labrador and Newfoundland, **Wilfred Grenfell** (see ST ANTHONY'S), appears unsympathetically in *The White Eskimo* as 'Dr Tocsin'. Horwood was elected Labrador's first member of the Newfoundland House of Assembly, sitting as a Liberal from 1949 to 1951.

NEW HARBOUR

Ron Pollett was born and raised in this fishing village in Trinity Bay, and by the age of sixteen had qualified as a teacher. Three years later he left teaching to work in a pulp-and-paper mill in Grand Falls, and in 1923 he immigrated to New York. Although Pollett never again lived permanently in Newfoundland, he was a frequent summer visitor from the early 1930's through 1951. In July 1946 his essays on Newfoundland life began appearing in the *Atlantic Guardian* and quickly made him one of the island's best-loved writers. Collected in *The Ocean at My Door* (1956), Pollett's writings express the Newfoundland exile's nostalgia for outport life and a highly personal sense of bewilderment at the loss of traditional communal values in modern urban life.

NEW HARBOUR

But what makes me happy, now that I'm getting up to the age when a man sits around in his socks and ruminates over his past—what makes me happy is to be able to look backward on a childhood and youth spent in an outport. Being reared in an outport—at least in my kind of Newfoundland village—I count a distinct privilege for anybody.

—Ron Pollett,
'There's No Place Like an Outport,'
The Ocean at My Door (1956)

NEW MELBOURNE

In March 1936 a small girl named Lucy Harris was lost for eleven days in the woods near this tiny community on the Bay de Verde at the northern tip of Newfoundland's Avalon Peninsula. She survived and was found, and **Margaret Duley** used the incident as the basis of a central episode in her novel *Cold Pastoral* (1939). (See ST JOHN'S.)

NORTH WEST RIVER, LABRADOR

On 15 July 1903 the ill-fated expedition of Leonidas Hubbard set out from North West River, then a Hudson's Bay Company post, to explore the Labrador interior. Although Hubbard perished, his companion **Dillon Wallace** lived to record the adventure in one of the finest books in the literature of exploration, *The Lure of the Labrador Wild* (1905). Dillon's book records each step of a journey in which faulty preparation and bad luck quickly turned a youthful adventure into tragedy. A day after leaving North West River, at the junction of Lake Melville and Grand Lake, the two Americans and a guide entered the unnavigable Susan River, mistaking its mouth for that of the Nauskapi River. Their goal was to reach Fort Chimo, Que., on Ungava Bay via Lake Michikamau near Churchill Falls. They sighted Michikamau from a rise on 9 Sept., but did not reach it. On 15 Sept. they decided to turn back, and on 18 Oct. Hubbard, weakened by starvation and exposure, had to be left behind in his tent in the valley of the Susan River, while the two healthier men raced for Grand Lake, barely managing to survive. In 1905 Hubbard's wife Mina returned to Labrador and took up the exploration of the interior, mapping rivers there. She included Hubbard's diary in her book *A Woman's Way Through Labrador: An Account of the Nauscapee and George Rivers* (1908).

PARADISE RIVER, LABRADOR

In 1775 **George Cartwright**—a British trapper, explorer, and merchant who was the first important writer on Labrador—established the shore settlement of Paradise on Sandwich Bay. He also named the river at whose mouth the community is situated. His principal work, *A Journal of Transactions and Events, during a Residence of Nearly Sixteen Years on the Coast of Labrador* (1792), shows that although the Labrador coast impressed him as awe-inspiring but dreary, he found the countryside around the deep bays, such as Sandwich, beautiful and fertile. (See also CHARLES HARBOUR, CARTWRIGHT.)

PASS ISLAND

Ted Russell came to this community in Hermitage Bay as a teacher in 1920, immediately after completing his education at Memorial College in ST JOHN'S, and began a fifteen-year period of teaching in small communities throughout Newfoundland. Russell's fictional 'Pigeon Inlet', home town of the character Uncle Mose and the setting of Russell's sketches collected in *The Chronicles of Uncle Mose* (1975) and *Tales from Pigeon Inlet* (1977), is probably modelled on Pass Island, which lies off Newfoundland's southern coast west of the Burin Peninsula. (See also COLEY'S POINT.)

Portugal Cove, *c.*1909

PETTY HARBOUR

One of Newfoundland's most famous folksongs, 'The Petty Harbour Bait Skiff', by the ST JOHN'S balladeer **John Grace**, commemorates a fishing boat from this picturesque rock-bound cummunity that was lost on 7 June 1852 with four of its crew of five. Grace's lyric records that 'The Lord preserved young Menchion's life.' Petty Harbour is about 10 miles from St John's.

PORTUGAL COVE

Every second Sunday for two years, from 1905 until early 1907, **E.J. Pratt** preached to the Methodist congregation of this village on the east shore of Conception Bay, about ten miles northwest of ST JOHN'S. Pratt was then pastor of the nearby congregation on Bell Island, where he completed three years of student preaching. His first book, *Newfoundland Verse* (1923), contains many poems—including 'The Passing of Jerry Moore' and 'The History of John Jones'—that were inspired by the life of the Portugal Cove fishermen and their families. Pratt recalled that the most difficult duty of his ministry was to report the loss of a husband or son to the village women. (See also WESTERN BAY.)

In May 1973 Portugal Cove saw the founding of the province's leading literary publisher, Breakwater Books, named for the harbour breakwater beyond which Bell Island can be seen. Now located in St John's, Breakwater Books publishes works by Percy Janes, Harold Horwood, Irving Fogwill, Al Pittman, and many other leading Newfoundland writers.

Wilfred Grenfell: 'Jack and I on Strathcona'

ST ANTHONY

Although French and Basque fishermen had settled at St Anthony, near the northern tip of Newfoundland, this harbour was virtually deserted in 1892 when **Dr Wilfred Thomason Grenfell** first visited it as a medical missionary. Grenfell produced a stream of books about Labrador, the people of Newfoundland, and the work of his mission, beginning with *Vikings of To-day* (1895) and ending with *A Labrador Logbook* (1938). One of his most interesting books is *Adrift on an Ice-Pan* (1909), a vigorously written account of Grenfell's own brush with death at St Anthony. On Easter Sunday 1908 he set off by dog-sled to treat a patient and was stranded on a shrinking ice pan when the ice broke up under him as he was crossing an arm of the sea. Grenfell was able to survive for a day and night by killing three of his dogs for food and warmth for himself and his remaining dogs: he was finally rescued by local fishermen. He commemorated the dogs by a plaque in a hall of the International Grenfell Association's chief hospital in St Anthony: 'TO THE MEMORY OF/THREE NOBLE DOGS / MOODY / WATCH / SPY / WHOSE LIVES WERE GIVEN / FOR MINE ON THE ICE / APRIL 21st 1908'.

Besides scientific, historical, and promotional books on Labrador, Grenfell wrote stories based on his experiences there, including *The Harvest of the Sea* (1905), *Down to the Sea* (1910), and *Tales of the Labrador* (1916). Grenfell died at St Anthony in 1940; his ashes, and those of his wife, are buried under a granite marker on Fox Farm Hill, a wooded hill near the town that overlooks the hospital and is reached by a footpath. A plaque commemorating Grenfell has been placed at the hospital (named the Curtis Memorial Hospital). The Ontario-born novelist **Norman Duncan** (see EXPLOITS ISLAND) depicted the famous missionary in *Dr. Grenfell's Parish: The Deep Sea Fishermen* (1905), and made him the model for the central character in *Doctor Luke of the Labrador* (1904).

In 1920 Elisabeth Bristol, a Vassar College student-volunteer to the Grenfell Mission at St Anthony, was struck by the folksongs she heard in northern Newfoundland and spent much of her summer collecting the lyrics. Encouragement from professors at Vassar led in 1929 to the Vassar College Folklore Expedition, consisting principally of Bristol, now Mrs **Elisabeth Greenleaf**, and a musicologist, Mrs **Grace Yarrow Mansfield**. Their volume, *Ballads and Sea Songs of Newfoundland* (1933), was the first systematic collection by outside scholars of Newfoundland folk materials. (See also SALLY'S COVE, TWILLINGATE.)

ST ANTHONY

Every one on our coast in winter has to have a dog team, no matter how poor he is, in order to haul home his firewood. In summer there is no time and there are no roads, while in winter the snow makes the whole land one broad highway. There is no better fun than a "randy" over the snow on a light komatik. At this time even our older people go on "joy rides," visiting along the coast. Many a moonlight night, after the day's work is over, when the reflection from the snow makes it almost as light as day, an unexpected but welcome visitor comes knocking at one's door, asking for a shake-down just for the night.

—Wilfred Grenfell, *Labrador Days* (1919)

Wilfred Grenfell's Hospital, Port Anthony, 1910

ST JOHN'S

The most easterly city on the American continent, St John's is also one of the oldest. Permanent settlement began soon after John Cabot's visit on the feast day of St John the Baptist in 1497, and after 1500 St John's was used regularly as a fishing port. In the first letter written in English from the New World to Europe, dated 3 Aug. 1527, Captain John Rut of the *Mary of Guildford* informed Henry VIII that he had counted twelve ships fishing out of St John's harbour. Jacques Cartier and other explorers had described Newfoundland, but the earliest literature to be inspired by the island came from **Stephen Parmenius**, a young Hungarian humanist who was with the 1583 expedition of Sir Humphrey Gilbert, who landed at St John's and formally took possession in the name of Elizabeth I on 5 Aug. During the voyage and the days spent here, Parmenius wrote letters describing the terrain and climate. A Latin poem—translated into English and reprinted as *The New Found Land of Stephen Parmenius*—was written before he left Europe. Gilbert left St John's harbour after seventeen days; Parmenius drowned when Gilbert's ship the *Squirrel* was lost with all hands on the return voyage to England. Today a plaque set into the base of the Newfoundland War Memorial commemorates Gilbert's landing; its text was written by Rudyard Kipling:

> *Close to this commanding and historic spot Sir Humphrey Gilbert landed on the fifth day of August, 1583, and in taking possession of the new found land in the name of his Sovereign Queen Elizabeth thereby founded Britain's overseas empire.*

Robert Hayman, an acquaintance of Ben Jonson and Michael Drayton, visited Newfoundland regularly from 1618 to 1628 as governor of the Bristol merchants' plantation at Bristol's Hope (now HARBOUR GRACE) in Conception Bay. His *Quodlibets* (1628) was the first book of English poetry written in North America. A vigorous proponent of Newfoundland colonization—he attempted to have the island's name changed to 'Britaniola'— Hayman was familiar with St John's but is associated most with Harbour Grace, where he wrote his book. A century later a poet named **Butler Lacy** published *Miscellaneous Poems Compos'd at Newfoundland* (1729), a book that details the harshness of life in St John's at that time.

Admiral **John Byron**, grandfather of the poet **Lord Byron**, was governor of Newfoundland from 3 May 1769 until mid-1772 (see also LOUISBOURG, N.S.; CHALEUR BAY, N.B.). In 1814 Lord Byron married Annabella Milbanke, a niece of Vice-Admiral Mark Milbanke, who was governor of Newfoundland from 1789 to 1792. One of Byron's schoolmates, Alexander Bannerman, was another governor of Newfoundland, serving from 1857 to 1864. His wife, the former Margaret Gordon of CHARLOTTETOWN, P.E.I., was the first love of Scottish writer **Thomas Carlyle** and the original of the character Blumine in his best-known work *Sartor Resartus* (1833-4). The Bannermans lived at Government House, a Georgian structure that was built on Military Road between 1825 and 1829 for £40,000 and that was almost certainly the most expensive private residence in North America.

Theatre began in St John's with the establishment of the Amateur Theatre in a converted store building at 206 Water St, two doors east of McMurdo's Lane; the theatre opened on 14 Mar. 1817 with a play entitled 'The Fair Penitent'. The first theatre built in the province, Theatre Newfoundland, was constructed in 1822–3 on what was then Gallow's Hill—a site occupied today by the triangular building at the corner of Queen's Rd and Duckworth St; its first production, on 17 Feb. 1823, was a popular melodrama, 'The Castle Spectre'.

On the site of the Amateur Theatre was later situated the residence of **William Carson**, one of Newfoundland's most important public figures in the early nineteenth century. Instrumental in obtaining representative government for the colony, Carson gave the first literary expression to the island's political sentiments in *Reasons for Colonizing the Island of Newfoundland, in a Letter Addressed to the Inhabitants* (1813). His gravestone can be seen in the churchyard of the Anglican Cathedral of St John the Baptist at the corner of Duckworth St and Church Hill.

The scientist **William Epps Cormack**, born in St John's in 1796, was the author of one of Newfoundland's first books of literary merit, *Narrative of a Journey across the Island of Newfoundland* in 1822, extracted in a Scottish journal in 1824 and published as a book in St John's in 1856. This was a record of Cormack's 1822 expedition on foot across Newfoundland (see also MILTON, SMITH SOUND). Cormack, whose merchant father died when he was seven, returned to Scotland with his family and was educated as a scientist at the University of Edinburgh; he resettled in St John's about 1821. Although he wrote little besides his *Narrative*, his concern for the Beothuk people, who were nearly extinct by 1821, led him to participate in an event that has often been written about: he discovered Nancy Shanawdithit, the last Beothuk known to colonists, in the TWILLINGATE home of John Peyton, who had captured her in 1819 with the encouragement of Governor Sir Charles Hamilton in one of the government's ill-conceived attempts to contact and preserve the tribe. Shanawdithit came to St John's and lived in Cormack's home, where she dictated the traditions of her people and practised traditional arts and crafts in order to leave a record of the Beothuk. **James Patrick Howley**'s *The Beothuks or Red Indians: The Aboriginal Inhabitants of Newfoundland* (1915), gives this picture of Shawnawdithit at St John's:

> *A gentleman put a looking glass before her and her grimaces were most extraordinary, but when a black pencil was put into her hand and a piece of white paper laid upon the table, she was in raptures. She made a few marks on the paper apparently to try the pencil; then in one flourish she drew a deer perfectly, and what is most surprising, she began at the tip of the tail.*

Her deerskin robe, which she painted herself, is on display in the Newfoundland Museum on Duckworth St opposite Cathedral St. Shanawdithit died of tuberculosis in Cormack's home on 6 June 1829 and was buried in the churchyard of St Mary the Virgin, an old stone church on the south side of St John's harbour that was torn down during the 1959–64 harbour redevelopment. However, a monument near Southside Rd, just east of the Long Bridge over the Waterford River, commemorates the church and Shanawdithit's burial there; the exact location of her unmarked grave is unknown. By 1836 Cormack had left Newfoundland and was pioneering in Australia; he later lived in England and California and died in British Columbia in 1868. His St John's home was destroyed in the great fire of 9 June 1846, which consumed the entire downtown section. It is likely that some of his childhood was spent in a house on the site of present-day Victoria Park on Water

THE BEOTHUK

In 1828 a final effort was made to open communication with a remnant of [the Beothuks] which were supposed to still survive. An expedition was organized which penetrated to their last retreat at Red Indian Lake. Only their graves and the mouldering remains of their wigwams were found, but no living Beothik. Silence deep as death reigned around. There were fragments of their canoes, their skin dresses, their storehouses, the repositories of their dead; but no human sounds were heard, no smoke from wigwams mounted into the air, their camp-fires were extinguished, and the sad record of an extinct race was closed for ever.

—Moses Harvey, *Newfoundland as it is in 1894* (1894)

St W; in 1805 a woman named Janet Cormack, believed to be his mother, had title to a plot of land adjacent to the old St John's Hospital, which stood on this site.

Poems, Written in Newfoundland (London, 1839) by **Henrietta Prescott**, daughter of Captain Henry Prescott, governor of the colony from 1834–41, observes the scenery of Newfoundland with a romanticism similar to that of Cormack's *Narrative.* **Oliver Goldsmith**, one of Canada's early poets, was stationed in St John's from 1848 to 1853, while employed by the British Army commissariat; his literary career, however, was far behind him by this time (see HALIFAX, N.S.; ST ANDREWS, SAINT JOHN, N.B.).

ST JOHN'S

Awake, dear child! the sun hath long since risen;
Awake! the smile of Spring is on the earth;
The streams have broken from their icy prison
To fill the valleys with a voice of mirth;
The little waves creep slowly o'er the ocean,
To cast their glist'ning spray upon the shore;
Full many a white-sailed ship is now in motion,
And many a boatman gaily plies his oar,
Awake! Is this a time to sleep,
When joy is on the Earth, and music in the Deep?
—Henrietta Prescott,
'A Spring Morning in Newfoundland,'
Poems, Written in Newfoundland (1839)

In the second half of the nineteenth century the most prominent man of letters in St John's was the Rev. **Moses Harvey**, a native of Armagh, Ireland, who came to the city in 1852 at the age of thirty-two. He was pastor of St Andrew's Free Presbyterian Church, at the corner of Cathedral and Duckworth streets, until 1878, when he retired and devoted himself entirely to writing. A popular figure, he was voted a lifetime annuity by his congregation. In St John's, Harvey became a tireless producer of works on the history and advantages of Newfoundland, and collections of essays on Victorian intellectual preoccupations. His books include *Lectures, Literary and Biographical* (1864) and *Where Are We and Whither Tending? Three Lectures on the Reality and Worth of Human Progress* (1886). His most important writing on Newfoundland is a series of books on the colony's history, geography, and natural resources published between 1878 and 1902; they include *Newfoundland; The Oldest British Colony, Its History, Its Present Condition, and Its Prospects in the Future* (1883), written in collaboration with the English writer Joseph Hatton. On 8 July 1892 Harvey was in the basement of St Andrew's Church attending the distribution of prizes to students of the St John's General Protestant Academy when news came that a fire, which had started in dry brush on the western outskirts, was approaching the city centre. Harvey helped to evacuate the building and watched as efforts to save the church and its neighbourhood failed. He then rushed to his house (gone) at 3 Devon Row, where the residents were wetting down buildings in hopes of protecting them. The fire's progress was finally halted in the block immediately west of Harvey's home. The author died in St John's on 3 Sept. 1901.

The period 1850–1914 saw the major flowering of the 'St John's ballads', a unique tradition of songs and popular poems by local folk singers and poets. Among these writers are two seamen from the Riverhead section of the city, **John Doyle**, author of 'The Huntingdon Shore', and **John Grace**, famous for the haunting song 'The Petty Harbour Bait Skiff'; **Johnny Quill**, a shoemaker at Maggotty Cover on Water Street East, whose songs include 'Betsy Mealey's Escape'; the carpenter **Johnny Quigley**, who wrote 'Jack Hinks' and 'John Picco'; and **Jimmy Murphy**, author of many songs and poems of the seal hunt. The tradition descended to recent times in the writings of **M.A. Devine**, a member of a locally renowned family of poets and antiquarians, and **Dan Carrol** of Patrick Street, author of 'The Master-Watch'; Carrol was also a woodcarver whose work can still be seen in some St John's buildings.

The most famous of the balladeers was **Johnny Burke**, 'the Bard of Prescott Street', who was born in 1851, probably at 10 King's Rd. The son of a master mariner drowned in an 1865 accident, Burke first gained wide notice through his hit operetta, *The Battle of Foxtrap*, which opened on 2 Feb. 1881 at the Total Abstinence Hall, on Duckworth Street opposite the top of McBride's Hill. This high-spirited entertainment concerned the attempt in June 1880 of the residents of Fox Trap, a Conception Bay community, to stop the railway from being built through their town. Although Burke's *métier* was the broadside ballad and folksong, he wrote two other topical operettas: *The Runaway Girl from Fogo*, which put new words to the music of *The Runaway Girl*, an English operetta; and *The Topsail Geisha*, which gave similar treatment to the English stage hit *The Geisha*. Among Burke's most famous songs are 'Cod Liver Oil', 'Trinity Cake', 'We Must Close Our Little Shop on Sunday Morning', 'Teapots at the Fire', 'She's Never Been There Before', and 'The Kelligrews' Soiree' (see KELLIGREWS). Burke became a city institution for his ability to dash off a topical song or ballad. Often, on the morning after some dramatic event, he would set

The house of Johnny Burke, St John's

up a table on Water St in the vacant lot east of the O'Dwyer's building, where he worked as a clerk, to sell hastily printed broadsides of a poem on the subject; he would attract the attention of passers-by by loudly playing records on an old-fashioned gramophone with a large horn. Later in his life Burke helped his sister Annie operate a grocery store at 74 and afterwards at 62 Prescott St (named for Governor Prescott, father of the poet Henrietta Prescott), and lived with her in rooms at the back of the shop (now gone). People often crowded the kitchen there to hear Burke sing, recite his works, or hold forth wittily on current events. Here he continued to write both folksongs and topical ballads, such as 'Water Street Disturbance', 'The Sealers' Strike', 'The July Fire', and 'Terrible Disaster of the South West Coast: Lives and Property Carried Away by the Tidal Wave' (1926). These compositions were printed on one side of a 5 × 12-inch broadside or song sheet and sold for two to five cents in Burke's store, or hawked by children in the streets. The St John's broadside ballads persisted during the decade following Burke's death in 1930. Although they ceased after the Second World War, folksongs and poems in this tradition are still composed. Examples are the verse of **Michael Harrington**, poet and Newfoundland historian, story-teller and broadcaster, and editor of the St John's *Evening Telegram* during the 1960s. For many years he lived at 12 Dartmouth Place.

Mike Harrington broadcasting on his daily radio program, 'The Barrelman', September 1951

During the heyday of the St John's ballads many other literary activities were occurring in the city. The New Brunswick-born novelist **Theodore Goodridge Roberts**, who lived in Newfoundland from 1899 to 1902, founded and edited at St John's a short-lived journal, *The Newfoundland Magazine* (1899–1900). Roberts first began writing his thirty adventure novels in Newfoundland; many have Newfoundland subjects and reflect his knowledge of outport life, the history of the island, and its Indian lore. His Newfoundland fiction includes his first novel *The House of Isstens* (1900), *The Toll of the Tides* (1913; reprinted as *The Harbor Master*, 1968), and *Brothers in Peril: A Story of Old Newfoundland* (1905), which attempts to portray sixteenth-century Beothuk Indian life. (See also FREDERICTON, N.B.; DIGBY, N.S.) In July 1901 the printer John J. Evans, who lived at 34 Prescott St in the early years of the century, brought out the first issue of his *Newfoundland Quarterly*, an important vehicle for Newfoundland writers that is still published, although Evans died in 1944. The year 1901 also saw the composition of the 'Ode to Newfoundland' by governor Sir **Cavendish Boyle**, who arrived in St John's on 16 June 1901 and governed until 1904. The 'Ode' became the colony's anthem.

In 1892, when **E.J. Pratt** was ten, his father came here to serve as minister of the Cochrane Street Methodist Church and young Ned Pratt witnessed the great fire of 8 July 1892; the Pratts had arrived on the very day of the fire. The family remained in St John's until 1895, living in the Cochrane Street Church manse on Military Rd. During this period Pratt had as a teacher J. Alexander Robinson, a Newfoundland poet and later the founder of the *St. John's Daily News*. After 1895 Pratt's father left St John's to serve a succession of small communities, but in 1897 Ned returned to the capital, where he worked for three years as an assistant in Sclater's Drapery, which stood on Water St opposite Queen St; during those years he lived with his aunt Sophie Knight at 24 Leslie St. In 1898 he was at the harbour to see the arrival of the bodies of forty-eight sealers from the *Greenland* who had been frozen to death in the ice fields. In 1900 he returned to school, attending St John's Methodist College for two years to complete his high-school matriculation and prepare for the ministry. The College building on Long's Hill burned down in 1925 and was replaced on the same site by the present Holloway School, which was named after Pratt's beloved teacher at the Methodist College, principal Robert E. Holloway. Also known as the best photographer of nineteenth-century Newfoundland, Holloway died in 1904; a book of his photographs was published posthumously in London in 1910. Holloway did much to instil in Pratt the respect for scientific accuracy and careful observation that is so much a part of his poetry. On 15 Dec. 1901 he took his class, including Pratt, to hear the Italian physicist Count Guglielmo Marconi speak at the Newfoundland House of Assembly. The following day it was announced to the world that Marconi had received the first transatlantic wireless message on 12 Dec. from Cornwall, Eng., by means of a wire aerial taken aloft by a kite from Signal Hill, the historic fortified site on a 500-foot rise on the east side of the entrance to St John's harbour, south of the downtown section. The ruins of the old hospital building that was Marconi's laboratory can be seen on Signal Hill. In 1902, after graduating from the Methodist College, Pratt left St John's for a teaching job in MORETON'S HARBOUR.

The young E.J. Pratt, with friends

Margaret Duley

(See also BELL ISLAND, CAPE RACE, CLARKE'S BEACH, PORTUGAL COVE, WESTERN BAY; TORONTO: 3, Ont.)

Two other events of literary interest associated with St John's in the last two decades of the nineteenth century are the birth of **John Murray Anderson** and the arrival of Sir **Wilfred Grenfell**. Anderson, who became the greatest Broadway producer next to Florenz Ziegfeld, was born in St John's in 1886. His father, John Anderson, had a shop in the Grace Building, on Water Street at Beck's Cove, next to Bowring Brothers' store. John Murray Anderson began his career by planning and producing Barnum & Bailey's 'Greatest Show on Earth' for many years; he then went to Broadway, where his yearly 'Almanac' reviews introduced and employed many legendary stars. Sir Wilfred Grenfell, the medical missionary and author, arrived in St John's on 9 July 1892, the day after the great fire that had virtually levelled the city. He came to direct the Royal National Mission to Deep Sea Fishermen, a function he had performed in Britain on the North Sea; in 1913 he established the International Grenfell Association, based in ST ANTHONY, to support his efforts on behalf of Newfoundland and Labrador fishermen and their families. He is honoured by a statue near the Confederation Building on Confederation Parkway.

The novelist **Margaret Duley** was born in St John's in 1894, a daughter of a wealthy English-born jeweller, Thomas J. Duley, and Tryphena (Soper) Duley, who came from a CARBONEAR mercantile family. The Duleys lived at 51 Rennie's Mill Rd, where Margaret Duley, who never married, lived for most of her life and wrote her four novels. She

Margaret Duley's house, St John's

received her early education in St John's, including one year at the Methodist College. In 1913 she enrolled in the Royal Academy of Drama and Elocution in London but returned home at the outbreak of the First World War; subsequently she made frequent visits to London. Duley apparently began her career as a novelist out of economic necessity after the Depression had affected her father's business. Her three novels with Newfoundland settings all contain portrayals of outport life, which she came to know at her mother's family's home at Carbonear: *The Eyes of the Gull* (1936), *Highway to Valour* (1941), and *Cold Pastoral* (1939), which is mostly set in St John's. Her last novel, which is not set in Newfoundland, was *Novelty on Earth* (1942), and her last book, *The Caribou Hut; The Story of a Newfoundland Hostel* (1949), was based on her experience of helping to run a hostel for servicemen in St John's during the Second World War. At the end of her life Duley lived briefly at 66 Topsail Rd. She died in obscurity in St John's in March 1968. There is a national historic plaque in her honour in Queen Elizabeth II Library at Memorial University.

At the age of one, **Joseph ('Joey') Smallwood** was brought to St John's from his native village, GAMBO. Smallwood attended Bishop Feild College until he was 15 and then left to become a journalist. He worked from 1915–20 for the *St. John's Evening Telegram*, and from 1920–5 worked for newspapers in New York before returning to St John's where he became a champion of labour causes and of union with Canada. Smallwood's first book was *Coaker the Newfoundlander* (1927), a biography of Sir William Coaker, founder of the Fisherman's Protective Union. he also edited *The Book of Newfoundland*, of which six volumes have appeared to date, two each in 1937, 1967, and 1975. Often called the 'only living father of Confederation', Smallwood was appointed premier immediately after union was declared on 31 Mar. 1949; he led the provincial Liberal Party to power in the election of 1951 and was not defeated until 1971. His career, closely involved with every aspect of modern St John's and Newfoundland, is recounted in his autobiography *I Chose Canada* (1973). Smallwood is also the author of *Dr. William Carson* (1978), a biography of the pioneer St John's physician, public figure, and author.

In 1937 the St John's playwright **Grace Butt** founded the St John's Players and soon produced her own first play, *The Road Through Melton*. Other plays by Butt include *New Lands* (1947), a cavalcade of Newfoundland history produced to celebrate the 500th anniversary of the landing of John Cabot, and *A Part of the Main* (1949), which won the O.Z. Whitehead Award as the best one-act play in the International Play-writing Competition of the Dublin (Ireland) Theatre Festival, where it was first produced. For many years Butt lived and wrote at 46 Cowan Ave. Many of her plays have been produced but not published; manuscripts of them are held in the Newfoundland Reference Collection, Provincial Reference and Resource Library, in the Arts and Culture Centre on Prince Philip Drive (near the campus of Memorial University). Another contributor to indigenous Newfoundland drama, through the genre of the radio play, was **Ted** [Edward] **Russell**, who was widely known for his 'Uncle Mose' stories of outport life. Born in 1904 in COLEY'S POINT, Russell completed his high-school education at Bishop Feild College in St John's and then attended Memorial College (the forerunner of Memorial University, it then occupied a building on Parade Street), qualifying as a teacher in 1920. Russell spent fifteen years teaching in remote Newfoundland communities (see PASS ISLAND) before joining the Newfoundland magistracy in 1935; he became Director of Co-operatives in 1943 under the commission government. During 1949–51 he was Minister of Natural Resources in Premier Joseph Smallwood's cabinet, and from that time until his death in 1977 was associated primarily with St John's. Russell's longtime home was at 1 Stoneyhouse St. From 1954 to 1960 he broadcast about 800 of his 'Uncle Mose' stories about outport life and people over CBC radio in St John's. Published selections of these include *The Chronicles of Uncle Mose* (1975), *Tales from Pigeon Inlet* (1977), and *The Best of Ted Russell* (1982). As an outport native, Russell knew and respected the traditional life of the islanders, but as a progressive public servant he was not sentimentally opposed to change; he once wrote of his Uncle Mose stories: 'I could tell an equal number far less amusing, but they are better left untold.' One of Russell's radio plays, *The Holdin' Ground* (1972), has been published separately, and another appears in *The Best of Ted Russell*. Very late in life Russell decided to return to teaching, whereupon he stopped writing, which he called a 'hobby'.

Another literary alumnus of Memorial College is **Arthur Scammell**, born in 1913 in CHANGE ISLANDS, who attended the old Parade Street campus in the early 1930s. After further education at St Francis Xavier University, he taught in Newfoundland

St John's today

schools (see WOODY POINT) for six years; in 1939 he went to Montreal to attend McGill University. He lived away from Newfoundland for the next thirty-one years, but returned often for summer visits. Scammell wrote the famous song, 'The Squid-Jiggin' Ground', during his boyhood at Change Islands. In Montreal, in Jan. 1945, he founded *The Atlantic Guardian, A Magazine of Newfoundland* (1945–57), which published much of his own best work and that of **Ron Pollett** (see NEW HARBOUR). *My Newfoundland* (1966) contains a selection of Scammell's stories and poems.

The novelist **Percy Janes** was born in St John's in 1922 but was raised in CORNER BROOK, where his father, a blacksmith, found work in the Bowater Company's pulp-and-paper mill. Janes returned to St John's during 1938–40 to attend Memorial College and then left for Montreal, beginning a world-wandering existence that kept him away from Newfoundland until the early 1970s (see LAKEFIELD, Ont.). 'I am willing to bet,' he has written, 'that I have lived in more sordid, single housekeeping rooms in more great cities of the world than any other Canadian writer.' A grandson of Skipper Bill Janes, once notorious for his smuggling exploits along Newfoundland coasts, Janes began his novel of industrialized Newfoundland, *House of Hate* (1970), while living in London, Eng. Although set mainly in Corner Brook (the 'Milltown' of the book), *House of Hate* also draws on the Janes family's experiences in St John's. The first chapter describes a scene in which Sir Edward P. Morris, Prime Minister of Newfoundland, 'appeared on the Court House steps facing Water Street in company with a real English lord and announced to a cheering crowd that the contract had been signed and work would begin almost immediately' on the plant that is now owned by Kruger Inc. and operated under the name of Corner Brook Pulp & Paper Co. After the publication of this sombre novel Janes returned to Newfoundland, building himself a house in ST THOMAS, but also keeping an address in St John's. His other books about Newfoundland include collections of poetry (*Light and Dark*, 1980) and short stories (*Newfoundlanders*, 1981). His novel *Eastmall* (1982) further explores the impact of modernization and economic development on Newfoundland, specifically St John's; it concerns the planning and building of a huge fictional commercial development, 'Eastmall', in the area bounded by Plymouth Road, Duckworth Street East, and Quidi Vidi Road.

The novelist **Harold Horwood** is a descendant of a well-to-do, politically prominent St John's family. He was born on 2 Nov. 1923 in his grandparents' house at 134 Campbell Ave and spent his childhood there and in the adjacent house of his own family, 140 Campbell. After receiving his high-school education at Prince of Wales College in St John's, he decided not to attend university but to prepare himself in his own way for a literary career. In Nov. 1945 he and his brother Charles founded the experimental literary periodical *Protocol* (1946–8), a vehicle for new ideas that had reached Newfoundland during the Second World War; the magazine, which continued for seven issues, was published from 134 Campbell Ave. During this period Horwood also worked as a union organizer in St John's, and in 1949, at twenty-six, was elected as a Liberal member to the first provincial House of Assembly. From 1952 to 1958 he was a reporter and an influential social and political commentator with the St John's *Evening Telegram*. In 1960 Horwood founded and edited the short-lived weekly newspaper the *Examiner* and in 1961 finally left his Campbell Street address for BEACHY COVE, where he wrote eight books and remained until 1978; he now lives in UPPER CLEMENTS, N.S. Horwood's major books include two novels, *Tomorrow Will Be Sunday* (1966) and *White Eskimo; A Novel of Labrador* (1973), and a book of nature observation and reflection, *The Foxes of Beachy Cove* (1967). (See also NAIN, Labrador.) A third novel, *Remembering Summer*, was published in 1987.

Harold Horwood

Other contemporary writers associated with St John's are Ray Guy, Michael Cook, Des Walsh, and Jay Macpherson. Born in ARNOLD'S COVE in 1939, **Ray Guy** has become a story-teller in the nostalgic and humorous vein developed by Ted Russell, Arthur Scammell, and Ron Pollett. After attending Memorial University here and Ryerson Polytechnical Institute in Toronto, Guy (like Harold Horwood) first gained prominence in Newfoundland as a columist for the St John's *Evening Telegram*. (He now writes for the *Sunday Express*.) His books—all of which are compilations of stories, sketches, and essays from columns—are *You May Know Them as Sea Urchins, Ma'am* (1975), *That Far Greater Bay* (1976; winner of a Stephen Leacock Medal for humour), and *Beneficial Vapours* (1981). Guy lived at 343 Hamilton Ave for many years; his present home is on Holbrook Ave. The English-born playwright **Michael Cook** came to the city in the mid-1960s and has since worked at Memorial University, where he is an Associate Professor of English. Cook began his playwriting career with *Colour the Flesh the Colour of Dust* (1972), a historical drama set in St John's. His plays all deal with Newfoundland history or the impact of contemporary developments on the island's traditional ways of life; published collections are *Tiln & Other Plays* (1976) and *Three Plays* (1977). Cook's longtime home in St John's was at 130A Waterford Bridge Rd; recently he has lived on Monkstown Rd. Prominent among Newfoundland's younger writers is **Des Walsh**, who was born in St John's in 1954 and whose poems first appeared in the anthology *Voices Underground* (1972), edited by Harold Horwood; some of Walsh's poetry is collected in *Milk of Unicorns* (1974). In 1970 Walsh lived at 360 Topsail Rd and in the late 1970s and early 1980s at 4 Fermeuse St; his present home is on Trinity St. The poet **Jay Macpherson**, who was born in England, came to St John's with her mother and brother in 1940, when she was nine. The family's house, called 'Bank House', was on Duckworth St. Macpherson attended Bishop Spencer College, a high school that stood at the corner of Bond and Flavin streets but was discontinued in 1959 (the building was used as an elementary school until 1972). She lived in St John's until 1944, when her family moved to Ottawa. She now lives and teaches in TORONTO (3), where her first book, *The Boatman*, was published in 1957.

ST THOMAS

After spending more than thirty years outside Newfoundland, **Percy Janes** returned to his native St John's in the 1970s but soon moved to this Conception Bay village, where he built the small house he lives in. His books written in St Thomas include *Light and Dark* (1980), *Newfoundlanders* (1981), and *Eastmall* (1982). (See also CORNER BROOK, ST JOHN'S.)

SALLY'S COVE

In 1920 **Elisabeth Bristol**, an American student at Vassar College, came here as a summer volunteer teacher in Dr Wilfred Grenfell's Mission (see ST ANTHONY). Her stay led eventually to *Ballads and Sea Songs of Newfoundland* (1933), one of the most important early field collections of folk literature and music. Bristol, who had been awakened to the importance of folk songs by hearing John Lomax lecture at Vassar, was serenaded on her first night in Sally's Cove by a group of young people singing the old ballad 'Thomas and Nancy'. During two further summers of teaching at Sally's Cove, Bristol actively collected songs, making such noteworthy finds as versions of the British ballads 'Babylon', 'The Unquiet Grave', and 'Young Barbour'. In 1929, as Mrs **Elisabeth Greenleaf**, she returned to Newfoundland with a musicologist, Mrs **Grace Yarrow Mansfield**; as the 'Vassar College Folklore Expedition' the two produced their famous *Ballads and Sea Songs of Newfoundland*, a landmark of twentieth-century folklore studies. Their material was collected almost entirely from the north part of the island, especially around TWILLINGATE and along the western 'Straits coast' near Sally's Cove and Sandy Cove. Sally's Cove is 13 miles north of Bonne Bay, along Highway 430.

SMITH SOUND

This long inlet in Trinity Bay was the eastern starting-point of a trek across Newfoundland made by **William Epps Cormack** and recorded in *Narrative of a Journey Across the Island of Newfoundland in 1822* (1856), which first appeared in a Scottish journal in 1824. The son of a merchant, Cormack was born in ST JOHN'S but returned as a child to Scotland with his family after his father's death. He studied natural history at the University of Edinburgh and then returned to Newfoundland in 1822, setting out on his journey on 5 Sept. accompanied by a Micmac guide, Joseph Sylvester. The two men reached St George's Bay on Newfoundland's west coast on 2 Nov. Marks of this journey remain in names for features of Newfoundland topography, such as the Jameson Hills east of Meelpaeg Lake, named for Cormack's teacher Robert Jameson, Regius Professor of Natural History at the University of Edinburgh. Cormack eventually left Newfoundland; after living in Australia, New Zealand, England, and the United States, he died in British Columbia.

> SMITH SOUND
>
> *The hitherto mysterious interior lay unfolded below us, a boundless scene, an emerald surface, a vast basin. The eye strides again and again over a succession of northerly and southerly ranges of green plains, marbled with woods and lakes of every form and extent, a picture of all the luxurious scenes of national cultivation, receding into invisibleness. The imagination hovers in the distance, and clings involuntarily to the undulating horizon of vapour, far into the west, until it is lost.*
>
> —William Epps Cormack, *Narrative of a Journey across the Island of Newfoundland in 1822* (1824)

TWILLINGATE

Twillingate, on an island north of Exploits Bay, was the base for folksong collecting in July 1929 of the 'Vassar College Folklore Expedition', consisting of Mrs **Elisabeth Greenleaf** and Mrs **Grace Yarrow Mansfield**. Their work resulted in the first important collection of Newfoundland traditional songs by outside scholars, *Ballads and Sea Songs of Newfoundland* (1933), a classic of twentieth-century folklore studies. The two authors collected in the Twillingate region at such places as Fleur de Lys, Fogo Island, and Fortune Harbour, and then on the west coast of the island around SALLY'S COVE.

The Twillingate museum preserves the diaries of John Peyton, in whose Twillingate home Shanawdithit, the last Beothuck Indian to have contact with non-Indians, lived until she was discovered and brought to St John's by William Cormack (see SMITH SOUND, ST JOHN'S). In 1827, while dying of tuberculosis in Cormack's St John's home, she painfully recorded her knowledge of the traditions and customs of her vanished people.

Shanawdithit and the last days of the Beothuks are the subject of Peter Such's novel *Riverrun* (1973), which is partly set near Twillingate. (See also ELLIOT LAKE, NORTH BAY, TORONTO: 7, Ont.)

WESTERN BAY

The poet **E.J. Pratt** was born on 4 Feb. 1882 at the Methodist manse in this village on the North Shore of Conception Bay; he remained in Newfoundland for the next twenty-five years. His father, the Rev. John Pratt, was a Methodist minister, and the moves required by his church every two years took the family to many villages on Conception Bay: Bonavista, Cupids, Blackhead, BRIGUS, Fortune, BAY ROBERTS, and Grand Banks, with a three-year interlude (1892–5) in St John's, where John Pratt was a minister at Cochrane Street Methodist Church. E.J. Pratt's Newfoundland background can be seen in much of his writing, especially the early poems collected in *Newfoundland Verse* (1923), *Verses of the Sea* (1930), and *Many Moods* (1930). A national historical marker on the post office grounds in Western Bay commemorates the poet's birth here.

WOODY POINT

The poet and folk-song writer **Arthur Scammell** taught here and at a series of other villages—Harbour Deep, Harbour Buffet, Belleoram, and Pinchard's Island—between 1933 and 1939. He then moved to Canada to pursue his teaching career, and over a thirty-one-year period he returned to Newfoundland only for summer visits. Woody Point, on the south shore of Bonne Bay facing Gros Morne (2,644 feet), is featured in one of the most widely known contemporary Newfoundland poems, Scammell's 'Gros Morne—Bonne Bay':

I am the great mountain,
I stand at the entrance of the west
Always on guard; long years have I stood
Motionless, waiting for men to gaze
Up from the level seas, waiting
While chaos swirls about my feet,
The chaos that men love. . . .

Nova Scotia

ALBION MINES

See STELLARTON.

AMHERST

The seat of Cumberland County, Amherst is in the heart of the Chignecto region and of **Will R. Bird** country. Bird was born nearby on 11 May 1891 in the tiny village of East Mapleton and educated at the Cumberland County Academy in Amherst. Nearly all of his novels and short stories—chiefly historical romances portraying the lives of Yorkshire immigrants to Nova Scotia in the eighteenth century—concern the Chignecto region. The trilogy *Here Stays Good Yorkshire* (1945), *Tristram's Salvation* (1957), and *Despite the Distance* (1961) traces the fortunes of a Chignecto family at the time of the American Revolution. An early work with a twentieth-century setting, *Maid of the Marshes* (1935), is set in the Tantramar marshes, which stretch from Amherst to SACKVILLE, N.B. Bird's novel *The Passionate Pilgrim* (1949) is set in the Chignecto region at the time of the Acadian Expulsion. His 27 books include two histories of the Chignecto region: *A Century at Chignecto: The Key to Old Acadia* (1928) and *Done at Grand Pré* (1955).

The British writer and painter **Wyndham Lewis** (1882–1957), who sometimes described himself as an Anglo-Canadian, was born on his father's yacht as it lay offshore of Amherst. He lived in TORONTO (2) and WINDSOR, Ont., during much of the Second World War, and drew on his feelings of exile and isolation during that period for his novel *Self-Condemned* (1954), which is set in Canada.

ANNAPOLIS ROYAL

Annapolis Royal traces its origin to the PORT ROYAL of Champlain and de Monts. It was established in 1605 and was the oldest successful settlement by Europeans in what is now Canada. Champlain's *Habitation* at Port Royal, on the north side of the Annapolis Basin and east of here, was burnt by the Virginian Captain Samuel Argall in 1613. After England's Charles I had returned the site to France, the French in the 1630s built their new Port Royal, fort and settlement, at Annapolis Royal. It was captured in 1710 by New Englanders, who named the village Annapolis Royal and the fort Fort Anne; from then until the founding of Halifax in 1749, Annapolis Royal was the capital of Nova Scotia. Today Annapolis Royal is a village of less than 1,000 inhabitants. Adjacent Fort Anne National Historic Park contains excavated fortifications, reconstructions, a library, and a museum.

Annapolis Royal: a Poem (1788) by **Roger Viets**, was one of the first books of verse published in Canada. A Loyalist clergyman of the Church of England serving at Digby, Viets wrote it to encourage the Nova Scotia Loyalists by celebrating their cultural heritage and the promise of their new land.

Another Loyalist clergyman, **Jacob Bailey**, was parish priest at Annapolis Royal from 1782 until his death in 1808. During this period he wrote sermons, travel essays, two incomplete novels, satirical poems in the manner of Samuel Butler's *Hudibras*, and an extraordinary religious and historical poem, 'The Adventures of Jack Ramble, the Methodist Preacher', which was left incomplete, though it ran to over 9,000 lines. Much of this writing, however, has remained unpublished. A selection from Bailey's journals and letters, *The Frontier Missionary*, was published in Boston in 1853.

Annapolis Royal's most distinguished literary resident was **Thomas Chandler Haliburton**, who came here to practise law in 1820 and remained until 1829, when he was appointed to succeed his father as a judge of the Inferior Court of Common Pleas at his native WINDSOR. From 1826 until 1829 he represented the constituency of Annapolis Royal in the House of Assembly. Though Haliburton had not yet begun his career as a writer of fiction and humour or developed his famous character Sam Slick, during his years here he produced his first notable work, *A General Description of Nova Scotia* (1823). Expanded as *An Historical and Statistical Account of Nova Scotia* (1829), this book contained a sympathetic and imaginative description of the expulsion from GRAND PRÉ of the Nova Scotia Acadians upon which Longfellow based his poems *Evangeline: A Tale of Acadie* (1847).

ANTIGONISH

Literary associations in Antigonish cluster around St Francis Xavier University, which was established here in 1855, and especially around its extension program, which was founded in 1921 and grew into the Antigonish Movement of co-operative economic self-help for local communities. A radical Maritime poet with an interest in Christian socialism, **Kenneth Leslie**, who was born in PICTOU, devoted his favourite composition, 'O'Malley to the Reds', to Father Moses Michael Coady (1882–1959), head of the university's extension department from 1929 and guiding spirit of the Antigonish Movement. This gave the title to Leslie's selected poems, *O'Malley to the Reds and Other Poems* (1972). (See also HALIFAX.) **Joe Wallace**, a Communist versifier, attended the university about 1908–11 and began writing his socially committed verse after a year's imprisonment in Petawawa, Ont., in 1941–2, following the prohibition of the Canadian Communist Party. Two selections of his poems from the 1940s and 1950s have been published: *A Radiant Sphere* (1964) and *Joe Wallace: Poems* (1981). (See also HALIFAX.)

The Antigonish Review, a literary magazine edited for many years by Father R.J. Macsween, is published at St Francis Xavier.

BADDECK

Novelist **Hugh MacLennan** spent the summer of 1940 at Baddeck, on the shore of Bras d'Or Lake. He and his first wife Dorothy Duncan stayed at a cottage called 'Three Chimneys', and there he began writing his first novel, *Barometer Rising* (1941). The book reveals MacLennan's intimate knowledge of HALIFAX, where he grew up, and centres on the disaster of 5 Dec. 1917, when that city was devastated by the explosion in its harbor of the French munitions ship *Mont Blanc*. (See also GLACE BAY; MONTREAL: 6, NORTH HATLEY, Que.)

BARRINGTON

Barrington's Old Meeting House, a historic site administered by the Cape Sable Historical Society and the Nova Scotia Museum, is Canada's oldest remaining non-conformist place of worship, having been built by New England Nonconformists about 1765. A plaque on a boulder in the graveyard honours Edmund Doane and his wife Elizabeth Payne Doane, the maternal grandmother of the American playwright and actor **John Howard Payne** (1791–1852), known as the author of the words of the song 'Home, Sweet Home'. In 1961 the Nova Scotia novelist **Evelyn M. Richardson** and her husband moved to Barrington and built a house on the foundation of the Doanes' house, where she lived until her death in 1976. Among Mrs Richardson's books is the popular memoir *We Keep a Light* (1945; rpr. 1973). Barrington is on Highway 3, near the southwestern tip of Nova Scotia. (See also BON PORTAGE ISLAND, EMERALD ISLE.)

BLOMIDON

North of this tiny village is Cape Blomidon, which juts sharply into Minas Basin and was the home of Glooscap, the mythical hero of the Micmacs and other eastern Algonkian Indian nations. The myths associated with him are retold by **Cyrus Macmillan** (see WOOD ISLANDS, P.E.I.) in *Canadian Wonder Tales* (1974), a combined edition of two books that were originally published in 1918 and 1922. It is said that Glooscap arrived mysteriously from the sea in a huge stone canoe, created the Indians and animals, married Queen Summer to the giant Winter, won several crucial victories over evil powers, such as the Spider Man, and sailed away from Cape Blomidon promising to return. Cape Blomidon is a 670-foot elevation; 'The Lookoff', east of the village, gives a spectacular view of the Minas Basin and six river valleys.

BON PORTAGE ISLAND

This island near Cape Sable was once owned by **Evelyn M. Richardson** and her husband, Morrill Richardson, who were lighthouse-keepers here from 1926 until 1961, when they retired to BARRINGTON. In the keeper's house Mrs Richardson wrote her popular books, including two novels of closely observed Nova Scotia coast life, *Desired Haven* (1953) and *No Small Tempest* (1957), and a non-fiction work, *We Keep a Light* (1945), which won a Governor General's Award. Toward the end of the Richardsons' residence on the island the federal government tore down the lighthouse that figures in *We Keep a Light*, and the couple lived in a different house that still stands; it, and the island, were deeded by the Richardsons to Acadia University. (See also BARRINGTON, EMERALD ISLE.)

BRIDGETOWN

The novelist **Ernest Buckler**, who died in 1984, spent the last several years of his life in Bridgetown at the Mountain Lea Lodge. This village of about 1,000 inhabitants, located on the Annapolis River and Highway 1, is in the heart of the Annapolis Valley, which Buckler made his own literary province in *The Mountain and the Valley* (1952), *The Cruelest Month* (1963), and his memoir of a rural Nova Scotia childhood, *Ox Bells and Fireflies* (1968). Buckler was born 18 miles southeast of Bridgetown in DALHOUSIE WEST. He lived most of his adult life in CENTRELEA.

CENTRELEA

In the late 1930s the novelist **Ernest Buckler** bought a farm and house at Centrelea in the Annapolis Valley, 4 miles west of BRIDGETOWN on Highway 201, and only about 20 miles from his birthplace, DALHOUSIE WEST. Here he lived for four decades and wrote his two novels, *The Mountain and the Valley* (1952) and *The Cruelest Month* (1963), and his collection of descriptive sketches of life in the Annapolis Valley, *Ox Bells and Fireflies* (1968). Centrelea, just south of the river, lies between North and South Mountains, the names given to the ranges of low hills that form the valley. These hills serve as models for the mountain that is a symbol of hope to the protagonist of *The Mountain and the Valley*, the story of a frustrated writer who struggles to express his vision in the midst of a rural existence that both inspires and oppresses him.

Ernest Buckler in front of his house, Centrelea

Buckler spent almost his entire life in the Annapolis Valley, in fact within 20 miles of Centrelea. He was born in 1908 in Dalhousie West in the South Mountains, where his family had a farm; during his childhood the family may also have farmed in the North Mountains. Buckler earned his B.A. from Dalhousie University, HALIFAX, when he was only twenty, and two years later received an M.A. in philosophy from the University of Toronto. He stayed in Toronto for another six years, working as an actuary, and in 1936 returned to the Annapolis Valley to work on his family's farm. Soon afterward he acquired his own farm at Centrelea. Buckler's house—on the north side of Highway 201 where it bends through the hamlet —is a modest farmhouse of traditional Nova Scotia style, dating from about 1865, with a centre gable and decorative pillars on the corners. It is privately owned.

CHESTER

Charles Ritchie, the former diplomat turned diarist, has a summer home at Chester, which is at Mahone Bay, on Highway 3 west of Halifax. Ritchie's books include *The Siren Years: A Canadian Diplomat Abroad* (1974, winner of a Governor General's Award) and *More Undiplomatic Diaries, 1962–1971* (1983), in which he describes Chester. (See also HALIFAX; OTTAWA, Ont.)

CORNWALLIS

In 1779 the Loyalist clergyman and writer **Jacob Bailey** immigrated to Nova Scotia, serving as parish priest here until 1782. A prolific writer, most of whose works remain unpublished, he wrote some of his interesting verse satires at Cornwallis. Selections from his letters and journals were published as *The Frontier Missionary* at Boston in 1853. Cornwallis is on Highway 1 on the south shore of the Annapolis Basin. (See also ANNAPOLIS ROYAL.)

DALHOUSIE WEST

Ernest Buckler was born in 1908 in this village south of BRIDGETOWN. The region of the Annapolis Valley, between Dalhousie West and Bridgetown, provides the background of the places and people in his three highly regarded works: the novels *The Mountain and the Valley* (1952) and *The Cruelest Month* (1963) and his sketches of a rural childhood, *Ox Bells and Fireflies* (1968). (See also CENTRELEA.)

DARTMOUTH

Dartmouth, sister-city of HALIFAX, occupies the east shore of Halifax harbour. The Dartmouth Heritage Museum, on Wyse Road near Park Avenue, contains the Howe Room, a re-creation of the study of **Joseph Howe**, the pre-eminent nineteenth-century Nova Scotia politician who was also a poet, journalist, and polished orator. Howe's *Poems and Essays* (1874) were published the year after his death; *The Speeches and Public Letters of the Honourable Joseph Howe* appeared in 1858.

The early Nova Scotia poet and editor **Mary Jane Katzman** (1828–90) was born in Preston, now within Dartmouth, and was a Dartmouth resident most of her life. Her father, Christian Conrad Katzman, came here in 1821 and built Maroon Hall (no longer standing). The name of the house is mentioned on its owner's headstone in Christ Church Cemetery; it stood on the crest of the present Dartmouth Memorial Gardens.

Katzman's poetry was praised by Joseph Howe in 1845 when she was only seventeen, and in 1852–3 she was the editor of the short-lived but influential *Provincial*, an important nineteenth-century magazine in the Atlantic provinces. Katzman published widely in magazines but issued no book during her life. A collection of her poems, *Frankincense and Myrrh* (Halifax, 1893), and her *History of the Townships of Dartmouth, Preston, and Laurencetown* (Halifax, 1893), appeared posthumously. She married William Lawson in 1869 and died in Halifax. Like her father, she is buried in Dartmouth's Christ Church Cemetery.

Helen Creighton's house, Dartmouth

The folklorist and author **Helen Creighton** was born here on 5 Sept. 1899 and spent most of her life at 'Evergreen', a large house overlooking Halifax harbour. 'Evergreen', to which Creighton's family moved in 1919 after having occupied two houses in Portland Street, is now a provincial historic site; it is at 26 Newcastle St. In 1926 Creighton was 'Aunt Helen' on radio station CHNS in Halifax and in that same year joined the Canadian Authors' Association; she was its president in 1962. Her books include *Traditional Songs from Nova Scotia* (1950), *Bluenose Ghosts* (1958), *Gaelic Songs in Nova Scotia* (1964), and her autobiography, *A Life in Folklore* (1975).

Helen Creighton records songs with William Gilbie of Sambro, N.S., July 1959

DIGBY

Roger Viets, author of the first book of poetry published in Canada, *Annapolis Royal: A Poem* (1788), was a Loyalist clergyman who had charge of Trinity Church in Digby from the late 1770s until his death in 1811.

The novelist and poet **Theodore Goodridge Roberts** settled in Digby in 1945 and died here on 24 Feb. 1953. His body was returned to FREDERICTON, N.B., to be buried near the graves of his brother Sir Charles G.D. Roberts and his cousin Bliss Carman. Roberts was the author of many historical romances, novels of mystery and wartime adventures, and tales of Newfoundland, such as his best-known novel *The Harbormaster* (1912; rpr. 1968). Desmond Pacey, in an introduction to the 1968 reprint of this book, states that during Roberts' last years, those spent in Digby, the author was 'desperately poor, and was eking out a precarious existence by selling adventure stories to the pulps . . .' (See also ST JOHN'S, Nfld.)

EAST MAPLETON

This hamlet in southern Cumberland County was the birthplace on 11 May 1891 of the novelist **Will R. Bird**, who is best known for his trilogy of novels tracing the fortunes of a Chignecto family at the time of the American Revolution: *Here Stays Good Yorkshire* (1945), *Tristram's Salvation* (1957), and *Despite the Distance* (1961). Bird was educated at AMHERST and has lived in HALIFAX for many years. His former home in East Mapleton is standing and can be pointed out by local residents. East Mapleton is 20 miles south of Amherst on a sideroad running south from Highway 2.

EMERALD ISLE

The novelist **Evelyn M. Richardson** was born on this small island near Cape Sable in May 1902 and was brought up at nearby Clark's Harbour, Cape Sable Island. Her family moved to Halifax in 1917. On 14 Aug. 1926 she married Morrill Richardson on Emerald Isle. That same year the Richardsons bought nearby BON PORTAGE ISLAND, where Mrs Richardson—the author of *We Keep a Light* (1945), which won a Governor General's Award—developed her writing career. (See also BARRINGTON.)

ESKASONI ISLAND

The Micmac poet **Rita Joe** lives on this island opposite the village of East Bay, Cape Breton Island. Her poems are collected in *The Poems of Rita Joe* (1978). The book was published by Abenaki Press, founded by the HALIFAX poet Andrew Merkel.

FALMOUTH

The family of the preacher and poet **Henry Alline** came to Falmouth in 1760 from Newport, Rhode Island, when Alline was eleven; his father was among 113 settlers granted property in the district in 1758–9 under Governor Charles Lawrence's offer of free land to immigrants. Alline's long process of self-education and conversion, recorded in his journals, culminated in a vision of light that came to him after a walk in the fields around Falmouth on Sunday, 26 Mar. 1775. Returning to his house, he chanced to read Psalm 38 in the King James Bible. 'My whole soul,' he wrote, 'that was a few minutes ago groaning under mountains of death . . . was now filled with immortal love.'

Maintaining Falmouth as his base, Alline travelled throughout much of Nova Scotia and what is now New Brunswick, as well as St John's Island (now Prince Edward Island), and, in the last months of his life, New England. At Falmouth, besides his journal, he wrote many of his hymns and sermons and probably his theological works. All of his writings are associated with his preaching, which began in 1776. His first volume of *Hymns and Spiritual Songs* (Halifax, 1782) entitles him to be considered the first Canadian poet of note. The second volume (Boston, 1786) was written during a lengthy illness near the end of his life; he was travelling to Boston to publish this work when he died at North Hampton, New Hampshire. Alline's theological writings, including *The Anti-traditionalist* (1783), reflect his dissenting 'divine light' Protestant outlook and were unpalatable to both Anglicans and Calvinists. They struck a chord, however, with the common people of the day and in the United States contributed to the founding of the Freewill Baptist movement. *The Life and Journal of the Rev. Mr. Henry Alline* appeared in Boston in 1806.

Joseph Howe's poem 'The Wreath', which the author dates 'Falmouth, May 10, 1869', records a 'starlight night, and homeward ride / Beside the lonely Avon River'. Falmouth, on Highway 1, is situated on the west bank of the Avon and faces WINDSOR.

GLACE BAY

The novelist **Hugh MacLennan** was born in this Cape Breton mining community on 20 Mar. 1907, though he calls Halifax his home town because he moved there with his family when he was seven. MacLennan recreated the spirit of his birthplace in *Each Man's Son* (1951), which tells of one Cape Breton boy's escape from a life in the mines. The novel blends a psychological portrait of the Scottish Highlanders who settled the Cape, among them MacLennan's own ancestors, with a keen physical detailing of the contast between the landscape's beauty and the grim features of a company town. Called Broughton in the novel, Glace Bay, with its rows of tenement houses and the human 'anthill' of the colliery, was typical of early twentieth-century coal-mining towns in the Maritimes and still retains much of that flavour. MacLennan's biographer, Elspeth Cameron (in *Hugh MacLennan: A Writer's Life*, 1981) reports that the MacLennan home was a small house that stood about a mile inland from the coast on the top of a knoll and was encircled by a brook. It is no longer standing. MacLennan's illustrious writing career—he is a five-time winner of the Governor General's Award, having been honoured for both novels and non-fiction—has been primarily associated with MONTREAL: 6; see also NORTH HATLEY, Que.

Visitors today can learn about Glace Bay's history at the Miner's Museum, Quarry Point, where retired miners act as guides. The museum affords an opportunity to dig for coal in the Ocean Deeps Colliery, a mine specially opened for museum use in a vein of coal extending beneath the Atlantic floor.

Philippe Hébert's statue of Evangeline. Behind is the chapel commemorating the Church of St Charles

GRAND PRÉ

This quiet village in Kings County, on the south shore of Minas Basin, is near the site of the original Grand Pré, an important Acadian community in the eighteenth century. The site is today in Grand Pré National Historic Park, which commemorates the Expulsion of the Acadians in 1755 and 1758. That event is the subject of *Evangeline: a Tale of Acadie* (1847), the epic verse-romance by the American poet **Henry Wadsworth Longfellow**. Grand Pré Park, just north of the village, contains a statue of Longfellow's imaginary heroine, Evangeline, sculpted by Philippe Hébert and his son Henri, descendants of deported Acadians. Portraying Evangeline as a girl from one side and as an old woman from the other, it stands before a replica of the parish church of St Charles, which is built on the foundation of the original building (where the deportation order was read to the Acadians in 1755) and which houses a bust of Longfellow and a collection of Acadian artifacts.

GRAND PRÉ

In the Acadian land, on the shores of the Basin of Minas,
Distant, secluded, still, the little village of Grand Pré
Lay in the fruitful valley. Vast meadows stretched to the eastward,
Giving the village its name, and pasture of flocks without number.
Dikes, that the hands of the farmers had raised with labor incessant,
Shut out the turbulent tides . . .

—Henry Wadsworth Longfellow, *Evangeline*

Longfellow never visited Grand Pré. A Boston minister, Horace L. Conolly, had heard a story of two young Acadian lovers separated by the Expulsion and approached the novelist Nathaniel Hawthorne to write a book based upon it; Hawthorne declined, but the idea appealed to his friend Longfellow, who began writing in 1845, working from published accounts of the Expulsion, especially Thomas Chandler Haliburton's *Historical and Statistical Account of Nova Scotia* (1829; see ANNAPOLIS ROYAL, HALIFAX).

Grand Pré National Historic Park is largely the result of the dedication of a little-known poet who devoted his life to studying the history of his Acadian heritage. **John Frederic Herbin** was a descendant of the Robischaud family, which had been driven from Grand Pré and later resettled in the former Acadie. A native of St Mary's Bay, Herbin lived for a while in the United States but in the late nineteenth century returned to Wolfville, three miles from Grand Pré. It was Herbin who first searched out many of the ancient Acadian sites in the region. He discovered the foundation of the church of St Charles and its rectory and in 1908 helped to erect a memorial stone cross, using stones from the original church building; it marks the site of what is believed to be an old Acadian cemetery. Herbin's greatest contribution, however, was to acquire possession of the ground on which the original village of Grand Pré had stood and to refuse to give it up except on condition that it become a monument to the dispersed Aca-

FROM 'THE RETURNED ACADIAN'

Along my father's dykes I roam again,
Among the willows by the river-side.
These miles of green I know from hill to tide,
And every creek and river's ruddy stain.
Neglected long and shunned our dead have lain
Here, where a people's dearest hope has died.
Alone of all their children scattered wide,
I scan the sad memorials that remain.

—John Frederic Herbin

dians. In 1920 the Evangeline statue was completed, and later in the decade the Societé Nationale de l'Assomption erected on the site of St Charles Church the chapel that became the focal point of the park. Herbin's passion for the melancholy fate of his ancestors was expressed in his poetry, which also reflects his custom of wandering for long hours through the marshes and along the dikes of the region. Herbin died while walking along the trail that his ancestors had followed from Grand Pré to their point of embarkation at present-day Horton Landing.

Bliss Carman's first published book of verse was *Low Tide on Grand Pré* (1893),

GRAND PRÉ

Was it a year or lives ago
We took the grasses in our hands,
And caught the summer flying low
Over the waving meadow lands,
And held it there between our hands?
—Bliss Carman, *'Low Tide on Grand Pré'*

whose title lyric is often considered his finest poem. Other poems in the volume also depict Grand Pré, its streams and neighbouring uplands, the characteristic willow trees of the region, and the old Acadian dikes (seen best at Horton Landing), which were built to hold back the Bay of Fundy tides in Minas Basin and transform marshes into farmland. Carman absorbed the landscape here, and its melancholy associations, during his yearly summer visits to his cousin Charles G.D. Roberts while the latter was teaching at nearby WINDSOR from 1885 to 1895. He portrays the Expulsion of the Acadians in his novels *The Forge in the Forest* (1896) and *A Sister to Evangeline* (1898).

Joseph Howe's poem 'Acadia', published posthumously in 1874 and written many years earlier, touches briefly on the Expulsion of the Acadians; although it does not mention Grand Pré by name, it celebrates the landscape of this Minas Basin area.

Grand Pré figures in *Rose à Charlitte* (1898), a romance by **Marshall Saunders** that is set during the time of the Acadian Expulsion and that was written following the highly successful publication of her *Beautiful Joe* (1894). (See also MILTON, HALIFAX; TORONTO: 6, Ont.) Grand Pré is prominent in the most important contemporary work of Acadian literature, *Pélagie-la-charette* (1979), by **Antonine Maillet** (see BUCTOUCHE, N.B.). The story of an old woman who leads a group of Acadians from the southern United States back to their homeland after the Expulsion, it also offers—like all of Maillet's works—a re-creation and celebration of the Acadian language, an offshoot of sixteenth-century French that preserves many archaisms. *Pélagie-la-charette* was the first book by a foreign author ever to win the French Prix Goncourt. An English translation by Philip Stratford, entitled *Pélagie: the return to a homeland*, was published in 1982.

GRAND PRÉ

'And this I say to all the children of Acadie: Never touch Grand-Pré, but forever keep its memory green in your hearts and blood.'
—Antonine Maillet, *Pélagie-la-Charrette* (1979; tr. Philip Stratford, 1982)

GRANVILLE FERRY

A Victorian house in Granville Ferry known as 'The Moorings' is operated as a guest-house by the novelist and short-story writer **H.R. Percy**, who lives in a cottage nearby. A native of England, and the founding chairman of the Writers' Federation of Nova Scotia, he is the author of two novels, *Flotsam* (1968) and *Painted Ladies* (1983), and a collection of stories, *The Timeless Island* (1960). Granville Ferry is on Highway 1, just across the Annapolis River from ANNAPOLIS ROYAL; it is near UPPER CLEMENTS, the home of the novelist **Harold Horwood**.

Not far from Granville Ferry is 'Browhill Cottage', the home in later life of **Andrew Merkel**, an amateur poet and one of the chief members of the Song Fishermen (see HALIFAX). Browhill Cottage is on the road between Granville Ferry and Port Royal National Historic Park. It stands about half a mile from the *Habitation*, the reconstruction of Champlain's fort, and can be identified by the name of its present owner on the mailbox, Professor Barry Moody. It was during his years at Browhill Cottage, after he retired from the Canadian Press, that Merkel founded Abenaki Press, which has published many Nova Scotian and other eastern-Canadian books.

GREAT VILLAGE

The American poet **Elizabeth Bishop** lived here for much of her childhood with grandparents; their house can be pointed out by local residents. Bishop wrote of her Nova Scotia upbringing and family in many poems. Her work is collected in *Elizabeth Bishop: The Complete Poems, 1927–1979* (1982). See also her story 'In the Village' in her book *Questions of Travel* (1965). Great Village is on Highway 2 just north of Cobequid Bay, the eastern end of Minas Basin.

HALIFAX

Many reminders of a distinguished literary past are scattered throughout this historic seaport. One of the earliest is a plaque in Province House, seat of the Nova Scotia legislature, recalling the establishment in 1751 of Canada's first printing press by the Boston printers John Bushell and Bartholomew Green Jr. Green soon died and Bushell became the colony's first King's Printer. On 23 Mar. 1752 he published the first number of Canada's first newspaper, the

Halifax, 1749

Halifax Gazette; its office was at the corner of Grafton and Duke Sts.

The enterprising publisher and printer **Anthony Henry**, a veteran of the siege of Louisbourg, came to work for Bushell in 1760 and, when Bushell died in 1761, took over the press and his duties as King's Printer. After being dismissed as King's Printer in 1766 for permitting his apprentice Isaiah Thomas to write articles for the *Gazette* that were critical of the Stamp Act, Henry immediately founded the *Nova Scotia Chronicle and Weekly Advertiser*, Canada's first independent newspaper, and drove the semi-official *Gazette* out of business. By 1770 Henry was again acting as King's Printer and in 1778 received an official commission to the post; one of the earliest surviving documents of Canadian publishing, it is preserved in the Legislative Library, Province House, 1451 Barrington St.

Henry published several notable books and pamphlets. One of his series of almanacs, the *Nova-Scotia Calendar or an Almanack for 1776*, contained Canada's first book illustration, a woodcut view of Halifax. He also published *Two mites on some of the most important and much disputed points of divinity...* (1871) by **Henry Alline**, the early poet and preacher (see FALMOUTH). Another important Halifax publication during this era was *Annapolis Royal: A Poem* (1788), the first separate volume of poetry published in Canada; it was written by **Roger Viets**, a Loyalist Anglican minister who was parish priest of DIGBY from 1785 to 1811.

Anthony Henry Holland, godson of Anthony Henry, founded *The Acadian Recorder*, which published one of Canada's earliest important literary works, **Thomas McCulloch**'s series of sixteen satirical letters by the fictional lame farmer Mephibosheth Stepsure. The original series was published between 22 Dec. 1821 and 11 May 1822. It appeared in book form in Halifax as *Letters of Mephibosheth Stepsure*—but not until 1862, nineteen years after McCulloch's death. McCulloch was the first principal of Dalhousie College, the forerunner of Dalhousie University, originally situated on the Grand Parade (a square between Duke and Prince streets on the north and south, and Barrington and Argyle Streets on the east and west), where City Hall stands today. An early faculty member was Abraham Gesner, inventor of kerosene, who wrote several books on the geology of Nova Scotia; he was professor of Natural History at Dalhousie at the time of his death in 1864. (See also PICTOU.)

The novelist **Douglas Smith Huygues**, primarily associated with SAINT JOHN, N.B., lived in Halifax in 1840–1, where he contributed poetry to the Halifax *Morning Post* under the pseudonym 'Eugene'. *Agrimou: A Legend of the Micmac*, his novel of the Acadian Expulsion and of the destructive consequences for the Micmac Indians of European settlement of the Maritimes, was published in Halifax in 1847. Also present in Halifax in 1840–1 was **Philippe-Ignace-François Aubert de Gaspé**, the son of one of Quebec's most important early writers, **Philippe-Joseph Aubert de Gaspé**, author of *Les Anciens Canadiens* (1863; see also QUEBEC CITY, SAINT-JEAN-PORT-JOLI, Que.). Aubert de Gaspé the younger was an important author himself, for he had written a work often considered the first French-Canadian novel, *L'Influence d'un livre* (1837), although it is believed that his father helped him with it. He died in Halifax on 7 Mar. 1841.

The novelist and poet **James DeMille** was professor of history and rhetoric at Dalhousie from 1865 until his death in 1880. Most of his novels were written in Halifax, though all were published in New York, Boston, or London after serial appearance in foreign magazines. DeMille wrote little about Nova Scotia, preferring foreign and historical settings for his novels, among the best known of which are *Helena's Household: A Tale of Rome in the First Century* (1868) and *The Dodge Club* (1869), a series of comic sketches about American tourists in Italy. *The Lily and the Cross* (1874), however, is a historical romance of Louisbourg, and a series of boys' books—about the Brethren of the White Cross (B.O.W.C.)—are drawn from DeMille's childhood experiences in the Minas Basin area (see WOLFVILLE.) His posthumous work of science fiction and satire, *A Strange Manuscript Found in a Copper Cylinder* (1888), is the most original pre-twentieth-century novel to be published in the Atlantic provinces. The Dalhousie Library contains manuscripts of several of DeMille's novels.

James DeMille

The DeMille house, Halifax

Cornelius O'Brien, the Roman Catholic Archbishop of Halifax from 1882 until his death in 1906, was also well known as the author of such works as *After Weary Years* (1885) and *Aminta—A Modern Life Drama* (1890), a long philosophical poem. In 1882 O'Brien became a charter member of the Royal Society of Canada, which he served as president in 1896. (See also CHARLOTTETOWN, P.E.I.)

Marshall Saunders, author of *Beautiful Joe* (1894), was born in MILTON in 1861 but spent much of her youth and early adulthood in Halifax, where she was educated and where she began her writing career. Her father, a Baptist clergyman, lived in a house, still standing (but now much renovated), at the southeast corner of Carleton St and Spring Garden Rd and this was Marshall Saunders' home while she was in Halifax; she is said to have had an aviary here. In the early 1890s she moved to Boston, beginning her many years of restless travel, though until 1909 she was often in Halifax; she finally settled in TORONTO: 6, Ont. in 1916. (See also MEAFORD, Ont.)

Lucy Maud Montgomery studied English literature for a year at Dalhousie University in 1895–6. For most of the academic year she boarded at the Halifax Ladies' College (now gone), which stood on Barrington Street at the corner of Harvey Street; that part of Barrington Street was called Pleasant Street. Montgomery returned to Halifax in 1901–2 when she accepted a job as a proofreader and reporter on the *Daily Echo*, the

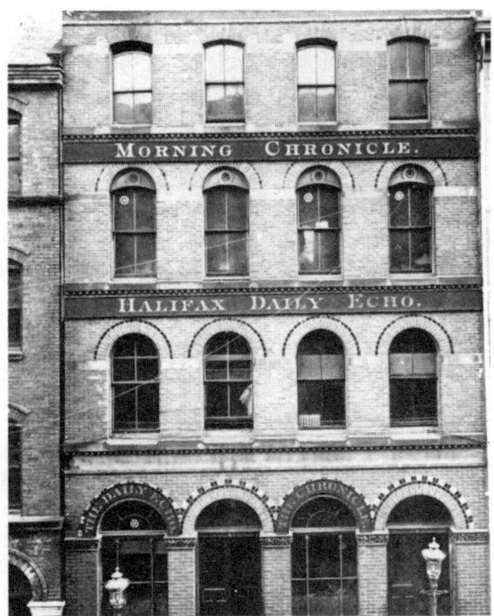

The *Daily Echo* office, Halifax, when L.M. Montgomery worked here

afternoon newspaper of the Halifax *Morning Chronicle*, whose building stood on Prince St. She stayed briefly at the Women's Christian Association but on 18 Nov. 1901 began boarding at 23 Church St, and on 1 May 1902, near the end of her residence in Halifax, moved to 25 Morris St. Montgomery published stories and poems in many periodicals during this period and wrote a column for the *Daily Echo*, 'Around the Tea Table', which contained miscellaneous items on fashion, diet, subjects of local interest, and the like. In the late spring of 1902 she returned to CAVENDISH, P.E.I., to take care of her grandmother.

While a student at Dalhousie, Montgomery was encouraged in her writing by one of her professors, **Archibald MacMechan** (1862–1933), who had come to Dalhousie as a professor of English in 1889. Although not influential as a creative writer, MacMechan played an important part in the formation of Canadian literature through his critical works, his essays, and especially his seminal study, *Headwaters of Canadian Literature* (1924). MacMechan taught at Dalhousie until shortly before his death on 7 Aug. 1933. In the 1890s MacMechan lived at 12 Lucknow Terrace, now Lucknow St. His long-time home, from about 1900, was a house at 72 Victoria Rd; its site is now occupied by an apartment building. Besides scholarly works and editions of English authors, MacMechan published *Sagas of the Sea* (1923), *Old Province Tales* (1924), and *Red Snow on Grand Pré* (1931). A volume of his poems, *Late Harvest* (1934), was published posthumously.

The Public Archives of Nova Scotia on South Street, on the grounds of Dalhousie University, contains an extensive collection of historic publications and related items. One of the principal exhibits is the printing press on which **Joseph Howe** printed *The Novascotian* from 1827 to 1840, when he sold it. A native of Halifax and a son of the King's Printer, John Howe, Joseph was born in 1804 in a house whose gatepost alone is preserved, on its original site at 5956 Emscote Dr. In 1828 Joseph Howe purchased *The Novascotian* and in its pages undertook a campaign for political reform. Charged with libel for his attacks on the province's magistrates and legislative council, Howe delivered a six-hour speech in his own defence at the old Courthouse, now called Province House, on 2 Mar. 1835; he was acquitted and elected to the legislative assembly in the following year. (A statue of Howe stands in front of Province House, which is on George Street, a short street running east from Halifax Citadel National Historic Park.) This event is regarded as an important victory for the principle of freedom of the press in Canadian history. Howe's activities combined journalism, publishing, oratory, politics, and the writing of verse. He was premier of Nova Scotia from 1861 to 1863; after his initial opposition to Confederation, he accepted a seat in John A. Macdonald's first federal cabinet. He returned to Halifax from Ottawa in 1873 as lieutenant-governor of the province, but he died at Government House only three weeks after taking office. Howe found time to write a considerable body of verse, as well as travel notes. Many of his voluminous writings were never published, but a collection of them, *Poems and Essays*, appeared posthumously in 1874; it includes a long poem on his native province entitled 'Acadia', and many shorter pieces memorializing Nova Scotia scenes and places. Howe was constant and energetic in his support of Nova Scotia writers, particularly in the pages of *The Novascotian*. He was the centre of a circle of writers and professional men—including, among others, Oliver Goldsmith, Beamish Murdoch, William Annand, Thomas Akins, and Thomas Chandler Haliburton. Together they formed 'The Club', which met regularly at Howe's home and contributed articles to *The Novascotian*. Halifax honours Joseph Howe and his times with a festival every September.

Joseph Howe

Beamish Murdoch, born in Halifax in 1800, was active in The Club from 1829 to 1831. He had been editor (from 1826 to mid-1827) of the important early literary journal, *The Acadian Magazine; or Literary Mirror*; he was also editor of *The Acadian Recorder* for several years. His publications include a *History of Nova Scotia* (1865–7), an *Epitome of the Laws of Nova Scotia* (1832–3), published by Howe, and a pamphlet on the famous fire of 1825 in Miramichi, N.B. **William Annand**, born in Halifax in 1808, worked with Howe on *The Novascotian* and later established his own newspaper, the *Morning Chronicle*; late in life he bitterly opposed, in the *Chroncile's* pages, Howe's final decison to support Confederation. Annand is named as the editor of Howe's *Speeches and Public Letters* (Halifax, 1858), although Howe himself was largely responsible for its preparation. **Thomas Akins** was articled in the law practice of Beamish Murdoch, and as Record Commissioner of the House of Assembly in 1857 became the first archivist of the province. Akins, the author of *History of Halifax City* (1847), lived in the small one-storey cottage on Brunswick St at Cornwallis that has been remodelled and is now an architect's office.

Another member of The Club, **Oliver Goldsmith**, was grandnephew of the Anglo-Irish poet of the same name. Born in 1794 in ST ANDREWS, N.B., Goldsmith came to Halifax with his parents in 1800. His father was the city's first assistant commissary general to the British Army. After attempting several other jobs in Halifax, Goldsmith went to work for the commissariat in 1810 and, apart from one brief European journey, worked there in positions of increasing importance until 1833, when he left Nova Scotia. During his Halifax years he wrote for *The Novascotian*, participated in amateur theatricals, and published his most famous poem, *The Rising Village* (1825), 528 lines in pentameter couplets celebrating the struggles and achievements of Nova Scotia settlers. Goldsmith tells the story of his years in Halifax in his brief *Autobiography*, which was first discovered and published in England in 1943.

Thomas Chandler Haliburton

Next to Howe himself, The Club's most distinguished member was **Thomas Chandler Haliburton**, who came to Halifax from ANNAPOLIS ROYAL in 1826 as that constituency's representative to the legislative assembly, where he served until 1829, when he was appointed to the Inferior Court of Common Pleas and took up residence in WINDSOR. Howe published Haliburton's *Historical and Statistical Account of Nova Scotia* (1829), which influenced the writings of Francis Parkman and provided Henry Wadsworth Longfellow with the account of the Acadian Expulsion upon which he based his *Evangeline: a Tale of Acadie* (1847). Haliburton's most famous work, *The Clockmaker; or, the Sayings and Doings of Sam Slick, of Slickville*, was published in book form by Howe in 1836 after its original serial appearance in *The Novascotian*. Haliburton's international popularity began soon afterwards when the book was pirated, to Howe's great financial detriment, by a London publisher. After several years in the Nova Scotia Supreme Court, Haliburton moved in 1856 to England, where he served in Parliament, wrote several political studies of Canada, and acted as chairman of the Canadian Land and Emigration Company (see HALIBURTON, Ont.). He died in 1865.

HALIFAX

The entrance to this noble harbour, the best, perhaps, in America, is exceedingly beautiful: such portions of the landscape as are denuded of trees exhibit a very high state of cultivation; while the natural sterility of the cold, wet and rocky soil of the background is clothed and concealed by verdant evergreens of spruce, fir, pine, and hemlock. On either hand, you pass formidable fortifications, and the national flag and the British sentinel.

—Thomas Chandler Haliburton, *The Old Judge; or, Life in a Colony* (1849)

The poet and editor **Mary Jane Katzmann**, a native of the Township of Preston (near DARTMOUTH), was helped to prominence by Joseph Howe's praise of her in 1845. Canada's foremost female editor of her day, she directed the twenty-four issues of an important journal, *The Provincial; or Halifax Monthly Magazine*, from January 1852 to December 1853. She died at Halifax in 1890, and two of her books appeared in 1893: *Frankincense and Myrrh* (poems) and *History of the Townships of Dartmouth, Preston, and Lawrencetown*. Among the writers Katzmann published in the *Provincial* was **Mary Eliza Herbert**, a native Haligonian. She and her half-sister **Sarah Herbert**, prolific writers of verse and of sentimental and moral fiction, were literary fixtures of nineteenth-century Halifax. Their joint book of poetry, *The Aeolian Harp* (1857), was very popular.

From 1863 to 1877 **George Monro Grant** was pastor of St Matthew's, the oldest Presbyterian church in Canada, located on Barrington St between Bishop and Salter. Grant lived in the fine stone house on Barrington at the corner of Bishop. Its address is now 1359 Barrington, although Grant's address was 239 Pleasant St. (The former Pleasant St, which ran from Point Pleasant to Salter, has been made into the southern end of Barrington St.) In the summer of 1872 Grant set out from Halifax as secretary to Sandford Fleming's expedition to find a route for a transcontinental railway. Grant's diary of this epic journey was published in 1873 as the travel classic *Ocean to Ocean*. (See also STELLARTON; KINGSTON, Ont.) Also associated with Halifax is **Basil King**, a native of CHARLOTTETOWN, P.E.I., who was educated at King's College, WINDSOR, and who served from 1884 to 1892 as curate and later as rector of St Luke's (Anglican) Cathedral. King's home here was at 73 Birmingham St. King moved from Halifax to Cambridge, Mass., where his writing career began in 1900. He set his popular novels of morals and manners in the affluent milieu of New York and Boston familiar to readers of Edith Wharton and Henry James. The single exception is one of his best books, *In the Garden of Charity* (1903), a story of Nova Scotia fishing people.

The house of George Monro Grant, Halifax

Amelia Fytche, a novelist and feminist writer of the late nineteenth century, lived and wrote in the house at 5206 Tobin St; this was the home of her father, a doctor, who spelled the family name 'Fitch'. Among Fytche's works are *A Kerchief to Hunt Souls* (1899). The poet **Frances Bannerman** and the novelist **Alice Jones** were both daughters of Alfred Jones, Lieutenant-Governor of Nova Scotia in 1900–6, and spent much of their lives at the Jones home, 'Bloomingdale'; it is now the Waegwoltic Club, which stands on extensive grounds on the shore of the Northwest Arm at the foot of Cobourg Rd; its address is 6549 Cobourg Rd. From about 1905 until her death in 1933, Alice Jones lived in France; her novels include *Bubbles We Buy* (1903) and *Marcus Holbeach's Daughter* (1912). Frances Bannerman was the author of *Milestones* (1899). Their sister-in-law, **Susan Jones**, was also an author, who wrote romantic novels such as *The Fascinating Mr. Savage* (1926); she was a lifelong Halifax resident.

The home of Alice Jones and Frances Bannerman, Halifax

Among the literary curiosities of Halifax, two stand out. **Anna Harriette Leonowens**, celebrated British governess to the children of the King of Siam and author of *The English Governess at the Court of Siam* (1870), lived in the city with her daughter from 1878 to 1897; her career was the basis for Margaret Landon's novel *Anna and the King of Siam* (1944). While in Halifax, Leonowens helped found the Victoria School of Art and Design, forerunner of the Nova Scotia College of Art. The Victoria School was at 1744 Argyle St, opposite the Grand Parade; the building, which dates from 1817, is now the Five Fishermen Restaurant. In the 1890s Leonowens lived at 235 Pleasant St (now part of Barrington St); this house was almost opposite the George Grant house at 1359 Barrington. The Lenoir Building, 1663 Hollis St—the oldest remaining structure in a group of nineteenth-century buildings that formed the cultural and political heart of Victorian Halifax—was the home of the Acadian lawyer Peter H. Lenoir, who acted as legal adviser to Victor Hugo's daughter, Adèle, when she came to Halifax in 1861 in pursuit of a Lieutenant Pinsent of the British Army, with whom she was in love. This was the subject of a film by François Truffaut, *L'histoire d'Adèle H.* (1975).

The Dartmouth-born writer and folklorist **Helen Creighton** attended Halifax Ladies' College, enrolling in 1914; she endured the Halifax Explosion of 1917 while a student there. In 1926 she returned to the city as a broadcast storyteller: she told her versions of folklore under the name 'Aunt Helen' on radio station CHNS. In September 1939 Creighton began a brief period as dean of women at King's College, 6350 Cobourg Rd; she maintained her home, 'Evergreen', at DARTMOUTH, but had an apartment on the King's College campus. The poet **Fraser Sutherland** (*Strange Ironies,* 1972), born in Pictou, attended King's College in the mid-1960s.

Halifax was the centre of activity for the **Song Fishermen**, a group of Maritime poets who often met to socialize, travel the Atlantic Provinces, and exchange their works mainly in the 1920s. The group included Charles G.D. Roberts, Bliss Carman, Kenneth Leslie, Charles Bruce, Robert Norwood, Eliza Ritchie, Ethel Butler, Evelyn Tufts, Stewart MacAulay, and others. Its moving spirit and most faithful member was **Andrew Doane Merkel**, an amateur poet who was also Atlantic Superintendent of the Canadian Press from 1918 to 1947. For much of his life he lived at 50 S. Park St, which was the primary meeting-place of the Song Fishermen and a centre for other Nova Scotia writers as well. (His house, which is still standing, is now number 1150.) The Song Fishermen were able to print their occasional broadsides on the Canadian Press mimeograph machine until the news agency ordered them to stop, about 1930. (See also GRANVILLE FERRY.)

Some of the other Song Fishermen were also Halifax residents. **Eliza Ritchie** (*Songs of the Maritimes*, 1931) had a house near the Northwest Arm. **Kenneth Leslie**, born in PICTOU, received his bachelor's degree from Dalhousie in 1912. He completed graduate studies in the United States, then married Elizabeth Moir, daughter of a prominent Halifax candy merchant, and lived in the city during the 1920s and 1930s. After publication of *By Stubborn Stars and Other Poems* (1938), winner of a Governor General's Award, he edited a radical political magazine in New York but returned to Halifax in 1949, having been branded a communist by Senator Joseph McCarthy. After his return, Leslie edited *New Man*, a Christian socialist magazine, and at various times worked as a Baptist lay preacher, teacher, and taxi driver. In the 1960s he lived at 6454 Almon St; in 1969 he moved to his last home, 1074 Wellington St. Leslie edited a selection from his various collections of poetry, *O'Malley to the Reds and Other Poems* (1972), before he died in 1974. (See also ANTIGONISH.)

Charles Bruce, a native of PORT SHOREHAM and well known for his poems and fiction about the Channel Shore district of Nova Scotia, was one of the most active members of the Song Fishermen. After graduating from Mount Allison University and publishing his first collection of poems, *Wild Apples*, in 1927, Bruce came to Halifax to work for the Canadian Press under Merkel; by 1945 he had risen to become General Superintendent of the agency at TORONTO (7). He lived first at 105 Granville St and afterwards at 282 Tower Rd; he was at the latter address when he published his second book, *Tomorrow's Tide* (1932). Charles Bruce's son, **Harry Bruce**—a well-known journalist and author of *The Short Happy Walks of Max MacPherson* (1968), *Lifeline* (1977), and *Each Moment As It Flies* (1985), among other books—lives on LeMarchant Street. **Joe Wallace**, the communist versifier (*The Golden Legend*, Moscow, 1958), was a native of Pictou but spent many years in Halifax. Before joining the Communist Party in 1921, Wallace founded an advertising agency in Halifax. Around the time of the First World War he lived at 294 North St and in 1919 moved both his home and his agency to Jollimore, a suburb on the south shore of the Northwest Arm. Wallace, who died in 1975, spent much of his last fifty-five years as a wandering proselytizer for communist views. (During the Second World War he was interned at Petawawa, Ont.) Another writer associated briefly with Halifax was **Ernest Buckler**, who received his bachelor's degree from Dalhousie University in 1928 (one year before Hugh MacLennan). His fiction dates from the 1950s and 1960s, when he was living at CENTRELEA.

The most disastrous event in the city's history, the Halifax Explosion—caused by the collision of the Norwegian freighter *Imo* with the French munitions ship *Mont Blanc* in Bedford Basin in December 1917—is the subject of a classic Canadian novel, *Barometer Rising* (1941), by **Hugh MacLennan**. Born in GLACE BAY, Cape Breton Island, MacLennan came to Halifax with his family in September 1915 and lived here until 1929, when he graduated from Dalhousie and went to Oxford University on a Rhodes Scholarship. (His only other period of residence in Halifax was a brief one in 1932, when he applied unsuccessfully for a teaching position at Dalhousie.) MacLennan's family first lived in a house on Morris St. By 1917, after several changes of residence, the MacLennans were established at 197 S. Park St, where they remained until 1927. This house, now 1583 S. Park St, is occupied by a beauty salon and is owned by CBC Halifax, which is

The boyhood home of Hugh MacLennan, Halifax

next door. MacLennan attended a Halifax grammar school, Tower Road School, and during the explosion was one of many children spared serious injury from flying glass in school buildings because Halifax schools

HALIFAX

An old man who a few hours before had left his wife and two beautiful daughters in their comfortable cottage in the destroyed area and had gone into the south end of the city on business, returned to find only the smoking ruins of his happy home, and after long effort recovered all that was left of his wife and daughters, the charred remnants of those he had parted from a few hours before.... Seeking in vain in the destroyed region for any receptacle for the remains he finally found ... an old sack ... He nearly filled it with all that was left and staggering under the weight of his burden and his sorrow ... he marched off, like Atlas of old, doomed to carry the load the fates had imposed.

—Archibald MacMechan, FRSC, director, Halifax Disaster Record Office, report on the Halifax Explosion, 1917

The aftermath of the Halifax Explosion, December 1917

did not begin in those days until 9:30 a.m. When the explosion occurred a few minutes after 9 a.m., MacLennan was at home in the bathroom, where his mother had sent him to wash his knees before leaving for school. MacLennan's childhood experience of this grim event became the inspiration of *Barometer Rising*. (See also MONTREAL: 6, NORTH HATLEY, Que.)

MacLennan attended Halifax County Academy after grammar school. Another graduate of this now-defunct high school was the novelist **Evelyn M. Richardson**, who attended from 1917 until 1920 and later (like Marshall Saunders and L.M. Montgomery) spent a single year at Dalhousie University. In 1926 she returned permanently to her native region, the Cape Sable area of coastal southwestern Nova Scotia, where she wrote her novels and the popular *We Keep a Light* (1945). (See also EMERALD ISLE, BON PORTAGE ISLAND, BARRINGTON.)

> HALIFAX
>
> *One clear, cold December morning, while the boys were playing on the packed ashes about the school, and the first fight of the day was brewing, there was a roar past all hearing, and we saw the windows of the school burst inward and the trees toss, and a teacher stagger out the front door with blood streaming from her face.*
>
> —Hugh MacLennan, 'Portrait of a City', *Cross-Country* (1949)

Two prominent regional and historical novelists, **Will R. Bird** and **Thomas Raddall**, have been residents of Halifax. Bird, who was born in East Mapleton, near Amherst, in 1891—is known for his novels of Yorkshire settlers in the Chignecto region. His works include a trilogy of novels: *Here Stays Good Yorkshire* (1945), *Tristram's Salvation* (1957), and *Despite the Distance* (1961). His papers are in the Dalhousie University Library. Bird lives on Marlborough Avenue. Raddall, a three-time Governor General's Award winner for his fiction and non-fiction, was born in 1903 in England and brought to Halifax in 1913. The family lived in a small wooden house on Chebucto Rd, near Chebucto School, which Raddall attended. On the day of the Halifax Explosion the school was used as a temporary morgue. His family's house was damaged by the blast and a piece of a ship's davit from the *Mont Blanc* was found on the roof. Too poor to attend university, Raddall in 1918 enrolled in the Canadian School of Telegraphy, which was on Prince St. This training enabled him to embark on an adventurous life of many occupations, most of them associated with seafaring. By 1920 he was able to buy his mother a house on Duncan St. but in 1923, after a year spent in Halifax, he went to Milton and soon established his own home nearby at LIVERPOOL, where he still lives. Raddall is often in Halifax, however; a close friend of Andrew Merkel and other Halifax writers, he used the city as a base from which to establish his career as a professional writer after the Second World War. His popular novels include *His Majesty's Yankee* (1942) and *The Nymph and the Lamp* (1950). He won Governor General's Awards for his first collection of short stories, *The Pied Piper of Dipper Creek and Other Stories* (1939); for his spirited chronicle of his hometown, *Halifax, Warden of the North* (1948; rev. 1965); and for a popular history, *The Path of Destiny: Canada from the British Conquest to Home Rule, 1763–1850* (1957).

Ray Smith, born in Inverness, Cape Breton Island in 1941, received his bachelor's degree from Dalhousie University in 1963. Since then he has lived mainly in MONTREAL (8), but his best-known book, *Lord Nelson Tavern* (1974), is a group of linked stories about university friends—patrons of the tavern of the Lord Nelson Hotel at the corner of Spring Garden Rd and S Park St—who continue to affect each other's lives as the years pass. The noted science-fiction writer **Spider Robinson**, who was born in the United States in 1948, has lived in Nova Scotia since 1974, settling in 1981 in Halifax, where he lives on Henry St. His books include *Antinomy* (1980) and *Melancholy Elephants* (1984); he is a three-time winner of the Hugo Award.

Dr **Arthur Lister Murphy**, for many years chief surgeon at Victoria General Hospital, was also a playwright. A winner of the Canadian Drama Award (1962), he was playwright-in-residence at Dalhousie University in 1977–8 and often supplied television plays to the CBC and to U.S. networks. He is the author of *Three Bluenose Plays* (1984). Until his death in 1985, Murphy lived on Tupper Grove, in the Victorian mansion of Sir Charles Tupper. Now this house is the home of **Marjory Whitelaw**, editor of the *Journals of Lord Dalhousie* (1983) and of *Letters from Nova Scotia* (1986), an anthology of early travel writing about the province.

'The Bower', which stands on spacious grounds at 5918 Rogers St, is one of the oldest houses in Halifax and was the childhood home of the former diplomat and popular diarist **Charles Ritchie** (*The Siren Years: A Canadian Diplomat Abroad*, 1974, and other volumes) of OTTAWA. (See also CHESTER.) The house was built by John Halliburton, a United Empire Loyalist who emigrated from Rhode Island, as a summer home for his family. It was later the home of his son, Sir Brenton Halliburton, who is primarily known as Chief Justice of Nova Scotia (1833–60) but who was also a writer. His works included *Observations on the Importance of the North American Colonies to Great Britain* (1825) and *Reflections on Passing Events: A Poem* (1856).

The childhood home of Charles Ritchie, Halifax

Robert Norwood

HUBBARDS

The poet **Robert Norwood** grew up in the rectory (now demolished) of the Anglican church at Hubbards, where his father was the rector. Also an Anglican clergyman, Robert Norwood served, from 1917 until his death in 1932, in Philadelphia and in New York, where he became known as an eloquent preacher; but he summered at Hubbards, where he did much of his writing. Norwood's works written in whole or in part at Hubbards include at least six volumes of poetry and six prose works on religious themes. Important among them are a collection of lyrics, *Mother and Son* (1925), and *Issa* (1931), a long meditative poem about Jesus. Norwood died suddenly in 1932 in New York just after returning from Hubbards. It is on the South Shore of Nova Scotia, on Highway 3 west of Halifax. (See also NEW ROSS.)

LIVERPOOL

The house of **Simeon Perkins**, famous as a diarist of Nova Scotia in the late eighteenth and early nineteenth centuries, is maintained here as a historic site by the Nova Scotia Museum; it is located off Highway 103. A Connecticut merchant, Perkins settled in Liverpool in 1763 and built his house in 1766. He kept his diary from that year until the War of 1812, providing a detailed record of life in colonial Liverpool over a period of half a century. Among the exciting events Perkins records are his leading role in the defence of the southern Nova Scotia coast against American privateers during the Revolution, in the organization of retaliatory raids, and in the successful battle against a group of invading Americans from Salem, Mass., in 1780. The diary, which also notes visits to Liverpool by the poet and preacher Henry Alline of FALMOUTH, was lost for many years but was discovered in 1897 in Liverpool and is now held in a bank vault; a typewritten copy, bound in several volumes, is on display in the house. *The Diary of Simeon Perkins: 1766–90* was published in three volumes by the Champlain Society in 1948–61. **Thomas Raddall** of HALIFAX—who now lives in Liverpool at 44 Park St—drew freely upon the diary in writing his novel *His Majesty's Yankee* (1942).

> LIVERPOOL
>
> *1769 Friday, June 16th,—Arrive at Liverpool, all well. No death, except the wife of Thomas Bee. Find the people employed in fishing, building, and lumbering. Capt. Wilson of White Haven, England, is building a ship of 250 tons. Stephen Collins is building a schooner of 30 odd tons. I think the place is improving.*
>
> —Simeon Perkins, *The Diary of Simeon Perkins: 1766–1790*

The early Nova Scotia poet **John McPherson** was born in Liverpool in 1817 and spent most of his brief, difficult life in the nearby farming district of North Brookfield, where in childhood he went to live with an uncle after his parents died. McPherson's abilities were recognized there by a young schoolteacher and poet, Angus Gidney, who in the late 1830s became an editor in Halifax and introduced McPherson to the city's literary life. Unable to support himself in Halifax, McPherson returned to North Brookfield, where he taught and contributed poetry to many periodicals. He died in his uncle's home on 26 July 1845; his poems were published posthumously in *Poems, Descriptive and Moral by John McPherson* (Halifax, 1862).

A distinguished literary native of Liverpool (who grew up in LOCKEPORT) is the poet and editor **John Sutherland**, who was born here on 21 Feb. 1919. After his mother died, Sutherland and his sister went to live with their grandparents at Lockeport, where he spent much of his childhood and where he is buried. Sutherland's literary activity occurred primarily in MONTREAL (5), where in 1942 he dropped out of McGill University to found *First Settlement* magazine and press.

LOCKEPORT

Born in LIVERPOOL, the poet and editor **John Sutherland** spent much of his childhood here. He and his sister came here, after his mother died, to live with their grandparents, whose large house on Crest St is now the Harbour View Rest Home. Later Sutherland lived with his father in SAINT JOHN, N.B., and studied at Queen's University in Kingston, Ont., and McGill University in MONTREAL (5). Although he did not graduate, he settled in Montreal, where he founded and directed the influential magazines *First Statement* (1942–5) and *Northern Review* (1946–56). Lockeport is on the southwestern coast of Nova Scotia.

The Simeon Perkins house, Liverpool

The King's Bastion, Louisbourg

LOUISBOURG

In 1760 Commodore 'Foul Weather' Jack Byron, grandfather of Lord Byron, was in charge of demolishing the huge French fortress and town of Louisbourg so that the installation, which had been captured by New Englanders in 1758, could never again be recaptured and used by France. Byron performed his task so thoroughly that the site was nothing more than a grassy knoll and a stone quarry for two hundred years, until the restoration of Louisbourg was begun in 1961. It was the largest archaeological reconstruction ever undertaken and is now the centre of the twenty-square-mile Louisbourg National Historic Park.

Nérée Beauchemin's poem 'Le cloche de Louisbourg' kept the memory of the great fortress alive in French Canada during the nineteenth century. The bell, saved from the destruction and taken to Halifax, was later acquired by Montrealers and placed in the Musée du Château de Ramezay. (See YAMACHICHE, Que.)

Louisbourg has fascinated English-language authors. The early Maritime novelist and poet **William Charles M'Kinnon**, who was born near North Sydney in 1828, made Louisbourg at the time of General James Wolfe's successful 1758 seige the setting of his novel *St Castine* (1850). **James De Mille's** novel *The Lily and the Cross; a Tale of Acadia* (1874) relates the rescue of a Frenchwoman from Louisbourg at the time of the fighting; it is the only novel that De Mille, a native of SAINT JOHN, N.B., set in the Maritimes. (See also HALIFAX, WOLFVILLE.) More recently the novelist **Thomas Raddall**, primarily associated with HALIFAX, made the Seven Years' War in North America, and the events culminating in the capture of Louisbourg, the subject of his novel *Roger Sudden* (1944). **Jack Grey's** play *Chevalier Johnston* (1964) portrays French attempts to defend the fortress, and **Christopher Moore's** *Louisbourg Portraits* (1982; winner of a Governor General's Award) recreates the daily life of the fortress through biographies of people who lived there.

MILTON

This village, just north of LIVERPOOL on the Mersey River, was the birthplace in 1861 of **Marshall Saunders**, author of the famous 'autobiography' of a dog, *Beautiful Joe* (1894), and other novels, many of them about animals. Saunders was the daughter of E.M. Saunders, Baptist minister of Milton and an eminent clergyman who moved his family to HALIFAX in 1867; she was educated in that city. A plaque on the Masonic Hall in Milton commemorates the author's birth here. (See also MEAFORD, TORONTO: 6, Ont.)

NEW GLASGOW

The lyric poet **George Frederick Cameron**, whose verse was published posthumously in *Lyrics of Freedom, Love and Death* (1887), was born in 1854 in this town on the East River, south of Pictou Harbour. Little is known of Cameron; the volume's brief preface, written by the poet's brother Charles, states that 'the author of the following poems, the eldest son of James Grant Cameron and Jessie Sutherland, was born in New Glasgow, Nova Scotia, September 24th, 1854. He received his preliminary education at the High School of his native town, and had read the greater part of Virgil and Cicero in the original before his fourteenth year. Even at this age he employed most of his spare time in poetry.' The Cameron family moved to Boston, Mass., in 1869, where George Frederick studied and later practised law and contributed poems to periodicals. In 1882 he returned to Canada and entered Queen's University in KINGSTON, Ont., where he studied and worked as a journalist until his death in 1885. *Lyrics of Freedom*, edited by Charles Cameron, appeared in Boston two years later. Charles stated that its 296 pages represented only a quarter of his brother's poetic production; the rest has never been found.

NEW ROSS

New Ross was the birthplace in 1874 of **Robert Norwood**; his father was serving here as the Anglican rector. Norwood grew up mainly in HUBBARDS and attended King's College, WINDSOR, where his poetry earned the praise and encouragement of Charles G.D. Roberts. An Anglican clergyman as well as a writer, Norwood served mainly in New York City but summered in Hubbards.

PICTOU

The Rev. **Thomas McCulloch**, author of *Letters of Mephibosheth Stepsure*, came to Pictou with his family in Nov. 1803. A learned Presbyterian minister with medical training, McCulloch was on his way to serve a congregation in Prince Edward Island, but members of the pioneer lumbering and shipbuilding community of Pictou wanted him to stay here; they convinced him that a late-season voyage to Prince Edward Island should be avoided and by the following spring had persuaded him to become pastor of a local Presbyterian congregation. In 1806 McCulloch used bricks from Scotland to build his Sherbrooke Cottage; now called McCulloch House, it is part of the Nova Scotia Museum Complex and is located at Pictou off Highway 106. Here McCulloch wrote *Letters of Mephibosheth Stepsure*, which appeared in the *Acadian Recorder* in HALIFAX between 22 Dec. 1821 and 11 May 1822, and in Jan. and Mar. 1823. The first of these two series appeared in book form in 1862, nineteen years after McCulloch's death; both series have been reprinted as *The Stepsure Letters* (New Canadian Library, 1960). Written in the voice of an imaginary lame Nova Scotia farmer, these humorous moral and political essays—good-natured, yet often iconoclastic—influenced the Sam Slick Writings of Thomas Chandler Haliburton (see WINDSOR). McCulloch's other works, all written at Pictou, include books on liberal education and Calvinist theology and *Colonial Gleanings: William and Melville* (1826), which contains two moral tales aimed at encouraging hard work in Nova Scotia immigrants.

As early as 1805 McCulloch had envisaged a non-sectarian institution of higher learning for Nova Scotia but was opposed by the Council of the Provincial Legislature, which favoured King's College (founded in 1790) in Halifax, where degrees were granted only to those who subscribed to the articles of the Church of England. Finally, in 1816, Pictou Academy was incorporated—the word 'college' could not be used because the province would not give degree-granting powers. Throughout the nineteenth and early twentieth centuries the academy was an educational force in the province. One of its graduates was **Frank Parker Day**, a native of SHUBENACADIE, whose novels of Nova Scotia include *Rockbound* (1928; rpr. 1973) and *John Paul's Rock* (1932). (See also YARMOUTH.)

Pictou was the childhood home of the novelist **Albert Hickman**, who was born in 1877 in Dorchester, N.B.; after graduating from Harvard University in 1899 he lived in SAINT JOHN, N.B., until the First World War ended and he moved his marine engineering firm to the United States. His novel *The Sacrifice of Shannon* (1903) was based on his experience of the yachting activities of Pictou's well-to-do residents and his own knowledge of shipyards and shipbuilders. A pioneer in speedboat technology, Hickman developed his work early in the century from experiments conducted at Pictou. His *Canadian Nights* (1914) contains stories set here.

Pictou Academy, Pictou

The Thomas McCulloch house, Pictou

The poet **Kenneth Leslie** was born in Pictou on 1 Nov. 1892. Winner of a Governor General's Award for *By Stubborn Stars and Other Poems* (1938), Leslie is primarily associated with HALIFAX, but his best poetry concerns Nova Scotia fishing and farming people and the seascapes and coastal landscapes he knew from his childhood here. His family home still stands at 16 Willow Street.

PLEASANT BAY

Near this seaside Cape Breton village on the Cabot Trail is a monument to the 'Canadian Boat Song', one of Canada's most famous nineteenth-century poems, which proudly recalls the Scots Highland heritage of many of the country's early settlers. About four miles east of Pleasant Bay, along the Cabot Trail, stands the Lone Shieling—a stone replica of the type of hut used by Highland crofters tending sheep in the Scottish hills—with a plaque bearing the best-known stanza, including the line from which the 'Canadian Boat Song' takes its more familiar subtitle, 'The Lone Shieling':

From the lone shieling of the misty island
Mountains divide us, and the waste of seas—
Yet still the blood is strong, the heart is highland,
And we in dreams behold the Hebrides.

This poem, which was published anonymously in 1829 in Scotland in *Blackwoods Magazine* (and was included in the first *Oxford Book of English Verse*, edited by Quiller-Couch), should not be confused with 'A Canadian Boat Song' by the Irish poet Thomas Moore (see STE-ANNE-DE-BELLEVUE, Que.). 'The Lone Shieling' has been attributed to the Scottish novelist John Galt (see CAMBRIDGE, Ont.); to Galt's associate, William ('Tiger') Dunlop (see GODERICH, Ont.); and to David Macbeth Moir of Musselburgh, Scot., who is said to have drawn his inspiration and information for the poem from Galt's writings on Canada.

PORT ROYAL

Modern Port Royal (formerly Lower Granville), on the north shore of the Annapolis Basin, is named after the first successful European settlement in North America—and, incidentally, is the birthplace of drama and poetry in what is now Canada. Port Royal National Historic Park contains a reconstruction of the *Habitation*—the original Port Royal—built in 1605 (three years before the founding of Quebec) by Samuel de Champlain, the Sieur de Monts, and the Sieur de Poutrincourt. At Poutrincourt's invitation Marc Lescarbot (*c.* 1570–1642), a

> *We spent this winter very pleasantly, and had good fare by means of the Order of Good Cheer, which . . . consisted of a chain which we used to place with certain little ceremony about the neck of one of our people, commissioning him for that day to go hunting. The next day it was conferred upon another, and so on in order. All vied with each other to see who could do the best, and bring back the finest game. We did not come off badly, nor did the Indians who were with us.*
> —Samuel de Champlain, *Voyages* (1613)

A reconstruction of the Habitation, Port Royal

Parisian lawyer, spent the winter of 1606–7 at Port Royal and became the poet, dramatist, and historian of New France's earliest years, in what was called Acadie (Acadia). On 25 Aug. 1606 he addressed a long poem of farewell to the members of Poutrincourt's second expedition who were returning to France and leaving Lescarbot among the party that was to winter at the fort. Almost certainly the first poem in a European language written north of the Mexican frontier, it was translated by F.R. Scott as 'Farewell to the Frenchmen Returning from New France to Gallic France' in his *Poems of French Canada* (1977). Lescarbot's Acadian poems—including the masque 'Le Théâtre de Neptune', whose performance at Port Royal on 14 Nov. 1606, partly on the shore and partly in the water, was the first theatrical presentation in North America—were published in *Les Muses de la Nouvelle France* (Paris, 1609). Lescarbot's writings also include his important *Histoire de la Nouvelle France* (1609, 1611–12, 1617–18), which contains his own version of French exploration from 1604 to 1615 and a collection of earlier French accounts of voyages to the New World. Lescarbot, along with Nicholas Denys (see BATHURST, COCAGNE, N.B.), is chiefly responsible for creating the myth—persistent in subsequent literature—of Acadia as a God-given land of plenty, the site of a new Golden Age to be created by the flowering of French culture in the virgin territory. Passed down through Thomas Chandler Haliburton, this idea found literary expression in Longfellow's *Evangeline: a Tale of Acadie* (1847; see WINDSOR, GRAND-PRÉ).

PORT ROYAL

M. de Poutrincourt reached Port Royal on November 14th 1607, where we received him joyously and with a ceremony absolutely new on this side of the ocean. . . . I bethought me to go out to meet him with some jovial spectacle, and so we did. And since it was written in French rhymes, made hastily, I have placed it among the Muses of New France, *under the title of "Neptune's Theatre", to which I refer the reader.*

—Marc Lescarbot, *The History of New France* (1617–18)

Samuel de Champlain wrote of Port Royal in the first volume of his *Voyages* (1613), which covers his voyages from 1604 to 1612, the year before the English destroyed the first Port Royal (see ANNAPOLIS ROYAL). Champlain describes (as does Lescarbot) the Ordre de Bon Temps (Order of Good Cheer), which he established during the winter of 1606–7. (See also QUEBEC CITY, Que.)

PORT SHOREHAM

Charles Bruce was born on 11 May 1906 in the fishing hamlet of Port Shoreham on the north shore of Chedabucto Bay. Although there is no longer a community here, Port Shoreham still appears on Nova Scotia maps. It was 6 miles east of Boyleston on Highway 344 and lay on the shore south of the road. Charles Bruce's family house is still standing: it is just south of the road, on the slope overlooking the site of Port Shoreham. The house is now owned and used in the summer by Charles Bruce's son **Harry Bruce**, who is also a writer. It can be pointed out by local residents.

Charles Bruce spent his childhood and adolescence at Port Shoreham, attending high school at Guysborough Academy in nearby Guysborough, the county seat. In 1923 he went to SACKVILLE, N.B., to attend Mount Allison University; while there he wrote his first book of poems, *Wild Apples* (1927). Upon graduating in 1927 Bruce worked for the Canada Press in HALIFAX and overseas before becoming the news agency's general superintendent in 1945; thereafter he lived mainly in TORONTO (7), Ont. All Bruce's poetry and fiction portrays the landscape and people of the Channel Shore— the part of mainland Nova Scotia near the Strait of Canso. His best-known book of verse, *The Mulgrave Road* (1955), which won a Governor General's Award, takes its name from the town of Mulgrave and the road running through it along the east side of the Strait of Canso, just north of Port Shoreham. Though Bruce evokes the local farming tradition, the life of the fishermen and their families inspires his most vivid descriptions. Bruce also wrote *The Channel Shore* (1954), a chronicle novel tracing three generations in the history of a South Shore Nova Scotia family, and *The Township of Time* (1959), a group of interrelated short stories set along the Channel Shore and spanning the period 1786–1950.

RIVER BOURGEOIS

Since 1975 **Farley Mowat** has made his summer home at 'The Brickery' on a secluded 150-acre farm near this Cape Breton Island hamlet on St Peters Bay. Here he wrote his widely acclaimed reminiscence of the Second World War, *And No Birds Sang* (1979). At the River Bourgeois Museum is Mowat's schooner, *Happy Adventure*, which he describes as his 'sometime residence 1953–1963'. Aboard this boat Mowat took a trip from Newfoundland to Expo '67 in Mon-

The house at Port Shoreham where Charles Bruce grew up

treal, described in *The Boat Who Wouldn't Float* (1968), which won a Stephen Leacock Medal for Humour. (See also BURGEO, Nfld.; PORT HOPE, Ont.)

RIVER JOHN

The folklorist **William Roy Mackenzie** was born on 14 Feb. 1883 in this Pictou County community and spent his childhood here. In 1902 he graduated from Dalhousie University, Halifax, and continued his education in the United States. He was the earliest important scientific collector of oral folk literature in Canada, gathering and preserving songs throughout his native province. His books, published while he was living in the United States, include *The Quest of the Ballad* (1919) and *Ballads and Sea Songs from Nova Scotia* (1928). Mackenzie returned to Nova Scotia in 1952, spending summers in River John and winters in Halifax until his death in 1957.

SABLE ISLAND

Lying 190 miles east of Halifax, Sable Island has for centuries been a threat to Atlantic shipping owing to its shoals and the currents and storms off the island. A colony was attempted in 1598, but five years later only eleven of the fifty original settlers were still alive; they were removed from the island. **Joseph-Charles Taché**, who was both a politician and a student of folklore, collected stories of ghosts and failed expeditions in *Les Sablons (L'Île de Sable et l'Île Saint-Barnabé)*, 1885. (See also KAMOURASKA, Que.)

The novelist **Thomas H. Raddall** served as a telegrapher on Sable Island from 2 Apr. 1921 to 22 Apr. 1922, during which time he published stories based on island legends, including 'The Singing Frenchman'. Sable Island is also the setting for Raddall's contemporary novel *The Nymph and the Lamp* (1950), in which telegrapher Matt Carney returns to the island with a young woman from Halifax, only to drive her away when he discovers that he is going blind. (See HALIFAX.)

The Hungarian poet **Stephen Parmenius** (1541–83), who wrote in Latin, accompanied Sir Humphrey Gilbert to Newfoundland and was drowned when Gilbert's ship went down with all hands in a storm off Sable Island on the return voyage to England. Parmenius' life, his writings from Newfoundland, and some other work are available in English in *The New Found Land of Stephen Parmenius* (1972), edited and translated by David Quinn and Neil Cheshire. (See ST JOHN'S, Nfld.)

ST ANNS

This Nova Scotia centre of Highland Gaelic culture was the home of **Angus McAskill**, the Cape Breton Giant, who enters literary history through the curious book *Angus McAskill—The Cape Breton Giant: A Truthful Memoir* (1899) by the versifier **James P. Gillis**. McAskill, who was 7 feet 9 inches tall and weighed over 400 pounds, operated a mill in St Anns and died here in 1863 at thirty-eight; he is buried in nearby Englishtown. The Giant McAskill–Highland Pioneers Museum in St Anns displays belongings of its most famous resident.

Gillis, one of the great eccentrics of Canadian letters, wrote songs and doggerel verse in both English and Gaelic; Gillis's story is told in William Arthur Deacon's mock-critical book on four poetasters, *The Four Jameses* (1927; rev. ed. 1953; rpr. 1974). Gillis lived for many years in a house on Mount Young overlooking Lake Ainslie, east of St Anns. Born at either Strathlorne or Broad Cover Intervale, he was raised by an uncle at Upper Margaree. From 1888 to 1904 he taught in Nova Scotia schools and was at Kiltarlity School in 1899 when his McAskill biography appeared. After a few years of wandering, during which he attended Truro Normal School and Dalhousie University and worked as a watchman at Simpson's in Regina, Sask., he settled in the St Anns area, where he was often visited by other regional writers (Robert Norwood, Thomas Raddall, and Helen Creighton, among others).

SHELBURNE

Cape Breton-born novelist **William Charles M'Kinnon** died in 1862 while serving as a minister on the Methodist circuit at Shelburne. He was thirty-four and had begun his writing career in 1848 with a book of poems, *The Battle of the Nile*. After several journalistic ventures in Nova Scotia and the United States, he began to publish historical novels with Nova Scotia backgrounds, including *St. Castine* (1850), set at LOUISBOURG. Disappointed by the financial failure of his novels, M'Kinnon entered the Methodist ministry in 1854 and in his last years wrote only theological works.

The Loyalist poet **Joseph Stansbury** lived in Shelburne immediately after the American Revolution, from 1783 to 1785. A native of England, Stansbury was operating a successful china shop in Philadelphia when agitation for revolution began. He supported the English cause against American independence, acting as Benedict Arnold's go-between with British Army headquarters. After the war he tried life in Shelburne but left after two years of hardship. His poem 'To Cordelia' expresses his disappointment at life in Nova Scotia; he died in New York in 1809. His poems are collected in *The Loyal Verses of Joseph Stansbury and Dr. Jonathan Odell* (1860).

Novelist **Hugh Hood**, of MONTREAL (6), took Shelburne as the model for the Nova Scotia town of Barringford in his novel *White Figure, White Ground* (1964). Hood's grandfather was the first mayor of Shelburne, taking office in 1907. (See also TORONTO: 5, Ont.)

SHUBENACADIE

The novelist **Frank Parker Day** was born in 1881 in this village southwest of Truro and spent his childhood here before attending Pictou Academy, Mount Allison University, Oxford University, and the University of Berlin. Although Day did not begin his writing career until the 1920s, when he was teaching at American universities, most of his books are based on his knowledge of the land and people of his native province. His work includes *Autobiography of a Fisherman* (1927) and two novels of Nova Scotia: *Rockbound* (1928; rpr. 1973) and *John Paul's Rock* (1932). (See also YARMOUTH.)

Alden Nowlan spent his youth (until age 14) in this house at Stanley

STANLEY

Alden Nowlan was born in this tiny rural settlement in 1933; the place is now merely a rural route (see WINDSOR). He attended a local school through grade five, the end of his formal education. He lived in Stanley during the 1930s and 1940s and renamed it Ketepaska Creek in his autobiographical sketch 'Growing Up in Ketepaska Creek: a Retrospective'. Stanley is 12½ miles northeast of Windsor on the Kennetcook River. Nowlan's childhood home is still standing. A very simple house, now painted green, it is on the south side of Highway 236 about one mile west of Stanley.

STELLARTON

There is a national historic plaque in Stellarton to **George Monro Grant**, who was born in the tiny settlement of Albion Mines on 22 Dec. 1835. This community sprang up when a mine was established in the early nineteenth century about 2 miles south of the village of New Glasgow; Albion Mines no longer exists; its site is occupied by Stellarton. Grant was the son of James Grant, a teacher, who came from Banffshire, Scotland, to Nova Scotia in 1826 and obtained work in Albion Mines. Educated at Pictou Academy and Glasgow University, George Monro Grant became a prominent man of letters and principal of Queen's University. He was the author of the travel classic *Ocean to Ocean* (1873), an account of his experiences as secretary to Sandford Fleming's exploratory trip from the Great Lakes to the Pacific in search of a route for a transcontinental railway. Grant was the literary editor of *Picturesque Canada* (1882–4), for which he wrote several of the historical and descriptive chapters on Canadian western regions. He was the grandfather of the philosopher George Grant. (See HALIFAX; KINGSTON, Ont.)

UPPER CLEMENTS

The Newfoundland-born writer **Harold Horwood** lives in this village, which is near Annapolis Royal. Since moving here in 1978 he has published a selection of short stories, *Only the Gods Speak* (1979), and *Tales of the Labrador Indians* (1981) among other books. Horwood and his wife designed both the solar house in which they live and its extensive grounds. (See also BEACHY COVE, ST. JOHN'S, Nfld.)

WESTPORT

This village on Brier Island, at the extreme western end of St Mary's Bay, was the childhood home of **Joshua Slocum**, author of *Sailing Alone Around the World* (1900), a classic of travel and adventure writing. The book recounts Slocum's voyage of April 1895–June 1898, which began and ended at Newport, R.I., where he then lived. Born in Annapolis County in 1844, Slocum lived in Westport until he was sixteen. He became a renowned captain of sailing vessels and undertook his adventure when the decline of sail put him out of work. He accomplished the journey in an oyster sloop, the *Spray*, which he himself had converted for his purposes. A decade after his successful circumnavigation of the globe Slocum was lost at sea in his ship. He is memorialized by a plaque in Westport.

WINDSOR

This historic shipping town, at the junction of the St Croix and Avon rivers on an arm of Minas Basin, is the birthplace of Canada's first internationally known literary figure,

'The Residence of Judge Haliburton', Windsor. Engraving, 1842, after a sketch by W.H. Bartlett, *c.*1838

Thomas Chandler Haliburton. The son of a local judge, Haliburton was born on 17 Dec. 1796; the family house, in which his father was also born, had been floated down-river to Windsor from Red Bank, N.S. Haliburton attended the Windsor grammar school and King's College, both of which were then housed in the same building. He left Windsor in 1820 to practise law in Annapolis Royal but returned in 1829 to succeed his father as judge of the Inferior Court of Common Pleas. This ended an eventful period during which he represented Annapolis Royal in the Provincial Assembly and frequented his friend Joseph Howe's literary group, The Club, in HALIFAX; but it marked the beginning of his active career as a humorist. In 1841 he became a member of the Supreme Court of Nova Scotia. Windsor remained Haliburton's home until 1856, when he moved to England.

Construction began in 1834 on 'Clifton', the fifteen-room house Haliburton built in Windsor on a site overlooking the Avon River. Here he wrote the first stories about Sam Slick, the moralizing Yankee clock pedlar whose appearance in *The Clockmaker* (1836) brought the author enormous popularity in Canada, Britain, and the United States. With its surrounding landscaped gardens planned by Haliburton and his wife Louisa, 'Clifton' was a renowned social centre frequented by Joseph Howe and other Nova Scotia luminaries. Visited in 1836 by the American poet and journalist Nathaniel Parker Willis (1806–1867) and the English artist-author William Henry Bartlett (1809–1854), it was described, with an accompanying engraving, in their *Canadian Scenery Illustrated* (1842).

Today 'Clifton' is the Haliburton Memorial Museum. Surrounded still by its lovely grounds, it stands on Clifton Avenue and is furnished with period pieces and artifacts from the 1830s and 1840s. The Nova Scotia government acquired the property in 1939 after it had been occupied by several private owners, one of whom added to the library a fireplace constructed with stones from the original French fortification at LOUISBOURG. Haliburton's desk is on display, along with a Sam Slick clock and many Sam Slick cartoons illustrating the sayings Haliburton

The Haliburton house today

coined for his character, including 'stick in the mud', 'jack of all trades and master of none', 'upper crust ', and 'six of one, half a dozen of another'. Virtually all of Haliburton's literary output belongs to this time and includes two more collections of Slick sketches, *The Clockmaker* (1838 and 1840); *The Attaché; or, Sam Slick in England* (1843); *The Old Judge; or, Life in a Colony* (1849); and several other creative, political, and historical works. Clifton is open from 15 May to 15 Oct. (9:30 a.m. to 5:30 p.m.).

King's College, founded in 1788, was the first English-language institution of higher learning in what is now Canada; in 1885 it hired the New Brunswick poet and nature writer **Charles G.D. Roberts** as Professor of English and French, and later of English and Economics. Roberts continued at the school until 1895 and lived at 'Kingscroft', a house (still standing) on the edge of the college forest. He had already published his first book, *Orion, and Other Poems* (1880), but much of his best poetry was written during his decade at 'Kingscroft' and appeared in *In Divers Tones* (1886) and *Songs of the Common Day* (1893). Roberts drew on his knowledge of the Windsor area in other works, including two novels of the Acadian Expulsion (see GRAND PRÉ) and the novel *By the Marshes of Minas* (1900). (See also DOUGLAS, FREDERICTON, SACKVILLE, N.B.; TORONTO: 1, Ont.)

While he was at King's, Roberts was visited at 'Kingscroft' by his cousin **Bliss Carman**. It was on the first of these visits, in 1886, that Carman became acquainted with nearby GRAND PRÉ and had the mystical experience recorded in his best poem, 'Low Tide on Grand Pré', which he wrote in Windsor. It became the title poem in a poetry collection that was published in New York in 1893. (See FREDERICTON, N.B.)

'Kingscroft', the house of Charles G.D. Roberts, Windsor

King's College graduates include the three most prominent of several clergyman writers of the Maritimes: Basil King, Hiram A. Cody, and the poet Robert Norwood. **Basil King** was educated here in the late 1870s and early 1880s; he left just before Roberts began to teach here. His writing career began in 1900 in Cambridge, Mass., where he had been an Anglican priest for eight years before failing eyesight forced him to retire. Nearly all his many novels concern wealthy eastern Americans in international plots of the type developed by Henry James and William Dean Howells, but this third novel, *In the Garden of Charity* (1903), portrays the lives of Nova Scotia fishermen and their families. (See also HALIFAX; CHARLOTTETOWN, P.E.I.) Just after Roberts' departure, **Hiram A. Cody**, the New Brunswick adventure novelist and exponent of 'muscular Christianity', was a student at King's for two or three years before he was ordained in 1898 as an Anglican priest. (See CODY'S, SAINT JOHN, N.B.). **Robert Norwood** was born in 1874 in NEW ROSS, 18 miles southwest of Windsor. He attended King's College in the 1890s and had Charles G.D. Roberts as a professor. Roberts encouraged his writing, and Norwood published his first volume, *Driftwood* (1898), as a result; it was a joint effort with his college roommate. Norwood was ordained in the Anglican Church in 1898, and after serving widely in Nova Scotia, Quebec, and Ontario, he went to New York City in 1917, where he became noted as an eloquent preacher; he continued to summer in Nova Scotia (see HUBBARDS). Norwood wrote many books expressing his liberal theology, several collections of verse (e.g., *His Lady of the Sonnets*, 1915; *Mother and Son*, 1925), and a number of dramatic, narrative, and reflective poems, notably *Issa* (1931), a long meditative work exploring his conception of Jesus. Norwood died in New York in 1932.

In 1887, during Roberts' professorship, King's College awarded the Akins Historical Award to **Mary Jane Katzmann**, a poet who was born in Preston and worked in Halifax, for her *History of the Townships of Dartmouth, Preston, and Lawrencetown* (1893).

Windsor was the birthplace of poet **Grizelda Tonge** (c. 1803–25), about whom little is known. Her early death—and an apparent premonition of it in her poem 'Lines Written at Midnight' (1825)—caused her to become for nineteenth-century Nova Scotia writers the epitome of the sensitive romantic poet cut off in youth. Joseph Howe contributed to her legend in his articles 'Western Rambles' (1828) and 'Nights with the Muses' (1845).

WINDSOR

The first of May gives new lodgers to new houses, and a simultaneous exchange of tenants takes place, while those who do not remove out of their tenements appear to abdicate nearly every room in them; for what is called the general 'house-cleaning' has commenced. Paint and white-wash brushes are busy everywhere; floors, ceilings, walls, and furniture, defiled by the smoke of a long winter, undergo a general purification, to the infinite fatigue of servants, and the unspeakable annoyance of the male part of the household, who are expelled by mops, brooms, and scrubbing-brushes from their homes.

—Thomas Chandler Haliburton, *The Old Judge; or, Life in a Colony* (1849)

WOLFVILLE

Many of Wolfville's literary associations cluster around Acadia University. Located on an attractive 250-acre campus in the centre of town, it was founded as a Baptist college in 1838. The university's Vaughan Memorial Library holds the sermons, journals, and other papers of **Henry Alline**, the FALMOUTH preacher and poet who was one of Canada's earliest literary figures and whose religious ideas attracted many followers who called themselves 'New Lights'.

The novelist **James De Mille**, born in 1833 in SAINT JOHN, N.B., was raised here and educated at Wolfville's Horton Academy and at Acadia College. In 1859 he married Elizabeth Ann Pryor, daughter of Acadia's first president, and taught classical languages and literatures at the college from 1860 to 1865; thereafter he was a professor at Dalhousie College in HALIFAX. Remembered chiefly for his posthumous utopian fantasy novel, *A Strange Manuscript Found in a Copper Cylinder* (1888; rpr. 1969), De Mille wrote almost all of his many popular novels in Halifax. The only novel likely to have been written in Wolfville was his first, *The Martyr of the Catacombs; a Tale of Ancient Rome* (1865). However, De Mille used the Wolfville area and his childhood experiences here in a series of juvenile novels—including *The 'B.O.W.C.'* (1869) and *The Boys of the Grand Pré School* (1870)—about a group of boys who called themselves the Brethren of the White Cross.

The poet and historian **Arthur Wentworth Hamilton Eaton** was born in 1849 in Kentville, about 5 miles southwest of Wolfville, and attended Acadia in the late

1860s. Although he completed his studies in the United States and spent most of his life as a clergyman and writer in Boston and New York, Eaton wrote many of his poems on Nova Scotia subjects and published several historical studies of his native province. He wrote four volumes of verse and a volume of selected poems, *Acadian Ballads and Lyrics in Many Moods* (1930); among his historical works is *History of King's County, Nova Scotia* (1910).

Wolfville's traditions of literature, scholarship, and Baptist theology were carried on by **Watson Kirkconnell** a poet, translator, and linguist in command of fifty languages, and a leading expert on the poetry of John Milton. President of the university from 1948 until 1964, Kirkconnell retired in Wolfville, although in 1966 he returned to the university to serve for two years as head of the English department. His books of poetry written here include *Centennial Tales and Selected Poems* (1965), *The Flavour of Nova Scotia* (1976), and *The Coronary Muse* (1977), which was composed in hospital and published in the year of his death. Kirkconnell produced many other works while living here, including anthologies of poetry he had translated from many languages, three volumes of source studies on Milton's major poems, and his autobiography, *A Slice of Canada* (1976). (See also PORT HOPE, Ont; WINNIPEG, Man.) During most of his years in Wolfville, Kirkconnell lived in the president's house at Acadia, a mansion in the Grecian Revival style dating from 1852; it stands at 362 Main St. When he retired as president, he moved to another historic house (still standing) at 101 Main St.

The President's house, Acadia University, Wolfville, where Watson Kirckconnell lived

The home of John Frederick Herbin, Wolfville

Wolfville was the home of the poet **John Frederick Herbin**, who was instrumental in the creation of Grand Pré National Historic Park at nearby GRAND PRÉ. Although an English-speaker, Herbin was a descendant of Acadians and was passionately interested in his heritage. Born near Wolfville, he lived for a short time in the United States but returned to his native region and settled in Wolfville, where he worked as a jeweller and optician. His jewellery store is still run by the Herbin family on Main St. His home, a Cape Cod cottage that was built in 1831, is at 89 Main St. Herbin was a tireless researcher into the traces of Acadian culture and history in the Wolfville area, and it was he who discovered many of the sites now preserved in Grand Pré National Historic Park. His works in verse and prose, including *Jess of the Marshes* (1921), largely concern the Acadians and the Grand Pré region. Herbin died at Grand Pré in 1923 while on one of his favourite walks through the historic sites he had identified.

The nineteenth-century novelist **Carrie Jenkins Harris** lived in Wolfville. She was the author of several works of fiction, including *Mr. Perkins of Nova Scotia; or The European Adventures of a Would-Be Aristocrat* (1891). Harris died in 1903. Wolfville has also been home to a historian of New Brunswick, **Esther Clark Wright** (*The St. John River and Its Tributaries*, 1966), and to the poet **Don Domanski** (*War in an Empty House*, 1982), who is a native of Sydney, N.S.

YARMOUTH

For many years the novelist **Frank Parker Day** lived in Yarmouth in the house that stands at 11 Chestnut St. A native of SHUBENACADIE, Day was educated at Pictou Academy, Mount Allison University, Oxford University (where he was a Rhodes scholar), and the University of Berlin. After teaching at the University of New Brunswick from 1909 to 1912, he taught until 1933 in American universities; during the First World War he served in the Canadian Army and helped organize the Cape Breton Highlanders (185th Battalion). Day began his writing career with *River of Strangers* (1926); he produced two other novels, *Rockbound* (1928) and *John Paul's Rock* (1932). *Rockbound* depicts life in a primitive South Shore fishing village and was based on one of the islands in Chester Basin and the families living on it. *John Paul's Rock*, the story of a Micmac Indian who is a fugitive from the law, demonstrates Day's intimate knowledge of Nova Scotian terrain and wildlife, as does his *Autobiography of a Fisherman* (1927). Day died in 1950.

The Yarmouth County Historical Museum, 22 Collins St., houses a 400-pound stone bearing an inscription that has been interpreted as proof of Norse visits to this part of North America. Discovered here in 1812, the Yarmouth Stone is 3 feet long, 2 feet wide, and 18 inches thick. One expert who translated its markings believes that it was a monument from Leif Ericsson to his father Eric the Red; others, however, believe they are of Indian origin or simply the result of weather. (See L'ANSE AUX MEADOWS, Nfld.)

Prince Edward Island

ALBERTON

John Hunter Duvar, Prince Edward Island's best-known nineteenth-century poet, died in Alberton in 1899; the site of the present Mill River Golf course near here was formerly 'Hernewood', the estate where Duvar lived the life of an English country gentleman. Originally named John Hunter, he was born in Scotland in 1821 and immigrated first to Halifax, coming to PEI in 1857. Here he changed his surname because the name John Hunter was very common among island residents. Hunter Duvar was the author of many lyrics, long poems, and poetic dramas, including *The Enamorado: A Drama* (1879), *The Emigration of the Fairies and The Triumph of Constancy* (1888), *De Roberval* (1888), and *Annals of the Court of Oberon* (1895). His best poem, 'The Emigration of the Fairies', is a humorous epic recounting the discovery and settlement of 'Hernewood' by Hunter Duvar and his family. He established the estate in 1857. (See also O'LEARY CORNER, SUMMERSIDE).

It was, in truth, a quiet shady place,
A nook apart from traffic's toil and moil;
Nor fair nor market, but unbroken face
Of lush green pastures on a fertile soil,
Well clothed with wealth of woods, by nature's bounty,
And known as Hernewood all throughout the county;

For the blue herons there would build their nests
High up on the tall tops of withered pines,
And sit there with their bills upon their breasts,
Or on one leg erect would stand in lines,
Fishing along the inlet's marish sedges,
Like sculptured ibises on old Nile's edges.

—John Hunter Duvar,
The Emigration of the Fairies (1888)

BAY FORTUNE

This community on Prince Edward Island's east coast was once a summering place for American theatre people. Among them was the New York playwright **Elmer Harris** (1878–1966), who based his play *Johnny Belinda* (1940) on events that occurred in the nearby hamlet of Dingwell's Mills. A hit of the 1940–1 Broadway season, the play tells of the rape of a deaf-mute girl and the consequences when her child, Johnny Belinda, is taken from her. Harris set his play in nearby Souris; a 1948 Hollywood film version changed the setting to Cape Breton Island, N.S.

Another frequent summer resident here was the San Francisco-born playwright and theatrical producer **David Belasco** (1854–1931), who wrote the plays on which two of Puccini's operas were based: *Madame Butterfly* (1900) and *The Girl of the Golden West* (1904). A sundial on private property on Abell's Cape was erected here by Belasco and Mrs Leslie Carter, who had starred in his play *Du Barry* (1901), in memory of Charles Flockton, an English-born actor who had a home in Bay Fortune.

BELMONT

In 1896–7 **Lucy Maud Montgomery** taught elementary school in this rural community on Malpeque Bay, near Summerside. Montgomery arrived on 16 Oct. 1896, and a few days later she described in her journal the one-room school where she taught: 'The school is situated on the bleakest hill that could be picked out. The view from it is magnificent, looking out over the head-waters of Richmond Bay.' She boarded about half a mile from the school in the home of Mr and Mrs Simon Fraser. Her discomfort and dissatisfaction while at Belmont are conveyed in her journal entries reproduced in *The Selected Journals of L.M. Montgomery, Vol. I: 1889–1910* (1985). Belmont was the second of three island schools at which Montgomery taught; the previous year she had served at BIDEFORD, and the following year she taught at LOWER BEDEQUE. (See also CAVENDISH, CHARLOTTETOWN, FRENCH RIVER, MONTAGUE, NEW LONDON, PARK CORNER.)

L.M. Montgomery, aged 30

Montgomery's photograph of the manse where she lived at Bideford

BIDEFORD

Lucy Maud Montgomery taught for one year (1894–5) at the one-room school in this town on the island's north shore. Bideford was the first of three Prince Edward Island villages where Montgomery worked as a teacher after graduating from Prince of Wales College, CHARLOTTETOWN. Montgomery's starting salary here was $179.58 a year plus $50 in supplements. The school, she wrote in her journal, was 'bleakly situated on a very bare-looking hill'. While at Bideford she boarded at the Methodist parsonage, a quarter-mile from the school, with the Rev. and Mrs J.F. Estey. It was here that Mrs Estey flavoured a cake with liniment and served it to a visiting minister, who ate his piece uncomplainingly—the origin of a famous episode in *Anne of Green Gables* (1908). (See also BELMONT, CAVENDISH, FRENCH RIVER, LOWER BEDEQUE, MONTAGUE, NEW LONDON, PARK CORNER.)

CAPE TRAVERSE

This scenic region, just southeast of Port Borden, is the setting for the Prince Edward Island portion of **Marian Engel**'s novel *The Glassy Sea* (1978), which also has settings in LONDON and elsewhere in south-

Montgomery's photograph of 'the old home', Cavendish

western Ontario, Engel's native province. A novel of a woman's spiritual quest, it begins with its Ontario-born narrator living 'in exile' at Cape Traverse; just before it was published, Engel stayed and worked at the Cape Traverse home of CHARLOTTETOWN publisher **Libby Oughton**, which has been a working resort for many Canadian writers. New Brunswick poet **Fred Cogswell** has set many poems in the Cape Traverse area. (See also TORONTO: 7.)

CAVENDISH

Lucy Maud Montgomery (1874–1952), author of *Anne of Green Gables* (1908) and numerous other 'Anne' books, lived here for many years at the home of her maternal grandparents, Alexander and Lucy Woolner Macneill. Another Cavendish house that she frequently visited as a child has been transformed into Green Gables House, the principal memorial and museum on the island that honours Montgomery as the province's most widely known author.

On 14 Sept. 1876 L.M. Montgomery's mother died at her parents' home, and immediately afterwards the future novelist—not yet two years old—came to live with the Macneills while her father pursued his business interests. The Macneill house (gone) lay between two apple and cherry orchards about half a mile from Cavendish Capes, a picturesque stretch of low capes along the island's north shore. It was at Cavendish that Montgomery attended school from the ages of six to fifteen in a whitewashed low-eaved building that stood in a spruce grove across the road from her grandparents' gate.

Before her grandfather's death on 5 Mar. 1898 Montgomery spent much time outside Cavendish, first to visit her father for about a year (1889) in PRINCE ALBERT, Sask., then as a student in CHARLOTTETOWN and HALIFAX, and as a teacher in three Prince Edward Island towns. In Mar. 1898 she returned to Cavendish to help her grandmother manage the home and run the town post office, although she left again in 1901 to take a position with a Halifax newspaper. After a single winter away she again went back to live with her grandmother, remaining until the old lady died on 10 Mar. 1911. She then moved to the PARK CORNER home of an aunt and uncle, Annie and John Campbell. In 1906 Montgomery became engaged to the Rev. Ewan MacDonald, who was serving as pastor of the Presbyterian Church of Cavendish; they were married on 5 July 1911 in Park Corner. Their graves, marked by a single stone, can be seen in the Cavendish cemetery near the present Green Gables Home.

Montgomery had been publishing poems and stories in periodicals for nine years when she returned to Cavendish in 1898 after her grandfather's death. It was here, between May 1905 and Jan. 1906, that she wrote *Anne of Green Gables*. On 15 Apr. 1907 she received a letter from the L.C. Page Co. in Boston, accepting her manuscript for publication; it had previously been rejected by four firms. Cavendish provided many of the most memorable features for the fictional landscape of the Anne books. While at Cavendish, Montgomery also published *Anne of Avonlea* (1909), *The Story Girl* (1911), and *Kilmeny of the Orchard* (1910).

Montgomery's novel *The Golden Road* (1913) dealt in part with the 'Yankee Storm' that on 3–4 Oct. 1851 destroyed more than 70 American fishing schooners just off the coast near Cavendish. This disaster was the subject of the best-known work of another Cavendish writer, the poet **Elizabeth Newell Lockerby**. Born on 12 Sept. 1832, Lockerby lived in Cavendish until 1862. She then lived in Charlottetown and, after her marriage in 1874, in Indianapolis, Indiana, where she died in 1884. Lockerby's two volumes of poetry were *The Wild Brier* (1866) and *Oak Leaves* (1869). The former contains her 'George and Amanda', a 60-page narrative poem about the 'Yankee Storm'. (See also LEASKDALE, NORVAL, TORONTO: 7, Ont.)

Montgomery's photograph of the Ernest Webb house, Cavendish (now the Anne of Green Gables House)

This evening I spent in Lover's Lane. How beautiful it was—green and alluring and beckoning! I had been tired and discouraged and sick at heart before I went to it—and it rested me and cheered me and stole away the heartsickness, giving peace and newness of life.

I owe much to that dear lane. And in return I have given it love—and fame. I painted it in my book: and as a result the name of this little remote woodland lane is known all over the world. Visitors to Cavendish ask for it and seek it out.

—The Selected Journals of L.M. Montgomery, *vol. 1, 1 August, 1909, Cavendish*

Montgomery's photograph of 'Lovers' Lane', Cavendish

CHARLOTTETOWN

Charlottetown was the birthplace on 24 Aug. 1798 of **Margaret Gordon**, the first love of the Scottish essayist and philosopher **Thomas Carlyle**; she is the 'Rose Goddess' Blumine of his *Sartor Resartus* (1833–4). Granddaughter of Walter Patterson, the first British governor of the province, Margaret was the daughter of Alexander Gordon, a doctor with the Forty-second Regiment stationed in the town. (Margaret's name can be seen in the baptismal register of St Paul's (Anglican) Church, 203 Richmond St, where she was christened in Sept. 1799; established in 1747, St Paul's is Charlottetown's oldest Protestant church.) Alexander Gordon returned with his family to Scotland, where he died in 1803. Margaret and her sister Mary were raised by an aunt, a Mrs Usher, in Kirkcaldy, Scotland, where the twenty-two-year-old Carlyle came as master of the burgh school in 1816 and where he met and fell in love with Margaret. His prospects did not please Mrs Usher and he withdrew his suit. Margaret wrote him several parting letters that have become famous: 'Genius will render you great. May virtue render you beloved! Remove the awful distance between you and ordinary men, by kind and gentle manners; deal mildly with their inferiority. . . .'

Later in life Carlyle referred bitterly to Margaret's marriage on 14 Jan. 1824 to Alexander Bannerman, a banker, wine merchant, and manufacturer of Aberdeen, 'some rich, insignificant, Aberdeen Mr. Something, who got into Parliament, was knighted, and later was sent out to Nova Scotia' as governor. Carlyle was mistaken: Sir Alexander Bannerman was governor of Prince Edward Island from 1851 to 1854. He arrived on 8 Mar. 1851, and his wife joined him on 19 May. They lived in Government House (near the harbour at Victoria Park Roadway and Pond Road) until 10 June 1854, when Bannerman left to take up the governorship of the Bahamas. While in Charlottetown, Lady Bannerman went to visit the house of her birth (gone), which stood on a tract of land on the York River, about half a mile from Government House. Sir Alexander Bannerman was governor of Newfoundland from 1857 until 1864 (when he died in England), and his wife was one of the central personalities of ST JOHN'S in that period.

Novelist **Samuel Douglas Smith Huyghue** was born in Charlottetown in 1816, during his father's military posting there, but was educated at SAINT JOHN, N.B. His literary activity is connected with that city, with HALIFAX, and to a lesser degree with Australia, where he moved in 1852 after eight years' residence in England. Charlottetown was the main centre of activity for the colourful **John LePage**, the 'Island Minstrel'. Born at Pownall in 1812, he was a teacher, first at rural Lot 49, then for many years at Malpeque, and finally in Charlottetown's Central Academy. (Amalgamated with the Normal School, the Central Academy became Prince of Wales College in 1860). LePage published numerous newspaper and broadsheet poems, and brought out two large volumes in Charlottetown: *The Island Ministrel: A Collection of the Poetical Writings of John LePage* (1860) and *The Island Minstrel . . . Volume II* (1867). Besides songs, elegies, and personal poems, these books contain public and satirical poems on scores of P.E.I. events of the day, and celebrations of the island's landscape and events of its history. LePage died in Charlottetown on 8 Jan. 1886, and his son Thomas LePage, also a master at Prince of Wales College, succeeded him as a prominent public versifier.

Elizabeth Newell Lockerby's *The Wild Brier: or Lays by an Untaught Minstrel* was published in Charlottetown in 1866 by George Brenmer, printer and bookseller, of Prince St. Born in 1832 in CAVENDISH, a daughter of John Lockerby, senior elder of Zion Presbyterian Church (gone), Elizabeth Lockerby came to Charlottetown in 1862 and studied painting with Mrs W.W. Irving of Grafton St. The frail and commonplace lyrics of her book are overshadowed by its centrepiece, a 60-page narrative poem entitled 'George and Amanda—a sketch from real life'. It tells the story of the 'Yankee Storm', a sudden and powerful storm that on 3–4 Oct. 1851 destroyed an American fishing fleet off Cavendish Shoals. Lockerby published a second book, *Oak Leaves* (1869), and lived in Charlottetown until 1874, when she married; she died ten years later in Indianapolis, Indiana.

Cornelius O'Brien was born in NEW GLASGOW on 4 May 1843 and came to Charlottetown about 1870 to attend St Dunstan's (Roman Catholic) College, which occupied the site at University and Belvedere Avenues that is now the campus of the University of Prince Edward Island. After further study in Rome, O'Brien returned to teach at St Dunstan's from 1871 to 1873. In 1873–4 he was principal priest of St Dunstan's Cathedral; this was the second wooden St Dunstan's, built in 1849 and occupying the same site on Great George St (at Sydney St) as today's basilica. O'Brien's many works include the long philosophical poem *Aminta—A Modern Life Drama* (1890) and *After Weary Years* (1885). In 1882 O'Brien was appointed fourth Archbishop of HALIFAX and also became a charter member of the Royal Society of Canada, which he served as president in 1896. (See also INDIAN RIVER.)

Another Catholic bishop, **Francis Clement Kelley**, was also a literary alumnus of St Dunstan's. Born in 1870 in VERNON RIVER, he came as a child to Charlottetown and received his early education at Queen's Square School (gone). He then attended St Dunstan's, the Séminaire de Nicolet, and Université Laval, and was ordained in 1893. A prolific author of fiction and non-fiction, he was a bishop in Michigan and in Mexico, founded the Catholic Church Extension Society of the United States in 1905, and sometimes served the United States and Mexico in a diplomatic capacity. Among his works were *The City and the World and Other Stories* (1919), *Pack Rat: A Metaphoric Fantasy* (1942), and a volume of autobiography, *The Bishop Jots It Down* (1939). In 1943 he donated 5,000 books and a fund of money to St Dunstan's for the building of a new library; the structure now housing the administrative offices and library of the University of Prince Edward Island was erected in 1963 and dedicated to Kelley.

Charlottetown's most famous clergyman author was **William Benjamin Basil King**, who was born here on 26 Feb. 1859. His intelligence was noticed by an Anglican minister, the Rev. George Wright Hodgson, who made it possible for King to study at St Peter's Cathedral grammar school (gone) in Charlottetown and afterwards at King's College, WINDSOR, N.S. After serving as rector of St Luke's Cathedral, Halifax, he went in 1892 to Cambridge, Mass., where he wrote his many novels; he died there in 1928. Among Basil King's books are *The Inner Shrine* (1908), *The Wild Olive* (1910), and *The Dust Flower* (1922). *In the Garden of Charity* (1903)—his only novel that does not deal in a moralistic way with the wealthy Boston–New York world of Henry James—has a Maritime setting among Nova Scotia fishing people.

Hodgson, King's benefactor, is remembered in the Hodgson Memorial Chapel of St Peter's Cathedral (Rochford Square, Rochford and Fitzroy Sts); the chapel is decorated with the magnificent murals painted by a Charlottetown resident, **Robert Harris**, who was a poet as well as a painter. Born in 1849 in Wales, he came to Charlottetown with his family in 1856. He attended Prince of Wales College about 1863, when it was a high school; it was at 72–90 Weymouth St, at the corner of Grafton. His life as an artist took him to many cities throughout Canada, the United States, and Europe, but he always retained his contacts with Charlottetown. President of the Royal Canadian Academy for thirteen years, Harris died on 27 Feb. 1919 and is buried in St Peter's Cemetery in the suburb of Parkdale, just northeast of Charlottetown. The Confederation Centre of the Arts, Queen and Grafton Sts, stands on the site of the former Robert Harris Memorial Gallery and houses 1,500 of that gallery's works, including a large collection of Harris's paintings. Harris is best known for *The Fathers of Confederation*, a painting that was housed in the Ottawa Parliament Buildings and destroyed in the fire of 1916. It was originally meant to depict the Charlottetown Conference at Province House, Grafton and great George Sts, where on 1 Sept. 1864 the provincial delegates agreed to begin the three-year series of meetings that led to Confederation. However, Harris was obliged to paint the picture so that the harbour of Quebec City, where the key conference was held in Oct. 1864, was seen from the window of Charlottetown's Province House. Harris's *Verses by the Way* (1920) and his memoir, *Some Pages from an Artist's Life* (n.d.), were both published by the Irwin Printing Co., which is still in operation at 19 Richmond St. His poetry celebrates the landscape of the Island. (See also MONTREAL: 3.) **Sir Joseph Pope** was a student at Prince of Wales College in 1865–70. Pope's father, William H. Pope, had been a delegate to both the Charlottetown and Quebec Conferences. The Pope family lived about a mile outside Charlottetown. Joseph Pope left school at fifteen for a position in the provincial treasury after an election of 1870 that resulted in a government of which his uncle, James Pope, was premier and his grandfather Joseph Pope was treasurer. Young Joseph Pope rose steadily in government service. From 1882 to 1891 he was private secretary to Sir John A. Macdonald and, as Macdonald's literary executor, wrote a memoir of the prime minister, among other books. Sir Joseph Pope died in Ottawa in 1926.

Montgomery's photograph of Prince of Wales College, Charlottetown

Other writers who attended Prince of Wales College are **Lucy Maud Montgomery** and **Andrew Macphail**. Montgomery entered the college in 1893 (it had been opened to women in 1879) and completed two years' work in a single year. She received her teacher's certificate on 8 June 1894 in a ceremony at the Charlottetown Opera House (gone), 77 Grafton St, at which she delivered a prize-winning essay she had written on Shakespeare's Portia; it was later published in the Charlottetown *Guardian*. The editors of the *Selected Journals of LM. Montgomery* (Vol. I, 1985) have identified the house at which Montgomery boarded when she was a student as that of Mrs Barbara McMillan, 24 Hillsborough St. It was near the harbour and about five blocks from Prince of Wales College. (See also BELMONT, CAVENDISH, FRENCH RIVER, LOWER BEDEQUE, MONTAGUE, NEW LONDON.) Five years earlier there had appeared in the pages of the Charlottetown *Daily Herald* the first published work by Montgomery, a poem she had written while visiting her father in PRINCE ALBERT, Sask. The original manuscript of Montgomery's *Anne of Green Gables* (1908) is in the museum in the Confederation Centre for the Arts, and a collection of the author's letters is housed in the library of the University of Prince Edward Island. (Sir) **Andrew Macphail**, a native of ORWELL, attended Prince of Wales College for two years around 1880; he also taught in island schools for three years and then went on to earn a B.A. in 1888 at McGill University, with which he was associated for the rest of his life. Macphail always praised the fine classical education he had received at the college. He is remembered with a plaque on the building at Grafton and Weymouth Sts (now Holland College, a community college) that housed Prince of Wales College until 1969, when it was merged with St Dunstan's University to form the present university on the former St Dunstan's campus. In the time of Montgomery and Macphail the college was a wooden structure. A new building erected in 1899 on the same site was destroyed by fire and rebuilt in 1932. Another literary alumnus who studied in the 1899 building was the historian **Edgar McInnis**, who was born in Charlottetown in 1900 and educated at Prince of Wales College, the University of Toronto, and Oxford University. McInnis won two Governor General's Awards for historical works—*The Unguarded Frontier* (1942) and *The War*, a six-volume account of the Second World War—and also wrote two volumes of poetry based on his experiences in the First World War: *Poems from the Front* (1918) and *The Road to Arras* (1920), both published in Charlottetown by the Irwin Printing Co.

Several twentieth-century poets are associated with St Dunstan's University and its successor, the University of Prince Edward Island. The Quebec poet **Alain Grandbois** spent one tumultuous and ill-adapted year here as a student of philosophy in 1919. He lived in the university's Dalton Hall and was remembered for instituting a protest over residence food. (See ST-CASIMIR-DE-PORTNEUF, Que.) The Acadian poet Father **Adrien Arsenault** has taught at St Dunstan's and UPEI since 1952 except for brief periods of study abroad. His books include *Psalms from the Cistercians* (1978) and *Icons of Poverty and Riches* (1980); he lives at Blanchard Hall on the U.P.E.I. campus. The poet **A.P. Campbell**, born in Souris in 1912, was educated at St Dunstan's and at Fordham University in New York, and taught for many years at the University of Ottawa. His poems, inspired by his Prince Edward Island heritage, were collected in *Red Clay Soil* (1976). A native of Toronto, the poet **John W. Smith** has been an Island resident since 1967, teaching at Prince of Wales College and UPEI. His books include *Winter in Paradise* (1972) and *Of the Swimmer among the Coral and of the Monk in the Mountains* (1976); he lives on Fitzroy St.

Milton Acorn, Prince Edward Island's best-known contemporary poet, was born in Charlottetown on 30 Mar. 1923 of working-class parents, a fact on which he based some of his best poetry and also some of his informal forays into autobiography.

Milton Acorn autographing books in Grossman's Tavern, Toronto, 16 May 1970, after receiving the 'People's Poet' award

The first home of Acorn's youth was on Park Terrace. Later the family lived at 103 North River Rd, then in another house on N. River Road in the countryside near Inkerman Shore, and from Acorn's fifteenth year at 219 Hillsborough St. Acorn served in the Second World War, during which he received a severe head wound, entitling him to a veteran's disability pension that helped support him in later life. After the war Acorn worked at trade and labouring jobs in the Maritimes and Quebec while beginning to write. When he was thirty-two he sold his carpenter's tools in Montreal and devoted himself to poetry. A peripatetic writer, Acorn was long absent from his native province except for visits, living in MONTREAL (6), TORONTO (2), and VANCOUVER. Among his collections of poetry are *I've Tasted My Blood: Poems 1956–1968* (1969), *Jackpine Sonnets* (1977) and *Dig Up My Heart: Selected Poems of Milton Acorn 1952–1953* (1983). Striking features of Acorn's work are its lyrical descriptions of nature, with Prince Edward Island as a frequent subject, and its portraits of common people, many of them Islanders. Acorn won a Governor General's Award for *The Island Means Minago* (1975), containing poetic evocations of the province's history, landscape, and people; Minago is an old Indian name for Prince Edward Island.

In 1981 Acorn moved back to Charlottetown, living first (and longest) at 26 Donwood Drive in the suburb of Parkdale, and later at 187 Weymouth St and 206 Dorchester St. He died of diabetes and heart disease on 20 Aug. 1986 and is buried near his mother, Helen Acorn, in St Peter's Cemetery on St Peter's Rd.

DINGWELL'S MILLS

American playwright **Elmer Harris** based his famous play *Johnny Belinda* (1940)—later a film—on events that occurred here. The town's Johnny Belinda Pond is named for the drama. Harris was one of many American theatre people who summered in this BAY FORTUNE district during the first half of the century; he had a summer home in FORTUNE BRIDGE.

DUVAR

This farming community, 3 miles north of O'Leary, was named for **John Hunter Duvar**, Prince Edward Island's best-known nineteenth-century poet, the author of *The Emigration of the Fairies* (1888) and other works. Hunter Duvar, who was also a federal fisheries inspector in the province, lived at 'Hernewood', his estate near ALBERTON.

FORTUNE BRIDGE

Cyrus Macmillan—whose retellings of the Glooscap cycle and other eastern Indian legends were collected in *Canadian Wonder Tales* (1918) and *Canadian Fairy Tales* (1922), and combined in *Canadian Wonder Tales* (1974)—died in Fortune Bridge on 29 June 1953. Macmillan was born in WOOD ISLANDS. **Elmer Harris**, the American playwright who based his play *Johnny Belinda* (1940) on events that occurred at nearby DINGWELL'S MILLS, had a summer home here. He also summered at BAY FORTUNE.

FRENCH RIVER

This fishing community in the heart of Anne of Green Gables country commemorates Anne and her creator, **Lucy Maud Montgomery**, in 'Anne's House of Dreams', a house on Hwy 20 that depicts the home of Anne and Gilbert Blythe as newlyweds. (The famous heroine's marriage occurs in *Anne's House of Dreams*, 1917, the third sequel to *Anne of Green Gables*, 1908.) Among the exhibits at the French River house, which was built in 1973, are scale models of buildings associated with Lucy Maud Montgomery and the Anne novels, including a model of the old Presbyterian church at CAVENDISH.

INDIAN RIVER

The philosophical poet **Cornelius O'Brien**, a NEW GLASGOW native who became Roman Catholic archbishop of HALIFAX, was parish priest from 1874 to 1882 at this town on Hwy 20 near the east shore of Malpeque Bay. During this period he published his first book, a theological work entitled *Philosophy of the Bible Vindicated* (1876).

The Bedeque school (in August 1982), where Montgomery taught

LOWER BEDEQUE

Lucy Maud Montgomery taught primary school in this small community at Bedeque Bay during the 1897–8 school year. This was the last of three Island villages at which the future novelist taught after graduating from Prince of Wales College, CHARLOTTETOWN; the other two were BIDEFORD and BELMONT. While here, Montgomery boarded with Mr and Mrs Cornelius Leard and became involved in a mutual infatuation with their son Herman, whom she considered—despite her strong attraction to him—completely unsuitable as a potential husband. She willed herself to conquer her feelings and was aided in this to some extent when the death of her grandfather, Alexander Macneill, on 5 Mar. 1898 obliged her to leave Lower Bedeque for CAVENDISH before the end of the school year.

Montgomery's birthplace, New London, with her son, Dr Stuart Macdonald, standing in front (August 1982)

MONTAGUE

The Garden of the Gulf Museum is located at 2 Main St in Montague, a village near Georgetown on the island's eastern shore. Among the museum's exhibits are letters by **Lucy Maud Montgomery**, author of *Anne of Green Gables* (1908), who was born at NEW LONDON and spent much of her life at CAVENDISH.

NEW GLASGOW

The Roman Catholic bishop and poet **Cornelius O'Brien** was born in New Glasgow on 4 May 1843 and spent his childhood here. After studying at St Dunstan's College, CHARLOTTETOWN, and in Rome, he was a teacher and parish priest in Prince Edward Island for ten years before being appointed fourth Archbishop of HALIFAX in 1882. O'Brien's many works included *Aminta—A Modern Life Drama* (1890), a long philosophical poem, and a memoir, *After Weary Years* (1885).

NEW LONDON

This village on the shore of the Southwest River, near London Bay, was called Clifton when **Lucy Maud Montgomery** was born here on 30 Nov. 1874 in a small green-trimmed frame house next door to which Montgomery's father owned a store that today is a gas station. The house is now a provincial historic site and museum dedicated to the author of *Anne of Green Gables* (1908). Preserved here are her wedding dress and shoes, a replica of the blue chest that appears in *The Story Girl* (1911), and her scrapbooks. Montgomery lived in Clifton for less than two years. On 14 Sept. 1876 her mother died of tuberculosis, and Lucy Maud went to live with her maternal grandparents in CAVENDISH.

ORWELL

Sir Andrew Macphail was born in Orwell on 24 Nov. 1864. His home—the setting of his autobiographical reminiscence, *The Master's Wife* (1939; rpr. 1977)—is the centrepiece of Sir Andrew Macphail Provincial Park and stands at the end of a majestic tree-lined drive. Macphail was brought up and received his grammar-school education here. After two years at Prince of Wales College, CHARLOTTETOWN, and three years' teaching in Prince Edward Island schools, he went to McGill University and earned his B.A. in 1888. He was associated with McGill and MONTREAL (3) for the rest of his life, though he never lost touch with his native province. After his father's death in 1905 he summered each year at his Orwell home. *The Master's Wife*, which is both a nostalgic memoir and an elegant history, evokes early Orwell and the life of Protestant settlers in the mid-nineteenth century and brings to life the personalities and accomplishments of Macphail's parents, William Macphail and Catherine Moore Smith—the Master (a PEI school inspector) and Master's wife of the title. Macphail also wrote a novel, a play, several volumes of polished essays and short biographies, and a long essay on John McCrae that appeared in the posthumous *In Flanders Fields and Other Poems* (1919). He also edited an important literary quarterly, the *University Magazine*, from 1907 to 1920. In 1921 he published the first translation of Louis Hémon's *Maria Chapdelaine*. (It was followed, and superseded, within a few months by the translation of William Hume Blake. The two men had originally wished to collaborate but were unable to agree on stylistic matters; Blake's poetic translation has been enduringly popular, but Macphail's is more accurate.) Macphail called *Maria Chapdelaine* 'the book that has interested me most in all my lifetime'; like his own writings, it expresses a strong belief that human life, to be healthy, must remain close to the soil and to family and community values. The pioneer life celebrated by Macphail in *The Master's Wife* is documented in the nearby reconstructed nineteenth-century village of Orwell Corner, which contains buildings (store, church, post office, school, houses, and farm buildings) that have been brought together and restored to recreate an Island pioneer community.

The Macphail house in the Sir Andrew Macphail Provincial Park, Orwell

Presently Earl Grey asked me to go for a walk, saying he wanted to hear all about my books etc. We went through the orchard and followed a little winding path past the trees until we came to a small white building. 'Let's sit down here,' said His Excellency, squatting down on the steps. Accordingly, I 'sat', too—since there did not exactly seem to be anything else I could do. I could not say to Earl Grey 'This is the Macphail water closet'—although that is what it was!! I suppose Earl Grey didn't know there were such places in existence. It was a neat little building, painted white, and even had a lace curtain in the window—likely put on for the occasion. And that is where His Excellency and I sat for half an hour and had our heart to heart talk. He never let the conversation lag, for he could ask a 'blue streak' of questions. He asked me to send him an autographed copy of Kilmeny *and my poems and was altogether delightful to me. But I was suffering so acutely from a suppressed desire to laugh that I hardly knew what I was saying. The Earl thought I was nervous and asked me if I had been rather dismayed at the idea of meeting him and when I said, 'Yes, I've been in a blue funk,' he laughed and said 'But you won't feel that way any more, will you.' I said 'No', but I really think if we had sat there much longer I would have gone into hysterics—and never been able to explain why. I was mortally afraid that some poor unfortunate was cooped up in the house behind us, not able to get out; and I beheld with fascinated eye straggling twos and threes of women stealing through the orchard in search of the W.C. and slinking hurriedly back when they beheld the Earl and me gallantly holding the fort!*

—*The Selected Journals of LM. Montgomery*, vol. 2, 16 September 1910, Cavendish.

A distinguished professor of the history of medicine and a major in the Canadian Army medical services during the First World War, Macphail was knighted in 1918. He died in 1938. *The Master's Wife*, which he considered his finest work, was published the next year.

The house in Park Corner where Montgomery lived in 1911. Now the Anne of Green Gables Museum.

PARK CORNER

The Anne of Green Gables Museum at Park Corner is in the house where **Lucy Maud Montgomery** lived from Mar. 1911 to 5 July 1911, when she was married in the front room to the Rev. Ewan MacDonald, a Presbyterian minister. The house belonged to Montgomery's aunt and uncle, Annie and John Campbell, and stood near the home of her paternal grandfather, Senator Donald Montgomery, which was across the road. As a child Montgomery was a frequent visitor to both houses.

RUSTICO

The Rev. **Georges-Antoine Belcourt** (1803–74), author of the first French-Ojibwa dictionary, is remembered by a monument in this village at the intersection of Hwys 6 and 243, inland from Prince Edward Island National Park. A native of Quebec, Belcourt was pastor of St Augustine's (Roman Catholic) Church here from 1859 to 1869. He came to the parish after more than twenty years of missionary work in the area of the Red and Assiniboine rivers. The monument to Belcourt stands between his church and its parish hall, which houses a small museum. This brown sandstone two-storey building dates from 1864, when it was the Farmers' Bank, which Belcourt helped found. (This was the smallest bank ever chartered in Canada and the first founded on credit-union principles.) Belcourt's dictionary was published after his death by the famous prairie missionary priest, the Rev. Albert Lacombe (see ST ALBERT, Alta).

SOURIS

American playwright **Elmer Harris** made Souris the setting of his well-known play *Johnny Belinda*, which was a hit on Broadway in 1940 and later a film. It was based on events that happened south of here, however, in a district where Harris had a summer home. See also BAY FORTUNE, DINGWELL'S MILLS, FORTUNE BRIDGE.

SUMMERSIDE

With a population of about 10,000, Summerside is the second-largest city in Prince Edward Island and the seat of Queens County. Here, from 1875 to 1879, **John Hunter Duvar** edited a newspaper, the *Summerside Progress*, and had his work *The Enamorado, a Drama* (1879) published by the firm of Graves and Company. *The Enamorado* was the first important book of original poetry published by Hunter Duvar, a Scottish immigrant who became the province's best-known nineteenth-century poet. Hunter Duvar, who had been a British correspondent for the Associated Press of New York, left newspaper work in 1879, when he became Dominion inspector of fisheries, a post he held until 1889. He then retired to his estate, 'Hernewood', near ALBERTON.

Summerside was the birthplace of **William Henry Pope Jarvis** (1876–1944), a journalist and writer who spent his professional life in Ontario and western Canada and described those locales in his volumes of local-colour fiction: *Letters of a Remittance Man to His Mother* (1908), *Trails and Tales in Cobalt* (1908), and *The Great Gold Rush* (1913).

The American poet **Mark Strand** was born in Summerside on 11 April 1934 and spent his early life here. Strand's Prince Edward Island childhood, especially his experiences on St Margaret's Bay, are described in such poems as 'Poor North', 'Shooting Whales', and 'Where Are the Waters of Childhood?' from *Selected Poems* (1980).

TIGNISH

L'Impartial, the first and only Acadian newspaper ever published in Prince Edward Island, was founded in Tignish in 1893 by Gilbert Buote and his son François Joseph Buote, and was published through the early 1900s. About 1900 the newspaper printed what is believed to be the only French-language novel ever to appear in PEI, *Placide, un homme mystérieux*, a romantic crime story about a young Acadian detective invited to go to New York by the city's police, who are baffled by a group of criminals operating there. Nothing is known of the author but a pen-name, 'Paul'.

VERNON RIVER

This village on Hwy 3 in eastern Queens County was the birthplace and childhood home of **Francis Clement Kelley** (1870–1948), a Roman Catholic bishop who was also a prolific writer of fiction, anecdote, ecclesiastical history and biography, theological and ethnological works, and autobiography. Among his books were *The City and the World and Other Stories* (1919), *Pack Rat: A Metaphoric Fantasy* (1942), and a volume of autobiography, *The Bishop Jots It Down* (1939). In 1905 Kelley founded the Catholic Church Extension Society of the United States, serving as its president for twenty years; the same year he founded the society's *Extension Magazine* and became its editor. Educated partly in CHARLOTTETOWN, he was a benefactor of St Dunstan's College there; a principal building of the University of Prince Edward Island is named after him.

WOOD ISLANDS

This community in southeastern Queens County was the birthplace on 12 Sept. 1882 of **Cyrus Macmillan**, author of *Canadian Wonder Tales* (1918) and *Canadian Fairy Tales* (1922), two lavishly illustrated books for children published in England. (Some fifty years later the stories in these books were combined in one volume and reissued as *Canadian Wonder Tales*, 1974.) Educated at McGill and Harvard Universities, Macmillan taught at Prince of Wales College, Charlottetown, before joining the staff of the English Department of McGill. He always maintained his close association with his native province, even serving as Member of Parliament for Queens County from 1940 to 1945 while he was Dean of Arts and Sciences at McGill (1940–7). (See also PASSAMAQUODDY BAY, N.B., BLOMIDON. N.S.; MONTREAL: 3, Que.)

New Brunswick

BATHURST

Nicolas Denys (1598–1688) built a fortified habitation called Nepisiguit on this site in 1652, after a former post on Cape Breton Island had been destroyed by fire. At Nepisiguit Denys wrote his two-volume *Description . . . des costes de l'Amérique septentrionale* (1672; English translation, 1908). The most interesting and important book about the early history of the region, it contains the fullest account of the war in 1645 at Portland Point (in SAINT JOHN) between Charles de Saint-Etienne de La Tour and Charles de Menou, Sieur d'Aulnay-Charnisay. This conflict occurred when Aulnay-Charnisay, lieutenant to the governor of Acadia, was not appointed to succeed the governor, Isaac de Razilly, after his death in 1635. La Tour challenged Aulnay-Charnisay's authority, and a French court ensured there would be strife by partitioning Acadia between them in such a way that the chief fort of each was in the territory granted to the other. A feudal war resulted, with Denys also entering the fighting in defence of his fur and fishing posts. The most famous incident of this war, recorded in Denys's book, took place at present-day Saint John, where Aulnay-Charnisay attacked Fort La Tour while La Tour was absent. It was stoutly defended by Madame La Tour, but she was finally taken prisoner and died in captivity; part of the garrison was imprisoned and part hanged. Aulnay-Charnissay died in 1650 and afterwards his widow was pillaged once by Denys and twice by her husband's chief creditor, Emmanuel Le Borgne. Ironically, under the pressure of these events Madame d'Aulnay-Charnissay in 1653 married Charles de La Tour, who had returned to Acadia. The first volume of Denys's work recounts this colourful story and other events of Acadian history and describes Acadian settlement, the fisheries, and manners and customs of the Indians; the second volume is a detailed account of the natural history of the region, with special attention to animals, fish, vegetation, and climate. A huge willow tree planted after Denys's death is said to mark his grave near the shore where the Nepisiguit River enters CHALEUR BAY. There is also a cairn in honour of Denys at Bathurst.

The Acadian poet and *chansonnier* **Calixte Duguay** (*Les Stigmates du silence*, 1975), now a resident of MONCTON, was for years a teacher of French-Canadian literature at the Collège de Bathurst.

BUCTOUCHE

Novelist and playwright **Antonine Maillet** was born in this Acadian fishing community on New Brunswick's east coast, one of nine children of schoolteaching parents—although her father left that profession to become manager of the Irving general store here. The store appears in 'Nouël', one of the sixteen monologues that make up *La Sagouine* (1971; English translation 1979), which first gained Maillet a large audience. Maillet attended elementary school in Buctouche and received her later education in Memramcook, MONCTON, and MONTREAL (16). After receiving her B.A. and M.A. from Collège Notre-Dame d'Acadie in Moncton, she taught elementary school in Richibucto, north of Buctouche, before becoming a university teacher at her Alma Mater; at its successor, Université de Moncton; and at Université Laval. (When Maillet taught elementary school she was a nun, with the name in religion of Soeur Marie-Grégoire.) She now lives in Montreal, on a street named after her. Maillet's first work of fiction, *Pointe-aux-Coques* (1958), is a chronicle of a year in a New Brunswick fishing village; the narrator is named Cormier, Maillet's mother's maiden name, and the book reflects the author's experience of both Buctouche and Richibucto. (Maillet left her religious order after publishing this book.) Her other works include *Don l'Orignal* (1972; *The Tale of Don l'Orignal*, 1978), winner of a Governor General's Award, and *Pélagie-la-Charrette* (1979; *Pélagie: The Return to a Homeland*, 1982), the first book by a foreign writer to win the French Prix Goncourt.

Antonine Maillet

FROM 'LA SAGOUINE'

This is a true story. The story of La Sagouine, *a scrubwoman, a woman of the sea, who was born with the century, with her feet in the water. Water was her fortune: the daughter of a cod fisherman, a sailor's girl, and later the wife of a fisherman who took oysters and smelts. A cleaning woman also, who ends up on all fours, with her bucket in front and her hands in the water.*

That is where I found her, between her mop and her rags, bending over the pail of dirty water that has been collecting for half a century all the dirt of the country.

—Antonine Maillet, *La Sagouine* (1971; tr. Luis de Céspedes, 1979)

CHIPMAN

Elizabeth Brewster was born on 26 Aug. 1922 in this town on the Salmon River, about 5 miles north of Grand Lake, and lived here until her family moved to HAMMTOWN in 1930. Brewster—whose books of poetry include *East Coast* (1951), *Lillooet* (1954), *Passage of Summer* (1969), *Sometimes I Think of Moving* (1977), and *The Way Home* (1982)—has written two novels, *The Sisters* (1972) and *Junction* (1983), and a collection of short stories, *It's Easy to Fall on the Ice* (1977). Much of her poetry and fiction is set in New Brunswick. (See also FREDERICTON, MINTO, SUSSEX.)

COCAGNE

I found there so much with which to make good cheer during the eight days which bad weather obliged me to remain there. All my people were so surfeited with game and fish that they wished no more, whether wild geese, ducks, teal, plover, snipe, pigeons, hares, partridge, salmon, trout, mackerel, smelt, oysters and other kinds of good fish. All I can tell you of it is this, that our dogs lay beside the meat and fish, so much were they satiated with it. The country there is as pleasing as the good cheer.

—Nicolas Denys, *Description . . . des costes de l'Amérique septentrionale* (1672; tr. W.F. Ganong, 1908)

COCAGNE

This village north of Shediac, at Cocagne Harbour, was given its old French name (from *pays de cocagne*, which means 'land of plenty') by **Nicolas Denys**, the seventeenth-century French colonizer and trader in Acadia who wrote the most important seventeenth-century account of what is now New Brunswick (see BATHURST).

CODY'S

Situated just south of the Trans-Canada Highway on the Canaan River, near its entrance into Washedemoak Lake, Cody's was the birthplace, on 3 July 1872, of Archdeacon **Hiram A. Cody**, author of twenty-three adventure novels that sought to convey a Christian moral message, and of a biography of Bishop William Carpenter Bompas, *An Apostle of the North* (1908). Cody was ordained an Anglican priest in 1898 and served in parishes in New Brunswick, in the West, and in the Yukon, and became rector of St James Church, SAINT JOHN. Some of his novels reflect not only his knowledge of the history of New Brunswick but also his experiences in western Canada. His notable works include *The Frontiersman: A Tale of the Yukon* (1910), *The Fourth Watch* (1911), *The Long Patrol: a Tale of the Mounted Police* (1912), *The King's Arrow: a Tale of United Empire Loyalists* (1922), and *The Stumbling Shepherd* (1929). The author's house at Cody's still stands and is a provincial historic site; it is privately owned. (See also GRAND FALLS, GREENWICK; WHITEHORSE, Y.T.)

DOUGLAS

On 10 Jan. 1860 **Charles G.D. Roberts** was born in the parish of Douglas, 10 miles north of Fredericton and now part of the city, though his family soon moved to the old Westcock parsonage of St Ann's, near SACKVILLE, where his father, Canon George Goodridge Roberts, was parish priest. Canon Roberts was probably the first priest at Douglas. The first Anglican church here, which is no longer standing, was built in 1854 and in its earliest years did not have an incumbent.

In the summer of 1895 **Pauline Johnson** toured New Brunswick and stayed in Canon Roberts' home in FREDERICTON. On this occasion Charles—who was living in WINDSOR, N.S., at the time—visited his father. He took Pauline for a morning drive along the Saint John River, turned north into the parish of Douglas, and, from a high ridge called Crock's Point, pointed out the house where he was born. Johnson memorialized the occasion in her poem 'The Douglas Shore', the manuscript copy of which she sent to Roberts.

The Jonathan Odell house, Fredericton, from the grounds of the Cathedral

EAST CENTREVILLE

Fred [Frederick William] Cogswell was born in 1917 in this tiny community north of Woodstock. He lived here until 1939 and received his early education in local schools; the schools are gone, but the Cogswell family house still stands. Cogswell, whose poetry often celebrates landscape and rural people, says of East Centreville: 'To this area I'm indebted for my knowledge of rural life and ways, and for the first attention I paid to natural surroundings.' Since 1945 Cogswell has been associated almost continuously with the University of New Brunswick in FREDERICTON, where he lives. The first of his thirteen volumes of poetry, *The Stunted Strong* (1954), concerns rural New Brunswick, specifically Carleton County and its farming heritage. Among Cogswell's other books are *A Long Apprenticeship: Collected Poems* (1980), and *Selected Poems* (1983). He is also a translator of French-Canadian poetry, a founder and editor of the *Fiddlehead*, a literary magazine, and founder and editor of Fiddlehead Poetry Books, which published 300 titles from 1959 to 1981 under his direction; it continues to publish.

FREDERICTON

The capital of New Brunswick officially received its name in 1785 from Governor Thomas Carleton when it was laid out for settlement by Loyalist immigrants. Its literary history, however, stems from the previous year, when Jonathan Odell arrived here, and continues unbroken to the present, encompassing the late-nineteenth-century literary flowering that has earned it the name of the Poets' Corner of Canada. Sir Charles G.D. Roberts and Bliss Carman, Fredericton's most famous literary residents, are only two of many writers who were born or lived here and give this historic city of stately elms a literary importance out of all proportion to its small size.

A New Jersey Loyalist, **Jonathan Odell** went to England in 1783 and arrived at Fredericton in November 1784, having been appointed secretary of the Province of New Brunswick, which had been established in that year to accommodate the influx of Loyalists into what was previously Nova Scotia territory. Odell was one of the best North American poets of the colonial period and the most effective of the Loyalist satirists. The American Revolution evoked his finest work, and in 1780 Odell's *The American Times* was published in New York and London; but in New Brunswick he continued to write satires, including verses inspired by the War of 1812 and by Governor Carleton's absences from the province after 1803. His satires were collected in *The Loyal Verses of Joseph Stansbury and Dr. Jonathan Odell* (Albany, 1860). The house Odell had built for himself in 1785 still stands at 808 Brunswick St; now the residence of the Anglican dean of Fredericton, it is probably the most important house in the province for its influence on subsequent domestic architecture. Odell, who was both a physician and an Anglican priest, served as provincial secretary until 1812, when the office passed to

Julia Catherine Beckwith Hart

his son. He died at Fredericton in 1818 and is today memorialized by the city's 300-acre Odell Park.

Julia Catherine (Beckwith) Hart, the first native of what is now Canada to write and publish a novel, was born in Fredericton in 1796. Her father, Nehemiah Beckwith, was a business partner of Benedict Arnold, who was at Fredericton from 1787 to 1791 and leased lots lying between 102 Waterloo Row and the present Government House (238 Waterloo Row); the older back part of the present house at 102 Waterloo Row is believed to have been on the property in Arnold's and Beckwith's time. In Fredericton Julia Beckwith began her first novel, *St Ursula's Convent; or, The Nun of Canada*, when she was only seventeen. In 1820 she moved to KINGSTON (Ont.), and in 1824 the novel was published there in an edition of 165 copies. In the same year she married George Hart and moved with him to the United States, where she published *Tonnowonte; or The Adopted Son of America* (1824–5). In 1831 the Harts returned to Fredericton, where Mrs Hart lived until her death in 1867, working on an unpublished novel, *Edith; or, The Doom*. She is buried in the Old Protestant Burial Grounds; her grave is at the corner of Sunbury and George Sts. The Harts lived in a house (gone) facing this cemetery on the Brunswick St side.

Besides working on *Edith; or, The Doom*, Mrs Hart published short fiction in the *New Brunswick Reporter and Fredericton Advertiser*, which was founded in 1843 and edited by the poet and and journalist **James Hogg**. He lived for a time in the 1840s and 1850s in the back cottage (the front gable end had not yet been built) of the house at 725 George St. In 1825 Henry Chubb of Fredericton printed Hogg's *Poems, Religious, Moral and Sentimental*, the first book of poetry published in the province. Hogg's newspaper also published the verse of the early Fredericton poet **Peter John Allan**, who died in his youth and whose romantic verse foreshadowed the achievement of the Confederation Poets. Born in England in 1825, he came to Fredericton as a child and briefly attended King's College (later the University of New Brunswick), which had been proposed in 1785 and received a Royal Charter on 10 Feb. 1829. In 1843 Allan began to publish verse in the *New Brunswick Reporter* but died suddenly in 1848 before he could issue a volume; his work was collected in *The Poetical Remains of Peter John Allan* (London, 1853). Allan lived in a house on King St where the Centennial Building now stands.

What is perhaps New Brunswick's oldest literary memento is housed in the Legislative Library, in the back of the Legislative Building, which stands with other government buildings at the northeast corner of King and St John Sts. It is a rare 1783 printed copy of the Domesday Book. (For seven centuries, until the printing of an edition in the 1780s, this ancient document existed in a single handwritten copy.) The Legislative Library also holds a precious complete set of John James Audubon's *Birds of America* (1834). Its four volumes, each more than 3 feet high, contain 435 hand-coloured pictures. The American author, artist, and naturalist observed and painted 'The Pine Finch' on the grounds of Fredericton's Old Government House in 1830. Audubon was a guest of Lieutenant-Governor Sir Howard Douglas but must have been entertained by the administrator, for Douglas was then in England preparing the Maine boundary case. The Old Government House, the home of colonial governors and then of provincial lieutenant-governors until 1892, is now the provincial headquarters of the Royal Canadian Mounted Police; it is located on Woodstock Rd, which is the continuation of King St, west of Smythe St.

In the grounds of the University of New Brunswick, whose campus begins at the south end of University Ave, Charles G.D. Roberts, Bliss Carman, and Francis Joseph Sherman are honoured by a tall monument that stands before the University's Harriet Irving Library. Dedicated on 15 May 1947, it was the idea of the poet Alfred Bailey, a long-time professor and administrator at UNB; the famous phrase 'Poets' Corner of Canada'—suggested by Dr J.C. Webster—appears on a bronze plaque.

Christ Church Cathedral, Fredericton, in the 1860s

Charles G.D. Roberts—who was born at DOUGLAS, N.B., and spent his childhood at SACKVILLE—came to Fredericton with his family in 1874, when he was fourteen. His father, Canon George Goodridge Roberts, was the pastor of St Anne's Church (at Westmoreland and George Sts), the parish church of Fredericton from its completion in 1849 until 1960. Canon Roberts was a classical scholar who taught languages at the Collegiate School (in the 800 block of George St, it is now gone); he was also rector of the city's magnificent Christ Church Cathedral, built in 1845–53, which occupies its own block of grounds facing Church Street, between Brunswick and King Sts. He and his family lived in the Georgian-style brick rectory at 734 George St, a house that Frederictionians call 'the birthplace of Canadian literature'. Roberts' mother, Emma Wetmore Bliss, and Bliss Carman's mother

The Roberts rectory, Fredericton

were sisters; the Bliss family had come from the Massachusetts Bay Colony and was related to the family of Ralph Waldo Emerson. Inspired by the Collegiate School's distinguished headmaster, George Parkin, Carman and Roberts wrote their earliest poems in the George St rectory. They may have been joined by Barry Straton, who was a first cousin to both of them and a lyric poet, and by their younger contemporary Francis Joseph Sherman. Charles G.D. Roberts lived in the house until 1879, when he graduated from the University of New Brunswick with 'honours in mental and moral science and political economy', a scholarship in Latin and Greek, and a medal for Latin prose composition. He then became headmaster of Chatham Grammar School. In 1880, while he was living at Chatham, his first book of verse, *Orion and Other Poems*, was published in Philadelphia; it incorporated the youthful poetry written at the Fredericton rectory. Roberts never returned permanently to Fredericton, but he and his family are known to have lived for a while in a house at 177 University Ave; this may have been in 1884, between his resignation as editor of Goldwin Smith's *The Week* in TORONTO (1) and the beginning of his ten-year teaching career at King's College, WINDSOR, N.S.

All of Canon Roberts' children were literary. Besides Charles, they included William Carman Roberts, a staff member of the *Literary Digest* for nearly forty years; Elizabeth (Roberts) Macdonald, a poet; and the youngest, Theodore Goodridge Roberts, who was born at the rectory on 7 July 1877. **Elizabeth Roberts Macdonald** lived at 'Little Glencoe', 745 George St, which was bought in 1872 by her grandfather Dr George Roberts, who had been headmaster of the Collegiate School before George Parkin's tenure. Here Elizabeth wrote her own poems and encouraged her son, Goodridge Macdonald, and his friends to write while they were children playing on the porch. (Among Goodridge Macdonald's collections of poetry are *The Dying General and Other Poems*, 1946, and *Beggar Makes Music*, 1950.) **Theodore Goodridge Roberts** left the University of New Brunswick in 1898 to become a war correspondent in the Spanish-American War for the New York *Independent*, which, with Bliss Carman as its literary editor, had already published his early poems. He married in 1903, lived for a time in Fredericton, and then spent periods in Barbados (where his first son, Goodridge Roberts, the distinguished painter, was born), England, France, Ottawa, Toronto, and other parts of Canada; he finally settled

Bliss Carman's home in Fredericton, 1906

in DIGBY, N.S., where he died in 1953. Roberts was a prolific author of adventure stories and historical romances; his most notable book, first published as *The Toll of the Tides* (1913) and now known as *The Harbor Master* (1968), is set in Newfoundland, where he lived for two years, and Labrador. (See ST JOHN'S, Nfld.) He also wrote poetry that is suffused with a sense of the Saint John River and the silent forests and backwoods country that flank it. His poems first appeared in *Northland Lyrics* (Boston, 1899), a family volume also containing work by his older brothers William Carman and Charles and by his sister Elizabeth Roberts Macdonald. His own poems were collected in *The Leather Bottle* (1934). T.G. Roberts lived for a time at 895 Charlotte St, which has also been the home of his daughter, the poet **Dorothy (Roberts) Leisner**, and of poet Alfred Bailey (see below); the house once belonged to Bailey's grandfather, Loring Bailey, a distinguished scholar. Dorothy Roberts produced much of her poetry in the house; her work is collected in *Dazzle* (1957), *In Star and Stalk* (1959), and *Twice to the Flame* (1961).

Bliss Carman was born on 15 Apr. 1861, probably in the old back portion (built before 1844) of the house now standing at 809 George St (the information comes from Alfred Bailey's grandmother, who was a friend of Carman's mother and assisted at the poet's birth). Carman's boyhood home, however, was the interesting house at 83 Shore St, which has its back to the street and faces a garden; a plaque marks it as a national historic site. Carman graduated from the University of New Brunswick in 1881 and in 1882 went to Oxford and then Edinburgh universities. He returned to Fredericton in 1883 and for three years dabbled in school-teaching, law, real estate, and even manual labour, working as a chainman on a railroad survey. In 1886 he went to Yale University for postgraduate study. He lived the rest of his life in the United States, settling in 1908 in New Canaan, Conn., where he died on 8 June 1929 after returning from a reading tour in British Columbia. Carman was the author of over fifty collections of poetry—including *Low Tide on Grand Pré* (1893), *Songs from Vagabondia* (1894), *Sappho: One Hundred Lyrics* (1904), and *Echoes from Vagabondia* (1912)—and numerous books of essays. Much of his poetry is rooted in his experience of the area around GRAND PRÉ, N.S., during ten summer visits (1886–95) with Charles G.D. Roberts while the latter was teaching at King's College, Windsor.

Bliss Carman in 1891

The third member of the Poets' Corner, **Francis Joseph Sherman**, was born in Fredericton in 1871; his childhood home, now gone, stood on St John St in the half-block now occupied by the Playhouse (at the southwest corner of Queen St and St John). Sherman was taught by George Parkin and Bliss Carman at the Collegiate School and entered the University of New Brunswick at fifteen; but financial difficulties forced him to withdraw before completing his studies. He joined the Merchants' Bank of Halifax and rose through postings at WOODSTOCK, Fredericton, and Montreal until he was stationed in Havana, where he was largely responsible for extending the bank's influence throughout Cuba and the West Indies. He returned to Canada in 1912 to work at the head office of the bank (which in 1901 had become the Royal Bank of Canada) in Montreal. Sherman's work appeared in seven small volumes published between 1896 and 1900 and was collected by Lorne Pierce in *The Complete Poems of Francis Sherman* (1935), with a foreword by Charles G.D. Roberts.

All three of the Poets' Corner poets are buried close together in Forest Hill Cemetery, on Forest Hill Road near the university. In addition, Theodore Goodridge Roberts, who died in Digby on 24 Feb. 1953, is buried here near his brother Charles G.D. Roberts and his cousin Bliss Carman. There is some question about the contents of Bliss Carman's grave. Miles B. Dixon, a member of the executive council of New Brunswick at the time of Carman's death, was sent to New Canaan to bring Carman's ashes back for interment. This was duly accomplished. However, Dixon once stated that when he arrived in Connecticut he found that Carman's ashes had already been scattered over the Hudson River and that he had brought back some ashes from a furnace to fulfil his commitment.

Fredericton had many additional literary associations in the late nineteenth and early twentieth centuries. **Barry Straton** was another notable lyric poet of the Frederictonian generation born in the 1860s and 1870s. Straton lived most of his life in the house that stands at 736 Brunswick St; his collections of verse include *Lays of Love* (1884). From 1867 to 1869 the British author **Juliana Horatia Ewing** and her husband, Major A. Ewing, made their home in the Golden Ball Inn (gone), which stood just upriver from the present residence of the president of the University of New Brunswick (58 Waterloo Row). Mrs Ewing called the building, which was not yet an inn, 'Reka Dom'—Russian for 'River House'; she wrote some of her poetry under the old willows on the river bank and mentions the house in three of her prose works, especially *Mrs Overtheway's Remembrances* (1869), which describes her life here. While stationed in Fredericton Major Ewing played the organ at Christ Church Cathedral and wrote his famous hymn 'Jerusalem the Golden'.

The Roberts tombstone in Forest Hill Cemetery, Fredericton

The house with three front doors at 117 Westmoreland St was once the home and grocery of Joseph Armour, whose daughter **Maria Armour** published romantic novels in the 1880s. From 1910 until 1912 the novelist **Frank Parker Day** lived at 177 University Ave, where Charles G.D. Roberts and his family lived for a time. He was a professor of English at the university during this period and had not yet embarked on his fiction career, which includes two novels set in his native Nova Scotia: *Rockbound* (1928) and *John Paul's Rock* (1932). (See also SHUBENACADIE, YARMOUTH, N.S.)

A statue of **Robert Burns**, erected in 1906, stands in The Green, a park at King and Church Sts overlooking the Saint John River. It is said that when the Fredericton Society of St Andrew first approached the Anglican bishop of Fredericton for permission to place a statue of 'the bard' on the nearby grounds of Christ Church Cathedral, the bishop agreed, assuming that the bard in question must be Robert Browning. When he learned of his mistake he adamantly refused permission because Burns was a 'drunken lecher': hence the present location.

No literary figure from Fredericton was better known to Canadians than the children's story-teller and broadcaster **Mary Grannan**, whose home stands at 345 Brunswick St. The creator of the *Just Mary Stories* and of the 'red-haired moppet Maggie Muggins' and her friend Fitzgerald Fieldmouse was born in Fredericton in 1902 and died here in 1975; her home had been in her family since 1839. She was a Fredericton teacher who gained national fame as a radio story-teller for children. Her broadcasts, from which her books were developed, were heard on CBC radio from 1939 to 1962. The 'Just Mary' and 'Maggie Muggins' stories were published in several volumes in the 1940s and 1950s.

The poet and historian **Alfred Bailey**, who was born in QUEBEC CITY in 1905 and passed his earliest years there and in Tadoussac, Que., came to Fredericton with his family and spent his childhood in the house at 895 Charlotte St, mentioned above, where

Fredericton in the 1860s

Theodore Goodridge Roberts and Dorothy (Roberts) Leisner have also lived. He graduated from the University of New Brunswick with a B.A. in 1927 and became a professor of history in 1937. He wrote six volumes of poetry, including *Miramichi Lightning: The Collected Poems of Alfred Bailey* (1981), and several important books and essays on ethnography and cultural history. Besides his poetry, his most important contribution to Fredericton's literary life is his major role in the founding in 1945 of the *Fiddlehead*, a poetry magazine that is still being published and now contains fiction and reviews as well as poetry. It was founded by a group that met at Bailey's home at 701 Churchill Row. Bailey is now a professor emeritus.

Desmond Pacey, who joined the university as professor of English in September 1944, became a member of the *Fiddlehead* group before the first issue was published on 27 Feb. 1945. All of Pacey's published verse, except his children's poems, appeared in the first seven numbers, and has never been collected. Known primarily as an influential critic, Pacey published two collections of stories, *The Picnic and Other Stories* (1958) and *Waken, Lords and Ladies Gay* (1974), and two volumes of children's poems. He was vice-president academic of the university from 1970 to his death in 1975. His house was at 249 Winslow St. (See also BRANDON, Man.)

Among the younger writers influenced by Bailey and Pacey at the University of New Brunswick are Robert Gibbs, Elizabeth Brewster, and Fred Cogswell. Born in Saint John in 1930, **Robert Gibbs** now teaches English at the university. He is closely associated with the *Fiddlehead*, which he edited for many years from its campus offices in the Observatory, an 1851 structure (Canada's oldest astronomical observatory) that is also known as the Brydone-Jack Building after William Brydone-Jack, another of the teachers of Charles G.D. Roberts and Bliss Carman at the Collegiate School. Robert Gibbs' five poetry collections include *The Road from Here* (1968) and *All This Night Long* (1978).

Poet and novelist **Elizabeth Brewster**, born in 1922 in CHIPMAN, N.B., attended the University of New Brunswick as an undergraduate from 1942 to 1946, living at 458 Needham St. She then left Canada to study abroad; on her return she took a library degree at the University of Toronto. For three years, 1965–8, she was associate librarian of the Legislative Library (at King and St John Sts, mentioned above) and lived in a house on University Ave. Fredericton appears in many of her poems, which are collected in six volumes and several pamphlets. The city appears under its own name in her novel of a girl's coming of age in the Maritimes, *The Sisters* (1974), and is the model for Georgetown in *Junction* (1983), her unusual novel of time travel in early twentieth-century Canada. It is also a location for 'A House Full of Women' in her story collection *It's Easy to Fall on the Ice* (1977).

Fred Cogswell—poet, publisher, translator, anthologist, and critic—was born in EAST CENTREVILLE in 1917. After serving in the Second World War he received a B.A. from the University of New Brunswick in 1949 and an M.A. in 1950, and a doctorate from Edinburgh University in 1952. A professor of English at the University of New Brunswick, Cogswell edited the *Fiddlehead* from 1952 to 1967. In 1959 he inaugurated Fiddlehead Poetry Books, which he published first in conjunction with the magazine and later on his own; this imprint has appeared on over 300 titles, including first or early volumes by many subsequently important poets from the Maritimes and throughout Canada. Cogswell has produced thirteen volumes of poems, from *The Stunted Strong* (1954) to *Selected Poems* (1983), and six books of translations from the French, including three anthologies of French-Canadian poetry in English and *The Complete Poems of Émile Nelligan* (1983).

In 1965–6 **Norman Levine** was the University of New Brunswick's first writer-in-residence. The experience is reflected in 'Thin Ice', the title story of a 1979 collection, and in his novel *From a Seaside Town* (1970). In 1969 **Alden Nowlan** took up the position of writer-in-residence and retained it until his death in the summer of 1983, at fifty. His home was at 676 Windsor St. Nowlan wrote vigorously in Fredericton, producing an autobiographical novel, *Various Persons Named Kevin O'Brien* (1973); a 1970 selection of poems from his early volumes; four new collections of poems, including *I Might Not Tell Everybody This* (1982);

Alden Nowlan

a travel book; and a collection of his widely admired feature journalism. In addition he collaborated with Walter Learning on three plays—*Frankenstein* (1976), *The Dollar Woman* (1972), and *The Incredible Murder of Cardinal Tosca* (1978)—which were produced by Theatre New Brunswick at the Playhouse and elsewhere in the province. Nowlan's friend **Leo Ferrari**, also a Fredericton poet, was the founder and president of the Flat Earth Society, now an internationally famous joke that is said to have originated from conversations between Ferrari and Nowlan in Nowlan's living-room.

Near Nowlan's home on Windsor St is that of the poet **M. Travis Lane**, author of *Homecomings* (1977) and *Divinations and Shorter Poems 1973–1978* (1980). A research associate of the University of New Brunswick's Department of English, she is one of several writers now active in the city, most of them grouped around the university. Another is **Kent Thompson**, the American-born poet, novelist, and short-story writer who is a professor of English and creative writing and who edited the *Fiddlehead* from 1967 to 1971 and in 1974. Among his novels are *The Tenants Were Corrie and Tennie* (1973) and *Shacking Up* (1980), both set in Fredericton.

The novelist **David Adams Richards**, born in 1950 in NEWCASTLE, N.B., studied in the early 1970s at St Thomas University, a Roman Catholic institution that shares the campus of the University of New Brunswick. He attended an informal writers' workshop that met in a converted ice-house on the campus and there knew Kent Thompson, Alden Nowlan, Fred Cogswell, and others. He wrote his first novel, *The Coming of Winter* (1974), as an undergraduate; when the manuscript was accepted by Oberon Press, Ottawa, he left school before completing his degree in order to become a full-time writer. Richards' novels, which all depict the Miramichi Valley and NEWCASTLE, include *Blood Ties* (1976) and *Lives of Short Duration* (1981). He has been writer-in-residence at the University of New Brunswick since 1984.

A literary benefactor to Fredericton who also had ties to NEWCASTLE was **Max Aitken, Lord Beaverbrook**, financier, newspaper magnate, adviser to Winston Churchill, British peer, and writer. He was born in Maple, Ont., and brought up in Newcastle; his dedication to New Brunswick is well known. His brief attendance at the University of New Brunswick in the 1890s resulted in a life-long love for the university and the city. The Playhouse was built by Beaverbrook in 1964; Theatre New Brunswick was founded through the agency of the Beaverbrook Canadian Foundation in 1969. His donations to the university include a set of chimes that play the tune of the New Brunswick folk song 'The Jones Boys' every hour and a collection of his books, housed in the Harriet Irving Library, which contains first editions of Charles Dickens and H.G. Wells. Beaverbrook died in 1964. His house in Fredericton, 238 Waterloo Row, has been the Government House of New Brunswick since 1975.

GRAND FALLS

A poem by **Hiram A. Cody**, Archdeacon of SAINT JOHN, recalls the legend and exploits of 'Main John' Glasier, the first man to drive logs over Grand Falls, the spectacular 80-foot plunge made by the Saint John River in the centre of this town on the Trans-Canada Highway. Cody's folk-style ballad about this pioneer lumberman of the Madawaska region portrays him thus:

Don't you see the 'Main John' striding in the lead?
Clear-eyed, strong and fearless, kith of Bluenose breed;
First to bring the timber drive through the wild Grand Falls;
First to sight the Squattook Lakes where the lone moose calls.
Haunter of the silent ways,
Spirit of the glen,
Dauntless as in olden days,
Glasier leads his men.

Glasier, the discoverer of Squatec Lake, Que., was elected to the New Brunswick legislature in 1861 and appointed to the Canadian Senate in 1868. The title 'Main John', said to have originated as a name of respect for Glasier, was applied by lumbermen to their leaders throughout eastern North America.

The Grand Falls were the subject of one of the earliest poems based on Canadian experiences, Adam Allen's 'A Description of the Great Falls of the River St. John, in the Province of New Brunswick', from Allen's book *The Gentle Shepherd*, published in England in 1725.

Grand Falls, *c.*1900

GRAND MANAN ISLAND

In 1925 the American novelist **Willa Cather** built a cottage on Grand Manan Island, the largest of the Bay of Fundy islands, and often summered there. The cottage still stands near North Head, a community on the north-eastern coast of Grand Manan; it can be pointed out by local residents.

GREENWICK

The Rev. **Hiram A. Cody**, novelist and poet, who later became Archdeacon of Saint John, was rector at Greenwick from 1897 to 1904. Afterwards he served in the Yukon, where several of his books are set. (See also CODY'S, GRAND FALLS, SAINT JOHN; WHITEHORSE, Y.T.)

HAMMTOWN

This small Queen's County community in the Washademoak Lake area was the childhood home of the poet **Elizabeth Brewster** from 1930 to 1934. Brewster, whose native town of CHIPMAN is about 30 miles north of here, attended the Hammtown School between the ages of eight and twelve. Washademoak Lake and Hammtown are the models for Moss Lake and the surrounding area in Brewster's novel *The Sisters* (1974), a semi-autobiographical story of a girl's coming of age in the Maritimes. Chipman and Hammtown may have served as models for the village examined in her early poem 'Lillooet: a Canadian Village'.

HARTLAND

Alden Nowlan began his professional careers as poet and journalist in this village of 1,000 north of Woodstock and just east of the Trans-Canada Highway (Highway 2). Born near WINDSOR, N.S., Nowlan came to Hartland in 1952, when he was hired as a reporter by the Hartland *Observer*, of which he later became the editor; the newspaper still publishes from the Main St building in which he worked. While here, Nowlan published his five earliest poetry collections—*The Rose and the Puritan* (1958), *A Darkness in the Earth* (1959), *Under the Ice* (1960), *Wind in a Rocky Country* (1961), and *Things Which Are* (1962)—before leaving Hartland in 1963 to join the SAINT JOHN *Telegraph-Journal*.

To win his job on the *Observer* the nineteen-year-old Nowlan, whose formal schooling ended with grade five, backed up his fictitious claim to a high-school education and a year's journalistic experience with a few occasional articles he had had published in the Windsor, N.S. *Tribune*. (See also FREDERICTON, SAINT JOHN, SUSSEX; STANLEY, N.S.)

'THESE ARE THE TREES . . .'

These are the trees: alive, the sluggish light
stationed in their moist hearts; they do not fight
the axe-blade, though they'll break an axeman's back
and look benevolent. The centuries
have made a violent marriage here, the men
wedded by violation to the trees,
so they reflect each other, taking in
strange qualities. The men assume at length
the stubborn stance of trees, their dogged strength.

—Alden Nowlan, 'These Are the Men Who Live by Killing Trees,' *Under the Ice* (1960)

KINGSTON

Walter Bates, the American-born author of *The Mysterious Stranger* (1817), settled in 1783 in Kingston, the oldest of New Bruns-

The cover of *The Mysterious Stranger*

wick's United Empire Loyalist settlements, and for many years served as sheriff of King's County. *The Mysterious Stranger*, which went through many editions in the United States and England, tells the story of Henry More Smith, alias 'Henry Moon', a thief whose exploits and ingenuity captured the nineteenth-century imagination. Smith was held for a time in Bates' jail but was pardoned and resumed his criminal activities in the United States. Bates drew on his own experience and that of other Connecticut Loyalists to write an account of present-day Kingston's chief monument, Trinity Anglican Church, which was erected by the Loyalists in 1789 and is still in active use. It appears in W.O. Raymond's *Kingston and the Loyalists of the 'Spring Fleet' of A.D. 1783 . . .* published in 1889 in Saint John.

MEDUCTIC

Excavations at Meductic have uncovered remnants of a fort that the Etchemin Indians (generally called the Malecites) built to defend themselves against their enemies the Mohawks. **John Gyles** (1680?–1755), the son of a New England judge, was captured at Pemaquid, Maine, when only nine years old and held captive here for six years, thus becoming the first English-speaking resident of what is now New Brunswick. Although treated as a slave, Gyles managed to keep a diary. This became the basis of his vivid account of his captivity, *Memoirs of Odd Adventures, Strange Deliverances, etc., in the Captivity of John Gyles, Esq.* (1736), which was edited and republished in Saint John in 1875 by James Henry Hannay (1842–1910), a newspaper editor and local historian. Gyles is the subject of a non-fiction narrative, *The Ordeal of John Gyles* (1966), by the essayist and humorist Stuart Trueman.

MEDUCTIC

After some miles' travel we came in sight of a large cornfield, and soon after of the Maliseet fort, to my great surprise. Two or three squaws met us, took off my pack, and led me to a large hut or wigwam, where thirty or forty Indians were dancing and yelling around five or six poor captives, who had been taken some months before from Quochech, at the time Major Waldron was so barbarously butchered by them.

—John Gyles, *Memoirs of Odd Adventures . . .* (1736)

MINTO

This community of about 4,000 persons is portrayed under the name 'Clearview' in New Brunswick poet **Elizabeth Brewster**'s *The Sisters* (1972), a partially autobiographical novel of a Maritime childhood and youth. Minto lies southeast of Brewster's home town, CHIPMAN, on Highway 10, in the dairy and livestock region to the east of Grand Lake. (See also FREDERICTON, SUSSEX.)

MONCTON

The family of **Northrop Frye**, literary theorist and critic, moved here in 1918, when Frye was six, from his birthplace in SHERBROOKE, Que. Taught at home by his mother, who had been a high-school teacher, Frye entered grade four in Moncton's old Victoria School, on Weldon St at Park, at the age of eight. He later attended Aberdeen High School on Botsford St, which has been an elementary school since 1935. The Frye family house stood on Pine St. On 27 Feb. 1927 the first Moncton Public Library was opened in the Archibald House at the foot of Archibald St; Frye was then fourteen and by the age of fifteen his reading here had given him a sound basic knowledge of ninteenth-century English literature and the first stirrings of his critical ideas. Frye's piano teacher, Dr George Ross, also had his home (where he taught) on Archibald St. On graduating from Aberdeen High School, Frye won a scholarship to a local business college, and later entered a national speed-typing contest held at Massey Hall, Toronto, placing second with eighty words a minute. That year, 1929, he enrolled in Victoria College, University of Toronto, with which he has been associated ever since, latterly as Chancellor. Among Frye's many influential books are *Anatomy of Criticism* (1957) and *The Great Code: The Bible and Literature* (1982). *The Bush Garden: Essays on the Canadian Imagination* (1971) is a collection of his writings on Canadian literature. (See TORONTO: 3, Ont.; WINNIPEG, Man.)

Moncton's population is about one-third French-speaking, and the city is a centre of the renaissance of Acadian culture. The writers who have contributed to this movement have been mainly grouped around several Moncton institutions: *L'Évangéline*, 80 Church St, the French daily newspaper that employed literary writers and published literary work; the Université de Moncton, the only Acadian university; and the only Acadian book publisher, Éditions d'Acadie. Founded in 1973, it was located through the mid-1980s at 120 Victoria St; it is now at 207 Robinson St. *L'Évangéline*, which was forced to close in the early 1980s, encouraged Acadian national identity and literature for well over a century by publishing many works of historical and literary interest. It twice reprinted Pamphile Lemay's translation of Longfellow's *Evangeline*, in 1887 and 1933.

The university's Centre d'Études Acadiennes houses, among its many documents, the unpublished manuscript of the play *Les Acadiens de Philadelphie* by **Pascal Poirier** (see SHEDIAC), which was successfully performed in Ottawa in 1875; the manuscript, believed lost in the 1916 fire that destroyed the Parliament Buildings in Ottawa, was recently discovered in Charlesbourg, Que. The Centre holds many other papers of Poirier, an early man of letters, whose work includes *Origine des Acadiens* (1874) and *Le Parler franco-acadien et ses origines* (1928), which attempts to analyse Acadian speech as a language rather than a dialect.

The poet and film-maker **Léonard Forest**, born on 17 Jan. 1928 in Chelsea, Mass., of Acadian parents, was brought to Moncton before the age of two and received his early schooling here. Since 1956 he has lived in Montreal and worked for the National Film Board, but most of his films concern Acadia, where they have been shot. Éditions d'Acadie has published his two volumes of poetry, *Saisons antérieures* (1973) and *Comme en Florence* (1979), winner of the Prix France-Acadie. The best-known modern Acadian poet is **Ronald Després**, who was born on 7 Nov. 1935 in Lewisville, a suburb just east of Moncton, and attended Moncton's Collège l'Assomption. In 1954 he went to Paris to study music and philosophy and contributed his 'Esquisses Parisiennes' to *L'Évangéline*; returning in 1956, he worked one year for the newspaper. In 1957 he became a parliamentary translator in Ottawa and in 1973 was charged with creating the present Translation Bureau of the Department of the Secretary of State. Deprés's poetry collections are *Silences à nourrir de sang* (1958), *Les Cloisons en vertige* (1962), and *Le Balcon des dieux inachevés* (1968); a selection, including more recent work, is *Paysages en contrebande* (1974).

Raymond LeBlanc, born at St-Anselme, studied philosophy at the Université de Moncton and while there helped to found Éditions d'Acadie; his book of poems, *Cris de terre* (1973), was the first published by the new press. LeBlanc also wrote for *L'Évangéline*. The poet **Hermé-négilde Chiasson**, born on 7 Apr. 1946 and brought up in St-Simon, received a B.A. from the Université de Moncton in 1967, and after further studies (see SACKVILLE) returned to teach at the university. Éditions d'Acadie published his influential *Mourir à Scoudouc* in 1974. The poet and *chansonnier* **Calixte Duguay**, for many years a high-school teacher in BATHURST, came to Moncton to produce the French-language music program 'Encore Debout' on CBC radio; his poems are collected in *Stigmates du silence* (1975). The poet **Guy Arsenault** is a Moncton native and resident who was born here on 2 Feb. 1954. His *Acadie Rock* was one of the earliest publications of Éditions d'Acadie, appearing in Dec. 1973.

Also briefly associated with Moncton was **Antonine Maillet**, the pre-eminent Acadian writer, author of *La Sagouine* (1971), *Pélagie-la-Charrette* (1979), and many other works. A native of BUCTOUCHE, Maillet studied during the 1960s in Moncton at Collège Notre-Dame d'Acadie, where she received her B.A. and M.A.

NEWCASTLE

One of the principal towns in the Miramichi district, Newcastle is associated with the preservation of northeastern New Brunswick's heritage of folk songs and literature. A large collection of these materials is held in the Old Manse, 255 Mary St, where the first curator was the folklorist **Dr Louise Manny**.

Max Aitken, Lord Beaverbrook (1879–1964), born in Maple, Ontario, grew up in the Old Manse. A London newspaper magnate and influential member of the British government during both the First and Second World Wars, Beaverbrook gave the province a large library, which is housed in the Manse, and in 1947 encouraged and enabled Dr Manny to begin research that led to *Songs of Miramichi* (1968), co-authored with a musicologist, James R. Wilson.

Newcastle holds an annual folksong festival at the end of June and beginning of July, when singers from throughout the region perform traditional and composed songs reflecting the ethnic diversity of the Miramichi region: old French ballads of the Acadians, Irish street songs and country ballads, traditional Scotch and English ballads, American folksongs and songs of the Revolutionary and Civil wars, and indigenous New Brunswick songs set to the old melodies. The visitor is almost certain to hear 'The Jones Boys', whose tune Beaverbrook liked so much that he gave the University of New Brunswick a set of chimes that play its chorus every hour:

The Jones boys,
They built a mill
On the side of a hill,
And they worked all night
And they worked all day,
But they couldn't make that gosh-darn
sawmill pay.

Newcastle was the birthplace in 1950 of the novelist **David Adams Richards**, who has continued to live here. Richards' father was the former owner of the Newcastle Opera House, which he converted to a motion-picture theatre around 1921; the Opera House has since been sold and converted to other uses. The family later operated two local movie theatres, now closed. Richards' highly regarded novels—*The Coming of Winter* (1974), *Blood Ties* (1976), and *Lives of Short Duration* (1981)—are all set in Newcastle and the Miramichi region, although the city and the river are unnamed in his work. Richards lived until 1984 in a white frame house near the city's central park, which contains a bust of Lord Beaverbrook; he is now writer-in-residence at the University of New Brunswick, FREDERICTON.

NEWCASTLE

The night air smelled of autumn, the autumn burnings—a tinge of smoke lying on the dark air and over the cut fields on both sides of the roadway, so that everything seemed full with it, and autumn warm.

And the town had that faintness of smoke to it between the rows of small houses and sheds, the burning of leaves in barrels. It was a quiet night, a good night for walking in the streets, through the side streets after dark, or out along the wharf.

—David Adams Richards, *The Coming of Winter* (1974)

NEW RIVER BEACH

The poet **P.K. Page** lived here for a period during the late 1930s, in a house called 'Pat's House' (not named for the poet), where she wrote her early prose romance *The Sun and the Moon* about a young wife in communication with mysterious forces that threaten her husband. The story, published under the name 'Judith Cape' in 1944, after Page had moved to Montreal, was reprinted under her own name in *The Sun and Moon and Other Fictions* (1973). (See also MONTREAL: 5, Que., VICTORIA, B.C.)

PASSAMAQUODDY BAY

This bay in the northwest shore of the Bay of Fundy enters literature through **James De Mille**'s humorous poem 'Sweet Maiden of Passamaquoddy', which makes fun of the tongue-twisting Micmac and Etchemin place-names throughout New Brunswick and begins:

Sweet maiden of Passamaquoddy,
Shall we seek for communion of souls
Where the deep Mississippi meanders,
Or the distant Saskatchewan rolls?
Ah no! in New Brunswick we'll find it—
A sweetly sequestered nook—
Where the sweet gliding Skoodawabskooksis
Unites with the Skoodawabskook . . .

Visitors here can still see the 'little Fundy fishing boats/With gunwales painted green' pictured in 'The Ships of Yule' from *Echoes from Vagabondia* (1912) by **Bliss Carman** (see FREDERICTON).

It has been argued that the Norsemen visited Passamaquoddy Bay and that Grand Manan Island and other features of the local coast and waters are recognizable from descriptions in the sagas relating to America (see L'ANSE AUX MEADOWS, Nfld.).

According to Eastern Algonkian legend the islands in Passamaquoddy Bay—Deer, Moose, and the group of islets called the Wolves—were created by the Algonkian culture-hero Glooscap when he came upon a pack of wolves killing a moose and a deer; to stop the slaughter he transformed them into islands. The myths and folklore of the Micmac and Etchemin (or Malecite) tribes that inhabited New Brunswick (and other eastern regions) can be read in **W.H. Mechling**'s *Malecite Tales* (1914), **Silus Tertius Rand**'s *Legends of the Micmacs* (1894), and **Cyrus Macmillan**'s *Canadian Wonder Tales* (1918) and *Canadian Fairy Tales* (1922), which were reissued in one volume under the title *Canadian Wonder Tales* in 1974. (See also WOOD ISLANDS, P.E.I.; BLOMIDON, N.S.; MONTREAL: 3, Que.)

ROTHESAY

The poet **P.K. Page** lived in Rothesay, just north of Saint John, during the 1930s. She

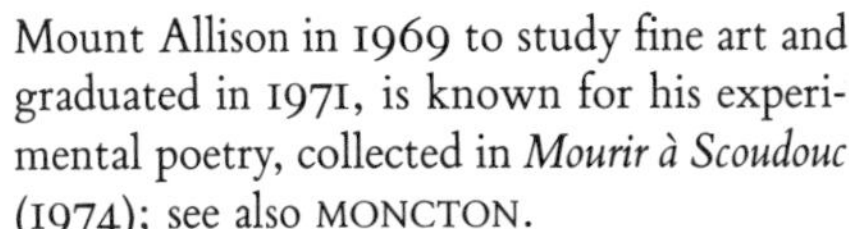

came here from Alberta, after graduating from high school in 1934, to take a job as a shop assistant in the Saint John retail firm of Manchester, Robertson, Allison. Page wrote some of her earliest published work in New Brunswick before moving to Montreal in the early 1940s. (See also NEW RIVER BEACH; MONTREAL: 5, Que.; VICTORIA, B.C.)

Rothesay was the home of the popular essayist and local-colour writer **Stuart Trueman** from 1940 until 1983, when he retired from the Saint John *Telegraph-Journal* and moved to nearby Hampton. Among his books of warm reminiscences about his life and his home province are *You're Only as Old as You Act* (1969), which won a Stephen Leacock Medal for humour, and *The Wild Life I've Led* (1976). During the 1940s he lived at 59 Crown St. He also lived at 24 Wentworth St and 68 Mecklenburg St.

SACKVILLE

Charles G.D. Roberts spent most of his boyhood here; his home until the age of fourteen was the old Westcock Parsonage of St Ann's (Anglican) Church, where the poet's father, the Rev. Goodridge Roberts, served until he moved to FREDERICTON. The parsonage overlooked the Tantramar Marshes, 80 square miles of former marsh converted to fertile grassland by old Acadian dykes that still shield it from the sea. Roberts' experiences here contributed much to his work in both poetry and fiction and led directly to one of his masterpieces, the poem 'The Tantramar Revisited' from *In Divers Tones* (1887).

Mount Allison University, which evolved from a Wesleyan Methodist boys' school founded here in 1840, has brought other writers and literary associations to Sackville. **Charles Bruce**, a native of PORT SHOREHAM, N.S., received his B.A. from Mount Allison in 1927, the year of publication of his first poetry collection, *Wild Apples*, most of which was written here. Bruce, who won a Governor General's Award for his collection *The Mulgrave Road* (1951), was influenced by the poetry of Roberts. From 1961 to 1965 **Elizabeth Brewster**, a native of CHIPMAN, worked as a librarian at Mount Allison; several poems in her first major collection, *Passage of Summer* (1969), are set here. Since the 1970s the Ontario-born poet **Douglas Lochhead** has been director of Mount Allison's Centre for Canadian Studies. His book *High Marsh Road* (1980) evokes the Tantramar region. The Acadian poet **Herménégilde Chiasson**, who entered Mount Allison in 1969 to study fine art and graduated in 1971, is known for his experimental poetry, collected in *Mourir à Scoudouc* (1974); see also MONCTON.

FROM 'THE TANTRAMAR REVISITED'

Here where the road that has climbed from the inland valleys and woodlands,
Dips from the hill-tops down, straight to the base of the hills,—
Here, from my vantage-ground, I can see the scattering houses,
Stained with time, set warm in orchards, meadows, and wheat,
Dotting the broad bright slopes outspread to southward and eastward.
Wind-swept all day long, blown by the southeast wind.

—Charles G.D. Roberts

The poet **John Thompson**—who died in 1976 at thirty-eight, apparently a suicide—came here in 1966 and taught in the English department of Mount Allison. His two books of poems, *At the Edge of the Chopping There Are No Secrets* (1973) and *Stilt Jack* (1978), were written during his years here, and both draw on his experience of the Tantramar Marsh country, where he lived in an old farmhouse that burned down just before his death. This incident is referred to in some of the poems of *Stilt Jack*.

Oliver Goldsmith

The Westcock Parsonage, Sackville, painted by Goodridge Roberts from a description by Charles G.D. Roberts

FROM 'THE RISING VILLAGE'

Happy Acadia! though around thy shore
Is heard the stormy wind's terrific roar;
Though round thee Winter binds his icy chain,
And his rude tempests sweep along thy plain,
Still Summer comes, and decorates thy land
Of fruits and flowers from her luxuriant hand;
Still Autumn's gifts repay the laborer's toil
With richest products from thy fertile soil;
With bounteous hand his varied wants supply,
And scarce the plants of other suns deny.
How pleasing, and how glowing with delight
Are now thy budding hopes! How sweetly bright
They rise to view! How full of joy appear
The expectations of each future year!

—Oliver Goldsmith

ST ANDREWS

This old United Empire Loyalist town on PASSAMAQUODDY BAY was the birthplace, on 6 July 1794, of **Oliver Goldsmith**, the first native-born Anglo-Canadian poet to publish a volume of poems, *The Rising Village* (London, 1825); it was reprinted in Saint John in 1834. Goldsmith was the son of Loyalists, and the poem, which narrates the establishment and growth of a Loyalist community in the Maritime wilderness, reflects Goldsmith's experience of the Annapolis Valley, N.S., rather than what is now New Brunswick; Goldsmith's family moved shortly after his birth, although he returned briefly to his native province, working in 1833–4 for the commissariat of the British Army in SAINT JOHN. Goldsmith was a grandnephew of the Irish poet Oliver Goldsmith, author of *The Deserted Village* (1770), on which *The Rising Village* was modelled. A national historic plaque at the St Andrew's post office commemorates Goldsmith's birth here. (See also HALIFAX, N.S.)

St Andrews is the home of the Scottish-born novelist **David Walker**, who first came to Canada in 1938 as aide-de-camp to Governor General Lord Tweedsmuir (see OTTAWA, Ont.) Walker immigrated in 1947 after a military career in Britain. Two of his novels, *The Pillar* (1952) and *Digby* (1953), won Governor General's Awards; probably his most popular books have been *Geordie* (1950) and *Harry Black* (1956), both of which were made into films, and *Come Back, Geordie* (1966). Walker's home is 'Strathcroix', an old farmhouse about 3 miles from St Andrews that the author has renovated.

SAINT JOHN

Saint John takes its name from the Saint John River, which was discovered and named by Samuel de Champlain on the feast day of St John the Baptist, 24 June 1604; the event is recorded in the first volume of Champlain's *Voyages* (1613). The city next appears in Canada's exploration literature in Nicolas Denys's *Description ... des costes de l'Amérique septentrionale* (1672), our chief source for the semi-legendary conflict between Charles La Tour, who built a fortified trading post here in 1631, and Charles de Menou, sieur d'Aulnay-Charnisay, both of whom had claim to the title of lieutenant-general. La Tour's fort was on Portland Point on the north bank of the mouth of the Saint John River. Determined to displace La Tour, Aulnay-Charnisay took advantage of La Tour's absence from the fort in April 1645 to attack it. After a gallant defence led by La Tour's wife, the fort fell; Madame La Tour died in captivity in June. La Tour, however, had his revenge. After Aulnay-Charnisay drowned in 1650, La Tour went to France and succeeded in becoming governor of Acadia. Returning to North America in 1653, he married Aulnay-Charnisay's widow. Portland Point and the site of Fort La Tour is within modern Saint John at the harbour.

The poet **Oliver Goldsmith**, grandnephew of the famous Irish author of the same name, lived in Saint John from 1833 to 1844. Born in ST ANDREWS in 1794, he moved at a young age to Nova Scotia; most of his literary activity occurred in HALIFAX, where he was a friend of Joseph Howe and a member of The Club. His major work *The Rising Village* (1825), a long poem in heroic couplets exploring the difficulties and rewards of establishing British civilization in the wilderness of Nova Scotia, was first published in London, but in 1834 Goldsmith published in Saint John a second edition that included some additional poems; his only other work was a brief *Autobiography*, which was not published until 1943. An employee of the commissariat of the British Army from 1810, Goldsmith was transferred to Hong Kong in 1844; he worked in ST JOHN'S, Nfld., from 1848 to 1853 and died in England in 1861. Another early Saint John man of letters, **George Edward Fenety**, was also a protégé of Joseph Howe. Born in Fredericton in 1812, Fenety spent seven years in Halifax as a writer and business manager for Howe's newspaper, the *Novascotian*. In 1839 he moved permanently to Saint John, founding the first penny newspaper in the Maritime provinces, the *Commercial News*, which operated until 1863 and was known as the *Morning News*, among other names. Fenety, who followed Howe in championing reform causes, wrote a satirical novelette, *The Lady and the Dressmaker; or, A Peep at Fashionable Folly* (1842), and a biography of his early mentor, *Life and Times of the Hon. Joseph Howe* (1896).

Other major contributors to the literary life of Saint John in the mid-nineteenth century were the novelists **Douglas S. Huyghue** and May Agnes Fleming, and the poet William Murdoch. Huyghue was born in 1816 into a military family in CHARLOTTETOWN, P.E.I., but spent his childhood and received his early education in Saint John. After a brief period in Halifax, he returned to Saint John for the years 1841–4. During this time he published, as a serial in the Saint John periodical the *Amaranth*, one of the best early novels produced in the Maritimes, *Argimou: A Legend of the Micmac* (1842). Sympathetic to Indian culture and its plight in the face of European encroachment, Huyghue is known to have helped organize and present an exhibition of Indian artifacts in Saint John in the early 1840s. In 1844 he immigrated to England, where he published another novel of Canada, *The Nomades of the West; or Ellen Clayton* (1850); in 1852 he moved to Australia, where he spent the last thirty-nine years of his life. **William Murdoch** was born in 1823 in Paisley, Scotland, and came to New Brunswick in 1854, at first working at the marine station on Partridge Island near the Saint John Harbour. In 1865 he joined the *Morning News* of Saint John and lived here until his death in 1887. As a poet Murdoch was an imitator of Burns, producing rollicking ballads on patriotic, political, and other themes. His books, all published in Saint John, include *Poems and Songs* (1860), its greatly expanded second edition (1872), and a collection entitled *Discursory Ruminations, A Fireside Drama, Etc., Etc.* (1876). The novelist **May Agnes** (née Early) **Fleming**, probably the first professional writer native to the Maritime Provinces, was born in Saint John on 15 Nov. 1840. She was educated at the Convent of the Sacred Heart in Saint John and while still a schoolgirl sold her first story to the New York *Mercury*. Fleming became an enormously popular writer of romance novels employing standardized plot elements and character types and mostly taking place in Europe and the United States. A few, however—such as *Kate Danton; or, Captain Danton's Daughters*, (1876)—are set in Canada, primarily in Quebec, which provided an exotic background for British and American readers. In the mid-1870s Fleming moved with her four children to Brooklyn, N.Y.,

May Agnes Fleming

where she died on 26 Mar. 1880. Her writings were so popular that they continued to be reprinted long after her death, and new Fleming romances were apparently ghost-written under her name.

In the 1860s Saint John gave rise to several important literary periodicals, notably *Stewart's Literary Quarterly* (1867–72). Born in the United States, **George Stewart** Jr. received his education in London, Ont., and in Saint John, where at sixteen he founded Canada's first stamp collectors' magazine. In 1867, when he was only nineteen, he established *Stewart's Literary Quarterly*; it was the only Canadian magazine of its time to rely entirely on original contributions (as opposed to reprinted ones) and one of the few to pay its contributors, among whom were Charles Sangster and Alexander McLachlan. After his magazine had succumbed in 1872 to financial pressures, Stewart remained in Saint John for six years as city editor of the *Daily News* and literary editor of the *Weekly Watchman*. Thereafter he worked as an editor in Toronto and QUEBEC CITY.

James De Mille, the best-known nineteenth-century Maritime novelist, was born in Saint John in 1833 but spent much of his childhood in the Minas Basin area of Nova Scotia and received his early education in WOLFVILLE, N.S. In the late 1850s De Mille returned to Saint John, where for several years he was a bookseller. He went back to Nova Scotia, however, to teach at Acadia College in Wolfville from 1860 to 1865 and then at Dalhousie College, HALIFAX, until his death in 1880. A prolific novelist, De Mille did not begin publishing his fiction until after he left Saint John, although his first novel, *Martyrs of the Catacombs* (1864), was written in Saint John in 1858. His affection for New Brunswick emerges in his poem 'Sweet Maiden of Passamaquoddy' (see PASSAMAQUODDY BAY), which makes comical use of the province's tongue-twisting place names.

The novelist **Albert Hickman** was born in Dorchester, N.B., in 1877 and reared in PICTOU, N.S., but he lived in Saint John from 1899 until after the First World War, during which time he produced all of his creative writing. Hickman operated a marine-engineering firm in Saint John, which he moved to New England after the war. His fiction includes *The Sacrifice of Shannon* (1903), a novel with a Nova Scotia background, and *Canadian Nights* (1914), a collection of novelettes and stories; one of these, 'An Unofficial Love Story' (1909), is set in Saint John.

The writer most closely identified with Saint John is the Rev. **Hiram A. Cody**, rector of St James (Anglican) Church from 1910 until his death in 1948. He lived at 280 St James St. Born in 1872 in nearby CODY'S, N.B., he was educated at the Saint John Grammar School and at King's College, WINDSOR, N.S.; he was ordained in 1898 and served in GREENWICK, N.B., from 1897 until 1904. All of Cody's twenty-three popular novels were published during his years in Saint John, beginning with *The Frontiersman: A Tale of the Yukon* (1910). Among his other Canadian novels are *The Long Patrol; A Tale of the Mounted Police* (1912) and *The King's Arrow: A Tale of United Empire Loyalists* (1922). Also a poet, Cody captured many aspects of Saint John and New Brunswick history in his locally familiar rollicking ballads. In 'The Port of Saint John' he celebrates the city's seamen and the shipbuilding industry, which began in 1769 and has given the city its economic base and its character ever since. (See also WHITEHORSE, Y.T.) Today, Saint John resident **William Edward Daniel ('Dan') Ross** carries on the city's tradition of popular novelists. Ross turned to writing in middle life, and since 1950 has produced over 350 Gothic romances and some 600 short stories both under his own name and under many pseudonyms. In the 1950s and '60s he lived at 1281 Manawagonish Rd.

The Rev. Hiram A. Cody

'THE PORT OF SAINT JOHN'

The finest wooden sailing-ships were built upon my shore,
The roaring Marco Polo *and the bounding* Beejapore;
The Flying Cloud, *the* Guiding Star *and other far famed ships,*
Designed and built by Saint John men, went smoking from their slips.

—Hiram A. Cody, *Songs of a Bluenose* (1925)

The essayist **Stuart Trueman**, formerly a prominent Saint John newspaperman, began as a cartoonist for the *Evening Times-Globe* in 1928 and retired in 1971 after twenty years as editor of that newspaper and its sister publication, the *Telegraph-Journal*. For many years he lived in nearby ROTHESAY. The author of many volumes combining local history, reminiscence, and reflection, Trueman received a Stephen Leacock Medal for humour for *You're Only as Old as You Act* (1969). During Trueman's years as editor one of his subordinates was the poet **Alden Nowlan**, who came to the *Telegraph-Journal* from the HARTLAND *Observer* in 1963 and was news editor from 1965 to 1968, when he moved to FREDERICTON as writer-in-residence at the University of New Brunswick. While in Saint John Nowlan published only one book, *Bread, Wine and Salt* (1967), which won a Governor's General Award. He lived at the Mitchell Apartments, on the Park Ave extension, from 1965 to 1968.

The poet **P.K. Page** came to New Brunswick in 1934 after graduating from high school and had her first job at the Saint John firm of Manchester, Robertson, Allison (no longer in existence). Until moving to MONTREAL (5) in the early 1940s she lived in ROTHESAY and later in NEW RIVER BEACH. The editor, critic, and poet **John Sutherland** is another writer associated with Montreal who lived for a time in Saint John. Born in 1919 in LIVERPOOL, N.S., he spent four years (1937–41) at his parents' home in Saint John, convalescing from tuberculosis of the kidney, which he had contracted while attending Queen's University in Kingston, Ont. Sutherland was the editor of two important literary magazines, *First Statement* and *Northern Review*. Some of his own writings are collected in *John Sutherland: Essays, Controversies and Poems* (1972). The poet **Robert Gibbs**, born here in 1930, is now a professor of English at the University of New Brunswick, Fredericton; he is the author of four volumes of poems, including *All This Night Long* (1978).

ST STEPHEN

The Ontario-born poet **Wilfred Campbell** served from 1888 to 1890 as rector of Trinity Anglican Church here. He published his first book, *Snowflakes and Sunbeams* (1888) in

St Stephen in order to help with fund-raising for a local charity event; and his second book, *Lake Lyrics and Other Poems* (Saint John, 1889), was partly written here. His years in St Stephen, therefore, coincide with his earliest period as a published poet, even though he had begun to write poetry long before coming here and most of his best work is based on his experience of the region around Georgian Bay in Ontario. (See also KITCHENER, OTTAWA, WIARTON, Ont.)

FROM 'INDIAN SUMMER'

Now by great marshes wrapt in mist,
Or past some river's mouth,
Throughout the long, still autumn day
Wild birds are flying south.
—William Wilfred Campbell

SHEDIAC

This Acadian fishing port, famed for its lobsters, was the home of *Le Moniteur Acadien*—a newspaper, founded in 1867, that was the first vehicle for Acadian literature and opinion after the Expulsion of the Acadians in 1755. It continued to publish into the early twentieth century. Early in its history *Le Moniteur Acadien* contributed to the Acadian literary revival by reprinting **Pamphile Lemay**'s 1866 translation of Longfellow's *Evangeline*.

A national historic monument in Shediac honours five Acadian men of letters associated with *Le Moniteur*, the most prominent of whom are **Pascal Poirier** (see also MONCTON) and **Placide Gaudet**. Poirier—a poet, dramatist, and historian who lived in Shediac—was the first Maritime-born Acadian author to publish a book, *Origine des Acadiens* (1874); he also produced an early study of Acadian speech, *Le parler franco-acadien et ses origines* (1928). Gaudet, the most thorough and accurate of early Acadian historians, was the author of *Le Grand Dérangement* (1922). The others named on the monument are Israel Landry, who founded *Le Moniteur* in 1867, Ferdinand Robidoux, who succeeded him as editor, and John Clarence Webster, an author of historical works. One of Canada's most distinguished doctors and scientists, Webster was an international authority on gynaecology and obstetrics.

SUSSEX

Elizabeth Brewster, who was born at CHIPMAN, lived here from 1938 to 1942 and attended Sussex High School. Sussex, under the fictional name of 'Milton', figures prominently as the site of the wartime military camp in *The Sisters* (1972), her partly autobiographical novel of a Maritime girl's growing up. Brewster's story, 'A House Full of Women', collected in *It's Easy to Fall in the Snow* (1977), is also set partly in Sussex. (See also FREDERICTON, HAMMTOWN, MINTO.)

The Dollar Woman (1972), a play by **Alden Nowlan** (see also HARTLAND, SAINT JOHN) and Walter Learning that premièred in Jan. 1977 at Theatre New Brunswick, Fredericton, recalls the nineteenth-century pauper auctions that took place at the Sussex railway station in the heart of town—now a centre for local artisans. Paupers auctioned by the county became virtual slaves of the families who bought them. Sussex, located on Highway 1 and the Kennebecasis River, 40 miles northeast of Saint John, is the largest town in King's County.

Tappan Adney in the Far North

UPPER WOODSTOCK

The Old Carleton County Courthouse, a two-storey frame structure erected in 1833, is now the museum of the Carleton County Historical Society, located in this village 2 miles north of WOODSTOCK on Highway 103. One of its exhibits recalls the career of New Brunswick writer **Edwin Tappan Adney**, who was a journalist, artist, naturalist, and student of Indian culture. Adney's books include one of the best eyewitness accounts of the Klondike Gold Rush, *The Klondike Stampede of 1897–98* (1900), based on his experiences as a correspondent for *Harper's Illustrated Weekly* of New York.

WOODSTOCK

Woodstock was the home of the poet, nature writer, and physician **Dr George Frederick Clarke**, whose house was made a provincial historic site in 1979; it is privately owned and occupied. Clarke was the author of *The Saint John River and Other Poems* (1933), *Too Small a World* (1958), *Six Salmon Rivers and Another in Canada* (1960), and *Song of the Reel* (1963).

After leaving the University of New Brunswick for financial reasons, the poet **Francis Joseph Sherman**, a native of FREDERICTON, came to Woodstock in 1887 to work in the Woodstock branch of the Merchants' Bank of Halifax (later the Royal Bank of Canada); Sherman remained here until 1892. He published seven slim volumes of verse from 1896 to 1900. They were collected in the posthumous *Complete Poems of Francis Sherman* (1935).

Quebec

AUSTIN

Since 1974 the novelist **Mordecai Richler** has divided his time between his house in this village on Lake Memphremagog, in the Eastern Townships, and his home in MONTREAL (6). Here Richler has worked on several of his best-known books, principally *Joshua Then and Now* (1980) and the children's story *Jacob Two-two Meets the Hooded Fang* (1975), which was made into a film.

BAIE COMEAU

Baie Comeau is named for the bay on which it is situated, which in turn is named for **Napoléon-Alexandre Comeau**, a naturalist and the author of an autobiography, *Life and Sport on the North Shore of the Lower St. Lawrence* (1909). Comeau was primarily associated with the Godbout River and is buried in GODBOUT, 30 miles east of Baie Comeau. Le Musée de Baie-Comeau, at 43 rue Mance, contains many books and documents relating to Canada's early exploration literature, including the four volumes of **Samuel de Champlain**'s *Voyages* (1603, 1613, 1619, 1632); the seventy-three volumes of **R.G. Thwaites**'s historic edition of the *Jesuit Relations and Allied Documents* (1896–1901); an early catechism written for the Montagnais Indians in their language; and a copy of the original 1720 edition of Rear-Admiral Sir **Hovenden Walker**'s *A Journal; or, Full Account of the Late Expedition to Canada*. Walker's book tells of his ill-fated expedition of August 1711 against Quebec, when forty ships carrying 5,000 men under his command were wrecked in fog on the St Lawrence near Baie Comeau; Walker and the survivors then returned to England. Baie Comeau is on Hwy 138 on the north shore of the St Lawrence, about 100 miles northeast of Tadoussac. Prime Minister **Brian Mulroney**, born in Baie Comeau on 20 Mar. 1939, is the author of *Where I Stand* (1983). (See also GODBOUT).

BEAUCEVILLE EST

The house of the poet **William Chapman** is preserved and marked with a plaque at 277 av. Lambert in Beauceville Est, on the Chaudière River in Beauce County, midway between Lévis and the Maine border. Born at St-François-de-la-Beauce on 13 Dec. 1850, Chapman became a Montreal businessman and journalist as well as a patriotic and landscape poet in the manner of Louis Fréchette, Octave Crémazie, and Pamphile Lemay; among his volumes were *Les Québecqoises* (1876), *Les Feuilles d'érable* (1890), and *Les Rayons du nord* (1910). His best poems celebrate the Quebec landscape: 'La Beauce', for instance, portrays his native region. Chapman died in OTTAWA on 23 Feb. 1917. (See also MONTREAL: 9)

BEAUHARNOIS

When the novelist **Albert Laberge** was born in Beauharnois, on the south shore of the St Lawrence, in 1877, his farming family had occupied the same land since 1659. Laberge's *La Scouine*, a bleak view of the Beauharnois region in the nineteenth century, was printed privately in 1918 in an edition of only sixty copies. The first 'realist' novel to appear in Canada, it was considered so shocking in Quebec that the full text was not printed until 1972. (A translation, *Bitter Bread*, was published in 1977.) Laberge produced much of his realistic fiction from 1896 to 1932, while working as a sports writer and art critic for *La Presse* in MONTREAL (11), though only *La Scouine* was published before his retirement in 1932 to CHÂTEAUGUAY, a village just east of Beauharnois. Laberge's other works are collections of stories, critical essays, and prose poems; they include *Visages de la vie et de la mort* (1936), *Quand chantait le cigale* (1936), *Scènes de chaque jour* (1942), and *Le Dernier Souper* (1953).

Beauharnois was also the home town of the poet and man of letters **Eugène Seers**, who was born here on 28 Nov. 1865 and received his early schooling at home. He went to MONTREAL (10) to attend high school, and his literary career is associated with that city. Although he wrote important poetry and criticism, he is chiefly known as the editor of the poems of Émile Nelligan. Seers wrote under the name **Louis Dantin**.

BELOEIL

In 1963, at the age of seventy-four, the poet **Paul Morin** died in poverty and obscurity at this old and scenic village east of Montreal on the west shore of the Richelieu River. A poet in the Parnassian manner, Morin's reputation rests on two collections, *Le Paon d'émail* (1911) and *Poèmes de cendre et d'or* (1922), winner of the 1923 Prix David. Beset by a series of misfortunes, including a fire in MONTREAL (13) in 1956 that destroyed his papers and his few possessions, he wrote little in the last thirty years of his life. In the early 1960s the republishing of his two books and the appearance of a volume collecting later work, *Géronte et son miroir* (1960), demonstrated his importance in Quebec letters but did little to call attention to the poet himself.

Paul Morin

Beloeil was the birthplace in 1862 and the childhood home of the novelist **Ernest Choquette**. Choquette became a doctor, with a practice just across the river, in St-Hilaire, where he was elected mayor several times. He was the author of three novels of rural life, including *La Terre* (1916), and a collection of stories and sketches, *Carabinades* (1900). He died in 1941.

BOUCHERVILLE

Boucherville, which is across the St Lawrence River from Montréal-Est, was the home of the eighteenth-century man of letters **Joseph Quesnel**, who produced an early and isolated example of French-Canadian drama, the musical play *Colas et Colinette; ou Le Bailli dupé*, performed in MONTREAL (9) in 1790 and published (without music) in

1812. (It was recorded for Radio-Canada in 1968.) A native of Saint-Malo, France, Quesnel was arrested and taken to Halifax by the British after they had captured a provisions ship bound for New York under his command. He was permitted to settle in Lower Canada and spent the rest of his life in Boucherville, where he became a wealthy fur merchant and pursued his literary interests. Many poems by Quesnel were published in newspapers, but his most interesting works are his dramas *Colas et Colinette*, *L'Anglomanie* (a satire on 'Anglomania', the tendency of young French Canadians to adopt English ways), and *Les Républicains français* (a savage satire on French republicanism). The latter two plays, neither published nor performed during Quesnel's lifetime, first appeared in 1965 and 1970 respectively, when they were printed by the magazine *La Barre du jour*; they still await book publication. Quesnel, who was also a musician, left the score for another projected but unwritten musical play; he died in Boucherville in 1809. His house at 386 Bd Marie-Victorin, which dates from 1750, is now a provincial historic monument.

CABANO

Near this picturesque village, on Lake Témiscouata southeast of Rivière du Loup, **Archibald Stansfeld Belaney** began his writing career. Known by his adopted Indian name of **Grey Owl** (Wa-sha-Quon-Asin), Belaney had been a trapper, hunter, and wilderness guide, but in 1926 he met an Iroquois woman, Anahareo, who inspired in him a revulsion against hunting and a passion for the conservation of wildlife and landscape. At a time when the beaver seemed on the verge of extinction, Anahareo and Grey Owl adopted two baby beavers and journeyed to Cabano with them to find a place where they could live in safety. This quest is the subject of his most famous book, *Pilgrims of the Wild* (1935). Grey Owl remained at Cabano until 1930, when the Canadian government appointed him an honorary park warden and assisted him in his conservation efforts, first at RIDING MOUNTAIN NATIONAL PARK, Man., and then, permanently, at Lake Ajawaan in PRINCE ALBERT NATIONAL PARK, Sask. A mile from Cabano on Hwy 232 the museum of Fort Ingall contains a section on Grey Owl. This restored fort is near the site of the cabin on Lake Témiscouata in which Grey Owl wrote the magazine articles and stories in the late 1920s that led to his fame as a nature writer and to the publication of his first book, *Men of the Last Frontier* (1929). Cabano is on the Trans-Canada Highway. (See also COBALT, TEMAGAMI, Ont.)

Anahareo and Grey Owl while they were living near Cabano

CACOUNA

The family of **Émile Nelligan** spent nearly every summer during the poet's childhood and youth in this village—a popular nineteenth-century beach resort—on the south shore of the St Lawrence just above Rivière du Loup. In the summer of 1896 the sixteen-year-old Nelligan summered here along with Denys Lanctot, a young poet he had met the previous spring; at that time he had also met a number of writers associated with the fledgeling École littéraire de Montréal, including Eugène Seers ('Louis Dantin'), Joseph Melançon ('Lucien Ranier'), and Arthur de Bussières. (See MONTREAL: 10.) At Cacouna, Nelligan began publishing his first known poems, and it is likely that some, if not all, of them were written here. These nine poems, which all appeared in Montreal's *Le Samedi*, were 'Rêve fantasque', 'Silvio Corelli pleure', 'Nuit d'été', 'La Chanson de l'ouvrière', 'Nocturne', 'Coeurs blasés', 'Mélodie de Rubinstein', 'Charles Baudelaire', and 'Beatrice'. It is believed that during at least a few of their vacations here the Nelligans stayed at St Lawrence Hall, a famous resort hotel at 500 rue Principale that was demolished about sixty years ago.

CARILLON

Situated on Hwy 344 west of Laval at the Long Sault, above the mouth of the Ottawa River, Carillon is the reputed site of the heroic battle waged by Adam Dollard des Ormeaux (1635–60) and sixteen Frenchmen against hundreds of Iroquois in May 1660; Dollard's remarkable defence, which

The Abbé Groulx, holding his *Dollard, est-il un mythe?* (1960)

lasted eight days, was for many years thought to have discouraged an Iroquois attack on Ville Marie (Montreal). This event is the subject of **Archibald Lampman**'s lyric-narrative poem 'At the Long Sault: May, 1660', which was included in the posthumous *At the Long Sault and Other New Poems* (1943). Dollard also figures in a series of works, beginning with *Si Dollard revient* (1919), by Abbé **Lionel Adolphe Groulx**, Quebec historian and nationalist, who made Dollard the representative hero of French-Canadian nationalism. Dollard des Ormeaux is commemorated by a monument that stands near the river; by a group of monoliths to the seventeen French heroes in Dollard des Ormeaux Park near the Carillon Canal; and by the Maison Desormeaux at 36 and 38 rue Principale.

The melody of 'O Canada' was composed here by Calixa Lavallée in 1880. (See also ST-PLACIDE.)

CAUGHNAWAGA

Kateri Tekakwitha, a Mohawk convert to Roman Catholicism, died here on 17 Apr 1630 at the age of 24. She is buried on the Caughnawaga Indian Reverse, in a white marble tomb in the mission church of Saint-François-Xavier, erected in 1717. A statue of her stands outside the Reserve's Tekakwitha School. Beatified by the Catholic Church for her saintly and heroic life, Tekakwitha has been the subject of many biographies; she figures prominently in the novel *Beautiful Losers* (1966) by **Leonard Cohen** (see MONTREAL: 7). The old fieldstone priests' house next to the church contains several books of historic interest: a genealogy of Caughnawaga Indian families back to 1700 prepared by Bishop Guillaume Forbes (Archbishop of Ottawa, 1928–40); an Iroquois grammar and French-Iroquois and Iroquois-French dictionaries by Fr Joseph Marcoux; and a Seneca dictionary by Fr Jacques Bruyas.

CHÂTEAUGUAY

The novelist **Albert Laberge** had a summer home in Châteauguay, a village near MONTREAL (II) on the south shore of the St Lawrence, from 1932 until his death in 1960. A native of nearby BEAUHARNOIS, Laberge became the pioneer of fictional realism in Quebec with his novel *La Scouine* (1918; trans. Conrad Dion, *Bitter Bread*, 1977). He worked on all his other published writings at Châteauguay, although after 1932 he also worked in MONTREAL (II) and maintained a home there. His later books include *Visages de la vie et de la mort* (1936) and *Fin de roman* (1951), collections of stories; and *Hymnes à la terre* (1955), sketches and prose poems.

'La Victoire de Chateauguay' is the best-known poem of **Joseph Mermet**, a Frenchman who spent the years 1813–16 in Canada, mostly at KINGSTON, Ont., with a Swiss regiment that had come to fight the Americans. 'La Victoire de Châteauguay' narrates, in a vague and elevated style, the battle that occurred southwest of here on 26 Oct. 1813 when 460 Canadian Voltigeurs under Charles-Michel de Salaberry defeated a larger American force, saving Montreal from attack.

CHICOUTIMI

Two of Quebec's most influential twentieth-century writers, **Jean-Charles Harvey** and Father **Félix-Antoine Savard**, received their basic 'cours classique' at the Séminaire de Chicoutimi, and both studied for the priesthood, although their subsequent careers took very different directions. (The seminary property, which overlooks the St Lawrence, is at the northeast corner of Bd. Jacques-Cartier and rue Bégin.) Born in LA MALBAIE in 1891, Harvey attended the seminary from 1905 to 1908. Thereafter he lived primarily in QUEBEC CITY and in MONTREAL (15), where he was a Jesuit scholastic (1908–15), and studied at Université de Montréal before becoming a novelist, a social critic, and a journalist renowned for defending freedom of thought and for tackling the Roman Catholic clergy on its behalf. Among his six books of fiction, the most important are the novels *Marcel Faure* (1922) and *Les Demi-civilisés* (1934; trans. John Glassco, *Fear's Folly*, 1982).

Charles Gill at Cap Éternité, 1908

Savard, born in 1896 in QUEBEC CITY, lived in Chicoutimi from his childhood until 1927. Educated at the Séminaire de Chicoutimi, he was ordained in 1922 and taught for five years. He also served at parishes in the diocese for four years before establishing a new parish at CLERMONT, where he stayed until 1945 and where he began his literary and folkloric work. This first parish was at Bagotville, south of Chicoutimi on Hwy 327. A poet, fiction-writer, and memoirist, Savard is best known for his novel *Menaud, maître-draveur* (1937; trans. Richard Howard, *Master of the River*, 1976), the story of a lumberman and his family in the Charlevoix region were Clermont is located.

Chicoutimi stands on the south shore of the Saguenay River at the point where deep-water navigation ends. In the early twentieth century the poet and painter **Charles Gill** visited the city several times as he collected impressions of the Saguenay and Lac St-Jean country for an epic cycle of poems, which he did not live to complete. Filled with admiration for the landscape of the river and the spirit of its pioneers, Gill wrote of them in the literary tradition of *le terroir* ('the countryside'). In Nov. 1907 he read parts of his 'Cap Éternité' to an audience in Montreal; he is known to have travelled to Chicoutimi and the Saguenay in Aug. 1908, on one of several trips during which he sought inspiration for his work. Gill died in the influenza epidemic of 1918. His poetry was published posthumously in *Le Cap Éternité: poème suivi des Étoiles filantes* (1919). From Chicoutimi there are eight-hour boat cruises on the Saguenay to Cap Éternité. (See also MONTREAL: II, PIERREVILLE, SOREL.)

CLERMONT

In 1931 the priest and author **Félix-Antoine Savard** established the parish of St-Philippe in Clermont, which is just northwest of La Malbaie on the Malbaie River. He was responsible for the building of its church and rectory, where he lived and wrote until he left Clermont in 1945. The parish of St-Philippe still exists at 20 rue des Erables, but the buildings have been destroyed by fire and rebuilt twice since Savard's time. Here he began his literary career and wrote two of his most important works, notably *Menaud, maître-draveur* (1937), the story of a log driver who attempts unsuccessfully to oppose the economic encroachment of English-speaking owners in the Malbaie region. This famous novel has led to the nickname of 'le pays de Menaud' for the Charlevoix Counties (East and West). Savard revised his book five times, and two of the versions have been translated into English as, respectively, *Boss of the River* (1947) and *Master of the River* (1976). Another important work Savard wrote at Clermont was *L'Abatis* (1943), poetic memoirs in prose and verse of his experiences among pioneers in the Abitibi region of northwestern Quebec. Active in recruiting people from Charlevoix for this settlement effort, he often accompanied them to Abitibi. During his years at Clermont, Savard also began to assemble folklore materials, an activity that led to the establishment of folklore archives of Université Laval. (See also QUEBEC CITY, ST-JOSEPH-DE-LA-RIVE.)

COATICOOK

The poet **Alfred DesRochers** lived in Coaticook in 1927–8 while he was founding and operating his short-lived weekly newspaper *L'Étoile de l'est*. During this period DesRochers's first book, *L'Offrande aux vierges folles* (1928) was published, and he must also have been working on his second and most important collection of poems, *À l'ombre de l'Orford*, which appeared the following a year. (See also ST-ÉLIE D'ORFORD.)

DESCHAMBAULT

For three months in the summer of 1940 the poet **Alain Grandbois** lived in the Hôtel Deschambault, where he was one of the few guests, and wrote *Les Voyages de Marco Polo* (1940); his permanent home at the time was QUEBEC CITY. The book, which won the Prix David of the province of Quebec, was the first important work produced in Canada by the forty-year-old Grandbois, who is best known as a poet. He had previously written only a biography of Louis Jolliet, *Né à Québec* (1933), published in Paris, and *Poèmes* (1934), a pamphlet that appeared in an edition of 150 copies in Hankow, China. Although Grandbois's book about the famous Italian traveller was completed in Deschambault, the project was apparently conceived during a trip to the Far East in 1933–4 and begun as early as 1936. (See also MONTREAL: 15, ST-ALBAN, ST-CASIMIR-DE PORTNEUF; CHARLOTTETOWN, P.E.I.)

ESCOUMINS

This town was the birthplace on 13 Jan. 1889 of **Blanche Lamontagne-Beauregard**, the first prominent French-Canadian woman poet and one of Quebec's leading poets of the *terroir*—regional literature that depicted rural people's ties with the soil. When she was eight her family moved to a rural area in Bas Québec, at Cap Chat, not far from the Gaspé Peninsula. After studying at Université de Montréal, Lamontagne-Beauregard returned to the Gaspé and remained here for the rest of her life. Her poetry, celebrating the Gaspé's intermingling of land and sea, of farming and fishing ways of life, appeared in many collections, including *Visions gaspésiennes* (1913), *La Vieille Maison* (1920), and *Ma Gaspésie* (1928).

Escoumins was also the home of the writer and journalist **Robertine Barry** (1863–1910). Barry was for many years on the staff of *La Patrie* and wrote under the pseudonym 'Françoise', but left in 1901 to found a bi-monthly review, *Le Journal de Françoise*, which she edited until her death in 1910. A collection of her stories and sketches, *Fleurs Champêtres*, was published in 1895; one of her stories, 'La Gothe and Her Husband', appears in *Stories by Canadian Women* (1984). Barry, whose home was the town's Hôtel Bellevue, was a friend of Émilie-Amanda (Hudon) Nelligan, the mother of the poet **Émile Nelligan**. Although Robertine was eighteen years older than Émile Nelligan, he fell platonically in love with her when he met her in Montreal. She became the model for his image of the dark-haired woman, and his feeling for her gave rise to the famous sonnet 'Rêve d'artiste', in which she is called his 'soeur angélique', 'soeur éternelle', and 'soeur d'amitié dans le règne de l'Art'.

Escoumins is on Hwy 138, east of Quebec City on the north shore of the St Lawrence.

FORT CHIMO

Gabrielle Roy based her novel of an artist in the Canadian North, *La Montagne secrète* (1961; trans. *The Hidden Mountain*, 1962), on accounts of René Richard, an artist who lived in the Northwest Territories and was a frequent visitor to her home in QUEBEC CITY. The settings in the novel extend from Great Slave Lake to the Ungava Peninsula, where the hidden mountain of the book's title is located. During the summer of 1961 Roy visited Fort Chimo on Ungava Bay. For a week she explored modern Fort Chimo Town and the older abandoned site of Old Fort Chimo across the Koksoak River. The visit provided material for a novel and three short stories of Eskimo life that are collected in *La Rivière sans repos* (1970). The volume bears the title of the novel, which tells of an Eskimo girl raped by an American soldier stationed at Fort Chimo who finds herself cut off from her people because of the child she has borne. The novel was translated into English by Joyce Marshall with the title *Windflower* (1970).

R.M. Ballantyne (1825–94), the Scottish author of adventure novels for children, worked in Canada, largely in the North, in 1841–7, and was at Fort Chimo. He used his knowledge of the region in *Ungava: A Tale of Esquimaux Land* (1857).

FOSTER

The poet and memoirist **John Glassco** owned a house and lived and wrote here (dividing his time latterly between Foster and Montreal) from 1946 until his death in 1981; the house is still owned by his widow. Born in 1909 in MONTREAL (4), Glassco came to Foster in 1935 after spending 1928–32 in Paris, where he contracted tuberculosis and had to return to Montreal. (In 1937 he bought a house in KNOWLTON.) In Foster he founded the Foster Horse Show in 1951 and served as mayor from 1952 to 1954. The landscape and rural culture of the Eastern Townships are prominently featured in his poetry, published in *The Deficit Made Flesh* (1958), *A Point of Sky* (1964), and *Selected Poems* (1971), which won a Governor General's Award. Glassco's best-known book, *Memoirs of Montparnasse* (1970), is a reminiscence of his years in Paris and of the glittering French and expatriate literary communities there. Glassco is also known as translator of the *Complete Poems* (1962) and *Journal* (1962) of **Hector de Saint-Denys Garneau** (see STE-CATHERINE-DE-FOSSAMBAULT) and as editor of *The Poetry of French Canada in Translation* (1970).

John Glassco in 1970

With F.R. Scott and A.J.M. Smith, John Glassco organized the Foster Poetry Conference, which was held on 12–14 Oct. 1963 at the Glen Mountain Ski Chalet, West Boulton (near Foster). The proceedings were published in *English Poetry in Canada* (1965) edited by Glassco.

GODBOUT

Godbout was home for more than four decades to **Napoléon-Alexandre Comeau**, naturalist and author of *Life and Sport on the North Shore of the Lower St. Lawrence* (1909). The book, published simultaneously in French and in a translation by Nazaire LeVasseur, contains Comeau's keen observations as a naturalist and explorer, and an account of his adventurous life. Born in 1848 in Saguenay County, the son of a Hudson's Bay Company factor, he spent his life trapping and hunting along the Godbout River as a federal game warden and fisheries officer in the area. His book also recounts legends of the Montagnais Indians and his observations and experiences in Labrador.

Comeau died in 1923 and is buried in Godbout in a commemorative mausoleum bearing a plaque that reads, 'Humble child of the north, from the book of nature he learned much to the great benefit of his folk and country.' Baie Comeau is named for him; 30 miles west of Godbout on Hwy 138 is the city of Baie Comeau, named for the bay, and founded in 1936.

HULL

Henri-Marie Desjardins, a poet and member of the *École littéraire de Montréal* (see MONTREAL: 10), was born in June 1874 in nearby Pointe-Gatineau but lived much of his life in Hull, where his father, the notary Paul Thomas Desjardins, moved his family in 1887. An undistinguished student at the Séminaire de Ste-Thérèse-de-Blainville in 1887–91, he spent the years 1891–9 in Montreal, where he mixed enthusiastic participation in bohemian literary activities with desultory college and university studies. He was the leader of a circle of young *littérateurs* called the 'Groupe des six éponges' ('sponges'—an allusion to the French idiom for 'drink like a fish'), because during its brief existence (the winter of 1894–5) it regularly convened in taverns on rue Sainte-Catherine. This group was the immediate forerunner of the *École littéraire*, of which Desjardins was an original member. Called home by his father in 1899 to enter upon his career as a notary, Desjardins at first continued to visit Montreal for meetings of the *École littéraire*, but he gradually ceased his literary activities under the pressure of personal problems. In 1905 his wife died after only one year of marriage. Depressed and in financial difficulties, Desjardins struggled to overcome a drinking problem in order to earn money to leave to his widowed mother. He died of heart disease on 9 Feb. 1907 and is buried in Hull in Notre-Dame Cemetery. Desjardins' poems have never been collected in book form.

Other writers connected with Hull are the early Upper Canada poet **Adam Hood Burwell**, who was an Anglican missionary to Hull from 1832 to 1836, when he was expelled from the Anglican Church for doctrinal irregularity (see KINGSTON, Ont.); the poet **Jeannine Bélanger**, Sister Marie-Joséfa, born in Hull in 1915 and author of two collections, *Stances à l'éternel absent* (1941) and *Le Visage dans la roche* (1941; see OTTAWA, Ont.); and **Pierre Ballois**, who published his modern-day parables, *Les Escoumins suivi de Chicoutimi et de le Coureur* (1973), from his home at 67 rue Chouinard.

During the late 1940s **Yves Thériault** worked as an announcer and writer at radio station CKCH in Hull. It was here that the prolific author wrote his first sketches for radio and published his first stories, which appeared in Jean-Charles Harvey's *Le Jour*. (See MONTREAL: 16, RAWDON.)

JOLIETTE

A native of MONTREAL (17), **Gustave Lamarche**, CSV, was for many years a professor at the Collège de Joliette. He contributed to the development of theatre in Quebec with his school drama troupe, Les Paraboliers du Roi, which toured the province extensively from 1939 to 1947. Of over fifty plays Lamarche wrote on religious themes for presentation by the troupe (he acted in many of them, as well as directing), his most successful was *Jonathas* (1935). Two of his works were presented in Montreal as outdoor performances attended by audiences of more than 100,000: *La Défaite de l'enfer* (1938) and *Notre Dame de la Couronne* (1947). Lamarche also published poetry, including *Palinods* (1944), and edited the magazine *Carnets Victoriens* from 1935 to 1955.

Poet and playwright **Rina Lasnier**, born in 1915 in ST-GRÉGOIRE-D'IBERVILLE, has lived here for many years, after a long career in MONTREAL (16). Devoted to religious themes, Lasnier's many volumes of poetry include *La Salle des rêves* (1971), which won the first A.J.M. Smith prize for Canadian poetry. Her plays, including *Le jeu de la voyagère* (1941), which is based on the life of Marguerite Bourgeoys, are drawn from the religious history of Quebec.

The novelist **Yves Thériault**, who lived west of here at RAWDON, during his later years, died in the Joliette hospital in 1983.

KAMOURASKA

This picturesque village, on the south shore of the St Lawrence opposite LA MALBAIE, is the setting of **Anne Hébert**'s celebrated novel *Kamouraska* (1970; trans. Norman Shapiro, 1974) and of the historical event upon which it was based: the murder on 4 Jan. 1839 of Antoine Tassy, the young seigneur of Kamouraska, by his wife and her lover. Hébert retains the names of the actual participants in this event, including that of her central character, Tassy's wife, Élisabeth d'Aulnières, but she says in a prefatory note, 'The real participants in the drama have lent it only their outermost, "official" gestures, as it were. From that point on, they ... have come to be imagined creatures all my own.' The novel is very much an evocation of the landscape and communities of the entire region. (See also QUEBEC CITY.)

Kamouraska was the birthplace in 1820 of **Joseph-Charles Taché**, the first important writer of short stories in French Canada. Taché was educated in QUEBEC CITY and belonged to the literary circle that met in Octave Crémazie's bookshop there. He became a doctor and practised, from 1845 until his death, in RIMOUSKI. There he wrote his *Forestiers et Voyageurs* (1865), stories attesting to his intimate knowledge of forest life among lumbermen, *coureurs de bois*, and Indians.

KÉNOGAMI

The French author **Louis Hémon** worked at Kénogami, 20 miles east of Alma on the Saguenay River, in Feb. and Mar. 1913 as a farm labourer while he was writing *Maria Chapdelaine* (1916). He was employed by the Price Brothers Co. here, presumably as a clerk and stenographer, positions he occupied in MONTREAL (12) both before and after his ten months in the Lac St-Jean region, which ended with his stay in Kénogami. Hémon lived at the Staff House Hotel, now gone. By 7 Apr. the novelist had returned to Montreal, where he typed his book and mailed it to Paris; it was first published as a serial in *Le Temps* in Jan. and Feb. 1914. Hémon was killed in a railway accident at CHAPLEAU, Ont. in July 1913. (See also PÉRIBONKA.)

KINGSMERE

A house called 'The Pink House' in Kingsmere, near Ottawa and Hull, was **P.K. Page**'s first home after her marriage to William Arthur Irwin in 1950. Irwin was then commissioner of the National Film Board (NFB), for which Page had been working since 1946 as a scriptwriter. The couple lived here until Irwin was appointed ambassador to Australia in 1953; his later service as ambassador to Brazil and to Mexico kept Page abroad through 1964. The years spent with the NFB in OTTAWA and those at Kingsmere produced the poems collected in Page's *The Metal and the Flower* (1954), which won a Governor General's Award.

Kingsmere is best known as the site of the estate of Prime Minister William Lyon Mackenzie King and for the fantastic series of artificial ruins, called 'The Cloisters', which he constructed on his grounds. These ruins figure in the story 'Kingsmere' in Gwendolyn MacEwen's book *Noman* (1972)

A ruin at Kingsmere

and in her novel *Julian and the Magician* (1961). King collected many of the pieces that went into the building of his ruins from various historic buildings that had been demolished or damaged, among them the Canadian Parliament Buildings, which burned down in 1916, the Bank of British North America, which once stood on Wellington St in Ottawa, and the bomb-damaged British Houses of Parliament at Westminster.

KNOWLTON

William Henry Drummond practised medicine from 1885 to 1888 in the village of Knowlton, now incorporated into Lac-Brome, a town of 4,000 in Brome County in the Eastern Townships, near the Vermont border. He came to Knowlton from STORNOWAY and in 1888 moved back to MONTREAL (2), where he had received his medical training, to establish a private practice. He is well known for his once very popular dialect poems about life in rural Quebec in *The Habitant and Other French-Canadian Poems* (1897) and other volumes. (See also ST-EUSTACHE: COBALT, Ont.)

The poet and memoirist **John Glassco** lived just outside Knowlton with his friend Graeme Taylor from 1937 to 1946. He bought a large house that he commemorated in his poem 'The White Mansion'. While living here Glassco delivered the mail, and milk produced on his farm. From Knowlton they moved to FOSTER, also in the Eastern Townships.

LAC-BROME

See KNOWLTON.

LACHINE

Lachine was the birthplace in 1915 of the American novelist **Saul Bellow**, who lived at 158 8th Ave until he was three. The public library here was named the Bibliothèque Municipale Saul Bellow in 1984. From 1918 to 1924 Bellow lived in central Montreal at 1092 rue Saint-Dominique; since then he has lived in Chicago.

From 1846 until his death in 1848 Dr **William 'Tiger' Dunlop** was the superintendent of the Lachine Canal. His *Recollections of the American War, 1812–14* appeared serially in the *Literary Garland and British North American Magazine*, June–Nov. 1847. While working here Dunlop lived in the former hamlet of Côte-Saint-Paul; his home was at GODERICH, Ont.

Located at the south-central point of Montreal Island, Lachine is a part of metropolitan Montreal.

LAC ST-PIERRE

A widening of the St Lawrence River between Trois Rivières and Sorel, Lac St-Pierre is the setting for one of **William Henry Drummond**'s most famous poems, 'The Wreck of the Julie Plante'. Drummond based the poem on a story he had heard from an old lumberman at Bord-à-Plouffe, near ST-EUSTACHE, where he began work as a telegraph operator in 1869. The poem's refrain directly echoes the words of the man who told Drummond the story; during his account he repeated 'An' de win she blow, blow, blow!' over and over. Before it appeared in Drummond's first book of poems, *The Habitant and Other French-Canadian Poems* (1897), the poem was well known from magazine publication.

FROM 'THE WRECK OF THE JULIE PLANTE'

On wan dark night in Lac St. Pierre,
De win' she blow, blow, blow,
An' de crew of de wood scow' 'Julie Plante'
Got scar't an' run below—
For de win' she blow lak hurricane,
Bimeby she blow some more,
An' de scow bus' up on Lac St. Pierre
Wan arpent from de shore.
—William Henry Drummond

LA MALBAIE

This city of about 4,000 inhabitants, some 160 miles northeast of Quebec City on the St Lawrence River, was so named by Champlain in 1608 after a low tide had beached his ships. It was the birthplace in 1845 of **Marie-Louise-Félicité Angers**, who, under the pseudonym 'Laure Conan', was French Canada's first woman novelist and one of Canada's most important nineteenth-century writers of fiction. After studying briefly in Quebec City, she returned to her family home in La Malbaie, where she spent the rest of her life, except for a period from 1893 to 1898 when she lived at the Monastery of the Precious Blood in St-Hyacinthe. The first Canadian to write novels of psychological analysis, she concentrated on religious and patriotic subjects with a single theme: the loss or willing sacrifice of immediate happiness in pursuit of a difficult ideal. Her most admired novel is *Angéline de Montbrun* (1884; trans. Yves Brunelle, 1974). The Musée Régional Laure Conan, 30 rue Patrick Morgan, displays some of her belongings and other items of literary interest, such as a cassock that belonged to the historian and man of letters, Canon Lionel Groulx, who wrote a preface to *Angéline*. A small monument on the grounds of the Quebec

The Angers house in La Malbaie, *c.*1927

Ministry of Transport at 628 rue Saint-Étienne marks the spot where Laure Conan's house stood. Her grave is marked with a cenotaph in La Malbaie Cemetery, about two miles from downtown. Laure Conan died on 6 June 1924 in the Hôtel-Dieu Hospital, Quebec City.

Félix-Antoine Savard, author of *Menaud, maître draveur* (1937; trans. Richard Howard, *Master of the River*, 1976), had two of his first three assignments as a parish priest in La Malbaie and nearby Ste-Agnès. (See also CHICOUTIMI, CLERMONT, ST-JOSEPH-DE-LA-RIVE.) La Malbaie was the birthplace in 1891 of the novelist and editor **Jean-Charles Harvey**, author of *Les Demi-civilisés* (1934; trans. John Glassco, *Fear's Folly*, 1982). He was educated in CHICOUTIMI and spent his later life in Quebec City and MONTREAL (15). **William Hume Blake** was a frequent visitor to La Malbaie and the surrounding region and portrayed them in several chapters of his book *In a Fishing Country* (1922). A lover of the Quebec countryside and of traditional *habitant* life, Blake is best known for his 1921 translation of Louis Hémon's *Maria Chapdelaine* (1916).

Charlevoix Counties (Est and Ouest), as well as the Charlevoix Coast (the north shore of the St Lawrence River from Beaupré to the Saguenay), are named after the Jesuit historian François-Xavier de Charlevoix. On the instructions of his superiors, Father Charlevoix made an exploratory tour from 1719 to 1721 of all of France's American colonies, recording his findings in his *Histoire et description générale de la Nouvelle France* (1744).

LA POCATIÈRE

The Collège de Ste-Anne-de-la-Pocatière numbers among its alumni two of French Canada's most important writers. The Abbé **Henri-Raymond Casgrain** attended the college during the 1840s before completing his education at QUEBEC CITY, where he went on to become a founder of the *Mouvement littéraire de Québec* and the author of many critical and historical works. The south-shore St Lawrence village of La Pocatière, in Kamouraska County, is only a short distance south of Casgrain's birthplace, RIVIÈRE-OUELLE. A century and a half later, in 1903, the writer and anthropologist **Marius Barbeau** received his B.A. from the college, and went on to complete his education at Université Laval in Quebec City and at Oxford University. Modern folklore studies in Canada originated with Barbeau and saw their fullest flowering in his voluminous writings (see OTTAWA). In his work in French Canada, he is a successor of Casgrain, who had early insisted on the importance of folklore as a basis of a French-Canadian national literature and had himself written versions of traditions from the Rivière-Ouelle area. (See also STE-MARIE-DE-LA-BEAUCE.) Another literary student of the college here was the poet 'François Hertel' (**Rodolphe Dubé**), who was born in Casgrain's home town of Rivière-Ouelle in 1905 and studied here and at the Séminaire de TROIS-RIVIÈRES before entering the Jesuit order in 1925. The author of philosophical works and novels, Hertel was primarily a poet; a selection of his many collections is *Poèmes d'hier et d'aujourd'hui* (1967); since 1947 he has lived in France. The historic Collège de Sainte-Anne-de-la-Pocatière is located at 100 4ième ave.

LA TUQUE

Félix Leclerc, poet and *chansonnier*, was born on 2 Aug. 1914 in La Tuque, a city in Champlain County north of Trois-Rivières. Leclerc is often regarded as the original *chansonnier*, a poet-composer-performer of uniquely Québécois stamp who helped inspire succeeding generations of poets who have sung and recited their own works to Quebec and worldwide audiences. Leclerc's *Pieds nus dans l'aube* (1946) is a memoir of his happy childhood in La Tuque, where he lived until 1928, when he began his secondary-school education in OTTAWA. His books include *Le Hamac dans les voiles* (1952), selections from his first three books of short stories; fables and poems; and *Le Fou de l'île* (1958), tales that have been translated by Philip Stratford as *The Madman, the Kite and the Island* (1976).

La Tuque is the first known stop on the journey by the French novelist **Louis Hémon** into the North, an experience that resulted in his novel *Maria Chapdelaine* (1916). Hémon left his job in MONTREAL (12) in mid-June 1912, and stopped briefly here and in Roberval. By 13 July he was at PÉRIBONKA.

LENNOXVILLE

Bishop's College, the forerunner of Bishop's University, was founded at Lennoxville in 1843 by George Mountain, Anglican bishop of Quebec. Lennoxville is south of Sherbrooke on Hwy 143 in the Eastern Townships. **William Henry Drummond** (*The Habitant and Other French-Canadian Poems*, 1897) graduated from the medical school of Bishop's College in 1884, but at that time the medical school was in MONTREAL (2). (See also KNOWLTON, LAC BROME, LAC ST-PIERRE, ST-EUSTACHE, STORNOWAY; COBALT, Ont.)

Both Canon **Frederick George Scott** and his son **F.R. Scott** attended Bishop's College. The elder Scott received his B.A. in 1881 and his M.A. in 1884 before going to London to attend King's College. His first publication, the privately published *Justin and Other Poems*, appeared the following year and was also a part of his first collection, *The Soul's Quest and Other Poems* (1885). Scott was the author of several other volumes of verse, a novel, and a memoir of his service as chaplain to the Canadian First Division in the First World War, *The Great War as I Saw It* (1922). A native of Montreal, he was for many years rector of St Matthew's Church, QUEBEC CITY. F.R. Scott, born in the St Matthew's rectory, received a B.A. from Bishop's in 1919 before going to Oxford University as a Rhodes Scholar. On his return to Canada, Scott pursued his two great interests, law and poetry. From 1924 until his death in 1985 he lived in MONTREAL (4). His first book of poems, *Overture*, was published in 1945. (See also NORTH HATLEY.)

A decade after Scott, the poet **Ralph Gustafson** received his B.A. from Bishop's University. After receiving his M.A. the following year, 1930, he too went on to study at Oxford University. Gustafson's first book of poems, *The Golden Chalice* (1935), won Quebec's Prix David. After many years in New York he returned to Bishop's in 1960 as professor of English and poet-in-residence, posts he held until he retired in 1979. He now lives in NORTH HATLEY. His many books published during the years at Bishop's include *Sift in an Hourglass* (1966), *Ixion's Wheel* (1969), *Selected Poems* (1972), *Corners in Glass* (1977), and *Fire on Stone* (1974), winner of a Governor General's award. (See also LIME RIDGE.)

Other writers associated with Bishop's University are **D.G. Jones** and **Michael Ondaatje**. Jones taught here from 1961 to 1963, when he joined the faculty of the Université de SHERBROOKE. Before coming to Lennoxville Jones had published his first collection of poems, *Frost on the Sun* (1957); in 1961 *The Sun Is Axeman* appeared. (See also MONTREAL: 7, NORTH HATLEY; BANCROFT, GUELPH, KINGSTON, LAKEFIELD, Ont.) The poet and novelist Michael Ondaatje (*The Collected Works of Billy the Kid*, 1970, winner of a Governor General's award) has lived most of his life in Canada in TORONTO (7), but studied at Bishop's from 1962 to 1964 before obtaining his B.A. from the University of Toronto in 1965.

Festival Lennoxville, a six-week summer festival of plays and stage performances held at the university's 650-seat Centennial Theatre, opened on 8 July 1972 with a revival of Mavor Moore's *The Ottawa Man*. It closed in mid-summer 1982. Its archives are at the university.

LÉVIS

The house where **Louis Fréchette** spent his childhood is at 229 rue St-Laurent in this city on the south shore of the St Lawrence River, opposite Quebec City. Fréchette became the unofficial poet laureate of Quebec, and it was through his work that French-Canadian literature first received significant attention in France and the rest

McGreer Hall (1846), the oldest building on the campus of Bishop's University

Louis Fréchette in 1874

of Europe. A seventh-generation Canadian, he unsuccessfully attended several secondary schools and at fifteen went to Ogdensburg, N.Y., where he worked as a labourer, before returning to Canada and graudating from the Collège de Nicolet in 1859 (see NICOLET). From 1864 to 1866 Fréchette practised law in Lévis and founded two Liberal newspapers. He then spent five years in self-imposed exile in Chicago, where he wrote the bitter satirical verse-attack on his countrymen and their society, *La Voix d'un exilé* (1868). He was angered not only by the terms of Confederation and by the Conservative government, but by the plight of the artist in Canada, manifested in the almost complete lack of attention to his first book of poems, *Mes loisirs* (1863), the first volume of lyric poetry ever published in Quebec. Working in Chicago as both a journalist and a railway employee, Fréchette lost most of his manuscripts of five years in the Chicago fire of 1871 and in that year returned to Lévis. He sat in the House of Commons from 1874 to 1878 as Liberal member for Lévis, but was not returned. About 1877 he moved to MONTREAL (9), where he spent the rest of his life. The most important public event in nineteenth-century French-Canadian letters was the awarding by the French Academy on 5 Aug. 1880 of a Prix Montyon to Fréchette's *Les Fleurs boréales. Les Oiseaux de neige* (1879). His major work, however, is *La Légende d'un peuple* (1887), a series of poems recounting the history of French Canada.

The Fréchette house, Lévis

LIME RIDGE

Ralph Gustafson—the author of many collections of poems, including *Fire on Stone* (1974), which won a Governor General's Award—was born on 16 Aug. 1909 in this small village near SHERBROOKE, at the home of his grandfather, who was superintendent of the lime kilns. Gustafson now lives in NORTH HATLEY.

LONGUEUIL

Frère **Marie-Victorin**, FÉC (Brothers of the Christian Schools), taught at the Collège de Longueuil in the late teens of this century, during which period he wrote and published his two collections of highly polished stories and sketches, *Récits laurentiens* (1919) and *Croquis laurentiens* (1920); the former was translated by James Ferres as *The Chopping Bee and Other Laurentian Stories* (1925). Although he remained associated with the Collège de Longueuil, Marie-Victorin (born Conrad Kirouac) became professor of botany and founder of the *Institut botanique* of the Université de Montréal in 1920; in 1931 he founded the Montreal Botanical Gardens. Of his many botanical works, the most important deals with the same Laurentian Mountains region that gave rise to his *Flore laurentienne, illustré de 22 cartes et de 1800 dessins* (1935), an important scientific work that combines botanical precision with a poet's insight and knowledge of the resources of his language. (See also MONTREAL: 15, QUEBEC CITY, ST-JÉROME-DE-TERREBONNE.)

LONGUEUIL

The road leaving Quebec which winds between hawthorn hedges towards Petite Rivière and Ancienne Lorette, crosses a country as old as the French pioneer's axe in America.

It has kept from the beginning, an air of rustic nobility, with vast historic farms, where riches are hereditary and constant, and it has quiet hamlets at the crossroads, which retain deliciously endearing old French names.

Near at hand, the River Saint Charles, bordered with choke-cherries, alders and white asters, rolls languidly with little bubbles over its smooth stones. Two roads, North and South, span it by turns, and with a single arch, on charming little old-fashioned bridges. Through the foliage, one guesses at, rather than sees, secluded houses and ancient mills built under the French regime.

—Marie-Victorian, *Croquis laurentiens* (1920; tr. James Ferres, 1925)

Dr **Jacques Ferron** (1921–85)—prolific short-story writer, novelist, and playwright—came to Longueuil in 1949 to live and practise medicine as a family doctor among local working-class people. He lived at 931 rue Bellerive and had an office at 1285 chemin de Chambly. With several friends Ferron operated Éditions d'Orphée, a small press that produced fine editions and published Ferron's books before the advent of Les Éditions parti pris in 1964. Ferron's earliest works were satirical plays. In 1951 he published his first novel, *La Barbe de François Hertel*, which satirizes the poet and philosopher 'François Hertel' (Rodolphe Dubé; see RIVIÈRE-OUELLE). Ferron's first major work, the short-story collection *Contes du pays incertain* (1962), received a Governor General's Award; a translation of Ferron's stories by Betty Bednarski, *Tales from the Uncertain Country* (1972), contains selections from this book and additional stories that were published with it in a second edition (1968). Other works by Ferron that have been translated include *Cotnoir* (1965; trans. by Pierre Cloutier, *Doctor Cotnoir*, 1973); *La Nuit* (1965; trans. by Ray Ellenwood, *Quince Jam*, 1977); and *Le Saint-Elias* (1972; trans. by Pierre Cloutier, *The Saint Elias* (1975). (See also LOUISEVILLE, RIVIÈRE-LA-MADELEINE, TROIS-RIVIÈRES.) A politicial activist, Ferron was a member of the separatist party Le Rassemblement pour l'indépendance

Jacques Ferron

nationale (RIN), and in the mid-1960s was overwhelmingly elected to the Quebec National Assembly as an RIN candidate. With his column 'Ce bordel de pays', he was an important contributor to the magazine *parti pris*, which identified the issues of Quebec literature and Quebec independence. The magazine's publishing house, Les Éditions parti pris, which was founded in Feb. 1964, published two of Ferron's novels, *La Nuit* (1965) and *Papa Boss* (1966).

In Longueuil Ferron was an important influence on another resident of the city who became a writer and an activist, **Pierre Vallières**, author of *Nègres blancs de l'Amérique* (1968; trans. by Joan Pinkham, *White Niggers of America*, 1971). Vallières spent his adolescence in Longueuil—his father was a railway mechanic employed in the CPR Angus Shops—and was later arrested in New York for demonstrating in front of the United Nations on behalf of the Front de Libération du Québec (FLQ): while awaiting extradition to Canada in the Manhattan House of Detention for Men he wrote much of *Nègres blancs*, in which he pays tribute to Ferron and recalls that 'Ferron's office was near my home, and I often went to him for treatment. . . . I never went home without a few newspapers the doctor had given me.' Published by Les Éditions parti pris, Vallière's book vividly evokes his home here, which was at 1197 Saint-Thomas, near the corner of Briggs.

One of the founding members of *parti pris*, the poet **Paul Chamberland** was born in Longueuil in 1939. His father was a designer for a linoleum manufacturer, Dominion Oilcloth, located in Montreal just across the Jacques-Cartier Bridge. Primarily associated with MONTREAL (18), Chamberland received his secondary education from the Holy Cross Fathers at the Séminaire Ste-Croix and later attended the Collège Saint-Laurent, 625 Bd Ste-Croix, Ville St-Laurent. His most famous book was the long poem of 1960s nationalist and separatist sentiment in Quebec, *L'Afficheur hurle* (1965; trans. by Malcolm Reid in his book *The Shouting Signpainters: A Literary and Political Account of Quebec Revolutionary Nationalism*, 1972, which takes its title from Chamberland's poem). Chamberland's other works include *L'Inavouable* (1968) and *L'enfant doré* (1981).

LOTBINIÈRE

A plaque in this village, on the south shore of the St Lawrence west of Lévis, commemorates the birth in 1837, near Lotbinière, of the poet **Pamphile Lemay**. The plaque stands before the 'chapelle de procession' a quarter-mile west of the beautiful St-Louis-de-Lotbinière church. In addition to his copious verse, seen at its best in the sonnet sequence *Les Gouttelettes* (1904), Lemay published three novels and other prose works; a translation in 1884 of William Kirby's *The Golden Dog* (1877); and a translation in 1865 of Longfellow's *Evangeline* (1847), which he revised in 1912. Lemay spent much of his life in OTTAWA and QUEBEC CITY; he worked as a parliamentary translator in Ottawa and then as librarian of the Quebec legislature. After retiring in 1892, he lived at Deschaillons, west of Lotbinière, and died there on 11 June 1918.

Pamphile Lemay

LOUISEVILLE

Among several historic eighteenth-century stone houses in this industrial town west of TROIS-RIVIÈRES, one dating from 1760 is the Maison Gagnon, the childhood home of the early folkorist and musician **Ernest Gagnon**. A member of the mid-nineteenth-century literary school of Quebec City that centred on François-Xavier Garneau, Octave Crémazie, and the Abbé Henri-Raymond Casgrain, Gagnon earned his place in literary history by collecting and publishing *Chansons populaires du Canada* (1865). This and another book of French-Canadian songs, George T. Lanigan's *National Ballads of Canada Imitated and Translated from the Originals* (1865), were the first efforts to gather Canadian folk lyrics and preserve them in literary form. Gagnon, who was born in Rivière-du-Loup on 7 Nov. 1834, received his musical education in France and spent most of his life in QUEBEC CITY, where he was organist at the Basilica and, from 1875 to 1905, a provincial civil servant. Besides his book of folksongs, his writings include contributions to Quebec local history, including that of the Louiseville area.

The playwright, novelist, and physician **Jacques Ferron** was born in Louiseville on 20 Jan. 1921 and spent his childhood and youth here, receiving his high school education in nearby TROIS-RIVIÈRES. His writing and medical careers are associated with MONTREAL (18), LONGUEUIL, ST LAMBERT. Among Ferron's most important books is *Contes du pays incertain* (1962; 2nd edn 1968), which won a Governor General's Award. A selection of the stories, *Tales from the Uncertain Country* (1972), was translated by Betty Bednarski. Although Ferron did not make his home here, his many works—especially his fiction—abound in references to his youth and to his father, who was a local lawyer and political organizer. Ferron died in 1985.

MAGDALEN ISLANDS

From 1967 to 1975 **Farley Mowat** spent the summer months in a century-old farmhouse on Île de Grande Entrée, one of the Magdalen Islands, a sixty-mile-long archipelago of twelve islands in the Gulf of St Lawrence. The increasing popularity of these beautiful fishing islands finally drove Mowat to find a new summer home on Cape Breton Island. Mowat: 'When I first went to the Magdalens, you never saw a tourist. Last year, there were over a hundred thousand. A hundred thousand. I had tour buses stopping at my gate. This is the home of Farley Mowat, the famous author. Can you imagine it?' (See also BURGEO, L'ANSE AUX MEADOWS, Nfld.; RIVER BOURGEOIS, N.S.; BELLEVILLE, PORT HOPE, Ont.; SASKATOON, Sask.; KEEWATIN BARRENS, N.W.T.)

MAGOG

The Auberge de l'Étoile, an inn and motel at 1133 rue Main ouest in Magog—in the Eastern Townships—is the setting of an important scene in **Hubert Aquin**'s novel *L'Antiphonaire* (1960; English trans. *The Antiphonary*, 1973). (See also MONTREAL: 18.)

Near Magog, at the northern end of Lake Memphremagog, the poet **A.J.M. Smith** had a lakeshore cottage where he spent the summers until his death in 1980. From the late 1930s Smith was a professor at Michigan State University but did much of his writing and editing during his summers here. His books include *News of the Phoenix and Other Poems* (1943, Governor General's Award), *Collected Poems* (1962),

A.J.M. Smith in the woods near Magog

The Classic Shade: Selected Poems (1978), and a book of critical essays, *Towards a View of Canadian Letters* (1973). He was also known as an editor of influential anthologies, including the *Book of Canadian Poetry* (1943; 2nd edn 1948; 3rd edn 1957) and *The Oxford Book of Canadian Verse: in English and French* (1960). (See also MONTREAL: 6.)

MONTREAL

The entry on Montreal is divided in keeping with the city's importance to literature in both English and French. An introductory section on explorers, founders, and early literary visitors is followed by seven sections on writers in English and eleven sections on writers in French. Within the English and the French parts of the entry the arrangement of material is approximately chronological.

Streets in Montreal have been renumbered at various times, so that addresses associated with writers of the nineteenth and early twentieth centuries are often different today. The original addresses, which are biographically important for these authors, are given, and wherever possible, present-day addresses or locations have been added.

1. EXPLORERS AND FOUNDERS: EARLY LITERARY VISITORS

In the autumn of 1535 **Jacques Cartier** reached the large island in the St Lawrence River on which Montreal is now situated and found there the Indian village of Hochelaga. *The Voyages of Jacques Cartier* (English translation, 1924), which are of uncertain authorship, record how on 2 Oct. 1535 Cartier named the island's central mountain Mont Royal, an event commemorated by a plaque on the Chalet de la Montagne in the Parc Mont-Royal. (The eastern portion of this park was designed by the famous American nineteenth-century landscape architect and author **Frederick Law Olmstead** (1822–1903).) **Samuel de Champlain**'s first volume of his *Voyages* (1612; trans. in *The Works of Samuel de Champlain*, 1922–36) records his visit of 1611, during which he built a wall to test the effects of the local weather on construction; on 25 May he named the location of his wall Place Royale, an event memorialized by a plaque at the site—the customs building in the Place Royale, at 165 rue de la Commune ouest. The city was founded in 1642 by Paul de Chomedy, Sieur de Maisonneuve, as a mission station, Ville-Marie. An early and entertaining annalist of the city's life was **Marie Morin**, who was born in Quebec City and moved to Montreal about 1670; she worked at the Hôtel-Dieu, the first hospital, built 1644. The site is marked by a plaque on the east side of rue Saint-Sulpice between Saint-Paul and le Royer. The modern edition of her *Annales* is entitled *Histoire simple et véritable* (1979). She died in Montreal in 1730.

Many of Montreal's early literary associations have to do with distinguished visitors. One of the most famous, **Benjamin Franklin**, was in fact not a visitor but an invader. American forces under Franklin occupied Montreal for seven months in 1775–6, withdrawing on 10 June. His headquarters were in the Château de Ramezay (now a museum) at 280 rue Notre Dame est; Franklin lived in a manor that once stood just west of the Château. During his brief residence, the author of *Poor Richard's Almanac* and the famous *Autobiography* and a signer of the Declaration of Independence brought Montreal its first printer, **Fleury Mesplet**, who published the first issue of the *Gazette du Commerce et Littéraire* on rue de la Capitale, east of Place Royale, on 3 June 1778. Falling afoul of the authorities for certain articles, Mesplet was imprisoned for three years, and after his release he founded the *Gazette de Montréal*, which he first published in French, and later in English as the *Montreal Gazette*; today it is a major daily newspaper. A plaque at 264 rue Notre-Dame ouest marks the site of the building where Mesplet died on 24 Jan. 1794.

Washington Irving visited Montreal several times on business during the early 1800s and knew the traders of the Northwest Company. He wrote about John Jacob Astor and 'Astoria' in *Anecdotes of an Enterprise Beyond Mountains* (1836), which tells also of the Nor'westers and of their annual gathering for the 'Grand Portage' at STE-ANNE-DE-BELLEVUE, an event that also inspired the Irish poet Thomas Moore's 'A Canadian Boat Song'. It is not known exactly where Irving stayed in Montreal, but he almost certainly would have visited Astor's fur warehouse, still standing at the intersection of rues Sainte-Hélène and Vaudreuil; the Northwest Company warehouses standing at the rear of 169 Place Jacques-Cartier; and the home of the Northwest Company co-founder and leader Simon McTavish, a striking house with a *porte cochère* that stands on rue Saint-Jean-Baptiste, between Notre-Dame est and Saint-Paul.

Charles Dickens visited the city for several days, on his North American tour of 1842, arriving in late May. He stayed at Rasco's Hotel, 281–95 Saint-Paul (the building is still standing but has been converted to other uses), and read from his works at the Theatre Royal, which stood across the street; there his wife Catherine acted, along with an amateur company, in a dramatic performance. On 12 Nov. 1940 the City of Montreal gave his name to the street that touches the east wall of Rasco's Hotel; it is the shortest street in Montreal. The historian **Francis Parkman** was only a twenty-year-old undergraduate, a year short of his bachelor's degree from Harvard, when he first visited Montreal in 1843, but he had already conceived his epic history of North American explorers, the great fur empires, and the struggle between France and England for control of the continent. He visited again in 1856, when he also toured Quebec City and parts of Nova Scotia. Montreal figures throughout much of his nine-volume work, *France and England in North America*; its early history is recounted in *Pioneers of France in the New World* (1865) and *The Old Régime in Canada* (1874), as well as in the volume on Frontenac and elsewhere.

At 408 rue Saint-Jacques stood the Ottawa Hotel, where **Harriet Beecher Stowe**, author of *Uncle Tom's Cabin* (1852) and numerous other books, stayed in 1869. Her family abounded in clergymen, and one of the objects of her visit was to hear the preaching of her brother Thomas Beecher, a Methodist minister. Mrs Stowe was one of several literary visitors to remark on the large number of churches in the city. In fact she wrote an article on this subject for an American magazine (reprinted on 1 June 1869 in the Montreal *Evening Telegraph and Daily Commercial Advertiser*) in which she commented that 'Montreal is a mountain of churches.' Her article makes clear that she liberally sampled the religious services available in a city where, as she put it, 'Every shade and form of faith is . . . well represented in wood or stone, and the gospel feast set forth in every form and shape to suit the spiritual appetite of all inquirers.' She is known to have attended the Church of St John the Evangelist, which stood at the corner of Dorchester and Saint-Urbain, and St Gabriel Church, a Presbyterian church (now gone) that was built in 1792 on rue Saint-Gabriel at the west end of the Champ-de-Mars, on land now occupied by the New Court House. **Mark Twain**, visiting the city in 1881, made the famous comment, 'This is the first time I was ever in a city where you couldn't throw a brick without breaking a church window.'

A great writer with a more substantial association with Montreal is the English novelist and controversialist **Samuel Butler**. He had already published *Erewhon* (1872) when he came to the city in 1874 to revive a company in which he had invested, the Canada Tanning Extract Company; during Butler's time in Montreal, it had its offices in the Exchange Bank building that stood at 102 rue Saint-François-Xavier. The company failed and Butler returned to England, where he precipitated an international dispute when he published, in *The London Spectator* for 18 May 1878, his 'A Psalm of Montreal'. This facetious poem records how Butler one day saw a taxidermist stuffing an owl in a prominent place in the display rooms of the Museum of the Montreal Natural History Society (then at 32 University Ave), and then discovered a plaster copy of the Discobulus (Discus Thrower) hidden away in a back room of the museum:

Stowed away in a Montreal lumber room
The Discobolus standeth and turneth his face to the wall;
Dusty, cobweb-covered, maimed and set at naught,
Beauty crieth in an attic and no man regardeth:
O God! O Montreal!

The poem was reprinted in the *Canadian Spectator* on 1 June 1878 and was answered in the following issue by an anonymous and amateur attempt in verse to reply to the 'Heathen Londoner'. Butler told the story of the incident in *The Note-Books of Samuel Butler* (1915). In 1881 'fit place' was found for the plaster Discobolus when it was donated to the Art Association of Montreal and housed in its gallery, at the corner of Ontario and Sherbrooke. Touring Canada in 1913, the poet **Rupert Brooke** remembered the controversy of a quarter-century earlier and viewed the statue. In *Letters from America* (1916) he wrote: 'I have to report that the Discobolus is very well, and nowadays, looks the whole world in the face, almost quite unabashed.'

Most of these early literary sites of Montreal are located in the old city, 'Vieux Montréal,' an area bounded approximately by Saint-Antoine and de la Commune on the north and south, by Berri and McGill on the east and west. All street numbers given in this area are the ones in present use; many are unchanged from the early days of the city.

2. THE EARLIEST ENGLISH WRITERS TO WILLIAM HENRY DRUMMOND

'Vieux Montréal' was also home to most of the city's first English-language writers. Among them were the poets George Longmore, Levi Adams, Adam Kidd, and W.F. Hawley, all of whom (with the possible exception of Hawley) were born in the ten years from 1793 to 1803 and were active in the 1820s. A native of Quebec City, **George Longmore** produced almost all his poetry in the period 1820–4, during which he was stationed with the British army in Montreal. His work in Canada consists primarily of two long poems, *Tecumthé*, which appeared in the Dec. 1824 issue of the *Canadian Review and Literary and Historical Journal*; and *The Charivari; or Canadian Poetics: A Tale After the Manner of Beppo*, which was published in book form, also in 1824. Originally a rural European wedding celebration, the charivari in Montreal took a unique form in the early nineteenth century. At the time of society weddings, mobs would take to the streets and demand gifts of money and drink from wealthy bridegrooms. Longmore's poem is based on an actual charivari of 1823 that got out of hand; a man was shot dead and a house was destroyed in the incident. **Levi Adams**, born in 1802, became an articled law clerk in the Montreal office of F.P. Bruneau in 1822 and was admitted to the bar in 1827. He died in June 1832, one of the first victims of the Montreal cholera epidemic witnessed by Susanna Moodie during her voyage of immigration to Upper Canada (now Ontario) and described in *Roughing It in the Bush* (1852). Adams' major work was a book-length poem, *Jean Baptiste: A Poetic Olio* (1825), set in the Montreal of the day. **Adam Kidd** and **William Fitz Hawley**, both of whom lived at various times in Quebec City as well as Montreal, were here in the late 1820s and were involved

Montreal, showing the Bank of Montreal, 1870.

in a literary controversy. Hawley's *Quebec, The Harp, and Other Poems* (1829) was unfavourably reviewed, apparently by Kidd, in the Montreal newspaper the *Irish Vindicator*, to which the two writers contributed. Then, when Kidd published his poem *The Huron Chief* (1830), it was bitterly criticized, possibly by Hawley, in Mesplet's *Gazette*. In addition, Kidd was attacked in the streets of Montreal and publicly beaten by the son of the British consul to New York and an accomplice; Kidd had criticized the consul in a footnote to his poem.

Many of these early Montreal works in English were published by the Lovell Printing and Publishing Company, 23 and 25 rue Saint-Nicholas, which also published the *Literary Garland* (Dec. 1838–Dec. 1851), perhaps the most prominent literary magazine of its time. Edited by John Gibson, brother-in-law of the printer John Lovell, it published writers such as Susanna Moodie, the novelist John Richardson, and the poet Charles Mair, all of Upper Canada, and the Montreal novelist Rosanna Leprohon. The *Garland*'s predecessors in the Montreal literary world included the *Canadian Magazine and Literary Repository* (1823–5) and the *Canadian Review and Literary and Historical Journal* (1824–6).

In 1836 Montreal was involved in an international religious controversy when a New York newspaper, the *American Protestant Vindicator*, published, first in the magazine and then as a book, *Awful Disclosures of Maria Monk*. Anonymously written, it purported to be an exposé dictated by a young women subjected to immoral practices 'during a residence of five years as a novice, and two years as a Black Nun, in the Hôtel Dieu Nunnery at Montreal'. The nunnery in question was connected with the first Hôtel-Dieu, which was founded in 1644 at the north corner of rue Saint-Paul and rue Saint-Sulpice and which remained there until it was moved in 1866 to its present location on Pine Ave (av. des Pins). An inspection of the Hôtel-Dieu and other evidence almost immediately discredited the book, which nonetheless continued to be reprinted until the early twentieth century and became the most widespread piece of anti-Catholic propaganda produced in North America.

The poet **Charles Heavysege** immigrated to Montreal from England in 1853; he was then thirty-seven. His first known address here was 75 rue Saint-Constant, where he lived in 1857; about this time he was working as a woodcarver. In 1855 Heavysege published the second, revised edition of his dramatic poem *The Revolt of Tartarus*, originally published in London and Liverpool in 1852. His most important work, *Saul: A Drama in Three Parts*, appeared in 1857 and was probably written, at least in part, at his rue Saint-Constant address. Eventually Heavysege found work as a journalist, writing first for the Montreal *Transcript* (13 rue Hospital), in its day the Montreal English daily with greatest circulation, and then for the *Daily Witness* (218 and 220 St James St). Heavysege was working for the *Daily Witness* by 1865 and continued to do so until his death in 1876. In 1861 he lived on Aylmer at number 5 (renumbered 15 during his time there) and then at number 11; these houses were near the corner of Aylmer and Sainte-Catherine. About 1869 he moved briefly to Dorchester, and later lived at 304 Saint-Urbain (this address was then near the corner of Sherbrooke), and 203 Bleury, a house that was in the present-day 1400 block near the corner of Mayor. Heavysege's last two important works were also verse dramas: *Count Filippo; or The Unequal Marriage* (1860), written at 106 rue Saint-Constant, and *Jepththah's Daughter* (1865), written or at least completed at 15 Aylmer; his Gothic novel *The Advocate* was also published in Montreal in 1865. Some of Heavysege's work has been reprinted in *Saul and Selected Poems* (1967).

Thomas D'Arcy McGee, born in 1825 in Ireland, came to Canada in 1857 from the United States, where he had been living since 1848. In Montreal he became a champion of the Irish population, establishing a newspaper, the *New Era*, and making his home from 1858 at 220 rue Saint-Antoine; in that year he was elected to the House of Assembly as an independent, representing the Place Rodier riding. In 1858 he prepared his single volume of poetry, *Canadian Ballads and Occasional Verses* (1858); these and other poems were assembled after his death in *The Poems of D'Arcy McGee* (1869). McGee had produced fiction and criticism in Ireland and the United States; in Canada, besides his poetry, he wrote polemics in favour of Confederation, which were published in such works as *Speeches and Addresses, Chiefly on the Subject of British American Union* (1865). In 1865 he was elected to the first Canadian parliament; on 7 Apr. 1867 he was assassinated in OTTAWA by Patrick James Whelan, a Fenian whose cause McGee had opposed in seeking to rally Irish support for Confederation. His funeral was held at Montreal's Saint Patrick's Church, 460 Dorchester West, on 13 Apr., which would have been his forty-third birthday. The funeral is commemorated by a plaque on the exterior of the church; McGee's pew, number 240, also bears a plaque in his memory. One of

Thomas D'Arcy McGee, *c.*1867

McGee's best-known poems was 'Our Ladye of the Snowe', about the old church of Notre-Dame-des-Neiges, which was on the south face of Mont Royal. In 1897 **Rudyard Kipling**, who may have known McGee's poem, wrote a poem entitled 'Our Lady of the Snows: Canadian Preferential Tariff, 1897', expressing Canada's nationhood and its growing independence *vis-à-vis* Great Britain. Kipling's poem contains the once-famous lines, 'Daughter am I in my mother's house, / But mistress in my own', which were often used to express the relationship of the two countries. Kipling travelled across Canada in 1906–7, and in 1907—the year he was awarded the Nobel Prize for literature—he received his first honorary degree from McGill University.

Rosanna Leprohon was, like McGee, an Irish-Catholic writer both by her birth and by the thematic interests of much of her work. Born Rosanna Mullins, the daughter of a well-to-do Montreal merchant, she first began to publish serialized stories in the *Literary Garland* in 1848. When she was sixteen her family's house was on Wellington, east of McGill, and the Mullins business was at 55 Commissioners (renumbered 67 after 1845). At this time, she was attending the Convent of the Congregation of

Notre Dame, where the sisters encouraged her to write; the convent stands at 6–12 rue Saint-Paul ouest and 1–5 Commissioners. In 1851, the year the *Literary Garland* ceased publication, she married a doctor, Jean-Lucien Leprohon, by whom she had thirteen children. After their marriage they spent a few years in Saint-Charles and then returned to Montreal, taking up residence at 51 rue Saint-Radegonde, at the corner of rue Lagauchetière. (Saint-Radegonde no longer exists; this address was near Victoria Square at Craig and Bleury.) Mrs Leprohon occupied this house until her death in 1879, and here wrote most of her many works, including the novels *Antoinette de Mirecourt; or, Secret Marrying and Secret Sorrow* (1864) and *Armand Durand; or, A Promise Fulfilled* (1868), as well as poems that were collected by John Lovell and published after her death in *The Poetical Works of Mrs. Leprohon* (1881). Leprohon's two major novels, as well as the earlier serial 'The Manor House of Villerai' (1859), were also popular in contemporary French translations.

George Lanigan, born in 1846 in Saint-Charles, was educated in Montreal and became a journalist here. In 1865 he published a book of metrical translations of French-Canadian songs, *National Ballads of Canada Imitated and Translated from the Originals*, using the pseudonym 'Allid'. A proponent of annexation to the United States, Lanigan moved to New York in 1869 and while working for the New York *World* wrote his famous humorous poem 'The Ahkoond of Swat: A Threnody' (included in A.J.M. Smith's *Book of Canadian Poetry*, 1957). In Montreal in the late 1860s Lanigan lived at 982 Sainte-Catherine (now in the 2300 block near Mansfield). Until 1868 he was editor of the *Canadian Monthly*, and in 1869 he founded (with Hugh Graham, later Lord Atholstan) the Montreal *Star*. Lanigan returned to the United States in late 1869 and remained there until his death in 1886.

William Douw Lighthall was born in 1857 in Hamilton, Canada West (Ontario), but came to Montreal as a child. A novelist, poet, and anthologist, he is best known for compiling *Songs of the Great Dominion: Voices from the Forests and Water, the Settlements and Cities of Canada* (1889). When Lighthall assembled this important early anthology, he was living at 913 Dorchester W. and working for the legal firm of Lighthall and Macdonald. Lighthall was educated at Montreal High School and McGill University and practised law in Montreal and Westmount until 1944. From 1900 to 1903 he was mayor of Westmount; he was also a founder of the Union of Canadian Municipalities and in 1918 was president of the Royal Society of Canada. From the 1890s until his death in 1954 he lived primarily at his home 'Châteauclair' at 14 Murray Avenue, Westmount. His first novel, *The Young Seigneur; or, Nation Making* (1888), was written at his Dorchester address; *The False Chevalier; or, The Lifeguard of Marie Antoinette* (1898) and *The Master of Life: A Romance of the Five Nations and Prehistoric Montreal* (1908) were written at 'Châteauclair'. There too he collected his poems under the title *Old Measures* (1922) and wrote three books that drew on his amateur archaeological research into the Indian village of Hochelaga and on his great historical knowledge of Montreal.

W.H. Drummond

The poet and physician **William Henry Drummond**, born in Ireland in 1854, immigrated to Montreal with his family in 1864. When his father died less than two years later he discontinued his private education to help his family, working as a telegraph operator at ST-EUSTACHE, where he made the acquaintance of the French-Canadian *habitant* farmers and woodsmen who provided material for nearly all his poetry. Eventually he was able to resume his studies; he graduated from Montreal High School at twenty-two, attended McGill University, and received his medical degree from Bishop's College, in 1883. After rural practice in KNOWLTON and STORNOWAY, in 1888 he established his first Montreal practice from an office in the family home at 240 rue Saint-Antoine, at the corner of rue des Seigneurs. In 1894 Drummond, now married, moved his home and practice to 249 (now 1181) Mountain St—to a house once occupied, in 1865, by Jefferson Davis, president of the Confederate States of America. Here Drummond wrote much of the poetry for which he is known, and which was extremely popular before and after the turn of the century. At the urging of friends he collected his first 'habitant' poems—genial verse monologues in a diction resembling the heavily French-flavoured, somewhat broken English that farmers and lumbermen had used with him—in *The Habitant and Other French-Canadian Poems* (1897). This was followed by similar volumes: *Phil-o-Rum's Canoe, and Madelaine de Verchères* (1898); *Johnnie Courteau, and Other Poems* (1901); *The Voyageur, and Other Poems* (1905); *The Great Fight* (1908), which was published by his wife the year after his death; and *The Poetical Works of William Henry Drummond* (1912), which was introduced—as *The Habitant* had also been—by Louis Fréchette, French Canada's most respected poet of the time. A 1926 selection of Drummond's work, *Habitant Poems*, was reprinted in 1959. By the early 1900s Drummond had moved his Montreal office to 1009 Dorchester; in addition to practising medicine he was serving as professor of medical jurisprudence at the Bishop's College medical school (corner of Jeanne Mance and Ontario). In 1907 he died of a cerebral hemorrhage in COBALT, Ont., where his brother owned a mining operation; Drummond had gone there to help combat an outbreak of smallpox. He is buried in Mont Royal Cemetery near family members.

Drummond's house on Mountain St became a literary meeting place. An evening there in the autumn of 1898, as recalled by the novelist Arthur Stringer, gives something of the mood of writers convinced they were witnessing the birth of a new Canadian literature. Stringer wrote: 'As the light came on, the second man rose to his feet. He had been squatting on the floor, boy-like, with a couple of sofa pillows under him, his hands linked tranquilly over his knees, his face turned toward the river bend beyond the heated city crowned with its luminous haze of dust. This second figure was Archibald Lampman, the purest poet, the greatest apostle of beauty who ever drew the breath of life in the Dominion of Canada. I peered at him and thought of Browning's line: "And so you once saw Shelley plain [*sic*]." '

3. LEACOCK AND HIS CIRCLE. THE CANADIAN AUTHORS' ASSOCIATION

Sir **Andrew Macphail** came to Montréal in the mid-1880s to study at McGill University (B.A., 1888; M.D., 1891). He practised medicine in the city until 1907, also teaching at William Henry Drummond's Alma Mater, Bishop's College medical school (corner of Jeanne Mance and Ontario), from 1893 until 1907. In 1907 he became McGill's first professor of the history of medicine and in the same year founded an important literary quarterly, the *University Magazine*, which he edited until 1920. From the 1890s Macphail's home was at 216 Peel, where he lived alone from his wife's death in 1902 until his own in 1938. During this period he wrote a novel (*The Vine of Sibmah: A Relation of the Puritans*, 1906), a biography (*Three Persons*, 1929), polished essays (*Essays in Puritanism*, 1905; *Essays in Fallacy*, 1910), and works on war history, religion, and medicine; he also made the first translation of Hémon's *Maria Chapdelaine* (trans. 1921; superseded later the same year by William Hume Blake's translation). Macphail's most important book is *The Master's Wife*, an autobiographical reminiscence of pioneer settlers in his native Prince Edward Island that describes the experiences of his father, who was a school inspector, and his mother. This book was published posthumously in 1939; like some of his others, it was written partly in Montreal and partly in his childhood home at ORWELL, P.E.I., where Macphail spent his summers after his father's death in 1905.

Major John McCrae

A friend of Macphail who shared both his medical profession and literary interests was **John McCrae**, who wrote the famous war poem 'In Flanders Fields'. The two men belonged to the Montreal Pen and Pencil Club, along with the painter Robert Harris (see CHARLOTTETOWN, P.E.I.), who was also a poet and memoirist; Stephen Leacock became a member of this group about 1906. A native of GUELPH, Ont., McCrae lived in Montreal from 1900 to 1914—after 1904 near Andrew Macphail at 190 Peel. In Montreal McCrae was associated with Montreal General Hospital (536 Dorchester West), the Alexandra Hospital (on rue Charron in the Pointe Saint-Charles district), and the Royal Victoria Hospital (432 Pine Ave.). McCrae's 'In Flanders Fields' first appeared in *Punch* in Dec. 1915; it had been written in the spring of that year after the second battle of Ypres. In 1915 McCrae left the front to serve at the military General Hospital in Boulogne, where he died of pneumonia on 27 Jan. 1918. Macphail collected and edited McCrae's only published volume, *In Flanders Fields and Other Poems* (1919), providing a long biographical essay on the physician-poet.

Another close friend of Macphail was the humorist **Stephen Leacock**, who came to Montreal in 1903 to teach economics and political science at McGill. Leacock and his wife Beatrix first lived in a flat near the McGill campus but moved in 1911 to their home of many years at 165 Côte-des-Neiges (the number of the house was changed during Leacock's lifetime to 3869; after his death the house was sold and was eventually torn down to make room for an expansion of Montreal General Hospital). In 1906 Leacock published a textbook, *Elements of Political Science*, his first book and, as it turned out, the most profitable he ever wrote. It was not until 1910 that he published his first book of humour, *Literary Lapses*, made up of pieces he had written for the most part during the 1890s. Privately published in an edition of 3,000 copies at Leacock's own expense and at the initiative of his brother George, it was sold out during the summer of 1910, almost wholly in Montreal. One of its purchasers was John Lane, publisher of the Bodley Head Press of London, who regularly visited Montreal to search for antique steel-engraved prints. He discovered the book in a Montreal train station and after reading it in England telegraphed Leacock from London to offer a British edition, which appeared (somewhat expanded) in the fall of 1910; thereafter Leacock's international popularity never flagged as he produced a book of humour nearly every year until his death in 1944. Notable among them are *Sunshine Sketches of a Little Town* (1912; based on ORILLIA, Ont.), *Arcadian Adventures with the Idle Rich* (1914; based in part on Montreal), *Nonsense Novels* (1911), *Moonbeans from the Larger Lunacy* (1915), *Short Circuits* (1928), *My Remarkable Uncle* (1942), and *Last Leaves* (1945). Besides humour, Leacock found time to write numerous books and articles on history, political science, economics, social theory, literature, and biography, as well as a history of Montreal (*Montreal: Seaport and City*, 1942) and an unfinished memoir, *The Boy I Left Behind Me*, which was published in 1946 two years after his death.

Stephen Leacock, *c.*1920. A detail from a group portrait of the Political Economy Club, McGill University

Leacock's literary work was done both at his summer house in Orillia and in the Côte-des-Neiges house. Here he customarily slept out of doors, even during winter, in a covered veranda, rose about 5 a.m., wrote for two hours before breakfast, and then walked to the McGill Arts Building, which housed his classroom and office. The other focal point of his life in Montreal was the University Club, which he had helped found in the spring of 1908; it first occupied quarters on Dorchester, but in 1913 it moved into its own new building on Mansfield, where it stands today. The 'Leacock corner' in the club, where the humorist had his customary chair, is today presided over by a portrait of him. The Redpath Library at McGill contains the Leacock Room, with a complete collection of his published writings and collections of his letters, manuscripts, and other material relating to him.

One of Leacock's close friends in Montreal was the essayist and editor **Bernard**

K. **Sandwell** (1876–1954), who had been a student of Leacock's at Upper Canada College in TORONTO (3, 7). From 1905 to 1911 Sandwell worked for the Montreal *Herald*, first as a reporter while lodging at 76 Victoria, and later as the *Herald*'s drama critic, when he lived at 276 Pine Ave W. It was Sandwell who arranged the meeting between Leacock and Edward Beck, managing editor of the *Montreal Star*, out of which grew the 1912 series of sketches for the *Star* that made up *Sunshine Sketches of a Little Town*. After 1911 Sandwell worked for the *Financial Times* in Montreal and in 1919 became an associate professor in the McGill Department of Economics and Political Science, which was headed by Leacock. Sandwell's essays were collected in *The Privacity Agent and Other Modest Proposals* (1928) and *The Diversions of Duchesstown and Other Essays* (1955). He left Montreal in 1923 to become head of the English department of Queen's University, KINGSTON, Ont.; he was later editor of *Saturday Night* (1932–51).

The popular novelist **Frank Packard**, born in 1877, spent his childhood at 5 rue Durocher. The family later moved to 33 Rosemount Ave in Westmount. Packard was educated at Montreal High School, 197 Peel, and at McGill (B.Sc., 1897), and then spent thirteen years out of the country. In 1910 he married and settled in Lachine at 611 rue Saint-Joseph (in the mid-1920s the number became 609). There he wrote most of his best-selling crime novels and books of short stories, such as *The Wire Devils* (1918), *Jimmie Dale and the Phantom Clue* (1922), and *The Big Shot* (1929). Few of his books have Canadian settings, but *Doors of the Night* (1922) and *The Hidden Door* (1933) are set on the North Shore of the St Lawrence. Packard died in 1942.

The Canadian Authors' Association, the oldest writers' organization in Canada, was founded in 1921 in Montreal by Stephen Leacock, B.K. Sandwell, the critic **Pelham Edgar**, and **John Murray Gibbon**, who became the CAA's first president. In the late summer of 1921 Leacock hosted a dinner for the three other writers at the University Club, and there the group discussed the organizing of opposition among Canadian writers to a proposed change in the country's copyright laws. (The change, which was never adopted, would have prevented Canadian authors from collecting royalties on Canadian editions of books that had been first published by foreign publishing houses.) Soon after this dinner Leacock left for a British speaking tour that kept him out of Canada for four months, but Gibbon, Sandwell, and Edgar approached other writers and met an overwhelming response: they found they would have to make accommodations for about 100. The meeting and a dinner were held on 7 Dec. 1921 in the Hôtel Place Viger. In discussions it became clear that the writers attending would agree to found a permanent organization if its constitution and by-laws could be written while they were still together. The three men worked through the night to prepare the necessary documents, which they presented to the group on 8 Dec. Approval was voted and thus the Canadian Authors' Association was formed. Gibbon, Sandwell, and Edgar conferred the distinction of being a charter member on Leacock *in absentia*.

Gibbon worked in Montreal as general publicity agent of the CPR from 1913 to 1945. Among his works were *Steel of Empire: The Romantic History of the Canadian Pacific, the Northwest Passage of Today* (1935); *Canadian Mosaic: The Making of a Modern Nation* (1938), winner of a Governor General's Award; a four-volume collection of French-Canadian folk songs (1928); and five novels. **B.K. Sandwell** was the CAA's first secretary and held this post until he left Montreal in 1923; he was also editor of the CAA's publication, the *Canadian Bookman*, which as *Canadian Author and Bookman* is still published (see NIAGARA-ON-THE-LAKE, Ont.). The CAA and *Canadian Bookman* offices were at 70 McGill College Ave; Sandwell lived in the early 1920s at 701 Shuter. One of the noteworthy early events sponsored by the CAA was the crowning of Bliss Carman as Canada's unofficial poet laureate in 1921, at the beginning of his tour of western Canada. In 1937 the CAA established the Governor General's Awards, in co-operation with Governor General Lord Tweedsmuir (John Buchan, himself a noted novelist). Originally the CAA intended to be a bilingual and bi-national organization—**Louvigny de Montigny** was one of the moving spirits in its creation. Although he lived in OTTAWA at that time, de Montigny maintained an office at 30 St James (room 61), as the Canadian representative of the *Association des auteurs de France*. In 1938 he helped transform the French wing of the CAA into the independent *Société des Écrivains canadiens*.

4. THE 'McGILL FORTNIGHTLY REVIEW' GROUP

In 1921 **A.J.M. Smith**, a nineteen-year-old freshman, persuaded the McGill student council to provide funds for a *Literary Supplement* to the *McGill Daily* and then made it a lively magazine, publishing his own poems and contributions from distinguished faculty members such as the psychologist Otto Klineberg, as well as from other students. A year later the student council withdrew its grant. The *McGill Daily* was located in the McGill Union Building, 328 Sherbrooke St W. In 1924 **F.R. Scott** came to McGill to study law, having completed studies at Oxford as a Rhodes scholar. The following year Scott and Smith became the main founders of the *McGill Fortnightly Review*, which was planned and edited at 989 Atwater Ave in Apt. 16, the apartment of Arthur Percy Rushton Coulborn, an English student who belonged to the editorial group. Scott and Smith chose as managing editor an eighteen-year-old sophomore, **Leon Edel**, who later became the influential biographer of Henry James. The *McGill Fortnightly Review* published from 1925 to 1927. At McGill during this period, and on the fringe of the *Fortnightly* group, were the poets **John Glassco** and **A.M. Klein**. Glassco, son of the university's bursar, did not contribute, although he was known to Scott, Smith, and Edel. Klein was younger than the others, entering as a freshman in the last year of the magazine. He submitted poems and impressed Scott and Smith, but was not published because, as Leon Edel tells it, he refused to remove from his submitted poem the word 'soul', judged romantic and old-hat by the editors. Another important member of the group was **Lew** [Louis] **Schwartz**, who was not a writer but later became an important publisher. With Scott and Leo Kennedy he founded and edited the *Canadian Mercury* (1927–9) and after the Second World War went to New York, where he published trade magazines and eventually became president of the publishing house of Abelard-Schumann. It was Schwartz who discovered, and brought into the group its final important member, the poet **Leo Kennedy**. Schwartz had noticed in the 'lonely hearts' column of the *Montreal Star* (to which he himself contributed anonymous tongue-in-cheek missives) certain letters of a marked literary quality appearing over the name 'Helen Lawrence'. He sought out the author and thus met Kennedy, a product of the Irish-Catholic working-class neighbourhood of Verdun. Kennedy was never a McGill student, but he began to associate with other members of the group at the Student Union and became an important part of the Canadian poetic revival in Montreal in the 1920s and early 1930s.

F.R. (Frank) **Scott** (the son of Canon **Frederick George Scott** of QUEBEC CITY, himself a poet in the style of the 'Confederation' group, who was born at 9 Bonaventure, Montreal, on 7 April 1861), born in

1899, was the oldest member of the Montreal group. After graduating from the law faculty of McGill and returning to McGill to teach in 1928 (he was dean to law from 1961 to 1964), he became a prominent political theorist, constitutional expert, and an important poet. During the years of the *McGill Fortnightly Review* Scott lived at 848 Tupper St (Apt. 3) and during the years of the *Canadian Mercury* at 22 Highland Ave. At these addresses he wrote some of the poems in his first collection, *Overture* (1945). Scott's later house on Clarke Ave (see below) became one of the best-known literary addresses in Montreal.

A.J.M. Smith was born in Westmount in 1902 of English immigrant parents, who lived at 215 Elm Ave, Westmount. In his second year at Westmount High School he was taken to England; he returned in 1920 and finished high school in 1921. In the fall of that year he entered McGill as a science student, although he soon switched to literature. During the period of the *Literary Supplement* and the *Fortnightly Review*, Smith lived with his parents at 79 Chesterfield Ave, Westmount. As an undergraduate Smith (along with Edel and other members of the group) had as a teacher **Cyrus Macmillan**, then recently appointed head of the English Department and living at 836 Oxender Ave. He is remembered today for his retellings of the Glooscap legends and other eastern Algonkian folklore, collected most recently in *Canadian Wonder Tales*, (1974); see WOOD ISLANDS, Prince Edward Island. At McGill, Smith also knew **Lancelot Hogben**, later famous as the author of popular works on science. A biology professor, Hogben was an Englishman who had associated with the Bloomsbury group in London; he published poems in the *McGill Fortnightly Review* under a pseudonym.

In 1927 Smith went to Edinburgh for doctoral work in English literature. When he returned to Canada he was unable to find a teaching post and eventually joined the English department of Michigan State College (now University). He remained there for the rest of his life and became an American citizen, but he kept in close touch with the Montreal group—particularly Frank Scott—and spent his summers near MAGOG in the Eastern Townships. Smith was an important figure in Canadian literature, not only for his poetry collections—*News of the Phoenix and Other Poems* (1943), winner of a Governor General's Award; *Collected Poems*, (1962); *The Classic Shade: Selected Poems*, (1978)—but also for his critical writings and his many influential anthologies, especially the *Book of Canadian Poetry: A Critical and Historical Anthology* (1943, 1948, 1957). In the thirties the Montreal group's chief members—Smith, Scott, Leo Kennedy, and A.M. Klein—joined with the Toronto writers **E.J. Pratt** and **Robert Finch** to produce the influential anthology *New Provinces: Poems of Several Authors* (1936). Smith and Scott were the editors.

A.M. Klein was born in the Ukraine in 1901, but was a lifelong Montrealer from 1910, when his family immigrated to Canada. Klein attended McGill from 1926 to 1930 (at this time his family lived at 4267 Clark) and the law faculty of the Université de Montréal from 1930 to 1933. He practised law in the city until 1954, when personal and emotional problems ended his writing career and prompted him to become a virtual recluse. After being called to the bar in 1933, Klein set up his law practice at 276 St James St (room 203). His home in the early 1930s was at 4455 Saint-Urbain, and he was living there at the time of *New Provinces*. In 1935 he married his childhood sweetheart, Bessie Kozlov; the couple lived first at 4353 Saint-Urbain. His poems of the 1920s and 1930s, many of them written here, were collected in his book *Hath Not a Jew . . .* (1940). Remaining in the forefront of the new poetry, he associated during and after the Second World War with the young poets of *First Statement* and *Preview* magazines. His other poetry collections were *The Hitleriad* (1944) and *The Rocking Chair and Other Poems* (1948), which won a Governor General's Award. Throughout the 1940s, Klein lived at 4857 rue Hutchison. His novel

A.M. Klein, *c.*1933

F.R. Scott, 1955

The Second Scroll (1951) was based on a fact-finding trip in 1950 to Israel and to Jewish refugee camps in Europe on behalf of the Canadian Jewish Congress. Klein returned to McGill University in 1945–8 as a special lecturer in poetry. From 1950 until his death in 1956 he lived at 236 av. Querbes, Outremont.

At the time when *New Provinces* was published F.R. Scott was a professor of law at McGill and was living at 5653 Oxenden Ave. A.J.M. Smith, seeking a teaching position in Canada, was probably staying with his parents, who at this time lived at 329 Grosvenor Ave, Westmount. Klein wrote at his av. Querbes address. The fourth member of the group, Leo Kennedy, was working as an advertising copywriter and living in Outremont at 635 Querbes. This was also his address at, or shortly after, the time of the publication of his single volume of poems, *The Shrouding* (1933; rpr. 1975). Later Kennedy moved to the United States and did not return to Montreal to live until 1978. Leon Edel also settled in the United States in the late 1930s, becoming a distinguished biographer of Henry James and the author of such books as *The Psychological Novel 1900–50* (1955) and *Stuff of Sleep and Dreams: Experiments in Literary Psychology* (1982).

After the cessation of the *McGill Fortnightly Review* in 1927, Scott, Kennedy, and Louis Schwartz founded the *Canadian Mercury* (1927–9), also an influential literary journal, which published many of the new poets of the time, both from Montreal and elsewhere. At this period, F.R. Scott lived at 22 Highland Ave; Louis Schwartz was apparently still living with his family at 1536 rue Saint-Antoine. By the early 1940s Scott had established his permanent home at 451 Clarke Ave, Westmount, which for forty years thereafter was one of the focal points of literary activity in Montreal. Here and at his home in NORTH HATLEY, he prepared many of the books for which he is known, including three winners of Governor General's Awards: *The Collected Poems of F.R. Scott* (1981), *Poems of French Canada* (1977), and *Essays on the Constitution: Aspects of Canadian Law and Politics* (1977). During the 1930s, through his work in the Co-operative Commonwealth Federation (CCF), Scott met French-Canadian writers such as the novelist and editor of the weekly *Le Jour*, **Jean-Charles Harvey**, and the slashing social satirist 'Jean Narrache', who under his real name, **Émile Codèrre**, was a pharmacist and later professor of pharmaceutical legislation at the Université de Montréal. In 1942 he met **Hector de Saint-Denys Garneau** at his Clarke Street house, when Garneau was visiting briefly at his family's home nearby in Westmount. The two poets exchanged books, Scott offering *New Provinces* and Garneau a copy of his only book published during his lifetime, *Regards et jeux dans l'espace* (1935). Then during the 1950s Scott held regular meetings in his house to encourage contact between English and French writers. This activity is reflected in Scott's translations in *Poems of French Canada*.

Another modernist poet working in Montreal but not associated with the McGill group was **Ronald G. Everson**, who came to Montreal in 1936 to join a public relations firm. By 1938 he had become its president and went on to become one of Canada's leading public-relations practitioners; in 1963 he retired from his firm of Johnston, Everson and Charlesworth and continues to live half of each year in Montreal. Although he published his poems widely in magazines from the 1930s, his first book was *Three Dozen Poems* (1957). Other collections are *Incident on Côte des Neiges and Other Poems* (1966), *The Dark Is Not So Dark* (1969), and *Selected Poems 1920/1970* (1970).

5. THE 'PREVIEW' AND 'FIRST STATEMENT' GROUPS

Like the 1920s, the 1940s were years of ferment and renewal for English-Canadian poetry, with Montreal writers in the forefront. The magazine *Preview* published twenty-three issues here from March 1942 until 1945. The principal editor, British immigrant Patrick Anderson, was joined on the editorial board by Frank Scott and P.K. Page, and in 1944 by A.M. Klein, who had been a contributor from the magazine's early issues.

P.K. [Patricia Kathleen] **Page** came to Montreal at the beginning of the 1940s from New Brunswick (see SAINT JOHN, N.B.) and remained here until 1946, when she went to work for the National Film Board in OTTAWA. For most of her years in Montreal she lived in a boarding house at 1484 Sherbrooke W. (the building still stands but has been converted to another use). It was here that Page wrote 'The Landlady' and most of her other well-known early poems. Her first collection was *As Ten as Twenty* (1944); in 1944 she also published her romance of the supernatural, *The Sun and the Moon*. Towards the end of her time in Montreal, Page rented the apartment of the novelist Hugh MacLennan (Apt. 4, 1178 Mountain St), while MacLennan was out of the city on a Guggenheim Foundation grant.

Patrick Anderson, the moving force behind *Preview*, came to Montreal from Britain in 1940 and for six years taught at Selwyn House, a private school at 95 Côte-St-Antoine, Westmount; in 1948–50 he taught at McGill University. His last year as a permanent resident of Canada was 1950, after which he lived primarily in England, achieving prominence as a writer of autobiographical and travel books (*Search Me: The Black Country, Canada and Spain*, 1957). In 1977 Anderson returned to Montreal for a year as a visiting professor, and his *Return to Canada: Selected Poems* (1977) was published during that time. He died in 1979.

Preview published, in its few mimeographed pages, many of the best young writers of the time; one it rejected was the critic and poet **John Sutherland**, who in 1942 was a McGill undergraduate. As a result, Sutherland began a rival magazine, *First Statement*, in September of that year; the editorial board consisted of Sutherland, his sister Betty Sutherland, his future wife Audrey Aikman, and others. In 1943 he was joined by the young Montreal poets Irving Layton and Louis Dudek; the magazine's first issue appeared in January of that year. An altogether independent figure, Sutherland left McGill (after less than one year of studies) when he founded *First Statement*. In the early days of the magazine it was mimeographed, like *Preview*, and Sutherland produced it from his room in a boarding house on Stanley St. He then had a job as a night clerk at the Windsor Hotel on Peel St. By May 1943 Sutherland had acquired a printing press to improve the appearance of his magazine and had rented an office: Room 18, 207 Craig St W. There he set type and met with members of his editorial board and contributors, including Miriam Waddington, who was then living in Toronto but who soon came to Montreal and remained here from 1945 until 1960. In Nov. 1943 Sutherland and Audrey Aikman were married; they then took an apartment at 3575 rue Durocher, where Sutherland wrote much of his influential criticism and his poetry. He never published a volume during his lifetime, but Miriam Waddington collected some of his work in *John Sutherland: Essays, Controversies and Poems* (1972).

By late 1945 *Preview* had published twenty-three issues and *First Statement* thirty-three. In December the two magazines merged under the editorship of Sutherland, and the resulting magazine was called *Northern Review*. At the same time Sutherland founded his First Statement Press; at his office he and his friend hand-typeset and printed first books by Irving Layton (*Here and Now*, 1945), Patrick Anderson (*A Tent for April*, 1945), Raymond Souster (*When We Are Young*, 1946), and Miriam Waddington (*Green World*, 1946). The joining of the two magazines created a volatile editorial board that included Sutherland, Scott, Layton, Anderson, Aikman, and A.M. Klein in Montreal, with other editors such as Dudek, A.J.M. Smith, P.K. Page, and Dorothy Livesay participating from long range. Most of the editorial board resigned in 1947 to protest Sutherland's sarcastic review of Robert Finch's *Poems* (1946), winner of a Governor General's Award. Sutherland carried on with the magazine until his death in 1956, moving it to Toronto in 1955.

Louis Dudek was born in Montreal in 1918, a son of Polish immigrants, and was brought up in the working-class east end of the city, a circumstance reflected especially in his early social-protest poetry. He attended McGill in the late 1930s, graduated in 1940, and for the next three years worked in advertising and journalism. Until his early twenties he lived in his parent's home at 2360 rue Bercy, a street about fifteen blocks east of Parc Lafontaine. After graduate studies in New York from 1943 to 1951, Dudek taught literature at McGill until 1982; he has lived latterly on Ingleside Ave, Westmount. Among his books of poems are *East of the City* (1946), *Europe* (1955), *Atlantis* (1967), and *Selected Poems* (1979). An indefatigable small-press publisher, Dudek collaborated with Raymond Souster and Irving Layton in the influential Contact Press (1952–67), founded his McGill Poetry Series in 1956 with Leonard Cohen's first book of poems, and in the mid-1960s (with R.G. Everson and others) formed Delta Publishing out of his earlier *Delta* magazine.

Irving Layton was another author who grew up in Montreal's east end; he moved

Louis Dudek, *c.*1980

there with his parents shortly after his birth in 1912 in Rumania. Like A.M. Klein and the novelist Mordecai Richler, Layton attended Baron Byng High School, at 4251 St Urbain St near the corner of rue Rachel (the building has been converted to other uses); he graduated in 1929. Layton then took a degree in agriculture from Macdonald College, served in the Second World War, and in 1943 returned to Montreal, where he entered McGill for graduate work in economics. His association with Sutherland was formed quickly. In 1943 Layton married Sutherland's sister, Betty; at that time the poet was working as a proofreader for the Montreal *Gazette*. Sutherland published Layton's first book, but the early work for which he is best known was written at 8035 Kildare Rd, where Layton lived from 1950 to 1958 while teaching English at the Herzliah School, a Hebrew school for boys. The poems from this period are gathered in various collections, especially *In the Midst of My Fever* (1954), *The Cold Green Element* (1955), and *The Bull Calf and Other Poems* (1956). In 1955 Layton became a part-time lecturer at Sir George Williams University (now part of Concordia University), where Sutherland had taught a few years earlier. From 1959 to 1968 he lived at 5731 Somerled in the Notre-Dame-de-Grâce district, and there wrote the poems collected in *Balls for a One-Armed Juggler* (1963), *Periods of the Moon* (1967), and *The Shattered Plinths* (1968). His *A Red Carpet for the Sun* (1959) won a Governor General's Award. Layton spent 1969–78 in TORONTO (7) as a professor of English at York University; he now lives on Monkland. His recent books of poetry include *Europe and other Bad News* (1981) and *A Wild Peculiar Joy, 1945–1982* (1982).

At a party to mark the end of *Preview* in 1945 members of *Preview* group amused themselves by posing for this portrait. Front: Patrick Anderson. Centre: Peggy Anderson, P.K. Page. Rear: Kit and Neufville Shaw, Bruce Ruddick, F.R. Scott.

Innumerable Layton poems evoke Montreal and places there with which he has been associated. 'Gothic Landscape', for instance, recollects his Jewish boyhood and rue Sainte-Elizabeth, where he grew up. 'Schoolteacher in Late November' was written while he was teaching at the Herzliah School, at the corner of Esplanade and Rachel; the building has now been converted to other uses. Like Klein, Layton was also associated with the old Jewish Public Library on Esplanade just north of Duluth, which has also been converted to other uses.

6. HUGH MACLENNAN. WRITERS AFTER 1940

The novelist **Hugh MacLennan** came to Montreal in the fall of 1935 as a teacher at Lower Canada College, 4090 Royal at the corner of Notre-Dame-de-Grâce; the latter street is portrayed in his 1953 essay 'The Best-Loved Street in Canada', and the high school is satirized as Waterloo School in his novel *The Watch That Ends the Night* (1959; GGA). On 22 June 1936 he married the writer **Dorothy Duncan** (1903–57) and the couple settled at 5265 Côte Saint-Luc in the Notre-Dame-de-Grâce district. By the early 1940s they had moved to the apartment at 1178 Mountain St that was later sublet for a year by P.K. Page while MacLennan was out of the city on a Guggenheim Foundation grant.

MacLennan spent the summer of 1940 at BADDECK on Bras d'Or Lake, Cape Breton Island, N.S., and there he began his first novel, *Barometer Rising* (1941), which was completed in Montreal. Here he also wrote *Two Solitudes* (1945), which received the first of five Governor General's Awards given to MacLennan's work, three for fiction and two for non-fiction. In 1942 the MacLennans began summering in NORTH HATLEY, and in 1945 he bought a house, 'Stone Hedge', there. On the strength of the success of *Two Solitudes* MacLennan retired from Lower Canada College in 1945; in 1951 he began teaching part-time at McGill University and earned additional money by working summers for the National Film Board.

Hugh MacLennan, *c.*1980

In 1957 Dorothy MacLennan died; although MacLennan finished his novel *The Watch That Ends the Night* that year, it was not published until 1959. By that time he was living at 1535 Summerhill Ave, Apt. 206, with his second wife, the former Frances Aline Walker of Montreal, whom he married on 15 May 1959. His novels since then have been *Return of the Sphinx* (1967) and *Voices in Time* (1980), a futuristic story set in Montreal.

Born in TORONTO (5), novelist **Gwethalyn Graham** spent most of her adult life in Montreal, and here wrote her two novels, *Swiss Sonata* (1938) and *Earth and High Heaven* (1944), which both won Governor General's Awards. Both deal with racial tension, especially anti-Semitism; *Earth and High Heaven* is set in Montreal during the Second World War. Graham died in 1965; her last home was Apt 17, 4652 Sherbrooke W.

Like the playwright and novelist Michel Tremblay, **Mordecai Richler** has made Montreal's ethnic east end the best-known

The young Gwethalyn Graham

part of Canada to non-Canadian readers. Richler's fictional world centres on St Urbain St. The poor, ethnic, largely Jewish and English-speaking neighbourhood of which Richler writes lay just to the west of Tremblay's Plateau Mont Royal. It was bounded approximately by Park and Saint-Laurent ('the Main') on the east and west, by Bernard and avenue du Mont Royal on the north, and by Pine (avenue des Pins) on the south. Richler lived at 5257 Saint-Urbain until 1944, when he was thirteen. He graduated from Baron Byng High School (as had A.M. Klein and Irving Layton), which appears as 'Fletcher's Field High School' in *The Apprenticeship of Duddy Kravitz* (1959), *St Urbain's Horsemen* (1971), and *Joshua Then and Now* (1980). After dropping out of university Richler spent 1951–2 in Europe, where he wrote his first novel, *The Acrobats* (1954); he lived in England from 1959 to 1972, when he returned to live permanently in Montreal. He now lives on Sherbrooke W.

Mordecai Richler, *c.*1980

The novelist **Sinclair Ross** was transferred in April 1946 to the Montreal head office of the Royal Bank, which had employed him previously in small-branch banks in his native Saskatchewan, beginning in ABBEY, Sask., in 1924, when he was sixteen. In Montreal Ross worked at 360 St James until 1962, when the offices were moved to Place Ville Marie. From 1959 Ross was a member of the advertising department; he retired on 31 Jan. 1968, spent the following twelve years in Greece and Spain, and now lives in Vancouver. Ross wrote his most important novel, *As for Me and My House* (1941), while he was working for the Royal Bank in WINNIPEG, but it did not attract widespread attention until 1957, when it was reprinted in the New Canadian Library. From early in his Montreal period Ross lived at 3450 rue Durocher, Apt. 30, which was within walking distance of his office. Here he wrote his second novel, *The Well* (1958), and some of the short stories collected in *The Lamp at Noon and Other Stories* (1968). Ross's other work includes the novels *Whir of Gold* (1970), set in Montreal, and *Sawbones Memorial* (1974). Another important novelist who came to Montreal in the early post-war period was **Brian Moore**, who was born in Ireland in 1921. He lived in Montreal from 1948 to 1959, working from 1948 to 1952 as a reporter for the Montreal *Gazette*. His first three novels were written here: *Judith Hearne* (1955), *The Feast of Lupercal* (1957), and *The Luck of Ginger Coffey* (1960), which is set in Montreal and won a Governor General's Award. Since 1959 Moore has lived primarily in California, but he has kept his Canadian citizenship; his later novels include *Catholics* (1972), *The Great Victorian Collection* (1975; GGA), and *The Mangan Inheritance* (1979).

After serving in the Second World War, the poet **Earle Birney** returned to Canada in 1945 as supervisor of the Central European section of the CBC's International Service in Montreal; in the same year he published his second poetry collection, *Now Is Time*. From 1946 to 1948 Birney was editor of the Canadian Authors' Association literary journal, *The Canadian Poetry Magazine*; in 1946 he returned as a professor to his Alma Mater, the University of British Columbia (see VANCOUVER). The Newfoundland writer **Arthur Scammell** (*My Newfoundland*, 1966) came to Montreal in 1939 to study at McGill, and stayed here for thirty-one years, becoming a teacher and eventually head of the English department of Mount Royal High School in the Town of Mount Royal. Scammell lived at 1330 Lombard Crescent, Apt. 56, in Mount Royal. While here he helped found the important Newfoundland magazine the *Atlantic Guardian* (1945–57). In 1940 the Newfoundland novelist **Percy Janes** (*House of Hate*, 1970) was also in Montreal briefly, but in 1942 he joined the navy here and served for four years in the medical corps. (See also CHANGE ISLANDS, CORNER BROOK, ST JOHN'S, Nfld.)

The Montreal-born short-story writer and novelist **Mavis Gallant** (née Young) worked in the late 1940s as a writer for the National Film Board and the *Montreal Standard*, where she was employed when the *New Yorker* accepted her first story. On the strength of this she left her job in 1950 and went to Europe. She has lived in Paris since the early 1950s, writing such highly regarded books as *My Heart Is Broken* (1964; rpr. 1982), *The End of the World and Other Stories* (1973), and *Home Truths: Selected Canadian Stories* (1981), winner of a Governor General's Award, and the novel *A Fairly Good Time* (1970). Another Montreal novelist was the eminent neurosurgeon and scientist **Wilder Penfield**, who came to the city in 1928 as professor of neurosurgery at McGill and founded the Neurological Institute in 1934; there he did his ground-breaking work on the causes of epilepsy and the biochemical functioning of the brain. Penfield lived at 4302 Montrose Ave, Westmount, and directed the Institute until he retired in 1960. He was the author of two historical novels, *No Other Gods* (1954) and *The Torch* (1960),

Farley Mowat and Dr Wilder Penfield exchanging their latest books, 1 Nov. 1963

and a book of essays and reflections, *The Second Career* (1963). Avenue Docteur Penfield forms the northwest boundary of the McGill campus.

Milton Acorn lived in Montreal from 1956 to 1959, at 75 Somerville. His friends here were Irving Layton and **Al Purdy** (see AMELIASBURG, Ont.), who was also a Montreal resident briefly. It was in 1956 that Acorn decided to sell his carpenter's tools, abandoning the trade that had supported him since the Second World War, and devote himself to poetry. Purdy later edited Acorn's *I've Tasted My Blood: Poems 1956 to 1968* (1969). (See also CHARLOTTETOWN, P.E.I.; TORONTO: 2, Ont.; VANCOUVER, B.C.) The novelist **Elizabeth Spencer**, an American, came to Montreal with her husband in the late 1950s and lived in Lachine and then in Montreal in an apartment building, 'Le Trianon', at 2300 Saint-Mathieu. She taught Creative Writing at Concordia University until 1986, when she and her husband moved to Chapel Hill, North Carolina. Her novels written in Canada include *The Light in the Piazza* (1960) and *The Salt Line* (1984); *The Stories of Elizabeth Spencer* appeared in 1981. The novelist **Scott Symons** lived in Montreal in 1960–1, working as a reporter for *La Presse*. During this period, and another brief stay in 1965–6, he completed his first novel, *Place d'Armes: A Personal Narrative* (1967; repr. 1978). Place d'Armes, around which the novel is set, is at rue Notre-Dame and rue Saint-Sulpice in Vieux Montréal.

The novelist and short-story writer **Hugh Hood**, who has lived in Montreal since 1961, has treated the city in detail in the title story of *Flying a Red Kite* (1962), in the linked sketches of *Around the Mountain: Scenes from Montreal Life* (1967), in the novel *A Game of Touch* (1970), and in others works. A professor of English at the Université de Montreal, Hood has lived on Hampton Ave since 1967. (See also TORONTO: 5) The novelist **Eric Koch** settled in Montreal at 9 Anworth in 1971, when he was appointed head of CBC English Radio Services here, and stayed until his retirement about six years later, when he returned to Toronto. His novels include *The Leisure Riots* (1973) and *The Last Thing You'll Want to Know* (1976).

The novelist **John Buell**, born in 1927 in Montreal, was educated at the Université de Montréal and teaches at Concordia University. While living at 4937 Westmore he published his first suspense novel, *The Pyx* (1959); it was filmed in Montreal in 1973. In 1962, when *Four Days* was published, Buell lived at 5171 Westmore. His other novels are *The Shrewsdale Exit* (1972) and *Playground* (1976).

Montreal's famous exposition, Expo '67, was the end-point of **Farley Mowat**'s voyage by sail up the St Lawrence from his then home in BURGEO, Nfld. The journey is the subject of his *The Boat Who Wouldn't Float* (1968), winner of a Stephen Leacock Medal for Humour.

7. WRITERS MAINLY ASSOCIATED WITH McGILL AND CONCORDIA UNIVERSITIES

'The troubadour of St Catherine Street', **Leonard Cohen**, was born in Montreal in 1934, a son of Nathan B. Cohen, general manager of the Freedman Company, a men's and boys' clothier at 372 St Catherine W, fifth floor. This firm was one of two (the other being L. Cohen & Son Coal Ltd., 40 Prince) belonging to the patriarch of the Cohen family, Lyon Cohen (1868–1937), a prominent Jewish community leader and philanthropist who in 1897 founded Montreal's *Jewish Times*. In the year of Leonard Cohen's birth his family was living at 4028 Vendôme but soon moved to the house where he spent most of his childhood and youth, 599 Belmont Ave, Westmount. Cohen attended Roslyn Avenue School, 4699 Westmount Ave, and Westmount High School (where A.J.M. Smith had studied). At McGill University Cohen studied under Louis Dudek, who published the young poet's first collection, *Let Us Compare Mythologies* (1956), as the initial title in the McGill Poetry Series. Until 1963 Cohen remained primarily in Montreal, writing and working in his family's business, although he briefly attended graduate school at Columbia University, New York. Until 1960 his main residence was his family's home; after 1960 he lived for some time in an apartment on Pine Ave. Since 1963 he has lived in California, on the Greek island of Hydra, and in New York, with frequent stays in Montreal. Cohen's books written before leaving Montreal in 1963 are his first collection of poems; his second and perhaps most popular collection, *The Spice Box of Earth* (1961); and his first novel, *The Favorite Game* (1963). His many books since then include his second novel, *Beautiful Losers* (1966) and his *Selected Poems* (1968), which was awarded a Governor General's Award (declined). Many of his poems and songs—in 1965 he began a successful international career as a singer-songwriter—are about Montreal, and others are based on autobiographical incidents that occurred here. His famous poem-song 'Suzanne Takes You Down', for instance, was inspired by the wife of the Quebec sculptor Armand Vaillancourt; of Suzanne Vaillancourt, Cohen said, 'We were never lovers, but she gave me Constant Comment tea in a small moment of magic.' She is not to be confused with Suzanne Elrod, the mother of Cohen's two children; 'the song conjured her', he has commented.

Leonard Cohen, *c.*1970

The short-story writer and novelist **Norman Levine** attended McGill from 1946 until 1949, receiving both a B.A. and an M.A.; while here he edited the *Forge*, the student literary periodical. Many of his short stories—including 'The English Girl', 'Class of 1949', and 'I'll Bring You Back Something Nice'—have Montreal settings; they are collected in such volumes as *Selected Stories* (1975) and *Thin Ice* (1979). (See also ST-PAUL-ÎLE-AUX-NOIX; OTTAWA, TORONTO: 5, WAWA, Ont.)

The poet **D.G. Jones** (*A Throw of Particles: New and Selected Poems*, 1983) attended McGill from 1949 to 1952 and met Patrick Anderson, Louis Dudek, Irving Layton, and John Sutherland during this period. (See also NORTH HATLEY, SHERBROOKE; BANCROFT GUELPH, Ont.) In 1952–3 the poet **Jay Macpherson** attended the McGill library school, then located at a downtown building since converted to other uses; she had just published her first book, *Nineteen Poems* (1952). (See also ST JOHN'S, Nfld.; OTTAWA, TORONTO: 3, Ont.) VANCOUVER-born poet **Daryl Hine** was a McGill classics and philosophy student at this time; his first book, *Five Poems* (1954), was published in Toronto by Macpherson under her Emblem Books imprint. Since 1958 he has lived abroad, primarily in the United States, and from 1958 to 1968 was editor of *Poetry*, Chicago. His books include *The Devil's Picture Book*

(1961), *Resident Alien* (1975), and *Selected Poems* (1980). In 1954 the Alberta novelist **Robert Kroetsch** (see HEISLER, Alta.) came to McGill to study and to meet Hugh MacLennan; he received an M.A. in 1956 and went on to further education in the United States. The novelist **Marian Engel** (*Bear*, 1976) attended McGill from 1955 to 1957. (See TORONTO: 7, Ont.)

The novelist **Adele Wiseman** (*The Sacrifice*, 1956; rpr. 1968) lived in Montreal from 1964 to 1969, first at 1217 Drummond, Apt 21. In 1964–5 she taught at Sir George Williams University (which was amalgamated with Loyola College in 1974 to form Concordia University), and afterwards at McGill for the rest of her years in Montreal; she now lives in TORONTO (7). Like McGill, Concordia has employed many writers. The novelist **Clark Blaise** (*Lunar Attractions*, 1979) taught there in the sixties and seventies. Poet **George Bowering** taught at Sir George Williams, while living on Grosvenor, from 1967 to 1971. It was during this period that his books *Mountain Foot* (1968) and *The Gangs of Kosmos* (1969) were jointly awarded the 1969 Governor General's Award. Other teachers or writers-in-residence have included Margaret Atwood, poet Frank Davey (*Selected Poems: The Arches*, 1980), John Newlove, and novelist **John Metcalf** (*General Ludd*, 1980), a resident of Montreal since 1969 who also taught at Loyola College, Sherbrooke W. and Broadway. Metcalf's books include the novel *Going Down Slow* (1972) and a collection of essays, *Kicking Against the Pricks* (1982). *Dreams Surround Us* (1977) is a collection of Metcalf's stories and John Newlove's poetry. The poet **Fred Cogswell** (see FREDERICTON, N.B.) was a visiting professor here in 1967–8, and at that time acquired a knowledge of French-Canadian literature that has resulted in his volumes of translations, principally *The Poetry of Modern Quebec* (1976) and *The Complete Poems of Émile Nelligan* (1983). The poet **Gary Geddes** (*Letter of the Master of Horse*, 1973; *War Measures and Other Poems*, 1976; *The Terracotta Army*, 1984) has for many years taught in the English Department at Concordia. The editor of several well-known literary anthologies, the founder of Quadrant Books, and the present publisher of Cormorant Books, he lives in Dunvegan, Ontario.

8. NEW WRITERS IN ENGLISH

One of the mainsprings of new English-language writing in Montreal is Véhicule Press, which during its heyday in the 1970s and early 1980s had offices—used also as a meeting-place and gallery—at 61 Sainte-Catherine W. Véhicule was the centre of a group of literary magazines and presses (including Delta, New Delta, Cross Country, Maker, and Signal, among others) that were interconnected, in some cases organizationally and in other cases informally, by the sharing of personnel. Most of the writers associated with Véhicule are poets and editors; they include **Ken Norris** (*The Book of Fall*, 1979), **Michael Harris** (*Grace*, 1975), **André Farkas** (*Murders in the Welcome Café*, 1977), **Artie Gold** (*before Romantic Words*, 1979), and **Raymond Filip** (*Hope's Half-Life*, 1983).

The Hungarian-born Farkas teaches at John Abbott College (in Ste-Anne-de-Bellevue), which employs or has employed as teachers many of Montreal's leading younger writers. Prominent among them is **Peter Van Toorn**, who was born in The Hague in 1944 and has lived in Montreal since 1954. His collections of poetry include *In Guildenstern County* (1973) and *Mountain Tea and Other Poems* (1984). Poets **David Solway** (*The Road to Arginos*, 1976, *Selected Poems*, 1982) and **Claudia Lapp** (*Dakini*, 1974) also teach at John Abbott.

Other centres of literary activity include The Word bookstore, 469 Milton, with its long-running reading series and sporadic publishing program, and the Mansfield Book Mart (no longer in operation), 2065 Mansfield, which also published literature and monographs. In the early 1970s Fred Louder and the poet **Robyn Sarah** (*Anyone Skating on That Middle Ground*, 1985) founded and edited their magazine *Versus* (defunct) and Villeneuve Press from their home at 375 rue Villeneuve ouest; the press and a new magazine, *Four by Four* are now published from their present home on Hutchison St, near the original address. Villeneuve has produced books by Montreal writers including August Kleinzahler, Brian Bartlett, Jack Hannan, and Robyn Sarah.

In 1969 five fiction writers—**Hugh Hood**, Clark Blaise, Ray Fraser, John Metcalf and **Ray Smith**—formed the Montreal Story Tellers, a performance group that gave readings from 1970 to 1975. None of these writers were Montreal natives; today only Hood (see TORONTO: 5, Ont.) and the Nova Scotia-born Smith (see HALIFAX, N.S.) still live here. Some of Montreal's recent writers, including Brian Bartlett and novelist **Lorris Elliott** (*Coming for to Carry*, 1982), have studied in the graduate program of the Department of English Studies, Universite dé Montreal, directed by Hood. Another graduate of Université de Montreal—he holds degrees in arts education and law from that institution and from Harvard, McGill, and Boston universities—is the novelist **Edward O. Phillips**. Born in Westmount in 1931, Phillips is the author of the serious crime novels *Sunday's Child* (1981) and *Where There's a Will . . .* (1984). Hood has presented the work of Sarah, Bartlett, Phillips, Elliott, and eight other writers in the Véhicule Press anthology *Fatal Recurrences: New Fiction in English from Montreal* (1985).

9. EARLY WRITERS IN FRENCH

French-Canadian literature in Montreal begins with the musical play *Colas et Colinette, ou Le Bailli dupé* by **Joseph Quesnel**, a French-born fur merchant and littérateur who made his home in BOUCHERVILLE; the comedy was performed in 1790 in Montreal by a troupe Quesnel helped found, and was published in Quebec City in 1808 or 1812. Quesnel was the author of at least two other plays, unpublished during his lifetime, and of poems and songs that appeared in newspapers. The early poet and historian **Michel Bibaud** was born on 20 Jan. 1782 at what is now 4505 chemin de la Côte-des-Neiges; the site is marked by a plaque. Educated at Montreal's Collège Saint-Raphael, Bibaud published the first French-Canadian book of poems, *Épîtres, Satires, Chansons, Épigrammes*, in 1830. He also wrote *Histoire du Canada* (1844) and several works meant to encourage the development of mathematics, science, and the arts in Quebec. For much of his life Bibaud lived at 37 Little St James St; the house, near the corner of Saint-Laurent, was later renumbered and the street renamed St James (now rue Saint-Jacques). Bibaud died in Montreal on 2 Aug. 1857. The novelist **Patrice Lacombe**, born in the village of Lac-des-Deux-Montagnes in 1807, became a Montreal notary in 1830 after graduating from the Collège de Montreal (1931 Sherbrooke W.). Until his death in 1863 he worked as an accountant for the Collège de Montreal and lived at 356 rue Lagauchetière, near the corner of Saint-Urbain. There he wrote his influential novel *La Terre paternelle* (1846), which became the prototype of the French-Canadian *roman paysan*, or 'novel of rural life'.

For the rest, the earliest French-Canadian literary activity in Montreal was carried on by orators and journalists. **Louis-Joseph Papineau**, the leader of the 1837–8 *Patriote* rebellion, was renowned for both the style and delivery of his speeches, some of which are preserved in such works as G. Filteau's *Histoire des patriotes* (2 vols, 1938–42). Papineau was born in 1785 and lived much of his life in the house that still stands at 44 rue Bonsecours. Papineau's daughter Azélie married the artist and novelist **Napoléon Bourassa**, author of the popular *Evangeline*-like tale of the Acadian Expulsion, *Jacques et Marie* (1866). The couple came to live with Papineau and on 1 Sept. 1868 their son Henri was born in the house on rue Bonsecours. A pre-eminent politician, **Henri Bourassa** was also an author and the founder in 1910 of the important newspaper *Le Devoir* (at 211 rue Saint-Sacrement). Much influenced by his grandfather, he continued Papineau's classical tribune-style oratory into the present century and was the author of many political pamphlets. Another important early figure in the Montreal newspaper world was **Denis-Benjamin Viger**, 'le père de la presse canadienne', who was born (in 1774) and spent his youth in the Viger house at 410 Place Jacques-Cartier, at the corner of rue Saint-Amable. Viger was the founder of *Le Spectateur* and was also associated with *Aurore du Canada* and *La Minerve*, two other early periodicals. The author and journalist **Honoré Beaugrand** founded the newspaper *La Patrie* in 1878 in a house (gone) whose location is marked by a plaque on rue Saint-Gabriel, between Notre-Dame and Sainte-Thérèse; the house had earlier belonged to the fur trader and explorer Simon Fraser. Among Beaugrand's books are a polemical novel in defence of French-Canadian residents in the United States, *Jeanne la Fileuse* (1878), and *Lettres de voyage* (1889).

During the latter part of the nineteenth century Montreal replaced Quebec City as the centre of French-Canadian letters. The shift can be marked by the move to Montreal in 1877 of **Louis Fréchette**, the leading poet of the day. A native of LÉVIS, Fréchette had been one of the members of the *Mouvement littéraire de Québec* and thus one of the founders of French-Canadian literature. His *Mes loisirs* (1863), published in QUEBEC CITY at his own expense, had been the movement's first book of poetry, and the first volume of lyric verse ever published in Quebec. In Montreal Fréchette made his home at 306 Sherbrooke E.; the building still stands and is marked with a plaque. Ardent in his political beliefs, Fréchette was elected a Liberal MP from Lévis in 1874, but was defeated twice after coming to Montreal, in 1878 and 1882. His literary work here was more successful. In 1880 *Les Fleurs boréales. Les Oiseaux de neige* (1879) was awarded a Prix Montyon by the *Académie française* in Paris. This was the first honour of its kind ever bestowed on a Quebec author and brought international attention not only to Fréchette but to French-Canadian literature in general. Working in his study on Sherbrooke, Fréchette wrote a famous sequence of long historical poems for *La Légende d'un peuple* (1887), his major work; the verse collection *Feuilles volantes* (1890); several plays and collections of prose sketches; and the posthumous *Poésies choisies* (1908). One of his public acts in Montreal was to promote the erection of a monument (at the corner of Saint-Laurent and Crémazie) to Octave Crémazie, a central figure of the *Mouvement littéraire* and Fréchette's associate in his youthful days in Quebec City; the monument was erected on 24 June 1906. Fréchette counted among his many honours the honorary presidency of the *École littéraire de Montreal* (organized 1895), the group of young writers who turned Quebec's literature in a new direction after more than thirty years' domination by the romanticism of the *Mouvement littéraire de Quebec*. Fréchette died in Ottawa of a stroke on 31 May 1908 and is buried in Montreal in the Notre-Dame-des-Neiges Cemetery.

The home of Louis Fréchette, Montreal

The poet **William Chapman**, a patriotic and romantic writer and a belated disciple of the Quebec City movement, lived in Montreal at 10 rue Saint-Constant about 1890. In 1890 he published *Les Feuilles d'érable*, his second book. (See BEAUCEVILLE EST.)

Louis Riel spent two lengthy periods in Montreal, the first being for his education here in 1858–66. He enrolled at the Séminaire de Saint-Sulpice, on rue Saint-Sulpice at rue de Brésoles in Vieux Montréal; It is Montreal's oldest building and is still occupied by the Sulpician order. Riel graduated to the Collège de Montréal, where he was preparing for the priesthood when he left in 1865 to read law under a Montreal lawyer, Rodolphe LaFlamme. In 1865–6 he lived with his uncle, John Lee, at Mile End, then a village north of the city. Riel's youthful poems, mainly school exercises, include verse fables in the manner of Lafontaine. In 1866 he left the city and in 1868, after an interval of which nothing is known, he returned to his home in ST VITAL, Man.

Fréchette's study, Montreal

The young Louis Riel in Montreal *c.*1866

After the Red River Rebellion of 1869–70, Riel was elected to Parliament from Manitoba on three separate occasions in 1873–4. He visited Montreal on his trips to Ottawa to attempt to take his seat in the House of Commons, which expelled him each time. The third expulsion, in Feb. 1875, was accompanied by a decree of banishment from Canada for five years, and Riel began a period of penniless wandering through the northeastern United States with clandestine visits to Montreal and elsewhere in Quebec. He began to exhibit signs of mental disorder and was brought to the home of John Lee in Mile End. On 6 Mar. 1876 Riel was committed, under the name 'Louis David', to the St-Jean-de-Dieu hospital for the insane, 3929 Notre-Dame E., where Émile Nelligan was later a patient and where, in modern times, Dr Jacques Ferron worked. Riel had apparently written no poetry since 1866 but began to produce verse again under the spur of his difficult period in this asylum and the asylum of Saint-Michel-Archange, Beauport (near Quebec City), where he was transferred on 19 May 1877; he was released as cured on 23 Jan. 1878. After 1876 poetry frequently appears in Riel's papers. Some of it was selected by Riel's brothers and published as *Poésies religieuses et politiques* (1886) after Riel's execution in 1885. The only book he published during his lifetime was *L'Amnistie* (1874), his view of the Red River Rebellion, including its background and aftermath. These and his many other writings have been published and translated in *The Collected Writings of Louis Riel* (5 vols., 1985). (See ST-BONIFACE, WINNIPEG, Man.)

10. THE ÉCOLE LITTÉRAIRE. ÉMILE NELLIGAN
'Four lawyers, an engraver, two journalists, a doctor, a bookseller, five students, a notary and a painter gathered on a green carpet strewn with manuscripts: that is the 'École littéraire.' Thus in his book *Un Mot au lecteur* (1900) Charles Gill described a typical meeting of the *École littéraire de Montréal*. The movement was founded on 7 Nov. 1895 in the city recorder's chamber of the Palais de Justice, 1 Notre-Dame est. Germaine Beaulieu was made the first president and Louvigny de Montigny the first secretary; also present were Jean Charbonneau, Albert Ferland, Edouard-Zotique Massicotte, Joseph Marie-Séraphin Melançon, Henri Desjardin, and several others. Charbonneau, Melançon, and Desjardin had all known one another as high-school students at the Collège Sainte-Marie, and Desjardin (see HULL) had informally headed the *École littéraire*'s predecessor group. This was the humorously named *Groupe des six éponges*, composed of Desjardins and several other university students of 'decadent' literary tastes and manners who met during the winter of 1894–5 to drink beer and lead a writer's life in the cafés of rue Sainte-Catherine, especially the Café Ayotte and the Petit Procope, now long gone.

In the earliest days of the *École littéraire* its members met alternately in the home of Germaine Beaulieu, 77 rue Saint-Hippolyte, and of Testard de Montigny (the city recorder and Louvigny's father) at the corner of Sherbrooke and Saint-Denis. The role of principal founder of this group, which gave French-Canadian literature fresh impetus and a new direction, is generally accorded to **Jean Charbonneau**. Born in Montreal in 1875, Charbonneau was a carpenter's son who developed his literary interests at the Collège Sainte-Marie (142 rue Bleury when he attended it; the number was changed by 1910 to 232). At the time of the *École*'s founding he was a law student at Université Laval's Montreal branch, which was at 185 rue Saint-Denis, the street where the author lived much of his life. In 1905 he lived at 309-B rue Saint-Denis and had law offices (with the firm of Dagenais and Charbonneau) in the New York Life Insurance Building, 11 Place d'Armes; later in offices at 71-A rue Saint-Jacques and 92 rue Notre-Dame est he practised law in Montreal for more than fifty years. By 1907 Charbonneau lived at 787 (now 3975) Saint-Denis, where he wrote his first volume of verse, *Les Blessures* (1912). His next home, at 938 (now 4169) Saint-Denis, saw the writing of his most significant volumes of poetry, *L'âge de sang* (1921), *Les Prédestinés* (1923), and *L'Ombre dans le miroir* (1925), as well as his principal philosophical work, *Des Influences françaises au Canada* (1916–20), for which he was crowned a laureate of the *Académie française* in 1922. About 1925 Charbonneau moved to 151 av. Laval. In 1935, when the movement he had done much to found and guide had run its course, Charbonneau wrote its history: *L'École littéraire de Montréal*.

Jean Charbonneau, *c.*1930

Fitfully active over a span of forty years, the *École* had its golden age during five short months in 1898–9. On 29 Dec. 1898 and 24 Feb., 7 April, and 26 May 1899 the group held public readings, all but the second (at the Monument National, 1182 rue Saint-Laurent) occurring at the Château de Ramezay, 280–90 Notre-Dame est, which had become a museum in 1896 through the efforts of the Montreal Archaeological Society (its vice-president at the time was William Douw Lighthall). These public readings were prominent events, widely noticed, but in retrospect the most important thing about them was the appearance at all of them of the nineteen-year-old poet **Émile Nelligan**, who presented thirteen of his poems. Although the *École*'s devotion to the Parnassian and Symbolist movements of France was a departure from the romanticism of the Quebec City school, the readings were well received—except for Nelligan's. A review on 11 Mar. 1899 in *Le Monde illustré* by the visiting French critic E. de Marchy praised all of Nelligan's fellow poets and associates in the second reading; Nelligan alone received

The young Émile Nelligan, with an inscription from Charles Gill to Albert Lozeau

thinly veiled criticism. This review is said to have occasioned his writing of 'Romance du vin', one of his most famous poems, and his defiant reading of it at the last of the *École*'s public evenings on 26 May. Greeted with unprecedented applause, this was one of the most famous events in French-Canadian letters.

Born on 24 Dec. 1879 at 602 rue Lagauchtetière, Émile Nelligan was baptized the following day, Christmas, at St Patrick's Church, 460 Dorchester W.; this baptism, like Thomas D'Arcy McGee's funeral, is commemorated by a plaque at the church. In Aug. 1887 the Nelligan family moved to an apartment at 112 Laval, where they remained until 1892. In these first two homes Nelligan led the happy childhood and experienced the idyllic relationship with his mother that are such prominent features of his poetry. In 1892 the Nelligans moved to 260 av. Laval, where the poet lived until he was committed to a mental institution. At this address he wrote most of the poems collected by his friend 'Louis Dantin' (Eugène Seers) in *Émile Nelligan et son oeuvre* (1904) and republished, along with fragments written during Nelligan's long hospitalization and other uncollected pieces, in *Poésies complètes*, 1896–1899 (1952). Nelligan received his elementary education at l'École Olier in the avenue des Pins, the same school later attended by the novelist Hubert Aquin. On 2 Sept. 1890 he was enrolled as a day pupil at the Institut Mont-Saint-Louis, 144 Sherbrooke E. and in Sept. 1893 entered the Petit Séminaire de Montréal. On 2 Mar. 1896 he became a pupil at the Collège Sainte-Marie, and during the following summer, between 13 June and 19 Sept., his first nine poems were published in *Le Samedi* under the pseudonym 'Émile Kovar'; these poems, or at least some of them, are thought to have been written at CACOUNA, a Gaspé resort where the Nelligans often spent the summer. Émile ended his schooling when he left the Collège Sainte-Marie in Mar. 1897—determined, against the wishes of his father, to make poetry his career. This may have been in part the result of his presentation by the young writer Arthur de Bussières to the *École littéraire* in Feb. 1987. Virtually all of Nelligan's poetry was produced in a concentrated period of less than three yars, from spring 1896 until autumn 1899. Having felt threatened by madness at the end of the summer of 1899, Nelligan was admitted on 9 Aug. to the Retraîte Saint-Benoît, 4140 Notre-Dame E., where he was diagnosed as suffering from *dementia praecox*. He

Émile Nelligan in early middle age

remained in this institution until 23 Oct. 1925 when, after the death of his sister Gertrude, he was transferred to the public wing of the Saint-Jean-de-Dieu Hospital for the Insane, 3929 Notre-Dame E. Here he died on 18 Nov. 1941; he was buried on 21 Nov. in the Notre-Dame-des-Neiges cemetery on Mount Royal. While in hospital Nelligan maintained an undeviating passion for literature, as **Dr Ernest Choquette** (see BELOEIL) attested after visiting him in 1909. The poet often organized literary evenings among the inmates, at which he would read, but the five notebooks that remain from his last forty-two years contain little besides reworded versions of his own early work and poems by his favourite French authors.

There were many interesting personalities among the founders and early members of the *École littéraire*. **Arthur de Bussières** was born on 20 Jan. 1877 in Montreal and attended the École Saint-Jean-Baptiste in rue Saguinet, where he was a classmate of the poet Albert Lozeau. At eighteen he took rooms of his own at 543 Saint-Laurent, and from that time until his death from appendicitis in 1913 he supported himself as a painter of buildings and store windows. He published his poems beginning in 1896 but never a collection. **Édouard-Zotique Massicotte**'s outstanding eccentricity was that he used dozens of pen-names—separate sets for verse and for prose—to publish the immense volume of his writings. Born in Montreal on 24 Dec. 1867, he was an *École* participant in 1895–1900. From 1898 to 1905 he edited *Le Monde illustré*, the French-language sister publication of Georges-Édouard Desbarats's *Canadian Illustrated News*. Massicotte was later the librarian of Sainte-Cunégonde de Montréal and, from 1911 until his death in 1947, the director of the Montreal judicial archives.

Joseph-Marie-Séraphin Melançon, born the son of Moïse Melançon, a papal zouave, on 15 Oct. 1877, entered the Collège Sainte-Marie in 1889 and there met Lozeau, Charbonneau, and Desjardins. He was a participant in the *École littéraire* for two years after it was founded but thereafter was occupied with studies for the priesthood. He was ordained on 22 Dec. 1900 by Msgr. Paul Bruchési, then a well-known author. For the rest of his life he served various parishes and women's religious communities in Montreal and Outrement, including

Émile Nelligan, 1924

in 1904–12 the parish of St-Louis-de-France, where he had as a parishoner his friend and fellow poet **Albert Lozeau**. In 1931, while he was chaplain to the nuns at the Maison-Mère d'Hochelaga, he wrote his book *Avec ma vie*, which was honoured by the *Académie française*. Melançon published his poems under the name 'Lucien Rainier'. **Albert Ferland** was born in Montreal in 1872 but spent most of his childhood near Lac Simon, Labelle County, where his father bought a farm after the family business failed. A graphic artist as well as a poet, Ferland set up a studio in 1894 in rue Notre-Dame. After 1910 he was a designer of stamps for the federal post office department. After two undistinguished volumes of early verse, Ferland became a leading proponent and practitioner of the poetry of the *terroir*, the countryside, in such volumes as *Les Horizons* (1908) and *Le Terroir* (1909).

During his hospitalization Émile Nelligan was taken at least once for a day-long visit to the summer home at Ahuntsic of **Gonzalve Desaulniers**; there is a famous photograph of him taken in Desaulniers's garden there. Desaulniers, a noted jurist who became chief justice of the Province of Quebec in 1923, was in 1895 the oldest and the most influential member of the *École littéraire*; his poetry, with its Lamartinian romanticism and its careful craftsmanship, formed a bridge between the new writers and the school of Fréchette and Crémazie. During the period of Desaulniers's close association with the *École*, through the first decade of the present century, he was a practising lawyer and lived at 328 Sherbrooke E. until 1905, and afterwards at 362 Sherbrooke E. For forty years he laboured over his poems before finally publishing his single collection, *Les Bois qui chantent* (1930). He died on 5 Apr. 1934 at the age of seventy.

Man of letters and journalist, **Louvigny de Montigny** was, along with Charbonneau and Desaulniers, one of the *École*'s most faithful adherents. Born on 1 Dec. 1876 at ST-JÉRÔME-DE-TERREBONNE, he graduated from the Collège Sainte-Marie and Université Laval's Montreal branch. From 1890 or earlier he lived in the family home at 154 Saint-Denis (now in the 3300 block), at the corner of Sherbrooke. (In 1895 his father, Testard de Montigny, who was city recorder of Montreal, named it 'Montée du Zouave'.) Subsequently the address was listed as 241 Sherbrooke E. About 1895 Louvigny de Montigny began his journalistic career, working for the dailies *La Presse*, *La Patrie*, and *Le Canada*, before founding and directing the *Gazette municipale*. In the early 1900s or before he lived first at 763 av. de l'Hôtel de Ville and later, with his widowed mother, on av. Laval. In 1910 de Montigny became translator to the Canadian Senate and moved to OTTAWA, where many of his books were written. These include the belletristic *Au pays de Québec* (1945) and his romance *L'Épi rouge* (1953).

Eugène Seers ('Louis Dantin') with Alice Lemieux (Mme Rosaire Dion-Lévesque)

Many other writers were associated with the *École littéraire*. **Eugène Seers** was not only Nelligan's friend and editor but also, under the pseudonym **Louis Dantin**, the author of influential poetry and literary criticism. Born in 1865 in BEAUHARNOIS, he was educated at the Collège de Montréal, (1181 Sherbrooke before 1900; later the number was 841 Sherbrooke W.) and in 1883 went to Europe. There he studied, taught, and in 1888 became a priest. In the early 1890s he returned to Montreal, associated with the *École littéraire*, became a friend of Nelligan, and edited and introduced the poet's works. In 1908 he broke with the Church and entered self-imposed exile first in Boston and then in Cambridge, Mass., where he worked for Harvard University press from 1919 to 1938 and died in 1945. There most of his books were written, including his major work, the first and second series of *Poètes de l'Amérique française* (1928, 1934), and his numerous volumes of poetry, including *Le Coffret de Crusoé* and the posthumous collected edition, containing more than 5,000 poems, *Poèmes d'outre-tombe* (1962). His chief production during the *École littéraire* years was *Franges d'autel* (1899), a volume of religious poems.

11. LATER WRITERS OF THE ÉCOLE LITTÉRAIRE

The collapse of Nelligan and the publication in 1900 of *Les Soirées du Château de Ramezay*, a group anthology, concluded the *École*'s first period of activity. It revived again about five years later, with Charbonneau, de Montigny, Gill, Albert Lozeau, and Albert Laberge as its most prominent adherents. A painter and poet, **Charles Gill** came to Montreal in 1894 after four years in Paris, during which he studied painting under Jean Léon Gérôme at the École des Beaux Arts and frequented the Café Procope, where Verlaine presided. Born in SOREL, he had been educated (1882–4) at the Collège Sainte-Marie in Montreal and had lived part of his adolescence (1886–90) at 642 rue Saint-Denis (now in the 3800 block), where his family took up residence after his father was appointed a judge of the Superior Court here. In the spring of 1894 Gill opened a studio at 946 rue Saint-Denis (now in the 4100 block), where in 1898–1900 he wrote the poems delivered at the *École*'s literary evenings and published in *Les Soirées du Château de Ramezay*; he had attended his first meeting of the *École* on 21 May 1896 at the home of a notary, Pierre Bédard. In Sept. 1896 he was made a professor of art at the École Normale Jacques Cartier (Sherbrooke E. and Parc Lafontaine), and taught subsequently at the Monument National and the École des Arts et Métiers. On 10 Oct. 1902 Gill was elected

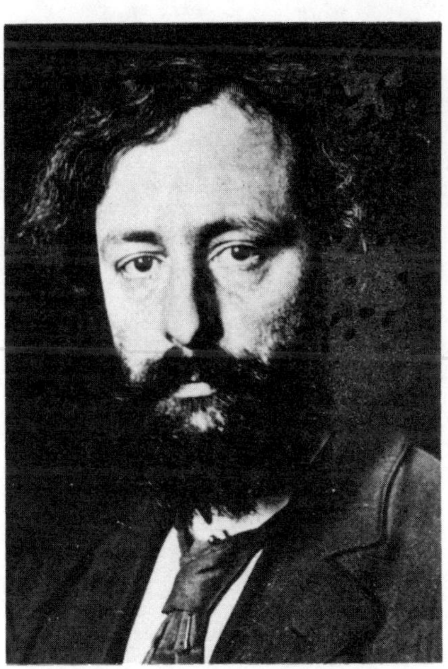

Charles Gill

vice-president of the *École Littéraire*, and in 1904, living at 502 Parc Lafontaine, he was writing the first version of his poem 'Le Saint-Laurent'. On 8 Nov. 1907 Gill read parts of his *magnum opus*, 'Le Cap Éternité', at a meeting of the *École*. Early in 1908 he was living at 42 rue Chambord. He left this address in Feb. 1913 for quarters in the rue Drolet, where he lived with the novelist **Georgine Bélanger**, whom he had married on 12 May 1912; they were separated on 24 Oct. 1913. Under her pen-name 'Gaétane de Montreuil', Bélanger was the author of a novel, *Fleur des ondes* (1912). Gill left Bélanger in financial distress, which resulted in a seizure of his goods from the rue Drolet; in 1916 his landlord is known to have seized two of his paintings for unpaid rent. On the night of 8–9 May 1917 he fled from the rue Drolet to 431 rue Saint-Laurent, which was apparently his last home. On 16 Oct. 1918 Gill died in the Hôpital Notre-Dame, 1560 Notre Dame est, a victim of the influenza epidemic of that year. His poems were published posthumously in *Le Cap Éternité: poème suivi des Étoiles filantes* (1919), and his *Correspondance* appeared in 1969. (See also CHICOUTIMI.)

The man who wrote the introduction to *Le Cap Éternité* was Gill's close friend, the poet **Albert Lozeau**, son of the chief clerk of the Superior Court. Born in Montreal in 1878, Lozeau contracted Pott's disease (partial destruction of spinal vertebrae by a tubercular infection) at the age of thirteen. Bedridden from 1896, although in later life he was able to sit up, he remained in his father's household throughout his life. His earliest

Albert Lozeau

home was in the rue Rachel. From 1888 to 1913 the Lozeau family lived at 468 av. Laval. At this address Lozeau suffered the attack of tuberculosis that left him paralysed; he was living here in 1904 when he was inducted by friends into the *École littéraire*, whcih subsequently often read, and commented favourably on, his poems at its meetings. And it was here that Lozeau wrote his first book, *L'Âme solitaire* (1907), with its distinctive elegiac note and its moving evocation of the poet's resignation over his enforced distance from the world: 'Je regarde ma vitre avec un plaisir calme.' After 1903 the family lived at 604 av. Laval, where Lozeau produced two volumes, *Le Miroir des jours* (1912) and *Lauriers et Feuilles d'érable* (1916). He was elected to the Royal Society of Canada in 1911 and in 1912 was made an officer of the *Académie française*. His last home was at 343 rue Drolet, where the family moved in 1918. He died in 1924, just before the publication of his *Poésies complètes* (1925–6).

Another close friend of Charles Gill was the novelist and short-story writer **Albert Laberge**, credited with introducing realism into the French-Canadian novel of rural life with his *La Scouine* (1918; trans., *Bitter Bread*, 1977). A native of BEAUHARNOIS (like Eugène Seers), Laberge attended the Collège Sainte-Marie but was expelled in 1892 before completing his studies, after confessing to the 'sin' of reading the fiction of the French Naturalists. He read these books in the library of his uncle, Dr Jules Laberge, who lived at 289 Saint-Denis (now in the 3400 block). The expulsion began a difficult four-year period for Laberge, during which he worked as a store clerk and simultaneously studied law at the firm of Le Blond de Brumath & A. Bonin, 4 Saint-Laurent, a firm that specialized in preparing apprentice lawyers. However, Laberge did not go into law. In 1896 he began his thirty-six-year journalistic career with *La Presse* (51 St James, near the corner of Saint-Lambert), where he was first a sports writer, later sports editor, and finally an art critic. Also in 1896 he began to attend meetings of the *École littéraire*, although he did not join formerly until 5 April 1909. Laberge apparently began working on *La Scouine* around 1899, publishing extracts in periodicals in the early 1900s (some of these pieces were condemned by Catholic priests) and bringing out the completed novel in a limited edition of only sixty copies in 1918. In 1900 Laberge was living at 52-A Aylmer, and during the succeeding twenty years he also occupied 39 Balmoral and 23 av. Christophe-Colomb; in 1918 he was living at 31 rue Boyer. Laberge apparently limited his privately published

Albert Laberge

edition of the historic novel to so few copies because he feared being condemned for having portrayed Quebec country life as brutish and demoralizing. It was not until he retired in 1932 that he published his six volumes of short stories, including *Visages de la vie et de la mort* (1936), and another six volumes collecting prose poems, memoirs, sketches, and art criticism. His home from the year of his retirement until his death in 1960 was at 5355 rue Hutchison; he also had a summer house at CHÂTEAUGUAY.

Laberge's qualms about publication may have been due in part to the example of another irreverent young novelist and Laberge's colleague at *La Presse*, **Rodolphe Girard**, who lost his job over a novel. Just two years Laberge's junior, Girard was born in 1879 in TROIS-RIVIÈRES and came to Montreal with his family in 1891, graduating from the Collège de Montréal in 1898. In 1900 he joined *La Presse* and published his first novel, *Florence*, which he quickly followed with a book of short stories and, in 1904, with his best-known work, *Marie Calumet* (trans. 1976, from Girard's expurgated text of 1946); during this period Girard was living at 228 rue Saint-Hubert and later at 195 rue Saint-Urbain; he may also have had other addresses. A high-spirited, satirical, and somewhat scatological novel of country life, *Marie Calumet* was publicly denounced by the Archbishop of Montreal, with the result that Girard was dismissed by *La Presse*; from 1904 he lived and worked in OTTAWA.

12. LOUIS HÉMON IN MONTREAL

Another event of great importance for the French-Canadian novel occurred in Montreal almost eight years after the *Marie Calumet* controversy and much more quietly —at the time it went entirely unnoticed. The French novelist **Louis Hémon**, who had arrived in Quebec City on 18 Oct. 1911, made his way to Montreal a few days later. By 28 Oct. he was living at 1230 rue Saint-Hubert, but in December he took lodgings at 419 rue Saint-Hubert, apparently to be nearer his work. He had obtained a position as a bilingual stenographer with the Security Life Insurance Company of Canada. Until the end of 1911 it was housed in an office building at 282 rue Sainte-Catherine W.; at the beginning of 1912 it moved to the Imperial Bank Building at 286 St James, near the corner of McGill. Hémon was employed by the company from mid-November 1911 until 15 June 1912; his weekly salary was $15. In late June he left for the Lac-Saint-Jean country, where he gathered impressions and began his classic novel, *Maria Chapdelaine* (1916; trans. 1921); see PÉRIBONKA.

About 7 Apr. 1912 Hémon returned to Montreal from KÉNOGAMI, where he had worked about two months, and took a position with Lewis Brothers, one of Montreal's oldest hardware firms, which had a large building at 20–42 Bleury; he took lodgings at 201 Saint-Christophe (today this address is number 1213). At Lewis Brothers the novelist typed his masterpiece, requesting and obtaining from his manager permission to use a desk and typewriter each day for one hour before opening and one hour after closing. Working steadily in this manner, he managed in several months to type *Maria Chapdelaine* in duplicate, and upon completion sent it to *Le Temps* of Paris, which serialized it from 27 Jan. to 19 Feb. 1914. It did not gain immediate attention and was not published in book form until an edition was prepared in Montreal in 1916 at the instigation of Louvigny de Montigny; not until 1980 was Hémon's text published in its original form, without editors' changes. Hémon never knew of his book's publication. In July he left Montreal and began the westward trek during which he was killed in a railway accident at CHAPLEAU, Ont.

Louis Hémon

13. THE 'NIGOG' GROUP

Le Nigog, Quebec's first fine-arts magazine, was founde in 1918 by a group of writers, artists, and musicians who met on Thursday evenings in the home of architect Fernand Préfontaine, 432 Wood Ave., Westmount. Modernist and internationalist in its outlook, *Le Nigog* (from an Indian word meaning 'fishing spear') stirred controversy by attacking Quebec's predominantly regional writing; it published poetry and articles on all the arts. The magazine printed fewer than 500 of its twelve numbers, all issued in 1918 and paid for by Préfontaine; it had offices at Apt. 17, 182 Sainte-Catherine E, a commercial building

Writers associated with *Le Nigog* include **Robert Laroque de Roquebrune**, one of the founding group, the poet Paul d'Équilly Morin, Roquebrune's cousin Jean-Aubert Loranger, an the essayist Marcel Dugas. Robert Laroque, who used 'de Roquebrune' (a name from his family's history) as a pen-name and later added it to his own, was born in 1889 at the manor house of L'ASSOMPTION, near Montreal, where he was educated. In 1919 he went to work for the Canadian Public Archives in Paris, where he remained for most of his life. His masterpiece is his autobiography of his early childhood, *Testament de mon enfance* (1951; trans. as *Testament of My Childhood*, 1964), which reveals that Roquebrune drew heavily on family history for the plots and characters of his three novels of Canadian history; *Les Habits rouges* (1923), *D'un océan à l'autre* (1924, a novel of Louis Riel), and *Les Dames Le Marchand* (1927). Roquebrune's cousin **Jean-Aubert Loranger** was born in 1896, a son of the Hon. Louis O. Loranger, judge of the Superior Court, and spent his childhood at 59 Saint-Denis; in the early 1900s the family moved to 286 Prince Arthur (after 1910 the address became 230 Prince Arthur W. and today it is 400). His poems (*Les Atmosphères*, 1920; *Poëmes*, 1922) were vital statements of the avant garde initiated by *Le Nigog*, but his short stories (*Contes*, 1970) are traditional regional works of the 'terroir' school. **Marcel Dugas**, one of French Canada's most accomplished belletrists, was educated in Montreal, studied law at the city's branch of Université Laval, and later worked here as a journalist and theatre critic. He went to Paris in 1910, returned to Montreal during the First World War, and afterwards lived again in Paris until 1940, working with Roquebrune at the Canadian Public Archives. In 1919 Dugas published *Apologies* (expanded as *Littérature canadienne: aperçus*, 1929), which contains essays on his friends from the *Le Nigog* period and earlier, including Paul Morin, Roquebrune, René Chopin, and Albert Lozeau. Essays collected in *Approaches* (1942) and other books pay tribute to later writers: Loranger, Robert Choquette, Hector de Saint-Denys Garneau, Alain Grandbois, and others.

Paul Morin, a Montreal native, graduated from the Collège Sainte-Marie and the law faculty of Université Laval at Montreal and was admitted to the bar in 1910 at the age of twenty. In the following year, while engaged in doctoral work on Longfellow at the Sorbonne in Paris, he completed an published his first book of poems, *Le Paon d'émail*. Many of the poems in it were doubtless written and polished at 2046 av. du Parc, where Morin lived around 1910. After returning from Paris he taught at McGill in 1914–15 and for two years in the United States, after which he married and settled permanently in Montreal. He helped found *Le Nigog* and published a second volume, *Poèmes de cendre et d'or* (1922). In Montreal Morin established his home at 4635 Sherbrooke, Westmount; he lived there through the thirties and practised law at 437 Saint James W. After 1930 he was beset with increasing financial difficulties and by personal tragedies, including his wife's death in 1952. The result was an almost complete cessation of his publishing activities. Later in the 1950s he lived in reduced circumstances in an apartment in the northern suburb of Pointe-aux-Trembles; on 16 Apr. 1957 a fire destroyed most of his few possessions, including manuscripts of poetry and the typescript of an edition of Montaigne in modern French that he was preparing. Late in life Morin saw the publication of *Paul Morin: textes choisis* (1958); a final collection of poems, *Géronte et son miroir* (1960); and the reissuing of his two earlier volumes under the title *Oeuvres poétiques* (1961). Nevertheless he died in almost complete obscurity in BELOEIL in 1963.

The poet **René Chopin**, born in 1885 in Sault-au-Récollet on the Rivière des Prairies, was educated at the Collège Sainte-Marie and became a notary, although he

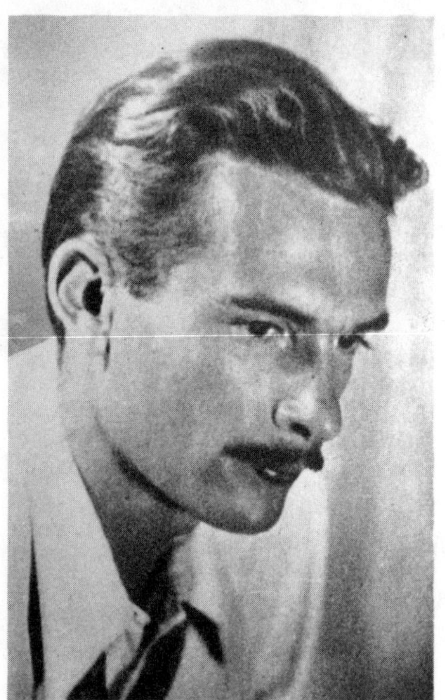

Hector de Saint-Denys Garneau

studied music in Paris and briefly thought of pursuing a career as an operatic tenor. From about 1910 until his death in 1953 he practised as a notary and occupied himself with poetry and religious introspection. He published his first book, *Le Coeur en exil* (containing the famous 'Paysages polaires', trans. in *The Poetry of French Canada in Translation*, 1970), in 1913; after 1910 he made his home at 801 Bd. Gouin. His second and final collection was *Dominantes* (1933).

14. THE 'LA RELÈVE' GROUP

Hector de Saint-Denys Garneau was born in Montreal on 13 June 1912; his father, Paul Garneau, was manager of a branch of the Royal Bank, and the family was living at 64 Côte Saint-Luc. A great grandson of the historian Francois-Xavier Garneau and grandson of the poet Alfred Garneau (see QUEBEC CITY), Saint-Denys Garneau spent most of his childhood at STE-CATHERINE-DE-FOSSAMBAULT, but in 1923 his family returned to Montreal, settling at 353 Olivier, Westmount. At this address the poet lived for most of the years between 1923 and 1937, when he began to isolate himself more and more, staying at the family's Ste-Catherine-de-Fossambault home; after 1941 he lived there in almost complete seclusion. In his Montreal years he studied at both the Collège Sainte-Marie and the École des Beaux Arts (3450 Saint-Urbain), but had to abandon his formal education owing to an illness that left him with the heart damage that led to his death in 1943. In 1933 he was one of a group of young writers (including Robert Charbonneau, Jean Le Moyne, André Giroux, and Robert Élie) who founded the important intellectual review *La Relève*. At his Olivier Avenue home Garneau wrote many of the poems collected in *Regards et jeux dans l'espace* (1937), and there he prepared the book for publication; it was his only book to be published during his lifetime. Since then have appeared *Poésies complètes* (1949), including a large group of posthumous poems entitled *Les Solitudes*; his *Journal* (1954); and *Lettres à ses amis* (1961). John Glassco has translated both the *Journal* (1963) and the complete poems (*Complete Poems of Hector de Saint-Denys Garneau*, 1975).

Two of Garneau's closest friends and associates were Jean Le Moyne and Robert Élie. **Jean Le Moyne**, a distinguishd essayist and now a senator, was born in Montreal on 17 Feb. 1913, a son of Dr Médéric Le Moyne of 257 Sherbrooke E.; later in Le Moyne's youth, including the mid-1930s period of *La Relève*, the family's address was 379 Sherbrooke E. Le Moyne writes of his father and of the atmosphere of intellectual and religious inquiry in his home in *Convergences* (1961), which collects essays from *La Relève* and after. This book won a Governor General's Award and was translated by Philip Stratford (with slightly altered contents) as *Convergence: Essays from Québec* (1966). As a journalist Le Moyne was associated with *La Presse* (1941–3); *Le Canada*, where he was assistant city editor and literary critic; and the Canadian Press. In 1951 he joined Radio-Canada in Montreal and was editor-in-chief of *La Revue Moderne* from 1953 to 1959; during this period he lived at 643 av. Champagneur, Outremont. In 1969 he moved to OTTAWA as a member of the prime minister's staff; he has been a senator since 1982. Le Moyne (with Élie) edited all three of Saint-Denys Garneau's posthumous books. **Robert Élie** is also a writer whose influence was felt at the time of *La Relève* but his books were published primarily after the Second World War. He was born in 1915 in Pointe-Saint-Charles—one of the industrial 'grey zones', comprising factories and poor working-class neighbourhoods —in Montreal's east end. Like Le Moyne he was associated with *La Presse* and *Le Canada*, as well as with Radio-Canada during the 1940s and 1950s. In 1958 he became director of l'École des Beaux Arts; his home was at 3664 Northcliffe. Élie's most important novel is *La Fin des Songes* (1950; trans. *Farewell My Dreams*, 1954, by Irene Coffin). In the sixties and early seventies Élie held government posts in Ottawa and Quebec City. He died in 1973 and his collected works (*Oeuvres*) appeared in 1979.

Of the group that contributed to *La Relève* (1934–40), **Robert Charbonneau** was the principal founder and the one most dedicated to the magazine. After it had published 48 numbers, it was he who reorganized it in 1941 as *La Nouvelle Relève* (1941–8, 55 numbers). Born in Montreal in 1911, he (like Garneau, Le Moyne, and Élie) was a product of the Collège Sainte-Marie. He too earned his living by journalism: *La Presse* (1934–7), *Le Droit* (1937–8), and *Le Canada* (1938–42); he worked on *Le Canada* with Élie and just before the arrival of Le Moyne. His autobiographical novel *Chroniques de l'âge amer* (1967) is fundamentally a memoir of the literary generation of *La Relève* in the years 1934–6. In 1941, while working at *Le Canada*, Charbonneau made his home at 6517 rue de Normanville. At this address he founded Les Éditions de l'Arbre, an influential venture that published books banned by the Vichy government in France and important young Quebec writers, including Roger Lemelin and Yves Thériault. It was by associating *La Relève* with Les Éditions de l'Arbre that Charbonneau created *La Nouvelle Relève*, which, like its predecessor, published not only Canadian but also French writers. It was also at this home that Charbonneau completed his first novel, *Ils possèderont la terre* (1941), which he had begun in 1936 while recuperating from pleurisy; the book was awarded Quebec's Prix David. By 1944– 5 Charbonneau was directing his publishing firm and magazine from Apt. 10, 5976 Côte Saint-Antoine; during this time he published his philosophical essay *Connaissance du personnage* (1944); his novel *Fontile* (1945), winner of the Prix Duvernay; and his sole poetry collection, *Petits Poèmes retrouvés* (1945). Charbonneau was forced to discontinue both *La Nouvelle Relève* and Les Éditions de l'Arbre in 1948, the year that saw publication of his most important novel, *Les Désirs et les jours*. He worked as a journalist and Radio-Canada executive in the 1950s and 1960s and died in 1967.

15. OTHER FRENCH-CANADIAN WRITERS, 1918–1940

It was not only through such movements as those surrounding *Le Nigog*, *La Relève*, and Les Éditions de l'Arbre that Montreal contributed to French-Canadian literature between the wars. At least one member of the earlier regional literature left his mark on the city. This was Brother **Marie-Victorin**, who was born Conrad Kirouac in 1885 in Kingsey Falls, Quebec, and took the name by which he is known in 1901 upon entering the Order of the Brothers of Christian

Schools. He became a professor of botany at Université de Montréal in 1920 and taught there until his death in 1944. Marie-Victorin's best-known literary works are *Récits laurentiens* (1919), traditional tales of the *terroir* genre translated by James Ferres as *The Chopping Bee and Other Laurentian Stories* (1925), and *Croquis laurentiens* (1920). He won fame for his many botanical works; he was the founder of the Montreal Botanical Gardens and is remembered by a statue to the right of its entrance, at the northeast corner of Sherbrooke and Bd. Pie IX. Before joining the Université de Montréal, where he founded the Institut botanique de Montréal, Marie-Victorin taught at the École de Saint-Léon in Westmount and the Collège de Longueuil.

Another traditional novelist of the period was the Frenchwoman **Marie Le Franc**. Born in 1879 in Brittany, she came to Montreal to marry Armand Bessette, a journalist. The marriage did not take place, but she remained until 1926 and began her literary career here with two volumes of poems and her first novel, *Grand-Louis l'innocent* (1925), winner of France's Prix Fémina; it was translated by George and Hilda Shively as *The Whisper of a Name* (1928). After the mid-1920s Le Franc returned to Brittany but continued to spend much time in Canada, which figured largely in her many literary works, including *La Randonnée passionée* (1930), descriptive of the scenery of Saint-Maurice, Que.; *La Rivière solitaire* (1934), set in Témiscaming; *Visages de Montréal* (1934); and *Pêcheurs de Gaspésie* (1938). Like Marie-Victorin, she excelled in the evocation of Laurentian forests and landscapes. A lake in the Mont-Tremblant district of the province is named for Marie Le Franc.

Among the many Montreal writers in the literary vanguard of the time was **Émile Coderre**. A 1919 pharmacology graduate of the Université de Montréal, he associated briefly with the *École littéraire* in 1912–3 but did not find his mature poetic style until *Quand j'parl' tout seul* (1933), which he published under the pseudonym 'Jean Narrache' (from *j'en arrache*, meaning 'I'm having trouble making a living'). When he wrote this book he was living at 2015 University. *Quand j'parl' tout seul* and its sequel (*J'parl' pour parler*, 1939) sympathetically describe Montreal's poor and sarcastically dissect the bourgeoisie and social ills. Coderre was one of the earliest writers to use urban French-Canadian slang, with its distinctive admixture of gallicized English words; later termed 'joual' (from a common pronunciation of 'cheval', horse), this slang became an important tool of the *parti pris* writers of the sixties and seventies. The popularity of the Jean Narrache books was such that Coderre became a major presence in the theatre and especially on radio, for which he wrote the well-known 'Rêveries de Jean Narrache' (1940–1) and 'Zigzags à travers mes souvenirs' (1956). Coderre's knowledge of the Depression poor was gained during his years as manager of a pharmacy in the twenties and thirties. A distinguished pharmacologist, he was editor-in-chief of the *Pharmacien* (1939–42), secretary of the *Collège des pharmaciens* (1945–60), and professor of pharmaceutical legislation at the Université de Montréal (1953–61). His long-time home in later life was at 3416 Patricia. He died in 1970.

Philippe Panneton ('Ringuet')

Philippe Panneton, physician and author, was born on 31 Apr. 1895 in TROIS-RIVIÈRES and settled in Montreal in 1916 to complete his medical studies at Université Laval's Montreal branch (it became the independent Université de Montréal in the year of his graduation, 1920). He spent three years studying in Paris and on his return to Montreal embarked on his literary career under the pseudonym **Ringuet**, his mother's maiden name. In 1924 his first book, *Littératures . . . à la manière de . . .* was published. Containing parodies of various writers, it was written with **Louis Francoeur** (1895–1941) who was a distinguished journalist; there is a monument to Francoeur in Parc Lafontaine, west of rue Calixa-Lavallée. In 1934 Panneton was living at 3553 av. du Parc; in that year he took a trip that inspired his later history of pre-Columbian Mexico, *Un Monde était leur empire* (1943). However, his first novel was the apex of his literary career and one of the turning-points in French-Canadian literature. This was *Trente Arpents*, published in 1938, when Panneton was living at 374 Sherbrooke W.; it was the labour of nine years, and was written both here and at Panneton's earlier home. Set in TROIS-RIVIÈRES in 1887–1932, it is a tragic story of the rural Quebecker's hard life on the land and of the breakdown of traditional ways in a changing province. Its realism was extremely influential because, although *Trente Arpents* had been anticipated in this regard by *La Scouine*, Panneton's work was widely circulated and immediately acclaimed, whereas Laberge's remained unknown. *Trente Arpents* was translated as *Thirty Acres* (1940) by Felix and Dorothea Walter; it received a Governor General's Award, the Prix David, and the Prix des Vikings of the *Académie française*. It spelt the beginning of the end for the long dominance of the novel of idealized country life that had begun with Patrice Lacombe. Panneton was an oculist and taught from 1942 at the Université de Montréal, where in 1945 he became professor of the history of medicine. He published three other novels, a volume of short stories, and works of history and memoirs. In 1956 he became ambassador to Portugal; he died in Lisbon in 1960.

Panneton, Coderre, and the many other writers who were associated, as students or teachers, with the Université de Montréal in its first two and a half decades were indebted, directly or indirectly, to **Édouard Montpetit**, an economist, man of letters, and humanist who was chosen secretary general of the university when it was made an independent institution in 1920. In addition to economic works, he produced collections of his essays and papers such as *Le Front contre la vitre* (1936) and three volumes of *Souvenirs* (1944, 1949, and 1955); the first of these memoirs, subtitled 'Vers la vie', was published by Charbonneau's Éditions de l'Arbre. Montpetit made his home at 5594 av. Plantagenet, Outremont. He died on 27 Mar. 1954 and is remembered by a statue at the main entrance of the Université de Montréal, at 2415 av. Édouard Montpetit.

Also active in transforming the regional and rural novel was **Germaine Guèvremont**, born Germaine Grignon on 16 Apr. 1893 in ST-JÉRÔME. In 1935 she came from SOREL to Montreal with her husband, who became a city employee, and in 1938 her writing was published for the first time—in the magazine *Paysana*, to which she contributed until 1945. Guèvremont and her husband lived for many years at 1010 Sherbrooke E. and here, out of an intimate knowledge of the Sorel area, she created her first novel, *Le Survenant* (1945). This book and its successor, *Marie-Didace* (1947), were translated together as *The Outlanders* (1950) and won a Governor General's Award and many other honours. Guèvremont died in Montreal on 21 Aug. 1968 and was buried in Sorel with her husband. She was a first cousin of the journalist and novelist 'Valdombre', Claude-Henri Grignon. (See SAINT-ADÈLE.)

Another major novelist in Montreal from the mid-1930s was **Jean-Charles Harvey**. From 1922 until 1934 he was the editor of *Le Soleil* in Quebec City, where he wrote and published his most famous novel, *Les démi-civilisés* (1934; trans. by John Glassco as *Fear's Folly*, 1982). It was denounced by Cardinal Villeneuve on 26 Apr. of that year; although Harvey made a public apology and withdrew the book from sale, he was dismissed from *Le Soleil* on 30 Apr. In 1936 he came to Montreal, where he founded the weekly *Le Jour* (1937–46), and by the early 1940s he had established his home at 4371 Draper. Harvey's works, many of them written in Montreal, include *Les Grenouilles demandent un roi* (1942, essays; trans. *The Eternal Struggle*, 1943); a volume of poems, *La Fille du silence* (1958); and *Des bois . . . des champs . . . des bêtes* (1965), a collection of short stories. From 1953 to 1966 he edited *Le Petit Journal* and *Le Photo Journal*; he died in 1967.

Born in Manchester, New Hampshire, the poet **Robert Choquette** came to Montreal with his family in 1913. He was a son of Dr Alfred Choquette, and the family is believed to have lived for some time in an apartment at 2070 av. du Parc. He was probably still living with his family when, at twenty, he published his first collection of poetry, *À travers les vents* (1925), enthusiastically received for its epic sweep. By the early 1930s Choquette was living on his own at 180 Côte Sainte-Catherine, Outremont, where he may have written his second, equally celebrated volume, a long lyric-epic poem entitled *Metropolitan Museum* (1931). While living at that address he published *Poésies nouvelles* (1933), usually considered one of the most important French-Canadian books of the decade, and began the nineteen years' labour that led to his *Suite marine* (1953), a twelve-canto poem in his lyric-epic manner. The long gestation of *Suite marine* and its formal perfection are in part the result of Choquette's reaction to criticism of his early books for their uncertain versification. While living in Outremont in the 1930s Choquette also embarked on his long career as an author of radio plays (and, later, television plays), including 'La Pension Velder' (1938–42 and 1957–61). From 1928 to 1931 Choquette was secretary and librarian of the

Robert Choquette, *c.*1949

École des Beaux Arts, 3450 Saint-Urbain, where many writers worked or studied. **Charles Gill** taught there. The poet **Paul Morin**, while maintaining his career as a lawyer, also served as secretary and librarian of the school from 1922 to 1930, overlapping Choquette's tenure. **Saint-Denys Garneau** was a student during the period when Morin and Choquette were present. Later, the poet **Paul-Marie Lapointe** studied there in the late 1940s; the poet and critic **Guy Robert** taught there; and **Robert Élie** was the school's director from 1958 through the early 1960s.

The development of French-Canadian letters between the wars led to the founding at Montreal in 1944 of the *Académie canadienne-française* by Victor Barbeau. The charter members included Choquette, Robert Charbonneau, Canon Lionel Groulx, Rodolphe Dubé ('Francois Hertel'), Panneton (who served as president 1947–53), the poet Rina Lasnier, and Marius Barbeau (see OTTAWA). Two other founding members, the historical novelist **Léo-Paul Desrosiers** and the poet Alain Grandbois, came to Montreal during the war years. Desrosiers had studied law at Université de Montréal before going to Ottawa, where he worked as a journalist and as French editor of the *Proceedings and Orders of the House of Commons* ('Hansard') from 1928 to 1941. In 1941 he came to Montreal as librarian of the Bibliothèque Municipale de Montréal and lived at 5627 Canterbury. At this time he was already known for his novels *Nord-Sud* (1931) and *Les Engagés du Grand Portage* (1939; trans. *The Making of Nicolas Montour*, 1978, by Christina van Oordt). In 1941 he published *Les Opiniâtres*, a tale of daily life in New France; this was followed by *Sources* (1942) and *L'Ampoule d'or* (1951). He retired from the library in 1953; his later works include a long trilogy of novels embodying his spiritual philosophy (1958–60); he died in 1967.

In 1942 **Alain Grandbois** came to work as a bibliographer at the Bibliothèque Saint-Sulpice, 1700 Saint-Denis; in 1944 the year he helped found the *Académie*, he published at the age of forty-four his first major collection of poetry, *Les Îles de la nuit*. During the period when this peripatetic writer was based in Montreal (1942–55) he also produced his second volume of poems, *Rivages de l'homme* (1944), and translated Merrill Denison's *The Barley and the Stream: The Molson Story* (1955) as *Au pied du courant* (1955). In the early 1950s he lived on Lincoln, then a quiet residential oasis running between Sherbrooke and Sainte-Catherine. After 1956 Grandbois lived in MONT-ROLLAND and QUEBEC CITY. (See also ST-CASIMIR-DE-PORTNEUF, DESCHAMBAULT; CHARLOTTETOWN, P.E.I.)

In their Montreal jobs both Desrosiers and Grandbois were successors of **Aegidius Fauteux**, a journalist, historian, man of letters, and librarian who occupied an important place in Montreal literary life and is remembered with plaques at the Bibliothèque Nationale (successor of the Bibliothèque Saint-Sulpice) on Saint-Denis and the Bibliothèque Municipale, 1210 Sherbrooke E. Trained as a lawyer, Fauteux first made his career in journalism, rising to become editor-in-chief of *La Presse*. In 1912 he left this profession to become the first librarian of the Bibliothèque Saint-Sulpice, where he remained until 1931. After that he was librar-

Alain Grandbois

ian of the Bibliothèque Municipale until his death in 1941; his position was filled by Desrosiers. Fauteux's many historical works include *Les Origines de l'imprimerie au Canada* (1930) and *Les Patriotes de 1837–1838* (1950).

16. FRENCH-CANADIAN WRITERS AFTER 1940

Many of the writers who founded the *Académie canadienne-française* belong as much to the post-war period as to the period between the wars. The poet **Rina Lasnier**, whose mature work belongs to the 1950s and 1960s, was educated in England and at the Pensionnat de Saint-Jean and the Collège Marguerite Bourgeoys in Montreal. Between 1930 and 1936 she studied at Université de Montréal, worked as a journalist for *Canada français* and the *Richelieu* (where she edited the women's page for three years), and taught literature at the Pensionnat de Saint-Jean. From 1936 she was a student at the École de Bibliothécaires, where the subject of her bio-bibliographic thesis was Victor Barbeau, the French-Canadian nationalist writer and linguist who was later to become the primary founder of the *Académie canadienne-française*. In 1943 Lasnier won the Prix David for three works: *Images et Proses* (1941), *Jeu de la voyagère* (1941, a choral play), and *Les Fiançailles d'Anne de Noué* (1943, also a play). As a fully contemporary yet devoutly religious poet (she has served as secretary of *La Ligue catholique féminine* in Montreal), Lasnier has stood apart from many post-war trends. Her main poetry collections include *Présence de l'absence* (1956), *Mémoire sans jours* (1960), *Les Gisants* (1963), and *L'Arbre blanc* (1966). She now lives in JOLIETTE.

In 1939 **Gabrielle Roy**, a former drama student and Manitoba school teacher with an ambition to write, came to Montreal after travelling in Europe. She took a room near the bus station (at Maisonneuve and Berri) and began to work as a free-lance journalist, publishing her first articles and stories in Jean-Charles Harvey's *Le Jour* and in *La Revue Moderne*. In 1941 she was rooming on Dorchester near Green Avenue, a district at the top of a slope that overlooks the CPR tracks and the Saint-Henri neighbourhood, where Roy set her first and most famous novel, *Bonheur d'occasion* (1945; trans. as *The Tin Flute*, 1947, by Hannah Josephson; retranslated by Alan Brown with the same title, 1980). She once described her discovery of the poor working-class Saint-Henri district this way:

Gabrielle Roy in the 1960s

> *I used to choose as the goal of my walks the pretty avenues of Westmount and the slope of the mountain [districts just north of her apartment]. One day, by pure chance, by caprice if you will, I instead went south on rue Saint-Ambroise and found myself before I knew it in the very heart of Saint-Henri. What can I say? How can I give you the deep impression I suddenly received? It was like the lightning that strikes lovers; it was a revelation, an illumination.*

Saint-Henri is one of Montreal so-called 'grey zones', the oldest industrial districts, all located in the southwest of the island. The other two are La Petite Bourgogne and Pointe-Saint-Charles (the birthplace of Robert Élie), which lies just south of Saint-Henri across the Lachine Canal. Saint-Henri centres on Notre-Dame and lies between the Trans-Canada Hwy and the canal on the north and south, between Atwater and St-Rémi in the east and west. It retains many of the characteristics that Roy observed in 1941–5 and evoked so vividly in her novel. Her writing about Saint-Henri began with a series of four descriptive articles entitled 'Tout Montréal' published in June-Sept. 1941 in the *Bulletin des agriculteurs*, a farm publication that became Roy's chief employer. In 1947 Roy married Dr Marcel Carbotte, like herself native of ST BONIFACE, Man., and after travelling and studying in Europe the couple settled in QUEBEC CITY in 1950.

At the end of the Second World War *Le Jour* began publishing the first stories of another writer, **Yves Thériault**, who was then working as an announcer and scriptwriter at radio station CKCH in HULL; in 1945 he returned to Montreal as a scriptwriter for Radio-Canada. Born in 1915 in QUEBEC CITY, Thériault was only three when his family moved to Montreal. During his childhood his family lived in the English-speaking Notre-Dame-de-Grâce district, just west of Westmount. He was educated at the parish school, which was at 150 Nore-Dame-de-Grâce, and at the Collège Mont-Saint-Louis, Sherbrooke E. and av. Hôtel de Ville. However, he left school at sixteen and worked as a truck driver, a cheese seller, and an emcee in night clubs, among other occupations. Curious and rebellious, he sometimes preferred to attend the synagogues of his many Jewish acquaintances to the Roman Catholic church of his own upbringing; his intimate knowledge of the Jewish community of west-end Montreal is seen in his novel *Aaron* (1954), the first of a series in which Thériault examined minority groups in Canada. The cumulative effects of overwork and poverty led to a year and a half in a sanatorium at Lac-Édouard (near Lac Saint-Jean) during the late 1930s. Then followed his career as a radio announcer, which began in Montreal at CKAC and continued in several other cities, including Hull, before he returned to Montreal and established a permanent home at 4346 av. Girouard, in the heart of his childhood neighbourhood; Girouard forms the east boundary of Parc Notre-Dame-de-Grâce and is just four blocks west of Décarie. Thériault's first book, *Contes pour un homme seul*, appeared in 1944, and his first novel, *La Fille laide*, in 1950. He continued to work at other occupations to support himself while writing voluminously, until the success of *Agaguk* (1958; winner of the Prix de la Province de Québec and the Prix France-Canada; trans. by Miriam Chapin, 1967); he then became a full-time writer. His equally popular *Ashini* (1961; winner of a Governor General's Award; trans. by Gwendolyn Moore, 1972) was written at 4871 av. Victoria, his next address, as were several more books by French-Canada's most prolific serious writer. At the time of his Governor General's Award in 1961 Thériault was still having to support himself by such work as a daily lonely-hearts column, which he was then writing for *La Patrie* and which he later continued in *Le Nouveau Journal*.

During the 1960s Thériault spent two years working for the federal government in OTTAWA; after 1970 he lived first at ST-DENIS-DE-RICHELIEU and later at RAWDON. However, he always maintained his connection with his home neighbourhood in Montreal. After his death in 1983 at the hospital in JOLIETTE, he was cremated and his ashes interred privately, but on 28 Oct. 1983 a commemorative service was held for him at the Église de Notre-Dame-de-Grâce; among the six concelebrating priests was the Dominican father Georges-Henri Levesque (see QUE-

Roch Carrier, *c.*1970

BEC CITY). The poet Marie-José Thériault is Yves Thériault's daughter.

The novelist **Roch Carrier**, whose most characteristic work evokes his native village of STE-JUSTINE-DE-DORCHESTER, studied at Université de Montréal and settled here after completing a doctorate at the Sorbonne. In the mid-1960s he lived at 1836 rue Baile and acted first as resident playwright and then as secretary general of the Théâtre du Nouveau Monde, which staged his dramatizations of his novels, including his well-known *La Guerre, yes sir!* (1968; trans. by Sheila Fischman, 1970). Carrier, who now teaches at the Collège Militaire Royale de St-Jean, lives on Harvard Ave in west-end Montreal. Novelist and former head of the literary section of the Canada Council, Iraqi-born **Naim Kattan** lives in Montreal on rue Mira (4800 block). His novels include *Adieu, Babylon* (1975) and *Les Fruits arrachés* (1977), translated by Sheila Fischman as *Farewell, Babylon* (1976) and *Paris Interlude* (1979). Born in Montreal in 1927, the novelist **André Langevin** (see also THETFORD MINES) has worked for the CBC (primarily as a producer) since 1948. During the mid-1950s, when Langevin was producing his landmark novel *Poussière sur la ville* (1953; trans. by John Latrobe and Robert Gottlieb, *Dust over the City*, 1955) and *Les Temps des hommes* (1956), he lived at 4865 King Edward. The novelist **Roger Lemelin**, also a successful businessman in his native QUEBEC CITY, came to Montreal as president and publisher of *La Presse* in June 1972, charged with revitalizing the newspaper. He did so and in 1981 retired and returned to his writing career. While at *La Presse* Lemelin employed numerous literary writers, among them Hubert Aquin, who served as literary director of Éditions La Presse in 1975–6. Montreal is the current home of novelist **Antonine Maillet** (see BUCTOUCHE, N.B.), who was educated in part at the Université de Montréal. The foremost writer of Acadia, she is best known for *La Sagouine* (1971; trans. by Luis de Céspedes, 1979) and *Pélagie-la-Charette* (1979; trans. by Philip Stratford, *Pélagie: The Return to a Homeland*, 1982), which was the first book not written by a French native to win France's *Prix Goncourt*. She lives in Outremont on a street named for her. The French poet Robert Marteau now lives in an apartment at 3221 Forest Hill. In Canada he has published *Atlante* (1976; trans. by Barry Callaghan, 1979) with Gaston Miron's Éditions de l'Hexagone and *Traite du blanc et des teintures* (1978) with Giguère's Éditions Erta. A selection of his poems, mainly from earlier books, with translations, is *Salamander* (1979), translated by Anne Winters. **Marie-Claire Blais** has lived here for approximately half of each year (see also RICHMOND) since 1976, when she returned from an extended stay in the United States and France. In her apartment in an old Westmount house she has worked on such novels as *Les Nuits de l'Underground* (1978; trans. by Ray Ellenwood, *Nights in the Underground*, 1979), which displays her knowledge of east-end Montreal's shadow-world of bars and after-hours clubs, and *Le Sourd dans la ville* (1979; trans. by Carol Dunlop, *Deaf to the City*, 1980), which won a Governor General's Award. The poet **Jacques Brault**, born in Montreal in 1933, is a Université de Montréal professor in the Institut des Sciences Médiévales; his poetry collections include *Mémoire* (1965) and *Poèmes des quatres côtés* (1975), made up of French adaptations of poems by Margaret Atwood, Gwendolyn MacEwen, and two American poets.

17. FRENCH DRAMA IN MONTREAL

The post-war period saw the creation, primarily at Montreal, of modern French-Canadian theatre by such writers as **Gratien Gélinas**, Marcel Dubé, and Michel Tremblay. Born in 1909 in ST-TITE-DE-CHAMPLAIN, Gélinas received his senior matriculation at the Collège de Montréal, where he was a co-founder of the amateur theatrical group Les Anciens du Collège de Montréal. After studying at Montréal's École des Hautes Études Commerciales, Gélinas was a bookkeeper for the La Sauvegarde Insurance Company for eight years (1929–37). During this period he doggedly maintained his conection with drama, and in 1935–7 played Lionel Théberge in Robert Choquette's radio serial 'Le Curé de village'. At the same time he was developing his own character, Fridolin (for which he has been called 'the Charlie Chaplin of Quebec'), in monologues presented at the Mon Paris, a Montreal cabaret of the period. He first presented this character on stage in 1936 at the Théâtre Saint-Denis in his own revue entitled 'Télévise-moi-ça'. His immediate success allowed him to resign from the insurance company in 1937. That year he began writing and performing a Fridolin comedy series, *Le Carrousel de la gaîté* (renamed *Le Train de plaisir* in 1938), on radio station CKAC, where Yves Thériault had worked briefly during the same period. In 1938 Gélinas instituted his annual *Fridolinons Revue* and continued writing it and performing in it until 1946; recently this material has been republished in a series of volumes, e.g., *Les Fridolinades 1941 et 1942* (1981). By the late 1940s Gélinas had established his home at 5580 Woodbury; he was living and writing there when, on 22 May 1948, his play *Tit-Coq* premièred at the Monument National; it was published in French in 1950 and in an English translation by Kenneth Johnstone and Gélinas in 1967. Gélinas's first full-length play *Tit-Coq* gave a realistic picture of French-Canadian social situations and used the everyday language of working-class people; it is generally regarded as the beginning of contemporary French-Canadian drama. Gélinas was still living at 5580 Woodbury in 1956 when he revived the *Fridolinons Revue* and played Juvenal Bolduc in the television series of Roger Lemelin's *Les Plouffe* (see QUEBEC CITY); in 1957 he became founding director and president of the Théâtre de la Comédie Canadienne troupe, which played in the Gaiety Theatre (now gone) at 64 Sainte-Catherine W., near the present-day Place des Arts. In

Gratien Gélinas in the 1950s

1959 his second major play, *Bousille et les justes*, premièred on 17 Aug. (trans. *Bousille and the Just*, 1961). Gélinas has received numerous honours and served as president of the Canadian Film Development Corporation in 1969–78. He has lived in OKA in recent years.

One of his most important successors is the playwright **Marcel Dubé**, who was born on 3 Jan. 1930 at 2364 Logan E., a son of Eugène Dubé, an accountant. Like many of Montreal's earlier writers, Dubé was taught by the Jesuit fathers of the Collège Sainte-Marie, which he attended from 1943 to 1951 and where with friends he founded a theatrical society, La Jeune Scène; this group performed his first successful play, *De l'autre côté du mur*, in 1952 while Dubé was a second-year student at the Université de Montréal. In the following year, when his play *Zone* won all prizes at the Dominion Drama Festival, Dubé decided to devote all his time to drama. After attending theatre schools in Paris in 1953–4, he returned to Montreal and took an apartment at 7045 Fielding. Here, during the late 1950s, he produced his other major plays, especially *Florence* and *Un simple soldat*, both performed on TV in their first versions in 1957. In 1956 Dubé became a script-writer for the National Film Board, in 1958 an editorial board member of *Écrits du Canada français*, and in 1959 he was made president of the Federation of Canadian Authors and Artists. Among his important later plays is *Le Réformiste* (1977).

Today's most prominent French-Canadian dramatist—also a fiction writer—is **Michel Tremblay**, who was born in 1942 and brought up on the rue Fabre in the Plateau Mont Royal district, on which most of his writings draw for settings and characters. This district is east of Mont Royal; rue Fabre runs through Parc Lafontaine to Parc Père Marquette and continues north. Since 1974 Tremblay has lived just west of this district, on rue Davaar, Outremont. His major plays include *Les Belles-soeurs* (1968; trans. by Bill Glassco and John Van Burek, 1974), *L'Impromptu d'Outremont* (1980; trans. by Glassco and Van Burek, *The Impromptu of Outremont*, 1981), *À toi pour toujours, ta Marie-Lou* (1973; trans. by Glassco and Van Burek, *Forever Yours, Marie-Lou*, 1973), and *Hosanna* (1973; trans. by Glassco and Van Burek, 1974). Like his cycle of plays from *Les Belles-soeurs* to *Damnée Manon, sacrée Sandra* (1977; trans. by Glassco and Van Burek, 1979), Tremblay's most highly regarded novels depict the Plateau Mont Royal district: *La grosse femme d'à côté est enceinte* (1978) and *Thérèse et Pierrette à l'école des saints-anges* (1980; trans. by Sheila Fischman

Michel Tremblay

as *The Fat Woman Next Door is Pregnant*, 1981, and *Thérèse and Pierette at the École des Saints Anges*, 1982). Called 'chroniques du plateau Mont Royal' by their author, these works form part of a projected tetralogy. The most recent addition to the work is *Thérèse and Pierrette and the Little Hanging Angel* (trans. by Fischman, 1984).

Three other important Montreal dramatists are Père **Gustave Lamarche**, CSV, Robert Gurik, and Claude Gauvreau. Lamarche was born here in 1895 and educated in part at the Université de Montréal. He formed the drama troupe Les Paraboliers du Roi, which toured Quebec extensively from 1939 to 1947 and did much to create an interest in drama. In Montreal he staged large spectaculars, including *La Défaite de l'enfer* (1938) and *Notre-Dame-de-la-Couronne* (1947), that drew audiences of more than 100,0000. A choral dramatist influenced by his knowledge of Greek literature, Lamarche is perhaps best known for his play *Jonathas* (1935) and his collection of poems *Palinods* (1944). Since the 1940s he has lived and worked primarily in Joliette. One of the most widely produced of Quebec playwrights, **Robert Gurik** came to Montreal from France in 1950 and at first supported himself as an engineer, graduating from the Institut Polytechnique de Montréal in 1957. His plays include *Api* 2967 (1967; trans. by Marc F. Gélinas, 1974), *Hamlet, prince du Québec* (1968), and *Le Procès de Jean-Baptiste M.* (1972; trans. by Alan Van Meer, *The Trial of Jean-Baptiste M.*, 1974).

Born in 1925 in Montreal, **Claude Gauvreau**, like Marcel Dubé, attended the Collège Sainte-Marie and began his dramatic activity when he was thirteen, with the production there of his earliest play, *Ma Vocation*. He came to prominence for his participation in *Refus global* (1948), the artistic manifesto that was issued (in an edition of 400 copies) by the painters **Paul-Émile Borduas** and **Jean-Paul Riopelle**, by Gauvreau, and others. Borduas was the author of the main essay in the collection of mimeographed, typewritten pages enclosed in a portfolio created by Riopelle, who lived at 4089 av. DeLor; Gauvreau contributed three brief plays. A cry for intellectual freedom influenced by Dadaism and Surrealism, *Refus global* is translated by Ramsay Cook in his *French-Canadian Nationalism* (1969). Gauvreau's major play is *Les Oranges sont vertes* (1971); tragically, on the day in 1971 following his agreement to having the play produced in a cut version, Gauvreau committed suicide by leaping from the third storey of the house on rue Saint-Denis where he lived. He was 45. *Les Oranges sont vertes* was staged by the Théâtre du Nouveau Monde in 1972. Many of Gauvreau's writings—harsh, difficult, heavily indebted to surrealism, and exerting a marked influence on several later Quebec writers—were unpublished during his lifetime or appeared only after long delays. They were collected in *Oeuvres créatrices complètes* (1971), published by Éditions parti pris under Gérald Godin. *The Entrails* (1981) is a book of translations by Ray Ellenwood from Gauvreau's early poetry.

18. THE 'PARTI PRIS' GROUP

The Quebec separatist and literary magazine *parti pris* was published from Oct. 1963 through the summer of 1968. Its thirty-eight issues and its publishing house, Les Éditions parti pris, provided the principal forum for many young writers of the 1960s and some older ones as well. The magazine was first published at 7906 av. Champagneur, Outremont, in the apartment of Pierre Maheu, one of the magazine's most active non-literary writers; in 1964 it moved to its own office in the basement of a new apartment building at 2135 rue Bellechasse, Rosemount.

Among the most important participants in *parti pris* were Paul Chamberland, Jacques Renaud, André Major, and Gérald Godin. The poet **Paul Chamberland** lived at 1390 av. Van Horne, Outremont, and during the magazine's first year was a teacher at the Collège Saint-Denis. Dismissed for his political activities, he later worked as a writer for Hydro-Québec. His most important work during this period was the long poem *L'Afficheur hurle* (1965; trans. by Malcolm Reid in his *The Shouting Signpainters: A Literary and Political Account of Quebec Revolutionary Nationalism*, 1972, which takes its title from Chamberland's (poem.) The rue Saint-Christophe, which plays a large part in Chamberland's poem ('in Saint Christopher Street / in the street of truth / that life's step is resounding / a sound of madness in the shadows') runs parallel to Tremblay's rue Fabre a few blocks farther west.

Of Rosemount origins, **Jacques Renaud** was the son of a garment worker (his father was a collar folder in an overcoat factory); he attended Rosemount's École Louis Hébert, where one of his teachers was Arthur Major, the father of André Major, another of the *parti pris* writers. Renaud became the chief novelist of the movement and the first Quebec novelist to make a thoroughgoing use of 'joual' (an urban Québécois dialect larded with anglicisms) with his landmark novel *Le Cassé* (1964; trans. by Gérald Robitaille, *Flat Broke and Beat*, 1968). As a young bohemian intellectual Renaud had frequented the clubs La Paloma and El Cortijo, which were at 2096 and 2112 rue Clark respectively. La Paloma especially was the model for the restaurant in which a crucial scene of *Le Cassé* occurs, leading to the stabbing outside the restaurant of the drug-pusher Bouboule by the central character Ti-Jean. Renaud's La Paloma days are reflected in his early volume of poetry, *Electrodes* (1962); at the time his novel was published he lived in a basement apartment on Crescent.

André Major attended the Collège des Étudistes but was expelled in 1961 and received no further formal education. By 1965 he had already broken with the *parti pris* group and had joined the newspaper *Le Petit Journal*; he later became a prominent literary journalist with *Le Devoir*. His writings during his *parti pris* period include the novel *Le Cabochon* (1964), the story collection *La Chair de poule* (1964), and *Poèmes pour durer* (1969), a selected poems that includes work from volumes published as early as 1961 and 1962. Major has received a Governor General's Award for his novel *Les Rescapés* (1976). Born in 1942 in Montreal, Major spent his childhood and youth in Varennes, a nearby village on the south shore of the St Lawrence River. In his stories, especially 'La Semaine dernière pas loin du pont', he evokes Ville Jacques Cartier, near LONGUEUIL, which is also associated with the writings of Jacques Ferron and Pierre Vallières.

Gérald Godin came to Montreal from his native TROIS-RIVIÈRES and worked here as a journalist, first for *Le Nouveau Journal* and then for the Radio-Canada news-commentary program 'Aujourd'hui'. An early *parti pris* contributor, Godin succeeded the novelist Laurent Girouard (*La ville inhumaine*, 1964) as editor of Les Éditions parti pris in 1964, which brought out Godin's collection *Les Cantouques* in 1966. During this period Godin lived at 1627 Selkirk. (He subsequently entered politics and became Minister of Cultural Communities and Immigration.) As editor Godin gave Les Éditions parti pris a broader appeal by adding books by established writers to its list. These included *Élégies pour l'épouse enallé* by the veteran **Alfred DesRochers** (see COATICOOK, ST-ÉLIE D'ORFORD, SHERBROOKE), a book of elegies written after his wife's death in 1964; DesRochers lived in Montreal from 1953 and died here on 12 Oct. 1978. Les Éditions parti pris also published a book (*Le Monde sont drôles*, 1966) by DesRochers's daughter, the cabaret entertainer Clémence DesRochers, and works by older writers such as Claude Jasmin and Jacques Ferron.

From 1960 **Claude Jasmin** has worked as a journalist and critic for several Montreal periodicals, including *La Presse*, *Sept-Jours*, *Québec-Presse*, and *Le Journal de Montréal*, where he has been editor of the arts and entertainment section. His best known early novel is *Ethel et le terroriste* (1964; trans. by David Walker as *Ethel and the Terrorist*, 1965); a collection of short stories, *Les Coeurs empaillés*, appeared in 1967. In the early 1970s Jasmin announced his retirement from creative writing to devote himself to his column of cultural news and criticism in *Le Journal*. However, he immediately broke his announced literary silence with a series of three *récits*—autobiographical and reflective narratives. The first of these, *La Petite Patrie* (1972), recreates his childhood in the 1930s on the few blocks of rue Saint-Denis between Jean Talon and Bélanger. After nine years Jasmin returned to fiction with the novel *Revoir Ethel* (1976); it was followed in 1979 by the novel *La Sablière* (trans. by David Lobdell as *Mario*, 1985). (See also STE-ADÈLE.)

Jacques Ferron, a doctor who lived and practised in LONGUEUIL, specialized briefly during the 1960s in caring for the mentally retarded, working at the Saint-Jean-de-Dieu hospital where earlier Émile Nelligan had been a patient. Ferron's Éditions parti pris novel *La Nuit* (1965; trans. by Ray Ellenwood, *Quince Jam*, 1977) is set in part at Montreal's city morgue on rue Saint-Vincent. (See also LONGUEUIL, ST-LAMBERT.) Another *parti pris* writer was the young poet **André Brochu** (*Délit contre délit*, 1965), who is now a professor at Université de Montreal.

Besides Pierre Maheu's apartment and the magazine's later offices, *parti pris* meeting places included the École Normale Jacques-Cartier in Parc Lafontaine, which several of the writers had attended, and clubs and bars on Saint-Denis and Sherbrooke W., especially the Swiss Hut and the Asociación Española, which were at 394 and 485 Sherbrooke W. respectively. At 1247 Saint-Denis was the Librairie Déom, which in the fifties and sixties was headquarters for the poet **Gaston Miron**; there he published his Éditions de l'Hexagone, founded in 1953. Miron was perhaps the principal influence on young poets before and during the *parti pris* period, although no volume of his own poetry was published until 1970, when *L'Homme rapaillé* appeared. D.G. Jones and Marc Plourde collaborated on the translations published in *Embers and Earth: Selected Poems* (1984).

Gaston Miron in the late 1960s

Many of Miron's Hexagone books were designed by the surrealist poet, painter, and printer **Roland Giguère**, who in 1949 founded his own Éditions Erta and still operates it. Giguère won the Prix France Canada and the Grand Prix Littéraire de la ville de Montréal for *L'Âge de la parole: poèmes 1949–1960* (1965); some of his poems appear in English in *Mirror and Letters to an Escapee* (1977, trans. by Sheila Fischman).

Prominent poets who received early publication from Les Éditions de l'Hexagone include **Paul-Marie Lapointe** (*Choix de poèmes—arbres*, 1960), who became a journalist after studying at the École des Beaux-Arts and who has been since 1968 the director of radio programming for Radio-Canada. In the 1960s and 1970s Lapointe lived at 912 Dunlop. The Hexagone poets Jean-Guy Pilon (*Comme eau retenue: poèmes 1954–1963*, 1968) and Fernand Ouellette (*Poésie*, 1972) joined in 1959 with the poet Jacques Godbout (*Les Pavés secs*, 1958) and the novelist Hubert Aquin to found the important magazine *Liberté*. In 1959 **Hubert Aquin** was a producer with Radio-Canada and lived at 5553 Coolbrook. Born in Montreal in 1929, he grew up in the Parc Lafontaine district and attended the École Olier (Émile Nelligan's elementary school) and the Collège Sainte-Marie as well as the Université de Montreal. His first and most famous novel was written during four months from July to Nov. 1964 when, after being arrested for illegal possession of a firearm, he was transferred from Montreal Prison to the Albert Prévost Psychiatric Institute and held there for examination. The book that resulted was *Prochain Épisode* (1965; trans. by Penny Williams, 1967); the incident is also treated by André Major in his story 'Mental test pour tout le gang' in *La Chair de poule* (1965). After publishing three more influential novels by 1974 (including *L'Antiphonaire*, 1969; trans. by Alan Brown, *The Antiphonary*, 1973), Aquin ceased to write and on 15 Mar. 1977 committed suicide.

Jacques Godbout, who worked as a film-maker for the National Film Board, lived at 5761 av. Déom in the early 1960s. During this period he began writing his successful novels, including *L'Aquarium* (1962) and *Salut Galarneau!* (1967; trans. by Alan Brown, *Hail Galarneau!*, 1970). He has made a film about Aquin, *Deux épisodes dans la vie d'Hubert Aquin*. Like Aquin, **Jean-Guy Pilon** was a Radio-Canada producer in this period; he lived at 4111 Northcliffe, not far from the older writer Robert Élie (who lived at 3664 Northcliffe), who was then director of the École des Beaux-Arts. Another important poet of the post-war period, **Gilles Hénault**, was born in Montreal in 1920 and since 1939 has been extremely active as a journalist and in government. During the early 1960s, while working for *Le Devoir* and *Le Nouveau Journal* and as a writer for the Royal Commission on Bilingualism and Biculturalism, he was also producing two of his most important collections: *Voyages au pays de mémoire* (1959) and *Sémaphore* (1962). At this time Hénault lived at 319 Grosvenor, Westmount.

19. RECENT WRITERS

Michel Beaulieu, born in Montreal in 1941, was a member of the 'Quartier-latin' literary movement and edited the student publication *Le Quartier Latin* at the Université de Montréal in the early 1960s. In 1964 he published his first collection of poems, *Pour chanter dans les chaînes*, from his own Éditions Estérel, which he made into a seminal imprint—under it appeared many of the early titles of Victor-Lévy Beaulieu, Nicole Brossard, Raoul Duguay, and others. Beaulieu was a prolific poet, the author of three novels, a dramatist and theatre critic, a publisher, and—especially after 1977—a translator of works by English-Canadian writers into French. His many books of poems include *Visages* (1982), which won a Governor General's Award. *Spells of Fury* (1984) is a translation by Arlette Francière of his *Charmes de la fureur*. Beaulieu died suddenly of a heart attack in 1985.

The novelist and publisher **Victor-Lévy Beaulieu** was born in 1945 in a village near Rivière-du-Loup, and came at the age of 12 to Montréal-Nord. The northern region of the city is evoked in some of his books, where the suburb of Montreal-Nord becomes Morial-Mort. Beaulieu, who never completed high school, worked as literary director of Éditions du Jour and then, just after the October crisis, founded Éditions de l'Aurore, which produced about 80 books before its bankruptcy in 1975. Soon afterwards he founded the important VLB Éditeur, which he at first edited and published from his Montréal-Nord home on the bank of Rivière-des-Prairies; the firm now has offices in Montreal. Seven of his 13 novels compose a saga of a Quebec family; one of these is *Don Quichotte de la démanche* (1974; trans. by Sheila Fischman as *Don Quixote in Nighttown*, 1978), winner of a Governor General's Award.

The elusive novelist **Réjean Ducharme** was born on 13 August 1941 in St-Félix-de-Valois near Sorel; during his childhood his father worked as a taxi driver in Berthier. Ducharme has lived in or near Montreal since he left high school at Joliette before completing Grade 12. In 1966, the year of the publication of his novel *L'Avalée des avalés* (trans. by Barbara Bray as *The Swallower Swallowed* 1968), he was living in an east-end rooming house. He was last interviewed and photographed in 1969, when he agreed to talk to a reporter from a Paris newspaper who managed to track him down. Ducharme was then living on av. de l'Esplanade. *L'Avalée des avalés* won a Governor General's Award but the reclusive novelist did not appear to receive it.

The novelist **Yves Beauchemin**, author of *Le Matou* (1981; trans. by Sheila Fischman as *The Alley Cat*, 1986), was born in 1941 in Noranda. He spent his childhood in Clova and his high-school years in Joliette, and came to Montreal in 1962. After working for three years as a book editor, he joined Radio-Canada in 1969 as a researcher. He began writing novels during lunch hours and in intervals from his work in the bleak former carpet factory that serves as the Radio-Québec offices. His first novel was *L'Enfirouapé* (1974); he produced four versions of *Le Matou*, running to 4,000 pages, over a period of seven years before the book was finally published. *Du sommet d'un arbre* (1986) is a collection of radio scripts of Beauchemin's reminiscences and reflections that were broadcast over Radio-Canada from 1979 to 1985.

The novelist **Louise Maheux-Forcier**, daughter of a prominent Montreal banker, was a concert pianist until, at the age of 34, she launched her career as a writer with the *succès d'estime* of her first novel, *Amadou* (1963), written at her home in the Montreal suburb of Pierrefonds. Among her subsequent books are *Une Forêt pour Zoé* (1969), winner of a Governor General's Award, and *En toutes lettres* (1980); both were translated by David Lobdell in 1981 and 1982.

The dramatist, poet, and novelist **Jovette Marchessault** was born in 1938 and brought up in Montreal's Saint-Henri district; she left school in Grade 8 to work in textile mills but later became a visual artist and the author of the novel *La Mère des herbes* (1980) and the play *La Saga des poules mouillées* (1981). **Nicole Brossard**, a leading avant-garde and feminist writer, was born in Montreal in 1943; in 1965 she published her first volume of poems, *Aube à la saison*, and helped found the literary journal *La Barre du jour*. Brossard has twice won Governor General's Awards for poetry: in 1975 for *Mécanique jongleuse* and in 1985 for *Double Impression*.

MONT-ROLLAND

This village near Ste-Adèle was the home of poet **Alain Grandbois** from 1956 to 1960. Here he prepared one of his most important collections of poetry, *L'Étoile pourpre* (1957), which won Grandbois his second Prix Duvernay in 1958. (See also DESCHAMBAULT, MONTREAL: 15, QUEBEC CITY, ST-ALBAN, ST-CASIMIR-DE-PORTNEUF; CHARLOTTETOWN, PEI.)

NATASHQUAN

This fishing village on the north shore of the St Lawrence River, about 810 miles from Montreal, was the birthplace in 1928 of **Gilles Vigneault**, Quebec's most famous *chansonnier*. Natashquan is little changed from the time of Vigneault's childhood, when it contained about 100 houses and 400 inhabitants. His father was a fisherman who spent much of his life as a fisheries inspector; the Vigneault family still lives here, although Gilles Vigneault has lived elsewhere since leaving in 1941 to be educated at the Petit Séminaire de RIMOUSKI and Université Laval in QUEBEC CITY. He has often returned to his native village. One of his purely literary works is the poetry collection, *Natashquan:*

Gilles Vigneault

le voyage immobile (1976), which evokes the people, occupations, and landscape of the area. Vigneault's many other books of poetry include *Quand les bateaux s'en vont* (1965; winner of a Governor General's Award) and *Silences, poèmes 1957–1977* (1979). His *chanson* 'Mon pays' has been adopted by the Québec National Assembly as an anthem.

NICOLET

Nicolet owes its honourable place in French-Canadian literary history to its famous institute of classical secondary education, the Collège (later the Séminaire) de Nicolet. Its building, designed by the Abbé Jérôme Demers and erected in 1827–33, is at 350 rue d'Youville and today houses the training school for the Quebec Provincial Police.

Antoine Gérin-Lajoie, destined to become one of Canada's most important nineteenth-century men of letters, entered the college in 1837. Before graduating he had written 'Un Canadien errant', a song—which has entered folklore—in the voice of an exile from Quebec after the Rebellion of 1837–8, and *Le Jeune Latour* (1844), the first verse tragedy ever written and published in French Canada. A still more renowned graduate of the college was **Louis Fréchette**. While enrolled there he began writing poetry at the age of nineteen; he graduated in 1859. Among Fréchette's works was *La Légende d'un peuple* (1887), the most important volume of French-Canadian poetry to appear in the nineteenth century. As a student in Nicolet, Fréchette lived at the Maison Lemay, a house built in 1794. **Nerée Beauchemin** also attended in the 1860s, preparing for his medical studies at Université Laval. A country doctor for all his life in his native city of YAMACHICHE, Beauchemin published only two poetry collections, *Les Floraisons matutinales* (1897) and *Patrie intime* (1928). **Emile Codèrre** studied at the college from 1904 to 1912. Coming to know Montreal's poorest inhabitants in his professional capacity as a pharmacist, he found his true voice during the 1930s, expressing in his poetry sympathy for the poor, accurate observation of their lives, and biting protest against the bourgeoisie. After 1933 he published under the pseudonym 'Jean Narrache', taken from the phrase *j'en arrache*, 'I'm trying to make ends meet'. (See also MONTREAL: 15.)

Other literary graduates of the Collège de Nicolet include the Abbé **Jean-Baptiste-Antoine Ferland** and the journalist **Arthur Buies**. Ferland completed his education here in 1816–17 and taught at the college in 1822–8; he returned as prefect of studies in 1848 and was the college's superior in 1850–4, after which he served as professor of history at Université Laval, QUEBEC CITY, until his death in 1865. Ferland was the author of an important early history of French Canada and many other historical, biographical, and belletristic works. He was a co-founder of, and frequent contributor to, *Le Foyer canadien* (1863–6) and *Les Soirées canadiennes* (1861–5), important magazines in the early history of literature in Quebec. The colourful and peripatetic Buies completed his education about 1846; in the 1870s and 1880s he made himself widely known as a fiery anti-clerical journalist and publisher in Montreal and Quebec City. His books include *Chroniques: humeurs et caprices* (1873) and *Lettres sur le Canada* (1862–3). **Philippe-Ignace-François Aubert de Gaspé** was educated here in the early 1830s. With the help of his famous father, Philippe-Joseph Aubert de Gaspé, the younger Aubert de Gaspé wrote what is generally considered Quebec's first novel, *L'Influence d'un livre* (1837).

NORTH HATLEY

The poet **F.R. Scott** and the novelist **Hugh MacLennan** are among the many writers who have lived at North Hatley. Both have been summer residents here for many years, with permanent homes in MONTREAL (4, 6). Scott was for long regarded as the centre of the village's literary life, and its chief social event until he became ill in 1983 (he died on 31 Jan. 1985) was the annual birthday party held in the Scott house by Marian Scott, the poet's wife. This event has attracted many of North Hatley's literary residents as well as **A.J.M. Smith**, who had a summer home at MAGOG, **John Glassco**, who lived at FOSTER, and **Louis Dudek**, whose summer home is at WAY'S MILLS. The Scott house was originally bought with the journalist **Blair Fraser** and used by both families until Fraser's death in 1968. From a brother Scott also inherited another local house, a tiny cottage on Lake Massawippi, at whose northern tip North Hatley is situated. In the early 1960s Scott lent this cottage to **Leonard Cohen**, who wrote most of his novel *The Favorite Game* (1963) there. Cohen also wrote a *haiku* inspired by the silence at the lake; the poem was carved in slate by Cohen's friend, the sculptor Morton Rosengarten, who figures as a character in *The Favorite Game*. F.R. Scott received Governor General's Awards for his *Collected Poems* (1981) and for *Essays on the Constitution: Aspects of*

F.R. Scott on Lake Massawippi, 1971

Canadian Law and Politics (1977). (See also LENNOXVILLE, QUEBEC CITY.)

Hugh MacLennan's summer home, 'Stone Hedge' on Houghton St, looks down the full length of Lake Massawippi. Here the novelist wrote parts of *Two Solitudes* (1945; winner of a Governor General's Award), *The Precipice* (1948; winner of a Governor General's Award), and *Each Man's Son* (1951). MacLennan has won more Governor General's Awards (five) than any other author.

Lower on Houghton Street are the homes of three permanent literary residents: poets **D.G. Jones** and **Ralph Gustafson** and novelist **Ronald Sutherland** are MacLennan's neighbours on either side. Sutherland and Jones both teach at Université de SHERBROOKE. Gustafson has lived here since 1960 and has written here, in whole or in part, most of his best-known books of poetry, including *Ixion's Wheel* (1969), *Fire on Stone* (1974; winner of a Governor General's Award), and *Corners in Glass* (1977). Gustafson has based a number of poems, including 'Wednesday at North Hatley', on North Hatley and environs. Jones also draws on his experience here in *Phrases from Orpheus* (1967) and *Under the Thunder the Flowers Light Up the Earth* (1977; winner of a Governor General's Award). (See also BANCROFT, GUELPH, KINGSTON, LAKEFIELD, Ont.) Sutherland, a native of Montreal, came here when he joined the English Department of Université de Sherbrooke in 1959. He is the author of two novels, *Snow Lark* (1971) and *Where Do the MacDonalds Bury Their Dead?* (1976), and three influential books of criticism.

A.J.M. Smith and F.R. Scott posing behind suitable tombstones in the cemetery near North Hatley

Poet **Gérald Godin**, who was Quebec's Minister of Cultural Communities and Immigration under the Parti québécois government of René Lévesque, has been a summer resident of North Hatley since 1968; he owns (jointly with the singer Pauline Julien) a small hillside farm, where he was arrested under the War Measures Act during the 'October Crisis' of 1970. Godin is the author of five volumes of poetry, including *Poèmes et Cantos* (1962) and *Libertés surveillées* (1975). (See also TROIS-RIVIÈRES.) The novelist **Roch Carrier** was a summer resident for several summers in the late 1960s. Here he met translator **Sheila Fischman**, and this meeting resulted in the English translation of *La Guerre, yes sir!* (1968; trans. 1970). Another summer resident during the 1960s was poet and painter **Roland Giguère**, whose selected poems, *La Main au feu, 1949–1968* (1973), won a Governor General's Award (declined).

Among several younger writers who live in or near North Hatley are the poet **Michel Garneau**, winner of a Governor General's Award (declined) for his drama *Les Célébrations suivi de Adidou Adidouce* (1977), who has a log house in the nearby community of Tomifobia, and novelist **Robert Allen** (*The Hawryliw Process: Part I*, 1980, and *Part II*, 1981).

OKA

Gratien Gélinas, a leader in the development of the modern Quebec Theatre, has lived in this small village near Montreal since 1977, when he resigned his post as chairman of the Canadian Film Development Corporation. Beginning in 1934 Gélinas contributed as actor, director, and writer to plays for the stage and radio in MONTREAL (17), where he had lived since early childhood. Since retiring he has been preparing the texts of his Fridolin revues, presented at Montreal from 1938 to 1946, for book publication. Two of four volumes planned have been released: *Les Fridolinades 1945 et 1946* (1980) and *Les Fridolinades 1943 et 1944* (1981). Gélinas based his most successful play, *Tit-Coq* (first staged in 1948 and published in 1980), on material taken from some of the Fridolin revues . (See also ST-TITE-DE-CHAMPLAIN.)

PERCÉ

André Breton, the guiding spirit of the French Surrealist movement and one of the most influential figures in twentieth-century letters, came to Percé and the Gaspé Peninsula on 20 Aug. 1944. He was especially interested in Bonaventure Island, a sea-bird sanctuary two miles out to sea, and in the famous Percé ('pierced') Rock, also a bird sanctuary, named by Champlain in 1607 for

The house of Ralph Gustafson, North Hatley

the natural arch (60 ft high, 100 ft long) that the sea had worn through this enormous offshore block of limestone. Breton's trip was the occasion for one of his most important books, *Arcane 17* (1945), which was composed partly at Percé and partly at STE-AGATHE, and was completed, according to Breton, in exactly three months, on 20 Oct. 1944. Bonaventure Island, Percé Rock, the swarming birdlife of the region, and the local fishermen are basic and recurrent images in Breton's complex work, which mingles visionary prose, autobiography, occultism, and criticism of Quebec culture.

PÉRIBONKA

After coming to Canada from England in late 1911 and spending his first Canadian winter in QUEBEC CITY and MONTREAL (12), the French novelist **Louis Hémon** went north to the Lac St-Jean region and found work as a farm-hand. By 13 July 1912 he had arrived here and had met Samuel Bédard, with whom he agreed to live and work for $8 a month. He had Saturday afternoons off to spend at the village of Péribonka, whic is on the river of the same name near where it flows into the northern part of Lac St-Jean. Until September Hémon lived with Samuel and Laura Bédard and their two adopted sons, gathering impressions of the area, conceiving and drafting his classic novel *Maria Chapdelaine*.

AUTUMN COMES TO LAC SAINT-JEAN

Between the wet days there was still fine bright weather, hot toward noon, when one might fancy that all was as it had been: the harvest still unreaped, the changeless setting of spruces and firs, and ever the same sunsets of grey and opal, opal and gold, and skies of misty blue above the same dark woodland. But in the mornings the grass was sometimes white with rime, and swiftly followed the earliest dry frosts which killed and blackened the tops of the potatoes.

—Louis Hémon, *Maria Chapdelaine* (1916; tr. William Hume Blake, 1921)

Another member of the household was Bédard's unmarried sister-in-law, Éva Bouchard, who later became proprietor of the farm after the deaths of Samuel Bédard and of Éva's sister, Mme Bédard. The romantic belief has grown up that Hémon modelled his Maria upon Éva Bouchard, and that he was in love with her.

In September and November he assisted a surveying party in the region as a substitute for Samuel Bédard, and in December he spent his last Christmas with the Bédards before moving on to ST-GÉDÉON. Within half a year of leaving Péribonka, Hémon was killed in a railway accident at CHAPLEAU, Ont., on 13 July 1913; he had spent only eighteen months in Canada. (See also KÉNOGAMI, LA TUQUE, ROBERVAL.) Today the Bédard farmhouse, 3 miles east of the village beside the Péribonka River, is the Musée Maria Chapdelaine, housing photographs of Hémon, letters of Éva Bouchard, and historical items from the north Saguenay region. Éva Bouchard's grave is in the Péribonka parish churchyard.

Éva Bouchard

PETITE-RIVIÈRE-ST-FRANÇOIS

This village on the north shore of the St Lawrence River in Charlevoix County, southwest of Baie Saint-Paul, was for many years the summer home of novelist **Gabrielle Roy** and her husband Dr Marcel Carbotte. Roy came to know the people and land of Charlevoix County intimately, and she evokes them in *Cet été qui chantait*, a lyrical book of fictionalized reminiscences of her experiences around Petite-Rivière-St-François. Published in 1972, the book was translated by Joyce Marshall As *Enchanted Summer* (1976). (See also MONTREAL: 16, QUEBEC CITY; CARDINAL, MEADOW PORTAGE, ST-BONIFACE, ST-VITAL, Man.)

PIERREVILLE

This town on the St Francis River was the site of the country estate of the Hon. Charles Gill, a judge of the Superior Court in MONTREAL (11) and father of **Charles Gill**, who did much of his painting and writing during the summers, both in the garden of the house and in a garden shed he had adapted as a studio. Charles Gill's poetry was collected in *Le Cap Éternité: poème suivi des Étoiles filantes* (1919), published the year after Gill died in the influenza epidemic of 1918. (See also CHICOUTIMI, SOREL.)

POINTE-AU-PIC

The grave of **William Hume Blake**, translator of Louis Hémon's *Maria Chapdelaine*, is in the yard of Murray Bay Protestant Church in Pointe-au-Pic, just south of La Malbaie. Blake was the author of three books that combined fishing lore, praise of the Laurentian wilderness and habitant life, and

The Gill house at Pierreville

retellings of legends (including that of the Wendigo, or werewolf): *Brown Waters and Other Sketches* (1915), *In a Fishing Country* (1922), and *A Fisherman's Creed* (1923). His translation of Louis Hémon's *Maria Chapdelaine* appeared in 1921, a few months after a translation by Sir Andrew Macphail (see MONTREAL: 3; ORWELL, P.E.I). The two men had originally sought to collaborate, but, unable to agree on style, each published a separate translation; Blake's quickly became standard. Blake's love for the French-Canadian people, among whom he spent much time in the Malbaie area, was also expressed in his translation of *Chez Nous* (1914; Blake's translation, 1924), sketches of Quebec folkways and landscape by the legal expert, linguist, and author **Adjutor Rivard** (1868–1945). (See also TORONTO: 2, Ont.)

POVUNGNITUK

Yves Thériault's novel of the Inuit, *Agaguk* (1958), is set in an unnamed Inuit village of the Ungava Peninsula, and on the Ungava tundra, where Agaguk and his wife Iriook make a life for themselves alone. Povungnituk and its environs form the setting of *Agaguk*'s sequel, *Tayaout, fils d'Agaguk* (1969), in which Agaguk has become a settled Inuit and persuades his people to create stone carvings for trade; in Thériault's view this is a betrayal of Inuit culture that must be expiated in a violent confrontation between father and son. Povungnituk, a village of about 700, is situated at the mouth of the Povungnituk River on the east coast of Hudson Bay. (See also MONTREAL: 16, RAWDON, SAINT-DENIS.)

QUEBEC CITY

1. 1535 TO 1850.

North America's oldest city occupies the plain along a narrowing of the St Lawrence and St Charles Rivers (Lower Town, the commercial district) and the plateau of Cap Diamant (Upper Town, where fortifications and administration were located). Its distinguished literary heritage antedates its founding by Samuel de Champlain in 1608. The general site was known to the French by 1535–6, when **Jacques Cartier** wintered on the St Charles River and visited the Indian village of Stadacona nearby. The narrative of Cartier's travels (translated as *The Voyages of Jacques Cartier*, 1924) records the events of that winter, but whether Cartier himself wrote any of this material is a matter of dispute. Other early writings associated with the site of Quebec City include the account of its founding and earliest days in the second volume of the *Voyages* (1613) of **Samuel de Champlain** and many parts of *The Jesuit Relations and Allied Documents* (1616–73; English trans. 1896–1901). One of the most famous 'allied documents' is Father Claude Dablon's account of the famous voyage of discovery to the Mississippi River undertaken in 1673 by Father Jacques Marquette and **Louis Jolliet**. Jolliet was born in Quebec in 1645 and educated there by the Jesuits. A 1683 structure that once was his home, Louis Jolliet House, is the lower station of a funicular railway connecting Upper and Lower Towns. Jolliet is the subject of poet **Alain Grandbois**'s *Né à Québec: Louis Jolliet* (1933; English trans. *Born in Quebec*, 1964).

Marie de l'Incarnation, co-founder and first mother superior of the community of Ursuline sisters at Quebec City, was a writer of considerable literary stature. Her spiritual autobiographies are ranked among the classics of Christian mysticism, and her voluminous, lively letters are valuable both as social history and as literature. Examples of her work in English translation are *The Autobiography of Venerable Marie of the Incarnation, O.S.U.* (1964) and *Word from New France* (1967, selected letters trans. by Joyce Marshall). In a famous letter she tells of the fire of 1650 that destroyed her convent, built in 1641. Its site is marked by a plaque on a wall of the present Ursuline Convent at 12 rue Donnacona at rue des Jardins. The museum of the Centre Marie de l'Incarnation here preserves books and other artifacts that belonged to Marie, and there is a statue of her at rue Donnacona and rue Parloir.

QUEBEC CITY

Now that I have seen this country I recognize it as the one which Our Lord showed me in a dream six years ago. These great mountains, the vast areas, the site and the configuration, which were still engraved on my mind as at the time of the dream—all this was exactly as I had seen it, except that I don't see as much fog now as I did then. This greatly renewed the fervor of my vocation as well as my attraction, through a complete abandonment of myself, to suffer and to do whatever our Lord would wish of me in this new abode and manner of life which would be mine.

—Mother Marie de l'Incarnation, *La Relation de 1654* (tr. Dom Albert Jamet, 1964)

The city's first literary publications appeared in English after New France was ceded to Britain by the Treaty of Paris in 1763, and an English garrison and community were established here. The most important of the early writers here was **Frances Brooke**. Her husband, the Rev. John Brooke, became chaplain of the garrison in 1760, and Mrs Brooke joined him in 1763, remaining until they returned to England in 1768. She wrote the first Canadian novel, *The History of Emily Montague*. An epistolary novel made up of 228 letters, it was published in London in 1769 but is set mostly in Quebec of the 1760s. Probably the first volume of poetry produced in Quebec City was *Abram's Plains* (1789) by Thomas Cary, a newspaper editor. *Quebec Hill: or Canadian Scenery; A Poem* (1797) appeared in London under the name of J. Mackay; the authorship of *Canada: A Descriptive Poem* (1806), published in Quebec, is not known.

Attached to the garrison in the early nineteenth century were two near contemporaries, **Walter Henry** and **George Longmore**. Irish-born Henry, an army surgeon with advanced medical views, was posted to Canada in 1827 and soon became a prominent Canadian literary figure. A poet, author of at least one short story, and a newspaper contributor on sporting and political subjects, Henry lived mainly in Quebec City and was an officer of the Quebec Literary and Historical Society. He retired to KINGSTON, Ont., in 1855 and died there five years later. His two-volume memoirs, *Trifles from My Portfolio*, printed by William Neilson at Quebec in 1839, was followed by an expanded edition, *Events of a Military Life*, which appeared in London in 1843. George Longmore, two years younger than Henry, was born in Quebec City in 1793, the son of a British army doctor, and lived here until 1809, when a British Army commission took him to England. He was posted to MONTREAL (2) for the years 1820–4, his last stay in his native country, and wrote his Canadian works during this period. They include a long poem, *The Charivari; or Canadian Poetics: A Tale after the Manner of Beppo* (1824), and 'Tecumthé', a long poem on the famous Shawnee chief Tecumseh, which appeared in a Canadian magazine, also in 1824.

The tablet of the Golden Dog, now set above the entrance of the Upper Town post office at 3 rue Buade, links the colourful history of the French regime with Canadian literature in the nineteenth century. It inspired the title of William Kirby's novel *The Golden Dog (Le Chien d'or): A Romance of the Days of Louis Quinze in Quebec* (1877), based on events that occurred under the infamous last intendant of New France, François Bigot (which are also treated in Joseph-Etienne-Eugène Marmette's novel *L'Intendant Bigot*, 1872). Beneath its bas-relief

The tablet of the Golden Dog

of a dog couchant gnawing a bone, the tablet bears this inscription in old French:

Je suis un chien qui ronge l'o
En le rongeant je prend mon repos,
Un tems viendra qui n'est pas venu
Que je morderay qui m'aura mordu.

In his novel, Kirby translates this as

I am a dog that gnaws his bone,
I couch and gnaw it all alone—
A time will come, which is not yet,
When I'll bite him by whom I'm bit.

The stone was once set in the house of Nicolas Jacquin *dit* Philibert, a wealthy merchant, at the corner of rue Buade and Côte de la Montagne, where the post office is today. Enlarged in 1736 by Philibert, this early mansion had been built by a physician, Timothée

FROM 'THE GOLDEN DOG'

Our tale is now done. It ends in all sadness, as most true tales of this world do! There is in it neither poetic nor human justice. Fain would we have had it otherwise, for the heart longs for happiness as the eye for light! But truth is stronger as well as stranger than fiction, and while the tablet of the Chien d'Or *overlooks the Rue Buade; while the lamp of Repentigny burns in the ancient chapel of the Ursulines; while the ruins of Beaumanoir cover the dust of Caroline de St. Castin; and Amélie sleeps her long sleep by the side of Héloise de Lotbinière, this writer has neither courage nor power to deviate from the received traditions in relating the story of the Golden Dog.*

—William Kirby, *The Golden Dog* (1877)

Roussel, in the last quarter of the seventeenth century. Today experts believe the tablet was the work of Roussel, but nineteenth-century legend attributed it to Philibert, a leader of the so-called *honnêtes gens* (prominent citizens, including Montcalm), who opposed the ruinous profiteering of Bigot. Kirby and others thought the inscription referred to Philibert's implacable opposition to Bigot; the merchant was eventually murdered by one of the intendant's hangers-on, Le Gardeur de Repentigny. The characters and events in *The Golden Dog* are based on real people and events: the central figure is Pierre Philibert, son of Nicolas; two of Kirby's heroines entered the Ursuline Convent, and Madeline de Repentigny, who figures in the book, lit a votive lamp there in 1717 that has been kept burning ever since. Kirby, a resident of NIAGARA-ON-THE-LAKE, Ont., began writing *The Golden Dog* after a visit to Quebec City in 1865. Some years earlier the American author **Henry David Thoreau** visited the city and environs—from Wednesday, 25 Sept. 1850, until Thursday of the following week—and confessed: 'I fear that I have not got much to say about Canada, not having seen much; what I got by going to Canada was a cold.' However, this did not prevent him from writing a whole book about the experience, *A Yankee in Canada* (1866).

The earliest stirrings of an indigenous French-Canadian literature were centred to some extent on the Petit Séminaire de Québec. A plaque at the principal entrance to the Séminaire de Québec, rue de la Fabrique, commemorates the third centenary, in 1968, of the founding of the Petit Séminaire, direct ancestor of the adjacent Université Laval. The Abbé **Jérôme Demers**, born in 1774 in nearby Saint-Nicholas, was educated at the Séminaire and taught philosophy there from 1800 to 1842. He was the author of a philosophical work, *Compendium philosophicae* (1835), and the architect of the Séminaire de NICOLET, erected in 1827–33. Two literary students who would have studied under Demers were **Philippe-Joseph Aubert de Gaspé** and **Pierre Petitclair**. By birthright the future seigneur of ST-JEAN-PORT-JOLI, where he spent his childhood, Aubert de Gaspé was born in Quebec City in 1786 and returned here to attend the Petit Séminaire from 1798 to 1806. He studied law under Jonathan Sewell, chief justice of Lower Canada, practised law in Quebec City, and was appointed sheriff in 1816, but he was relieved of office in 1822 because of indebtedness to the Crown; during this period he lived at 34 rue Saint-Louis—the Maison Jacquet, built in 1675 and now occupied by the restaurant Aux Anciens Canadiens. Thereafter he lived at St-Jean, visiting Québec City frequently; he was imprisoned for debt here from 1838 to 1841. In his old age Aubert de Gaspé became one of the founders of French-Canadian literature as author of the historical novel *Les Anciens Canadiens* (1863; English trans., *The Canadians of Old*, by Sir Charles G. D. Roberts, 1890; rpt. 1974) and his *Mémoires* (1866).

His son, **Philippe-Ignace-François Aubert de Gaspé**, was also an important literary figure. He was born—one of thirteen children—in Québec City on 8 Apr. 1814, was educated at the Collège de Nicolet, and became a journalist. In Nov. 1835 he was jailed, following a fight with Edmund Bailey O'Callaghan, the Yamaska deputy to the legislative assembly. After his release in Feb. 1836 he avenged himself by leaving a bottle of asafoetida in the assembly chamber. Fleeing to St-Jean in company with Napoléon Aubin, another rebellious newspaperman and early French-Canadian littérateur, he spent about a year there with his father before the latter was imprisoned for debt. During that time, with his father's help, he wrote *L'Influence d'un livre* (1837), the first French-Canadian novel. He moved to HALIFAX to seek his fortune in journalism, and died there in 1841. **Pierre Petitclair**, an early dramatist, was born near Quebec City and lived here until 1838, after which he spent most of his life in Labrador. His *Griphon; ou La Vengeance d'un valet* (1837) is the earliest play known to have been published by a native French Canadian.

2. MOUVEMENT LITTÉRAIRE DE QUÉBEC

The establishment of a French-Canadian literature began in Quebec about 1860 and was heralded by the work of historian and poet **François-Xavier Garneau**. Born here in 1809, he trained and worked as a notary, and his historical and literary education was largely self-acquired. After travels in France and England, he returned to Quebec City in the early 1830s; became a partisan of the *patriote* cause; worked as a bank clerk, notary, and translator; and in 1844 became clerk of the city, retaining this position until just before his death in 1866. His authoritative study of Quebec's heritage, *Histoire du Canada depuis sa découverte jusqu'à nos jours* (3 vols, 1845–8), is said to have been inspired partly by his indignation at Lord Durham's remark (*Durham Report*, 1839) that French-Canadians were a 'people without history'. Garneau also wrote poetry—romantic evocations of landscape and of the aspirations of his people. A plaque on the Maison Hamel (named for its builder), at 14 rue Saint-Flavien, identifies the house in which Garneau lived from 1862 until his death on 3 Feb. 1866. Here also the novelist **Joseph-Étienne-Eugène Marmette** courted Garneau's daughter Joséphine, whom he married in 1868. Later the house was occupied by the minor poet and musician Napoléon Legendre, who often entertained the writer and composer **Ernest Gagnon**, organist of the Basilica and author of the first collection of French-Canadian folksongs, *Chansons populaires du Canada (*1865; see also LOUISEVILLE). Legendre died in the house in 1907. Remembrances of Garneau in his native city include a statue near the Porte Saint-Louis, and his elaborate monument in the Belmont Cemetery—the first ever erected in homage to a Quebec man of letters—which was in part the idea of author Pierre-Joseph-Olivier Chauveau, first premier (1867–73) of the Province de Quebec.

The Garneau house, Quebec City

Garneau was the forerunner and mentor of the *Mouvement littéraire de Québec*, a literary group that existed in Quebec City for approximately ten years, 1857–67, and had many important members, though it was primarily centred on the Abbé **Henri-Raymond Casgrain** and the poet **Octave Crémazie**. Crémazie was born in Quebec on 16 Apr. 1827; the only given names on his birth certificate are Claude-Joseph-Olivier, suggesting that 'Octave' was a name of his own adoption. A plaque at 60 rue Saint-Louis marks the site of the house in which he was born; in 1827 the address was 11 rue Saint-Louis. With his two brothers—Jacques, a lawyer and later professor at the law faculty of the new (organized 1852) Université Laval, and Joseph—Octave Crémazie operated the famous bookstore where members of the *Mouvement littéraire de Québec* first began to meet. It was opened in Jan. 1844 at 15 rue Saint-Joseph (today rue Garneau, located in the city's 'Latin quarter'), and moved within a year to 8 côte Sainte-Famille (called côte de Lery in 1845). In 1847 the shop moved to 12 rue de la Fabrique, where in the late 1850s it became the meeting-place of the young writers who were in the process of creating a new literature. That building still stands, marked by a plaque; today the address is 42 rue de la Fabrique. The Crémazie bookstore is the direct ancestor of La Librairie Garneau at 47–49 rue Buade, near the Upper Town post office, with its tablet of the Golden Dog.

The writers who met in the rue de la Fabrique bookstore—besides Crémazie, Casgrain, Garneau and Aubert de Gaspé—included the poet **Louis Fréchette** (see LÉVIS); the poet **Léon-Pamphile Lemay** (see LOTBINIÈRE); the novelist **Antoine Gérin-Lajoie** (see YAMACHICHE); the short-story writer and folklorist **Joseph-Charles Taché** (see KAMOURASKA and RIMOUSKI); the poet **Alfred Garneau** (son of the historian); the historian Abbé **Jean-Baptiste-Antoine Ferland**; and the doctor, professor, and man of letters **François-Alexis-Hubert LaRue**. At this time Taché lived at 16 rue Couillard, LaRue at 1 rue Saint-François, and Lemay at 23 rue de Lachevrotière. Two other important members of the *Mouvement littéraire* were Charles Gauldrée-Boilleau, the French consul at Quebec City, whose home was at 20 rue d'Auteuil, and **Étienne Parent**, who lived at 1 rue Laporte, an address that no longer exists. Parent was a journalist and the publisher of a newspaper, *Le Canadien*, on which he employed Aubert de Gaspé the younger. Also an expert in economics, he served at this time as under-secretary of Lower Canada and secured for F.-X. Garneau his position as city clerk.

The building that housed the Crémazie Bookshop

During the heyday of this group in the early 1860s it founded two important literary and intellectual magazines—*Les Soirées canadiennes* (1861–5) and *Le Foyer canadien* (1863–6)—and its members published many books of historical importance. These include Québec's first two volumes of poetry, Fréchette's *Mes loisirs* (1863) and Lemay's *Essais poétiques* (1865); Casgrain's early work in establishing the cultural history of Quebec and Qubec City, including his *Histoire de la Mère Marie de l'Incarnation* (1864); the first collection of French-Canadian short stories, Taché's *Forestiers et Voyageurs* (1863); Aubert de Gaspé's *Les Anciens Canadiens* (1863); and Gérin-Lajoie's novel *Jean Rivard* (1862–4).

The end of the *Mouvement littéraire* came in 1867, when the establishment of the

Dominion government at Ottawa drew away some of the authors who had been employed by the government of United Canada while it sat at Quebec City (1859–67). The disintegration had already begun in 1862, when Crémazie was forced to leave Canada to avoid imprisonment for debt. Taking the name Jules Fontaine, he fled to France and lived there for the rest of his life. He endured the Prussian siege of Paris, and later in the 1870s moved to Le Havre, where he died in 1879. The years of exile were almost entirely barren of poetry for Crémazie; but he wrote *Journal du siège de Paris* (1886), and his correspondence with Casgrain during this period constitutes the earliest French-Canadian literary criticism. His poems were collected in the *Oeuvres complètes de Crémazie* (1882). A man of learning (although his scholarship, alleged to include Sanskrit, has been exaggerated by his booster, Casgrain), Crémazie aspired with his bookstore to rival the best in France. In selection and quality he appears to have achieved his aim, but the small educated population of Quebec City at the time could not support the venture; thus his very love of poetry and literature resulted, in 1862, in his bankruptcy and exile in France.

Other members of the *Mouvement littéraire* who left Quebec City include Taché and Gérin-Lajoie, who had duties with the Dominion government and homes elsewhere. Ferland died in 1865, and in 1866 Fréchette, a passionate Liberal, entered five years of self-imposed exile in Chicago because of his opposition to Conservative-sponsored Confederation ideas. However, other important members of the group were longtime residents of the city. Chauveau, who in 1853 had already published *Charles Guérin*, one of the earliest and most influential French-Canadian novels, retired from politics in 1874 and in 1878 became a professor of Roman law at Université Laval. His later writings include a volume of poems, *Souvenirs et légendes* (1877), and a biography of F.-X. Garneau (1883). Chauveau lived at 22 rue Sainte-Anne, at the corner of rue du Trésor. Casgrain, who was vicar of the Roman Catholic Cathedral of Quebec, was the most powerful promoter of French-Canadian writers, both by material assistance and by the example of his own prolific work. The cathedral where Casgrain served is the Basilica of Notre-Dame-de-Québec, which stands at the southeast corner of rue Sainte-Famille and rue Buade. In 1874 Casgrain was forced by ill health, including failing eyesight, to give up active parochial work, but he managed to continue writing and editing until the late 1890s. Among his late books, *Pèlerinage au pays d'Évangeline* was crowned by the Académie française, and *Montcalm et Lévis* (2 vols, 1891, 1898) is considered one of his best historical works. Blind at the end of his life, he spent his last years in the Couvent du Bon Pasteur, a religious house in Quebec City. He died in 1904 and is buried in his native village, RIVIÈRE-OUELLE.

LaRue remained a professor of medicine at Université Laval from 1859 until his death in 1881; his home in later life was at 128 rue Sainte-Anne. His works include a satiric play written in collaboration with fellow doctor and writer Joseph-Charles Taché, *Le Défricheur de langue* (1859), and, much later, a volume of nostalgic essays about Quebec's main street, *Voyage sentimental sur la rue Saint-Jean: départ en 1860, retour en 1880* (1879). **Pamphile Lemay** was appointed librarian of the Quebec legislature in 1867, a post from which he retired in 1892. His many volumes of poetry include *Les Gouttelettes* (1904), generally considered his best work; in addition he wrote folkloric tales, novels, plays, and the standard translations of the two English works most important to nineteenth-century Quebec, Longfellow's *Evangeline: A Tale of Acadie* (first version of the translation published in 1865) and Kirby's *The Golden Dog* (trans. 1884). The address of Lemay's house, 23 rue de Lachevrotière, became number 63 in the later nineteenth century. Lemay lived there until about 1880; in 1890 his home was at 21 rue Burton, and a few years later he moved to the suburb of St-Jean Deschaillons.

The Séminaire de Quebec, founded in 1663 by Bishop François de Laval, educated many writers of the *Mouvement littéraire*: Crémazie, Chauveau, Casgrain, Taché, Alfred Garneau, and others. In 1852 the seminary founded Université Laval, at first housed in the seminary buildings, which occupy extensive grounds on rue Sainte-Famille; today the university's principal campus is in the western suburb of Ste-Foy. An important member of the *Mouvement littéraire*, co-founder of its magazines and author of many historical and biographical works, the Abbé Jean-Baptiste-Antoine Ferland was professor of history at Université Laval from 1855 until his death in 1865 (see NICOLET). During the early 1860s both LaRue and Taché were professors of medicine there.

An important late nineteenth-century literary graduate of the university was **Nérée Beauchemin**, the poet and country doctor of YAMACHICHE, author of *Les Floraisons matutinales* (1897) and *Patrie intime* (1928); Beauchemin received his medical degree here in 1874 but spent only his student years outside his native town. Sir **Adolphe-Basile Routhier**, whose home at 3325 rue Rochambeau in Ste-Foy (once an outlying village, now a part of metropolitan Quebec City) is a provincial historic site, graduated in law from Université Laval, practised in the city from 1861, and became a judge of the superior court of Quebec here in 1873. Author of 'O Canada', now the Canadian national anthem, he was not only a poet but a novelist, travel-writer, historian, legal theorist, literary critic, and indefatigable controversialist (see also ST-IRÉNÉE, ST-PLACIDE). The poet **William Chapman** (see BEAUCEVILLE EST) was educated at Université Laval and later worked in the city at various businesses and as a journalist; from 1898 to 1902 he owned a bookstore on rue Rideau. Chapman's books of poetry include *Les Québecquoises* (1876) and *Les Feuilles d'érable* (1890). **Marie-Victorin** (the name in religion of Conrad Kirouac), who moved to Quebec City as a child during the late 1880s, was educated at the parish church of St-Sau-

The Seminary at Quebec and Laval University, late nineteenth century

veur and the Académie Commercial—the school later attended by novelist Roger Lemelin. In 1901 he entered the Christian Brothers (Order of the Brothers of the Christian Schools). His teaching took him to the Laurentians, where he began careers as a writer and a botanist, finally settling in MONTREAL (15) as professor of botany at Université de Montréal. Marie-Victorin's literary writings include *Récits laurentiens* (1919; English trans., *The Chopping Bee and Other Laurentian Stories*, 1925). He was twice awarded the Prix David of the province of Quebec.

The French-language journalist Arthur Buies and the English-language journalist George Stewart Jr were important members of Quebec City's literary scene in the nineteenth century. **Arthur Buies** founded the anti-clerical newspaper *Le Réveil* here in 1876. His books include three volumes of his *Chroniques* (1873, 1875, 1878), collections of his periodical sketches of Quebec life and society. Less radical as the years passed, Buies wrote immigration literature for the Quebec government and died at Quebec City on 26 Jan. 1901. (See also NICOLET.) An innovative editor and an essayist, **George Stewart** Jr edited important magazines in SAINT JOHN, N.B., and Toronto, Ont., before settling permanently here in 1879. From 1879 to 1896 he edited the *Quebec Daily Chronicle*; his books include historical works and two volumes of *Essays from Reviews* (1892, 1893). Stewart's long-time home was at 146 rue Saint-Augustin. He died at Quebec City on 26 Feb. 1906.

The Rev. **Frederick George Scott** was the most prominent of Quebec City's English-Canadian authors in the nineteenth century. Born in Montreal, he was educated at Bishop's College, LENNOXVILLE, and ordained in the Anglican Church in England. In Quebec City he was rector of St Matthew's Church and lived with his family in the rectory; the buildings and the churchyard, on rue Saint-Jean at rue Saint-Augustin, are now provincial historical properties. Scott was made a canon of the Anglican cathedral of Quebec City in 1906 and archdeacon in 1925. Nationally beloved for his service in the First World War as chaplain of the Canadian First Division, he recorded his experience in a memoir, *The Great War As I Saw It* (1922). During his residence at St Matthew's rectory he wrote one novel and five volumes of poetry, including *My Lattice and Other Poems* (1894) and *Poems Old and New* (1900). As a poet he is associated mainly with the Confederation group—which included Archibald Lampman, Charles G. D. Roberts, Bliss Carman,

Padré Frederick George Scott on 'Dandy'

and Duncan Campbell Scott (no relation). Scott continued to write poetry throughout his long life; he died in 1944. His famous son, **F.R. Scott** (see MONTREAL: 4, NORTH HATLEY) was born in St Matthew's rectory on 1 Aug. 1899; on that day the father wrote in his diary, 'Small boy born at 5:10. Slept in the afternoon. Dined at Dobell's.' F.R. Scott spent his childhood in Quebec City before beginning his education at his father's *alma mater*, Bishop's College; but his literary career is associated with Montreal, where he spent his adult life.

3. THE TWENTIETH CENTURY.

In 1905 the poet and ethnologist **Alfred Goldsworthy Bailey** was born in a house at 37 rue Sainte-Ursule that had been in the family since it was built in Upper Town, just after the Conquest, by Richard Goldsworthy, a military engineer. The historian J.M. Wintemberg has argued that Stadacona was within a few hundred yards of this address. There is a picture of this house in Marius Barbeau's *I Have Seen Quebec* (1957), where it is incorrectly identified as the home of Mme de la Peltrie, patron of the Ursulines and co-founder with Mère Marie de l'Incarnation of their convent here. In fact, Mme de la Peltrie's house, which burned down in 1650, stood on the site of the present-day Marie de l'Incarnation Museum, on rue Donnacona at rue des Jardins. On 18 Oct. 1911 **Louis Hémon** arrived in Quebec from Liverpool and spent a few days here, soon moving on to Montreal. His impressions of the city are the subject of *The Journal of Louis Hémon* (English translation, 1924). See also KÉNOGAMI, PÉRIBONKA, ST-GÉDÉON; CHAPLEAU, Ont.)

Since early in this century Université Laval has educated future writers and attracted teachers of literary distinction. The folklorist and novelist **Marius Barbeau**, who was born in 1883 in STE-MARIE-DE-LA-BEAUCE, studied law at Laval and was admitted to the bar in 1907; but he left immediately for Oxford University as a Rhodes Scholar. His next important connection with Quebec City did not come until 1945, when he became a professor in the Faculté des Lettres of the university; even then, however, he maintained his residence in OTTAWA, where he lived throughout his life. The novelist **Ringuet** (Philippe Panneton) was a medical student at Laval, but transferred to the University's Montreal campus, where he obtained his degree in 1920. The poet **Alain Grandbois** was a law student at Laval from 1922 to 1924 and was admitted to the bar in Quebec City in 1925, although from 1924 to 1938 he travelled incessantly in Europe and the Far East, returning to his native province only for a few short visits. Grandbois lived in Quebec City from 1930 to 1942 and during this period published *Les Voyages de Marco Polo* (1940), largely written at DESCHAMBAULT. He returned in 1961, worked for the Quebec Museum (in National Battlefields Park, site of the Battle of the Plains of Abraham), and lived at 958 av. Moncton throughout the 1960s, the decade that saw the publication of his collected *Poèmes* (1963) and of *Selected Poems* (1964), trans. by Peter Miller. By 1975 Grandbois was living at 949 av. Casot. The novelist and dramatist **Jacques Ferron** studied medicine at Université Laval during the 1940s, and in 1949 began his practice on the Gaspé Peninsula before building his well-known practice in LONGUEUIL. He left his 1966–70 papers to the Quebec French National Archives here; these include the manuscripts of *Le Ciel du Québec* (1969), his longest work of fiction, which is set in Quebec in 1937–8, the centennial of the Patriote rebellion.

Two of Quebec's most prominent literary figures were long connected with Université Laval as faculty members: the Abbé **Lionel-Adolphe Groulx** and Father **Félix-Antoine Savard**. Groulx, who was appointed in 1915 to the chair of Canadian history, also wrote (under the pseudonym Alonie de Lestres) two novels, *L'Appel de la race* (1922) and *Au Cap Bomidon* (1932); selections of his writings in translation are found in *Variations on a Nationalist Theme* (1973), trans. by Susan Trofimenkoff. (See also CARILLON.) Savard was born in Quebec City in 1896, but at the age of two moved with his family to CHICOUTIMI. He did not return here until 1941, when he began to lecture in Quebec folklore at the university. Influenced by Marius Barbeau, he worked with the scholar and writer Luc Lacourcière to collect Quebec folksongs and stories, and this material formed the basis of the university's archives, which were established in 1944 through the two men's efforts; in the same year Lacourcière was given the new chair of folklore studies at the university. Savard maintained his home in ST-JOSEPH-DE-LA-RIVE while also teaching at Laval. In 1943 he became a full-time faculty member; in 1945 he became professor of French poetry; and in 1950 he was appointed dean of the Faculté des Lettres, a post he occupied until 1957. After an active retirement at St-Joseph, during which he wrote a number of works including *Le Barachois* (1959; winner of a Governor General's Award), Savard was forced by declining health to return to Quebec City. Here he lived at the Pavillon Saint-Dominique, a religious residence, until his death on 24 Aug. 1982, an event announced by *Le Devoir* with the words 'Menaud est mort', alluding to Savard's famous novel *Menaud, maître draveur* (1937; trans. by Richard Howard, *Master of the River*, 1976).

Both Groulx and Savard had a great influence on younger writers educated at Laval by virtue of their Quebec nationalism and, in Savard's case, by a distinguished literary *oeuvre*. Savard's best-known literary student is probably the poet and *chansonnier* **Gilles Vigneault**, who studied at Laval from 1945 to 1950, after attending the Petit Séminaire de RIMOUSKI, where he had first encountered Savard's writings. After graduating from Laval and teaching at several high schools, Vigneault returned to the university as a teacher and remained until his début in 1960 as a *chansonnier*. During this period he founded a literary magazine, *Émourie*, and a literary publishing house, Éditions de l'Arc, and published his first collection of poems, *Étraves* (1959). Vigneault's *Où la lumière chante* (1966) celebrates the city of Quebec. During the 1950s Vigneault lived at 148 rue Saint-Augustin. In the 1960s he lived at various addresses, including 1033 rue d'Artigny, 941 av. Bougainville, and 1335 rue Charles Huot. (See also NATASHQUAN.) Another important influence on Gilles Vigneault was of course **Félix Leclerc**, the originator of the Quebec *chansonnier* tradition. Leclerc's connection with Quebec City antedates Vigneault's presence here: he was an announcer at radio station CHRC in 1934–7. Leclerc's books include *Le Fou de l'île* (1958; trans. by Philip Stratford, *The Madman, the Kite and the Island*, 1976). (See also La TUQUE; OTTAWA, Ont.)

The novelist and anti-clerical controversialist **Jean-Charles Harvey** came to Quebec in 1922 to work on the newspaper *Le Soleil*, and from 1927 until April 1934 was its editor-in-chief; during that period he lived at 302 rue Fraser. He was removed from his position the day after the Archbishop of Quebec publicly condemned his important novel *Les Demi-civilisés* (1934; trans. by John Glassco, *Fear's Folly*, 1982). Appointed director of the Quebec office of statistics by Premier Louis-Alexander Taschereau, Harvey remained in the city for two more years. In 1935 his volume of short stories, *Sébastien Pierre*, continued the novel's satire of the clerical domination of education, and in Aug. 1936 Harvey was again fired, following the election of Maurice Duplessis as premier. Harvey then moved to MONTREAL (15).

Roger Lemelin, with Quebec's Lower Town behind him, in the 1950s.

Yves Thériault, Quebec's most prolific writer—mostly of novels and short stories—was born on 28 Nov. 1915 in Quebec City, the son of a carpenter, but he was brought up in Montreal, where the family moved in his early childhood. Among his many works are two well-known novels of the Inuit and Montagnais peoples, respectively: *Agaguk* (1958; winner of the Prix de la Province de Québec and the Prix France-Canada) and *Ashini* (1960; winner of the Prix France-Canada and a Governor General's Award); both books have been translated. **Anne Hébert**'s association with the city has been more intimate. Born on 1 Aug. 1916 in STE-CATHERINE-DE-FOSSAMBAULT, she spent a reclusive childhood and youth, punctuated by illness, both there and in Quebec City, where her father, the critic Maurice Hébert, worked in the Quebec government. In the late 1920s the family home was at 92 av. Turnbull. By 1932 the Hébert family lived at 342 rue Saint-Cyrille, and throughout the forties and fifties at 89 av. du Parc. During the 1950s Anne Hébert worked for the CBC and the National Film Board here, and in 1958 established her own home at 1705 av. du Parc, which was her address as late as 1965, although she was often in France. Since the mid-1960s she has lived primarily in Paris but has often returned for year-long visits or briefer stays. Among Hébert's many books, the best known perhaps are her *Poèmes* (1960; trans. by Alan Brown, 1975) and the novel *Kamouraska* (1970; trans. by Norman Shapiro, 1974). (See also KAMOURASKA.)

Roger Lemelin was born in 1919 in Saint-Saveur, a working-class neighbourhood of Quebec City's Lower Town that is situated at the foot of the *pente douce*, or 'gentle slope', joining Lower Town and Upper Town. Saint-Saveur is the setting of his largely autobiographical novel *Au pied de la pente douce* (1944; trans. by Samuel Putnam, *The Town Below*, 1948). Like the novel's protagonist, Denis Boucher (who had been called Roger in the manuscript), Lemelin was the second child of a family of eleven children, and had an older brother who died young from the combined effects of illness and an operation to remove ribs. The family lived in a frame house the father had built by hand. Lemelin studied at the Institut

Thomas, and the Académie Commerciale de Québec, and was an accomplished athlete; in 1936 he broke an ankle while preparing to compete in the Winter Olympics as a ski jumper and spent six years in a wheelchair, the period during which he began to write. His best-known novel, *Les Plouffe* (1948; trans. by Mary Finch, *The Plouffe Family*, 1950), is also a portrait of family life in Lower Town. The locales familiar to readers of these popular novels can be visited. Sites from *Au pied de la pente douce* include the rue Franklin and rue Montmagny district, scene of the escape of Denis Boucher's gang of apple-stealing youths in the opening chapter; rue Colombe, in which the homes of Boucher and his friend Jean Colin stood across from one another; and the rue Châteauguay, in which the novel's heroine, Lise Lévesque, lived. St Joseph's parish church, the construction of which forms a part of the novel, is at 633 rue Châteauguay, and the rival church of St Malo, which the novel's characters attended before they had a church of their own, is at 275 rue Marie de l'Incarnation. Roger Lemelin has always maintained a home in Quebec City; a successful businessman since the mid-1940s (he wrote his first novel while working at a lumber company of which he later became president and owner), he now lives on rue Saint-Félix in the western suburb of Cap Rouge. There he wrote the sequel to *Les Plouffe*, *Le Crime d'Ovide Plouffe* (1982). Lemelin's only extended period spent outside Quebec was from 1972 to 1981, when he was publisher of *La Presse* in Montreal.

Along with Lemelin's two novels of the 1940s, **Gabrielle Roy**'s *Bonheur d'occasion* (1945; trans. by Hanna Josephson, *The Tin Flute*, 1947; retranslated by Alan Brown, 1980) is credited with directing the course of Quebec fiction towards modern realism. A native of ST-BONIFACE, Man., Roy settled in Quebec City in 1950, and her husband, Dr Marcel Carbotte, established a medical practice here. Until her death on 13 July 1983, Roy lived with her husband in a brown brick apartment building at 135 Grand-Allée ouest. Here, and at her summer home at PETITE-RIVIÈRE-ST-FRANÇOIS, she wrote most of her many books, including *Alexandre Chenevert* (1955; trans. by Harry Binsse, *The Cashier*, 1955), *Rue Deschambault* (1955; trans. by Harry Binsse, *Street of Riches*, 1957), *La Route d'Altamont* (1966; trans. by Joyce Marshall, *The Road Past Altamont*, 1966), and her two works set in the far North, *La Montagne secrète* (1961; trans. by Harry Binsse, *The Hidden Mountain*, 1962) and *La Rivière sans repos* (1970; partial trans. by Joyce Marshall, *Windflower*, 1970). Among Roy's many honours were Governor General's Awards in 1947, 1957, and 1977. (See also MONTREAL: 16; MEADOW PORTAGE, Man.)

With Roy and Lemelin, **André Giroux** is an important creator of the modern Quebec novel of urban realism. He collaborated in the important review *La Réleve* (see MONTREAL: 14) but has spent much of his career in Quebec City, where he worked in the early 1950s for the provincial government and after 1957 as a writer for Radio-Canada. During the 1950s Giroux lived at 72 rue de la Colline. His major novels include *Au-delà des visages* (1948) and *Le Gouffre a toujours soif* (1953). He is widely known for his television series *14 rue des Galais*; rue des Galais is in the western suburb of Ste-Foy.

The playwright **Françoise Loranger**, a native of St-Hilaire who lived and worked in Montreal for many years, now lives on rue de la Corniche in St-Nicholas, opposite Cap Rouge on the south shore of the St Lawrence. Loranger won a Governor General's Award for her collection of plays *Encore cinq minutes suivi de Un cri qui vient de loin* (1967). The novelist and memoirist **Claire Martin** (née Montreuil) was born in Quebec City in 1914. She took her mother's maiden name in defiance of an unhappy childhood dominated by her father—as described in her most famous work, *Dans un gant de fer* (1965; trans. by Philip Stratford, *In an Iron Glove*, 1973). Also described in the book is her education here in the Ursuline Convent, and in that of the sisters of the Congrégation Notre-Dame. The continuation of Martin's memoir, *La Joue droite* (1966; trans. by Philip Stratford, *The Right Cheek*, 1975), received the Prix de la Province de Québec and a Governor General's Award. After completing her convent education, Martin had a career as a radio announcer, first on CKCV in Quebec City and later in Montreal. For many years she lived in OTTAWA, where she began to write, and in Paris, before taking up residence in Quebec City again in 1982. The poet **Cécile Cloutier**—author of *Chaleuils*, (1978; trans. by Alexandre Amprimov, *Springtime of the Spoken Word*, 1979)—was born in 1930 in Lower Town and received degrees from Université Laval; since 1966 she has been a professor of French at the University of Toronto. Another native of Lower Town is the novelist and poet **Marie-Claire Blais**, who was born on 5 Oct. 1939 in the parish of St-Pascal. The eldest of a family of five children living in a three-room tenement flat, Blais wrote her first novel at twelve. By sixteen she had dropped out of school and had begun a series of semi-skilled jobs. In the late 1950s she enrolled in evening courses at Université Laval, where she attracted the attention of Georges-Henri Lévesque, the Dominican priest noted for his influence on the cultural awakening of Quebec in the 1950s, and for having founded at Laval, in 1938, Canada's first school of social studies. (Lévesque had been a student of Félix-Antoine Savard when the latter taught at the Séminaire de Chicoutimi.) He encouraged Blais and arranged for her first publication, the novel *La Belle Bête* (1959; trans. by Merloyd Lawrence, *Mad Shadows*, 1960), which was soon followed by *Tête blanche* (1960 trans. by Charles Fullman, 1961). Guggenheim Fellowships in 1963 and 1964 enabled Blais to spend many years in Massachusetts and in France; since returning to Quebec she has established homes in MONTREAL (16) and RICHMOND.

The sociologist and poet *Fernand Dumont*, born in 1927 in Montmorency, near Quebec City, is now director of the Institut supérieur des Sciences humaines at Université Laval; his poetry is collected in *L'Ange du matin* (1952) and *Parler de septembre* (1970). The novelist **Jacques Poulin** was educated at Université Laval and has worked in the city as a commercial translator. His first three novels are set largely in Quebec City's Old Town; translated by Sheila Fischman as *The Jimmy Trilogy* (1979), they are *Mon cheval pour un royaume* (1967), *Jimmy* (1969), and *Le Coeur de la baleine bleue* (1970). Poulin has lived on chemin St-Louis in Cap Rouge for several years. **Antonine Maillet**, the most prominent Acadian author, received her Doctorat ès Lettres from Université Laval in 1970 and long taught literature and folklore at the university. She now lives in MONTREAL (16). (See BUCTOUCHE, N.B.)

RAWDON

During the last years of his life, **Yves Thériault** lived in this Laurentian village at 319 rue Metcalfe. Here he produced his longest

Yves Thériault

novel, *La Quête de l'ourse* (1980), an examination of primitive North American ways of life that continues the themes of his famous novels *Agaguk* (1958) and *Ashini* (1960). He also collected many of his short stories in two volumes, *La Femme Anna et autres contes* (1981) and *Valère et le grand canot* (1981). Thériault, who suffered a severe stroke in 1970, became ill in the summer of 1983 and died in August in the hospital of nearby JOLIETTE: the previous spring he had undertaken an arduous two-month tour of bookstores throughout Quebec to promote his books. Between 1979 and 1981 he added to his enormous and varied output five books for children based on Indian and Inuit material. (See also MONTREAL: 16, QUEBEC CITY, ST-DENIS.)

While living in Montreal and working as a journalist between 1939 and 1947, **Gabrielle Roy** spent her summers in Rawdon; the Rawdon district was the childhood home of Roy's mother, who had been born in the village of St-Alphonse. Roy once commented, 'Throughout my childhood in Manitoba the two names of Rawdon and Joliette were constantly striking my ear, penetrating into me, impregnating my sensibilities. It is possible that Rawdon and its region will appear in my next novel and play a marked role.' Although she worked on it sporadically for twelve years, Roy never completed this novel, which was to be an epic chronicle of the migration of Quebec *habitants* to the West in the nineteenth century. Her work on this material did bear fruit, however, in *La Route d'Altamont* (1966; trans. by Joyce Marshall, *The Road Past Altamont*, 1966) and in a long article, 'Mon héritage du Manitoba', collected in *Fragiles lumières de la terre* (1978; trans. by Alan Brown, *Fragile Lights of Earth*, 1982). During her summers in Rawdon, Roy worked on her famous first book, *Bonheur d'occasion* (*The Tin Flute*), which was published in 1945. (See also MONTREAL: 16, PETITE-RIVIÈRE-ST-FRANÇOIS, QUEBEC CITY; CARDINAL, MEADOW PORTAGE, ST-BONIFACE, ST-VITAL, Man.)

RICHMOND

The novelist **Marie-Claire Blais** lives in a century-old farmhouse on a 60-acre farm near Richmond, dividing her time between this home and an apartment in MONTREAL (16). Her books written at Richmond, where she has lived since the late 1970s, include *Le Sourd dans la ville* (1979; trans. by Carol Dunlop, *Deaf to the City*, 1980), which won a Governor General's Award, and *Visions d'Anna* (1982). Another literary resident of

The young Marie-Claire Blais

the same house is Blais's long-time friend, the American painter and author **Mary Meigs** (*Lily Briscoe: A Self-Portrait*, 1981). (See also QUEBEC CITY.)

RIMOUSKI

From 1845, Rimouski was the home of **Joseph-Charles Taché**, author, doctor, politician, and representative abroad of Canada and French-Canadian culture. He was born in KAMOURASKA and eduted in QUEBEC CITY. After coming to Rimouski to practise medicine, he was elected by acclamation to the legislative assembly, where he served for ten years. In 1855 and 1867 he represented Canada at world exhibitions in Paris and in 1855 was made a member of the French Légion d'honneur. The first important French-Canadian writer of short stories, Taché wrote three books of fiction and several important non-fiction works, most of which were produced at Rimouski. *Trois légendes de mon pays* (1861) retells folk materials representing three stages of Quebec's history. *Forestiers et Voyageurs* (1865), fictional and folk tales combined in a loose narrative framework, displays Taché's unparallelled knowledge of the lives of lumbermen and voyageurs of the 'pays d'en haut'; the book is so specific that it provides some of the best documentary evidence of this vanished way of life.

RIVIÈRE-LA-MADELEINE

From 1946 to 1949 **Jacques Ferron** practised medicine in this Gulf of Saint Lawrence village at Cap de la Madeleine on the northern shore of the Gaspé Peninsula. This was the period of his earliest published writings, including the plays *Le Licou* (1947) and *L'Ogre* (1948). More important to his subsequent literary work were the oral storytellers he met here and the folklore and traditions of the Gaspé; these elements are prominent in his mature writings. His fantastic tale *La Chaise du maréchal ferrant* (1972) is set in the Gaspé and makes use of the region's folklore; *Gaspé-Mattempa* (1980) is also based on Ferron's experience at Rivière-la-Madeleine. (See also LONGUEUIL, LOUISEVILLE, MONTREAL: 18, ST-LAMBERT, TROIS-RIVIÈRES.)

RIVIÈRE-OUELLE

This tiny community, on the south shore of the St Lawrence south of Kamouraska, was the birthplace of two of French Canada's most important writers: Abbé **Henri-Raymond Casgrain** and **Rodolphe Dubé**. Casgrain, who spent most of his life in QUEBEC CITY, was an indefatigable historian, critic, and promoter of the young French-Canadian literature. He began his writing career in 1860 with poems and retellings of Quebec folklore. One of his earliest publications was *Le Tableau de la Rivière Ouelle* (1860), his versions of legends from his native region. Born in 1831, Casgrain was a lover of all that was noble and heroic in history and claimed a noble lineage for himself, suggesting that he was descended from French warriors who had fought the Turks. Highly amused by this, the novelist and great jurist, Adolphe-Basile Routhier, author of the poem 'O Canada', traced the Abbé's family to an innkeeper in Quebec City's Lower Town who had married a Pawnee woman and made a living selling drink to the *voyageurs* of the '*pays d'en haut*'. 'It matters little', Routhier wrote to Casgrain, 'whether your great-grandfather was Casgrain the sabre-scarred veteran or Casgrain the sausage-vendor.' Casgrain's family home here, which often figures in his work, was the Manoir d'Airvault, also called the Manoir Casgrain.

Born in Rivière-Ouelle in 1905, Rodolphe Dubé has published all his many works under the pseudonym 'François Hertel'. He entered the Jesuit order in 1920 and was ordained in 1938 but left the priesthood in 1946 and moved a year later to France, where he now lives. Dubé is the author of four novels, two collections of short stories, and several philosophical works, as well as volumes of travel and autobiography. He is primarily a poet, however; his *Poèmes d'hier et d'aujourd'hui* (1967) gathers 100 poems from twelve collections published both before and after his self-exile from Quebec.

The Manoir Casgrain, Rivière-Ouelle

ROBERVAL

The French novelist **Louis Hémon** stayed briefly in Roberval on his travels in the Lac St-Jean region, from which he drew *Maria Chapdelaine*. He left MONTREAL (12) in mid-June 1912, paused briefly at LA TUQUE, and was in Roberval by 24 June. Here he stayed at the Hôtel Commercial, which was where the Roberval hospital now stands. By 13 July Hémon was in PÉRIBONKA.

RUPERT'S HOUSE

The novelist and nature writer **Fred Bodsworth** often visited this trading post on the eastern shore of James Bay during the 1950s while on assignment for *Maclean's*. He based the setting of his novel *The Strange One* (1959) on Rupert's House—which was founded in 1668 as the first Hudson's Bay Company fur-trading post and is still in operation—but moved his fictional settlement from the Quebec side of the Bay to the western shore, which lies in Ontario. Bodsworth's novel symbolically interweaves a romance between a Cree woman and a Hebridean biologist with the story of the mating of a Canada goose with a Hebridean barnacle goose. (See also TORONTO: 6.)

STE-ADÈLE

The novelist **Claude-Henri Grignon** was born in 1894 in this picturesque town, which is now a writers' and artists' colony. Grignon was educated partly at home, but from his high-school years until 1936 he lived mostly in Montreal, working there as a civil servant. In 1936 he returned to his native region, where until 1943 he published the important periodical *Les Pamphlets de Valdombre*, using his pseudonym 'Valdombre'. He was also mayor of Ste-Adèle from 1941 to 1951 and prefect of Terrebonne County. His important novel, *Un Homme et son péché* (1933; trans. by Yves Brunelle, *The Woman and the Miser*, 1978), written during his residence in Montreal, is a naturalistic evocation of the life of rural people in the Ste-Adèle region. The story of a miser, Séraphin Poudrier, it has been reprinted many times, was made into two films, and provided the basis for serials on both radio (1939–65) and television (1956–70).

The Village de Séraphin, two miles north of Ste-Adèle on Hwy 117, is a reconstructed nineteenth-century rural community that depicts Grignon's book and the way of life it describes. Séraphin's house conforms to descriptions in the novel. One house, L'auberge Joe Maltère, has been here since about 1850; other houses were moved here from other Quebec locations or have been newly built.

Grignon's other works include *Le Déserteur et autres récits de la terre* (1934) and *Précisions sur 'Un Homme et son péché'* (1936). This defence of the book's realism declares that it was based on actual events and persons in the Ste-Adèle area.

The popular novelist, short-story writer, critic, and television writer **Claude Jasmin** has a home here. A native of MONTREAL (18), he has written about Ste-Adèle in *Sainte-Adèle-la-vaisselle* (1974), a nostalgic autobiographical work that evokes a ten-month period in 1951 when the adolescent Jasmin worked here as a *laveur de vaisselle*—a dishwasher; Jasmin has also portrayed the Laurentian foothills area around Ste-Adèle in a book of fables for children, *Les Contes du Sommet-Bleu* (1980; trans. *The Dragon and Other Laurentian Tales*, 1987).

STE-AGATHE

André Breton, the French poet and father of the Surrealist movement, who was in exile in New York City from 1941 to 1946, lived at Ste-Agathe during part of the period from 20 Aug. to 20 Oct. 1944. There, and at PERCÉ, where he visited the Bonaventure Island and Percé Rock bird sanctuaries, he wrote one of his major prose works, *Arcane 17* (1945), which mingles visionary prose, autobiography, occultism, and criticism of Quebec culture. The title of Breton's book alludes to the seventeenth arcanum of the Tarot card deck, the Star, which represents the author's theme of hope and regeneration.

Ste-Agathe was the birthplace in 1928 of **Gaston Miron**, perhaps the most influential contemporary French-Canadian poet. (See MONTREAL: 18.)

ST-ALBAN

The family of poet **Alain Grandbois** had a summer home on a small lake near St-Alban, just northeast of the poet's home town, ST-CASIMIR-DE-PORTNEUF. Grandbois spent all his childhood summers at the lake—then called Lac Clair, but known today as Lac des Frères because of the monastic houses established on its shores. The lake and its environs had a permanent influence on Grandbois's poetry; in his first major collection, *Les Îles de la nuit* (1944), the poem 'Avec ta robe' alludes to an island in the lake as 'l'île de mon enfance'. Lac Clair appears as 'Lac Cristal' in a volume of short stories, *Marie de l'Hospice* (1945), by the poet's sister, **Madeleine Grandbois**. (See also DESCHAMBAULT, MONTREAL: 15, MONT-ROLLAND, QUEBEC CITY; CHARLOTTETOWN, PEI.)

STE-ANNE-DE-BELLEVUE

During the eighteenth and nineteenth centuries the 'fur brigades' of the great trading companies gathered here every year before heading west via the Ottawa River—an event described in the Irish poet **Thomas Moore**'s 'A Canadian Boat Song':

Faintly as tolls the evening chime,
Our voices keep tune and our oars keep time.
Soon as the woods on shore look dim,
We'll sing at St. Ann's our parting hymn.
Row, brothers, row, the stream runs fast,
The Rapids are near, and the daylight's past.

Moore visited Canada in 1804 and is said to have written his poem at Ste-Anne; set to music, it became one of the most popular nineteenth-century drawing-room ballads. (Another 'Canadian Boat Song', generally known by its subtitle, 'The Lone Sheiling', was published anonymously in Scotland in 1829 and has been attributed to, among others, John Galt and William 'Tiger' Dunlop; see CAMBRIDGE, Ont.; PLEASANT BAY, N.S.) At 153 rue Sainte-Anne is the Maison Thomas Moore, where Moore is thought to have stayed and where he may have written 'A Canadian Boat Song' and several other poems inspired by his Canadian visit; the house dates from 1798 and has been designated a provincial historic site. Moore was the guest here of the fur trader and explorer Simon Fraser, who built the house.

After graduating from high school in MONTREAL (5), the poet **Irving Layton** attended MacDonald College here during the years 1933–9, graduating with a B.Sc. degree in agriculture. Ste-Anne-de-Bellevue is on Hwy 401 just west of Montreal.

ST-CASIMIR-DE-PORTNEUF

On 25 May 1900 the poet **Alain Grandbois** was born in St-Casimir, a village pleasantly situated at the confluence of the Ste-Anne and Blanche Rivers. Grandbois spent his childhood and received his early education here, before attending high school, university, and law school in MONTREAL (15), QUEBEC CITY; CHARLOTTETOWN, P.E.I., and Paris. One of French Canada's most respected and influential modern poets, Grandbois did not publish his first major collection until 1944, when *Les Îles de la nuit* appeared; other important volumes of poems include *Rivages de l'homme* (1948), *L'Etoile pourpre* (1957), and the collected *Poèmes* (1963). *Selected Poems*, a selection of Grandbois's poems translated by Peter Miller, appeared in 1965. Grandbois also wrote many prose works, including *Les Voyages de Marco Polo* (1941). Among his honours are the Prix David, which he won three times, the Prix Duvernay (twice), and the Lorne Pierce Medal. The house where he was born, at 145 rue Tessier ouest, bears a plaque placed there by the Société des Poètes canadiens-français. (See also DESCHAMBAULT, MONT-ROLLAND, ST-ALBAN.)

STE-CATHERINE-DE-FOSSAMBAULT

This pleasant old village 25 miles northwest of Quebec City is associated with two prominent figures in French-Canadian literature:

Anne Hébert

Hector de Saint-Denys Garneau and Anne Hébert.

Born on 13 June 1912 in Montreal, Saint-Denys Garneau lived in Ste-Catherine from 1916 to 1922; the house his family bought here was the ancestral manor of Senator Antoine Juchereau-Duchesnay. Through his mother, Saint-Denys Garneau was a descendant of this ancient Quebec family, a member of which had received a seigneury for heroic action during the siege of Quebec City in 1690. On his father's side he was the grandson of the poet Alfred Garneau and the great-grandson of French Canada's pre-eminent historian, François-Xavier Garneau. From 1922 to 1939 Saint-Denys Garneau lived mainly in Montreal, where he was educated; in 1928 he suffered a serious illness that damaged his heart and forced him to withdraw temporarily from school and then to abandon his formal studies permanently in 1932. All of his work—consisting of a single book of poems, *Regards et jeux dans l'espace* (1937), the posthumously published *Poésies complètes*, and his *Journal* (1954)—was produced during the years 1935–9. Prey to a sense of guilt and self-doubt, he retired increasingly to his family's manor house at Ste-Catherine. He spent the winters of 1940 and 1941 there alone, and from 1941 until his death in 1943 lived there entirely. On 24 Oct. 1943, after a dinner party with family friends, he set out by canoe for an island where he had begun to build a small cabin. He suffered a heart attack en route but made his way to shore and went to the home of a farmer named Boucher to call his parents; the man, however, had no telephone, and Saint-Denys Garneau left. The next day some children found him lying dead near a small creek, his feet nearly frozen. Heart failure was the cause of his death at thirty-two. Garneau's writings were translated by John Glassco: the *Journal* in 1962 and the *Complete Poems* in 1975. (See also MONTREAL: 14.)

> SAINT-CATHERINE-DE-FOSSAMBAULT
>
> *When you look north from Quebec, to the north and north-west, your eyes glide over a wide valley, following it up the gentle incline to the Laurentian mountains bounding the horizon. Your gaze is led to the soft undulations of those peaks and remains hovering there in suspense. Boundless space lies beyond, mysteriously hidden and beckoning to us with a vague, enchanting appeal. Before this view we understand the* coureurs de bois, *those who have known already and for all time what leavetaking is—and why tarry now?*
>
> —Hector de Saint-Denys Garneau, *Journal* (1954; tr. John Glassco, 1962)

Garneau's cousin, **Anne Hébert**, was born here on 1 Aug. 1916, the daughter of a civil servant and literary critic, Maurice Hébert. She was educated almost exclusively by her parents; illness in childhood caused her to lead a reclusive life in Quebec City and in the village, where she spent four successive years of retirement in her family's summer home. At Ste-Catherine she was closely acquainted with Saint-Denys Garneau, and her work was affected by both his poetry and his sudden death. In the 1950s Anne Hébert worked for Radio Canada and the National Film Board, and began to make extended trips to Paris, where she has lived since the mid-1960s. Her poetry has been collected in *Les Songes en équilibre* (1942; winner of Quebec's Prix David), *Le Tombeau des rois* (1953), and *Poèmes* (1960; winner of a Governor General's Award). She has published short stories and plays but is best known for her five novels, three of which are set in Quebec: *Kamouraska* (1970), based on historical events in the village of KAMOURASKA (and giving rise to a 1973 film directed by Claude Jutra); *Les Enfants du sabbat* (1975), set in the 1930s and 1940s in the countryside outside Quebec City and based on research into local witchcraft practices; and *Les Fous de Bassan* (1982), a tale of violence set in a fictional Gaspé village, Griffin Creek. All have been published in English: as *Kamouraska* (1974), *Children of the Black Sabbath* (1978), and *Héloise* (1982). (See also QUEBEC CITY.) Complete translations of her two mature books of poems have been made by Alan Brown (1975) and A. Poulin Jr.

(1980); F.R. Scott published his influential translations of both Garneau and Hébert in *Saint-Denys Garneau and Anne Hébert* (1962) and *Poems of French Canada* (1977).

ST-DENIS

Sir **Thomas Chapais**, knighted in 1935 for his writings as a historian, was born here in 1858, a son of Jean-Charles Chapais, minister of agriculture in the first Dominion government and a Senator. Thomas Chapais was also a prominent public figure; a professor of history at the Université Laval, he was a conservative political theorist, editor of *Le courrier du Canada* in *1884–1901*, a Quebec senator, and member of three Quebec provincial administrations. His historical works include *Cours d'histoire du Canada: 1760–1867* (8 vols, 1919–33) and, in English, *The Great Intendant: A Chronicle of Jean Talon in Canada* (1914), based on an earlier work in French. A monument to Chapais stands in Saint-Denis near his former home; he died in 1946.

In 1968 the novelist **Yves Thériault** bought a small farm here that was his home in 1970 when he suffered a severe cerebral thrombosis that left him unable to speak or write. His difficult convalescence required several years; during and after his illness he lived at MONTREAL (16) and RAWDON. In 1968, the year he arrived here, Thériault published six books. While living here he wrote several of the novels that appeared from 1969 through 1976. These include *Antoine et sa montagne* (1969); set in 1835, it is about the conditions and events leading to the Rebellion of 1837 as experienced in a Richelieu River village, like St-Denis. St-Denis is northeast of Montreal on the Richelieu River and Hwy 133. A large statue of a *patriote* in a park here commemorates 12 men killed in the first fighting of the Rebellion, which occurred on 23 Nov. 1837. A cairn marks the battle's site, Maison Saint-German (gone), where *patriotes* under Dr Wolfred Nelson withstood a superior British force.

ST-ÉLIE-D'ORFORD

This farming and lumbering village near Sherbrooke was the birthplace on 5 Oct. 1901 of the poet **Alfred DesRochers**. His family moved away from St-Élie in 1904 but returned in 1907, and DesRochers, who lived here until 1914, received his early education in the village school. His second and best-known book, *À l'ombre de l'Orford* (1929), includes poems that describe and celebrate the annual round of travel into the forests and the work of St-Élie's lumbermen. It was awarded Quebec's Prix David in 1932; a third edition (1948) contained thirteen sonnets about St-Élie entitled 'Cycle du village' and the poem 'Ma patrie'. DesRocher's other books include *L'Offrande aux vierges folles* (1928), *Oeuvres poétiques* (1977), and a book of critical essays, *Paragraphes: entrevues littéraires* (1931). (See also SHERBROOKE.)

ST-EUSTACHE

The death of his father forced the young **William Henry Drummond** to interrupt his high-school education in Montreal and take a job in 1869 as a telegraph operator in this town on the St Lawrence, west of Montreal at the mouth of the Rivière des Mille Îles. He worked here until he could afford to resume his schooling in Montreal in 1876, at the age of twenty-two; in 1884 he earned a medical degree from Bishop's College. While at St-Eustache he made frequent visits to nearby Bord-à-Plouffe, a lumbering town on the Rivière des Prairies, that introduced Drummond to the oral poetic tradition of French-Canadian lumbermen, which he incorporated in dialect verse that became very popular. From Gédéon Plouffe he heard the legend of the shipwreck of a lumber scow on LAC ST-PIERRE, which he retold in 'The Wreck of the Julie Plante'. This and other poems were widely circulated in Canadian and American magazines before their publication in book form in *The Habitant and Other French-Canadian Poems* (1897). (See also KNOWLTON, MONTREAL: 2, STORNOWAY; COBALT, Ont.)

ST-GÉDÉON

For three weeks in Jan. and Feb. 1913 the novelist **Louis Hémon** lived in this village of fewer than 1,000 persons on the east shore of Lac St-Jean, south of Alma. His lodging was in a boarding house, long since demolished, that was owned by a man named Johnny Tremblay and was patronized by salesmen. Hémon left here some time after 9 Feb. (although he may have returned later for part of that month) to find a job in KÉNOGAMI. At St-Gédéon he worked on *Maria Chapdelaine* (first published in book form in 1916), which he had begun in notes and drafts made while he was living at PÉRIBONKA. It is at Saint-Gédéon that Hémon places the farm where the mother of his heroine, Maria, was born.

ST-GRÉGOIRE-D'IBERVILLE

The poet **Rina Lasnier** was born on 6 Aug. 1915 in St-Grégoire d'Iberville, which is southeast of Montreal in the Eastern Townships on Hwy 219. Lasnier moved to the city with her family as a child and attended school there, graduating from the Université de Montréal in 1930. A journalist for many years, she has also published several books of poetry, including *La Salle des rêves* (1971), which won the first A.J.M. Smith prize for Canadian poetry; and stories and plays, which have received many awards, including the Prix David (1943 and 1974) and the Prix Duvernay (1957). She now lives in JOLIETTE, north of Montreal.

ST-HILAIRE

After receiving his medical degree in 1886, the novelist **Ernest Choquette** practised medicine here until his death in Montreal in 1941. He was elected mayor of the village several times and in 1910 was appointed to the Quebec legislative council. A novelist of rural life, Choquette confined his literary career to the years between 1895 and 1910, although his last novel, *La Terre*, did not appear until 1916. His other novels are *Les Ribaud: une idylle de 37* (1898), a story of the *Patriote* rebellion, and *Claude Paysan* (1899). A book of stories and sketches, *Carabinades* (1900), reflects his experience as a country doctor at St-Hilaire, which lies on the east bank of the Richelieu River opposite BELOEIL, Choquette's birthplace.

ST-IRÉNÉE

This village of fewer than 800 persons, located southwest of La Malbaie on the St Lawrence River, was for many years the home of Sir **Adolphe-Basile Routhier**, jurist, novelist, poet, and writer. Routhier is best known as the author of 'Chant national'. He wrote it in 1880 and it was set to music by Calixa Lavallée later in the year. The poem appeared in Routhier's collection, *Les Échos* (1882). In an English translation by R. Stanley Weir (1908) it became known as 'O Canada'. With a modified English text and the original French words, it was officially adopted as Canada's national anthem in 1975. Routhier's house is a historic site. (See also CARILLON, QUEBEC CITY, ST-PLACIDE.)

ST-JEAN-PORT-JOLI

Philippe-Joseph Aubert de Gaspé, who in his old age wrote two of the most notable books in nineteenth-century French-Canada, is buried in the magnificent parish church of St-Jean-Port-Joli. He was the last of the ancient seigneurial line of Port-Joli and is

The mill on the property of Aubert de Gaspé, Saint-Jean-Port-Joli

memorialized by a marble plaque that marks his seigneurial pew in the church. A brass plaque elsewhere in the church lists his forebears, the seigneurs of Port-Joli and their wives, back to 1633.

Born in 1786 in QUEBEC CITY, Aubert de Gaspé spent his childhood at his family's ancestral manor at St-Jean-Port-Joli. He became a lawyer in 1811 and in 1816 was made sheriff of Quebec City, but was removed from office in 1822 owing to debt. Thenceforth he divided his time between St-Jean-Port-Joli and Quebec City, where in the 1850s and 1860s he was a member of the literary group that met in Octave Crémazie's bookstore. In 1837 his son **Philippe-Ignace-François Aubert de Gaspé** (1814–41) published *L'Influence d'un livre*, generally considered the first French-Canadian novel; the elder Aubert de Gaspé is thought to have contributed at least one chapter to it.

In 1863, at seventy-seven, Aubert de Gaspé published his historical novel *Les Anciens Canadiens*, a romance of the Seven Years' War in Quebec that draws on his own and his family's reminiscences to recreate the folk-ways, traditions, and seigneurial way of life of eighteenth-century Quebec. A translation by Charles G.D. Roberts, *Canadians of Old*, first published in 1905, is still in print. Aubert de Gaspé's *Mémoires* (1866), another fascinating document of social history, is even more successful as literature because the septuagenarian author was not hampered by unfamiliar novelistic conventions but was free to indulge his rambling style. Aubert de Gaspé died in Quebec City on 29 Jan. 1871 and was brought to his ancestral home for burial. Because his son had predeceased him, the seigneurial line of Port-Joli came to an end.

Both St-Jean-Port-Joli and its church, which stands prominently at a curve in Hwy 132, west of the village, are famous for the traditional Quebec wood sculptures they display. About two miles west of the village stands the Musée des anciens Canadiens; inspired by Aubert de Gaspé and his famous novel and recalling the region's history, it is open from June to November. The Aubert de Gaspé seigneurial manor is gone, but a plaque in the village now marks its location. The first manor was burnt down by the English in 1759. The second manor, the author's home, was built soon afterwards and some of its ruins were visible into the early twentieth century.

SAINT-JEAN-PORT-JOLI

The Seignorial manor, situated between the river St. Lawrence and the promontory, was only separated from the latter, by a large courtyard, the royalty road and the grove. It was a one-storied building with a steep roof, a hundred feet long, and flanked by two wings of fifteen feet, each projecting into the principal courtyard. A bake-house adjoining the kitchen to the north-east, served also as a wash-house. A little summer house, contiguous to a large drawing room to the south-west, gave some appearance of regularity to this mannor built after the old Canadian fashion. Two other out-buildings to the south-east, served, the one, as a dairy, and the other as a second laundry, containing a well which communicated by means of a water-pipe with the kitchen of the main building. Coach-houses, barns and stables, five little out-houses of which three were in the grove, a kitchen garden to the south-east of the manor, two orchards, one to the north, and the other to the north-east, completed a picture which will give some idea of this Canadian seigniorial residence, which the habitants *used to call the d'Haberville* village.

—Philippe Aubert de Gaspé (père), *Les Anciens Canadiens* (1863; tr. Georgina M. Pennée, 1864)

ST-JÉRÔME-DE-TERREBONNE

Several distinguished writers have been associated with St-Jérôme. It was the home of the de Montigny family and the birthplace on 1 Dec. 1876 of **Louvigny Testard de Montigny**, who spent only his earliest childhood here. De Montigny was one of the principal founders of the *École littéraire de Montréal* (see MONTREAL: 10) and a journalist in that city until he went to OTTAWA in 1910 as a translator to the Senate. His most important books include *La Langue française au Canada* (1916) and a collection of his plays, *L'Épi rouge* (1953). De Montigny's older brother, **Henri-Gaston**, who was born here on 27 May 1870, also became a writer and journalist in Montreal, co-founding with his brother the newspaper *Les Debats*. A collection of his prose poems and other writings was published posthumously as *L'Étoffe du pays* (1951). The father, **Benjamin Gaston Testard de Montigny**, was born here on 6 Oct. 1838 and was a prominent public figure and lawyer as well as a writer on legal and economic subjects. In 1873 he was appointed magistrate of Terrebonne, and in 1880 the family moved to Montreal, where he was city recorder. His works include *Histoire du droit canadien* (1869) and *La Colonisation: Le Nord* (1886).

The novelist **Germaine Guèvremont** was born Germaine Grignon in St-Jérôme in 1893 and received her early education here before completing her schooling in Montreal and Toronto. (She was a cousin of the novelist Claude-Henri Grignon, a native of nearby STE-ADÈLE.) After her marriage in 1916 Guèvremont lived in SOREL, which provides the background for her two well-known books, *Le Survenant* (1945) and *Marie-Didace* (1947); they were translated together as *The Outlanders* (1950), which won a Governor General's Award. She died in 1968.

Gratien Gélinas, the author of *Tit-Coq* (1950) and the founder of modern Quebec drama, received part of his elementary education at the Collège des Frères des Écoles (Brothers of the Christian Schools) in the early 1920s (see also MONTREAL: 17, OKA, ST-TITE-DE-CHAMPLAIN, TERREBONNE). A little earlier the writer and botanist Frère **Marie-Victorin** (Conrad Kirouac), a member of the same order, had held his first teaching position at this institution. It was here that he first began to pay systematic attention to the flora of Quebec, during an illness that forced him to retire temporarily from teaching; he subsequently became a distinguished botanist, professor of botany at Université de Montréal, founder of that city's famous Botanical Gardens, and author of many works on Quebec plant life. His creative works include *Récits laurentiens* (1919), trans. by James Ferres as *The Chopping Bee and Other Laurentian Stories* (1920). (See also LONGUEUIL, MONTREAL: 15, QUEBEC CITY.)

ST-JOSEPH-DE-LA-RIVE

Félix-Antoine Savard—priest, novelist, poet, and folklorist—established and for many years directed La Papeterie Saint-Gilles in this village on the north shore of the St Lawrence, opposite Île-aux-Coudres. The only mill in Canada employed in the hand manufacture of fine parchment-like paper, rivalling the chiné papers of France, China, and Japan, La Papeterie Saint-Gilles is one of several economic contributions Savard made to the Charlevoix region of northeastern Quebec. The area has been known as 'le pays de Menaud' since the publication in 1937 of his classic novel *Menaud, maître-draveur*, set in the La Malbaie area (see CLERMONT). La Papeterie Saint-Gilles is located at 304 rue Principale.

Savard lived here during his years as a teacher at Université Laval (1943–57). His *presbytère* was at 252 chemin de l'Eglise. After retiring from Laval he lived permanently at St-Joseph-de-la-Rive until his last three years, when illness forced him to return to QUEBEC CITY, where he died on 24 Aug. 1982. It was in St-Joseph-de-la-Rive that Savard wrote all his later works, including *Le Barachois* (1959), *Martin et le pauvre* (1959), *La Folle* (1960), and two two-volume works of autobiography: *Journal et Souvenirs* (1973, 1975) and *Carnet du soir intérieur* (1978, 1979). He is buried in the cemetery here.

STE-JUSTINE-DE-DORCHESTER

Novelist **Roch Carrier** was born in 1937 in this village in the Beauce area, south of Quebec City. Although he has lived elsewhere since completing high school—primarily in MONTREAL (16) and Longueuil—his hometown and region gave him a primary setting for his novels, including his first and most famous, *La Guerre, yes sir!* (1968; trans. by Sheila Fischman, 1970). Carrier's return to Ste-Justine in 1971 for the filming of a CBC documentary on his life and work, *The Ungrateful Land*, included a visit with his ninety-year-old grandfather, whose barn was a filming site. The experience gave rise to the novel *Il n'y a pas de pays sans grand-père* (1979) and to many of the stories in *Les Enfants du bonhomme dans la lune* (1979). These works have been translated by Sheila Fischman as *No Country Without Grandfathers* (1981) and *The Hockey Sweater and Other Stories* (1979).

ST-LAMBERT

Jacques Ferron, who lived and practised medicine for three decades in neighbouring LONGUEUIL, spent his last years in St-Lambert, on Oak Street; he died on 5 Jan. 1985. His later books include, notably, *Gaspé-Mattempa* (1980), which draws on his pre-Longueuil medical practice at RIVIÈRE-LA-MADELEINE in the Gaspé during the years 1946–9. Ferron won a Governor General's Award for his *Contes du pays incertain* (1962), selections from which were translated by Betty Bednarski as *Tales from the Uncertain Country* (1972). (See also LOUISEVILLE, MONTREAL: 18, TROIS-RIVIÈRES.)

STE-MARIE-DE-LA-BEAUCE

Ste-Marie, at the northern tip of Beauce County, was the birthplace on 5 Mar. 1883 of **Marius Barbeau**, the founder of modern folklore studies in Canada. Barbeau spent his childhood here before beginning his formal education at twelve; he graduated from the Collège de STE-ANNE-DE-LA-POCATIÈRE and from Université Laval, QUEBEC CITY. After further studies at Oxford University he settled in OTTAWA, where he lived from 1911 until his death in 1969. Barbeau wrote more than 100 books and pamphlets on folkloric subjects and collaborated on 60 more, as well as producing 600 journal articles. He used his knowledge of Indian culture in two novels: *The Downfall of Temlaham* (1928) and *Mountain Cloud* (1944).

STE-MARIE-DE-MONNOIR

The seigneury of Ste-Marie-de-Monnoir, today a tiny hamlet in Rouville County south of Montreal, is the setting of the novel *The Curé of St. Philippe: A Story of French-Canadian Politics* (1899; rpt. 1970) by **Francis William Grey** (1860–1939). A first cousin of the fourth Earl Grey (Governor General of Canada from 1904 to 1911), Grey emigrated from England to the United Sates, and while teaching in New York in 1885 married Jessie Rolland, daughter of Charles Octave Rolland, seigneur of Ste-Marie-de-Monnoir. It is not known how much time Grey spent at Ste-Marie, or if he ever lived in the district, but his novel shows an intimate acquaintance with the people, society, and politics of the Richelieu River region of Quebec in the 1890s. Grey worked from 1903 to 1913 in Ottawa, and in later life lived in Edinburgh, where he died. Also a poet and a playwright, Grey received the honorary degree of Doctor of Letters from the University of Ottawa in 1908.

ST-PLACIDE

A plaque marks the childhood home of Sir **Adolphe-Basile Routhier**, who was born and spent his childhood in this village on the north shore of the Ottawa River, west of Laval. The house, located on Hwy 344, which forms the main street of St-Placide, was the Routhier family home from 1847, the year of its construction, and has been designated a provincial historic monument. A noted jurist as well as a writer, Routhier is best remembered as the author of 'Chant national', a poem written in 1880 to a tune by Calixa Lavallée that is now the French version of 'O Canada' (see also CARILLON). Routhier's works include the volume of poems in which 'Chant national' appeared, *Les Échos* (1882), and two novels—*Le Centurion: roman des temps messianiques* (1909) and *Paulina: roman des temps apostoliques* (1918)—that were principally fictional embellishments of New Testament stories.

ST-SAVEUR-DES-MONTS

The novelist **Léo-Paul Desrosiers** made his home in this Terrebonne County village from 1952, when he retired from the public library in MONTREAL (15), until his death in 1967. The main work that he wrote here was a trilogy of novels expressing his philosophical and social-political views. Published in 1958–60, it has the overall title of its first volume, *Vous qui passez*; the second and third novels are subtitled *Les Angoisses et les Tourments* and *Rafales sur les cimes*. Here Desrosiers also wrote his study of Montreal's pioneer educator, Marguerite Bourgeoys, *Les Dialogues de Marthe et Marie* (1957). (See also OTTAWA.)

ST-TITE-DE-CHAMPLAIN

The actor and playwright **Gratien Gélinas**, author of *Tit-Coq* (trans., 1967) and *Bousille et les justes* (trans., 1961), was born here on 8 Dec. 1909. The town is on Hwy 159, about 30 miles north of Trois-Rivières. Gélinas grew up in MONTREAL (17). After several years of performing in amateur theatre troupes he played the role of 'Lionel Théberge' in the first Radio-Canada serial, *Le Curé de village* (1936), by Robert Choquette. Remembered particularly for his radio and stage appearances as 'Fridolin', which Gélinas made the centre of an annual revue from 1938 to 1946 at the Théâtre Monument National, he was chairman of the Canadian Film Development Corporation from 1969 to 1977. He now lives in OKA, near Montreal.

SHERBROOKE

Sherbrooke is the largest city in the Eastern Townships of Quebec. The novelist **Margaret Murray Robertson**, born in Scotland in 1823, lived here from 1836 to 1873. Her father was the pastor of Sherbrooke's Congregational Church, and she taught at the Sherbrooke Academy. Between 1864 and 1889 she published twelve novels on Christian moral themes, most of them set in Scotland and North America; in 1873 she moved to Montreal, where she died in 1897. Her novel *The Bairns; or Janet's Love and Service, A Story from Canada* (1870) is set partly in the Eastern Townships. The poet **Louise Morey Bowman**, born in 1882, was a lifelong Sherbrooke resident. A friend of the poet Frank Oliver Call (see LENNOXVILLE), she was an early champion of Imagism and the poetry of Ezra Pound in Canada; her books include *Moonlight and Common Day* (1922) and *Characters in Cadence* (1938).

Sherbrooke was the primary scene of the life and literary activity of the poet **Alfred DesRochers**. Born in ST-ÉLIE D'ORFORD in 1901, he came to Sherbrooke four years after ending his formal education in TROIS-RIVIÈRES in 1921. (He had spent several years of his adolescence here as an apprentice typesetter.) In 1925 he joined the newspaper *La Tribune* (1950 rue Roy) as a proofreader, then became a sportswriter and ultimately a translator. During his first years with *La Tribune* he published his early poems in the newspaper's women's pages. DesRochers lived in Sherbrooke and worked for *La Tribune* until 1952, with the exception of two periods: 1927–8, when he founded and operated his own weekly newspaper in COATICOOK, and 1942–6, when war service and a year of work in OTTAWA kept him away. In the late forties he lived at 15 rue Pacifique, and in the early fifties at 477 South Boven St. In 1953 he moved to MONTREAL (18) as a translator for Canadian Press. DesRochers, whose most characteristic work dates from his years in Sherbrooke and Coaticook, is one of Quebec's most important writers of the period between the wars. His major works are his first collection of poems, *L'Offrande aux vierges folles* (1928), *À l'ombre de l'Orford* (1929, winner of the Prix David in 1932), and an expanded third edition of the latter book, published in 1948. DesRochers's last major work, *Élégies pour l'épouse enallée* (1967), was written after the death in 1964 of his wife, the former Rose-Alma Brault, whom he married in Sherbrooke in 1925. He was awarded an honorary doctorate by Université de Sherbrooke in 1967. He died in Montreal in 1978.

Northrop Frye was born in Sherbrooke on 14 July 1912, a son of Herman Edward Frye, a salesman, and the former Catherine Maud Howard, a high-school teacher who had taught at Stanstead Collegiate, and who taught Frye to read and to play the piano by the time he was three. Early in Frye's life the family was shaken by the death of his elder brother in the First World War: he was killed by what is believed to have been the first bomb ever dropped from an airplane in combat. The family left Sherbrooke in 1917 and settled in MONCTON, N.B., the following year; Frye's career as an eminent literary critic, however, is associated almost wholly with TORONTO (3). His major books include *Anatomy of Criticism* (1957), *The Great Code* (1982), and *The Bush Garden* (1971), a collection of book reviews and essays about Canadian culture in which he speaks of spending his childhood and youth in two bilingual cities. (See also WINNIPEG, Man.)

Another important critic who is a native of Sherbrooke is **Gilles Marcotte**, who was born here in 1925. His career is primarily associated with Montreal, where he has been a professor at Université de Montréal since 1966. His critical works include *Une Littérature qui se fait* (1962). His novel *Le Poids de Dieu* (1962) has been translated by Elizabeth Abbott as *The Burden of God* (1964).

A native of Montreal, **Ronald Sutherland** has taught English at Université de Sherbrooke since 1959 and was chairman of its English Department from 1962 to 1974. He founded the university's graduate program in comparative Canadian literature in 1963. His novels include *Snow Lake* (1971) and *Where Do the MacDonalds Bury Their Dead?* (1976). Since 1963 the poet **D.G. Jones** (*A Throw of Particles*, 1983) has been a professor at Université de Sherbrooke, where in 1969 he founded Canada's only bilingual literary magazine, *Ellipse*, in which texts by English- and French-Canadian writers are printed in both languages. Both Sutherland and Jones are currently residents of NORTH HATLEY. The university's art gallery houses works by the poet and painter **Roland Giguère**, a native of MONTREAL (18) and former resident of North Hatley.

SOREL

Standish O'Grady, a Church of Ireland minister and early Canadian poet, settled on a farm here in 1836 and in 1841 published his only work, *The Emigrant*, a poem of more than 1,000 heroic couplets. The book also contained occasional poems, including 'Old Nick in Sorel'.

Sorel was the birthplace on 21 Oct. 1871 of the painter and poet **Charles Gill**, author of the uncompleted 'Le Cap Éternité', an epic-scale poem set on the Saguenay River. In Gill's childhood his family's home was at 80 rue Georges. Primarily an allegorical painter, Gill spent the years 1890–5 in Paris, studying under Jean-Léon Gérôme at the École des Beaux Arts and frequenting the Café Procope, where Verlaine sat enthroned. After returning to Canada he became a leading member of the *École littéraire de Montreal* and a friend of such literary figures as the poet Albert Lozeau and the novelist Albert Laberge. Gill taught art in MONTREAL (11) and did much of his own painting and writing at his parent's home in PIERREVILLE. He died in the 1918 influenza epidemic, and his writings were collected in *Le Cap Éternité: poème suivi des Étoiles filantes* (1919). (See also CHICOUTIMI, PIERREVILLE.)

The novelist **Germaine Guèvremont**, born in ST-JÉRÔME in 1893, came to Sorel in 1928 and lived here until 1935, when she moved to MONTREAL (15). She worked as a journalist for *Le Courrier de Sorel* and absorbed the impressions that became the material of her literary career. The rural people of the Sorel area and of the agricultural Sorel Islands in the Chenal du Moine (Monk's Channel) region of the St Lawrence are the subject of *En pleine terre* (1942), stories and sketches, and of *Le Survenant* (1945) and its sequel *Marie-Didace* (1947). *Le Survenant* received the Prix Duvernay, the Prix David, the French Prix Olivier-de-Serres and, in 1950, when it was combined with *Marie-Didace* and translated into English as *The Outlanders*, the Governor General's Award. Guèvremont was a cousin of Claude-Henri Grignon (see STE-ADÈLE).

STANSTEAD

The critic **William Arthur Deacon**, born in 1890 in PEMBROKE, Ont., lived in Stanstead from 1891 to 1907, when he graduated from Stanstead College, a private co-educational secondary school founded in 1872. Deacon then attended the University of Toronto and the University of Manitoba. As a literary critic he was associated with *Saturday Night* and the *Mail and Empire* (later the *Globe and Mail*), TORONTO (2, 6). The

The childhood home of William Arthur Deacon, Stanstead

poet **Duncan Campbell Scott**, born in 1862 in OTTAWA, received his high-school education at Stanstead College during the 1870s. He returned to Ottawa in 1879 to begin work in the civil service as a clerk in the Indian Branch (later the Department of Indian Affairs).

STORNOWAY

William Henry Drummond's first practice as a country doctor, which he held until 1885, was in this small village northwest of Lake Megantic on Hwy 161. Known in school as an athlete, he is remembered in local legend for fighting and defeating a Scottish bully named 'Red John', who challenged his athletic ability. In 1885 Drummond—who wrote dialect poems about French-Canadian *habitant* life that became very popular—bought the practice of a retiring physician at KNOWLTON in Brome County. (See also MONTREAL: 2, ST-EUSTACHE; COBALT, Ont.

TERREBONNE

Gratien Gélinas, the founder of modern theatre in Quebec, attended the École Séconddaire Saint-Sacrement, 901 rue Saint-Louis; he went from here to the Collège de Montréal, where he completed his senior matriculation in 1929. Gélinas's best-known play is the ground-breaking *Tit-Coq* (1950; trans. by Kenneth Johnstone and Gélinas, 1967), which used working-class French vernacular in a story about Quebec social conditions and the pressures on French Canada from the surrounding English-Canadian and American societies. Terrebonne is in the southeastern corner of Terrebonne County. (See also MONTREAL: 17, OKA, ST-JÉRÔME-DE-TERREBONNE, ST-TITE-DE-CHAMPLAIN.)

THETFORD MINES

Under the fictional name of 'Macklin', Thetford Mines is the setting of **André Langevin**'s famous novel *Poussière sur la ville* (1953; trans. by John Latrobe and Robert Gottlieb, *Dust over the City*, 1955). The book centres on a doctor and his efforts on behalf of the downtrodden working people of the mining town. (Langevin's wife is the daughter of a Thetford Mines doctor.) In 1965 *Poussière sur la ville* was made into a film, which was shot in Thetford Mines. (See also MONTREAL: 16.)

TROIS-RIVIÈRES

A monument in Champlain Park, at rue Royale and rue Radisson, honours several men of letters and poets associated with Trois-Rivières. It features a 2½-foot bust of **Benjamin Sulte**, a historian of French Canada and of the Trois-Rivières region in particular, who was born here in 1841. More highly regarded as a collector than as an analyst of historical information, Sulte is known primarily for his eight-volume *Histoire des Canadiens-français* (1882–4); he also produced two volumes of poems, *Les Laurentiennes* (1870) and *Les Chants nouveaux* (1876). Plaques on the monument memorialize three other writers. Born in nearby Baie-du-Febvre, the historian **Edmond Boisvert de Nevers** (Abraham-Edmond Boisvert), who is known for his lucid belletristic style, wrote *L'Avenir du peuple canadien-français* (1896) and *L'Âme américaine* (1900). He was an articling lawyer at Trois-Rivières but lived in Europe after 1888; he died in France in 1906. The subjects of two other plaques, **Antoine Gérin-Lajoie** and poet **Nérée Beauchemin**, were both born in nearby YAMACHICHE. Gérin-Lajoie is famous for two works of his youth—the poem *Un Canadien errant* (1842), which became a beloved folksong, and French Canada's first published tragedy, *Le Jeune Latour* (1844), written while he was still a student at the Collège de NICOLET—as well as for the influential novels *Jean Rivard: le défricheur* (1874) and *Jean Rivard: économiste* (1876), which convey the author's theories on the social and economic benefits of colonizing the wilderness. Beauchemin, perhaps the best of the nineteenth-century French-Canadian regional poets, spent almost his whole life in Yamachiche, where he was a country doctor. His verse is collected in *Les Floraisons matutinales* (1897) and *Patrie intime* (1928), both published here. A literary dinner at which Beauchemin was given a poet's crown was held in Trois-Rivières in 1930, when the poet was eighty; he died the following year.

What may be the second novel to have been published in Canada, *Matilda; or The Indian's Captive*, was published in Trois-Rivières in 1833. The author was **James Russell**, of whom nothing is known. The novelist **Rodolphe Girard**, author of *Marie Calumet* (1904), was born here in 1879 and attended the École Sainte-Ursule. His career as a writer is connected with MONTREAL (11), where his family moved in 1891, and with OTTAWA. Trois-Rivières was also the birthplace of **Philippe Panneton**, who under his pen-name Ringuet published the novel *Trente Arpents* (1938; trans. by Felix and Dorothea Walter, *Thirty Acres*, 1940); a landmark of realism in Quebec literature, it is set in the Trois-Rivières region in the years 1887–1932. Born in 1895, Panneton spent most of his life in MONTREAL (15), where he was a distinguished physician and the author of other books.

Several important writers have been associated with the Séminaire de Trois-Rivières, located at 858 av. Laviolette. The priest and author **Joseph Gérin Gélinas** taught here from his ordination in 1889 until his death on 24 Jan. 1927. His works include *Arthur Beaulac* (1914) and *En veillant* (1919). **Rodolphe Dubé**, born in RIVIÈRE-OUELLE in 1905, attended the Séminaire de Trois-Rivières in the early 1920s. Prominent as both a philosopher and a poet, he wrote under the pen-name François Hertel. **Clément Marchand** was also educated at the seminary; in 1932, at the age of twenty, he established his publishing house, Bien-

Public, here; among its publications were the first three books by Gérald Godin, also associated with the seminary. Marchand's own books of poetry include *Courrier des villages* (1940) and *Les Soirs rouges* (1947), both of which won the Prix David.

Trois-Rivières is also associated with other important twentieth-century poets. **Alfred DesRochers** attended the Collège séraphique of the Franciscan Fathers here from 1918 to 1921; this was the end of his formal education and he spent most of his life in the SHERBROOKE area and in Montreal. He is known for his poetry collection *À l'ombre de l'Orford* (see also ST-ÉLIE-D'ORFORD). The poet **Gérald Godin** was born here in 1938 and received his early education in the city, although he left school without graduating to work as a proofreader on the Trois-Rivières newspaper *Le Nouvelliste*, at 500 rue Saint-George. After experience as a journalist in Montreal, he entered politics and has twice been elected to the Quebec National Assembly; he was Minister of Cultural Communities and Immigration under the Parti Québécois government (see NORTH HATLEY, QUEBEC CITY). Godin's collections of poetry include *Poèmes et cantos* (1962) and *Libertés surveillées* (1975). Also associated with Trois-Rivières is **Jacques Ferron**, a native of nearby LOUISEVILLE, who received his high-school education at the Collège Brébeuf here. Author of *Contes du pays incertain* (1962; *Tales from the Uncertain Country*, 1972), which received a Governor General's Award, Ferron traces the origin of his opinions about the self-isolation of the French-Canadian upper classes and his consequent attraction to social and political activism to his years at the Collège Brébeuf. (See also LONGUEUIL.)

The poet **Gatien Lapointe** taught at the Université du Québec, Trois-Rivières from the mid-1960s until his death in 1983; during much of this time he lived at 3530 rue Notre-Dame. He founded and operated a small press, Les Écrits des Forges, devoted to publishing new and unknown poets. His books include *Arbre-radar* (1980) and *Corps et Graphies* (1981). Two other important authors lived briefly in Trois-Rivières while pursuing careers in radio. The novelist *Yves Thériault* was an announcer at CHLN here in the 1930s, and author and *chansonnier* **Félix Leclerc** was a script-writer at the same station in 1937–9.

VAUDREUIL

Canon **Lionel-Adolphe Groulx** was born in Vaudreuil on 13 Jan. 1878, and after a childhood spent here was educated at the Séminaire de Ste-Thérèse-de-Blainville (a village north of Montreal in Terrebonne County). Groulx's career as a writer, historian, and one of the most influential of all French-Canadian nationalists is primarily associated with Montreal, where he taught at Université de Montréal and edited the magazine *L'Action française*. Among his many works are *Notre Maître, le passé* (1936) and the monumental *Histoire du Canada français* (4 vols, 1950–2), considered the first important re-interpretation of the history of French Canada since François-Xavier Garneau's *Histoire du Canada* (1845–8). (See also CARILLON.)

WAY'S MILLS

The poet **Louis Dudek** and his wife Aileen Collins, who was editor of the influential magazine CIV/n (1953–5), have a summer and working home in this village at the southern end of Lake Massawippi. Dudek's collections of poems include *Atlantis* (1967), *Selected Poems* (1979), and *Continuation* (1981); he and Aileen Collins edit and publish D.C. Books. Morton Rosengarten, an artist and sculptor who figures as a character in Leonard Cohen's *The Favorite Game* (1963), also has a summer home and studio here. (See MONTREAL: 5, NORTH HATLEY.)

YAMACHICHE

In this town on the north bank of the St Lawrence west of Trois-Rivières stands the house of the poet **Nerée Beauchemin**, who lived his whole life in Yamachiche except for the years he spent at the Séminaire de Nicolet and Université Laval, where he received his degree in medicine in 1874. The house at 711 rue Sainte-Anne, in which he lived for over fifty years as a dedicated country doctor, is a Quebec historic monument. It has been preserved both inside and out and still bears traces of Beauchemin's medical and literary activities. Here he produced the two books that are generally regarded as the high point of French nineteenth-century poetry in Canada: *Les Floraisons matutinales* (1897) and *Patrie intime* (1928). Beauchemin also wrote scores of other poems that were published in magazines, many prose notes, and hundreds of alternative versions of the poems he chose to publish. After the appearance of his first volume, he seemed content to write for himself, perfecting his work and filing it away, until friends persuaded him to publish his second and most important book. His work is collected in *Nérée Beauchemin, son oeuvre* (1973–4). Characteristic of many Beauchemin poems is a combination of pure classical versification with the simplicity and melody of the folk song. Beauchemin's 'Cloche de Louisbourg' is probably the most widely known and anthologized French-Canadian poem of the nineteenth century. His simple devotion to his native place is captured in these lines from 'Patrie intime' (*Patrie intime*, 1928):

The Gérin-Lajoie house, Yamachiche

> *Mon rêve n'a jamais quitté*
> *Le cloître obscur de la demeure*
> *Où, dans le devoir, j'ai goûté*
> *Toute la paix intérieure.*

Another of Quebec's important early men of letters, **Antoine Gérin-Lajoie**, was a native of Yamachiche. He was born here in 1824 in a house that no longer stands; a historic plaque marks its site. In 1842, while a student at NICOLET, he wrote the verses of a song that has passed into folklore, 'Un Canadien errant', about a *patriote* banished from Quebec after the Rebellion of 1837. (The original can be read in *The Oxford Book of Canadian Verse*, 1960; an English version, 'From His Canadian Home', was written in 1927 by John Murray Gibbon.) In the same year Gérin-Lajoie wrote *Le Jeune Latour*, a three-act verse play that was the first tragedy written and published in French Canada. After an unsuccessful period seeking his fortune in the United States, Gérin-Lajoie returned to his native province; in 1856 he became a civil servant attached to the legislature of Quebec, and later worked in OTTAWA. He also resumed his literary career with two influential novels, *Jean Rivard, le défricheur* (1862) and *Jean Rivard, l'économiste* (1864). These form the saga of Jean Rivard, who carves a domain for himself from Quebec's virgin forest and by his example attracts other pioneers, who establish the village of Rivardville. The novels are thinly veiled treatises on the colonization of Quebec's empty territory, which Gérin-Lajoie recommended as the key to economic growth and independence from the United States.

Ontario

AGAWA BAY

In Lake Superior Provincial Park, on the northern shore of Agawa Bay, rock cliffs bear pictographs painted centuries ago by a triumphant Ojibwa chief who had led a war party across the lake to a victory nearby. The pictographs were described in 1851 by American ethnographer and Indian agent **Henry Rowe Schoolcraft** (1793–1864), who had seen only a birchbark reproduction. The description influenced **Henry Wadsworth Longfellow**'s *The Song of Hiawatha* (1855); the poem's section on 'picture-writing' relates Hiawatha's portrayal of 'The Great Serpent, the Kenabeek, / With his bloody crest erected, / Creeping, looking into heaven.' This reflects Schoolcraft's account of 'a kind of fabulous serpent resembling a saurian, having two feet and armed with horns', which he called Misshikinabik, or Great Serpent. Schoolcraft, who was at Sault Ste Marie, Michigan, when he heard of the pictographs, never saw them and did not give their location in his account. **Selwyn Dewdney**, who was not only a scientist but a respected author, known especially for his novel *Wind Without Rain* (1946), crowned a fourteen-month search in September 1958 with the discovery of the pictographs on the Lake Superior coast. Dewdney tells the story in *Indian Rock Paintings of the Great Lakes* (1962); he was able to identify his discovery with the pictographs used by Longfellow by comparing it with the description in Schoolcraft's *Historical and Statistical Information Respecting the History, Condition and Prospects of the Indian Tribes of the United States* (1851–7). (See also LONDON.)

An access road off Hwy 17 beyond the look-out over Agawa Bay leads to a wooden stairway from which most of the pictographs can be seen. They include mythological beasts, forest animals, canoes, and symbols recounting the Ojibwa journey and victory.

ALLISTON

From 1973 to 1980 **Margaret Atwood** lived on a farm near this small town on Hwy 89, northwest of Toronto. During her Alliston years she produced three poetry collections, *You Are Happy* (1974), *Selected Poems* (1976), and *Two-Headed Poems* (1978), a collection of short stories, *Dancing Girls* (1977); and a novel, *Life Before Man* (1970). Atwood shared the farm with **Graeme Gibson** (*Perpetual Motion*, 1982), the father of her daughter. She returned to TORONTO (3, 4, 6) in 1980.

AMELIASBURG

In 1957 the poet **Alfred Purdy** and his wife built an A-frame house on the shore of Roblin Lake, south of BELLEVILLE and just outside the village of Ameliasburg, in Prince Edward County. Gradually improved and elaborated over the years, the house has been the poet's home ever since, and its surroundings have provided him with material for some of his best-known writings. His first book of poems written at Roblin Lake, *The Crafte so Longe to Lerne* (1959), includes 'At Roblin Lake', the first of his poems to evoke the landscape and history around the village—once called Roblin's Mills after the nineteenth-century miller, Owen Roblin, who was the founding settler. Poems inspired by Roblin Lake appeared also in *The Cariboo Horses* (1965; winner of a Governor General's Award) and *Wild Grape Wine* (1969) and in the long poem *In Search of Owen Roblin* (1974), in which Purdy describes his relationship both to the Roblin Lake region south of the Bay of Quinte and to the adjacent region, 'the country north of Belleville' (the title of a well-known Purdy poem). At Ameliasburg can still be seen 'the old ruined grist mill / built by owen Roblin in 1842 / four storeys high with a wrecked mill wheel / cumbered by stones and time', and the 'graveyard near the millpond / beneath the busy black-topped road' containing Owen Roblin's red granite tombstone. (See also WOOLER.)

Al Purdy

AMHERSTBURG

The first native-born Canadian novelist, **John Richardson** (1796–1852), grew up in Amherstburg. His father, an army surgeon, was posted in 1802 to Fort Malden, built here in 1796 to protect the Canadian frontier on the western Lake Erie shore. Richardson entered the British 41st Regiment when the War of 1812 began and was stationed at Fort Malden, where he met Tecumseh, the famed Indian ally of the British. Richardson fought in several battles, but was captured by American troops at Moraviantown, near THAMESVILLE, and taken to an American prison camp. After the war he went to Europe with the regiment, but it did not arrive in time to fight Napoleon. Richardson remained in Europe for several years and published the first of many works that drew on his experiences during the War of 1812: *Tecumseh* (1829), an epic poem celebrating the famous chief, which was published in 1829 and widely praised. In 1832 he published *Wacousta; or, The Prophecy; A Tale of the Canadas*, a story of Old World betrayal avenged during frontier battles in America at the time of Pontiac's uprising (1763). The principal character was based in part on a man Richardson knew in Amherstburg. (As agent for the town's business interests in wilderness areas, this man had adopted Indian customs and the name Wagousta.) Richardson's early literary successes were followed by considerable difficulty both in his career and his personal life. He returned to Canada in 1838 as a reporter for the London *Times* to cover Lord Durham's fact-finding tour of post-rebellion conditions, but was fired for failing to follow the paper's editorial policy on Canada. He then returned briefly to Amherstburg, but soon moved to WINDSOR and then to BROCKVILLE. A national historic plaque in Amherstburg commemorates Richardson's connection with the town.

The Kingston-born poet **Charles Sangster** came to Amherstburg in 1849 to work as the editor of the weekly newspaper the *Courier*; by autumn, however, the paper had failed and Sangster returned to KINGSTON to work on the *Daily British Whig*. (See also OTTAWA.)

Today Fort Malden Historic Park contains a museum displaying artefacts from the fort's past and a restored barracks building from 1840. The original buildings from the War of 1812 days are gone, but some of the ramparts remain, providing a fine view of Lake Erie. The boulder from which Tecumseh exhorted the troops preparing to attack Detroit—a raid planned by Tecumseh and General Isaac Brock at Fort Malden—can still be seen on the park grounds.

Peter McArthur

APPIN

Peter McArthur (1866–1924), 'the sage of Ekfrid', was born on a farm near here and educated in local schools. The family's log house has been preserved and can be visited at DOON Pioneer Village. McArthur taught locally in 1887–8, studied and worked in TORONTO (1) for the next two years, and then worked until 1909 as a writer, editor, and advertising man in New York, with a brief period in London, Eng., (1902–4). When his New York advertising agency failed in 1909, he returned to the family farm in Ekfrid Township, where he began to write pastoral essays for the Toronto *Globe* and the *Farmer's Advocate*. In these he advocated a return to rural simplicity and became Canada's leading writer on the country's farm tradition. His chief works were collections of his columns polished for book publication: *In Pastures Green* (1915), *The Red Cow and Her Friends* (1919), *Around Home* (1925), *Familiar Fields* (1925), and *Friendly Acres* (1927). They display his humour, his vivid observation of farm life, and his unique style of personal essay, which he combined with fiction and, often, with elements of the animal fable. A plaque on Hwy 2 just west of Appin commemorates McArthur's association with this district.

THE JOURNALIST AND HIS FARM

Real farmers, according to their various natures, viewed my work with pity, contempt, ridicule, loathing, malevolence, mendacity, loquacity, jackassity, and every other capacity that people develop. Lecturers for the farmers' institutes made it a point to call on me when they were in the neighbourhood, and after the first shock was over proceeded to gather specimens of noxious weeds that they found it hard to get elsewhere. Government scientists came out of their way to see me, and gazed with awe at the neglected farm from which I had raised such a crop—of newspaper articles. Then they took out their cyanide bottles and began to collect rare specimens of bugs and pests, for I had all of them. Touring automobilists stopped to make a call, and when they went away I could hear them laughing as far off as the second culvert on the concession line.

—Peter McArthur, *In Pastures Green* (1915)

ATHENS

The novelist **Hugh Hood** has spent his summer vacations on Charleton Lake, near Athens, since 1967. Athens has been one of the main settings for several of Hood's novels in his New Age series, for which twelve volumes are planned. Hood's fictional town of Stoverville is closely based on the Athens-Brockville area; it figures prominently in *A New Athens* (1977)—the title alludes to Frances Brooke's statement in the *History of Emily Montague* that Canada will never become 'a new Athens rising near the pole' —and *The Scenic Art* (1984) as the home town of the central character, Matt Goderich. (See also TORONTO: 5; MONTREAL: 7, Que.)

BANCROFT

The poet **D.G. Jones** was born here on 1 Jan. 1929. Though he lived in Bancroft until 1954—when his first teaching post took him to the Royal Military College, Kingston—he spent most of every year away at school, beginning in 1942 when he was a boarding student at Grove School in nearby Lakefield. During the summers until 1968, Jones often worked at his family's cottage at Paudash Lake, just west of Bancroft. There he wrote

D.G. Jones

poems collected in his first three books, *Frost on the Sun* (1957), *The Sun Is an Axeman* (1961), and *Phrases from Orpheus* (1967). In 1953 the cottage was the site of an informal writers' conference attended by Jones, F.R. Scott, Irving Layton, Louis Dudek, A.J.M. Smith, and others. One of Jones's several poems about his native region is 'A Garland of Milne', evoking the painter David Milne, who lived at Bancroft in 1951–3, the last years of his life. (See also GUELPH; MONTREAL: 7, NORTH HATLEY, SHERBROOKE, Que.)

BELLEVILLE

Susanna Moodie moved to Belleville in 1840, when her husband John was appointed sheriff of Hastings County. Her literary career flowered here. Before the move she had been writing at her home in DOURO TOWNSHIP for John Lovell's Montreal magazine the *Literary Garland*, which in 1847 published several chapters of her most famous book, *Roughing It in the Bush*, (2 vols, 1852), based on the discouraging farming ventures of the Moodies at DALE'S CORNERS and in Douro Township. Moodie followed it with an account of life in Belleville, called *Life in the Clearings* (1853), which took a more optimistic approach to the experience of immigrants in Ontario. Both John and Susanna were writers. They assumed joint editorship in 1847 of the *Victorian Magazine*, founded in Belleville by John Wilson; the magazine failed in 1848 after twelve issues. A third Belleville book, *Flora Lyndsay; or, Passages in an Eventful Life* (1853), is the fictionalized story of Susanna Moodie's life in England and her trip to Canada. While living in Belleville she also published several Gothic romances, including *Mark Hurdlestone; or, The Gold Worshipper* (1853); *Matrimonial Speculations* (1854); *The Faithless Guardian* (1855); and *The World Before Them* (1868). Her long-time Belleville home stands at 114 Bridge St W. and now belongs to the author **Leo Simpson** (see below). The house is a national historic site and is marked with a plaque. Following her husband's death in 1869 Moodie left Belleville and lived alternately with her children in TORONTO (1) and with her sister, Catharine Parr Traill, in LAKEFIELD. She died in Toronto in 1885 and is buried near her husband in Belleville.

Sir Gilbert Parker, who was born in CAMDEN EAST, is honoured with a plaque at Corby Public Library, 223 Pinnacle St. Ordained in 1885, Parker served briefly as lay reader and deacon at St Thomas Anglican Church here before leaving Canada for a journalism career in Australia. His success there led him to London, where he published *Pierre and His People* (1892), a collection of adventure tales of the Northwest that became internationally popular, and many historical novels.

The poet **Al Purdy**, a native of WOOLER, was educated at Albert College in Belleville and in the late 1940s operated the Diamond Taxi Co. in nearby TRENTON. Purdy now lives in 'the country north of Belleville' at AMELIASBURG.

Farley Mowat was born in Belleville on 12 May 1921. He spent his first years in a third-floor apartment over the Corby (previously the Carnegie) Public Library (the building is still standing), where his father, **Angus Mowat**, worked as librarian. A native of nearby Trenton, Angus Mowat later took the family west to SASKATOON. He was a novelist as well as a librarian; his books include *Then I'll Look Up* (1938) and *Carrying Place* (1941). Farley Mowat's many works of non-fiction, beginning with *People of the Deer* (1952), include *The Regiment* (1955; 1973), the history of the Second World War regiment raised by the counties of Hastings and Prince Edward. (See also PORT HOPE; BURGEO, Nfld.,; RIVER BOURGEOIS, N.S.; MAGDALEN ISLANDS, Que.; KEEWATIN BARRENS, N.W.T.)

J.W.D. Moodie and Susanna Moodie (with an unidentified woman), *c.*1860

Susanna Moodie's house in Belleville

The comic novelist **Leo Simpson**, who came to Canada from his native Ireland in 1961, has lived in Madoc, north of Belleville, since 1972. He and his wife, a native of Belleville, have restored the Susanna Moodie house in Belleville, which they own. Simpson moved to the district in 1966 from TORONTO (2), where he worked for Macmillan's; he settled first in Queensborough Township before moving to Madoc. His first novel, *Arkwright* (1971), is set in Toronto, but both *The Peacock Papers* (1973) and *Kowalski's Last Chance* (1980) take place in the fictional town of Bradfarrow, modelled on Belleville.

BEWDLEY

A small memorial stone near Kidd's Corners, just south of Bewdley on Hwy 28, commemorates **Joseph Medlicott Scriven**, author of the hymn 'What a Friend We have in Jesus', and a preacher and private tutor in the Bewdley–Port Hope district for most of his life. He often stayed near Bewdley at the home of his friend James Sackville (the site is now unknown). Scriven drowned during such a stay on 10 Aug. 1886, at the age of sixty-six. Sackville found his body 'in the attitude of prayer' in the flume of a dam on a stream, now probably dried up, that led into Rice Lake. Scriven was buried at PENGELLEY'S LANDING near Bailieboro. (See also PORT HOPE.)

BIG TROUT

Fred Bodsworth drew on his knowledge of the landscape and customs of Indian communities at Big Trout Lake and Weagamow Lake to create the fictional setting for his novel *The Sparrow's Fall* (1967). Big Trout is about 200 miles south of Hudson Bay; both communities are accessible only by air. *The Sparrow's Fall* depicts the cultural dilemma of an Ojibwa couple imbued with the teachings of Christian missionaries but dependent for their survival upon killing animals. The book's action takes place in an Indian village that Bodsworth calls Wapanishee, on a lake of the same name. He blended the physical surroundings of Big Trout Lake and the Big Trout Indian community with customs of the Round Lake Ojibwa, who lived about 100 miles south of Big Trout; he had visited these people during the 1950s, while working as a writer for a Toronto magazine. (See also TORONTO: 6.)

BINBROOK

The writer and teacher **George Washington Johnson**—author of the poem 'When

You and I Were Young, Maggie', which became a famous song (by J.A. Butterfield)—was born on 19 Aug. 1839 in Binbrook, 10 miles southwest of Hamilton on Hwy 56, and lived in the Hamilton area much of his life. In nearby GLANFORD TOWNSHIP he met, and in 1864 married, the subject of his famous poem, Maggie Clarke, who died within a year. Johnson continued his career as schoolteacher; he was principal of Binbrook School, taught at Stoney Creek and Bartonville, became principal of Central High School in HAMILTON in 1875, and for many years was on the staff of Upper Canada College, TORONTO (7). 'When You and I Were Young, Maggie' was published in Johnson's first poetry collection, *Maple Leaves* (1864).

BISCOTASING

In 1910 **Archibald Stansfeld Belaney**, the nature writer and conservationist known as **Grey Owl**, moved from TEMAGAMI, Ont., to Biscotasing, the headquarters of the Mississauga Reserve. He worked as a guide and trapper in the region (including the area now contained in Mississauga Provincial Forest) until 1914, and then as a fire ranger; the following year he joined the Canadian Expeditionary Forces. In 1917 Belaney returned to the Mississauga River country, living the nomadic life of a trapper and guide. Formally adopted by the Ojibwa tribe, he was named Wa-sha-Quan Asin (Grey Owl), and was afterwards generally believed to be an Indian. In 1925 he left Biscotasing and moved farther north to an uninhabited region of Ontario, where he met an Indian woman, Anahareo, who persuaded him to become a protector of the beaver. His search for a place to establish a conservation area for beavers, threatened at that time with extinction, took him to CABANO in eastern Quebec, where he first began writing articles about nature and animals. (See also PRINCE ALBERT NATIONAL PARK, Sask.)

BLENHEIM

See RUSCOMB.

BOBCAYGEON

For many years the narrative poet **E.J. Pratt**, who lived in TORONTO (3) while studying and then teaching (from 1907) at the University of Toronto, summered near Bobcaygeon on Buckhorn Lake, northwest of Lakefield. Here, as a present for his wife on their fifth wedding anniversary in 1923, he wrote *The Witches' Brew* (1925), which makes use of the Pratt cottage and the surrounding landscape in its fanciful and comic portrayal of debauchery in the animal kingdom. His daughter Claire, in *The Silent Ancestors: The Forebears of E.J. Pratt* (1971), describes the poet at work at Bobcaygeon: 'In the summer the setting would change to our cottage at Bobcaygeon in what was then deep country stillness where he would settle comfortably, feet up, into a chair on the screened-in verandah, or in the green den he had built for himself fifty yards from the cottage and nearer the lake where there was nothing to disturb him but the occasional odious crow. I don't remember him ever using a pencil more than two inches long. His writing was equally tiny and would fill every millimeter of the page. And although it became shortly afterwards illegible even to himself, it gave him pleasure to see an overpopulated sheet of paper, giving itself utterly to the purpose for which it was made.'

The TORONTO (6) reviewer and satirist **William Arthur Deacon** bought land in the area in 1924 and built a cottage in 1928. His visitors over the years included his neighbour E.J. Pratt, Lorne Pierce (see TORONTO), Tom MacInnes (see VANCOUVER), and Frederick Philip Grove (see SIMCOE; RAPID CITY, Man.). **Arthur Phelps** (*A Bobcaygeon Chapbook*, 1922) took the occasion of a visit in 1926 to show Deacon Grove's manuscript of *A Search for America* (1927), which on Deacon's recommendation was submitted to Graphic Press in Ottawa. On the strength of his new relationship with Graphic Press, Grove himself came east in the fall of 1929 to settle in OTTAWA. He frequently visited Deacon at Bobcaygeon until 1935, when Deacon moved his summer home to Wilson's Point on Lake Couchiching.

BON ECHO PROVINCIAL PARK

Sixty miles northwest of Kingston on Hwy 41, Bon Echo Provincial Park includes a tract of land once owned by the writer **Merrill Denison** (1893–1975); in 1957 he donated it to the province as a memorial to his mother, Flora Denison. On the east side of Mazinaw Lake in the park is a mile-long wall of granite, rising 375 to 400 feet above the water, that bears 135 rock paintings similar to those found on the shore of Lake Superior at Agawa. On 25 Aug. 1919 Flora Denison and the American author Horace Traubel, biographer and literary executor of **Walt Whitman**, dedicated a portion of the rock called 'Old Walt' as a memorial to Whitman. Horace Traubel died here in September, shortly after the dedication. Merrill Denison, who ran a summer resort at Bon Echo for many years, drew on his experiences in northern Ontario for the stories in *The Unheroic North: Four Canadian Plays* (1932). Best known as a dramatist for stage and radio in the 1920s and 1930s, Denison also wrote a book of sketches about life at the resort: *Boobs in the Woods: 17 Sketches by One of Them* (1927). On 29 June 1955 'Old Walt' was the object of a pilgrimage in honour of the 100th anniversary of the publication of Whitman's *Leaves of Grass*. Sponsored by the Canadian Authors' Association, it included E.J. Pratt, Evelyn Fox Richardson, Helen Creighton, Guy Sylvestre, Yves Thériault, and other Canadian writers. (See also TORONTO: 3.)

Merrill and Muriel Denison at Bon Echo Inn

Merrill Denison was married to **Muriel Denison**, the author of *Susannah, a Little Girl with the Mounties* (1936), which was made into a popular film, *Susannah of the Mounted*, starring Shirley Temple.

BRANTFORD

E. Pauline Johnson, the daughter of a Mohawk father and an English mother, was born on 10 Mar. 1861 at Chiefswood, 10 miles east of Brantford in MIDDLEPORT. She attended Brantford Collegiate from 1875 to June 1877, when she left the school and lived in a boarding-house nearby. This was the end of her formal education. Following the death of her father in 1885, Johnson, with her mother and sister, lived first at Chatham and West Sts, then moved to 7 Napoleon St (now Dufferin Ave) in Brantford. Her poems first appeared in print in Oct. 1886 after she delivered a poem at the unveiling of the Joseph Brant statue in Victoria Park, a performance that was widely praised in the local newspapers. A successful career of public readings—in which she wore Indian dress when reading Indian poems—

The Mohawk Chapel, Brantford

began in 1892 after a very effective stage appearance in Toronto. She visited her family in Brantford regularly, but in 1909 she retired to VANCOUVER. Among her books are the well-known poetry collections *Flint and Feather* (1912) and *Legends of Vancouver* (1911). The Brant County Museum, 57 Charlotte St, displays Johnson memorabilia (along with

Pauline Johnson, *c.*1890

that of other local authors, including Sara Jeannette Duncan and Thomas B. Costain). There is also a granite memorial to Johnson at St Paul's, her Majesty's Chapel of the Mohawks on Mohawk St. Built in 1785 with a grant from George III, this was the first Protestant church in Ontario and contains the graves of Joseph Brant and his son John. Chiefswood is now a provincial museum.

Sara Jeannette Duncan was born in Brantford in 1861 at 96 West St. The First Baptist Church next door, at 70 West St, bears a provincial plaque to her. Educated at Brantford Collegiate, Duncan briefly attended the Toronto Normal School but in 1884 began a successful career as a journalist and, following her marriage in 1890, as a novelist. After a world tour in 1888, Duncan lived abroad. *The Imperialist* (1904), one of

The home of Sara Jeannette Duncan, Brantford

her two best novels (along with *Cousin Cinderella; or A Canadian Girl in London*, 1908), provides a faithful portrait of contemporary Brantford in the story of a young politician—a champion of imperial ties between Britain and Canada—who is campaigning in the fictional town of Elgin for a seat in Parliament. The young man wins the election but loses the seat when his own party asks him to resign. (See TORONTO: 1.)

The novelist and journalist **Norman Duncan** (no relation), who was born in nearby NORWICH, was raised in Brantford. After studying at the University of Toronto for three years he went to the United States to pursue a career in journalism, returning frequently to Canada, or visiting Newfoundland, on assignment for American publications. Most of his novels are based on sea adventures he encountered on the Labrador coast: they include *Doctor Luke of the Labrador* (1904) and *The Adventures of Billy Topsail: a Story for Boys* (1906). (See also EXPLOITS ISLAND, Nfld.)

The historical novelist and editor **Thomas B. Costain** was born in Brantford in 1885 and educated here. His first job was on the *Brantford Expositor*; he went on to work in Guelph and in TORONTO (7), where he was editor of *Maclean's* from 1914 until 1920, when he moved to the United States. After the success of his first novel, *For My Great Folly* (1942), he wrote several best-selling historical romances, including *The Black Rose* (1945). Among his books about Canada are *The White and the Gold: The French Reign in Canada* (1954), a work of popular history; *High Towers* (1949), the seventeenth-century adventures of the LeMoyne family; and *Son of a Hundred Kings* (1950), a story set in the Brantford area that follows the life of an orphaned boy during the 1890s.

BROCKVILLE

The seat of Leeds County, this city on the St Lawrence River was the scene of much of the literary activity of the early novelist, poet, historian, and journalist, Major **John Richardson**, who settled on a nearby farm in 1840 and in 1841 founded his *New Era, or Canadian Chronicle*, a literary weekly that failed the following year; he then published another short-lived newspaper at Brockville, the *Canadian Loyalist* (1843–4). Shortly thereafter, probably in 1845, he left Brockville, having been appointed superintendent of the police at the Welland Canal. Now known primarily as the author of the novel *Wacousta* (1832; see AMHERTSBURG), Richardson was the first Canadian novelist to gain an international reputation and the first native of Upper Canada to have his verse published in London, Eng. At least two of his most important books were published while he was in Brockville: *The Canadian Brothers; or, The Prophecy Fulfilled* (1840), a sequel to *Wacousta*'s account of the Indian uprising of 1763, and his historical work, *War of 1812* (1842), which had previously appeared in the *New Era*.

A plaque honouring Richardson and his connection with Brockville can be seen at Laura Secord Public School, Walnut and Queen Sts. (See THAMESVILLE, WINDSOR.)

CAMBRIDGE

The city of Cambridge was formed on 1 Jan. 1973 from several municipalities, including the city of Galt. William Dickson, who founded the settlement in 1816, changed its name to Galt, from Shade's Mills, in honour of his friend (and former Edinburgh schoolmate) **John Galt**, novelist, founder of nearby GUELPH, and commissioner of the Canada Company from 1826 to 1829. Galt visited the city named for him in 1827, but during his few years in Canada he lived in the Huron Tract, which the Canada Company was developing for British immigrants.

The novelist **Mazo de la Roche** moved

to Galt from TORONTO (2) in 1891; her family stayed at the Queen's Hotel, and she attended a private girl's school. She returned to Toronto in 1893. (See also MISSISSAUGA, OAKVILLE, SUTTON.)

The novelist **Robert Edward Knowles**, born in Maxwell, Ont., in 1868, was educated at Galt Collegiate and settled here permanently in 1898; he was the minister of Knox Presbyterian Church in 1898–1914. In their day Knowles's novels on moral and religious themes enjoyed sales that rivalled those of Ralph Connor and Lucy Maud Montgomery. New Jedboro, the city portrayed in his *St. Cuthbert's* (1905), is based on Galt. Knowles wrote seven novels, including *The Dawn at Shanty Bay* (1907) and *The Attic Guest* (1909). Ill health forced him to retire from the ministry in 1914; at that time he was living at 9 Melville St S. For many years he pursued a successful career as a journalist, writing columns for the Toronto *Star*, and as a lecturer. His home was at 92 Glenmorris St, where he was living when he died in 1946.

Hubert Evans, born in 1892 in VANKLEEK HILL, came here with his family in the late 1890s. In 1910 he dropped out of high school here to begin his career as a journalist on the Galt *Reporter*. His work as a novelist, poet, and writer of children's books is primarily associated with ROBERTS CREEK, B.C., but one of his most important novels, *O Time in Your Flight* (1979), is an autobiographical evocation of his boyhood in Galt.

The poet **Margaret Avison** was born in Galt in 1918. Since beginning her studies at Victoria College, University of Toronto, in 1936, Avison has lived mainly in TORONTO (3). Her poetry collections are *Winter Sun* (1960), which won a Governor General's Award; *The Dumbfounding* (1966); and *Sunblue* (1978).

CAMDEN EAST

One of the most popular novelists at the turn of the century, **Gilbert Parker**, was born on 23 Nov. 1862 in this Lennox and Addington County village about 20 miles northwest of Kingston. Son of a storekeeper and justice of the peace here, Parker was educated at the University of TORONTO (3) and moved to England in 1889. Many of his historical novels have Canadian settings and subjects; one of the most famous, *The Seats of the Mighty* (1896), is set in Quebec in 1757–9 and is based on the memoirs of Robert Stobo, who claimed to have shown Wolfe the cove from which the English commander was able to surprise the French on the Plains of Abraham. Parker, who was ordained a Church of England deacon in 1883 and for a short time served in this capacity at St Thomas Church, BELLEVILLE, also served from 1900 to 1918 in the British House of Commons as member for Gravesend. He was knighted in 1902 for his achievements in literature. *The Works of Gilbert Parker*, including prose and poetry, appeared in twenty-three volumes (1911–23).

A plaque honouring Parker and recalling his early life in Camden East has been erected at St Luke's (Anglican) Church on County Rd 4.

CANNINGTON

In 1962 the novelist and shorty-story writer **Timothy Findley** left his first profession, acting, to devote himself entirely to writing. In 1964 he moved to his present residence, 'Stone Orchard', a farm near Cannington, which is east of Lake Simcoe between Hwys 12 and 46. During his years here he has published *The Last of the Crazy People* (1967, his first novel), *The Butterfly Plague* (1969), *The Wars* (1977), *Famous Last Words* (1981), *Not Wanted on the Voyage* (1984), and *The Telling of Lies* (1986), as well as plays, screenplays, and television scripts. *The Wars* received a Governor General's Award in 1978. (See also KINGSTON, OTTAWA, STRATFORD, TORONTO: 5.)

CEDAR SPRINGS

The novelist **Arthur Stringer** (1874–1950) owned a fruit farm near Cedar Springs from 1903 to 1921, and during those years it was his principal residence. About 1914 he made a brief, unsuccessful attempt at farming near CALGARY, Alta; this experience became the basis of his most enduring accomplishment, a trilogy of novels—written at Cedar Springs—about the adjustment of a New England socialite to conditions on the Canadian Prairies after her marriage to a Scots-Canadian wheat farmer. The trilogy includes *The Prairie Wife* (1915), *The Prairie Mother* (1920) and *The Prairie Child* (1921). One of Stringer's few other books with a Canadian setting, *Lonely O'Malley* (1905), is based on his boyhood in CHATHAM, where he was born, and in LONDON. After 1921 Stringer lived in the United States and wrote primarily for an American audience. (In 1914 he scripted the famous film serial *The Perils of Pauline* starring Pearl White and Crane Wilbur; he had established himself, during a residence in New York in the late 1890s, as a producer of popular fiction, especially crime stories and sentimental romances.) Stringer's fruit farm here was on the shore of Lake Erie; Cedar Springs is on Highway 3 east of Leamington.

Arthur Stringer

CHAPLEAU

A memorial grave marker in the Roman Catholic cemetery at Grey and Birch Sts commemorates the French-born novelist **Louis Hémon** (1880–1913), who is buried here. The author of *Maria Chapdelaine* (1916) was killed about two miles west of Chapleau on 8 July 1913, when he was struck by a Canadian Pacific Railway express train.

When he was killed, Hémon was beginning a trip to the West to gather experiences for his literary work and was apparently intending to 'ride the rails'. Presumably he had arrived at Chapleau by this means. The novelist had conceived and begun his famous novel at PÉRIBONKA and KÉNOGAMI, Que., and had completed it at MONTREAL (12), mailing it to *Le Temps* in Paris, where it first appeared as a serial in Jan. and Feb. 1914. After he had dispatched his manuscript, he wrote to his mother in France on 24 June 1913 that he was leaving for western Canada that evening.

A plaque at Dufferin and Monk Sts also commemorates Hémon and his death. Among the guests at the dedication ceremony in Aug. 1938 were Hémon's daughter Lydia and his sister Marie.

CHATHAM

Both the Chatham-Kent Museum, 59 William St, and the Chatham Public Library, 120 Queen St, contain materials relating to Josiah Henson, a fugitive slave whose life was a major source for **Harriet Beecher Stowe**'s *Uncle Tom's Cabin* (1852). (Henson, who settled in nearby DRESDEN in 1830, is remembered there at Uncle Tom's Cabin

Museum.) Chatham was the terminus for the Underground Railroad, which smuggled escaped slaves out of the United States into Canada. The library also contains a plaque honouring **Jean McKishnie Blewett**, journalist and versifier, who died at Chatham in 1934. (See also SCOTIA, TORONTO (2).)

The popular novelist **Arthur Stringer** was born here on 26 Feb. 1874 and lived here until he was ten, when his family moved to LONDON. Stringer returned to the Chatham district in 1903 to buy a farm, 'Shadow Lawn', in nearby CEDAR SPRINGS. The farm remained his home, despite frequent absences, until 1921, when he sold it and moved permanently to the United States, where his work was in demand both in New York and in Hollywood. Most of the books that made Stringer popular during his lifetime—including the espionage thriller, *The Wire Trappers* (1906)—were written at Cedar Springs. He is best remembered now for a trilogy of novels on prairie life—*The Prairie Wife* (1915), *The Prairie Mother* (1920), and *The Prairie Child* (1921)—which are based to some extent on Stringer's unsuccessful attempts to start a grain farm in Alberta about 1914. In his novel *Lonely O'Malley* (1905) he wrote about his childhood in Chatham and London; he named the town in his book Chamboro.

CHATSWORTH

The novelist, feminist, and temperance advocate **Nellie McClung** was born Helen Letitia Mooney on 20 Oct. 1873 near this Grey County farming village south of Owen Sound. The youngest child of farmer John Mooney, Nellie spent the first seven years of her life on the 100-acre family farm on the Garafraxa Rd, 1 mile from the town. She attended Sunday school in Chatsworth but did not begin elementary school until 1880, when the family moved west in the hope of finding richer farmland in the new province of Manitoba. The McClung farmhouse at Chatsworth is no longer standing, but Nellie McClung provided a clear and nostalgic picture of it in her first volume of autobiography, *Clearing in the West* (1936): 'I have a wistful memory of the sunlit populous farmyard, over which fresh yellow straw drifted as the wind blew, and where I could rove at will, without a care or fear. The white house under the red maples, with bright sumach trees in front, threw back the sunshine in a dazzle that made me wink my eyes, but I loved to look at it.' Although she spent the rest of her life in western Canada, choosing the subjects of her books from her experiences there, McClung is remembered in her home town with a national historical marker on the west side of Chatsworth and with a provincial marker in front of the Chatsworth United Church on Toronto St (Hwy 10), near the intersection with Crawford St. (See also LA RIVIÈRE, WINNIPEG, Man.; CALGARY, EDMONTON, Alta.; VICTORIA, B.C.)

The Nellie McClung plaque at Chatsworth

CHEAPSIDE

The poet **Wilson MacDonald**, author of many collections of popular verse, whom Albert Einstein once called 'the greatest thing I found in Canada', was born on 5 May 1880 in a house in Cheapside that was demolished in the 1970s. MacDonald's father was a tailor and Baptist preacher whose advanced views so antagonized local residents that he was prompted to return to his trade. MacDonald, who lived in Cheapside until he was seven—when the death of his mother obliged him to live with his grandparents, ending the idyllic, formative period of his early childhood—rose to prominence with *The Song of the Prairie Land* (1918). He had a large readership during the following two decades for his romantic lyrics on the quest for beauty and for his bitter satires against modern materialist society.

About one mile east of Cheapside on Talbot (formerly Rainham) Rd are a provincial historical plaque commemorating the poet and the Wilson MacDonald Memorial School Museum. Built in 1872 and used as a school until 1965, the one-room museum now houses books, pictures, and artefacts pertaining to MacDonald and the Cheapside district. It is said that MacDonald was briefly a grammar-school student here, although his formal education is usually thought to have begun at the age of eight at Port Dover Public School. (See also PORT DOVER, TORONTO: 7.)

Alice Munro, *c.*1980

CLINTON

The novelist and short-story writer **Alice Munro**, a native of nearby WINGHAM, has lived on a farm near Clinton in the farming area east of Lake Huron since the late 1970s, when she returned after many years' residence on the west coast. Her books written at Clinton include *Who Do You Think You Are?* (1978), winner of her second Governor General's Award, and *The Progress of Love* (1987), winner of her third. (See also WINGHAM; VANCOUVER, VICTORIA, B.C.)

COBALT

Famous for its silver mines, this town near the northwest shore of Lake Timiskaming was a focus of activity during 1905–7 for two important writers, the poet William Henry Drummond and the nature writer Grey Owl. There is no indication that either man knew of the other.

William Henry Drummond came to Cobalt in 1905, after most of his books of poetry—amusing dialect verse, usually dealing with French-Canadian *habitant* life—had been published: *The Habitant* (1897), *Phil-o-rum's Canoe and Madeleine de Verchères* (1898), *Johnnie Corteau* (1901), and *The Voyageur* (1905). Drummond, who was a doctor, came here to help his brothers in a silver-mining venture at Kerr Lake, about 2 miles southeast of the town, devoting his medical skill to the miners and their families. In 1907, while he was in MONTREAL (2), smallpox broke out in the mining camp. Drummond hurried back to help combat the disease, and while working was stricken with a cerebral haemorrhage, from which he died on 6 Apr. 1907. He was buried in Montreal.

The Drummond cabin at the mine site was destroyed by fire early in the century; but the stone fireplace, which remained, was made into a monument to Drummond. It can be seen on its hilltop two miles south of the town near Kerr Lake; its plaque bears two lines from Drummond's 'Le Vieux Temps':

An' w'en he fin' me ready, for mak' de longue voyage
He guide me t'roo de wood hese'f upon ma las' portage.

A provincial historical plaque in Drummond's memory stands in Cobalt in Drummond Park at the corner of Silver St and Prospect Ave; it directs visitors to the site of the Drummond Mine.

Grey Owl—whose birth name was **Archibald Stansfeld Belaney**—had his first experience of the Canadian wild in the Cobalt-Latchford district to which he came in 1905, the year of his immigration to Canada. (Latchford is a few miles southwest of Cobalt near Lake Timiskaming.) During his brief sojourn here he was employed as a canoeman and packer, and was greatly helped in his adaptation to the North and its ways by an Ojibwa woman named Michelle, with whom he stayed during the winter of 1905–6. In the summer of 1906 he moved to TEMAGAMI.

Probably the best known of all Canadian mining songs is 'The Cobalt Song', the words of which were written here in 1910, by mining engineer L.F. Steenman, to the tune of 'Oh You Rousseau'. The song's refrain goes, 'For we'll sing a little song of Cobalt, / If you don't live there it's your fault'.

COBOURG

Of the many writers associated with Cobourg, the first to arrive was **Susanna Moodie**. According to her account in *Roughing It in the Bush* (1852), she and her husband disembarked from the *Prescott IV* about midnight on 9 Sept. 1832 and stayed at the Steamboat Hotel (no longer standing) until 22 Sept. The Moodies then left Cobourg to take possession of a farm northeast of Cobourg. (See DALE, Ont.)

Rhoda Anne Page, a popular romantic poet of the 1840s, was born on a farm near Newcastle, 10 miles east, and lived much of her life at a house called 'The Pines' in or near Cobourg; its location is now unknown. In Feb. 1856 she married William Bowes Faulkner, the ceremony probably taking place at St Peter's (Anglican) Church, Cobourg. The couple then moved to GORE'S LANDING.

St Peter's Church, still standing and in use at 118 King St E., is associated with **Archibald Lampman**, the foremost poet of the Confederation group. Lampman's father, who had been serving at Gore's Landing, came to St Peter's as curate in 1874. Until 1882 the family home was a three-storey brick house at 37 King St E., in part of which the elder Lampman opened a school. Archibald Lampman attended Cobourg Collegiate Institute until the age of sixteen. The school building, now converted to private apartments, stands at 117 King St E., directly across the street from St Peter's Church and rectory.

The school building of Lampman Sr today

In 1841 **Egerton Ryerson** came to Cobourg as the first principal of Victoria College, which had evolved out of Upper Canada Academy (founded in 1836) as a Methodist alternative to the Anglican Upper Canada College in Toronto. Ryerson, whose principal literary work is *The Loyalists of America and Their Times* (1880), became chief superintendent of education for Canada West in 1844, but the college remained an important part of Cobourg's civic life for another fifty years. In 1892 it moved to Toronto and became an affiliated college (Victoria College) of the University of Toronto. Its handsome Greek Revival building still stands in Cobourg at University Ave and College St.

Virna (Virginia) **Sheard**, née Stanton, who also published under the name Stanton Sheard, was born in Cobourg about 1865, although her family soon moved to Toronto, where she was raised. Her writings include children's books, historical and sentimental novels, and poetry collected in such volumes as *The Miracle and Other Poems* (1913), *The Ballad of the Quest* (1922), and *Fairy Doors* (1932). She died in 1943.

Also associated with Cobourg are several other authors, whose main achievements were in fields other than literature. The artist **Paul Kane** was born in Ireland and immigrated to Canada with his family in about 1819. He began his career by painting portraits in Cobourg, before living and studying in the United States and Europe until 1843. While in Cobourg he lived in a stuccoed frame house that still stands at 134 King St W.; it now houses a pizzaria. In 1846–8 Kane undertook an epic journey from TORONTO (1) to Vancouver Island and back; and the paintings, sketches, and journals of this experience formed the basis of his important book, *Wanderings of an Artist Among the Indians of North America* (1859; included in J. Russell Harper's *Paul Kane's Frontier*, 1971).

The actress **Marie Dressler** (1869–1934) originally Leila Koerber) was born in Cobourg on 9 Nov. 1896. In her two autobiographies, *The Life Story of an Ugly Duckling* (1924) and *My Own Story* (1934), she recounts how, in storybook fashion, she embarked on a theatrical career by running away from Cobourg at seventeen with a touring opera troupe. Her home at 212 King St W. is now a popular restaurant.

Charles Dickens visited Cobourg early in May 1842 and mentioned it in his *American Notes* (1843) as 'a cheerful, thriving little town'.

COLLINGWOOD

Edna Jaques, one of Canada's most prolific newspaper versifiers, was born on 17 Jan. 1890 on a farm near Collingwood. Her early years were spent at 130 4th St in a house built by her father. Central School, which she attended, is located at Maple and Fifth Sts. Jaques' autobiography, *Uphill All the Way* (1977), gives details of her youth in Collingwood. In 1902 the family moved to Saskatchewan, and although Jaques lived in Ontario from the early 1940s until her death in 1978, she was primarily associated with the prairies. Beginning in 1903 she published thousands of poems in newspapers and magazines in Canada, the United States, and Great Britain and collected her writings in eleven volumes, such as *Backdoor Neighbors*. Her verse inspired the parody poems that Paul Hiebert (see CARMAN, Man.) wrote for his satiric character Sarah Binks, 'the sweet songstress of Saskatchewan'. (See also BRIERCREST, Sask.)

Each June, Collingwood hosts the Blue Mountain Poetry Festival, which attracts many of the country's leading poets for readings and teaching sessions.

DALE

Near this small community at the intersection of Highway 28 and the Dale Road, is the site of **Susanna Moodie**'s farm, 'Melsetter', named after Melsetter in the Orkney Islands, the birthplace of Mrs Moodie's husband,

DALE

Just then, the carriage turned into a narrow, steep path, overhung with lofty woods, and, after labouring up it with considerable difficulty, and at the risk of breaking our necks, it brought us at length to a rocky upland clearing, partially covered with a second growth of timber, and surrounded on all sides by the dark forest.

"I guess," quoth our Yankee driver, "that at the bottom of this 'ere swell you'll find yourself to hum"; and plunging into a short path cut through the wood, he pointed to a miserable hut, at the bottom of a steep descent, and cracking his whip, exclaimed, " 'Tis a smart location that. I wish you Britishers may enjoy it."

I gazed upon the place in perfect dismay, for I had never seen such a shed called a house before. "You must be mistaken; that is not a house, but a cattle-shed, or pig-sty."

—Susanna Moodie, *Roughing It in the Bush* (1852)

John Wedderburn Dunbar Moodie. The property, now occupied by the privately owned Blyth Farm, is not open to the public but can be seen from a back road. Three miles east of Hwy 28, on the Dale Road, a partially paved road runs north from the Dale Road opposite the Hamilton Heights Golf Club. ('Melsetter' was about a mile north on this road, on the northeast corner of its intersection with another sideroad, where Blyth Farm now stands.) Mrs Moodie describes the family's life here from Sept. 1832 to Feb. 1834 in some of her most vivid sketches, found in the first two-thirds of *Roughing It in the Bush* (1852). She tells how she, her husband, and children were forced to move into a shack on their own property when the family that had been living in the farmhouse refused to give it up to its new owners. (See GORE'S LANDING.) The funeral of Phoebe, a daughter of this family, who was buried on the property, is described at the end of the sketch 'John Monoghan'; the burial ground is said to be enclosed now by a low fence on the Blyth Farm. (See also BELLEVILLE, DOURO TOWNSHIP, LAKEFIELD, TORONTO: I.)

DELTA

Lorne Pierce was born in Delta on 3 August 1890 and spent his childhood here. The family home is gone, but he is honoured with a plaque in the village. As editor of the Ryerson Press in TORONTO, Pierce assisted the careers of many writers; in 1926 he donated the Lorne Pierce medal in Canadian literature, which is awarded by the Royal Society of Canada. His books include *William Kirby: A Portrait of a Loyalist* (1929) and *English Canadian Literature* (1932).

The novelist **John Metcalf** lived in Delta in 1978–83; during this period he published his comic novel, *General Ludd* (1980); a book of essays, *Kicking Against the Pricks* (1982); and *Selected Stories* (1982). (See also OTTAWA; MONTREAL: 7, Que.) Delta is west of Brockville on Hwy 42.

DOON

Doon Pioneer Village, near Kitchener, is a re-created 1850s community that has on its grounds the log house in which **Peter McArthur** (1866–1924) was born and lived as a child. McArthur was born near APPIN on his family's farmstead in Ekfrid Township, Middlesex County. After a period as a freelance writer and magazine editor in New York and London, Eng., he opened an advertising agency in New York. When it failed in 1909 he returned to his father's farm and this house, where he began writing the humorous but penetrating essays on rural life that won him the title 'the sage of Ekfrid'. They were published in book form, beginning with *In Pastures Green* (1915).

Doon was also the birthplace of the painter Homer Watson (1855–1936), who lived most of his life here. He produced two of the most famous paintings in Victorian Canadian art: *The Pioneer Mill* (1880) and *The Flood Gate* (1900).

Doon Pioneer Village displays historic books that belonged to early southwestern Ontario settlers, including a 1560 Geneva Bible and an 1823 painted Pennsylvania Dutch Bible. Located northwest of Hwy 401 at interchange 34, the village is open daily, 10 a.m. to 5 p.m., from the first weekend in May to 31 Oct.

DOURO TOWNSHIP

Lying about 5 miles southeast of Lakefield, near Hwy 134, this was the centre of literary activity for the Strickland family members as a group. For five years (1834–9) Douro Township was home to Susanna Moodie, Catharine Parr Traill, and their brother, Samuel Strickland. Books based largely on their experiences here include Moodie's *Roughing It in the Bush* (1852), Traill's *The Backwoods of Canada* (1835), and Strickland's *Twenty-seven Years in Canada West* (1853).

The neighbouring properties of the three writers were near the site of Lakefield, clustered around the clearing made by **Samuel Strickland** on the shores of Katchewanooka Lake. Strickland had immigrated to Canada in 1825. After homesteading in Otonabee Township and working from 1828 to 1831 as a Canada Company officer at Guelph and Goderich, he settled in Douro Township and was soon joined by his sisters and their husbands. **Catharine Parr Traill** and her husband, Lieutenant Robert Traill, emigrated in 1832 and proceeded directly to the LAKEFIELD district, where they soon acquired property adjoining Strickland's. **Susanna Moodie** and her husband, John W.D. Moodie, also emigrated in 1832 but did not join Strickland and the Traills here until Feb. 1834. While here, Mrs Traill not only wrote her famous book, but contributed greatly to her family's solvency by selling short stories and sketches to American and English periodicals; and Mrs Moodie, in 1839, was invited to contribute to *The Literary Garland and British North American Magazine*, Montreal, where many of the chapters of *Roughing It in the Bush* appeared, beginning in 1847. In 1839 the Traills sold their farm and moved to Ashburnham, now a suburb of PETERBOROUGH. The following year the Moodies moved to BELLEVILLE after John Moodie was appointed sheriff of Hastings County. These six to seven years, spent in close association in Douro Township, served to launch Catharine Parr Traill and Susanna Moodie on their Canadian literary careers and provided much of the material for books written at other sites as well—especially, perhaps, Mrs Traill's first notable work as a naturalist, *Rambles in the Canadian Forest* (1859), which is based on her observations in the woods of Douro. (See TORONTO: I.)

The Journals of Susanna Moodie (1970) by Margaret Atwood, a sequence of poetic monologues based on Mrs Moodie's writings, makes reference to incidents that occurred in Douro Township.

How rapidly the face of this country changes. I left the woods of North Douro, 26 years ago. Only three houses all composed of logs and of the smallest dimensions were to be found within three miles of us. Now, my brother, who may be termed the Father and founder of the village of Lakefield, has a handsome commodious house and a beautiful garden which would amply satisfy the taste of any gentleman of moderate fortune, four of his five lads are married and settled near him. A neat village consisting of pretty well built houses, has sprung up like magic, where the lovely falls once foamed and thundered in the heart of the forest. The hand of industry has curbed the wild torrent and made it subservient to the wants of man. The stumps are almost all gone, and tasteful gardens full of bright flowers meet the eye in every direction. The place has already four churches, and they are busy building a very handsome new Episcopal church.

—Susanna Moodie, letter to Richard Bentley, 1865

DRESDEN

Uncle Tom's Cabin Museum, half a mile west of Dresden, preserves the house, church, and burial place of Josiah Henson, a fugitive slave whose life story inspired much of the plot of **Harriet Beecher Stowe**'s abolitionist novel, *Uncle Tom's Cabin* (1852). Born in 1780, Henson escaped to Upper Canada in 1830 and bought 200 acres of land near Dresden. He established the British American Institute in 1841, and in 1849 met Stowe during a trip to Boston. He died in 1883 and is buried near the house. Of the eight buildings on the museum grounds, four are historic structures, including Henson's house, dating from 1841, and his church (1850). The modern museum building displays mementoes of Henson and the British American Institute. The museum complex is open from 1 May to 31 Oct. daily from 10 a.m. to 6 p.m. It is located on County Rd 40, one mile north of County Rd 15; signs on Hwy 21 and in Dresden give directions. Beside the museum grounds is the Henson Family Cemetery, which contains Josiah Henson's grave and a national historic plaque commemorating him; this is still an active cemetery used by branches of the Henson family in the Dresden area. Across the road from the museum is the cemetery of the British American Institute. Henson wrote his own story of his experiences as a slave in *Truth Stranger Than Fiction: Father Henson's Story of His Life* (1858). (See also CHATHAM.)

The poet **Tom MacInnes** was born in Dresden on 29 Oct. 1867 and attended public school here, but he spent much of his childhood in NEW WESTMINSTER, B.C. Although he attended University in TORONTO (3), he lived most of his life on the west coast, especially in VANCOUVER. His books include *Lonesome Bar, a Romance of the Lost, and Other Poems* (1909), *In Amber Lands* (1910), and *In the Old of My Age* (1947).

EGYPT

This small community, in which **Stephen Leacock** spent his Canadian childhood, is now only an intersection where several modern farmhouses cluster near the Egypt Women's Institute, built in 1901. About 2 1/2 miles south of Hwy 48, Egypt lies at the intersection of York Regional Rd 18, known locally as Egypt Sideroad, and Concession Rd 4. The farm where Leacock's father, Peter Leacock, pursued his persistently unsuccessful career in agriculture and where Stephen lived from 1875 through his early high-school years, is on the northwest corner of the intersection, about 400 yards west of York 18 along the concession road. The former Leacock house—a large cement-clad frame structure that stood on a rise at the north end of the farm—burned down on 25 Feb. 1960. A rough tractor trail still leads from the concession road to the site of the house and its outbuildings, which figure prominently in Leacock's *The Boy I Left Behind Me* (1947).

ELLIOTT LAKE

This town, midway between Sudbury and Sault Ste Marie, was established in 1954 after uranium ore was discovered here. During the late 1950s the novelist **Peter Such** worked here as a miner in his summers while studying for his B.A. at the University of Toronto. His first novel *Fallout* (1969; rpr. 1978), which recounts the boom and collapse of local uranium mining, is a bitter indictment of that industry's impact on the environment and the native peoples of the Elliott Lake area. (See also TORONTO: 7; TWILLINGATE, Nfld.) The Elliott Lake Nuclear and Mining Museum portrays the industry's history in the area.

ERIN

Erin was the home from 1850 to 1877 of **Alexander McLachlan**. During his years here he published four of his five volumes of verse: *Poems* appeared in 1856, followed by *Lyrics* (1858), *The Emigrant and Other Poems* (1861) and *Poems and Songs* (1874). The latter two volumes made McLachlan one of the most important of Canada's early poets, especially interesting for his depiction of Ontario pioneer life. He was born in 1818 in Scotland, came to Canada in 1840, and farmed in Peel County (1840–44), in Downie township, Perth County (1844–7), and in North Easthope township, Perth County (1847–50); his first book was *The Spirit of Love and Other Poems* (1846). In 1850 he gave up farming and moved to Erin, where he supported himself by tailoring and by lecturing for the rural Mechanics' Institutes. In 1862, through his friend and admirer D'Arcy McGee, McLachlan was appointed an emigration agent to Scotland. In 1877 he moved to a farm in Amaranth township; he died in ORANGEVILLE in 1896. His last two books and some of his other poems including several from manuscripts, were published as *The Poetical Works of Alexander McLachlan* in 1900; this was reprinted in 1974 with an appendix containing additional poems.

The Porcupine's Quill, a prominent literary publisher since 1974, is at 68 Main St. Its co-owner and publisher is the poet **Tim Inkster** (*Letters*, 1976; *Blue Angel*, 1983). Erin, on Hwy 24, is northwest of Georgetown.

> DANIEL McMILLAN,
> REPUTED FOUNDER OF ERIN
>
> *He chopp'd, he logg'd, he clear'd his lot,*
> *And into many a darken'd spot*
> *He let the light of day;*
> *And through the long and dismal swamp,*
> *So dark, so dreary and so damp,*
> *He made a turnpike way.*
> *The church, the school-house, and the mill,*
> *The store, the forge, the vat, the kiln,*
> *Were triumphs of his hand;*
> *And many a lovely spot of green*
> *Which peeps out there, the woods between,*
> *Came forth at his command.*
>
> —Alexander McLachlan, from 'A Backwoods Hero', *The Poetical Works of Alexander McLachlan* (1900)

FLORENCE

Kildare Dobbs lived in Florence—a village of fewer than 200 people on the Sydenham River in southeastern Lambton County—while teaching during the 1952–3 term at nearby Lambton-Kent High School. Born in 1923 in Ireland, Dobbs emigrated in 1952, coming first to TORONTO (4), but almost immediately taking up his teaching post in Florence. The community inspired his fictional Venice, Ont., described in *Running to Paradise* (1962), which won a Governor General's Award. According to the chapter 'Views of Venice', Dobbs found himself in the small town because he was determined, upon arriving in Canada, to take the first job that appeared. He comments on the reluctance of people to believe that Venice, Ontario, really exists: ' "But," people say to me when I talk about it, "where on earth *is* Venice, Ontario?" I can tell by the way they ask that they think I have made it up. It is not in the gazetteer or on any railway line or on the road to anywhere. It is where it is, and to the people who live on its two streets it is naturally at the centre of the universe, the still centre where nothing happens but about which life and time revolve.'

GALT

See CAMBRIDGE.

GLANFORD TOWNSHIP

Maggie Clark, who inspired the poem 'When You and I Were Young, Maggie', lived in a square stone house still standing on lot 13, concession 5 of Glanford Township near Hamilton. The house is marked by a provincial historical plaque commemorating Maggie and the poem's author, her husband, **George Washington Johnson**. One mile north, on Twenty Mile Creek, stood the sawmill mentioned in Johnson's poem:

I wandered today to the hill, Maggie,
To watch the scene below:
The creek and the old rusty mill,
Maggie . . .

Johnson taught in 1859 at Glanford Section School No. 5, where Maggie was one of his pupils. They were married in 1864, the same year Johnson published *Maples Leaves*, which contained the Maggie poem. Shortly after, the couple moved to the United States, where Johnson worked as a newspaper editor. In 1865 Maggie, only twenty-three, died of typhus. She is buried near her former Glanford home in the White Church Cemetery, MOUNT HOPE. 'When You and I Were Young, Maggie' was set to music in 1866 by J.A. Butterfield.

GODERICH

The writer, pioneer, and physician **William 'Tiger' Dunlop** founded this city, now the largest Canadian port on Lake Huron, in 1827, and is responsible for the 'star' pattern of its plan—still one of the community's most striking features: eight major streets radiate from the angles of a central octagonal shaped common. In Dunlop's plan this common was named 'Duncan Place'. He originally called the settlement Gairbraid, a name it shared with his rambling log mansion (gone). Dunlop, his home, and his circle are extensively described in *In the Days of the Canada Company* (1896, rpr. 1972) by Robina and Kathleen Macfarlane Lizars, who lived at Stratford and whose family was related to Dunlop's. Dunlop arrived in Canada in 1813–14 as surgeon of the 89th Regiment and came to Ontario (then Upper Canada) permanently in 1826 as a forest warden and explorer for the Canada Company; in this capacity he was associated with the Scottish novelist John Galt, who founded GUELPH and after whom Galt was named (see CAMBRIDGE). Dunlop established his home at Goderich and fought for the rights of the settlers. He became inspector of the Canada Company's lands and settlements and, in 1833, its general superintendent; but, dissatisfied with its treatment of immigrants, he resigned in 1838. He was a reform member of the House of Assembly in 1841–6 and superintendent of the Lachine Canal from

'Tiger' Dunlop drawn by S.O. Tazewell of Goderich, for the *Canadian Literary Magazine*

1846 until his death two years later. Dunlop's writings—vividly descriptive, often humorous and satirical—include his *Statistical Sketches of Upper Canada, for the Use of Emigrants* (1832), which vividly describes nature and the joys of the outdoorsman's life in Upper Canada, while also conveying a cheerful disregard for facts and an absence of statistics. He also published *Recollections of the American War, 1812–14* (magazine publication, 1847; book, 1905). A Loyalist novel, *Two and Twenty Years Ago; A Tale of the Canadian Rebellion* (1859), has been attributed to him. Dunlop's grave lies just north of Goderich off Hwy 21; he is honoured by a plaque there, and by another in town in Harbour Park.

> A PIONEER HOME NEAR GODERICH
>
> *The log house was so close upon the bank that ingress and egress had to be given by the door looking toward the forest and future roadway. The kitchen was the first of the three large rooms, with big open fireplace, crane, Dutch oven and ingle-nook of old times. Divided by a screen, one part served the purpose of dining-room. Next came the drawing-room, furnished with skins of beasts—lamb, wolf, bear, calf and coon—rugs for the floor, or stretched upon seats made by the boys. . . . The whole house was thickly overgrown with grapevine, the French window of the drawing-room heavily framed with it. That window opened upon the bank, the river some seventy feet below, with wooded islands; and the wild roses whose succession of blooms made the whole summer beautiful, freshly picked, were all about the room so primitively furnished, yet which was decorated with miniatures and portraits that told of the life left behind.*
>
> —Robina and Kathleen Lizars, *In the Days of the Canada Company* (1896)

GORE'S LANDING

This tiny village built on scenic hills and ridges on the south shore of Rice Lake has carefully preserved a rich history that includes associations with many notable nineteenth-century writers and literary works. **Catharine Parr Traill** first visited here in 1840. She stayed with the Rev. George Bridges, an Anglican clergyman without incumbency, who had come from England by way of Jamaica and was persuaded to choose Canada as his permanent home partly by Mrs Traill's *The Backwoods of Canada* (1836). Bridges had built a unique octagonal six-storey house in which each storey was a single large room, which Mrs Traill, who had a passion for naming things, called 'Wolf Tower'. When the Traill family moved to Gore's Landing from Ashburnam (see PETERBOROUGH) in the spring of 1846, they lived in 'Wolf Tower' for a year. The house burned down in 1856; its site is now occupied by a private home called 'Tower Manor', at the north end of Tower Manor Road near the shore of Rice Lake.

In the spring of 1847 the Traills moved to a log house called 'Mount Ararat' that was built for them on a site at or near Gore's Landing. They then bought another farm, 'Oaklands', about a mile and a half south of the lakeshore on the west side of Traill Road; the large log house had been the home of Judge William Falkner. The foundation of the house and the barns that were part of the Traill farm still stand in fields near a high ridge that provides a spectacular view of Rice Lake. While living at 'Oaklands' Mrs Traill wrote two children's books: *The Canadian Crusoes. A Tale of the Rice Lake Plains* (1852) and *Lady Mary and Her Nurse; or, a Peep into the Canadian Forest* (1856); here also she did much of her work on Canadian flora. When the house burned down with all its contents in 1857, a manuscript on wildflowers was saved; this became *Canadian Wild Flowers* (1868). Shortly after the disastrous fire Catharine's husband, Thomas Traill, died, and the writer moved permanently to LAKEFIELD. *Canadian Wild Flowers* incorporated Mrs Traill's observations both at Gore's Landing and in the Douro woods at Lakefield.

'Old Joe R—' in *Roughing It in the Bush*

by **Susanna Moodie** was a Loyalist from New England, Joe Harris, who lived for a time in what is now the west wing of a clapboard house on the south side of Lander Road, several hundred yards west of Kelly Road, near Gore's Landing. In the chapter entitled 'Our First Settlement, and the Borrowing System', Moodie tells how, upon taking possession of their farm 'Melsetter' (see DALE), the Moodies found Old Joe and his wife Hannah living in the farm house. They refused to leave, forcing the Moodies to live through a difficult winter in a dilapidated shack on their own property.

GORE'S LANDING

There lies between the Rice Lake and the Ontario, a deep and fertile valley, surrounded by lofty wood-crowned hills, the heights of which were clothed chiefly with groves of oak and pine, though the sides of the hills and the alluvial bottoms gave a variety of noble timber trees of various kinds, as the maple, beech, hemlock, and others. This beautiful and highly picturesque valley is watered by many clear streams of pure refreshing water, from whence the spot has derived its appropriate appellation of "Cold Springs."

—Catharine Parr Traill, *Canadian Crusoes: A Tale of the Rice Lake Plains* (1852)

Rhoda Anne Page lived at Gore's Landing from the time of her marriage in COBOURG in Feb. 1856 until her death on 7 Dec. 1863. Page married William Bowes Falkner, a son of Judge William Falkner, whose farm, 'Oaklands', had been bought and occupied by the Traills. The poet and her husband lived in a one-and-a-half-storey log house on a farm at the northeast corner of County Rd 9 and Lew Harris Rd—diagnonally opposite the former 'Oaklands' farm. One of Canada's most widely read poets in the 1840s and 1850s, Rhoda Page began publishing in 1846 in the Cobourg *Star*, and afterwards her poems appeared in many other periodicals in Canada West and Canada East. Her 'Rice Lake by Moonlight: a Winter Scene' was the most frequently reprinted Canadian poem of the time. She published a small collection of poems in Cobourg in 1850, and the year after her death five of her poems appeared in the first important anthology of Canadian verse, E.H. Dewart's *Selections from Canadian Poets* (1864). Her gravestone, now almost illegible, can be seen in the churchyard of St George's (Anglican) Church, on the crest of a steep wooded hill on the south side of Church Hill Road. A nineteenth-century fieldstone church replaces the original clapboard structure, erected in 1847. (Mrs Traill attended the first service on 1 Jan. 1848.)

The original St George's Anglican Church at Gore's Landing, 1850. painted by William A. Johnson

In 1867, more than a decade after Rhoda Page died and Mrs Traill had left Gore's Landing for Lakefield, Archibald Lampman Sr, father of the poet **Archibald Lampman**, became the Anglican incumbent at PERRYTOWN and Elizabethville and began taking services at Gore's Landing in the absence of a resident clergyman. In 1868 he moved his family to Gore's Landing, taking up residence in the Weller Tavern (built by William Weller, the first mayor of Cobourg). Dating from about 1845, the tavern had been closed since 1864 and was draughty and in poor repair; the draughts and dampness were blamed for a serious illness suffered by the six-year-old future poet during the family's year-long residence there. The building (now covered with white aluminum siding) can be seen on the northwest corner of Plank Rd and the path now called Lampman Lane, one block south of the lakeshore.

While in Gore's Landing, where he lived until he was thirteen, the young Archibald Lampman attended a private school run by Frederick W. Barron, a former headmaster of Upper Canada College, Toronto, who in 1869 married the widow of Thomas Gore, after whom the village is named. The Barrons occupied Gore's house, 'Glenavy', and Barron conducted his school there. 'Glenavy'—located on the north side of Church Hill Rd, just west of St George's Church—was destroyed by fire in 1910; but its site can still be identified by the grove of locust trees in which it stood, and by a portion of the foundation still visible. The years at Gore's Landing first awakened Lampman to the experience of nature that informs his poetry. Writing at the age of thirty about this period of his childhood, he said: 'I remember a lake with a long mid-winter road running across its frozen surface marked with young cedars fading into the distance, an infinite dotted line, and I remember the jingling teams that would come by this track on the crystal Christmas mornings, bound for the little rough-cast church on the hilltop above the landing.'

The Lampman home at Gore's Landing today

GUELPH

Guelph was founded on 23 Apr. 1827 by the Scottish novelist **John Galt**, superintendent of the Canada Company from 1826 to 1829.

THE FOUNDING OF GUELPH

I do not suppose that the sublimity of the occasion was unfelt by the others, for I noticed that after the tree fell there was a funereal pause, as when the coffin is lowered into the ground; it was, however, of short duration, for the doctor pulled a flask of whisky from his bosom and we drank prosperity to the City of Guelph.

—John Galt, *Autobiography* (1833)

He designed the radial pattern of the city streets and lived with his wife in a log house in the new settlement in 1828–9; he then returned to England. A small model of the first house Galt built in Guelph, 'The Priory', stands in Riverside Park, where an elaborate clock garden and provincial plaque are dedicated to the city's founder. (There is another plaque in Royal City Park.) Galt tells the story of the founding of Guelph in his *Autobiography* (1833). His novel *Laurie Todd: or, The Settlers in the Wood* (1830) draws on

Galt's experiences with the Canada Company. (See also CAMBRIDGE.)

James Gay—the self-proclaimed 'Canadian poet laureate' and one of the four poets written about by William Arthur Deacon in *The Four Jameses* (1927)—settled at Guelph in 1834 and lived here most of his life. He first worked as a carpenter and later ran a gunsmith's shop in Market Square. It was in Guelph that Gay published his *Poems by James Gay: Written While Crossing the Sea in 1882* (1883). He died here in 1891 and was buried in St George's Woodlawn Cemetery.

John McLean, author of the travel classic *Notes of a Twenty-five Years' Service in the Hudson's Bay Company* (1849), retired to Guelph in 1845. He died here in 1890. His house at 21 Nottingham St is preserved as a historic site and is marked with a plaque.

John McCrae, author of 'In Flanders Fields', was born here on 30 Nov. 1872. His birthplace at 102 Water St is a national historic site. The bedroom and combined diningroom and kitchen are furnished as he knew them, and manuscripts and sketches by him are on display. Next door the McCrae Memorial Gardens contain a light burning in memory of the poet. McCrae was educated in Guelph and at the University of Toronto (see TORONTO: 3), where he graduated in medicine. After serving in the Boer War, he practised medicine in MONTREAL (3) for fourteen years before entering military service as an artillery brigade field surgeon. 'In Flanders Fields' was written in 1915 during the Second Battle of Ypres, where McCrae was serving in a front-line dressing station. The poem first appeared in *Punch* on 15 Dec. 1915. McCrae died of pneumonia in 1918 in Boulogne and is buried at Wimereux in northern France. *In Flanders Fields and Other Poems* was published the next year, with a memoir by Sir Andrew Macphail. (See also SHILO, Man.)

The McCrae home, Guelph, from the Memorial Gardens

Tablet at the City Hall, Guelph

The poet **Douglas Lochhead** was born in Guelph in 1922 but grew up in Fredericton and Ottawa. (See TORONTO: 3; SACKVILLE, N.B.)

The Guelph Reformatory has a literary association for having given the playwright **John Herbert** the unfortunate experience on which he based his play *Fortune and Men's Eyes* (1967; 2nd edn 1974). A native of TORONTO (7), Herbert served a six-month sentence there in 1946–7, when he was nineteen, as a result of being harassed by some local toughs and accused of homosexuality at a time when it was illegal. His play premièred off-Broadway on 23 Feb. 1967 and was filmed in 1971.

The University of Guelph was formed in 1964 out of the former Ontario Agricultural College; its most famous literary alumnus is **John Kenneth Galbraith**, who studied here from 1926 to 1931 and writes of the school in his autobiographical works *The Scotch* (1964) and *A Life in Our Times* (1981). (See also IONA STATION.) The poet **D.G. Jones** lived on Westmount Blvd from 1955 to 1961 while teaching at the agricultural college; during this period he published his first two volumes, *Frost on the Sun* (1957) and *The Sun is an Axeman* (1961). (See also BANCROFT; NORTH HATLEY, Que.) The university's McLaughlin Library houses, among other literary materials, the diaries of **Lucy Maud Montgomery**. Her son, Dr. E. Stuart Macdonald, closed these papers to public inspection until 1992, so that the scholar **Mary Rubio** could oversee their editing and publication in a suitable form. This work has begun to appear with publication of *The Selected Journals of L.M. Montgomery, Volume I: 1889–1910* (1985) and *Volume II: 1910–1921* (1987). Dr. Rubio and the other editor of the *Journals*, Dr **Elizabeth Waterston**, are both professors of English at the University of Guelph. (See also LEASKDALE, NORVAL, TORONTO: 7; CAVENDISH, CHARLOTTETOWN, NEW LONDON, P.E.I.)

HALIBURTON

This village and the surrounding Haliburton Highlands are named after the Nova Scotia-born humorist and judge **Thomas Chandler Haliburton** (see WINDSOR, N.S.). The district was first settled in 1864 by immigrants who had bought land from the Canadian Land and Emigration Co. (London, Eng.), of which T.C. Haliburton was then chairman. Haliburton had moved to London permanently in 1856, but his name still carried weight in Canada, where it was featured prominently in advertisements for settlers on more than 250,000 acres that the company had for sale. The Haliburton County Library, Dysart Branch, Mountain St, displays a historic nineteenth-century photograph of Haliburton. A provincial historical plaque commemorating the founding of the Village of Haliburton stands in Sam Slick Park, named for Haliburton's most famous humorous character, at the west end of the village on Hwy 121, at the foot of Head Lake.

Haliburton's second wife, Sarah, whom he married shortly after moving to England, donated an organ to St George's Anglican Church here. The original frame structure of the church, later destroyed by fire, was built on property donated by the Canadian Land and Emigration Co. The present church, erected in 1922 on the same site, stands on Mountain St on a hill overlooking Head Lake.

HAMILTON

George Washington Johnson, who wrote the words for the popular song 'When You and I Were Young, Maggie' was born in 1839 near Hamilton in BINBROOK TOWNSHIP. A schoolteacher in Hamilton, he was named principal of Central High School in 1875 and was on the staff of Upper Canada College, TORONTO (7), from 1891 to 1908. The author of three collections of verse, all published in the 1860s, he died in 1917 and is buried in Hamilton. In 1875–6 Johnson lived at 84 John St S., and later in the 1870s and early 1880s he lived at 78 Hughson St S.; his address in 1880–90 was 3 Young St. Upon his return from Toronto he lived at 36 Ray St N. from 1909 until his death.

The novelist and poet **Philip Child** was born in Hamilton in 1898 and lived most of his life in TORONTO (3), where he taught at Trinity College, University of Toronto. His books include the novels *Village of Souls* (1933) and *Mr. Ames Against Time* (1949), and *The Victorian House* (1951), a narrative poem.

The poet **George Johnston** was born here on 7 Oct. 1913. Educated at the University of Toronto, he taught at Carleton University, OTTAWA, from 1950 until his retirement in 1980. He now lives in Athelstan, Qué. His books of poetry include *The Cruising Auk* (1959) and *Happy Enough: Poems 1935–1972* (1972).

The popular novelist **Richard Rohmer** was born in Hamilton on 24 Jan. 1924. He lived in Hamilton at intervals throughout his childhood and attended high school in Fort Erie. After serving in the Second World War he attended school in WINDSOR, and since 1948 has lived in TORONTO (5). Among his novels are *Ultimatum* (1973); *Exxoneration* (1974), *Separation* (1976), and *Periscope Red* (1980); he has also published several works of non-fiction.

Hamilton was also the birthplace, on 8 Mar. 1935, of **Sylvia Fraser**. After attending local schools, she received her B.A. from the University of Western Ontario, London. Her first novel, *Pandora* (1972), is the story of a girl growing up during the Second World War in an Ontario steel town closely modelled on Hamilton.

Another Hamilton native, poet **David McFadden**, was born in 1940 and attended school here. In 1962 he started work as a proofreader at the *Hamilton Spectator* and in 1970 he became a reporter. His early books of poems were rooted in his Hamilton family life; these include *Letters from the Earth to the Earth* (1968) and *Poems Worth Knowing* (1971). McFadden left the paper in 1976 to work as a freelance writer and editor. The McFadden family home at the time of McFadden's birth was at 21 Somerset Ave; in the mid-1940s the family lived at 175 Balmoral Ave, Apt 1. From 1948 the McFaddens lived at 99 Barons Ave N. After going to work for the *Spectator*, McFadden lived at a number of addresses, including 1975 Barton St E. in the mid-1960s, 86 Garside Ave N. in 1967–9, and 9 Toby Cr. from 1970 to 1979. He now lives in TORONTO (6).

McMaster University, founded in Toronto in 1887, moved to Hamilton in 1930. Its staff and students have included many writers. **Watson Kirkconnell**, prolific translator and popularizer of Canadian immigrants' writing in languages other than French and English, was head of the English Department at McMaster from 1940 to 1948. (See WOLFVILLE, N.S.) Throughout his eight years in Hamilton, Kirkconnell lived at 31 Mt Royal Ave. In 1967 **Matt Cohen** was appointed lecturer in the Department of Religion, where he taught the sociology of religion; the following year he abandoned teaching for writing. McMaster graduates include the novelist **Marian Engel** (née Passmore) who received her M.A. in 1955. (See TORONTO: 2, 7.) The Mills Memorial Library of McMaster contains a collection of the papers of Margaret Laurence, David McFadden, Farley Mowat, John Coulter, and other Canadian writers, and archival material from McClelland and Stewart, Oberon Press, and the Writers' Union of Canada; the library also holds papers of several foreign authors, including Samuel Beckett, Anthony Burgess, and Bertrand Russell.

HARRINGTON WEST

Charles Gordon, who as 'Ralph Connor' was one of North America's most popular novelists at the turn of the century, came in 1870, at the age of ten, from Glengarry County to a small community named Zorra near Harrington West. Gordon's father, a minister, had been called to the Harrington Presbyterian congregation, and for the next twenty years Zorra was his family home. Now best known for his books about his Glengarry birthplace (see ST ELMO), Charles Gordon attended high school in the Zorra area, graduating in 1879. After teaching in local schools for eighteen months to earn money for his university tuition, he entered the University of Toronto in 1880. Gordon returned to Zorra in 1888–9 to help his ailing father with his parish duties; in 1890 his mother, one of the most important influences in Gordon's life, died here. Soon after, Gordon entered missionary work in the Northwest Territories (see CANMORE, Alta) and in 1895 accepted a call to St Stephen's Church near WINNIPEG, which remained his parish until his death in 1937. In his autobiography, *Postscript to Adventure* (1938) Gordon described Zorra in the 1870s: 'Roads had been graveled and swamps drained. The forests, alas for us boys, had been reduced to little wood lots, where nothing bigger or more dangerous than a woodchuck or a skunk could be found, and where the only game were a few timid partridges. The forest had given place to great wheat crops, turnip and potato fields, magnificent orchards.' Zorra no longer exists as a populated community.

> THE LOGGING BEE
>
> *The men with the axes went first, chopping up the half-burned logs into lengths suitable for the burning piles, clearing away the brushwood, and cutting through the big roots of the fire-eaten stumps so that they might more easily be pulled. Then followed the teams with their logging-chains, hauling the logs to the piles, jerking out and drawing off the stumps whose huge roots stuck up high into the air, and drawing great heaps of brush-wood to aid in reducing the heavy logs to ashes. At each log-pile stood a man with a hand-spike to help the driver to get the log into position, a work requiring strength and skill, and above all, a knowledge of the ways of logs which comes only by experience.*
>
> —Ralph Connor (Charles Gordon), *The Man from Glengarry* (1901)

HAWKESBURY

The poet **Tom Wayman** was born in Hawkesbury on 13 Aug. 1945 but has lived most of his life on the west coast. His family moved first to PRINCE RUPERT and then to VANCOUVER, where Wayman attended school. His books include *Waiting for Wayman* (1973), *A Government Job at Last* (1976), and *The Nobel Prize Acceptance Speech* (1981).

INGERSOLL

Known as the 'cheese' poet, **James McIntyre** lived for many years in Ingersoll. He moved here from ST CATHARINES in the second half of the nineteenth century and almost certainly was settled, with his furniture factory in operation, by 1866; it was in that year that the giant cheese, to which he dedicated his 'Ode on the Mammoth Cheese', was produced in Ingersoll. A provincial plaque in honour of the famous 7,000-pound cheese, the largest of its time, stands south of Ingersoll on Hwy 19, near the site of the factory where it was made.

The cheese was intended for display at a world's fair in Paris and was being shipped to a provincial exhibition in Toronto when McIntyre sang its praises:

> *We have seen thee, queen of cheese,*
> *Lying quietly at your ease,*
> *Gently fanned by evening breeze,*
> *Thy fair form no flies dare seize.*

The poem was published in *Musings on the Banks of the Canadian Thames* (1884); another book, *Poems of James McIntyre*, followed in 1889. McIntyre's furniture store burned down, but he remained a popular community figure, active in the Erskine Presbyterian Church and the town's fraternal organizations. He died at Ingersoll in 1906. McIntyre is one of the subjects in William Arthur Deacon's humorous *The Four Jameses* (1927).

IONA STATION

In 1964 the noted economist **John Kenneth Galbraith** published *The Scotch*, a memoir of his childhood in Elgin County, where he was born on 15 Oct. 1908. Galbraith has also written of his Ontario upbringing in his autobiography, *A Life in Our Times* (1981). His father had a farm 20 miles west of St Thomas, near the hamlet of Iona Station. The Galbraith farmhouse was on a county road named Hogg St, which runs from Currie Road to the Southwold Twp line about 3 miles west of Iona Station. Galbraith attended a one-room school, SS 104, in nearby Wallacetown, completing the eight grades in four years. In 1926 he entered the Ontario Agricultural College, GUELPH. During his student years he wrote a weekly column on agriculture for the St Thomas *Times Journal*. 'That $3 a week was the highest pay I've ever had, considering the marginal utility of money,' said Galbraith on a visit to Elgin County in the 1960s. Since 1931, the year he graduated from Ontario Agricultural College, Galbraith has lived in the United States where he taught at Harvard University; he has also been an economic adviser to the American government and ambassador to India.

KEENE

James Evans, the inventor of a syllabic alphabet still in use among the Cree Indians, came to Canada in 1823 from his native England and began teaching in the Methodist missions near Keene at Rice Lake in 1828. Ordained in 1833, Evans was named general superintendent of the northwest missions in 1840 and travelled to NORWAY HOUSE, Man., where he printed the first book using his new alphabet in 1841.

KINGSTON

The site of Kingston, on Lake Ontario at the mouth of the Cataraqui River, was visited by Europeans for the first time in 1615, when **Samuel de Champlain** discovered an Iroquois Indian camp here. In 1673 Frontenac, governor of New France, built a stockade on the western bank of the Cataraqui; the explorer La Salle replaced the building with stone bastions and named the site Fort Frontenac. The region remained in French hands until 1758, when the fort was captured by the British. Named Kingston by the United Empire Loyalists, who settled here in 1784, the town was fortified at Point Henry during the War of 1812. **Joseph Mermet**, an officer with the Swiss Régiment de Watteville at Kingston from 1813 to 1816, wrote many poems about the war and a soldier's life in Canada. The poems include a description of the Battle of Châteauguay and 'Les Boucheries: fêtes rurales du Canada', which recreates the ceremonies surrounding the preparation of a winter food supply. Mermet's poems are included in the magazine, *La Bibliothèque canadienne* (9 vols, 1825–30) edited by Michel Bibaud, and the anthology *Le Répertoire national* (4 vols, 1848–50) edited by James Huston. (See also CHÂTEAUGUAY, Que.)

St. Ursula's Convent; or, The Nun of Canada (1824) was the first novel by a native-born author to be published in British North America. A melodramatic tale of shipwreck, evil priests, and exchanged babies, the book was published by Hugh C. Thomson of Kingston. One hundred and forty-seven subscribers paid 9s. 4d. for the two-volume work, the first novel of **Julia Beckwith Hart**, a native of FREDERICTON, N.B., who had moved to Kingston in 1820 to live with an aunt. Hart had begun the novel when she was seventeen and based her story to some extent on personal observation of life in Quebec, where she frequently visited relatives while growing up. In Kingston she married, and ran a girls' boarding school before moving to the United States, where her second novel, *Tonnewonte; or The Adopted Son of America* (1825), was published. From 1831 Hart lived in Fredericton, where she often contributed stories to local periodicals. She died in 1867.

Kingston's most important early writer is **Charles Sangster**, who was born on 16 July 1822 at the naval yard on Point Frederick, the present site of the Royal Military College. Sangster's father was a joiner and shipbuilder in the Royal Navy. Raised in Kingston and in Pittsburgh Township, Sangster left school at the age of fifteen to work in the munitions laboratory at Fort Henry.

Charles Sangster

(Fort Henry was built in 1832–6 and has been restored as a provincial historic site.) He made cartridges there during the Rebellion of 1837; in 1839 he was transferred to the Ordnance Office, where he worked as a clerk for ten years. Dissatisfied with his superiors' refusal to promote him, Sangster found a job on an AMHERSTBURG newspaper in the summer of 1849. After it failed, Sangster worked as a proofreader and bookkeeper for Kingston's *British Whig* and later as a reporter for the *Daily News*. Most of Sangster's published poetry was written during his years as a journalist in Kingston. *The St. Lawrence and the Saguenay and Other Poems* (1856), his first book, shows his indebtedness to the English Romantics in tone and subject as he blends description of nature with retellings of Indian legends and events from British exploration and conquest. Sangster's second book, *Hesperus and Other Poems and Lyrics* (1860), lays greater emphasis on pride in Canadian history than on love of nature, with such poems as 'The Plains of Abraham', 'Death of Wolfe', 'Brock', and 'Song for Canada'. From 1868 to 1886 Sangster worked in OTTAWA for the Post Office. He

IN THE THOUSAND ISLANDS

XI.

On, through the lovely Archipelago,
Glides the swift bark. Soft summer matins ring
From every isle. The wild fowl come and go,
Regardless of our presence. On the wing,
And perched upon the bough, the gay birds sing
Their loves: This is their summer paradise;
From morn till night their joyous caroling
Delights the ear, and through the lucent skies
Ascends the choral hymn in softest symphonies.

—Charles Sangster, *The St. Lawrence and the Saguenay and Other Poems* (1856)

The house where Charles Sangster died

disliked his job (he complained that the work left him no time or energy to write) and again found himself passed over for promotion. On retiring in 1886 Sangster returned to Kingston to live with his nephew William at 398 Barrie St, where he died on 9 Dec. 1893; this house is still standing. He is buried in Cataraqui Cemetery and is honoured with a provincial historic plaque near his former home; the plaque is located on the Cricket Field near Court St, on the Barrie St side.

Adam Hood Burwell came to Kingston after being expelled from the Anglican priesthood in 1836 because his teaching departed from church doctrine. He lived here until his death in 1849, serving as a minister of the Catholic Apostolic Church ('Irvingite'). Born near Fort Erie in 1790, Burwell began publishing poetry in Upper Canada newspapers in 1816. Near the end of his life many of his poems and religious tracts were published in periodicals, including the *Literary Garland* of Montreal. A selection of his work was pulished in *The Poems of Adam Hood Burwell, Pioneer Poet of Upper Canada* (1963) edited by C.F. Klinck.

Barker's Canadian Monthly Magazine, published here in twelve issues from May 1846 to Apr. 1847, was the first pre-Confederation magazine written entirely by Canadians. It was published by **Edward John Barker**, who came to Kingston from England in 1832 and in 1834 founded the *British Whig* (the newspaper that employed Charles Sangster as proofreader beginning in 1849). *Barker's Magazine* published poetry, fiction, reviews, satire, articles on Canadian politics, and a novel, **John Swete Cummins**' *Altham: A Tale of the Sea* (1849). (Cummins, a native of Ireland, lived on Amherst Island, near Kingston, as agent for Lord Mountcashel; little is known of his life in Canada, but it is likely that he lived in this area in the 1830s and 1840s.) Instalments began to appear in Oct. 1846 in *Barker's*, but only two-thirds of the novel had been published before the magazine ceased operations. Cummins' story is set during the Napoleonic Wars and takes place, in part, in Halifax and Montreal.

The novelist **Grant Allen** was born in 1848 at his family home 'Alwington House' (gone) on Wolfe Island. His father was Joseph Antisell Allen, the first Anglican clergyman of Wolfe Island and the author of two books of poetry, *Day-Dreams of a Butterfly* (1854) and a *Tercentenary Poem on Shakespeare* (1864). Grant Allen was educated privately in Kingston, and studied at Merton College, Oxford, from 1868 to 1871. In the 1870s he settled in London to pursue a writing career but had no success until 1880, when he began writing magazine fiction. From that time until his death in 1899, Allen published more than forty works of fiction and thirty of non-fiction. His novels include *The British Barbarians; A Hilltop Novel* (1895), one of many he wrote to dramatize current social problems, and *An African Millionaire; Episodes in the Life of the Illustrious Colonel Clay* (1897), which is of interest to readers of detective fiction for its Raffles-like hero, who anticipated by two years E.W. Hornung's gentleman bandit. Allen's niece, **Agnes Maule Machar**, was also a popular novelist at the end of the nineteenth century. Machar was the granddaughter of Joseph Antisell Allen and the daughter of John Machar, minister of St Andrew's Presbyterian Church from 1827 to 1863 and principal of Queen's University from 1846 to 1853. Machar, who often wrote under the pen-name 'Fidelis', was born here on 23 Jan. 1837 and was a lifelong resident of Kingston. For many years the family lived at 25 Sydenham St; this was Agnes Machar's home until her death in 1927. Her career began with five children's novels, all with Canadian settings, including *Katie Johnson's Cross; A Canadian Tale* (1870) and *For King and Country; A Story of 1812* (1874). *Down the River to the Sea* (1894), one of her three novels for adults, is reminiscent of Sangster's *The St. Lawrence and the Saguenay*, presenting a journey from Niagara Falls to the Gaspé as part of its story. Machar also wrote two biographies, one of them about her father: *The Memorials of the Life and Ministry of the Reverend John Machar, D.D.* (1873). Her other works include two books of poetry, *Lays of the True North and Other Canadian poems* (1892) and the verse-drama *The Winged Victory* (1902); a history of the city, *The Story of Old Kingston* (1908); and many periodical essays and stories reflecting her strong commitment to social issues.

Agnes Machar's home on Sydenham St

The poet **Evan MacColl**, a native of Scotland, came to Kingston in 1850 and worked here as a customs officer. A friend of Charles Sangster, McColl wrote in both Gaelic and English and in 1883 published *Poems and Songs Chiefly written in Canada*.

The family of **Isabella Valancy Crawford** (*Old Spookses' Pass, Malcolm's Katie, and Other poems*, 1884) was discovered living at a country inn north of Kingston during the winter of 1861–2 and was invited by a member of the Strickland family to move to LAKEFIELD. The Crawfords had been forced to leave their home in PAISLEY because of a financial scandal; from Lakefield they moved to PETERBOROUGH. Crawford spent the last years of her life in TORONTO (I), where her book was published at her own expense.

Many writers were attracted to Kingston by Queen's University, founded in 1841. The poet **Charles Mair** (*Dreamland and Other Poems*, 1868) came twice, first as an undergraduate in 1856–7 (he was forced to leave university to work in his father's business), and again in 1867, when he studied briefly at the university's medical school. **George Monro Grant**, principal of the university from 1877 until his death in 1902, came soon after the publication of his best-known work, *Ocean to Ocean* (1873), an account of his experiences with the CPR engineer Sanford Fleming on a surveying trip across the Prairies to the Pacific. He lived on the university grounds. During his years at Kingston, Grant was also general editor of, and contributor to, *Picturesque Canada* (1882) and wrote several works on politics and religious questions, including *Imperial Federation* (1890) and *The Religions of the World* (1911). (See also HALIFAX, STELLARTON, N.S.) The poet **George Frederick Cameron** (born in NEW GLASGOW, N.S.) attended Queen's in 1882 and 1883, after several years' study in the United States. He

The Reverend George Monro Grant

was the prize poet of the university in 1883. In March of that year he was appointed editor of the *Kingston News*, a post he held until his death from heart disease in Sept. 1885. Cameron's last poems are dated in the month of his death. His *Lyrics of Freedom, Love and Death* was published posthumously in 1887. Cameron also wrote an opera, *Leo, the Royal Cadet* (1889), whose hero is a student at the Royal Military College in Kingston.

Eric Nicol—three-time winner of the Leacock Medal for Humour for *The Roving I* (1950), *Shall We Join the Ladies?* (1955), and *Girdle Me a Globe* (1957)—was born in Kingston on 28 Dec. 1919 and lived here until he was six, when his family moved to VANCOUVER.

The novelist and playwright **Robertson Davies**, who was born in THAMESVILLE, moved to Kingston in 1927 and lived for many years at the family home, 'Calderwood', on Union Street. The house is gone but the garden remains. His father owned the *Whig Standard* and Davies' brothers worked on this newspaper. After studies at Upper Canada College, TORONTO (3), Davies attended Queen's University from 1932 to 1935. When he returned from several years in England, he worked first as literary editor of *Saturday Night*, Toronto, and then in 1942 joined the staff of his father's Peterborough *Examiner*. During his years in PETERBOROUGH, Davies wrote a trilogy of novels about a university town he called Salterton, which was based in large measure on Kingston. In all three books—*Tempest-tost* (1951), *Leaven of Malice* (1954), and *A Mixture of Frailties* (1958)—Davies draws on his wide experience in the university community, the theatre, and newspapers.

Matt Cohen was born here on 30 Dec. 1942 and grew up in Ottawa. For many years he has divided his time between a home in TORONTO (3) and a farm north of Kingston at VERONA. Four of Cohen's novels—*The Disinherited* (1974), *The Colours of War* (1977), *The Sweet Second Summer of Kitty Malone* (1979), and *Flowers of Darkness* (1981)—are set in the fictional town of Salem, identified with this part of southern Ontario. Scenes in *The Disinherited* and *The Sweet Second Summer of Kitty Malone* take place in Kingston.

Pierre Berton (*The Mysterious North*, 1956) was a captain and instructor at the Royal Military College during the Second World War. He came to Kingston from Vancouver, where he had been city editor of the *News-Herald* before joining the army, and he returned to that city after his military service to become a feature writer for the Vancouver *Sun*. (See also KLEINBERG, TORONTO; DAWSON CITY, WHITEHORSE, Y.T.)

Timothy Findley, born in TORONTO, worked at radio station CKWS as a disc jockey in 1951 and 1952, but left Kingston in 1953 to pursue a career as an actor and script-writer before publishing his first novel, *The Last of the Crazy People*, in 1967. He won a Governor General's Award for *The Wars* (1977). (See also CANNINGTON, OTTAWA, STRATFORD.)

Queen's University has continued in the twentieth century to be a literary centre in Kingston. **Watson Kirkconnell** (*The Flying Bull and Other Tales*, 1940) received an M.A. in classics here in 1916. The editor and essayist **B.K. Sandwell** (*The Privacity Agent and Other Modest Proposals*, 1928) was head of the English department from 1923 to 1925. (See also TORONTO: 2; MONTREAL: 3, Que.). The journalist **Wilfrid Eggleston** (*The High Plains*, 1938) attended Queen's during the 1920s before joining the OTTAWA press corps. **Samuel Walter Dyde**, principal of Queen's Theological College, wrote four books of verse: *War Verse* (1924), *A Year* (1927), *The Highway* (1928), and *From My Gallery*) (undated). Queen's was one of three universities where the poet **E.J. Pratt** taught during the summers from 1930 to 1952. **Edward McCourt** (*Music at the Close*, 1947) taught English here during the 1938–9 school year. The playwright **Jack Gray** (*Bright Sun at Midnight*, 1957) was educated at Queen's during the 1940s. **Elizabeth Brewster** worked at Queen's University Library in 1951–2. She was living in Kingston when her first book, *East Coast* (1951), was published, and wrote her second book, *Lillooet* (1954), here. Her story, 'Comfort Me with Apples', is set in Kingston. Poet **D.G. Jones** studied at Queen's University from 1952 to 1954, when he received his M.A. His thesis adviser was the chairman of the English department, **George Whalley** (1915–83), who was also a poet (*No Man an Island*, 1948), a Coleridge scholar, and author of the posthumously published *Studies in Literature and the Humanities: Innocence of Intent* (1985) and of *The Legend of John Hornby* (1962). (For Hornby, see KEEWATIN BARRENS, N.W.T.). In the early 1950s Whalley lived at 106 Barrie St and in the late 1950s and the 1960s at 186 Union St W. For one year D.G. Jones taught at the Royal Mili-

George Whalley sailing off Garden Island, summer 1967

Douglas LePan in the 1950s

tary College before moving to GUELPH in 1955. He lived at Gananoque, east of Kingston on the St Lawrence River, while studying and teaching in the city. Another writer influenced by Whalley was the poet and novelist **Michael Ondaatje**, who studied here in 1965–7 (see below). Poet **Douglas LePan** (*The Net and the Sword*, 1953) taught at Queen's in the English department from 1959 to 1964 (he lived at 135 Centre St). Le Pan wrote *The Deserter* (1964), winner of a Governor General's Award for fiction, while in Kingston. **Joan Finnigan**, a native of OTTAWA, lived in Kingston from 1964 until the late 1970s, when she studied at Queen's and published several books of poetry, including *A Dream of Lilies* (1965), *Entrance to the Green-house* (1968), *It Was Warm and Sunny When We Set Out* (1970), and *In the Brown Cottage on Loughborough Lake* (1970). She also wrote the screenplay for the National Film Board movie *The Best Damn Fiddler from Calabogie to Kaladar* (1969). Finnigan still lives in the Kingston area.

Two prominent Queen's writers were successors to B.K. Sandwell in the post of chairman of the English department. **George Herbert Clarke** came to Queen's as chairman in 1925 and held the post until 1943. Clarke had published two books of poems before his years in Kingston: *Wayfaring* (1901) and *At the Shrine and Other Poems* (1914). While at Queen's he edited anthologies of wartime poetry from Canada and Britain, and several volumes of his own verse were published, including *The Hasting Day* (1930) and *Halt and Parley, and Other Poems* (1934). His *Selected Poems* (1954), published after his death in 1953, was edited by George Whalley, his successor in the Queen's English department. In the 1930s Clarke lived at 90 Alice St, in the 1940s at 90 Queen's Cres., and from 1951 until his death at 140 College St.

Gérard Bessette, one of Canada's most distinguished French-language novelists, lives on Frontenac Ave. Bessette came to Kingston in 1958 to teach at the Royal Military College; in 1960 he joined the French department of Queen's University, where he taught until 1979. Shortly before coming to Kingston he added the writing of fiction to his literary criticism and poetry (*Poems temporels*, 1954). His novels began with *La Bagarre* in 1958 (*The Brawl*, 1976), and include two winners of Governor General's Awards: *L'Incubation* (1965; *Incubation*, 1967) and *Le Cycle* (1971). Another French-language novelist associated with Kingston is **Adrien Thério**, who taught at the Royal Military College in the late 1960s. His novels include *Le Printemps qui pleure* (1962), *Le Mors aux flancs* (1965), *Soliloque en hommage à une femme* (1968), and *Un Païen chez les pingouins* (1970).

The poet and novelist **David Helwig** lives on Montreal St and taught for several years at Queen's. Helwig began teaching at the university in 1965, but left for a time to work as story editor for CBC-TV. A native of TORONTO (3), he first worked in Kingston teaching drama and creative writing, with his wife Nancy, at Kingston Penitentiary. Helwig has published several volumes of poetry, including *Figures in a Landscape* (1967), *The Sign of the Gunman* (1969), *The Best Name of Silence* (1972), and *A Book of the Hours* (1979). His many novels include a group of four set in Kingston: *The Glass Knight* (1976), *Jennifer* (1978), *It Is Always Summer* (1982), and *A Sound Like Laughter* (1983).

The winner of the 1981 $50,000 Seal First Novel Award for *The Ivory Swing*, **Janette Turner Hospital**, has lived for several years in Kingston, where her husand is Principal of Queen's Theological College.

Queen's University has a strong tradition of literary magazines, beginning with *Queen's Quarterly*, founded in 1893 by Principal **George Monro Grant**, who wrote in the first issue, 'We have such faith in truth that we believe that it needs only a fair field and time. We offer the fair field and we ask our readers to give the time.' The *Quarterly* was not solely a literary magazine, but rather a review of political and social issues. The first story ever published in it was Frederick Philip Grove's 'Snow'. *Queen's Quarterly* published the first stories of Sinclair Ross and Margaret Laurence; Ross went on to publish most of his eighteen stories in this magazine. Laurence's appearance was arranged by her former professor at United College, Winnipeg, Malcolm Ross.

Quarry, the student literary annual founded in 1952, has grown into a quarterly that publishes writers from across the country as well as Queen's students and faculty members. The transformation began in 1965 with two student editors, **Tom Marshall** and Tom Eadie, who determined in the fall of that year to attempt the change from one issue to four a year. Marshall, who has taught at Queens' since 1968 and lives on Victoria St, came to Kingston in 1957 to study at the university, where he received his B.A. in 1961. A student of history, Marshall edited the university newspaper and first published in *Quarry* in 1959. He returned to Queen's in 1964 as a graduate student and editor of *Quarry*, in which he featured writing by Quebec authors, including Cécile Cloutier and Gatien Lapointe. From 1964 to 1966, Marshall lived at 63 West St and wrote many of the poems that appeared in his first book, *The Silence of Fire* (1969). In the spring of 1965 *Quarry's* editor, Tom Eadie, drew on the Queen's community—including at that time George Whalley and David Helwig—and other Canadian writers such as Earle Birney, Raymond Souster, and Cécile Cloutier, to produce a very successful issue, which led to the plan the next fall to attempt a quarterly with national circulation. In the interim Marshall, Eadie, and Colin Norman (another recent editor of *Quarry*) produced *The Beast with Three Backs*, the first publication of Quarry press.

During the 1965–6 academic year Eadie and Marshall co-edited *Quarry* with the assistance of several guest editors, including David Helwig, **Michael Ondaatje**, and **Douglas Barbour**. Ondaatje appeared in the spring 1965 issue while still a student at the University of Toronto and then moved to Kingston to study for his master's degree at Queen's. During his one year here he lived at 318 William St. Ondaatje was then writing the poems that appeared in his first book, *The Dainty Monsters*, which was published in 1967 when he was teaching at the University of Western Ontario, LONDON. Associated for many years with York University in TORONTO (6), Ondaatje spends his summers north of Kingston at a cottage on the Skootamatta River. Barbour, then living at 2 Cooper St, was at Queen's as a doctoral student and became editor of *Quarry* in 1966–8 while Marshall was in London, England. Barbour, who received his Ph.D. from Queen's in 1976, has taught Canadian literature and creative writing at the University of Alberta, EDMONTON, since 1969. His first book of poems, *A Poem as Long as* *the Highway*, was published in 1971. Marshall, on his return from England, served from 1968 to 1970 as chief editor of the magazine. Another editor was **Gail Fox**, who published *Dangerous Season* with Quarry Press in 1969.

From 1968 to 1981 Tom Marshall lived at 8 Annandale Apts; his first book, *The Silence of Fire*, was published in 1969 and was followed by *Magic Water* (1971), *The Earthbook* (1974), and *The White City* (1976). *The Elements: 1960–1975* (1980) is a selection from his earlier books. He has also published several works of criticism and a novel, *Rosemary Gaol* (1978).

Queen's university is also the home of the Lorne Pierce Collection, housed in the Douglas Library. **Lorne Pierce**, editor of Ryerson Press in TORONTO (2) from 1922 to 1960, was educated at Queen's and donated a large collection of books, manuscripts, and correspondence to the university. The collection includes unpublished novels by Raymond Knister (*White Narcissus*, 1929); the prose of Isabella Valancy Crawford, along with her narrative poem, *Hugh and Ion* (1977), edited by Glenn Clever from a manuscript found by Dorothy Livesay at Queen's; the papers collected by Stan Dragland for *Wilson MacDonald's Western Tour 1923–4* (1976); and many other documents relating to the careers of Canadian authors associated with Pierce.

KITCHENER

The poet **William Wilfred Campbell** was born in Kitchener (then Berlin) on 1 June 1858, the second son of the Rev. Thomas Campell, an Anglican minister. A national historical plaque at Kitchener-Waterloo Collegiate commemorates Campbell's birth and honours him as the author of several of post-Confederation Canada's most influential volumes of poetry, including *Lake Lyrics* (1889), *The Dread Voyage* (1893), *Beyond the Hills of Dream* (1899), and *Collected Poems* (1905). When Campbell was only a year old, his family moved from Kitchener to WIARTON. (See also MEAFORD, OTTAWA, TORONTO: 3; ST STEPHEN, N.B.)

KLEINBURG

Journalist, broadcaster, and historian **Pierre Berton** has lived just outside the village of Kleinburg, northwest of TORONTO (2), for many years. Berton moved to Toronto in 1947 to work as an editor at *Maclean's* and has continued for 40 years an active career as journalist and broadcaster in the city while publishing a series of award-winning popular histories. Berton's first book, *The Mysterious North* (1956), was the first of three books for which he has won Governor General's Awards; the others are *Klondike: the Life and Death of the Last Great Goldrush* (1958) and *The Last Spike: the Great Railway, 1881–1885* (1971). *The Last Spike* is the second volume of Berton's history of the CPR; the first volume, *The National Dream: The Great Railway; 1871–1881* appeared in 1970. Berton has also published five collections of newspaper essays, one of which, *Just Add Water and Stir* (1959), won the Leacock Medal for Humour. He has surveyed Canada's place in modern social history with *Hollywood's Canada: the Americanization of Our National Image* (1975) and *The Dionne Years: A Thirties Melodrama* (1977), and after being long identified with his books on the Canadian frontier in the West and the North, Berton published a two-volume history of an eastern-frontier event, the War of 1812, in *The Invasion of Canada, 1812–1813* (1980) and *Flames Across the Border, 1813–1814* (1981). (See also KINGSTON; VANCOUVER, B.C.; DAWSON CITY, WHITEHORSE, Y.T.)

From 1972 to 1975 the novelist **Adele Wiseman** lived in Kleinburg, where she wrote her novel *Crackpot* (1974), set in her native WINNIPEG. (See also TORONTO: 7; MONTREAL: 7, Que.)

LAKEFIELD

The village of Lakefield, along with adjacent Douro Township, was a centre of literary and pioneering activity for **Catharine Parr Traill**, **Susanna Moodie**, and their brother, **Samuel Strickland**, all of whom lived here for varying periods between 1832 and 1899. Strickland was the first to settle in the district. In 1832 he acquired land and made a clearing on the shore of Katchewanooka Lake, now on the north side of Lakefield. There he was joined later in 1832 by Robert Traill and Catharine Parr Traill, who took adjoining property, and in February 1834 by John and Susanna Moodie (see DOURO TOWNSHIP).

'Westove' today

The three farms were not far from the present provincial historical plaque commemorating Susanna Moodie, which stands in Cenotaph Park on the north side of Water St, east of Bridge St. While living here Mrs Moodie wrote her best-known poem 'Sleigh Bells', and experienced the events and situations described in the later chapters of *Roughing It in the Bush* (1852). The Moodies moved to BELLEVILLE in 1840; but after the death of her husband in 1869 Mrs Moodie divided her time between Lakefield and TORONTO (1). While at Lakefield she stayed with her sister, Mrs Traill, at the latter's home, 'Westove'.

'Westove', Lakefield, the home of Catharine Parr Traill, *c.*1906

Catharine Parr Traill in 1867

Still standing and privately owned at 16 Smith St in Lakefield, Westove bears a provincial historical plaque in honour of Catharine Parr Traill. In 1839 the Traills moved to Ashburnam and GORE'S LANDING; in 1857 their house on Rice Lake was destroyed by fire, and shortly afterwards Thomas Traill died. Mrs Traill then returned to Lakefield, and in 1862 her daughters bought Westove, where she lived until her death in 1899. It was in Westove that she wrote the most important book of her later career and her chief work as a naturalist, *Studies of Plant Life in Canada* (1885).

Samuel Strickland is commemorated by a plaque in Christ Church (Anglican), 62 Queen St, Lakefield. This church was built, largely through his efforts, in 1853. During a trip to England in 1851 to raise funds for the project Strickland arranged for the editing and publication in London of his *Twenty-seven Years in Canada West* (2 vols, 1853). Written during his years as a pioneer in Douro Township, the second volume of this book contains an excellent account of the environment and conditions of early settlers in the Lakefield area. Strickland is buried in the churchyard of Christ Church.

Lakefield was also home for a time to one of the most important post-Confederation poets. **Isabella Valancy Crawford** moved here after her father, Dr Stephen Crawford, was convicted of misappropriating public funds while treasurer of PAISLEY Township. The dates of her residence in Lakefield are uncertain, but it is thought that she was living here by late 1862. She lodged for a time with Robert Strickland, a nephew of Mrs Traill and Mrs Moodie, and was a member of their circle. Several years later she moved to PETERBOROUGH.

In the spring of 1974 **Margaret Laurence** moved into her yellow brick house on Regent St, where she lived until her death on 5 Jan. 1987. In 1970, after several years in England, Laurence had bought a cottage on the Otonabee River, near PETERBOROUGH, where she spent her summers. After serving as writer-in-residence at the University of Western Ontario in London during 1973, she decided to remain permanently in Canada and settled in Lakefield. *The Diviners* (1974), the last novel in Laurence's 'Manawaka' cycle, was written mainly at her Otonabee cottage (named 'Manawaka' after her fictional town). It appeared about the time she was moving into her Lakefield home, but many details in it, based on Lakefield, show that Laurence already had an intimate knowledge of the city. Descriptions of the Lakefield and Peterborough areas are an important element in the novel, as is the mental relationship established with Catharine Parr Traill by Laurence's central character, Morag Gunn, a modern novelist who is depicted as living in a house dating from pioneer times and located near the scenes of the pioneer author's life. (See also NEEPAWA, Man.)

The poet **D.G. Jones**, whose books include *A Throw of Particles* (1983), was a student from 1942 to 1949 at Grove School, a private secondary school just north of Lakefield on Hwy 28. In 1949, after graduating from the University of Toronto, the novelist **Percy Janes** came to Lakefield to work as a tutor at Grove School, where he remained for a short time. His first novel, *So Young and Beautiful* (1958), concerns small-town Ontario life and is based in part on his

Margaret Laurence, *c.*1980

experiences here. (See also CORNER BROOK, ST JOHN'S, Nfld.)

LANARK

The poet **Charles Mair** was born in Lanark on 21 Sept. 1838 and lived here for most of the next thirty years. The house in which he lived for most of that time still stands on the west side of George St (the main street), one door north of Hillyer St. The exterior of this stone structure is relatively unchanged since Mair's time; it is today one of the buildings of Glenayre Kitten Ltd, a Lanark firm. This house is often incorrectly identified as Mair's birthplace, which stood on the opposite side of George St and was destroyed by fire. Mair is commemorated by a national

Christ Church, Lakefield

historic plaque at the Lanark post office. He attended elementary school in Paisley and boarded with his sister in Perth while attending high school. After one year at Queen's University in KINGSTON, he was called home to help in his father's general store. Though he disliked the work, he stayed for ten years. During that time he began writing poetry. In 1867 Mair left Lanark for the last time, to enter Queen's University Medical School; his first poetry collection, *Dreamland and Other Poems*, was published the following year. (See also OTTAWA; WINNIPEG, Man.; PRINCE ALBERT, Sask.; CALGARY, Alta.; VICTORIA, B.C.)

The Manse at Leaskdale today

LEASKDALE

This small village, about 8 miles north of Uxbridge on Concession Rd 7, was for fifteen years the home of **Lucy Maud Montgomery** (see CAVENDISH, NEW LONDON, P.E.I.). On 5 July 1911 Montgomery married the Rev. Ewan MacDonald, pastor of St Paul's Presbyterian Church, Leaskdale, in a ceremony at PARK CORNER, P.E.I. After a honeymoon in Britain, the couple came in Sept. 1911 to the manse at Leaskdale, which had been redecorated according to Montgomery's directions. Montgomery's two sons were born in the manse—a stuccoed brick house on the east side of Concession Rd 7—and there she wrote eleven of her twenty-two books, including *Anne of the Island* (1915), *Anne's House of Dreams* (1917), and the Emily series. Montgomery pursued the active career of a minister's wife until 1926, when her husband accepted a charge at NORVAL and Union, Ont. On 12 Feb. 1926 a farewell party was held for the family at St Paul's Church. Both the church and the nearby manse, which is now over 100 years old and carries a plaque recalling the Montgomery connection, are still in use.

LINDSAY

Ernest Thompson Seton (1860–1946), naturalist and author of such animal-story classics as *Wild Animals I Have Known* (1898), formed his deep love of wildlife and landscape as a boy in the countryside around this community just south of Sturgeon Lake. (Seton, who emigrated with his family from England, was born Ernest Evan Thompson, but in 1883 he adopted the family name Seton.) In Aug. 1866 his family bought 100 acres in the Township of Ops (west half of lot 15, concession X) and took up residence there. Four years later they moved to TORONTO (I). Seton's novel *Two Little Savages* (1906), which is set in the Lindsay area, is a semi-autobiographical account of the experiences of Seton and a young friend (a son of a local family named Blackwell) during the school holidays in 1876. The games that Seton and his friends played in the wild, described in *Two Little Savages*, were made part of boy-scout training in 1910 when Seton became a co-founder of the Boy Scouts of America and the author of the organization's manual. Seton is commemorated by a plaque at the Victoria County Historical Society Museum on Kent St W.

The historical novelist **W.G.** (William George) **Hardy** was born near Lindsay on 3 Feb. 1895 and spent his childhood in the district. While head of the Classics department of the University of Alberta, EDMONTON, he became known for meticulously authentic tales of biblical and Roman times, such as *All the Trumpets Sounded* (1942) and *The Bloodied Toga* (1979).

The novelist and humorist **Donald Lamont Jack** lived for many years in a house on Russell St E. until he moved from Lindsay in the mid-1980s. He is known for 'The Bandy Papers', a series of novels about the comic exploits of a preacher's son from the Ottawa Valley. The series includes *Three Cheers for Me* (1962), *That's Me in the Middle* (1965), *It's Me Again* (1975), and *Me Bandy, You Cissie* (1978). Jack won the Stephen Leacock Medal for humour in 1963, 1974, and 1979.

LONDON

Richard Maurice Bucke—biographer of Walt Whitman and author of a book famous in its time, *Cosmic Consciousness* (1901)—was raised on a farm near London, where his family had settled in 1838 after emigrating from England. Bucke attended London Grammar School but studied at home before entering McGill University's medical school; he graduated in 1862. After studying abroad, he practised medicine in Sarnia and London, settling here in 1877, when he was appointed superintendent of the city's Asylum for the Insane. He held that position until his death in 1902, by which time he had become one of the world's leading alienists. In Bucke's time the London Asylum for the Insane was on Governor's Rd, 2 miles outside the city. Bucke's home was on the asylum grounds. None of the nineteenth-century buildings remain, but the asylum's successor institution, the London Psychiatric Hospital, 850 Highbury Ave, commemorates Bucke in its Teaching and Research Museum, which contains a re-creation of the famous alienist's office.

A student of mysticism and an avid admirer of **Walt Whitman**, Bucke attributed to Whitman's poetry a mystical experience that convinced him of the hopeful order in the universe—which he proceeded to describe in his later writings. Whitman

L.M. Montgomery's photograph of the Manse at Leaskdale

Dr Bucke on the steps of the Superintendent's House of the London Asylum, *c.*1900

visited Bucke in London twice; the first visit in 1880 was described in *Walt Whitman's Diary in Canada with Extracts from Other of His Diaries and Literary Note-books* (1904). In 1883 Bucke published the first biographical study of his friend, *Walt Whitman*, which incorporated revisions made by the poet. As one of Whitman's literary executors, Bucke prepared several posthumous volumes of the poet's work and was one of the editors of the *Complete Writings of Walt Whitman* (10 vols., 1902). *Cosmic Consciousness: A Study of the Evolution of the Human Mind* (1901) was Bucke's most ambitious presentation of his conviction that mystical illumination about cosmic order united all the world's great thinkers—Homer, Christ, Blake, Whitman, and others—and provided hope of a future millenial age of universal harmony. The University of Western Ontario, founded here in 1878, owns a collection of Bucke's papers. Bucke was associated with the university for many years as professor of mental and nervous diseases. He died in 1902 and is buried in London in Mt Pleasant Cemetery.

The editor and journalist **George Stewart, Jr.** was three when his parents moved from New York City to London in 1851. Educated here and in SAINT JOHN, N.B., Stewart founded *The Stamp Collector's Monthly Gazette* (1865–7) there when he was sixteen. That was the beginning of a long career as editor of periodicals in Saint John—where he founded *Stewart's Literary Quarterly Magazine* (1867–72)—Toronto, and QUEBEC CITY.

Another childhood resident of London was the novelist **Arthur Stringer**, who moved here in 1884 from CHATHAM at the age of ten. In 1886 he entered London Collegiate Institute with the highest entrance examination marks ever recorded; while there he founded a school magazine called *Chips*. The brick house to which Stringer's family moved about 1890 still stands at 64 Elmwood Ave. Between 1884 and 1889 Stringer's father, Hugh, a carriage maker, maintained both his business premises and the family home at 143 King St. Although Stringer was often away from London after 1892, he was a sometime occupant of the Elmwood Ave house until 1899. After studying at the University of Toronto (1892–4) and at Oxford, Stringer began his newspaper career with the *Montreal Herald* (1897–8), moving on to New York. He returned to southern Ontario in 1903 when he bought a farm at CEDAR SPRINGS. Stringer's novel, *Lonely O'Malley* (1905), follows the career of an orphan boy growing up in Ontario in the 1880s, and is based on the author's childhood in Chatham and London.

A national historic marker dedicated to **Peter McArthur** can be seen in a roadside park on Hwy 2, east of the Hwy 80 intersection and west of London. McArthur grew up, and spent the last years of his life, on his family's farm in Ekfrid Township near APPIN, where he died in 1924. The many collections of his articles about Ekfrid—published in the Toronto *Globe* and the *Farmer's Advocate*—include *In Pastures Green* (1915) and *Friendly Acres* (1927). (See also DOON.)

The poet **Anne Wilkinson** (*Counterpoint to Sleep*, 1951) was born in TORONTO (5) but spent much of her childhood in London, where she was privately educated by tutors. Wilkinson wrote about life in London in her family history, *Lions in the Way* (1956), and in her autobiographical essay, 'Four Corners of My World', which first appeared in *The Tamarack Review* (20, Summer 1961), and was included in *The Collected Poems of Anne Wilkinson* (1968) edited by A.J.M. Smith.

In 1937 **Selwyn Dewdney** settled with his family in London, where he wrote his first novel, *Wind Without Rain* (1946), based upon his experiences as a teacher in OWEN SOUND. From 1937 to the late 1940s Dewdney taught at Sir Adam Beck College; in 1937–40 he lived at 517 William St, Apt 5, in 1941–4 at 74 Doulton St, and in 1945–56 at 1548 Dundas St. In the 1950s Dewdney taught art at Beal Technical School, where he had as students such future artists as Jack Chambers and Greg Curnoe; he and his wife worked as art therapists in London hospitals from 1953 to 1972. From 1957 until his death in 1979 Dewdney lived at 26 Erie Ave. Beginning in 1957 he was associated with the Royal Ontario Museum in TORONTO (4) as a researcher of native art and anthropology. Dewdney's *Indian Rock Paintings of the Great Lakes* (1966) describes his discoveries at AGAWA BAY, Ont. *Christopher Breton*, his second novel, was published in 1978.

Dewdney's youngest son, **Christopher Dewdney**, has published six books of poetry, many of which make extensive use of biological and geological images drawn from the London area. Born on 5 May 1951, Dewdney attended Victoria Public School and South and Westminster Collegiate Institutes; in the mid-1970s he lived at 27 Evergreen Ave and in 1979–80 at 161 Ridout St. His books include *A Paleozoic Geology of London, Ontario* (1973, 1974); *Spring Trances in the Control Emerald Night: Book I of A Natural History of Southwestern Ontario* (1978); and *Predators of the Adoration* (1983), a volume of selected poems. Christopher Dewdney credits his father with awakening him to the special aspects of nature he emphasizes in his poetry: 'On a summer evening, as we drove down into the Grand River valley near Paris, Ont., he explained that the limestone was almost entirely composed of the shells and skeletons of underwater creatures, millions of years old, compacted and turned to rock. His explanation transformed the rock into a miraculous substance.' (See also TORONTO (7).)

The novelist **Graeme Gibson** was born in London in 1934 and attended the University of Western Ontario. His first novel, *Five Legs* (1969), is set in London on the university campus and follows the tragic careers of a professor, Lucas Cracknell, and two of his students. One of these, Felix Oswald, appears again in Gibson's *Communion* (1971). Gibson's *Perpetual Motion* (1982) is set in rural Ontario during the nineteenth century; the hero, Robert Fraser, hopes to create a perpetual-motion machine. (See also ALLISTON.)

James Reaney, a native of nearby STRATFORD, has been a member of the English department of the University of Western Ontario since 1960; his longtime home is on Huron St. From 1960 to 1971 he published the magazine *Alphabet* whose nineteen issues are credited with providing an important outlet for young and unconventional poets, including Margaret Atwood, George Bowering, Bill Bissett, and b.p. nichol. Reaney edited and published the magazine and did much of the typesetting and printing. Before coming to London, Reaney had already published two books of poems, *The Red Heart* (1949) and *A Suit of Nettles* (1958; 2nd edn, 1975), both of which won Governor General's Awards. His books from London include *Twelve Letters to a Small Town* (1962), another winner of a Governor General's Award; *The Dance of Death at London, Ontario* (1972); *Selected Shorter Poems* (1975), and *Selected Longer Poems* (1976). Reaney began his distinguished career as a dramatist in 1953 with the libretto for the chamber opera by John Beckwith *Night-blooming Cereus*; it was published in *The Killdeer and Other Plays* (1962). Best known for *The Donnellys* (1976), a trilogy of plays about the murders of an Irish immigrant family in LUCAN in the 1880s, Reaney has also published *Colours in the Dark* (1969), *Listen to the Wind* (1972), and *Masks of Childhood* (1972). Reaney is married to the poet **Colleen Thibaudeau** (*The Martha Landscapes*, 1984). (See also TORONTO: 3.)

James Reaney at his printing press, *c.*1973

Other writers associated with the University of Western Ontario include the poet **R.A.D. Ford**, who graduated in 1938. Ford (*A Window on the North*, 1956) did graduate work at Cornell and in 1940 returned to Canada to enter the diplomatic service. (See also OTTAWA.) Ford's closest friend at university was Kenneth Millar, who was raised in southern Ontario but settled in the United States after serving in the Second World War. Under the pseudonym **Ross Macdonald** he wrote the Lew Archer detective novels, including *The Galton Case* (1959), which is based in some measure on Millar's own experience of childhood confusion between American citizenship and Canadian residence.

Alice Munro (*Dance of the Happy Shades*, 1980) attended the University of Western Ontario from 1949 to 1951 but left without a degree to marry James Munro; the couple moved to VANCOUVER, B.C. (See also CLINTON, WINGHAM; VICTORIA, B.C.)

George Bowering (*Burning Water*, 1980) lived at 650 Ayerswood Ave in 1966–7 while teaching at the university and working on his first novel, *A Mirror on the Floor* (1967). (See also MONTREAL: 7, Que.; BURNABY, VANCOUVER, B.C.) The writers-in-residence at Western have included **Harold Horwood** (1976–7), **Earle Birney** (1981–2), and **Margaret Laurence** (1973). The novelist **Lawrence Garber** is a long-time faculty member (see also TORONTO: 3). The university's library houses manuscripts and other papers of Richard Maurice Bucke, Sara Jeannette Duncan, and Peter McArthur, among others.

LUCAN

A trilogy of plays by **James Reaney**, *The Donnellys* (1973–5), is based on a violent feud that occurred in the late nineteenth century in Lucan, north of LONDON on Hwy 4. On 4 Feb. 1880 about thirty people attacked the James Donnelly farm—killing Donnelly, his wife, a son and a niece—and then destroyed the farm buildings. Another son was killed on the same night in a nearby town. Although the alleged participants were twice tried, no one was ever convicted of the deaths, which had resulted from a blood feud that James Donnelly had brought here from his home in Tipperary, Ireland. In 1857 Donnelly had killed a neighbour in the Lucan district over land rights, and although he served seven years for the murder, his sons continued to conduct violent disputes with local farmers while he was in prison. In St Patrick's Cemetery, Lucan, a granite tombstone marks the Donnelly burial place. Erected in 1966, it replaced the original black marker that had identified the family members as victims of murder. The story of the feud is also told by **Thomas P. Kelly** in *The Black Donnellys* (1954).

MEAFORD

This Georgian Bay community, the centre of a prosperous resort and fruit-growing region, was the birthplace of the classic children's novel *Beautiful Joe: an Autobiography* (1894), which is cast in the form of a dog's narration of his own life story. The book's author, **Margaret Marshall Saunders**, was inspired to write it during a visit to Meaford in 1892, apparently to meet the family of a Miss Moore, her brother's future wife. Miss Moore's father, William Moore, was a local miller, who owned the real Beautiful Joe; he told Saunders how he had saved the dog from a cruel owner who had cut off his ears and tail. The dog was probably still alive at this time, and Saunders is said to have spent

'Beautiful Joe',
from a private postcard of Marshall Saunders

as long as six months here, gathering material for the story suggested to her by this incident. The book was completed while Saunders, an avid and restless traveller, was staying in a small Massachusetts town near Boston that served as the model for the fictional Fairport, Mass., where she set *Beautiful Joe*.

Beautiful Joe Park, on Victoria Cres. near Big Head River, surrounds the burial place of Beautiful Joe. A provincial historical plaque has been placed on a stone marker over his grave. (See also TORONTO: 6; MILTON, HALIFAX, N.S.)

The poet **William Wilfred Campbell** spent part of his boyhood in Meaford. In 1867, when Campbell was nine, the family moved here so that his father, an Anglican clergyman, could serve Meaford and, at various times, other local towns, including Athens and Lansdowne. The Campbells remained at Meaford until 1871. Before and after this period they lived at WIARTON.

MIDDLEPORT

The poet **E. Pauline Johnson** was born on 10 Mar. 1861 in the mansion 'Chiefswood', which is at Middleport on Hwy 54 between Hwys 2 and 6 on the Grand River Reserve (1 mile east of Brantford). The house was

'Chiefswood' today

built in 1853 by her father, the Mohawk chief, George Henry Martin Johnson, for his English bride; the family took up residence in Dec. 1856. As a child Pauline swept the stairs in the square two-storey house and listened to Indian tales told by her grandfather John Smoke Johnson. She took part in ceremonies welcoming frequent royal visitors to the reserve, including Arthur, Duke of Connaught, Lord and Lady Dufferin, and the Marquis of Lorne and Princess Louise. Johnson was taught at home by governesses, with the exception of two years at a school on the reserve and two years as a boarder at Brantford Collegiate. Her father died in 1884, and the following year she moved permanently with her mother and sister to BRANTFORD, where, in 1886, Johnson's recitation at the unveiling of the statue of Joseph Brant in Victoria Park first attracted attention to her work as a poet.

A view of the Martyrs' Shrine from the reconstruction of Sainte-Marie-Among-the-Hurons

Chiefswood, one of the few Indian mansions surviving from before Confederation, was restored as a provincial historic site in 1961 and has been decorated with 1870s furnishings; it bears a provincial plaque dedicated to Pauline Johnson. The displays contain personal belongings of Johnson, including her christening dress, writing desk, and manuscripts of poetry. The house is open from Victoria Day to Labour Day. (See also WINNIPEG, Man.; VANCOUVER, B.C.)

MIDDLEVILLE

The novelist **Robert J.C. Stead** was born on 4 Sept. 1880 in Middleville, 20 miles north of Perth in Lanark County. After being raised on a homestead near CARTWRIGHT, Man., he returned to Ontario in 1919 to work as publicity director for the Department of Immigration and Colonization in OTTAWA. His novels—the most famous of which is *Grain* (1926)—draw on his many years in western Canada. (See also CALGARY, Alta.)

MIDLAND

About three miles east of Midland, on Hwy 12, stand two impressive monuments to the Jesuit missionaries of seventeenth-century Huronia, whose *Relations* provide much of the important early history and literature of Canada. Just south of Hwy 12, on a narrow plain on the east bank of the Wye River, stands the meticulously reconstructed Jesuit settlement, Sainte-Marie-among-the-Hurons. The Martyrs' Shrine of the Roman Catholic Church stands on a height just north of the road, a few hundred yards away.

Besides its faithful reconstruction of twenty-two buildings and other works, Sainte-Marie contains a modern museum and library; the entire complex abounds in artifacts and associations that point to the intense literary culture the Jesuits brought to this first European inland settlement in North America. Built in 1639, and burnt down in 1649 by the Jesuits themselves when they were forced to abandon it because of the Huron-Iroquois conflict, Sainte-Marie, and the mission to Huronia in general, are subjects of the central group of *Jesuit Relations*, covering the years 1632 to 1650. Most of the reports and letters in the *Relations*—addressed to the Provincial Father of the Society of Jesus in Paris—were written from Sainte-Marie by Fathers Paul Ragueneau, Paul Le Jeune, Jérôme Lalemant, Gabriel Lalemant, and Jean de Brébeuf. Brébeuf's famous Huron Christmas carol, 'Jesous Ahatonhia', may date from 1641 but was probably written at Quebec City while Brébeuf was sick in bed; it was, of course, intended for use in Huronia and must often have been sung there. A large stone marker on the floor of the church at Sainte-Marie marks the spot where researchers found a buried lead plaque with the inscription 'P. Jean De Brébeuf / Bruslé par les Iroquois / 17 mars l'an / 1649'. It is believed that Brébeuf was buried here and that his bones were moved by the Jesuits when they fled. The original plaque is on display in the museum, along with many other Sainte-Marie relics of literary significance, including Jesuit books from the years 1616 to 1661; a copy of the original Jesuit *Relation* for 1649; an original copy of Champlain's *Voyages*: original letters from Saint-Marie to the Jesuit General in Rome from Jérôme Lalemant (May 1642) and Paul Ragueneau (undated); and a Papal Bull dated February 1644, granting a plenary indulgence to visitors to the church at Sainte-Marie (this was renewed in 1926 by Pope Pius XI). The library of the

Huronia Historical Resource Centre, located here at Sainte-Marie, houses a large collection of books and copies of manuscripts by and about the Huronia Jesuits, including the seventy-three volumes of the R.G. Thwaites edition of the complete *Jesuit Relations and Allied Documents* (1896–1901) and a collection of manuscripts copied from holdings in the Public Archives of Canada, les Archives du Québec, and the Jesuit archives at Quebec City and St-Jérôme, Que.

The Martyr's Shrine contains various reminders of the literary Jesuits, including statues of Brébeuf inside and outside the church, and signs on the grounds bearing quotations from Ragueneau's *Relations*. To the right of the altar is a richly ornamented bronze reliquary containing relics of Brébeuf, Gabriel Lalemant, and Charles Garnier. The tiny fragment of Brébeuf's body—a gift to the shrine from the Jesuits of France—was taken across the Atlantic to Europe and returned nearly 300 years later to rest a short distance from its original burial place in Sainte-Marie. Just northeast of the church the grounds rise to a lookout over Georgian Bay and the end point of the 800-mile canoe route from Quebec City to Huronia. This high ground was the site of an outdoor mass celebrated on 15 Sept. 1984 by Pope John Paul II.

Sainte-Marie and Huronia form the setting for much of the epic poem *Brébeuf and His Brethren* (1940) by **E.J. Pratt**. (See TORONTO: 3; WESTERN BAY, Nfld.) Pratt was a careful researcher who insisted upon factual accuracy to lend realism to his poems, and he visited the excavations of Sainte-Marie while working on *Brébeuf*, even helping to unearth some of the palisades.

The town of Midland was the birthplace in 1937 of **Richard Wright**, whose novels include *The Weekend Man* (1970; rpr. 1977) and *Farthing's Fortune* (1976). *The Weekend Man* is set in a town named Middleburgh that is clearly modelled on Midland. (See also HAMILTON, TORONTO: 2.)

MISSISSAUGA

The centre of the southern-Ontario world created by **Mazo de la Roche** in her fourteen Jalna novels was the magnificent Whiteoaks family house, named Jalna after a military post in India. Although de la Roche denied that her Jalna was based on a real house, it is generally thought that the house called 'Benares', 1503 Clarkson Rd N., Mississauga, was the novelist's inspiration. The present house was built in the 1850s and is the third on the site. The veranda was added in the 1880s. Sold to the Ontario Heritage Foundation in 1968 by a descendant of the original owner, Arthur Harris, Benares is not open for tours because it is still privately occupied. De la Roche was familiar with the house because in Dec. 1924 she bought two lots, formerly attached to the house from the Sayers estate. On them she built 'Trail Cottage'. At the time she had already published *Explorers of the Dawn* (1922) and *Possession* (1923). Her novel *Delight* (1926) appeared while she was settling into Trail Cottage and finishing the manuscript of *Jalna* (1927). De la Roche only briefly lived year-round there; she usually had an apartment in TORONTO (2, 6, 7) as well, and after *Jalna*'s great success she also spent many years abroad. The cottage was sold in 1946. A remembrance of de la Roche's residence in the district was found near the intersection of Ravine Dr. and Jalna Ave, where a diamond-shaped gravestone marks the burial place of her dogs, Bunty, Sam, and Tam. From 1911 to 1915 de la Roche lived on her family's farm in the village of Bronte, now part of OAKVILLE. Oakville may be identified with the town of Stead in the novels, and two communities now part of Mississauga, Clarkson and Erindale, are also part of the geography of Jalna: they are linked to the fictional towns of Weddels and Evandale respectively. De la Roche's Jalna series included *Whiteoaks of Jalna* (1929), *Finch's Fortune* (1931), *The Master of Jalna* (1933), *Young Renny* (1935), *Whiteoak Harvest* (1936), *Whiteoak Heritage* (1940), *Wakefield's Course* (1941), *The Building of Jalna* (1946), *Mary Wakefield* (1949), *Renny's Daughter* (1951), *The Whiteoak Brothers* (1953), *Variable Winds at Jalna* (1954), and *Morning at Jalna* (1960). (See also CAMBRIDGE, NEWMARKET, SUTTON.)

'Benares' today

Mazo de la Roche at Traill Cottage

The family of poet **Dorothy Livesay** owned a summer house near Trail Cottage. 'Woodlot Cottage' was built in the 1930s by J.F.B. Livesay, Dorothy's father and head for many years of Canadian Press. De la Roche spoke fondly of her association with the Livesays in her autobiography, *Ringing the Changes* (1957); she was a special friend of Livesay's mother, Florence, sometimes spoken of as a model in some respects for de la Roche's character, Meg Whiteoaks. Woodlot Cottage is still standing, at 1219 Ravine Dr., Mississauga; the house is privately owned. In the 1920s and 1930s the Livesays lived in TORONTO (4), at 77 and 132 Walmer Rd, and later at 20 Rosemount Ave. Livesay's first books appeared during these years, *Green Pitcher* in 1928 when she was nineteen and *Signpost* in 1932. (See also WINNIPEG, Man.; VANCOUVER, B.C.)

The novelist **Josef Skvorecky**—who has lived in TORONTO since 1968, when he immigrated to Canada from his native Czechoslovakia— teaches at the University of Toronto's Erindale College, located in Mississauga. The college is a prominent setting, as Edenvale College, in Skvorecky's *The Story of an Engineer of Human Souls* (1983).

MORPETH

The Confederation poet **Archibald Lampman** was born on 17 Nov. 1861 at the rectory (gone) of Trinity (Anglican) Church, a quarter-of-a-mile south of this southwestern Ontario town near Lake Erie. He lived here until 1866, when his clergyman father was transferred to PERRYTOWN (see also GORE'S LANDING). Lampman died in 1899 in OTTAWA, where he had worked for several years in the federal civil service. On 13 Sept. 1930 friends of Lampman gathered at Trinity Church, 1½ miles east of Morpeth in Howard Township, to unveil a memorial cairn that had been financed by subscrip-

Duncan Campbell Scott at the dedication of the Lampman Memorial, Morpeth, 1930

tions collected over a period of two years—the first monument erected in Canada to the memory of a literary figure. The dedication ceremony was attended by Arthur Stringer, Nathaniel A. Benson, who had written an official poem for the occasion, and Lampman's close friend and literary executor, Duncan Campbell Scott. A more popular poem than Benson's about the cairn proved to be Wilson MacDonald's 'The Cairn at Morpeth', published in MacDonald's *A Flagon of Beauty* (1931); it was a tribute from one southwestern Ontario poet to another, for MacDonald was born in nearby CHEAPSIDE. Generally considered Canada's finest nineteenth-century English-language poet, Lampman published his poems in *Among the Millet and Other Poems* (1888) and *Lyrics of Earth* (1895); important posthumous collections are *At the Long Sault and Other New Poems* (1943) and *Lampman's Kate: Late Love Poems of Archibald Lampman* (1975). (See also PORT HOPE, TORONTO: 3.)

MOUNT HOPE

White Church Cemetery near Mount Hope contains the grave of Maggie Clark, who inspired the ballad, 'When You and I Were Young, Maggie', written for her by **George Washington Johnson** before their marriage in 1864. The poem, published in Johnson's collection *Maple Leaves* (1864), was set to music by J.A. Butterfield in 1866. Maggie died in 1865 in Cleveland, where the couple had moved when Johnson took an editorial position on the *Plain Dealer*. After his wife's death, Johnson returned to Ontario to work as a teacher and write novels. The story of Maggie Clark is told on a provincial plaque at her childhood home 3 miles west of Mount Hope in GLANDFORD TOWNSHIP. (See also BINBROOK TOWNSHIP, HAMILTON, TORONTO: 7.)

NEWMARKET

Although **Mazo de la Roche**'s birthplace is still often listed as TORONTO (2, 6, 7), the author of *Jalna* (1927) and *Whiteoaks of Jalna* (1929) was in fact born (on 15 Jan. 1879) in Newmarket, a town 30 miles north of Toronto. Her parents, William and Alberta Roche, were living in Alberta's family home on Prospect St, which has since been converted to a nursing home. William Roche's family, an important one in Newmarket, lived at the south end of Main Street, and his brother Danford operated a Newmarket store, the Leading House, where William worked. The Roche house on Main St was a converted bank, where the novelist recalled having played hide-and-seek in the safe; here also she briefly knew her paternal great-grandmother, Sara Danford Bryan, on whom she modelled the matriarch of the Jalna stories, Adeline Whiteoaks. In Mar. 1882 William Roche took his family to nearby Aurora to run Danford's store there but returned in 1883 to the Newmarket business. The family remained until 1885, when they moved to Toronto. A plaque in honour of Mazo Louise Roche (her original name) was erected in the Wesley Brooks Conservation Park in Newmarket.

NIAGARA FALLS

Poet **Tom Marshall** was born here in 1938 and lived at 703 MacDougall Cres. from 1944 to 1954. He attended Kitchener Street Public School, where he first began to write, and Niagara Falls Collegiate on Epworth Circle. Niagara Falls settings are featured prominently in his first book of poems, *The Silence of Fire* (1969), which is combined with three later books in his *Elements: Poems 1960–1975* (1980). (See also KINGSTON.)

Visitors to North America have commented on the city's most famous geographical feature, the Falls, ever since the first European account appeared in *Description de la Louisiane, nouvellement découverte au sud-ouest de la Nouvelle France* (1683). The author, Father **Louis Hennepin**, recorded his first view of the Falls on 6 Dec. 1678: 'Four leagues from Lake Frontenac [Lake Ontario] there is an incredible Cataract or Waterfall, which has no equal.' The majority of well-known authors who have since given their impressions of Niagara Falls have not shared Hennepin's enthusiasm or wonder. **Anna Jameson**, in *Winter Studies and Summer Rambles in Canada* (1838), wrote: 'What has come over my soul and senses?—I am no longer Anna—I am metamorphosed—I am translated—I am an ass's head, a clod, a wooden spoon, a fat weed growing on Lethe's bank, a stock, a stone, a petrifaction,—for have I now seen Niagara, the wonder of wonders; and felt—no words can tell what disappointment.' (See also TORONTO: 1.) **Oscar Wilde**, a century later, wrote: 'I was disappointed with Niagara—most people must be disappointed with Niagara. Every American bride is taken there, and the sight of the stupendous waterfall must be one of the earliest, if not the keenest, disappointments in American married life.' (See also TORONTO: 2.) Many others have been unimpressed: **Frances Trollope**, the English novelist and mother of novelist Anthony Trollope, who spent four days in the spring of 1831 on the Canadian side of the Falls; **Henry David Thoreau**, who visited them in May 1861; **Mark Twain**; and **John Steinbeck**.

Some authors, however, have been full of admiration. The American writer **Jack London** visited here in June 1894 and recalled the trip in *The Road* (1907). 'Once my eyes were filled with that wonderful vision of down-rushing water, I was lost.' **Henry James**, in *Portraits of Places* (1883), wrote, 'You purchase release at last by the fury of your indifference, and stand there gazing your fill at the most beautiful object in the world.'

NIAGARA-ON-THE-LAKE

Born in nearby QUEENSTON, the novelist **John Richardson** lived from 1796 to 1798 at officers' quarters in Fort George, where his father, an army surgeon, was stationed. Fort George was destroyed during the War of 1812 when the Americans attacked Niagara-on-the-Lake, but reconstructions of the fort's principal buildings are now a local tourist attraction.

William Kirby, author of the historical romance *The Golden Dog* (1877), lived from 1857 until his death in 1906 in a house at 130 Front St that bears a provincial plaque. Born in England in 1817, Kirby came to Canada in 1839 and settled soon after in Niagara-on-the-Lake. The Kirby house, built after American troops destroyed the town in the War of 1812, dates from about 1818.

William Kirby, c.1859

Although many of its elements have since changed, the centre-hall plan and the principal first-floor rooms are much the same. Kirby was the editor of the *Niagara Mail*, served from 1871 to 1895 as the town's collector of customs, and wrote several historical works, including *Annals of Niagara* (1896). *The Golden Dog*, which was very popular in its day and is still read in an abridged version, is set in Quebec City in 1748. Kirby also wrote two books of poems: *The U.E.: A Tale of Upper Canada* (1859) and *Canadian Idylls* (1894). He is commemorated by a national historic plaque at the town hall.

Malcolm Lowry lived in Niagara-on-the-Lake from Oct. 1944 to Feb. 1945; it was here that he finished the fourth and final version of *Under the Volcano* (1947). When Lowry's shack at DOLLARTON, B.C., burnt down on 7 June 1944, he and his wife, Margerie Bonner, came to OAKVILLE to live with Lowry's friend from Cambridge University days, Gerald Noxon. At the end of July the Noxons moved to Niagara-on-the-Lake, while Lowry stayed in Oakville at the house they had leased through September. He then moved into a rental cottage that the Noxons had found for him here. On Christmas Eve 1944 Lowry felt he had completed his novel and he and Margerie carried the manuscript to the Riverside Inn (now the Harbour Inn, 35 Melville St) to have a drink; there Lowry made a few notes in the margin of chapter 12 and declared, 'I've finished it.' In February Lowry returned to Vancouver; he made a few further revisions and dispatched his manuscript to an agent in June.

The poet **Irving Layton** lived at 9 Castlereagh St in 1979–82. (See TORONTO: 7; MONTREAL: 5, Que.)

Since 1962 Niagara-on-the-Lake has been home to the Shaw Festival, named after **George Bernard Shaw**. Founded by Brian Doherty, it gave its first performance at the historic town Court House (*c.* 1874) on 29 June 1962. In 1973 a new 820-seat festival theatre opened, but plays are still performed at the Court House as well.

NORVAL

The novelist **Lucy Maud Montgomery** lived at the Presbyterian manse, 402 Draper St in Norval, on Hwy 7 near Guelph, from Feb. 1926 until her husband Ewan Macdonald resigned the parish in late 1935. They had moved to Norval from LEASKDALE, where Macdonald had served for many years. Montgomery was very productive in the Norval manse, where she wrote *Anne of Windy Poplars* (1936), *Emily's Quest* (1927), *Pat of Silver Bush* (1933), and *Mistress Pat* (1935). The years at Norval were troubled by Macdonald's ill health and other family worries. By July 1936 the couple were settled in their last home: 210A Riverside Dr., TORONTO (7). (See also CAVENDISH, P.E.I.)

The Manse at Norval today

NORWICH

The novelist **Norman Duncan** was born on 2 July 1871 in Norwich, where his father was a merchant, but spent only the first few years of his childhood here. His father's uncertain business fortunes took the family to BRANTFORD, Fergus, and Mitchell. After studying for three years at the University of Toronto, Duncan moved to the United States in 1894; he became a prominent journalist for the New York *Evening Post* and later a professor at Washington and Jefferson University and the University of Kansas. He is best known for his stories and novels of the life of the Newfoundland and Labrador fishermen (see EXPLOITS ISLAND, ST ANTHONY, Nfld), whom he first came to know in 1900 when on an assignment to write on the subject for *McClure's Magazine*. Duncan's Newfoundland books include a collection of stories, *The Way of the Sea* (1903; rpr. 1970, 1982), a collection of essays on the missionary, physician, and writer Wilfred Grenfell, *Dr. Grenfell's Parish: The Deep Sea Fishermen* (1905), and a series of juveniles with a central character based on Grenfell. Duncan died in 1916 at Fredonia, N.Y., where he had retired; he is buried in Brantford. Norwich, on Highway 59, is southwest of Brantford.

OAKVILLE

Mazo de la Roche, creator of the Jalna novels, was associated with the Oakville area for many years. In 1911 she moved with her parents to a farm outside the village of Bronte, west of Oakville. The farm, called 'Rochedale', stretched from Hwy 2 just west of Cudmore Rd to the shore of Lake Ontario. The family left 'Rochedale' for Toronto in 1915 after de la Roche's father died, but life on the farm provided her with material for her novel *Possession* (1923), whose setting she called 'Foxleigh Farm'. In the 1920s she built a cottage in the community of Clarkson, now part of MISSISSAUGA. A house nearby was the model for the Whiteoaks family home, 'Jalna', in the famous series that began with *Jalna* in 1927. De la Roche drew extensively on the landscape between Oakville and Mississauga for the novels; the town of Stead in the books has been identified as a fictional rendering of Oakville. (See also NEWMARKET, SUTTON, TORONTO: 2, 6, 7.)

Novelist **Malcolm Lowry** lived in Oakville from June to September 1944, having come here to live with his friends, the Gerald Noxons, after his shack at DOLLARTON, B.C. burned down. The Noxons rented a large house surrounded by trees on the edge of Lake Ontario, and Lowry remained here until their lease ran out at the end of September, working on *Under the Volcano* (1947), although the Noxons themselves moved in July to NIAGARA-ON-THE-LAKE. Lowry followed them there in October.

The **T.V. Shevchenko** Museum and Memorial Park, 1363 Dundas St, contains 500 exhibits concerning the career of the Ukrainian cultural hero, who was born a serf in 1814 in the Ukrainian village of Morintsi. A founder in the 1840s of the Society of Saints Cyril and Methodius, dedicated to a unified republic of all Slavonic peoples, Shevchenko was arrested by the Russian government and kept under supervision for ten years to prevent him from writing. Pardoned in 1857, he died in 1861. Shevchenko was never in Canada, but Ukrainian Canadians remember his writings and his painting both here and in Winnipeg, where there is a statue on the grounds of the Manitoba legislature.

ORANGEVILLE

The humorist **Max Braithwaite** lived here at 51 Sunset Dr. from 1956 until 1969, when he moved to Toronto. In Orangeville, where he served for two years on the town council and took part in other community activities, he wrote some of his best-known books about growing up in Saskatchewan, including *Why Shoot the Teacher?* (1965) and *Never Sleep Three in a Bed* (1970). His *A Privilege and a Pleasure* (1973) is a satirical book about a small town near Toronto; called Goodston, it bears a resemblance to Orangeville. (See also BRANDY LAKE, STREETSVILLE, TORONTO: 4; ABERDEEN, EYRE, NOKOMIS, PRINCE ALBERT, VONDA, Sask.)

Archibald Lampman taught in the Orangeville High school in the fall of 1882, just after graduating from the University of Toronto. In 1883 he took a post in the Post Office Department, OTTAWA. In 1877 the poet **Alexander McLachlan** moved to a farm 7 miles west of Orangeville in Amaranth Township. By this time his poetic activity had ceased: his last and best volume was *Poems and Songs* (1874). In 1895, after the death of his son who worked the Amaranth Township farm, McLachlan moved into Orangeville itself, living in a brick house on Elizabeth St, where he died on 20 Mar. 1896. He is buried here in Greenwood Cemetery beneath a monument erected by public subscription in 1900. *The Poetical Works of Alexander McLachlan* was edited by E.H. Dewart and published in 1900 (rpr. 1974). Known in his day as 'the Canadian Burns', McLachlan provides some of the best existing verse descriptions of pioneer life and customs in the Ontario backwoods. (See also ERIN.)

ORILLIA

Stephen Leacock, who took Orillia as his model for the 'Mariposa' of his *Sunshine Sketches of a Little Town* (1912), first visited here in the 1890s when his mother, Agnes, was living in Orillia on Lake Couchiching, which adjoins Lake Simcoe at its northern end. Since 1876 the Leacock family had lived on a farm at EGYPT, near SUTTON, on the southern shore of Lake Simcoe; but in 1892, with the farm heavily in debt, Stephen Leacock moved his mother and younger brothers and sisters off the property. Agnes

Stephen Leacock in the garden at Old Brewery Bay, Orillia, 1939

lived in Sutton, Beaverton, and Orillia, until she settled in a lakeshore cottage near Sutton, where she lived until her death in 1942. Leacock met his wife Beatrix in Orillia in 1898 while she was staying with her mother at the Pellatt family summer estate, 'Southwood'. (Beatrix was a niece of Sir Henry Pellatt, the builder of Casa Loma in Toronto.) At the time of their meeting Leacock was preparing to leave his job at Upper Canada College, TORONTO (3, 7), in order to study economics at the University of Chicago. He and Beatrix were married in New York during the summer of 1900; after Leacock received his Ph.D. from the University of Chicago in 1903, he joined the faculty of McGill University, MONTREAL (3), where he taught economics until 1936. In 1908 he bought land on Lake Couchiching, where he planned to build his summer home. Naming the region 'Old Brewery Bay', Leacock and his brother Charlie built the first structure on the property during the first summer. Over the years the original 'cook house' grew into a substantial cottage. A very early riser, Leacock arranged an office for himself on the second floor of a boat-house on the lake, where he worked for several hours before breakfast in order to have the rest of the day free. Leacock filled his summer home with relatives—he had ten brothers and sisters, most of whom brought their own large families. While living here Leacock continued to write but declined to interrupt his summer with any other professional commitment.

Leacock's first book of humour, *Literary Lapses* (1910), was well received; but he established an international reputation with *Nonsense Novels* (1911). In 1911 he was commissioned by the *Montreal Star* to write a series of sketches on Canadian life. According to Leacock's friend, B.K. Sandwell, who helped to arrange the series, it was the first project of its type in Canada. Leacock took his subject largely from his experience of life in Orillia, concentrating on the town's reaction to the election of 1911, during which Leacock had campaigned vigorously in Orillia on behalf of the Conservative Party. In the original newspaper articles Leacock used the names of townspeople—a practice he abandoned, at the suggestion of an Orillia newspaper editor, for their book publication in *Sunshine Sketches of a Little Town* (1912). When *Sunshine Sketches* appeared, the people of Orillia tried to identify the characters and expressed resentment that Leacock had poked fun at the town—although Leacock insisted that they were really composite types rather than portraits of real people.

Scenes based on Leacock's life in Orillia—fishing exploits, gardening woes, summer parties—continued to appear in his writings, although no later book was devoted exclusively to the town. Leacock produced an average of one humour book per year, along with works on Canadian history and politics. After his compulsory retirement from McGill in 1936 he made a tour of Canada, which he described in *My Discovery of the West* (1937), winner of a Governor General's Award. He continued to divide his time between summers here and winters in Montreal. Remembrances of these later years are collected in Allan Anderson's oral history *Remembering Leacock* (1984). Leacock died in Toronto in 1944 after a brief illness and was buried at Sutton.

Leacock's summer house—now called the Stephen Leacock Memorial Home—is on Old Brewery Bay, off Hwy 12B. It is not the original house begun by Leacock in 1908, but a larger one built from 1926 to 1928. The nineteen-room white stucco dwelling has a spacious front veranda and grounds

Main Street, Orillia, *c.*1886

Leacock's summer home at Old Brewery Bay

leading down to Lake Couchiching. For many years after Leacock's death it was unoccupied. In the 1950s townspeople organized a campaign for the Orillia City Council to authorize the city's purchase and restoration of the property. The Memorial House was officially opened on 5 July 1958. Thousands of items—including Leacock's books, personal papers, and belongings—were acquired and catalogued, and are selectively displayed. The house is open for visitors from mid-June to Labour Day and guided tours are available. A national historic marker in Leacock's honour can be seen on the grounds. In 1946 the Stephen Leacock Medal for humour was established as an annual award for the best Canadian book in this genre. The Memorial Home is the site for banquet in honour of the year's winner.

The Orillia Public Library, 36 Mississauga St W., has a large collection of books by Leacock and displays a bronze bust of Leacock by Elizabeth Wyn Wood.

OSHAWA

The poet **R.G.** [Ronald Gilmour] **Everson** was born on 18 Nov. 1903 on a farm at the west end of Oshawa—then a much smaller town than it is today. The farm, just north of the Kingston Rd, had a trout stream on the property. Everson worked as a newspaper carrier in Oshawa until he was fourteen and then worked summers in the General Motors assembly plant here (Samuel McLaughlin's automotive company became General Motors of Canada in 1918). He lived in Oshawa until 1920, when he entered Victoria College, University of Toronto (see TORONTO: 3), where he began writing poetry and edited a literary magazine; later he financed his attendance at Upper Canada (Osgoode Hall) Law School by writing pulp mysteries and westerns. His books of poetry include *Three Dozen Poems* (1957), *Blind Man's Holiday* (1963), *Selected Poems 1920–1970* (1970), and a volume of selected and new poems, *Everson at 80* (1983). Since 1936 Everson has lived primarily in MONTREAL (4), where he headed a public-relations firm until his retirement in 1963.

OTTAWA

1. THE NINETEENTH CENTURY

In 1857 Ottawa was chosen as capital of the united Province of Canada by Queen Victoria, and construction on the Parliament Buildings began in 1860. From 1859 the peripatetic legislature of the Province sat in Quebec City, where the assemblage of talented persons it attracted contributed greatly to the creation of the *Mouvement littéraire de Québec*. Upon Confederation in 1867, when Ottawa became the capital of the new Dominion of Canada, writers came to the city as civil servants and journalists. Only later, when the concentration of governmental services and growing industries began to support a large urban population, did the city begin to produce native-born writers of note.

When the seat of government moved to Ottawa, two of the *Mouvement littéraire's* most important members came with it. **Antoine Gérin-Lajoie** became French translator to the Legislative Assembly in 1852 and moved in this post to Ottawa in 1865. He continued to hold it after Confederation and later became assistant librarian of the Library of Parliament; he retired in 1880 and died in Ottawa on 4 Aug. 1882. In the late 1860s Gérin-Lajoie lived on Besserer St east of Gloucester St; from the early 1870s until his death his home was at 300 Wilbrod St. During his years in Ottawa, Gérin-Lajoie produced his two famous didactic novels, *Jean Rivard: le défricheur* (1874), and its sequel *Jean Rivard, économiste* (1876), promoting colonization of Quebec's frontiers and the virtues of rural life to French Canadians. (See also YAMACHICHE, NICOLET, Que.). In 1864 **Joseph-Charles Taché** became deputy minister of agriculture for the Province of Canada, moving to Ottawa and retaining the office until he retired in 1888. Until the mid-1870s Taché lived on Bolton St between Sussex Dr. and Dalhousie St. While in Ottawa he published editions of his important works *Trois légendes de mon pays* (1876) and *Forestiers et Voyageurs* (1884), which had first appeared in Quebec City in 1861 and 1863 respectively. His *Les Sablons* (1885) recounts the history and folklore of Île de Sable and Île Saint-Barnabé and their environs (see SABLE ISLAND, N.S.). Taché died in Ottawa on 16 Apr. 1894; from about 1877 he lived at 16 Water St. (See also RIMOUSKI, Que.). Taché and Gérin-Lajoie were briefly joined in Ottawa by their former associate in the *Mouvement littéraire* and its most important poet, **Louis Fréchette**, who sat as a Liberal Member of Parliament for his hometown of LÉVIS, Que., from 1874 to 1878. On 31 May 1908, while visiting Ottawa from his home in MONTREAL (9), Fréchette died suddenly of a stroke; he had been preparing a definitive edition of his poems, which appeared posthumously as *Poésies choisies* (1908). Another member of the *Mouvement littéraire*, the poet **Alfred Garneau**, was appointed chief French translator to the Senate in 1873 and lived in Ottawa until his death in 1904; his longtime home here was at 288 Nelson Rd. In 1882 he edited the fourth edition of the *Histoire du Canada*, written by his father, the historian and poet François-Xavier Garneau. Alfred Garneau's own poetry was primarily the product of his youth in QUEBEC CITY; some of it was collected by his son, Hector, as *Poésies* (1904). Alfred Garneau was the grandfather of the poet Hector de Saint-Denys Garneau.

One of Joseph-Charles Taché's books written at Ottawa was *Les Histoires de M. Sulte—Protestation* (1883), a retort to critics of the historical ideas of **Benjamin Sulte**, historian and poet. Born and educated in TROIS-RIVIÈRES, Sulte came to Ottawa in 1867 as a translator to the House of Commons, and later served in the department of militia and defence, retiring in 1902 but remaining in Ottawa until his death on 6 Aug. 1923. His longtime home was at 304

Wilbrod St. Sulte published two volumes of verse, *Les Laurentiennes* (1870) and *Les Chants nouveaux* (1876), and wrote a French translation of 'God Save the King'; but he is known primarily for his many historical works, including *Histoire des canadiens-français* (8 vols, 1882–84). A selection of his research papers, first published in periodicals, was collected under the title *Mélanges historiques* (21 vols, 1918–34).

The poet, essayist, and politician **Thomas D'Arcy McGee** (*Canadian Ballads and Occasional Verses*, 1858) had been a member of the Legislative Assembly of the Province of Canada since 1858 before he was elected by his MONTREAL (2) riding to the first House of Commons after Confederation in 1867. On 7 Apr. 1868, returning to his lodgings at Sparks St (Mrs Trotter's boarding house) from an evening session of Parliament, he was shot to death as he turned the key in the lock of his front door. The murderer escaped, but McGee's assassination has generally been held to be the work of a Fenian; McGee often expressed strongly anti-Fenian and pro-Confederation views, and was one of the most important Fathers of Confederation. A statue to him stands on the grounds of the Parliament Buildings near the Centre Block; he was buried in Montreal. *The Poems of Thomas D'Arcy McGee*, collected by Mrs J. Sadlier, appeared in 1869.

Charles Mair, sometimes called the 'Canada First poet', arrived in May 1868 at Ottawa's Russell Hotel (gone) during a trip to arrange for the publication of his first book, *Dreamland and Other Poems*; it appeared in Montreal later that year, but a fire destroyed all but 200 copies before they could be distributed. While in Ottawa, Mair was one of the five originators of the patriotic Canada First movement. The others—Ottawa residents **George Taylor Denison**, **Robert Grant Haliburton**, Henry J. Morgan, and W.A. Foster—were all writers. Haliburton was a son of Thomas Chandler Haliburton (see WINDSOR, N.S.) and had published, among others works, *Voices from the Street: A Series of Poems* (n.d.). Denison—the author of two books on the theory of cavalry warfare and three volumes of memoirs—was, like Mair, a leading spokesman against the Métis during the Red River and North West Rebellions; both men served militarily in the latter. Mair did not remain long in Ottawa; later in 1868 he went to what is now WINNIPEG as paymaster to a road-survey party, and there his actions helped to precipitate armed conflict between the Métis and government representatives. (See also LANARK, WINDSOR; PRINCE ALBERT, Sask.; FORT STEELE, VICTORIA, B.C.)

Duncan Campbell Scott, with Rupert Brooke behind; the women are Mrs R.T.M. Scott (standing) and Mrs D.C. Scott

The poet **Charles Sangster**, called 'the poet laureate of colonial Canada' for his *The St. Lawrence and the Saguenay, and Other Poems* (1856) and *Hesperus, and Other Poems and Lyrics* (1860), came to Ottawa in 1868 to take up a $500-per-annum position in the postal department. For the last ten years of this period he lived at 281 Maria St (this street no longer exists); earlier he lived on Queen and on Boteler Sts. He retired in 1886 and returned to his native KINGSTON. He later claimed that eighteen years of unremitting desk work had not only caused a nervous breakdown that forced him to retire, but had prevented him from publishing a third volume of poems. (Sangster's manuscripts are in the McGill University Library, Montreal.) From 1883 until Sangster's retirement in 1886, the poet Archibald Lampman (see below) worked in the same postal department with him but took no notice of the older writer.

The novel *Honor Edgeworth; or Ottawa's Present Tense* by 'Vera', the pen-name of **Kate M.B. Bottomley**, appeared in 1882. A sentimental tale of society life in the capital as lived by civil servants, politicians, and members of established families, it was the first fictional portrayal of Ottawa. In 1888 **Sara Jeannette Duncan**, who had not yet embarked on her career as a novelist, came to Ottawa as the parliamentary correspondent of the Montreal *Star*; by 1889 she had left on the round-the-world cruise that resulted in her first book, *A Social Departure: How Orthodocia and I Went Round the World by Ourselves* (1890). (See also BRANTFORD.)

Duncan Campbell Scott, Archibald Lampman, and William Wilfred Campbell—the three Ontario-born members of the group of writers, born in the 1860s, who are called the Confederation Poets (the two others are Charles G.D. Roberts and Bliss Carman)—worked in Ottawa in the civil service and produced most of their literary work here. Scott, who was the first major writer born in Ottawa (on 2 Aug. 1862), entered the Department of Indian Affairs in 1879 and retired in 1932 as its deputy superintendent general. He lived at 108 Lisgar St for more than sixty years, until his death on 19 Dec. 1947. (A plaque marks the site of his home, now gone.) Scott's many works include *The Magic House and Other Poems* (1893), *New World Lyrics and Ballads* (1905), *Poems* (1926), and *The Green Cloister: Later Poems* (1935), and two volumes of short stories.

The British poet **Rupert Brooke** visited Canada from Mar. through Sept. 1913, and spent 11 days in Ottawa, most of them at Scott's home. Brooke arrived in Montreal, visited Quebec City, the Saguenay River and Tadoussac, Ottawa, Niagara Falls, Winnipeg, Calgary, Banff, Lake Louise, and Vancouver, before going to San Francisco. He came to Ottawa about July 10 and stayed for a day at the Windsor Hotel before presenting his introduction from John Masefield to Scott. He toured Ottawa with Scott and made excursions to Meach Lake and Kingsmere. In his account of his North American trip, published after his death in battle in 1915 as *Letters from America* (1916), he wrote: 'The streets of Ottawa are very quiet, and shaded with trees. The houses are mostly of that cool, homely, wooden kind, with verandahs, on which, or on the steps, the whole family may sit in the evening and observe the passers-by. This is possible for both the rich and the poor, who live nearer each other than in other cities. In general there is an air of civilisation, which extends even over the country round.' Brooke left Ottawa on 21 July.

OTTAWA

They told me, casually, that there was nothing but a few villages between me and the North Pole. It is probably true of several commonly frequented places in this country. But it gives a thrill to hear it. But what Ottawa leaves in the mind is a certain graciousness—dim, for it expresses a barely materialised national spirit—and the sight of kindly English-looking faces, and the rather lovely sound of the soft Canadian accent, in the streets.

—Rupert Brooke, *Letters from America* (1916)

Archibald Lampman obtained a position in the post-office department and moved

Archibald Lampman, 1895

to Ottawa in 1883. He lived first at 67 O'Connor St and was there when the inaugural issue of Goldwin Smith's *The Week* (6 Dec. 1883), edited by Charles G.D. Roberts, appeared with his poem 'A Monition', his first publication outside of college periodicals. (This poem was subsequently entitled 'The Coming of Winter'.) Lampman's favourite walks in Ottawa were to Rockcliffe, along the Russell Rd to Dow's Swamp, around the Hog's Back Locks, and at the Experimental Farm; all of these provided panoramas of the city, whose skyline is so often evoked in his poetry: 'The bell-tongued city with its glorious towers . . .' ('The City'). On 3 Sept. 1887 Lampman married Maud Playter and the couple used a legacy of hers to publish a private edition of Lampman's first book, *Among the Millet* (1888). The book immediately gave him a high place among Canadian writers, although he never published any volume commercially in Canada during his lifetime. By the early 1890s the Lampmans were living in a house on Florence St not far from Scott; the two men had been fast friends since Lampman's first months in Ottawa and often hiked, canoed, and vacationed together. A trip they made in the summer of 1890 to the lower St Lawrence resulted in Lampman's poem 'Sunset at Les Éboulements'. In the fall of 1892 Lampman moved to 369 Daly Avenue, where he completed his second volume of poems, *Lyrics of Earth* (Boston, 1895). Shortly after it appeared in early 1896, Lampman and his family moved to 187 Bay St, near the corner of Slater, but soon rented out this house and moved to the suburb of Britannia. He died on 10 Feb. 1899, and his death interrupted the publication of his third volume, *Alcyone* (1899); only twelve copies were issued. After Lampman's death his friend Scott became the keeper of his literary reputation, editing *The Poems of Archibald Lampman* (1900), with a memoir; *Lyrics of Earth: Songs and Ballads* (1925); *At the Long Sault and Other Poems* (1943, with E.K. Brown); and *Selected Poems of Archibald Lampman* (1947). Lampman's long-standing love for Katherine Waddell, a fellow clerk to whom he became attracted in 1889, is reflected in the poems collected in *Lampman's Kate: Late Love Poems of Archibald Lampman* (1975).

The Lampman house on Daly Avenue

During 1891 the poet **Wilfred Campbell**, having left the Anglican priesthood, also came to Ottawa to work in the civil service. At first he had only a clerking position in the office of the Secretary of State and was 'desperately poor', according to Lampman, who counted Campbell as one of his 'neighbours' during the time he was living on Florence St. Campbell's home through much of the 1890s and in the first decade of the twentieth century was at 24 Lisgar St. Campbell was already known as the author of *Lake Lyrics and Other Poems* (1889), and it was to help alleviate his poverty that Scott and Lampman conceived the idea of a joint literary and intellectual newspaper column, *At the Mermaid Inn*, which ran weekly in the Toronto *Globe* from 6 Feb. 1892 to 1 July 1893 (see TORONTO: 1). The first piece was Campbell's essay 'Mythology', which by referring to the cross as a 'myth' caused a public outcry that elicited an apology from the *Globe* and explanatory letters from Campbell himself. Among the books that Campbell produced while living at 24 Lisgar were *Beyond the Hill of Dreams* (1899) and *The Poems of Wilfred Campbell* (1905). In 1909 he joined the Dominion Archives as bibliographer. With improving fortunes he acquired property on high ground south of the city and just south of the Experimental Farm, in the district named City View. His home, on Merivale Rd, was called 'Kilmorie House.' Campbell's chief works written here were *Sagas of Vaster Britain: Poems of the Race, the Empire, and the Divinity of Man* (1914); a prose work, *The Beauty, History, Romance and Mystery of the Canadian Lake Region* (1910); and the first *Oxford Book of Canadian Verse*, which he edited in 1913. Campbell died on New Year's morning, 1919. In 1958 the Ottawa poet **Arthur Bourinot** published *At the Mermaid Inn*, a selection of columns by Scott, Lampman, and Campbell.

Scott, Lampman, and Campbell are all buried in Beechwood Cemetery, at Hemlock Rd and St Laurent Blvd. Campbell's plot was donated by William Lyon Mackenzie King, and the impressive Campbell monument was executed by Dr Tait Mackenzie. (Scott: see also STANSTEAD, Que. Lampman: see also COBOURG, GORE'S LANDING, MORPETH, PERRYTOWN, TORONTO: 3. Campbell: see also TORONTO: 3, WIARTON; ST STEPHEN, N.B.) A footnote to the story of the Confederation Poets in Ottawa is that the poet Loftus MacInnes, only son of the poet Tom MacInnes (see DRESDEN; VANCOUVER, B.C.), married Archibald Lampman's only daughter, Natalie (born 11 Jan. 1892); the couple lived in Ottawa.

2. 1900 TO 1939

After his novel *Marie Calumet* (1904) was condemned by the Bishop of Montreal, **Rodolphe Girard** was dismissed from his job at *La Presse* in Montreal and came to Ottawa, where he lived until his death in 1956. Girard worked for the Ottawa newspaper *Le Temps* from 1904 to 1907 and in 1908 joined the department of the secretary of state; in 1911 he became a translator to the House of Commons. During his first years in Ottawa, Girard lived at 328 Besserer St, where he wrote his novels *Rédemption* (1906) and *L'Algonquine* (1912). He served twice as president of the *Institut canadien-français d'Ottawa* (1907–8, 1912–14), founded the Ottawa branch of the *Alliance française* (1908), and became a lieutenant-colonel in the Canadian Forestry Corps during the First World War. Girard remained a prolific writer throughout his life, but the major publication of his later career was a revised, somewhat expurgated, version of *Marie Calumet* (1946); this he prepared at 371 Friel St, his home in the last decades of his life. (See also MONTREAL: 11.)

William Chapman came to Ottawa in 1902 to take up a position as translator to the Senate. During his fifteen years here he lived for a time at 184 Osgoode St and published *Les Aspirations* (1904), *Les Rayons du nord* (1910), and *Les Fleurs de givre* (1912)—collections of romantic poetry. In 1917, while living with his friends Alfred Saint-Laurent at 521 King Edward St and working on a book of poems that was to have been entitled *L'Éopée canadienne*, he died suddenly on 23 Feb. (See also BEAUCEVILLE EST, MONTREAL: 2, Que.)

Louvigny de Montigny, another founding member of the *École littéraire de Montréal*, arrived in Ottawa in 1910 as a translator to the Senate; in 1915 he became chief translator, a position he held until his death in 1955. De Montigny's early home in Ottawa was at 364 Chapel St; in the 1940s and 1950s, when he published his best-known works (*Au Pays de Québec*, 1945; and a collection of his plays, *L'Épi rouge et autres scènes du pays du Québec*, 1953), he lived at 129 Powell Ave and also had a house on Blue Sea Lake in the Gatineau region of Quebec, north of Ottawa. He was one of the principal organizers of the Canadian Authors' Association (1921) and *La Société des Écrivains Canadiens* (1922). Perhaps his most noteworthy literary accomplishment was to perceive the importance of Louis Hémon's *Maria Chapdelaine*, which had been serialized in 1914 in *Le Temps* of Paris. Through de Montigny's efforts it was published in book form in Montreal in 1916. He told the story of his discovery of Hémon's novel, and of its world-wide reception after its book publication, in *La Revanche de Maria Chapdelaine* (1937). (See also MONTREAL: 10.)

The anthropologist, folklorist, and writer **Marius Barbeau** settled in Ottawa in 1911 on his return from Oxford University, where he was a Rhodes Scholar. He joined the anthropology staff of the Museum Branch, Geological Survey of Canada; in 1927 this branch became the National Museum, at Metcalfe and McLeod Sts. Barbeau retired in 1949 but maintained his close association with the museum, serving as a consultant for another fifteen years and continuing to prepare museum publications; he died in Ottawa on 27 Feb. 1969. His home throughout most of his fifty-eight years in the city was at 260 McLaren St. Of his more than fifty books, many are of literary importance, including his two novels, *The Downfall of Temlaham* (1928) and *Mountain Cloud* (1948), and numerous folksong and folklore collections, such as *Folksongs of French Canada* (1925, with Edward Sapir), *Au Coeur de Québec* (1934), *L'Arbre des rêves* (1948; English edition, *The Tree of Dreams*, 1955), and *Huron-Wyandot Traditional Narratives in Translation and Native Texts* (1960). His twelve

Marius Barbeau in the 1930s

volumes of folk stories and legends retold for children were published as *Les Contes du grand'père sept-heures* (1950–53); a selection from them was translated by Michael Hornyansky as *The Golden Phoenix and Other French-Canadian Fairy Tales* (1958). Barbeau was a faithful lifelong participant in the activities of the Ottawa chapter of the Canadian Authors' Association; in 1944 he was a founding member of the *Académie canadienne-française*. (See also SAINT-ANNE-DE-LA-POCATIÈRE, SAINTE-MARIE-DE-LA-BEAUCE, Que.)

With another Ottawa writer, **Lawrence J. Burpee**, Barbeau was co-founder of the *Société historique du Canada*. Born in Halifax, N.S., on 5 Mar. 1873, Burpee came to Ottawa as a member of the civil service in 1890. From 1905 to 1912 he was librarian of the Ottawa Public Library, and thereafter—until his death in 1946—was Canadian secretary of the International Joint Commission. In his home at 22 Rideau Terrace, Burpee produced his books, mainly historical and geographical in subject, including *Sandford Fleming, Empire Builder* (1915), *On the Old Athabaska Trail* (1927), and *Jungling in Jasper* (1929). In 1930, just before the failure of the Graphic Press (see below), Burpee served as its president. Other English-language writers in Ottawa in the early years of the century include **Francis William Grey**, Edward William Thomson, and Robert Fontaine. The English-born Grey was first cousin of the fourth Earl Grey, who was governor general from 1904 to 1911. His chief work is the novel *The Curé of St. Philippe: A Story of French-Canadian Politics* (1899), based on events that took place at SAINTE-MARIE-DE-MONNOIR, Que. Settling in Ottawa in 1903, Grey taught at the University of Ottawa (1903–4) and then worked in the Dominion Archives, first as a clerk and then as a translator, until his retirement in 1913; there he must have been acquainted with William Wilfred Campbell. During at least part of his time in Ottawa, Grey lived at 87 Daly Ave. His books include a play about Frontenac, *Sixty-nine: A Series of Historical Tableaux* (1904) and *Love Crucified and Other Sacred Verses* (1902), which was published here. He died in Edinburgh in 1939. **Edward William Thomson**, a much-travelled writer and editor who was born in a rural area that is now part of Toronto, came to Ottawa in 1902 after ten years of literary journalism in Boston. A close friend of both Scott and Lampman, Thomson had selected the poems for Lampman's *Lyrics of Earth* (1895) at the poet's request and had secured publication of the book by the Boston firm of Copeland and Day. Thomson's Ottawa home was at 360 Concession St, which became 360 Bronson Ave when the street name was changed in 1909. Here he produced his collection of poems, *The Many-Mansioned House and Other Poems* (1909). In 1917, just after he had left Ottawa for Boston, where he died, there appeared his still-popular *Old Man Savarin Stories: Tales of Canada and Canadians*, a revised and expanded edition of a book first published in 1895. **Robert Fontaine** was born in 1907 in Massachusetts but was raised until the age of fifteen in Ottawa. His boyhood in Ottawa was the subject of the stories collected in *The Happy Time* (1945), which was turned into a radio series in the year of its publication, a Broadway musical in 1950, and a film directed by Stanley Kramer in 1952. The sequel, *Hello to Springtime* (1955), was less successful. In 1915 the poet **R.A.D. Ford** was born in Ottawa; he has spent most of his career outside Ottawa because of his postings as a Canadian diplomat. (Since 1968 he has been ambassador to Russia.) Ford's first volume, *A Window on the North* (1956), won a Governor General's Award; his other books are *The Solitary City* (1969) and *Holes in Space* (1979). (See also LONDON.)

Robert J.C. Stead, born in 1880 in MIDDLEVILLE, came to Ottawa from CALGARY, Alta, in 1919 to work as publicity director for the Department of Immigration and Colonization. From 1936 until he retired in 1946 he was superintendent of publicity for parks and resources in the Department of Mines and Resources; he died here on 26 June 1959. Stead's home for almost all his Ottawa years was at 193 Second Ave, where he wrote the novel generally considered his masterpiece, *Grain* (1926), as well as *The Smoking Flax* (1925), *The Copper Disc* (1931), and possibly *Dennison Grant* (1920). Stead produced no new book after 1931; during the last years of his life his home was at 703 Parkdale Ave. An active participant in the Canadian Authors' Association from its beginnings, Stead was its president in 1923. The meetings of the Ottawa chapter of the CAA brought together some of Canada's most prominent writers between the wars. De Montigny, Scott, Stead, and Barbeau—its early members—were later joined by Lawrence J. Burpee, Arthur S. Bourinot, Wilfred Eggleston, the novelist Madge Macbeth, Mackenzie King, Dr Esther Clark Wright, Irene Baird, and others. (See also CARTWRIGHT, Man.)

In 1923 the printer Henry C. Miller founded Graphic Publishers Ltd in Ottawa to publish literary books, primarily novels and essays. At this time Miller was manager of the Ottawa Composition Company and operated Graphic Publishers from his home at 1 Middleton Dr. The early books published by the press include *Shackles* by Madge Macbeth and a volume of poetry by Wilson MacDonald, *Out of the Wilderness* (1926). (See CHEAPSIDE). In 1927 it issued *A Search for America* by **Frederick Philip Grove**, his partly autobiographical story about the difficulties of European immigrants. In Dec. 1929 Grove and his wife moved to Ottawa from BOBCAYGEON so that he could take up a position as editor with Graphic Publishers; his official title was president of Ariston Press, a subsidiary of Graphic. Grove took a house in Eastview, east of the city on the site of the present National Research Council on Montreal Rd; he lived on Skead Rd, which no longer exists. While here he published a novel, *The Yoke of Life* (1930); his son Arthur Leonard was born on 14 Oct. 1930. In 1929, when Grove arrived, Graphic Publishers was located in its own offices at 171–5 Nepean St and Miller was serving as its president and manager. Grove was not at first aware that Graphic was in financial difficulties. By 1930 Graphic had moved to 50 Russell Rd, Overbrook (the district east of the Rideau River and south of Montreal Rd), and Lawrence Burpee was acting as president. During his fifteen-month tenure with Graphic, Grove felt shut out from the local literary community. He wrote that 'in Ottawa I lived in an isolation comparable to that of an Antarctic explorer' and complained that no Ottawa writer had ever called on him or his wife, singling out Scott and Burpee as offenders. Grove left Ottawa for SIMCOE in Mar. 1931 and Graphic Publishers was liquidated in May of the following year. In 1930 Graphic had sponsored its Canadian Novel Contest, with a prize of $2,500, a first in Canadian publishing and literary awards. It was Grove who encouraged Raymond Knister (see RUSCOMBE and STONEY POINT) to submit his novel, *My Star Predominant*, which was awarded the prize in 1931. However, the book was not published until 1934 because of Graphic's collapse; for the same reason Knister waited a long time for his money and never received all of it.

The novelist **Madge** (Mrs M.H.) **Macbeth**, née Lyons, was born in Philadelphia in 1878 and educated in London, Eng., but spent most of her adult life as an Ottawa resident at 324 Chapel St. Her long series of internationally popular novels, most of them initially published in England, included *Kleath* (1917), *The Patterson Limit* (n.d., probably 1922), *Shackles* (1926), *Shed of Circumstance* (1947), and *Volcano* (1963). Macbeth's two books published under the pseudonym 'Gilbert Knox', *The Land of Afternoon* (1924) and *The Kinder Bees* (1935), are satires on the political and social life of Ottawa. Macbeth also wrote travel books and reminiscences. Another member of the Ottawa literary community at this time was **Lloyd Roberts**, son of Charles G.D. Roberts, who was often visited by his father at his home 'Low Eaves' in Westboro, Ont., near Ottawa. Lloyd Roberts was a member of the Ottawa chapter of the CAA and in 1927 published a book of poems, *Along the Ottawa*. From 1925 to 1939 he was parliamentary correspondent for the *Christian Science Monitor*; his other literary works include a collection of verse, *I Sing of Life* (1937), and one of essays, *The Book of Roberts* (1923). He died in Toronto on 28 June 1966.

The poet, memoirist, and *chansonnier* **Félix Leclerc**, associated primarily with his native town of LA TUQUE, Que., spent six formative years in Ottawa: the four years of his high-school education at the Junioriat du Sacré-Coeur and his last two years of formal schooling at the University of Ottawa. He left in 1934 to begin his career in radio and theatre at Quebec City. Leclerc's books include his famous memoir of his childhood at La Tuque, *Pieds nus dans l'aube* (1946), and *Le Fou de l'île* (1958; English trans. by Philip Stratford, *The Madman, the Kite and the Island*, 1976, rpr. 1983). A major French-Canadian writer more closely associated with Ottawa was the novelist **Léo-Paul Desrosiers**, who lived here from 1929 to 1941 at 163 Mackay St while he worked as French editor of *Hansard*; in the 1920s he had been in Ottawa as parliamentary correspondent for the Montreal newspaper *Le Devoir*. In Ottawa Desrosiers produced three of his best-known historical novels—*Nord-Sud* (1931), *Les Engagés du Grand Portage* (1939, winner of the Prix David; trans. by Christina van Oordt, *The Making of Nicolas Montour*, 1978), and perhaps his finest work, *Les Opiniâtres* (1941)—as well as a number of other books. (See also MONTREAL: 15, ST-SAVEUR-DES-MONTS, Que.)

In 1925 **Bruce Hutchison**, a three-time Governor General's Award winner for his books on Canadian history and society, came to Ottawa from VICTORIA, B.C., as political reporter for his newspaper the *Times*. His most important books were written during the 1940s and 1950s, long after he had left Ottawa, but during the 1920s he was a prolific writer of pulp fiction (see also VANCOUVER, VICTORIA, B.C.) **Wilfrid Eggleston** came to Ottawa in 1929 as a

Sir Charles G.D. Roberts and Lloyd Roberts at 'Low Eaves'

correspondent for the Toronto *Star* and became president of the Parliamentary Press Gallery in 1933. He had published his single volume of poems, *Prairie Moonlight and Other Lyrics*, in 1927. In Ottawa he wrote two novels, *The High Plains* (1938; rpr. 1975) and *Prairie Symphony*, written in the 1940s but not published until 1978. Both books were probably written at 150 Metcalfe St, Apt. 20, where Eggleston lived in the late 1930s and early 1940s; he and his wife, **Magdalena Eggleston** (author of the novel *Mountain Shadows*, 1955), later lived at 234 Clemow Ave and 229 Powell Ave. It was in the Clemow Ave house that Eggleston wrote his important study of western-Canadian writing, *The Frontier and Canadian Letters* (1957). He was Canada's press censor during the Second World War; in 1947 he founded the Carleton University Department of Journalism and served as its director in 1958. He published his memoirs, *While I Still Remember*, in 1968. He died in June 1986. (See also TORONTO: 2; LETHBRIDGE, MEDICINE HAT, Alta.)

Arthur Bourinot, born in Ottawa on 3 Oct. 1893, was a lifelong resident of the city and a fixture of its literary community; his earliest book was *Laurentian Lyrics* (1915). Bourinot's longtime home was at 202 Cloverdale Rd, Rockcliffe Park, and there he produced numerous poetry collections, including *Under the Sun* (1939, winner of a Governor General's Award), *Selected Poems* (1935), *Collected Poems* (1947), and *More Lines from Deepwood* (1949). From about 1953 he lived at 158 Carleton Rd, Rockcliffe Park, and during the last fifteen years of his life published *Tom Thomson and Other Poems* (1954) and *To and Fro in the Earth: Poems* (1963), among other volumes. Much of his poetry concerns Ottawa, its people, history, and surrounding landscape. Bourinot was an indefatigable participant in and promoter of the Ottawa literary community, and published critical studies of Scott, Lampman, and other poets; a volume of the letters of Lampman and Thomson; two further volumes of Lampman and Duncan Campbell Scott letters; and his selection of the *At the Mermaid Inn* columns (1958) by Lampman, Scott, and Campbell. In addition he collaborated with Marius Barbeau and the painter Arthur Lismer in *Come a-Singing!* (1947), a collection of folksongs. Bourinot was a son of Sir **John George Bourinot**, clerk of the House of Commons, honorary lifetime secretary of the Royal Society of Canada, and author of many political and historical works, including *The Intellectual Development of the Canadian People: An Historical Review* (1881). Arthur Bourinot died in Ottawa on 17 Jan. 1969; his last address was 290 Acacia Ave, Rockcliffe Park.

The famous Scottish novelist **John Buchan**, first Baron Tweedsmuir, was Governor General of Canada from 2 Nov. 1935 until his death on 11 Feb. 1940 in Montreal. He occupied the official residence of the Governors General, Rideau Hall on Sussex Dr., and while in Canada produced several works, including the novels *The Island of Sheep* (1936) and *Sick Heart River* (1941), a historical study, *Augustus* (1937), and his autobiography, *Memory-Hold-the-Door* (1940). He approved the establishing of the Governor General's Awards in 1937.

In June 1938 novelist and women's-rights advocate **Nellie McClung** came to Ottawa for the unveiling of a plaque commemorating the famous 'persons case', in which she had participated. On 18 Oct. 1929, as the result of a petition from McClung and others, the Privy Council of Great Britain ruled that in section 24 of the British North America Act, dealing with appointment to the Senate, 'the word persons includes members of the male and female sex'. McClung writes of the 'persons case' in her third volume of autobiography, *The Stream Runs Fast* (1945). This plaque can be seen in the antechamber of the Senate, on the left wall as one enters. Another literary curiosity in the Parliament Buildings relates to the Memorial Chamber, on the second level of the Peace Tower, which was built as a memorial to the dead of the First World War. In the arch above the entrance door are engraved two lines

All's well, for over there among his peers
A Happy Warrior sleeps.

These lines were chosen by John Pearce, architect of the reconstruction of the Parliament Buildings after the 1916 fire, but he could not remember where he had seen them. In 1939 an obscure versifier and itinerant labourer named **John Ceridigeon Jones** came forward to claim authorship. Major C.J. Charlton, who had once known the Welsh-born Jones, sought him out in the flophouse where he was living on Lagauchetière St W. in Montreal, and Jones was able to prove that he had written the lines in a doggerel poem, 'The Returning Man', composed in 1919 or 1920 in Calgary and published in the *Calgary Albertan*. When this evidence had been presented, the department of Defence sent Jones $8; he died in obscurity in 1950 at SULTAN. The Memorial Chamber contains, carved in stone, the text of John McCrae's 'In Flanders Fields' and a French translation.

The poet, novelist, and critic **Margaret Atwood** was born in Ottawa in Nov. 1939 and until 1945 lived at 314 First Ave. Her father, Carl E. Atwood, was an entomologist attached to the Department of Agriculture. From early childhood Atwood accompanied her family each summer on trips into the bush of northern Ontario and Quebec, a yearly routine that continued after the Atwoods moved to Sault Sainte-Marie in 1945 and to TORONTO (3, 4, 6) in 1946.

The novelist and poet **Elizabeth Smart** was born in Ottawa on 27 Dec. 1913. Daughter of a prominent lawyer, Russell Smart, she spent her earliest childhood at 515 Besserer St; in 1916 the family moved to 15 Linden Terrace and by the late 1920s lived at 361 Daly Ave, only a few doors from one of the residences of Archibald Lampman. In 1935, after being educated at a private school and spending a year in England, Smart returned to Ottawa and worked for the *Ottawa Journal*, then at 233–7 Queen St. In 1939 and 1940 Smart lived at 'Cottrin Lodge', on the south side of The Driveway in Rockcliffe Park, where she began her famous novel *By Grand Central Station I Sat Down and Wept* (1945). She completed it in 1941 in PENDER HARBOUR, B.C., and there gave birth to her first child, by the English poet George Barker, whom she had met in California in the late 1930s and with whom she had travelled in the United States and Canada. After 1941 Smart lived primarily in England; she had three other children by Barker. Her other books are *A Bonus* (1977), poems, and *The Assumption of Rogues and Rascals* (1977), an extended work of poetic prose in the manner of her first work. Her journals—*Necessary Secrets*, edited by Alice Van Wart—were published in 1986. She died on 4 Mar. 1986.

The Smart house on Daly Avenue

3. SINCE 1945

The British Columbia novelist **Irene Baird** came to Ottawa in 1942 to work for the National Film Board, primarily in publicity and public relations. She was a civil servant for about twenty years, becoming chief of the Information Services Division of the Department of Indian and Northern Affairs in 1962. For at least part of Baird's years in Ottawa she lived at 122 Young St. Her novels *John* (1937), *Waste Heritage* (1939), and *He Rides the Sky* (1941) were written before she came to the city. *Climate of Power* (1971) appeared after she left and is based on her civil-service experience of dealing with the adverse effect on northern native peoples of well-meaning but short-sighted public policies. (See also VANCOUVER, VICTORIA, B.C.)

The poet **P.K. Page** came from Montreal to Ottawa in 1946 and worked as a script writer for the National Film Board. She lived first at 309 Daly St and later at 173 Daly. In 1950 Page married the commissioner of the NFB, William Arthur Irwin, who later became ambassador to Australia, Brazil, and Mexico. After their marriage the couple moved to nearby KINGSMERE, Que., where Page completed her volume *The Metal and the Flower* (1954), winner of a Governor General's Award; poems from the Ottawa years include 'Christmas Eve—Market Square', 'T-Bar', and 'Morning, Noon and Night'. (See also MONTREAL: 5, Que.; VICTORIA, B.C.) In 1944 the family of the poet **Jay Macpherson** came to Ottawa from ST JOHN'S, Nfld. They lived at 554 The Driveway, and Macpherson attended Glebe Collegiate Institute (1944–8) and Carleton University, from which she graduated in 1952. Her early poetry appeared in the chapbook *Nineteen Poems* (1952), published by Robert Graves's Seizen Press. (See also TORONTO: 3.) The British Columbia poet **Anne Marriott** (winner of a Governor General's Award for *Calling Adventurer*, 1941) worked in Ottawa from 1945 to 1949 as a script editor for the NFB, living for much of this period at 79 Blackburn Ave. In 1945 she published *Sandstone and Other Poems*; her book *The Circular Coast: New and Selected Poems* (1981) contains selections of her work from the 1940s and earlier. (See also PRINCE GEORGE, VICTORIA, B.C.) The prolific and popular versifier **Edna Jaques** worked in Ottawa from 1942 to 1947 for the Wartime Prices and Trade Board. The novelist **John Marlyn**, author of *Under the Ribs of Death* (1957) and *Putzi, I Love You, You Little Square* (1981), has worked in Ottawa since the late 1940s as a writer for the federal government. Born in Hungary, he was brought up in WINNIPEG, where his novels are set.

After living for twenty years in Paris, the French-Canadian belletrist and critic **Marcel Dugas** fled the Nazi occupation of France, settling in 1941 in Ottawa where he remained until his death in 1947. Dugas's publications include a memoir of his last days in occupied France, *Pots de fer* (1941); a collection of verse, *Salve Alma Parens* (1941); and an important collection of literary essays, *Approches* (1942). Dugas had been active in several literary movements in Montreal (particularly that surrounding the avant-garde review *Le Nigog*) and was the principal member of *Le Groupe des Sept* in Ottawa from 1943 to 1946. (See also MONTREAL: 13.) The poet **Alfred Desrochers** lived in Ottawa in 1945 when he became a translator for Parliament; later that year he was made secretary of the *Fédération Libérale Nationale*, but in 1946 he moved to Montreal. His enduring connection with Ottawa was through his association with a local poet. For many years Desrochers laboured over the Spenserian stanzas of his *Le Retour de Titus* (1963), about the Roman Emperor Titus who in AD 75 was forced by the Roman Senate to choose between his office and his love for Bérénice. Desrochers kept sending the completed stanzas to the Ottawa poet **Jeannine Bélanger**, who collected them, provided an introduction, and was instrumental in securing publication of the finished poem. Bélanger, born in Hull in 1915, became a nun with the name in religion of Sister Marie-Josefa; her own books of verse include *Stances à l'éternel absent* (1941).

The poet **George Johnston** joined the staff of Carleton University in 1949 and taught there until 1980. Now professor emeritus, he lives in nearby Athelstan, Que. Johnston's best-known book of poems is *The Cruising Auk* (1959), which contains a fancifully distorted portrait of Ottawa. He is the author of several other collections, including *Happy Enough: Poems 1935–1972* (1972) and *Auk Redivivus: Selected Poems* (1981), and has translated several Old Norse Sagas, including *The Greenlanders' Saga* (1976), which deals with the Norse discovery of what is now Canada. The poet **Elizabeth Brewster** worked as a librarian in the Carleton University Library in 1953–7; in this period she published her early poem based on her native New Brunswick, *Lillooet: A Canadian Village* (1954), which is included with other early poems in her first major volume, *Passage of Summer* (1969). (See also CHIPMAN, FREDERICTON, HAMMTOWN, SACKVILLE, SUSSEX, N.B.; KINGSTON, TORONTO, Ont.; SASKATOON, Sask.; EDMONTON, Alta.; VICTORIA, B.C.) The poet **Joan Finnigan** was born here on 23 Nov. 1928 (her parents lived in nearby Shawville, Que.) and attended Carleton. Her extensive knowledge of her native region is central to her books of poems, *A Reminder of Familiar Faces* (1978) and *Living Together* (1976), and to her collections of oral traditions and folkways, *I Come from the Valley* (1976) and *Giants of Canada's Ottawa Valley* (1981). (See also KINGSTON.) The poet and social critic **Robin Mathews** is a professor of Canadian literature at Carleton University. His books include *Language of Fire* (1976, poems) and *Canadian Literature: Surrender or Revolution* (1978).

The author and New Brunswick historian **Esther Clark Wright** lived for many years in Ottawa at 40 Island Park Dr. Her books include *The St. John River* (1949) and *Grandmother's Child* (1959). Another longtime resident of the city was the popular British novelist **Nicholas Monsarrat**, who lived in Rockcliffe from 1953 to 1956 while he was chief of British Information Services; he then lived at 85 Range Rd, until 1966, when he moved to Malta. He died in 1979. Among his books written here were *Canada Coast to Coast* (1955) and a novel, *The Nylon Pirates* (1960).

Norman Levine was born on 22 Oct. 1923 in Ottawa's Lower Town, the old section lying northeast of Parliament Hill between the Rideau Canal and the Rideau River. Levine's father, Moses Levine, was an Ottawa fruit pedlar, and at the time of Norman's birth the family lived in a house (now gone) on St Joseph St. The family's next house, 249 Guigues Ave, at the corner of King Edward Ave, still stands. Later Levine lived at 363 Murray St (gone) and attended York Street School. Ottawa sites and buildings, especially those in Lower Town, play a great part in Levine's narrative of a journey through Canada in the 1950s, *Canada Made Me* (1958), and in many of his short stories, collected in *One-way Ticket* (1961), *I Don't Want to Know Anyone Too Well* (1972), *Selected Stories* (1975), and *Thin Ice* (1979). The small park by the Rideau River at King Edward Ave and Cathcart St is identifiable in *Canada Made Me* and in the stories 'A Father' and 'In Lower Town'. In *Canada Made Me* Levine wrote: 'I like the lower towns, the place across the tracks, the poorer streets not far from the river. They represent failure, and for me failure here has a strong appeal.' Levine left school at sixteen and joined the Royal Canadian Air Force at eighteen; his overseas service began in 1944, and after the war he lived chiefly in St Ives, Cornwall, until his return to Canada in 1980. (See also TORONTO: 5, WAWA, Ont.; MONTREAL: 7, Que.)

Ottawa has recently instituted the position of poet laureate, and the first to receive the title (for the 1982–4 term) was **Catherine Firestone**, born here on 23 Oct. 1949;

her book *Daydream Daughter* (1976) received the A.J.M. Smith Prize for Canadian poetry awarded by Michigan State University. The poet **Seymour Mayne** (*The Impossible Promised Land: Poems New and Selected*, 1981) has taught English literature at the University of Ottawa since 1973. In 1979 the novelist **Jack Hodgins** came to the university, remaining for several years as writer-in-residence and visiting professor; in this period he wrote *The Resurrection of Joseph Bourne* (1980) and *The Barclay Family Theatre* (1981), both of which concern his native Vancouver Island. (See MERVILLE, NANAIMO, B.C.) The novelist **Matt Cohen** (*The Sweet Second Summer of Kitty Malone*, 1979) attended elementary school and Nepean High School in Ottawa between 1948 and 1960, but is mainly associated with the country north of KINGSTON, where he lives and where many of his novels are set. Ottawa figures in his novel *Flowers of Darkness* (1981).

The French-Canadian novelist, memoirist, and translator **Claire Martin** was an Ottawa resident for more than twenty years. She and her husband—Roland Faucher, a chemist and civil servant—lived for at least part of their Ottawa years at 141 Crichton St. They moved to France in 1972. Martin's books include her memoirs, *Dans un gant de fer* (1965) and *La Joue droite* (1966), which won a Governor General's Award. (Both were translated by Philip Stratford and published in one volume, *In an Iron Glove*, 1968 and later separately: *In an Iron Glove*, 1973, and *The Right Cheek*, 1975.) Martin also wrote the novels *Doux-amer* (1960) and *Quand j'aurai payé ton visage* (1962). She returned to Ottawa for a year in 1973 as writer-in-residence at the University of Ottawa. **Claude Aubrey**, born on 23 Oct. 1914 in Morin Heights, Que., came to Ottawa in 1949 and was made chief librarian of the Ottawa Public Library in 1953. His works during the 1940s were *Le Vengeance des hommes de bonne volonté* (1944) and *Miroirs déformants* (1945). During the 1950s he lived at 5 Southern Dr. and latterly on Claver St. He wrote several retellings of folklore, including *Le Violin magique et autres légendes du Canada français* (1968) and *Légendes du Canada français* (1977). Aubrey died in 1885. The novelist **Gérard Bessette** was long associated with KINGSTON as a Queen's University professor; upon his resignation in 1979 he came to Ottawa, where he lives on Lisgar St. Among his many novels is *L'Incubation* (1965; trans. by Glen Shortliffe, *Incubation*, 1967), which won a Governor General's Award. Bessette published a collection of his short stories, *La Garden-party de Christophine*, in 1980. The Acadian poet and novelist **Ronald Després** (see MONCTON, N.B.) came here in 1957 as a Parliamentary translator and in 1973 was charged with creating the present Translation Bureau of the Department of the Secretary of State; he lives in Ottawa. Selections of Despres' work from several previous volumes appear in his selected poems, *Paysages en contrebande* (1974). The essayist **Jean Le Moyne** came to Ottawa in 1969 as a member of the Prime Minister's staff and was made a Senator in 1980; his book of essays *Convergences* (1961) brought him prominence as a writer and a Governor General's Award; it was translated by Philip Stratford as *Convergence: Essays from Quebec* (1966). (See also MONTREAL: 14, Que.) Another writer long associated with Ottawa is the historical novelist **Hélène Brodeur**, who now lives on Long Island Dr. in Manotick, Ont. A winner of the Prix Champlain, she chronicles the life of the Franco-Ontarian people in her series of historical novels, called collectively *Chroniques du Nouvel Ontario*. They include *Le Quête d'Alexandre* (1981; trans., *Alexandre: A Saga of Northern Ontario*, 1983) and *Entre l'aube et le jour* (1983).

Other French-language writers associated with Ottawa are the poet **Cécile Cloutier** (*Cuivre et Soies*, 1964), who taught at the University of Ottawa in 1962–6, and the poet **Gilles Hénault** (*Signaux pour les voyants*, 1972), who was writer-in-residence there in 1974–5. Iraqi-born **Naim Kattan**, who has lived in MONTREAL (16) since 1954, also has a home in Ottawa. He joined the Canada Council in 1962 and until recently headed its Writing and Publication Section. Among his many works are the novels *Adieu, Babylone* (1975) and *Les Fruits arrachés* (1977), trans. by Sheila Fischman as *Farewell, Babylon* (1976) and *Paris Interlude* (1979). *The Neighbour and Other Stories* (NCL, 1982) is a selection of his short fiction translated from four collections. Poet **Fernand Ouellette**, primarily associated with his native city of MONTREAL (18), attended Ottawa's Collège séraphique des Capucins, leaving in 1947. Another native of Montreal, the poet **Pierre Trottier**, joined the Department of External Affairs here in 1949, but has lived mainly at foreign postings since 1951; since 1979 he has been Ambassador to UNESCO. Trottier's important book of poems, *Sainte-Memoire* (1972), includes a collection published in 1951, *Le Combat contre Tristan*; he is also the author of a famous book of essays on the French-Canadian identity, *Mon Babel* (1963).

The diplomat and diarist **Charles Ritchie**, born in HALIFAX, was based in Ottawa for many years, although he was often abroad on diplomatic assignments. His life from the 1920s through the 1960s is memorably portrayed in his diaries: *The Siren Years: a Canadian Diplomat Abroad 1937–1945* (1974, winner of a Governor General's Award), *An Appetite for Life: the Education of a Young Diarist* (1977), and *Diplomatic Passport: More Undiplomatic Diaries* (1981). **Sondra Gottlieb** wrote her novel *True Confessions* (1978)—about her WINNIPEG childhood during the 1950s—in Ottawa, where her husband was Under-Secretary of State for External Affairs; she now lives in Washington, D.C., where Allan Gottlieb is Ambassador to the United States. The novelist **Hugh Hood**, never an Ottawa resident, treats the city in detail in his *A Game of Touch* (1970) and *Black and White Keys* (1982). (See also ATHENS, TORONTO: 5; BARRINGTON, N.S.; MONTREAL: 6, Que.)

The poet and novelist **Joy Kogawa**, born in British Columbia, lived in Ottawa throughout the 1970s; she was a writer in the Prime Minister's office from 1974 to 1976 and writer-in-residence at the University of Ottawa in 1978. In Ottawa she wrote her poetry collections *A Choice of Dreams* (1974) and *Jericho Road* (1978); but she is best known for her novel *Obasan* (1981), which records her experience of the evacuation of Japanese Canadians during the Second World War. Kogawa now lives in TORONTO (4). The novelist and critic **John Metcalf** lives on Lewis St in Ottawa and has been writer-in-residence at the University of Ottawa. His books include the novel *General Ludd* (1980), *Selected Stories* (1982), and *Kicking Against the Pricks* (1982), a collection of essays. (See also DELTA.)

Ottawa is the home of several institutions of great literary interest. The Canada Council—which offers assistance to writers and Canadian-owned publishing companies—has offices at 255 Albert St. On the campus of the University of Ottawa is the Centre de Recherche en civilisation canadienne-française (Lamoureux Hall), with its extensive collections of manuscripts, documents, books, and pictures relating to French-Canadian literature. Perhaps most important are the National Library and the National Archives of Canada at 375 Wellington St. The National Library houses the most complete collection of Canadian books, including many extremely rare old volumes and manuscripts. The extensive manuscript collections of the National Archives contain papers of many twentieth-century writers, including Alfred G. Bailey, Arthur S. Bourinot, Robertson Davies, Gratien Gélinas, André Giroux, John Glassco, Charles Gordon (Ralph Connor), Roger Lemelin, Marie LeFranc, Marshall McLuhan, Claire Martin, Louvigny de Montigny, Gabrielle Roy, Laura Goodman Salverson, Félix-Antoine Savard, Marshall Saunders, F.R. Scott, Elizabeth Smart, Wilfred Watson, Phyllis Webb, Ethel Wilson, and J. Michael Yates.

OWEN SOUND

The novelist Mary Esther MacGregor, who wrote under the pseudonym **Marion Keith**, lived in Owen Sound during the 1940s and 1950s and is buried here in Greenwood Cemetery. The home in which she wrote three of her novels is approximately 14 miles north of Owen Sound on the Bayshore Road next to Lake Huron. MacGregor's life in this lakeshore farmhouse forms the basis of many scenes in *As a Watered Garden* (1946), *Yonder Shining Light* (1948), and *Lilacs in the Dooryard* (1952). MacGregor was born Mary Esther Miller in Rugby, Ont., in 1876. She married a Presbyterian minister, the Rev. Donald MacGregor, and in accompanying him to the many churches he served she gained the experience of rural and small-town Ontario that is the subject of her novels. The best known of them is *Duncan Polite: The Watchman of Glenoro* (1905), the story of the conflict between a minister and his congregation over a new church organ the minister wishes to install. After the Rev. MacGregor died in the 1950s, Mary MacGregor lived in Toronto; she published her last novel, *A Grand Lady*, in 1960. She died in 1961 and was buried next to her husband.

After completing his university education, the novelist **Selwyn Dewdney** taught high school in Owen Sound for several years during the 1930s. This experience was the background of his first novel, *Wind Without Rain* (1946). Dewdney was born in 1909 in PRINCE ALBERT, Sask.; after his brief residence here, he settled in LONDON, Ont. (See also AGAWA BAY.) The poet **William Wilfred Campbell** attended high school in Owen Sound, graduating in 1879. (See also KITCHENER, OTTAWA, WIARTON, Ont.; ST STEPHEN, N.B.)

PAISLEY

A provincial historical plaque near the old hose tower at Queen and Goldie Sts commemorates the Irish-born poet **Isabella Valancy Crawford**, author of *Old Spookses' Pass, Malcolm's Katie, and Other Poems* (1884). Crawford arrived in Canada in 1858 with her parents, Dr Stephen Crawford, the village's first doctor, and his wife Sydney. The precise dates of Isabella's residence in Paisley are uncertain; the family seems to have left under a cloud created by charges of

Isabella Valancy Crawford

misappropriation of funds against Dr Crawford, who was Paisley's treasurer; he was subsequently convicted. It is believed that the Crawfords left Paisley in mid-1861 and by Nov. 1862 had settled in LAKEFIELD.

The poet **Charles Mair** was educated in the 1840s at the Paisley schoolhouse, where his teacher was the Scot Robert Mason, a well-known pioneer educator. (See also KINGSTON.)

PALGRAVE

In 1946, after military service in the Second World War, **Farley Mowat** began to build a house on a wooded lot near Palgrave, which is located on Hwy 50 northeast of Toronto. He lived there until 1960, launching his writing career with several books based on his two years in the KEEWATIN BARRENS. These books include *People of the Deer* (1951), *Lost in the Barrens* (1956), and *The Desperate People* (1959). (See also BELLEVILLE, PORT HOPE; RIVER BOURGEOIS, N.S.; MAGDALEN ISLANDS, Que; RANKIN INLET, N.W.T.)

PEMBROKE

The critic and satirist **William Arthur Deacon** (*The Four Jameses*, 1927, rev. 1953, rpr. 1974) was born in Pembroke in 1890 but spent only his first nine months here. He was raised in STANSTEAD, Que., and after his education practised law in WINNIPEG, Man., before settling in TORONTO: 6, with which his career is primarily associated.

PENGELLEY'S LANDING

Two and a half miles east of Bailieboro is Pengelley's Landing and the Pengelley family cemetery, the burial place of **Joseph Medlicott Scriven** (1819–1886). A sixteen-foot monument to Scriven in the cemetery bears three stanzas of his most famous work, the hymn 'What a Friend We have in Jesus', which originated as a poem entitled 'Pray Without Ceasing'. A Plymouth Brethren preacher, Scriven was a graduate of Trinity College, Dublin, in his native Ireland. After settling permanently in Canada in 1847 he was employed during the 1850s as a tutor by Captain Robert L. Pengelley, a retired British naval officer. A roadside plaque near the cemetery marks a small frame house that occupies the site of the original Pengelley cabin where Scriven taught. The present structure dates to the nineteenth century and may have been built while Scriven was working with the family, some of whose descendants live nearby.

At the base of the large monument in the Pengelley cemetery are the graves of both Scriven and his fiancée Eliza Roche, a niece of Captain Pengelley. She died before the wedding, having contracted a chill after being baptized by immersion in Rice Lake, probably at Pengelley's Landing. The tragedy is sometimes said to have led to the writing of Scriven's famous hymn, which is often dated to 1857; however, there is evidence that Scriven showed it to

The Scriven tombstone, Pengelly's Landing

acquaintances as early as 1850. Scriven was buried next to Miss Roche after his death by drowning.

Pengelley's Landing is reached by following County Road 2 two and a half miles east from Bailieboro to Scriven Road, an unpaved road that leads south towards Rice Lake. A half-mile south is the Pengelley home and the cemetery, in sight of the lake. (See also BEWDLEY, PORT HOPE.)

PERRYTOWN

Now only a church stands on the site of what was, in the 1860s, a small community about 9 miles north of Port Hope and south of Millbrook on the Millbrook Rd. It was here that Archibald Lampman Sr came in 1866 as incumbent pastor of the Anglican congregations of Perrytown and Elizabethville; his son, the future poet **Archibald Lampman**, was four years old at the time. The elder Lampman began taking services in 1867 at GORE'S LANDING on Rice Lake, in the absence of a resident clergyman there, and later moved his family to that village, probably in 1868.

PETERBOROUGH

A provincial plaque on the grounds of Thomas A. Stewart Secondary School honours Stewart's wife, **Frances Stewart**, whose collected letters provide an interesting portrait of Peterborough in the era of its settlement, *c.* 1825. The Stewarts came from Ireland to the Otonabee River in Douro Township in 1822. Frances Stewart's letters to her adoptive parents were collected by her daughter, E.S. Dunlop, and published as *Our Forest Home: Being Extracts from the Correspondence of the Late Frances Stewart* (1889; 2nd edn, 1902).

According to Stewart, the founding of Peterborough made life much easier for all the settlers in the region. **Catharine Parr Traill** moved with her growing family to the Ashburnham area east of Peterborough from DOURO TOWNSHIP in 1839. Traill's husband Thomas was a friend of Thomas Stewart and of Peterborough's first physician, Dr John Hutchison. Hutchison's house, the first stone house built in the settlement, is located on Stewart St and was constructed in 1837 by the residents in an effort to keep the doctor from moving to Toronto. Before coming here Catharine Parr Traill published *The Backwoods of Canada* (1836), but she did little writing in Peterborough. She tried briefly to teach, but the financial troubles that had plagued the household for many years continued, and in 1846 the Traills moved to GORE'S LANDING, where a friend had offered them free use of a house. (See also LAKEFIELD.)

The family of the poet **Isabella Valancy Crawford** lived in Peterborough from 1870 until 1875. They moved here from LAKEFIELD, where they settled briefly after a financial scandal involving her father, a doctor, had forced the Crawfords to leave their first home in Canada, PAISLEY. Crawford lived in a house on a brick terrace opposite the market square. Three years later financial difficulties forced a move to a small cottage on Brock St. Following the death of her father in 1875, Crawford moved to TORONTO with her mother and invalid sister. In Toronto, Crawford published *Old Spookses' Pass, Malcolm's Katie, and Other Poems* (1884) at her own expense. Both narrative poems of the book's title were written in Peterborough. Crawford died in Toronto in 1887, but she was buried in Little Lake Cemetery here. A Celtic cross marks her grave.

Joseph Scriven's *Hymns and Other Verses* was published by James Stephens in Peterborough in 1869. The book contained ninety-four hymns and 21 verses of Scriptural paraphrases, but did not include Scriven's most famous poem, 'Pray Without Ceasing', which was set to music by Charles W. Converse and circulated around the world under the title 'What a Friend We Have in Jesus'. Scriven lived in the Rice Lake area south of Peterborough from 1844 until his death in 1886. (See also BEWDLEY, PENGELLEY'S LANDING, PORT HOPE.)

The poet **W.W.E. Ross** was born here in 1894 and educated at the University of Toronto. A geophysicist, Ross worked for many years at the Dominion Magnetic Observatory in the Toronto suburb of Agincourt. Called Canada's first modern poet, Ross published his first book, *Laconics*, in 1930, followed by *Sonnets* (1932) and *Experiment 1923–29* (1956). *Shapes and Sounds*, a selection of his poems edited by Raymond Souster and John Robert Colombo, was published in 1968. (See also TORONTO: 7.)

Robertson Davies came to Peterborough in 1942 from TORONTO (3, 6, 7), where he had been working as literary editor of *Saturday Night* after several years of study and theatre work in England. Davies joined the staff of the *Peterborough Examiner*, 400 Water St, which was owned by his father. In 1946, with his two brothers, Davies assumed ownership of the *Examiner* and became its editor. Until 1963, when he left Peterborough to become Master of Massey College in Toronto, he made his editorial work at the newspaper the foundation for a busy career as essayist, novelist, and playwright. Even after resigning as editor, Davies continued to be involved in the *Examiner's* operation until the paper was sold in 1968. In 1942–50 he lived at 572 Weller St, and in 1951–62 at 361 Park St N. Davies produced three collections based on his Saturday columns written for the *Examiner* under the pseudonym Samuel Marchbanks: *The Diary of Samuel Marchbanks* (1947), *The Table Talk of Samuel Marchbanks* (1949), and *Marchbanks' Almanack* (1967). The column appeared between 1943 and 1953 not only in the *Examiner* but in many other newspapers. During the Peterborough years Davies also wrote for *Saturday Night* (1953–9) and the *Toronto Star* (1959–62). Pieces from this body of work appear in *A Voice from the Attic* (1960) and *The Enthusiasms of Robertson Davies* (1979).

Davies' 'Salterton' trilogy was written in Peterborough, although the university town in which the books are set resembles KINGSTON more closely. The three novels are *Tempest-tost* (1951), *Leaven of Malice* (1954), and *A Mixture of Frailties* (1958). In the second book Davies uses his experiences as an editor to create the character of Gloster Ridley, editor of the Salterton *Evening Bellman*, who copes with town politics and social pressures while trying to make his paper accurate and useful.

Davies' theatrical experience in England provided the groundwork for his vigorous contribution to the development of Canadian drama. While living in Peterborough his work for the theatre ranged from masques written for students at his Alma Mater, Upper Canada College, to a dramatization of *Leaven of Malice*, which was called *Love and Libel* for its 1960 production but renamed *Leaven of Malice* for its theatrical revivals in 1973 at Hart House Theatre and in 1975 at the Shaw Festival, Niagara-on-the-Lake. Davies wrote three plays for the Crest Theatre, Toronto: *A Jig for the Gypsy* (1954), *Hunting Stuart* (written in 1955), and *General Confession* (written in 1956, but published along with *Hunting Stuart* in *Hunting Stuart and Other Plays*, 1972). Four of Davies' five one-act plays from the Peterborough period are collected in *Eros at Breakfast and Other Plays* (1949). In the fifth, *Overlaid* (1948)—his most frequently acted play—a struggle between a spirited father and his conservative daughter ends with a defeat for love of culture by the forces of respectability and religion. Davies' play *At My Heart's Core* (1950) draws on the history of Peterborough as three of the area's early women writers—Frances Stewart, Susanna Moodie, and Catharine Parr Traill—engage in personal rebellions against the backdrop of the Rebellion of 1837. (See also THAMESVILLE.)

The novelist **Margaret Laurence** (1926–87) bought a cottage on the Otonabee River during the summer of 1970 and called it Manawaka, after the name she gave to her hometown, NEEPAWA, Man., in her fiction. She eventually bought a house in LAKEFIELD, north of Peterborough, for her principal residence. She worked on her last novel—*The Diviners* (1974), the last novel in the 'Manawaka' cycle—at the cottage, and the Ontario town of McConnell's Landing in the book suggests connections with the Peterborough region. Laurence was writer-in-residence at Trent University, Peterborough (founded in 1963), in 1974, and in 1980 she was appointed chancellor of the university. (See also WINNIPEG, Man.; VANCOUVER, B.C.)

Richard Wright, a native of MIDLAND, wrote his second novel, *The Middle of a Year* (1973), while studying at Trent University. Wright lived in a rented house on the shore of Little Mud Lake, north of the city, and rose at 5:30 every morning to work on the novel. He graduated with honours in 1972. (See also ST CATHARINES, TORONTO: 2.)

PORT BURWELL

The novelist **Fred Bodsworth** was born on 11 Oct. 1918 in this small fishing port on Lake Erie. He attended Port Burwell Public and Continuation School from 1924 to 1936 (the building still stands); his formal education ended at the age of eighteen when he was forced to seek work. Bodsworth lived in Port Burwell until he was twenty-one, working as a reporter on a local newspaper, and still spends vacations in the area; he has lived in TORONTO (6) since 1943. His novels are *The Last of the Curlews* (1954; rpr. 1963), *The Strange One* (1959), *The Atonement of Ashley Morden* (1964), and *The Sparrow's Fall* (1967).

PORT CARLING

Max Braithwaite has lived on Brandy Lake near Port Carling since 1973, having moved here from TORONTO (4). A native of Saskatchewan, he is famous for his books about growing up on the Prairies, but he has lived in Ontario since the end of the Second World War. Two of his books are based on the Muskoka region, where Port Carling is situated. The first, *Lusty Winter* (1978), is set in the fictional town of Wolf Lake, and the second, *McGruber's Folly* (1981), in the fictional town of Port Perkins. (See also ORANGEVILLE, STREETSVILLE; ABERDEEN, EYRE, NOKOMIS, PRINCE ALBERT, VONDA, Sask.)

PORT CREDIT

The wildlife author and artist **Ernest Thompson Seton** lived in a cabin in Lorne Park west of Port Credit from 1887 until 1890. A native of England, Seton had first come to Ontario as a child of six (see LINDSAY). In his teens he was forced by ill health to abandon art studies abroad; he returned to Canada to live for several years in CARBERRY, Man., on his brother's farm. In the 1880s Seton began spending time in the United States on commissions, including extensive illustration work for *The Century Dictionary*. Upon completing this work he came to Port Credit, and after 1890 pursued a wandering life as artist and student in Europe, Canada, and the United States, where he settled in 1896. His first book, *Wild Animals I Have Known* (1898), established him as a popular author. (See also TORONTO: 1.)

PORT DOVER

Wilson MacDonald moved here from CHEAPSIDE to live with his grandparents in 1887, following the death of his mother. In 1888, at the age of eight, he began attending Port Dover Public School and then went on to Woodstock College and McMaster University, both at that time in TORONTO (7). After several years in the United States and Montreal, MacDonald settled permanently in Toronto. He published the first of his many collections of romantic verse, *The Song of the Prairie Land*, in 1918.

Raymond Knister moved in 1929 from TORONTO (2) to a farmhouse near Port Dover, where he wrote his novel *My Star Predominant*, based on the life of Keats. In 1930 the book received the first prize of $2,500 in the Canadian Novel Contest of Graphics Press in OTTAWA, but the collapse of the firm meant that Knister's novel was not published until 1934, two years after he drowned while on holiday at STONEY POINT. He is buried in Port Dover Cemetery on Hwy 6. Knister's first novel, *White Narcissus* (1929), an account of farm life based on his home region around RUSCOMB, was published while Knister was living in Port Dover. He moved to Montreal in 1931.

Raymond Knister

PORT HOPE

A cenotaph to **Joseph Medlicott Scriven**, author of the hymn 'What a Friend We Have in Jesus', stands at the northeast corner of Port Hope Memorial Park, opposite the Port Hope Library, 31 Queen St. The monument bears the text of Scriven's poem and directs visitors to the Scriven shrine, thirteen miles north at Pengelley's cemetery (see PENGELLEY'S LANDING).

Scriven came to Canada from his native Ireland in 1843 at the age of twenty-four and spent most of his life in the Port Hope–Bewdley district. In Port Hope he gathered a small Plymouth Brethren congregation and often preached in the market square in front of the Town Hall, which was built in 1851 and is still standing at 56 Queen St. For the last twenty years of his life Scriven lived in a house that can be seen at 54 Thomas St (on the southwest corner at Strachan St); the house is privately owned and still inhabited. Scriven's hymn was written by 1857, before he took this house, but he probably composed some of his other devotional lyrics there. Scriven's *Hymns and Other Verses* (PETERBOROUGH, 1869) did not contain his famous hymn; but it was included by a Port Hope minister, James Cleland, along with other Scriven writings, in *What a Friend We Have in Jesus and Other Hymns by Joseph Scriven* (Peterborough, 1895).

In September 1876 the fourteen-year-old **Archibald Lampman** entered Trinity College School, which occupies spacious grounds at the northeast corner of Ward and Deblaquire Sts. Lampman spent two years here, and during that period sent one of his earliest poems in a letter to his father at the family home in COBOURG. (See also MORPETH, OTTAWA.)

Port Hope was also the childhood home of the poet and professor **Watson Kirkconnell**, born here on 16 May 1895 in the family's house at 42 Bedford St. The young Kirkconnell attended Port Hope Public

School and lived here until 1908, when his father, headmaster of the Port Hope high school, accepted a similar post in Lindsay, Ont. Kirkconnell became the pre-eminent Canadian linguist of his day, mastering many languages and translating literature from Hungarian, Icelandic, and other languages that are seldom translated into English. A scholar of international note, especially for his investigations into the sources and backgrounds of Milton's poetry, he was also widely known for both his lyrics and his narrative poems in the tall-tale tradition. Kirkconnell won the Lorne Pierce Medal for achievement in Canadian literature in 1942.

Farley Mowat, having left BURGEO, Nfld, as a result of the incident he recounts in *A Whale for the Killing* (1972), established his home in Port Hope and still lives here for part of the year. He and his wife Claire lived at 25 John St before moving to their present home. (See also BELLEVILLE, PALGRAVE; RIVER BOURGEOIS, N.S.; MAGDALEN ISLANDS, Que.; KEEWATIN BARRENS, RANKIN INLET, N.W.T.)

PRESCOTT

The editor and novelist **Bruce Hutchison** was born here on 5 June 1901, but was taken as an infant to British Columbia and grew up in VICTORIA. (See also VANCOUVER.) The Hutchisons' house here stood on Dibble St.

QUEENSTON

Major **John Richardson**, Ontario's first internationally known novelist, was born at Queenston on 4 Oct. 1796, while his mother was visiting her family here. At the time Richardson's parents lived in the officers' quarters of Fort George in NIAGARA-ON-THE-LAKE, and they remained there until his father, an army surgeon, was posted to FORT ERIE and other stations; the family settled in AMHERSTBURG in 1802. In later life Richardson returned briefly to the Niagara Peninsula; in 1845–6 he lived in ST CATHARINES and worked as superintendent of the Welland Canal Police. A plaque honoring him stands in the yard of Laura Secord Public School at Walnut and Queenston Sts in Queenston. Richardson's works include his best novel, *Wacousta; or, The Prophecy: A Tale of the Canadas* (1832), and its sequel, *The Canadian Brothers; or, The Prophecy Fulfilled* (1840), and a long poem, *Tecumseh* (1828), all of which deal with the War of 1812 in the region around Detroit. (See also BROCKVILLE.)

ROCKWOOD

Rockwood was the birthplace in 1857 of **Agnes Ethelwyn Wetherald**, poet and journalist. She was the daughter of the principal of Rockwood Academy, where she was in part educated. The building that housed the Academy from 1850 until it ceased operation in the early 1880s is still standing and is marked with a plaque. Wetherald's career was primarily associated with TORONTO (1). Her collected *Lyrics and Sonnets* appeared in 1931; she died in 1940. Rockwood, on Hwy 7, is northeast of Guelph.

RUSCOMB

The novelist and poet **Raymond Knister** was born on 27 May 1899 on a farm near Ruscomb in Essex County. He spent much of his childhood and youth here. In 1919 he entered Victoria College, TORONTO (2), but ill health forced him to leave the university early the next spring and live on his father's new farm near Blenheim, 40 miles from Ruscomb. He worked on that farm for three years before moving to Iowa City, Iowa, where he began to publish poetry and edited a literary magazine; he returned to southern Ontario after a brief stay in the United States. Many of Knister's writings, including his first novel, *White Narcissus* (1926), have farm settings based on his life at Ruscomb and Blenheim. On 29 Aug. 1932 Knister drowned while swimming in Lake St Clair near STONEY POINT, where he and his wife had rented a cottage. (See also PORT DOVER; MONTREAL, Que.)

ST CATHARINES

From 1845 to 1846, while he was superintendent of the Welland Canal Police, the novelist Major **John Richardson** lived in Allenburgh, near St Catharines. His wife, Maria Drayson, died here and was buried in the Butler Burial Grounds of Niagara-on-the-Lake. A native of QUEENSTON, Richardson moved to St Catharines from BROCKVILLE, where he had founded two newspapers, both of which were forced to close.

The 'cheese' poet **James McIntyre** (1827–1906)—remembered in William Arthur Deacon's humorous critical work, *The Four Jameses* (1927)—lived here briefly before moving to his long-time home in INGERSOLL. He operated a furniture store in St Catharines, where he had moved after several years on southwest Ontario farms. A native of Scotland, he arrived in Canada in 1841. One of his poems was the 'Oxford Cheese Ode'.

The novelist **Richard Wright** was head of the English department of Ridley College here from 1975 to 1979 and still lives here. A native of MIDLAND, Wright moved to St Catharines from PETERBOROUGH, where he had written a novel and received a degree from Trent University. His books written in St Catharines include *Farthing's Fortunes* (1976) and *The Teacher's Daughter* (1982). Also associated with Ridley College are the novelist **Edward McCourt** (*Music at the Close*, 1947; rpr. 1966), who taught here in 1935–6 (see SASKATOON, Sask.) and the poet **Robert Finch** (*Poems*, 1946), who studied here in the 1920s (see TORONTO: 3).

St Catharines appears as 'Grantham' in **Howard Engel**'s tongue-in-cheek detective novels about a Toronto gumshoe, Benny Cooperman. Born in TORONTO (4) in 1931, Engel spent his childhood in St Catharines and graduated from St Catharines Collegiate. His books include *The Suicide Murders* (1980), *The Ransom Game* (1981), and *Murder on Location* (1982).

ST ELMO

The Rev. **Charles William Gordon**—who wrote many popular novels under the pseudonym **Ralph Connor**—was born on 13 Sept. 1860 at St Elmo (formerly Indian Lands), in historic Glengarry County in eastern Ontario. Gordon based many of his most famous books—including *The Man from Glengarry: a Tale of the Ottawa* (1901), *Glengarry School Days* (1902), and *The Sky Pilot* (1899)—on incidents from the ten years he spent here. In 1870 his father, the Rev. Daniel Gordon, who had been minister of the Presbyterian congregation of St Elmo, accepted a call to Zorra, Ont. (this community no longer exists; see HARRINGTON WEST). Charles Gordon never returned to live in the county that he recalled so vividly in his writings. In 1894 he became the minister of St Stephen's Presbyterian Church, WINNIPEG, where he remained until he died in 1937.

Gordon believed that his fiction was so successful because it was based on his own experiences. In his autobiography, *Postscript to Adventure* (1938), he asserted that 'All that is set down in *Glengarry School Days* is true. Our education began in the little log schoolhouse of great hewn pine logs, plastered at the cracks.' The lumbermen in *The Man from Glengarry* are drawn from his childhood memories of St Elmo, and Gordon recalls having ridden to school 'on the big timber sticks, sixty feet long and more, which were being hauled to the Scotch River to be floated down to the Ottawa when the ice broke, and thence by the St. Lawrence to Quebec for the British navy.'

A provincial historical plaque to Gordon stands in front of the Presbyterian church at the corner of County Rd 20 and Concession Rd 19, St Elmo.

ST JOSEPH'S ISLAND

The novelist **Marian Engel** spent the summer of 1969 on this island, in St Joseph's Lake 150 miles north of Thunder Bay, which she describes in her book *Islands of Canada*. A story about the island's history suggested part of the plot for Engel's novel *Bear* (1976), whose setting, on a Northern Ontario island estate called Penarth, is modelled to some extent on St Joseph's Island. (See also HAMILTON, SARNIA, TORONTO: 2, 7.)

SARNIA

An English visitor, **Amelia Frances Howard-Gibbon** (1826–74), drew Canada's first picture-book, *An Illustrated Comic Alphabet*, while living here in 1859. It was not published, however, until 1966; the original manuscript is in the Osborne Collection of Early Children's Books in Toronto. In 1971 the Canadian Association of Children's Librarians established a medal in Howard-Gibbon's name to be awarded annually for the best illustrations in a Canadian children's book.

The novelist **Marian Engel** moved to Sarnia with her family in 1945, when she was twelve, and lived here until 1952, when she enrolled at McMaster University, HAMILTON. (See also ST JOSEPH'S ISLAND, TORONTO: 2, 7; CAPE TRAVERSE, P.E.I.)

SCOTIA

Jean (McKishnie) **Blewett** was born on 4 Nov. 1862 in Scotia, Kent County, and was educated at St Thomas Collegiate Institute. For many years she contributed articles to the Toronto *Globe*, and later she joined the staff as head of the Homemaker's Department. She retired in 1925 and died in Chatham in 1934. Her books of poetry include *Out of the Depths* (1890), *Heart Songs* (1897), *The Cornflower and Other Poems* (1906), and *Poems* (1922). Blewett is honoured with a national historical plaque in Scotia.

SIMCOE

Frederick Philip Grove settled with his wife and infant son on a farm near Simcoe in 1931. He had moved there from OTTAWA following the collapse of Graphic Press, for

Mr & Mrs Frederick Philip Grove and Leonard

which he had been working since Dec. 1929. He planned to work the land, but by 1939 had sold the greater part of the property to a neighbour, retaining only the house and its yard. Grove described the house as 'a loose-jointed, ramshackle affair of eight rooms. . . . In places, one could see daylight through the walls from inside.' It was more than 125 years old when the Groves moved in, and repairs strained their limited income. In 1932 Catherine Grove opened a private school in the house to supplement the farm income; it soon became the family's primary source of money, and Catherine became well known for her success in teaching disabled children. Grove gave the school's French and German classes as well as working on the farm and continuing to write. In the provincial election of 4 Aug. 1943 he ran unsuccessfully as CCF candidate for Haldimand-Norfolk and served as honorary president of the local CCF. His books dating from the Simcoe period include *Two Generations: A story of Ontario* (1939), *The Master of the Mill* (1944), *In Search of Myself* (1946), which won a Governor General's Award, and *Consider Her Ways* (1947), his last book.

Two Generations is one of the few published works of Grove's set outside the Prairie provinces; but at the end of his life he was working on a series of novels set in a town called 'Rivers', which incorporates aspects of Simcoe, Hamilton, and Brantford. One story set in 'Rivers' was published (with many unauthorized editorial changes) in the magazine *Canadian Boys* as 'The Adventure of Leonard Broadus'. In 1982 *Canadian Children's Literature* published Grove's original text, preserved by his son Leonard, on whose childhood adventures the story is largely based. Rich in details of the geography of the Simcoe district near Lake Erie, the story alludes to Turkey Point, 15 miles west of the mouth of the Lynn River on Lake Erie, as the site of a hobo camp, and Patterson Creek, which in Grove's story resembles the Lynn more than the actual Patterson Creek near Simcoe. (Grove used the name 'Patterson' for his hero in *Two Generations*.) 'The Adventure of Leonard Broadus' contains, as its triumphant climax, the royal visit by King George VI and Queen Elizabeth to Hamilton on 7 June 1939. Grove had written his story before the Royal visit to Hamilton but with the intention of making this first visit to Canada by a reigning monarch a central event. However, he insisted on attending the actual ceremonies before finishing the story—though he made little use of the day's details. He immediately sent the manuscript to the Ryerson Press, Toronto, publishers of *Canadian Boys*.

During his lean years Grove once worked briefly at the Canadian Canners plant in Simcoe. There he is said to have met an Englishman, evidently educated and refined, to whom he put the question, 'What brought you here?' The man replied, 'Drink!' and then asked Grove the same question—to which the author answered, 'Literature'. A series of crippling strokes increasingly limited Grove's ability to travel and work. He died on 19 Aug. 1948, and after a service in his Simcoe house his body

The Grove house at Simcoe

was taken to RAPID CITY, Man., and buried beside that of his daughter Phyllis May. For several years afterwards Catherine continued the Simcoe school.

Grove's house, now considerably altered, is still maintained by his son as a summer residence.

SOUTHAMPTON

Poet **Wilfred Campbell** (*Lake Lyrics and Other Poems*, 1889) returned to the Bruce Peninsula area of his childhood in 1890 to serve as the Anglican minister of Southampton, west of OWEN SOUND on the shore of Lake Huron. Ordained in 1886, Campbell had served in parishes in the United States and at ST STEPHEN, N.B., before moving here. In 1891 he resigned his position and moved to OTTAWA to enter the civil service. (See also KITCHENER, WIARTON.)

STONEY POINT

On 29 Aug. 1932 **Raymond Knister**—poet, novelist, and short-story writer—drowned while swimming near Stoney Point. A native of RUSCOMB, he was vacationing with his wife and daughter at a cottage on Lake St Clair before starting a new job at the Ryerson Press in TORONTO (2). At the time of his death Knister had been away from his home region of southwestern Ontario since 1926, living in Toronto, PORT DOVER, and Montreal, Que. Much of his work was still in manuscript when he died. Knister's wife, Myrtle, began a diary at Port Dover that contains details of their last years, including the day of Knister's drowning, when, according to Myrtle, he said, 'I feel just like Keats did when he was just coming into his powers. I feel as though I am just coming into mine. The world is before us, Myrtle. We have everything we want and we are happy.'

STRATFORD

The poet and playwright **James Reaney** was born on 1 Sept. 1926 on a farm near Stratford at South Easthope in Perth County. He attended a one-room school at Elmhurst until the age of fourteen, when he entered Stratford Collegiate and Vocational Institute; throughout his childhood he went to church and Sunday School in the city. He left the district to attend school in WINNIPEG in 1949, but Stratford and the surrounding farm region recur in his work, including two poetry collections, *A Suit of Nettles* (1958) and *Twelve Letters to a Small Town* (1962). Reaney, who has lived in nearby LONDON since 1961, wrote *The Donnellys* (1975, 1976, 1977), a trilogy of plays about the Donnelly family killings in LUCAN, 20 miles west of Stratford. Reaney's play *Colours in the Dark* (1969) was staged in 1967 at the Stratford Festival.

The Stratford Shakespearean Festival was founded by a Stratford resident, Tom Patterson, with the encouragement of Tyrone Guthrie, who directed the productions in the first two seasons. It opened on 13 July 1953, with Alec Guinness starring in *Richard III*. It is open from June to October, and annual attendance at its three theatres now exceeds half a million: the largest of the three, the Festival Theatre, seats 2,258; the Avon Theatre, in use since 1956, was purchased by the festival in 1963 and seats 1,102; the Third Stage, designed for informal workshop presentations featuring new performers, opened in 1971. (The novelist **Timothy Findley** was an actor in the first season. See CANNINGTON, TORONTO: 5.) Although many of each year's productions are Shakespearian, the Stratford Festival also presents works of other playwrights. Canadian authors whose plays have been staged here include James Reaney; Tom Hendry, whose musical *Satyricon* was staged in 1969 (see also WINNIPEG, Man.); Roch Carrier, whose dramatization of his novel *La Guerre, Yes Sir!* had its English première in 1972; and in 1973, Michael Ondaatje (*The Collected Works of Billy the Kid*, 1973) and Henry Beissel (*Inook and the Sun*, 1973). John Herbert's *Fortune and Men's Eyes* was given its first dramatic reading on 1 Oct. 1965 at the Festival, before its off-Broadway success in 1967. In **Hugh Hood**'s novel *The Scenic Art* (1948), Stratford's first season provides the setting and basic situation; the wife of the novel's protagonist, Matt Goderich, is a member of the Shakespeare Festival's design team (see also TORONTO: 5; MONTREAL: 6, Que.).

Stratford was the birthplace in the nineteenth century of **Kathleen** and **Robina Lizars**, and it was here that they wrote their three jointly authored books. Two of these were graceful and amusing anecdotal histories: *In the Days of the Canada Company: The Story of the Settlement of the Huron Tract and a View of the Social Life of the Period, 1825–1850* (1896) and *Humours of '37: Grave and Grim. Rebellion Times in the Canadas* (1897). The third book is a satirical novel, *Committed to His Charge* (1900), that pokes fun at Stratford society through its story of the conflict between a new Anglican rector and the entrenched, overbearing Ladies' Auxiliary of his parish. The house in which the Lizars sisters lived and wrote stands at 11 Hamilton St; it is privately owned. Shortly after the turn-of-the-century the Lizars moved to Toronto, where they died; Robina on 26 Aug. 1918 and Kathleen on 20 Apr. 1931. Kathleen was also the author of a historical work, *The Valley of the Humber* (1913).

STRATHROY

Stephen Leacock spent the fall of 1888 at Strathroy High School studying for a certificate as a high-school language teacher. One of the students he taught in his practice classes was Arthur Currie, later commander of the Canadian Corps in the First World War and Leacock's principal at McGill University. Leacock graduated at Christmas 1888 and soon after received his first job, at the new UXBRIDGE High School. (See also EGYPT, ORILLIA, SUTTON, TORONTO: 3, 7; MONTREAL: 3, Que.)

Another Ontario humorist to graduate from the Strathroy High School certification program was **Peter McArthur**, who completed the course one year ahead of Leacock, in 1887. After six months' teaching, McArthur entered the University of Toronto; in 1890 he left to become a journalist and editor. Later McArthur helped to further Leacock's writing career by publishing several of Leacock's articles in the New York magazine *Truth*, which McArthur edited in 1895–7. (See also APPIN.)

STREETSVILLE

The humorist **Max Braithwaite** lived near here for ten years, from 1946 to 1956, in a house one mile north of town. Discharged from the navy at the end of the Second World War, Braithwaite became a freelance writer in 1945 and worked here on articles and scripts for magazines, radio, and television. For five years he was a member of the Streetsville School Board. In 1956 he moved to ORANGEVILLE, where he began writing novels, primarily about his early years in Saskatchewan including (*Why Shoot the Teacher* (1965), and *Never Sleep Three in a Bed*, (1970). (See also PORT CARLING, TORONTO: 4; ABERDEEN, EYRE, NOKOMIS, PRINCE ALBERT, VONDA, Sask.)

SULTAN

Near this remote settlement in the Algoma country, 30 miles from Chapleau, is the wilderness grave of **John Ceredigion Jones**, a Welsh-Canadian poet who is remembered for a single quotation:

> *All's well, for over there among his peers*
> *A Happy Warrior sleeps.*

These lines, engraved over an archway in the Peace Tower in OTTAWA, were chosen by the architect, John Pearson, who could not remember where he had seen them. The author of the lines was unknown until 1939, when Jones came forward and proved that they were from 'The Returning Man', a poem he had written in Calgary in 1919 or 1920 and published in the Calgary *Albertan*. As a result of this declaration, the Defence Department paid him $8, but Jones was lost sight of; he died at Sultan in 1950, at the age of sixty-four, while working at the McFadden Company lumber mill. A tireless doggerel versifier, he had immigrated to Canada in 1904 and travelled throughout the country, living by casual labour. The site of his grave was unknown until it was pointed out to Lester B. Pearson by the McFadden mill manager during Pearson's 1953 campaign visit to Sultan.

SUNDRIDGE

Sundridge was the birthplace in 1889 of **Mary S. Edgar**, author of the hymns 'God of All the Many Lands' and 'God Who Touchest Earth with Beauty', and of several books of verse and prose. Edgar's childhood home was the building that is now Langs Store, Main St: her parents operated it as a general store and lived in the apartment above. Edgar was an active promoter of scouting for girls and founded the Bernard Lake Camp for Girls, across Lake Bernard from Sundridge; the camp is still in operation. Edgar's books, many of which were connected with scouting, include *The Christmas Tree Bluebird* (1920), *Woodfire and Candlelight* (1945), and *Under Open Skies* (1955). She died in 1973; there is a cairn to her memory in Sundridge's High Rock Park, overlooking Lake Bernard. Sundridge is south of North Bay on Hwy 11 at its junction with Hwy 124.

SUTTON

Two of Canada's most popular authors, Stephen Leacock and Mazo de la Roche, are buried at St George's Anglican Church on Sibbald Point, 4 miles east of Sutton on the shore of Lake Simcoe.

Stephen Leacock is buried in a family plot that also contains the graves of his mother and many of his ten brothers and sisters. (He died in Toronto in the spring of 1944 after a brief illness.) The family farm was located at the now-vanished village of EGYPT, 4 miles from Sutton. The Leacocks came to Ontario in 1876 from their home in England, and Stephen Leacock lived on the

The Leacock tombstone, Sutton

farm until 1882, when he began his studies at Upper Canada College, TORONTO (3, 7). Sutton was the family's shopping town and the site of the nearest train station in Leacock's youth. The family attended St George's Church; in his autobiography, *The Boy I Left Behind Me* (1946), Leacock writes of the days when the present stone building, completed in 1877, was being built. The farm at Egypt remained Leacock's home during school vacations until 1892, by which time he was a teacher at Upper Canada College. In that year he moved his mother and eight younger brothers and sisters off the farm, which was greatly encumbered by debt. His mother, Agnes, lived in Sutton as well as in Beaverton and ORILLIA, where Leacock bought property for his summer home in 1908; for many years she had a cottage on Lake Simcoe near the Sibbald Estate east of the town. Leacock often visited his mother at the Lake Simcoe cottage during his own summer holidays at Orillia. Sutton (much transformed by the age of the automobile) is described in Leacock's sketch 'The Old Farm in a New Frame' in *My Remarkable Uncle* (1942).

Mazo de la Roche—who was born in NEWMARKET in 1879 to parents whose families were well represented in the towns lying between Lake Simcoe and Lake Ontario—lived most of her life in the TORONTO (2, 6, 7) area, but she spent many summers at Lake Simcoe. There is a memorial window dedicated to her in St George's Church. Her famous series of Jalna novels began in 1927 with *Jalna* and continued through thirteen more books; the last, *Morning at Jalna*, was published in 1960, the year before her death in Toronto. (See also MISSISSAUGA, OAKVILLE.)

TEMAGAMI

Grey Owl, the famous nature writer and conservationist whose real name was **Archibald Stansfeld Belaney**, lived from the summer of 1906 until 1912 in the Temagami area. This was his first permanent home in Canada after emigrating from his native England in 1906. He worked as a guide and trapper and lived closely with the Ojibwa Indians, who summered on Bear Island in Lake Temagami. It was while living with these Ojibwas that he underwent an adoption ceremony and received the name Wa-sha-Quon-Asin (Grey Owl). He married a member of the tribe, Angele Eguana, in 1910 but left her behind when he moved to BISCOTASING in 1912. Grey Owl is commemorated by a provincial plaque in the Finlayson Point Provincial Camping Grounds off Hwy 11, one mile south of the village of Temagami. (See also BISCOTASING, COBALT: CABANO, Que.; RIDING MOUNTAIN NATIONAL PARK, Man.; PRINCE ALBERT NATIONAL PARK, Sask.)

The poet **Archibald Lampman** made his last canoe trip to Lakes Temagami and Timiskaming with his brothers-in-law during the summer of 1896. Both lakes are described in sonnets he wrote during the trip. (See also GORE'S LANDING, OTTAWA, PERRYTOWN, PORT HOPE, TORONTO: 3.)

THAMESVILLE

The novelist and playwright **Robertson Davies** was born here on 28 Aug. 1913 and lived until 1919 in a house on Elizabeth St that is still standing. Thamesville was the model for Davies' fictional community Deptford, where he set much of the action of his 'Deptford Trilogy' novels: *Fifth Business* (1970), *The Manticore* (1972), and *World of Wonders* (1975). (See also KINGSTON, PETERBOROUGH, TORONTO: 3, 6, 7.)

Two miles west of Thamesville an inscribed boulder marks the spot where the Shawnee chief Tecumseh was killed in the Battle of the Thames on 5 Oct. 1813. During that battle the novelist Major **John Richardson**, who had known Tecumseh from earlier days at AMHERSTBURG, was captured by American troops. In 1828 Richardson published in London his *Tecumseh*, an epic poem celebrating his famous Indian acquaintance. Another Ontario writer, **Charles**

Mair, worked for many years on a verse-drama recounting the chief's alliance with the British during the War of 1812 and his death near present-day Thamesville; this was published in *Tecumseh, a Drama, and Canadian Poems* (1901). (See also WINDSOR.)

THUNDER BAY

Thunder Bay is the name given in 1970 to the amalgamation of Fort William and Port Arthur. The children's author **Sheila Burnford** settled in Port Arthur with her family in 1950; in the early and mid-1950s the Burnfords lived at 28 Winnipeg Ave. A native of Scotland, she became a Canadian citizen and divided her time between Port Arthur and a cottage on nearby Pass Lake until 1974, when she and her husband moved back to England. Burnford continued to spend summers at Pass Lake until her death in 1984 (at her home in Beaulieu, England). She is best known for her first book, *The Incredible Journey* (1961), the story of an adventurous trip through the northern-Ontario wilderness made by a trio of animals—a Siamese cat, an English bull terrier, and a Labrador retriever—determined to be reunited with their owners. From 1958-68 Burnford lived at 144 Summit Ave, and in 1969-71 at a succession of addresses: 9 High St, 73 Cumberland St, and 59 Court St. After her first book, Burnford published three non-fiction works: *Without Reserve* (1961), based on diaries kept during visits to Ontario Indian settlements; *Fields of Noon* (1964), a collection of articles about life in Port Arthur and Thunder Bay; and *One Woman's Arctic* (1973), impressions of life on Baffin Island gathered from visits over a two-year period. In 1972-4 she lived on Algoma St at Cameron St. An active outdoorswoman, Burnford did most of her writing at Pass Lake. After returning to England she published *Bel Ria* (1977), an animal story set in Europe during the Second World War. *The Incredible Journey* has been translated into twenty-five languages and was made into a Walt Disney film with the same title in 1963.

The author of another children's book that has had a wide readership, **Dorothy M. Reid**, lived near Fort William until her death in 1974. Her book, *Tales of Nanabozho* (1963), celebrates the creator-magician of the Ojibwa, Nanabozho—associated with the Sleeping Giant, a rock formation on Thunder Cape near Thunder Bay. Dorothy Reid was for many years head of the children's department of the Fort William Public Library.

TOBERMORY

The poet and philosopher **Francis Sparshott** has spent his summers since 1957 on Warner Bay, St Edmunds Township, near Tobermory on the Bruce Peninsula. Almost all his books have been written here, and references to landscape and animals in *The Rainy Hills* (1979) and *The Naming of the Beasts* (1979) are based on the Warner Bay region. *A Book* (1970), a satire of 'The Great Canadian Novel' published by Sparshott under the pseudonym 'Cromwell Kent', is set in St Edmunds Township. The beaver lodge in the story was at the upper end of William Henry Marsh. (See also TORONTO: 3.)

TORONTO

Metropolitan Toronto includes the cities of Etobicoke, North York, Scarborough, Toronto, York, and the Borough of East York. Because of the city's size and the great number of writers who have lived and worked here, the Toronto entry is divided into seven sections:

1. TORONTO BEFORE 1900
2. DOWNTOWN TORONTO SINCE 1900
3. THE UNIVERSITY OF TORONTO
4. THE ANNEX
5. ROSEDALE
6. TORONTO: EAST
7. TORONTO: WEST

1. TORONTO BEFORE 1900

Lieutenant-Governor John Graves Simcoe founded the new capital of Upper Canada, to be called York, in 1793. The first published accounts of this British settlement at Toronto Bay, on the northern shore of Lake Ontario, appeared less than twenty years later. *In Travels through the Canadas, Containing a Description of the Picturesque Scenery* (1807), **George Heriot**, deputy postmaster-general of British North America, praised the early growth of York, observing that it was a 'town which may be termed handsome, reared as if by enchantment, in the midst of a wilderness'. An even earlier account—not published until the twentieth century—appears in the diary of **Elizabeth Simcoe**, wife of the lieutenant-governor, who lived in York from 1793 until the couple returned to England in 1796. Mrs Simcoe praised the natural beauties of the area, but could say little of its building development; her three years were spent largely in elaborate British navy-issue canvas tents. Her complete account was published in 1965 in *Mrs. Simcoe's Diary*, edited by Mary Quayle Innis. Selections from her diary were published in *The Diary of Mrs. John Graves Simcoe . . . With Notes and a Biography by John Ross Robertson and Two Hundred and Thirty-seven Illustrations, including Ninety Reproductions of Interesting Sketches Made by Mrs. Simcoe* (1911). Unhappily for struggling York, the kind words from Heriot and Mrs Simcoe were the last the town received from the many British officials and important travellers who published accounts of their visits during the rest of the nineteenth century. **Francis Hall**, author of *Travels in Canada and the United States in 1816 and 1817* (1818), visited York after it had been occupied by American troops during the War of 1812. Before leaving, the American soldiers had burnt most of the buildings and heavily damaged the fort. Hall commented, 'I believe they did not leave one stone upon another, for they did not find one.' He thought the capital should be moved and charged that only investors in the area were preventing relocation of public officials to a more favourable site. **Edward Allen Talbot**, writing shortly after in *Five Years' Residence in the Canadas; Including a Tour through Part of the United States of America in the Year 1823* (1824), said that York was 'better calculated for a frog-pond or beaver-meadow than for the residence of human beings'. **John Galt**, superintendent of the Canada Company from 1826 to 1829, also had unkind words for York in his *Autobiography* (1833).

The lengthiest, most literate, and best-circulated criticism of the early years came from **Anna Brownell Jameson**, author of *Winter Studies and Summer Rambles in Canada* (1838). Jameson's husband Robert came to Upper Canada in 1833 as Attorney-General and after two years in the House of Assembly was named Vice-Chancellor in Mar. 1837. The Jameson marriage had not been happy; only four years after their wedding they separated, when Robert accepted a judicial appointment in Dominica in 1829. Still, Anna agreed to come to Canada in the fall of 1836 in anticipation of her husband's new post as Vice-Chancellor. She arrived in the city in Dec. 1836, to temporary rooms on

> FROM 'WINTER STUDIES AND SUMMER RAMBLES'
>
> *A little ill-built town on low land, at the bottom of a frozen bay, with one very ugly church, without tower or steeple; some government offices, built of staring red brick, in the most tasteless, vulgar style imaginable; three feet of snow all around; and the gray, sullen, wintry lake, and the dark gleam of the pine forest sounding the prospect; such seems Toronto to me now. I did not expect much; but for this I was not prepared.*
>
> —Anna Jameson, *Winter Studies and Summer Rambles in Canada* (1838; rpr. 1965)

Brock Street. By March the Jamesons were settled in their newly built house Lyndhurst; now gone, it stood on the south side of Wellington St west of Spadina Ave. According to *Winter Studies*, the house was not yet completed, but Jameson at first was hopeful that she would enjoy life there.

The long winter months convinced her, however, that she disliked Toronto intensely—its people, its amusements, its stores and public buildings, especially its pretensions. Jameson spent the summer months in a journey that took her to Niagara Falls, Hamilton, Brantford, Woodstock, London, St Thomas, Port Talbot, Chatham, and Detroit, and then proceeded north along Georgian Bay to Penetanguishene. From there she travelled by canoe and portage to Lake Simcoe and then home to Toronto. This journey—the 'summer ramble' of her book's title—proved much more enjoyable than life in the city; within a month Anna Jameson had left Toronto forever to return to England. An active participant in London literary life, Jameson was also an intimate in Goethe's family; best known for her appreciations of books and pictures, she is remembered primarily for the four-volume work, *Sacred and Legendary Art* (1852–61). The Royal Ontario Museum in Toronto possesses a large collection of her drawings, and the University of Toronto's Robarts Library has a book annotated by Jameson and several of her letters.

In 1834 the town of York was incorporated as the City of Toronto. The first mayor was the controversial journalist and editor of the *Colonial Advocate*, **William Lyon Mackenzie**. Just a few months after Jameson's departure he led an attack on Toronto that was the only battle of the Upper Canada Rebellion of 1837. After twelve years in exile in the United States, during which time he wrote *Mackenzie's Own Narrative of the Late Rebellion* (1838), Mackenzie spent the last years of his life in Toronto, where he was elected in 1851 to the House of Assembly. His house stands at 82 Bond St and has been restored as a historic site with early nineteenth-century furnishings. Although Jameson saw little indication of intellectual life in Toronto, there were some stirrings. John Galt's associate in the Canada Company, **William 'Tiger' Dunlop**—whose home was in GODERICH—founded the Toronto Literary Club in 1836. Irish-born artist **Paul Kane** had been brought to the town of York as a child in 1818 or 1819. After years of travel as a portrait painter and then study in the United States and Europe, he returned to Canada in 1845. He wrote an account of two years' painting in the Canadian northwest called *Wanderings of an Artist among the Indians of North America from Canada to Vancouver's Island and Oregon through the Hudson's Bay Company Territory and Back Again* (1859). The last years of his life were spent in Toronto at 56 Wellesley St E (still standing). The Royal Ontario Museum has a large collection of drawings and paintings by Kane, including many that date from the trip described in his book. A lavishly illustrated volume, *Paul Kane's frontier: including 'Wanderings of an artist among the Indians of North America' by Paul Kane* (1971), edited by Russell Harper, contains a definitive biography of Kane. (See also COBOURG; EDMONTON, Alta.)

The Mackenzie house on Bond St

Whereas Kane returned from European study determined to devote his art to the beauties of life he found in Canada, British visitors to Toronto during the 1840s continued to express disappointment with the city. In *The Canadas in 1841*, Sir **Richard Henry Bonnycastle** criticized the landscape surrounding Toronto and dismissed the city itself as of little value. 'The public amusements in Toronto are not of a nature to attract much attention,' he wrote. **Charles Dickens** passed through the city very briefly during his 1842 tour of North America. Although he complained in private letters of city politics and innkeepers, he had some praise for the development of the settlement in *American Notes for General Circulation* (1843): 'There is a good prison here; and there are, besides, a handsome church, a Courthouse, public offices, many commodious private residences, and a Government Observatory for noting and recording the magnetic variations.' Among others who complained as the decades passed were American novelist **William Dean Howells** (*The Rise of Silas Lapham*, 1886) in 1860 and English novelist **Anthony Trollope** who observed in *North America* (1862), 'Toronto is not a city generally attractive to a traveller.'

The steady stream of criticism found determined rebuttal in the work of the Rev. **Henry Scadding**, for many years the rector of the Church of the Holy Trinity. Born in England, Scadding came as a child to Canada in 1821; he received his early education at the newly founded Upper Canada College, then located on the south side of King St between Simcoe and John Sts (see 7. TORONTO: WEST). After studies at Cambridge and ordination in 1838, Scadding taught at Upper Canada College for several years before beginning his service at Holy Trinity. His best-known work of local history is *Toronto of Old* (1873), a survey of the city as it was during the 1840s, in which Scadding took pains to answer many criticisms of Toronto, including those found in Jameson's *Winter Studies and Summer Rambles*. After retiring from parish work Scadding devoted the last years of his life to his literary interests. Other works include *Toronto, Past and Present* (1884) with J.C. Dent, and *Toronto, Old and New* (1891) with G. Mercer Adam. Scadding's house is still standing at 6 Trinity Square near Holy Trinity Church in downtown Toronto.

The Scadding house

Dr Scadding showing the location of Simcoe's 'Castle Frank'

G. Mercer Adam was one of the most important editors and journalists of nineteenth-century Toronto. He was an associate of Goldwin Smith (see below) in the *Canadian Monthly and National Review* and *The Bystander*. In 1887 Adam published *An Outline History of Canadian Literature*; his works include a novel, *An Algonquin Maiden* (1886), written with Agnes Ethelwyn Wetherald, and contributions to *Picturesque Canada* (1882). In the late 1880s Adam lived at 184 Spadina Ave and in the 1890s at 196 Spadina Ave; he is commemorated by a plaque on an outdoor bench at Allan Gardens, at Jarvis and Gerrard Sts. In 1892 Adam moved to New York, where he died in 1912. His collaborator on *An Algonquin Maiden*, **Agnes Ethelwyn Wetherald**, was born in 1857 in ROCKWOOD. In the late nineteenth century she was on the staff of the Toronto *Globe*, but for most of her life she worked as a freelance journalist. Her *Lyrics and Sonnets* (1931) collected four earlier volumes of verse. She died in 1940 in Fenwick, Ont.

Susanna Moodie divided her time between LAKEFIELD, Ont., where her sister Catharine Parr Traill lived, and Toronto from 1869 until her death in 1885. Moodie's only literary work in these years was a revision of the manuscript of her first book about Canada, *Roughing It in the Bush*, for its first Canadian edition, which was published in Toronto by the firm of George Rose in 1871. In Toronto, Moodie lived with her children. Her daughter, Mrs J.J. Vickers, lived at 152 Adelaide St W.; and her son, Robert B. Moodie, lived at 17 Wilton Cr. Moodie died at her son's home and was buried in BELLEVILLE next to her husband, who had died in 1869.

Nature writer **Ernest Thompson Seton** was ten when his family moved from LINDSAY to Toronto in 1870. Educated at public schools on Elizabeth and Victoria Sts, Seton lived at several different addresses in his early years, but mostly at 17 Pembroke St, where his accountant father also had his business. After graduating from Toronto Collegiate (now Jarvis Collegiate at 495 Jarvis St), Seton studied at the Ontario College of Art, where he won a scholarship to study at the Royal Academy in England. Ill health forced him to return to Canada. After a brief stay in Toronto, he moved to his brother's homestead at CARBERRY, Man. During the next fifteen years Seton travelled widely, stopping frequently in Toronto. In the early 1880s his family's firm—Seton, Thompson & Co, 116 Bay St—listed him as a partner living in England. In the late 1880s Seton's family built a new house, Glen Cottage, at 86 Howard St (gone); Seton moved into it in the fall of 1892 and lived there for about a year, until he received his appointment as Manitoba's first Provincial Naturalist. In 1893 Seton met his long-time friend, **Pauline Johnson**, in Toronto. Her famous Indian stage dress, now on display in Vancouver, B.C., was a present from Seton. Before moving permanently to the United States in 1896, Seton had published *The Birds of Manitoba* (1891) and provided 1,000 illustrations for the *Century Dictionary*. He is best known for his many animal stories, which began with *Wild Animals I Have Known* (1898), and for *Two Little Savages* (1906). Seton is commemorated by Ernest Thompson Seton Park at Don Mills Rd and Overlea Blvd on the west branch of the Don River. In this area the young Seton once built a cabin in the woods; here he gained much of his early experience of nature, which determined his future careers in literature, art, and public life.

Charles Mair—a native of LANARK, Ont., who spent most of his life in the West—first came to Toronto in the spring of 1870 to bring news of the outbreak of the Red River Rebellion at WINNIPEG, Man. He spoke on 6 Apr. to a meeting at the St Lawrence Hall, calling for a military expedition to oppose the provisional government established by Louis Riel. In 1882 fear of a second rebellion brought Mair from his home in PRINCE ALBERT, Sask., to WINDOSR, Ont. During the next four years he was a frequent visitor to the home of his close friend, **George Taylor Denison**, Heydon Villa (now gone), on the west side of Dovercourt Rd between St Anne's Rd and the present Heydon Park Rd. Denison, the third generation of a noted Toronto family, was one of Mair's associates in the 'Canada First' group, founded in Ottawa in 1868; another member in Toronto was Goldwin Smith, who for a time headed the branch here but later left the movement. Canada First's headquarters in Toronto was the National Club, then at 98 Bay St and today at 303 Bay St, where there is a plaque commemorating the movement.

Educated at Upper Canada College and the University of Toronto (LL.B., 1861), George Taylor Denison was called to the bar in 1861. In 1866 he became lieutenant-colonel commanding the Governor General's Body Guard, a unit formerly known as 'Denison's Horse' for its founder, his grandfather. A writer on Canadian history and the military, Denison received the Czar of Russia's prize for the best work on cavalry and mounted operations for *A History of Cavalry, from the Earliest Times, with Lessons for the Future* (1877). From 1877 to 1923 Denison was senior police magistrate in Toronto. During the 1880s, when Mair was living in Windsor, Denison was an enthusiastic supporter of his friend's verse drama, *Tecumseh*, which was published in Toronto in 1886. Having thrust portions of Mair's manuscript into the hands of **Matthew Arnold** while the famous English poet was visiting Heydon Villa during his 1884 Canadian tour, Denison happily reported Arnold's words of praise to Mair. Later, Denison faithfully urged copies of *Tecumseh: A Drama* on friends and acquaintances at every opportunity and was the recipient of Mair's confidences when the book proved a failure.

Another stop on Matthew Arnold's Toronto tour was The Grange, home of the editor and literary critic **Goldwin Smith**. A native of England, Smith came to Toronto in 1871 with a long, distinguished career of university teaching and literary journalism

Goldwin Smith in front of The Grange

The Grange, *c.* 1867

behind him, both at Oxford and at the newly founded Cornell University in Ithaca, New York. Beginning in 1872, Smith took an active role in Canadian journalism, helping to found *The Canadian Monthly and National Review*. Under the pen-name 'A Bystander', he contributed to this and many other magazines during the next thirty years. In 1875 Smith married Harriet Boulton, the widow of William Henry Boulton (mayor of Toronto 1845–7), and moved to her home, The Grange, 24 Grange Rd. Built in 1817, The Grange stood on a 100-acre site stretching from Queen St E. to Bloor St. Today The Grange is still a city landmark as part of the Art Gallery of Ontario. Restored and furnished in the style of the 1830s, it is open daily (except Monday), from noon to 4 p.m., and may be entered either through the Art Gallery of Ontario or Grange Park to the south. During the time of Smith's residence the house was a centre of the city's intellectual life. In addition to *The Canadian Monthly*, Smith founded or helped to found several other Toronto publications, the most famous of them being *The Week*, which appeared from 1883 to 1896. Smith at first allied himself with the 'Canada First' group but later became an advocate of economic union with the United States; his view that annexation of Canada by the United States was inevitable made him unpopular with many people. Besides his political activities and his magazines, Smith wrote many books on literature, history, and social issues, including *Canada and the Canadian Question* (1891), *Essays on Questions of the Day* (1893), *Shakespeare the Man* (1899), and *Commonwealth or Empire* (1902).

Matthew Arnold—in his essay, 'Equality', published in *Mixed Essays* (1904)—spoke regretfully of leaving Goldwin Smith behind in what he regarded as the deadening cultural environment of Toronto. One enjoyable part of Arnold's visit to the city was his meeting with poet **Charles G.D. Roberts**, whom he greeted as 'the boy I wanted to meet' during a party at The Grange. Arnold knew the young New Brunswick writer through his first poetry collection, *Orion, and Other Poems* (1880). Roberts came to Toronto to edit *The Week*, which was located at 5 Jordan St. The poet lived at 147 Ontario St during 1883 and 1884 but left the city when he resigned from the magazine because he disagreed with Smith's political beliefs. Roberts went from Toronto to WINDSOR, N.S., where he taught at King's College until 1895; he then lived outside Canada, both in the United States and Europe, until 1925, when he returned to Toronto. He lived here until his death in 1943 and became a vital part of the city's literary community again; his home in 1925–43 was Apt B25, 197 Wellesley St: the Ernescliff building, which is still standing. Roberts bgan his publishing career with poetry but also distinguished himself as a writer of short stories, particularly about wild life. His first collection of these, *Earth's Enigmas*, appeared in 1896; along with Ernest

Sir Charles G.D. Roberts on the roof of Ernescliffe

Thompson Seton he is regarded as an inventor of the modern animal story. It was a genre he continued to practise throughout his life: one of his books after returning to Toronto was *Further Animal Stories* (1936). Roberts also published several books of poetry from Toronto after 1925, including *The Vagrant of Time* (1927), *The Iceberg, and Other Poems* (1934), *Canada Speaks of Britain and Other Poems of the War* (1941), and *Selected Poems* (1936). A veteran of many years of professional journalism during his years away from Canada, Roberts also published romances and works of non-fiction, including *A Standard Dictionary of Canadian Biography: The Canadian Who Was Who* (2 vols, 1934 and 1938), which he edited with Arthur L. Tunnell.

The Week published many of the period's most distinguished writers, including Archibald Lampman, Bliss Carman, William Wilfred Campbell, and **Arthur Stringer**, a native of CHATHAM, Ont., who attended the University of Toronto from 1892 to 1894 but left without graduating. Active in the 1892 student strike, Stringer was represented in *The Week* by the famous poem 'Indian Summer'. **Sara Jeanette Duncan**, a native of BRANTFORD, Ont., came to Toronto to attend the Normal School (50 Gould St, but only a remnant of the original 1851 building remains) and graduated in 1882. She taught until 1884, when she began her career as a journalist. Duncan was for a time literary editor of *The Week*; she later worked for the Toronto *Globe*, writing under the pen-name 'Garth Grafton'. Her novels include a portrait of her hometown, *The Imperialist* (1904). Another editor was Susie Frances Harrison, who wrote under the pen-name 'Seranus'. In her capacity as music and literary editor of *The Week*, Harrison once had to tell poet Isabella Valancy Crawford that the magazine did not pay for poetry. *The Week* helped Crawford to the extent of printing good notices of her only book, *Old Spookses' Pass, Malcolm's Katie, and Other Poems* (1884), and of her submissions in other publications. The poet and novelist **Susie Frances Harrison** (née Riley) was born in 1859 in Toronto. In 1879 she married a musician, John W.F. Harrison, and spent the next six years in Ottawa, where her first book, *Crowded Out and Other Sketches* (1886), was published. The family then returned to Toronto, living first at 145 College St, where she wrote her poetry collection, *Pine, Rose and Fleur-de-lis* (1891). Harrison's other books include a novel, *Ringfield* (1914) and the poetry collections *In Northern Skies* (1912) and *Penelope and Other Poems* (1932). In the early twentieth century the Harrisons lived

The John St building where the Crawfords lived on the second floor, 1929

at 25 Dunbar Rd and in the 1920s established a home at 212 Stratmore Blvd. Susie Frances Harrison died in 1935.

Isabella Valancy Crawford came to Toronto with her mother in 1876 from PETERBOROUGH, Ont. After three years in rooms at 180 Adelaide St W., they settled in an apartment over a grocery store at King and John Sts. Their address was 57 John St; although the number has since been changed, the building is still standing at the southwest corner. Crawford came to the city in hopes of supporting herself and her mother by her writing, but the obstacles were very great. Her first Toronto poem was published in *The National* in July 1876. 'Where, Love, Art Hid?' was the first of several poems accepted by Toronto periodicals, but when Crawford attempted to place a book manuscript she could find no publisher. Crawford arranged with James Bain & Son, 51 King St E, to finance the publication of her book herself. When it appeared in 1884, *Old Spookses' Pass* received good notices both in Canada and in England but sold only fifty copies. Crawford died on 12 Feb. 1887 in Toronto; her last words, spoken to her landlandy, were, 'What a trouble I am, Mrs Stuart.' She was buried in Peterborough.

The Crawford dwelling today (to be demolished)

During the 1880s visitors to Toronto included **Oscar Wilde**, during his 1882 tour, and **Walt Whitman**, who stopped during a journey on Lake Ontario and the St Lawrence River with his friend **Richard Maurice Bucke**, of LONDON, Ont. Unlike most literary visitors, Whitman enjoyed his day in Toronto in 1880 and praised the city and its harbour scenery in his diary, which was published in *Walt Whitman's Diary in Canada, with Extracts from Other of His Diaries and Literary Note-Books* (1904), edited by William Sloane Kennedy. Oscar Wilde visited Canada twice on lecture tours in 1882. From May 14 to May 31 he toured Quebec and Ontario, arriving at Montreal and then stopping at Ottawa, Quebec City, Montreal again, Kingston, Belleville, Toronto, Brantford, Toronto again, Woodstock, and Hamilton. Wilde was in Toronto May 24–5 and May 27–9, and was by all accounts cheerful and polite to all he met, although his appearances here aroused comment—both for his aesthetic philosophy and his affected manner. From Oct. 4 to Oct. 14, Wilde toured the Maritime Provinces.

Novelist **Mark Twain** came to Canada in 1881 but not to Toronto; rather he spent six months in Montreal to establish legal residence as a step towards gaining copyright protection for his books within the British Empire. Twain regarded Toronto publishers as 'pirates' because of their unauthorized editions of his work; among his targets was **John Ross Robertson**, founder of the *Daily Telegraph* (1866–71) and, in 1876, of the *Evening Telegram*. Born here on 28 Dec. 1841, Robertson devoted much of his newspaper fortune to philanthropy and to his collection of historical pictures, housed today in the Baldwin Room of the Metropolitan Toronto Library, 789 Yonge Street. Robertson's house, Culloden, is still standing at 291 Sherbourne St. In addition to publishing, Robertson wrote several books, including *Robertson's Landmarks of Toronto* (6 vols, 1894–1914). He also edited the first publication (1911) of selections from the diary of Mrs Simcoe.

Journalism and publishing were growing industries in the city during the 1880s. *Saturday Night* was founded in 1887 as *Toronto Saturday Night* by the Sheppard Publishing Company at 9 Adelaide St W. Over its 100 years of publication the magazine has been edited by many prominent writers, including B.K. Sandwell, Hector Charlesworth, and Robert Fulford. **Peter McArthur**—a native of Ekfrid Township, Middlesex County, Ont (see APPIN)—came to the city in 1887 to enrol in the University of Toronto but left without graduating in 1889 to begin work for the Toronto *Globe*. The *Globe* was then housed at 28 King St E. McArthur lived at 63 Mutual St while at the newspaper, but after one year he moved to New York. He worked as a journalist in New York and London until 1908, when he returned to the family homestead. For the *Globe*, McArthur wrote humorous articles about his life on the farm, many of which were collected in a series of books, including *In Pastures Green* (1915), *The Red Cow and Her Friends* (1919), and *Around Home* (1925).

From 6 Feb. 1892 until 1 July 1893, the *Globe*—at that time located at 64 Yonge St—published the column 'At the Mermaid's Tavern'. This weekly feature on literary subjects was a joint project undertaken by three writers then living in OTTAWA: **Archibald Lampman, William Wilfred Campbell**, and **Duncan Campbell Scott**. Campbell was the principal writer for the column and, according to Lampman, the one most in need of the income from the work.

Novelist and editor **Robert Barr** came from WINDSOR, Ont., to study at the Normal School in 1873 to obtain his permanent teaching licence. In 1875 he was named principal of Windsor Central School but left the following year to begin a journalism career in Detroit. Barr settled in London, where he became a successful novelist and magazine editor. One of his twenty novels, *The Measure of the Rule* (1907), describes his experiences at the Normal School. **Pauline Johnson** (*The White Wampum*, 1895) began her successful career as a stage performer in Jan. 1892, when she appeared on a program of local writers held at the Young Liberals' Club, Room 4, Richmond Chambers. A native of MIDDLEPORT, Ont., Johnson was living in BRANTFORD at the time of the Toronto appearance. Her work had appeared in the important anthology, *Songs of the Great Dominion* (1889), but the public notice of her Toronto performance persuaded her to attempt a stage career, which she pursued until 1909, when she retired to VANCOUVER, B.C.

2. DOWNTOWN TORONTO SINCE 1900

Downtown Toronto is here defined as the area bounded on the south by the Lakefront, on the north by Bloor St, on the east by Sherbourne St, and on the west by Spadina Ave—except for the northwest corner, which is treated separately because it is home to the University of Toronto.

Visitors to Toronto during the early twentieth century continued to find much fault with the city. One exception was British humorist **Jerome K. Jerome** who, in addressing the Canadian Club in 1905, expressed his pleasure in the city's welcome. **John Dos Passos** complained in a 1907 letter: 'Toronto on a Sunday morning—a beastly place.' **Rudyard Kipling** visited the same year and wrote in *Notes on a Recent Trip to Canada* (1908) that the city was 'consumingly commercial'. On the eve of the First World War, **Rupert Brooke** passed through Toronto and in *Letters from America* (1916) wrote: 'The only depressing thing is that it will always be what it is, only larger, and that no Canadian city can ever be anything better or different. If they are good they become Toronto.'

Throughout the nineteenth century, all or most of Toronto was contained in the area now considered 'downtown,' and that is where all writers lived. As twentieth-century expansion progressed, many writers settled in outlying areas; but the downtown area of the city remained the section most frequented by writers because of the concentration here of publishing houses, newspapers, magazines, the University of Toronto and other educational institutions, theatres, libraries, writers' organizations, and gathering places.

Although Rupert Brooke did not especially like Toronto, he did like its writers, whom he met at the Arts and Letters Club. Brooks was lionized in the club's original quarters in the old Assizes Building at 57 Adelaide St E. Founded in 1908, the club remained at this location until 1920, when it moved into its present premises in its building at 14 Elm St.

The author of the 'Jalna' novels, **Mazo de la Roche**, often said that she was born in Toronto, although her birthplace in 1879 was north of the city in NEWMARKET, and the family did not settle in Toronto until 1885. Still, Toronto remained the centre of de la Roche's life in Canada. She lived first at 113 John St and later on Victoria St and Wilton Ave. From 1893 to 1900, while a student at Parkdale Collegiate, she lived at 157 Dunn Ave. During her studies at the Ontario College of Art she lived at 469 Jarvis St, where in 1902 she sold her first magazine story to *Munsey's*. From 1911 to 1915 the family lived on a farm in the village of Bronte, now a part of OAKVILLE, Ont. After her parents died she lived at 89 Collier St. Her first book, a collection of short stories entitled *Explorers of the Dawn*, appeared in 1922 and was followed by her first novel, *Possession* (1923). Encouraged by her success, de la Roche bought land and built a cottage in MISSISSAUGA, Ont. which she occupied only briefly as a year-round home but kept as a summer house until the 1940s. She lived at several different addresses in Toronto for the rest of the year; she was at 86 Yorkville Ave late in 1926 when she received her prize cheque for *Jalna* (1927), the first book in the series that continued until *Morning at Jalna* (1960). After 1939 she lived in the northeastern suburbs (see 6. TORONTO: EAST) and in Forest Hill (see 7. TORONTO WEST).

Essayist and translator **William Hume Blake** was born in Toronto on 2 Nov. 1861, educated at the University of Toronto, and called to the Ontario bar in 1885. The grandson of 'Canada First' spokesman Edward Blake, he published several volumes of essays: *Brown Waters and Other Sketches* (1915), *In a Fishing Country* (1922), and *A Fisherman's Creed* (1923). He is best known for his translations of Louis Hémon's *Maria Chapdelaine* (1921) and Adjutor Rivard's *Chez Nous* (1924). Blake was for many years a partner in the law firm of Blake, Lash, Anglin and Cassels, with offices in the Bank of Commerce building on King St W at Jordan St (just west of Yonge St). In 1910–11 he lived at 30 Dale Ave; in 1912–14 at Apt 9, 41 Spadina Rd; in 1915 at 46 Maple Ave; and in 1916 at 49 Clarendon Ave. Blake spent much time in French Canada, especially in the Laurentians and at LA MALBAIE, Que. He died in Victoria B.C., in 1924 and is buried in Toronto.

Robert Service—working as a bank-teller in DAWSON CITY, Y.T.—mailed the manuscript of his first book, *Songs of a Sourdough*, to the Methodist Book and Publishing House (later the Ryerson Press) in 1907. He planned to use his Christmas-bonus money to pay for its publication, but because the typesetters working on the book greatly enjoyed the poems, editor William Briggs offered to have the firm bear the cost of publication. The book was a financial success when it was published in 1907 and established Service as a popular author in Canada and the United States.

In 1907 the Methodist Book and Publishing House was located at 29–33 Richmond St W; the publishing arm of the Methodist Church in Canada, it traced its origin to the *Christian Guardian*, a Methodist periodical edited in Toronto in 1829 by Egerton Ryerson. In 1907 the Rev. William Briggs, Service's editor, lived at 21 Grenville St. The publishing firm was located from 1915 to 1970 at 299 Queen St W; after the formation of the United Church in 1925 from the Methodist, Presbyterian, and Congregationalist denominations, it became the United Church Publishing House, and afterwards the Ryerson Press. It was sold to McGraw Hill in 1970.

Under the editorship of **Lorne Pierce**, the Ryerson Press became one of the chief publishing vehicles for the first generations

The young Lorne Pierce

of modern Canadian writers. Pierce received a B.D. degree from Victoria College in 1917 and became literary adviser to the press; in 1922 he was appointed editor, a post he retained until his death in 1961. A tireless promoter of Canadian literature, Pierce gave a first publishing opportunity to many of Canada's best-known literary figures. In 1925 he introduced both the Makers of Canadian Literature series and the Ryerson poetry chapbooks. In the early 1920s Pierce was living at 56 Wineva Ave and in the early 1930s at 233 Glen Grove Ave W; by 1935 he had established his long-time home, 5 Campbell Cres. in North York.

During the 1920s and 1930s many writers not only frequented the Arts and Letters Club but attended the luncheons, dinners, and lectures of the Toronto Writers' Club, founded in 1923 and presided over by Charles G.D. Roberts. From about 1928 it held its functions in a room in the Brown Betty Tea Rooms, 42 King St E, approximately opposite the King Edward Hotel; in the 1930s and 1940s, when William Arthur Deacon was a prominent member, it was at 99 Yonge St. The Club numbered among its members Roberts, E.J. Pratt, Merrill Denison, Raymond Knister, and **Arthur Heming**. An artist as well as an author, Heming travelled widely in northern Ontario and Manitoba, and in Labrador, and made his knowledge of nature and the north the basis of *The Drama of the Forests: Romance and Adventure* (1921) and *The Living Forest* (1925). In the 1920s Heming lived at 72 Madison Ave. Another author and artist of the period was **Bertram Brooker**, an active number of the Arts and Letters Club. An illustrator and abstract painter, he won the first Governor General's Award for fiction for his novel *Think of the Earth* (1936), an expression of his philosophy of eternal purpose working itself out in natural and even violent events. His *The Robber* (1949), also a philosophical novel, reinterprets the crucifixion of Christ by telling a story of Barabbas. His first novel, a mystery entitled *The Tangled Miracle* (1922), was written at his home at 44 Oakdene Cr; after the early 1920s Brooker lived at 707 Greenwood Ave. (See also POPLAR POINT, Man.)

Bertram Brooker with one of his paintings

Arthur Heming was associated with the painters of the Group of Seven, and sometimes worked in the Studio Building, built in 1913–14 by Lawren Harris and Dr Joseph MacCallum; it is at 25 Severn St, north of Bloor St in the Rosedale Ravine. One of its habitués was **J.E.H. MacDonald**, who exhibited some of his sketches at the Arts and Letters Club in 1911—an event that led directly to the founding of the Group of Seven, although the Group did not exhibit collectively until 1920. A collection of his poems, *West by East*, was published in 1933, the year after his death. **A.Y. Jackson**—another member of the Group of Seven—lived and worked in the Studio Building until the mid-1950s. (The famous painter Tom Thomson shared a studio with Jackson and in 1915 moved into a shack—since moved to the McMichael Collection Museum in Kleinburg—behind the building that was also occupied at various times by writers, including, in the 1930s, Earle Birney and Roy Daniells. Among the Studio Building's later occupants is the distinguished painter Harold Town.) Jackson's autobiography, *A Painter's Country*, was published in 1958. Jackson lived from 1955–68 in Ottawa and from 1968 until his death in 1974 in Kleinburg, where he is buried.

Many of Toronto's newspaper journalists have made contributions to literature, and many writers whose chief aims have been literary have supported themselves in Toronto with newspaper journalism.

Ernest Hemingway lived briefly in Toronto in 1920 and again in 1923–4. On the first occasion, he stayed at the home of Ralph Connable, an American executive for the Woolworth Stores in Canada, and was tutor to the Connables' slightly disabled son. The Connable home was the mansion that stands at 153 Lyndhurst Ave; Hemingway had a private cottage on the grounds. While here, Hemingway began writing for the *Toronto Star*, where he met Greg Clark. He attended many Toronto entertainments and social events with the Connables' daughter, Dorothy, and worked on rehabilitating his leg, damaged by shrapnel in the First World War, by skating on the flooded tennis court that stood between his cottage and the main house. Hemingway left Toronto soon after his contract with the Connables expired in May, but he maintained his con-

Hemingway's apartment building at 1599 Bathurst

nection with the *Star* through correspondence with Clark. Late in 1921 he was made a Paris correspondent. In the fall of 1923 he returned to Toronto, at the *Star*'s prompting, and for three months wrote articles for the *Star Weekly*. He and his wife Hadley stayed briefly at the Selby Hotel, 592 Sherbourne St, and then moved to the apartment building that stands at 1599 Bathurst St, above the Cedarvale ravine; the Hemingway's son John Hadley, was born on 10 Oct. 1923, while they were living here. At the *Star*, in 1923, Hemingway met **Morley Callaghan**, who spent his summers while a student at the University of Toronto as a reporter for the paper. Callaghan bought a copy of Hemingway's *Three Stories & Ten Poems* (Paris, 1923) at a bookstore near Bay and Bloor. Encouraged to write fiction by Hemingway, Callaghan began writing seriously in 1923. When Hemingway left the city he took some of Callaghan's short stories and helped to place them in expatriate magazines in Paris.

The old *Toronto Star* office—where Clark, Hemingway, and Callaghan worked—was at 18 King St W. In 1929 the *Star* moved to the new Star Building at 80 King St W., since demolished to make room for First Canadian Place; the newspaper has been located at 1 Yonge St since 1971. Other writers employed there have included poet and novelist **Wilfrid Eggleston** (see OTTAWA; MEDICINE HAT, Alta) and novelist **Hugh Garner**, who was a copy boy in 1929. **Greg Clark** began his career with the *Star* in 1911, and initiated his popular humorous column and human-interest feature stories after he had become an editor at the *Star Weekly*. These pieces have been collected in many volumes, including *Greg's Choice* (1968). Clark left the *Star* in 1947 but continued to write for the *Montreal Herald* and later for *Weekend Magazine*, which until its demise in the early 1980s had offices at Queen and Bay Sts (see 7: TORONTO WEST).

The tradition of author-journalists at the *Star* goes back at least to **Augustus Bridle**.

Gregory Clark

Born in England in 1869, Bridle grew up in Canada and for many years was an editor of the *Canadian Courier* (1908–30). Bridle then joined the staff of the Toronto *Star* as art, music, and drama editor. Author of one novel, *Hansen* (1925), he also published two collections of biographical essays: *Sons of Canada* (1917) and *Masques of Ottawa* (1921). Over his long career in Toronto Bridle lived at many different addresses, including 216 Dunn Ave, his home when he published *Hansen*; and 33 Nanton Ave, where he lived in the 1930s when working for the *Star*. Bridle died in Toronto in 1952.

The *Toronto Globe and Mail* carries on the literary tradition of George Brown's *Globe*. It was formed in 1936 by a merger of the *Globe* with the *Mail and Empire*, and in that year moved to a building at King and York Sts, which—like the *Star*'s 80 King St W building—has been replaced by First Canadian Place. In 1971 the *Globe and Mail* moved to 444 Front St W. Early in the century the *Globe* employed the poet **Jean McKishnie Blewett**. Born in 1862 in Scotia, Ont., Jean Blewett contributed to the *Globe* for several years before becoming editor of the paper's 'Homemaker's Department'. During the 1910s, she lived at 399 Keele St; in 1925, when she retired from journalism and moved to CHATHAM, Ont., her last address in the city was 592 Jarvis St. Blewett published several volumes of poetry, including *Heart Songs* (1897), *The Cornflower and Other Poems* (1906), *and Poems* (1922). **William Arthur Deacon** became literary editor of the *Mail and Empire* in 1928 and continued in that capacity with the *Globe and Mail* until 1960; he lived in the north-eastern section of the city (see 6. TORONTO: EAST). In 1960 Deacon was succeeded by **William French**, who still writes reviews and literary commentary for the newspaper.

Born in England, the well-known editor **B.K. Sandwell** was a student of Stephen Leacock's at Upper Canada College (see 7. TORONTO: WEST). He then attended the University of Toronto and in 1897 began his journalism career on the Toronto *News*. After several years in MONTREAL (3), Que., and a term as chairman of the English department at Queen's University, KINGSTON, Sandwell returned to Toronto, where from 1932 to 1951 he was the editor of *Saturday Night*. A highly-regarded humorist, B.K. Sandwell published *The Privacity Agent and other Modest Proposals* in 1925. Another collection, *The Diversions of Duchesstown and Other Essays*, appeared posthumously in 1955. While working in Montreal, Sandwell helped to arrange for the series of articles by Leacock that were collected in 1912 as *Sunshine Sketches of a Little Town*. During most of his long career with *Saturday Night* Sandwell lived downtown in apartment buildings on Spadina Rd. In the 1930s he lived at Apt 2, 72 Spadina Rd. In 1940–1 he lived at 87 St Clair Ave W.; but in 1942 he returned to Spadina, taking Apt 5 at 41 Spadina Rd (the same building in which William Hume Blake had lived in 1912–14), where he remained until his death in 1951.

Popular novelist **Arthur Hailey** came to Toronto from his native England in 1947 and worked on Maclean-Hunter publications, including *Bus and Truck Transport* and *Maclean's*, until 1953; during much of this period he lived at 2745 St Clair Ave E. His first novel, *Flight into Danger* (1958), was based on a teleplay with the same title presented on CBC in 1956. Hailey, who has lived for many years in the Bahamas, is the author of *Hotel* (1965), *Airport* (1968) and *Wheels* (1971). The well-known journalist and popular historian **Pierre Berton** also joined *Maclean's* in 1947 and remained with the magazine until 1958; from 1952 he was managing editor. In the 1940s Berton lived at 379B Donlands Ave; he has lived for many years in KLEINBURG, northwest of Toronto. Berton returned to *Maclean's* for one year in 1962 after four years with the Toronto *Star* as columnist and associate editor. From 1963 to 1973 he was the host of the 'Pierre Berton Show', and has continued to appear on several popular radio and television programs. **Peter C. Newman** was an editor for *Maclean's* in 1956–64 and its chief editor in 1971–82; since then he has lived in Cordova Bay, B.C. His many books—all vivid analyses of social and political history and of influential persons—include *Renegade in Power: The Diefenbaker Years* (1963), *The Canadian Establishment*, (2 vols, 1975, 1981), and *Company of Adventurers: An Unofficial History of the Hudson's Bay Company* (1985).

Novelist **W.O. Mitchell** (*Who Has Seen the Wind*, 1947) was fiction editor of *Maclean's* in 1948–51, and during this period lived at 140 Springdale Blvd, East York. Mitchell was in the city again in 1973–4 as writer-in-residence at the University of Toronto. (See CALGARY, CASTOR, EDMONTON, HIGH RIVER, Alta; WINNIPEG, Man; WEYBURN, Sask.)

The Canadian Broadcasting Corporation (CBC) was formed in 1936, and almost immediately its Toronto headquarters at 354 Jarvis St (the original Havergal College) became an important address for writers whose works were broadcast, or who were employed by the network as script writers. Two radio playwrights active in the city during the 1940s were **Lister Sinclair** and **Len Peterson**. Both were writers for 'CBC Stage', the successful drama series created by Andrew Allan in 1943. Sinclair graduated in 1942 from the University of British Columbia and joined the faculty of the Academy of Radio Arts, Toronto. A collection, *A Play on Words and Other Radio Plays* (1948), featured Sinclair's early work, including the satirical *We All Hate Toronto*. Associated for many years with the CBC, where he was executive vice-president from 1972 to 1974, Sinclair has written plays for the stage, including *Socrates* (1957) and *The Blood Is Strong* (1956). In the early 1950s Sinclair lived at 37 Glenavy Ave, North York; in the 1960s at 66 Victoria Park Ave, Scarborough; in the early 1970s at 25 Glen Oak Dr; and in the late 1970s at 51 Alexander St. Peterson, a native of REGINA, Sask., has produced over 1,200 scripts in a career spanning four decades in Toronto theatre. In addition to his work for the CBC, he has written adult and children's plays for the stage. Among his one-act plays for children produced at the Young People's Theatre are *Almighty Voice* (1974), presented in 1975, and *Billy Bishop and the Red Baron* (1975). His works for adults include *The Great Hunger* (1967), *Burlap Bags* (1972), *Women in the Attic* (1972), and *They're All Afraid* (1981). In the late 1940s Peterson lived 67 Charles St W and by 1950 had moved to 286 Bain Ave. He has lived since the mid-1950s in his home on Islington Ave. **Mordecai Richler**'s interpretation of the conditions and the atmosphere surrounding writers at the CBC in Toronto during the 1950s is vividly conveyed in early chapters of his novel *St. Urbain's Horseman* (1971). Richler worked for the CBC in 1952–9 before moving to England, where he remained until 1972. He now lives in his native MONTREAL.

Hungarian writers **George Jonas** and **Robert Zend** settled in Toronto in 1956. Jonas, born in 1935, began working for the CBC soon after coming to the city and has been associated with the corporation for many years as a television producer. His first books in Canada were the poetry collections *The Absolute Smile* (1967), *The Happy Hungry Man* (1970), and *Cities* (1973). Jonas wrote the librettos for *The European Lover* (1966) and *The Glove* (1973), both commissioned by the Canadian Opera Company. In the late 1960s and early 1970s Jonas lived in an apartment building at 392 Sherbourne St, and in 1972 moved to a building at 131 Bloor St W. He now lives on Cumberland St. His other books include *Final Decree* (1981), a novel, and *By Persons Unknown* (1977), non-fiction. Zend, who worked for many years for the CBC, was a cartoonist and columnist in his native Budapest before coming to Toronto. With co-translator John Robert Colombo, Zend published two books of his poetry, *Beyond Labels* (1972) and *From Zero to One* (1973). In the late 1960s and early 1970s Zend lived in an apartment building at 790 Eglinton Ave W; in the late 1970s and early 1980s he lived at 82 Hillcrest Dr. Zend died in Toronto on 27 June 1985 and in July his innovative book of poetry and graphic art, *OĀB*, was published; he is buried in Mount Pleasant Cemetery.

The tombstone of Robert Zend, Jiri Ladocha sculptor

Poet **Phyllis Webb** worked for the CBC for several years during the 1960s. In 1966 she originated the CBC program 'Ideas' and was its executive producer from 1966 to 1969. Her book *Naked Poems* appeared in 1965. In Toronto Webb lived in an apartment at 81–3 Isabella St. Her *Selected Poems* (1971) appeared after she had moved to SALTSPRING ISLAND, B.C., her present home.

Until his retirement as an executive producer in 1985, the literary and cultural programming of CBC Radio was vey much identified with editor **Robert Weaver**, who joined the network's Talks and Public Affairs Department in 1948 after graduating from the University of Toronto. Programs he has produced include 'Critically Speaking', 'Stories with John Drainie', and 'Anthology', which began in 1953. Weaver's programs have boadcast the works of many writers—including Mordecai Richler and Alice Munro—often providing them with their earliest significant exposure. In addition to his work as a producer Weaver has edited many anthologies of Canadian short stories, and, with William Toye, *The Oxford Anthology of Canadian Literature* (1973; 2nd edn, 1981). He was also the inspiring force behind *The Tamarack Review* (1956–82). Other founding editors were Kildare Dobbs, Millar MacLure, Ivon Owen, William Toye, and **Anne Wilkinson** (see 5. TORONTO: ROSEDALE).

John Robert Colombo (see 7. TORONTO: WEST) and the poet **Janis Rapoport** became editors in the 1970s. Born in 1946, Rapoport graduated from the University of Toronto and has published two books of poetry: *Within the Whirling Moment* (1967) and *Jeremy's Dream* (1974). Since *The Tamarack Review* ceased publication in 1982 Rapoport and her husband Douglas Donegani have edited and published the literary magazine *Ethos* from offices on Dupont St in the Annex neighbourhood.

The British painter and novelist **Wyndham Lewis** lived in Toronto from 1939–43—in hotels on Sherbourne St just south of Bloor St E. Lewis had been visiting New York at the outbreak of the Second World War. Unable to return to England, he settled here, living first at the Tudor Hotel, 559 Sherbourne St. After it burned down early in 1943 Lewis and his wife lived for a short time at the Selby Hotel, still standing at 592 Sherbourne St. (In that year Lewis accepted an offer to teach at Assumption College in WINDSOR.) While in Toronto Lewis supported himself largely by painting portraits. Toronto and Lewis's years here are scathingly portrayed in his novel *Self-Condemned* (1954).

Many of the novelists who have lived recently in the downtown area have worked at publishing houses and schools here. Comic novelist **Leo Simpson** came to Canada in 1961 from his native Ireland. He worked until 1966 as publicity director and editor at Macmillan & Co, then located in the building that stands at 70 Bond St, just south of Mackenzie House. (*Saturday Night*'s editorial offices are now in this building. Macmillan of Canada was acquired in 1978 by Gage Publishing Ltd and is now located at 146 Front St E. The late John Morgan Gray, the firm's head from 1946–73, published his memoirs, *Fun Tomorrow*, in 1978.) Leo Simpson set his first novel, *Arkwright* (1971), in Toronto, although it did not appear until he had left the city. During Simpson's years with Macmillan another future novelist, **Richard Wright**, also worked there. He joined the firm in 1959, shortly after graduating from Ryerson Polytechnical Institute, and served as a book salesman and later as an editor during the early 1960s. In the first years of this period he lived at 68 Prince Arthur Ave. Wright was living in an apartment building at 135 Rose Ave in 1965 and working for Macmillan when he published his first work, the children's book *Tolliver* (1965). Wright also worked for Oxford Canada before moving to HAMILTON. His novels include *The Weekend Man* (1970; rpr. 1977) and *Farthing's Fortunes* (1976). (See also MIDLAND.)

Novelist **Constance Beresford-Howe** teaches English at Ryerson. She had written four novels before arriving in Toronto in 1971 from Montreal, where she was born in 1922. In Toronto she has produced her best-known works, a loose trilogy of novels that portray women in contemporary social situations: *The Book of Eve* (1973), *A Population of One* (1977), and *The Marriage Bed* (1981).

Novelist **Marian Engel** lived downtown in 1964–67 at 16 Clarence Sq., which is east of Spadina Ave and south of King St, and in 1967–70 at 114 Pembroke St, south of Allan Gardens. In 1968, while living at Pembroke St, she published her first novel, *No Clouds of Glory* (reissued in 1974 as *Sara Bastard's Notebook*). At this address she also wrote much of *The Honeyman Festival* (1970); she has said that the house in this novel is based on houses she saw while canvassing for the New Democratic Party in downtown Toronto, especially the former home of Mazo de la Roche at 113 John St (see the early part of this article). Engel's home at Clarence Sq. (since converted to a townhouse) was a model for the house in *Lunatic Villas* (1981). She lived at these two downtown addresses during her marriage to former CBC producer **Howard Engel**, who has since become known as the author of the Benny Cooperman series of mystery novels (see 4. TORONTO: THE ANNEX and HAMILTON). In 1970–3 Marian Engel lived in the Annex, and from 1973 until her death in 1985 at 70 Marchmount Rd (see 7. TORONTO: WEST), the address with which her career is most associated.

Novelist **Stephen Vizinczey** published his best-known novel, *In Praise of Older Women*, in 1965; he was then living at 38-A Sherbourne St N, just north of Bloor St. The poet and novelist **Margaret Atwood** lived downtown for several years during the early 1980s. Her home at the time was 73 Sullivan St. During her years here Atwood published the poetry collection *True Stories* (1981) and the novel *Bodily Harm* (1981). (See also 3. TORONTO: UNIVERSITY OF TORONTO, 4. TORONTO: THE ANNEX, 6. TORONTO: EAST, ALLISTON, OTTAWA.)

One of the most interesting of downtown Toronto's recent literary residents was the poet **Milton Acorn**, a native of CHARLOTTETOWN, P.E.I., who moved here in the early 1960s from MONTREAL (6), where he had begun to publish his poetry. In 1962 he married the Toronto poet Gwendolyn MacEwen (see 4. TORONTO: THE ANNEX), but the marriage lasted only one year. His book *Jawbreakers* (1963) was published by Raymond Souster's Contact Press (see 7. TORONTO: WEST). Acorn then moved to Vancouver, but was back in the city by 1969, when his book *I've Tasted My Blood* was published. As it failed to win a Governor General's Award, Acorn was honoured by fellow writers on 16 May 1970 at Grossman's Tavern, 379 Spadina Ave, with a medal naming him 'The People's Poet'. Six years later he won a Governor General's Award for *The Island Means Minago* (1975). In Toronto Acorn lived briefly in an apartment at 555 Palmerston Ave, rooming there with poet James Deahl, but stayed mainly at the Waverly Hotel, 484 Spadina Ave. In 1981 he returned to Charlottetown, where he died in 1986.

Grossman's, the site of Acorn's famous 'People's Poet' award, is one of many restaurants, taverns, and coffeehouses that have from time to time served as Toronto literary meeting-places. The most important have been the Bohemian Embassy, which was at 7 Nicholas St, and the Selby Tavern, 592 Sherbourne St, still frequented by writers for its association with Hemingway, who liked to drink there during the First World War when he worked for the Toronto *Star*. Toronto's first important series of poetry readings was held from 1 June 1960 to 1 June 1966 by writer Don Cullen at his Bohemian Embassy coffeehouse. The series was revived on 1 June 1974 at Harbourfront, 235 Queen's Quay West, and ended on 26 to 29 Feb. 1976 with a marathon reading that lasted over seventy-five hours and included 150 poets. Since 1976 poet **Greg Gatenby** (*Growing Still*, 1981), who had revived the Bohemian Embassy series, has managed the weekly Harbourfront Reading Series. Since 1980 the series has sponsored yearly International Writers' Festivals, with readings by many distinguished authors. In the 1960s and 1970s many Toronto writers frequented the Village Book Store, which was long located at 29 Gerrard St W; since the mid-1970s it has been at 239 Queen St W.

A distinctive part of Toronto's downtown area is the Toronto Islands, situated on a low lying sandbar that lies opposite the city's downtown shoreline between Bathurst and Parliament. They are mainly given over to parkland but contain two small residential communities, Algonquin Island and Ward's Island, near their eastern extremity. In earlier times there were summer homes in many parts of the Islands.

Novelist and poet **Raymond Knister** (*White Narcissus*, 1929) first came to Toronto in 1919 when he entered Victoria College, University of Toronto; he left the following February because of illness. Knister returned to the city in 1926 and worked as a freelance writer. A friend of poet Wilson MacDonald, Knister met his future wife, Myrtle Gamble, at MacDonald's downtown Toronto apartment at 197 Wellesley St, the same building in which Charles G.D. Roberts (also a friend of Knister's) lived. The couple married in 1927 and moved to Hanlan's Point on the Islands. In the summer of that year, while living in a cottage (now gone) called 'Poplars', Knister finished *White Narcissus*, his first novel. Later the Knisters moved to Apt 3, 78 St Albans Rd, in Islington, where they found themselves living immediately above Wilfrid Eggleston, who was then working for the *Star*. An introduction to Roberts by Knister helped Eggleston enter the literary circle of Roberts' son Lloyd in OTTAWA, where Eggleston worked for many years. In 1929 the Knisters moved to PORT DOVER.

Novelist **Hugh Garner** lived in 1951–3 in a flat on Centre Island, where there are now no private homes. **Gwendolyn MacEwen** was living at 3 Second St, Ward's Island (house gone) when she published the book of poems *The Rising Fire* (1963) and her first novel, *Julian the Magician* (1963).

Victor Coleman, born in Toronto in 1944, grew up on the Island (he is a third-generation Islander) and in Montreal. He lived for many years at 25 Third St, Ward's Island. In 1965 Coleman founded the magazine *Island* and Island Press. In 1967 he became the editor of Coach House Press, 401 Huron St, which had been established in 1965; Coleman directed Coach House for nearly a decade, publishing many now-prominent authors and founding the company's literary magazine, *Is*. He also served for two years as director of A Space, 85 St Nicholas St (now converted to other uses), a Toronto centre for literary readings and performance art. (Founded in 1970, A Space moved in 1978 to 299 Queen St W, the former Ryerson Press building; since 1983 it has been at 204 Spadina Ave.) Coleman's poetry collections include *From Erik Satie's Notes to the Music* (1965), *One/eye/love* (1967), *Light Verse* (1970), *Strange Love* (1974), and *Traffic at Both Ends* (1978). Coleman has lived downtown since 1981.

Poet **Robert Sward** (*Half a Life's History: Poems New and Selected 1957–1983*, 1983) has lived on Wyandot Ave, Algonquin Island, since coming from British Columbia to Toronto in the early 1980s.

The concentration in (and near) downtown Toronto of theatres that produce new plays, and thus the presence here of many playwrights, are features of the area that date from a four-year period when four of the city's most important theatre companies were founded: Theatre Passe Muraille (1968), Factory Theatre Lab (1969), Toronto Free Theatre (1970), and Tarragon Theatre (1971). (Earlier playwrights, who did not live and work downtown, are treated in other sections of the entry: Merrill Denison, 3.

TORONTO: UNIVERSITY OF TORONTO; John Coulter, 6. TORONTO: EAST; John Herbert, 7. TORONTO: WEST; and Robertson Davies, 3. TORONTO: UNIVERSITY OF TORONTO and 6. TORONTO: EAST.)

David French moved to Toronto in 1945 from his birthplace, COLEY POINT, Nfld. He attended Rawlinson Public School, Harbord Collegiate, and Oakwood Collegiate, where he graduated in 1958. While at Harbord he sold his first short story to *The Canadian Boy*, a United Church publication. From 1958 to 1960 he worked as a mailboy at the CBC; after studying in California at the Pasadena Playhouse, French began working as an actor. He sold his first play, *Beckons the Dark River*, in 1962 to the CBC. French spent the years 1968–70 in REGINA, Sask., where he worked for the post office. In 1971 he submitted *The Keepers of the House*, an early version of *Leaving Home* (1977), to Bill Glassco at the Tarragon Theatre, 30 Bridgman Ave. Glassco, who has produced several plays by French at the Tarragon, staged *Leaving Home* in 1972. French's first play examines family conflict in a Toronto household of immigrants from Newfoundland; a struggle begins when the family's two sons decide to leave home. French's play *Of the Fields, Lately* (1975) is a sequel. Author of many scripts for television and radio, French has written several other plays for the stage, including *One Crack Out* (1976), *Jitters* (1980), *Salt-Water Moon* (1985), *The Riddle of the World* (unpublished), and a translation of Chekhov's *The Seagull* (1978). French divides the year between Toronto and a summer home in Prince Edward Island.

Jack Gray—educated at Queen's University, KINGSTON, and at the University of Toronto—worked as an assistant editor at *Maclean's* from 1953 until 1957, when he published his first play, *Bright Sun at Midnight*. It was followed by many others, including *Chevalier Johnson* (1964) and *Striker Schneiderman* (1970). Gray was secretary-general of the Canadian Theatre Centre from 1971 to 1973.

Jack Winter, a native of Montreal, studied at McGill and the University of Toronto before joining the Toronto Workshop Productions theatre company in 1962; in the 1960s and 1970s the company was located at 47 Fraser Ave. Associated with the workshop until 1967, Winter had two plays produced here, *Before Compiègne* (1964) and *Hey, Rube* (1966), and lived at 126 Castlewood Rd. **Ken Gass**, a native of ABBOTSFORD, B.C., came to Toronto after studying theatre in Vancouver at the University of British Columbia. He worked as a highschool teacher at Parkdale Collegiate and directed plays at Theatre Passe Muraille and John Herbert's Garret Theatre before joining the Factory Theatre Lab in 1970 as artistic director; the theatre was then at 94 Yonge St. He was also active from 1970 in Toronto's Festival of Underground Theatre. Gass's first full-length play was *Red Revolutionary* (unpublished), an adaptation of Charles Mair's verse drama *Tecumseh* (1886). Published works include *Hooray for Johnny Canuck* (1975), *The Boy Bishop* (published in *The Canadian Theatre Review*, 1976), and *Winter Offensive* (1978). In the 1970s Gass lived at 256 Withrow Ave.

Playwright **Carol Bolt** moved to Toronto from Montreal in the late 1960s and has been associated with George Luscombe's Toronto Workshop Productions and Paul Thompson's Theatre Passe Muraille. In the early 1970s Bolt's work for adults emphasized political and social issues, particularly those affecting workers' rights in the Canadian West. These plays include *Buffalo Jump* (1972), *Gabe* (1973), *Red Emma* (1974), and *Shelter* (1975). Her many plays for children began with *My Best Friend Is Twelve Feet High* (1972); others include *Cyclone Jack* (1972), *Tangleflags* (1973), *Maurice* (1974), and *Finding Bumble* (1975). Bolt's most successful play for adults, *One Night Stand* (1977), won three Canadian Film Awards in 1978 when it was adapted for television.

David Freeman was born here in 1947. A victim of cerebral palsy, he wrote his first drama when the CBC commissioned him to produce a script based on an article he had published about Toronto's Cerebral Palsy Workshop and other such institutions. The script was not produced, but it came to the attention of Bill Glassco, who produced a rewritten version of it, entitled *Creeps* (1972), at the Factory Theatre Lab in 1971; later in the same year Glassco made *Creeps* the first play at his newly founded Tarragon Theatre. Freeman—whose other works include *Battering Ram* (1974) and *You're Gonna Be Alright Jamie Boy* (1974)—moved to Montreal in 1975. In the same year **John Gray** moved from VANCOUVER, B.C., to compose music for the Theatre Passe Muraille. He spent only a few years here before returning to Vancouver, with which his career is primarily associated. Gray's musical plays produced in Toronto include *18 Wheels* (unpublished, produced in 1977) and *Billy Bishop Goes to War* (1981), which was written in collaboration with Eric Peterson and won a Governor General's Award.

Some of the companies mentioned have had several locations. Today, only Toronto Workshop Productions, 12 Alexander St, is within the downtown area as defined by this article. Nevertheless, because they are located on its fringes, all these theatres are essentially downtown institutions. The current premises of three are a few blocks west of Spadina Ave: Tarragon Theatre, 30 Bridgman Ave; Theatre Passe Muraille, 16 Ryerson Ave; and Factory Theatre Lab, 125 Bathurst St. The Toronto Free Threatre, 26 Berkeley St, is just east of Sherbourne.

Many institutions and organizations of literary importance are located in Toronto. Several are housed in the Artists' Alliance Building, 24 Ryerson Ave: the League of Canadian Poets, the Canadian Writers' Union, the Periodical Writers' Association, the Writer's Trust, and the Canadian Authors' Association. Toronto's central reference library, the Metropolitan Toronto Library, 789 Yonge St, contains the Baldwin Room collection of Canadian historical materials, the John Ross Robertson collection of written and pictorial material relating to Toronto, and a Canadian literature collection that is believed to hold a copy of every book published in what is now Canada before 1867, and a very extensive collection of those published between 1867 and 1900.

In 1949 Dr Edgar Osborne presented a collection of 2,000 children's books published in England before 1910 to the Toronto Public Library. The Osborne Collection of Early Children's Books is housed at Boys' and Girls' House, 40 St George St. The Lillian H. Smith Collection of Children's Books was founded in 1962 to supplement the Osborne Collection with books published in Canada, the United States, and the United Kingdom since 1910. The holdings now number more than 12,000 titles.

3. THE UNIVERSITY OF TORONTO

The University of Toronto's main campus—called the St George campus after the street that bisects it—is bounded on the north and south by Bloor and College Sts, on the west by Spadina Ave, and on the east by Bay St. Most of the authors associated with the University of Toronto that are discussed below are also associated with one (or more) of its several constituent colleges and universities.

University College. In the 1880s University College had several students who later distinguished themselves as writers. The poet **William Wilfred Campbell** studied at the University of Toronto from 1880 to 1883. After two years at University College in a liberal-arts program, he spent two years as a divinity student at Wycliffe College, the Anglican divinity school. Campbell was ordained in 1886, and from 1888 to 1890 was pastor at ST STEPHEN, N.B., but he resigned from the ministry in 1891 and joined the civil service in OTTAWA. His first book was *Snowflakes and Sunbeams* (1888).

Charles Gordon—who wrote under the pen-name **Ralph Connor**—graduated from University College in 1883 with a B.A. in classics and English. He returned to the university's Knox College to study theology, and graduated in 1887. (He was ordained in the Presbyterian ministry in 1890.) Gordon was inspired to work in the western missions by a lecture he heard in 1883, given at St Andrews Church (still standing at 75 Simcoe St) by Dr James Robertson, superintendent of missions. His first book, *Black Rock: A Tale of the Selkirks* (1898) appeared originally as a serial in the Toronto magazine *The Westminster*, a publication of the Presbyterian Church. (See also ST ELMO; BANFF, Alta; WINNIPEG, Man.)

Stephen Leacock attended the University of Toronto in 1887–8 but lack of money forced him to become a high-school teacher (see STRATHROY, UXBRIDGE). While teaching at Upper Canada College from 1889 to 1899 he studied at University College and received a B.A. in modern languages in 1891. Leacock also worked on the university newspaper, the *Varsity*, which published some of his earliest humorous pieces. (See also 7. TORONTO: WEST, ORILLIA; MONTREAL: 3, Que.) Another humorist, **Peter McArthur**, attended University College in 1888–90 but left without taking a degree to work for the Toronto *Globe* (see 1. TORONTO BEFORE 1900). As a successful magazine writer in New York during the 1890s, and especially as editor of the New York periodical *Truth* in 1895–7, McArthur first published many of the essays that were later collected in Leacock's first book of humour, *Literary Lapses* (1910). McArthur's own career as a humorist is primarily associated with his home in Ekfrid Township, Ont. (see APPIN). The editor and humorist **Bernard K. Sandwell** (who had studied under Leacock at Upper Canada College), graduated from University College in 1897 (see 2. DOWNTOWN TORONTO SINCE 1900; MONTREAL: 3, Que.).

Archibald MacMechan (*Headwaters of Canadian Literature*, 1924) graduated from University College in 1884. From 1889 until his death in 1933 he taught at Dalhousie University, HALIFAX, N.S. The poet **Tom MacInnes**, a native of DRESDEN, graduated from University College in 1889; he was then living at 30 Avenue Rd; but after he began to study law at Osgoode Hall he lived at 637 Spadina Ave. (See VANCOUVER, B.C.) **John McCrae**, the author of 'In Flanders Fields', received his B.A. from University College in 1894 and an M.B. from the University of Toronto in 1898. During several of his student years he lived at 329 Jarvis St. A native of GUELPH, McCrae spent most of his adult life in Montreal (3).

University College today

The poet **Earle Birney** received an M.A. from the University of Toronto in 1927 and began doctoral course work in 1932; he spent most of the early 1930s in the United States and England, studying and teaching. When his Ph.D. was awarded in 1936, he joined University College as a lecturer in English literature and was a member of the staff from 1936 to 1946. In 1938 he became literary editor of the *Canadian Forum*. In the late 1930s Birney lived downtown at 100 Gloucester St and later at 90 Millwood Ave in northeastern Toronto. In 1940 he moved back to the university area and lived at 40 Hazelton Ave; this was his address when, in 1942—just before beginning military service—he published his first book of poems, *David*, which won a Governor General's Award. (See also 6. TORONTO: EAST; BANFF, MORNINGSIDE, Alta; CRESTON, VANCOUVER, B.C.)

Born in 1900 in the United States, the poet **Robert Finch** was educated at Harbord Collegiate and University College (B.A. 1925). After studying in Paris, Finch joined the French Department in University College in 1928; he was a full professor from 1952 until he retired in 1968. (His office was at 20 Queen's Park Cr. W.) In the early 1930s Finch lived in East House, University College, and at 78 Grosvenor St and 292A St George St. In 1938 he moved to 33 Prince Arthur Ave, his address for many years; he lived there in 1946 when he published his *Poems*, which won a Governor General's Award. Finch was one of the six poets whose works were included in the important anthology *New Provinces* in 1936; the others were E.J. Pratt (see Victoria College, below), F.R. Scott, A.J.M. Smith, A.M. Klein, and Leo Kennedy (see MONTREAL: 4). Since 1961 Finch has lived in Massey College (see below). The poet and novelist **Douglas LePan** was born in 1914 in Toronto and educated at the University of Toronto Schools and University College (B.A. 1936). He then attended Oxford University, and in 1938–41 was an instructor in English literature at Harvard University. After many years' diplomatic service for the Canadian government—a period in which he published two collections of his poems, *The Wounded Prince* (1948) and *The Net and the Sword* (1953)—LePan returned to Toronto in 1964 to become principal of University College. He was University Professor in 1970–9 and in 1970 was named Senior Fellow of Massey College. LePan's novel *The Deserter* (1964) won a Governor General's Award; his later works include a memoir, *Bright Glass of Memory* (1979), and a book of poems, *Something Still to Find* (1982) (See also KINGSTON.)

Many other writers have attended or taught at University College. **Claude Bissell**, president of the University of Toronto in 1958–71, studied under Finch in the 1930s; Bissell is the author of several books, including *Halfway Up Parnassus: A Personal Account of the University of Toronto 1932–71* (1974). After leaving the President's residence he moved to Erskine Avenue. The Austrian-born novelist **Henry Kreisel** fled his homeland after the Nazi takeover in 1938, was sent in 1940 by British authorities to Canada, and was educated at Jarvis Collegiate and University College (B.A. 1946, M.A. 1947). (See EDMONTON.) The German poet **Walter Bauer** came to Toronto in 1952, received his B.A. from University

College in 1958, joined the German department, and taught there until he retired in 1976. Bauer published more than seventy books in German: poetry, novels, stories, children's books, and biographies, including studies of Grey Owl and the explorer de la Salle. Translations of his poetry include *The Price of Morning* (1968) and *A Different Sun* (1976).

The poet and dramatist **James Reaney** attended University College (B.A. 1948, M.A., 1949) and received a Ph.D. in 1958 (see LUCAN, STRATFORD). The poet **Colleen Thibaudeau** (*My Granddaughters Are Combing Out Their Long Hair*, 1978), who is married to Reaney, also graduated from University College in the late 1940s. Another graduate of this period was poet **Phyllis Gottlieb** (see 7. TORONTO: WEST). Novelist **David Lewis Stein** attended University College in the late 1950s and was an editor of the *Varsity*. His works include the novel *Scratch One Dreamer* (1967), and a non-fiction book, *Toronto for Sale: The Destruction of a City* (1972); for many years he has written for the Toronto *Star*. The novelist **Lawrence Garber** (*Sirens and Graces*, 1983) graduated from University College in 1962; since 1967 he has lived in LONDON, where he teaches at the University of Western Ontario.

KINGSTON native **Matt Cohen** has for several years divided his time between a home in Toronto and a farm in VERONA, north of Kingston. Cohen was a student at University College from 1960 to 1964, when he received his B.A. (M.A., 1965). He began as a student of science and mathematics but switched to sociology and philosophy; after leaving Toronto he taught the sociology of religion at McMaster University in Hamilton, Ont. Cohen began writing in 1963–4, when he was living at 55 Harbord St. Toronto is the setting for the title story of *The Expatriate* (1982) and for many of his stories.

Trinity College. **Archibald Lampman** attended Trinity when it was located at Queen St W. and Strachan Ave (it is now on Hoskin Ave, on the University campus) and lived in the college residence; he graduated in 1882. Active in campus life, especially in publications, he began contributing to *Rouge et Noir*, the college magazine, in Dec. 1880; he also edited several issues of the magazine *Episcopon* from Nov. 1881 to Mar. 1882. After graduating he lived briefly at 283 Jarvis St while looking for a job. He had hoped to find writing work, but by the fall he settled for a teaching position in ORANGEVILLE, Ont. The work was distasteful to him, and by December he had accepted a post as clerk in the new Post Office Department in OTTAWA. While a student at Trinity, Lampman was inspired by his first reading of Charles G.D. Roberts' *Orion, and Other Poems*:

> *Like most of the young fellows about me, I had been under the depressing conviction that we were situated hopelessly on the outskirts of civilization, where no art and no literature could be, and that it was hopeless to expect that anything great could be done by any of our companions, still more useless to expect that we would do it ourselves. I sat up most of the night reading and re-reading* Orion *in a state of the wildest excitement and when I went to bed I could not sleep. It seemed to me a wonderful thing that such work could be done by a Canadian, by a young man, one of ourselves.*

Lampman's first collection of poetry, *Among the Millet*, was published in 1888. Another Trinity student in the 1880s was the historical novelist **Gilbert Parker**. Born in 1862 in CAMDEN EAST, he studied here just before he was ordained an Anglican deacon in 1882. Parker's first publication was *Pierre and His People* (1892)—a collection of tales about the people of the Canadian Northwest—published in London, Eng., where he settled permanently in 1889.

Officers of the Trinity College Literary Institute, *c*.1880. Lampman is seated on the floor in the centre

The novelist and poet **Philip Child** received his B.A. from Trinity in 1921. After two decades of studying, teaching, and writing in the United States, England, and British Columbia, Child became professor of English at Trinity in 1942 and spent the remainder of his teaching career here. He died in Toronto in 1978. Child's works are the novels *Village of Souls* (1933), *God's Sparrows* (1937; NCL 1978), *Blow Wind, Come Rack* (1945), *Day of Wrath* (1945), and *Mr. Ames Against Time* (1949), which won a Governor General's Award; and the long narrative poems *The Wood of the Nightingale* (1965) and *The Victorian House* (1951). Child's home of many years was at 40 Heathdale Rd.

Dave Godfrey—born in 1938 in Winnipeg—attended Trinity briefly and finished his university education in the United States. In 1966 Godfrey moved back to Toronto to teach at Trinity, and the following year he co-founded the House of Anansi Press with Dennis Lee (see Victoria College). Godfrey was writer-in-residence at the University of Toronto's Erindale College in Mississauga in 1973–4 and a professor in York University's creative-writing program in 1977, before

Will R. Bird and Philip Child in the 1940s

being appointed chairman of the creative-writing department at the University of VICTORIA. While living in Toronto Godfrey published three books: *Death Goes Better with Coca-Cola* (1967), a story collection; *I Ching Kanada* (1976), a prose meditation; and the novel *The New Ancestors* (1970), which won a Governor General's Award. Novelist **Scott Symons**, who was born in Toronto in 1933, received his B.A. from Trinity College in 1955 (see 5. TORONTO: ROSEDALE). In 1955–7 the novelist **Austin Clarke** studied economics at Trinity (see 4. TORONTO: THE ANNEX).

St Michael's College. Founded in 1852, St Michael's (now the University of St Michael's College) is affiliated with the Roman Catholic Church and shares its campus with the Pontifical Institute of Medieval Studies, founded in the late 1920s. One of its guiding spirits was the French philosopher and author **Etienne Gilson** (1884–1978; *The Elements of Christian Philosophy*, 1960), who served for many years as the Institute's Director of Studies; while in Toronto Gilson lived on St Michael's campus in the house now called Gilson House on Elmsley Pl., opposite the building on St Joseph St that houses the St Michael's and Pontifical Institute libraries. Another French philosopher who taught at the Institute (1933–45) was **Jacques Maritain** (1892–1973; *Le Paysan de la Garonne*, 1966; Eng. trans. 1968).

Marshall McLuhan taught English at St Michael's College from 1946 until the year before his death at the end of 1980. McLuhan began an influential series of studies of communications theory in 1951 with *The Mechanical Bride: Folklore of Industrial Man.* He won a Governor General's Award for *The Gutenberg Galaxy: The Making of Typographic Man* (1962). Founding director in 1963 of the Centre for Culture and Technology at the University, McLuhan published further works on the impact of communications media on modern culture, including most notably *Understanding Media: The Extensions of Man* (1964). He was an editor from 1953 to 1959 of the magazine *Explorations*. A collection of his literary criticism, *The Interior Landscape: The Literary Criticism of Marshall McLuhan 1943–62* (1969), was edited by Eugene McNamara. During his first years at St Michael's, 1946–50, McLuhan lived just east of the College at 91 St Joseph St. The McLuhans then moved to 29 Wells Hill Ave and in 1968 to Wychwood Park. (See also 7. TORONTO: WEST).

The novelist **Sheila Watson** (*The Double Hook*, 1959) was one of McLuhan's doctoral students. She completed her thesis on

Marshall McLuhan, *c.*1946

Wyndham Lewis in 1965. Although Watson had begun the program in 1957, she did not spend the entire period in the city. In 1961 she joined the faculty of the University of Alberta, Edmonton. Watson and her husband, poet **Wilfred Watson**, were closely associated with McLuhan's work. Sheila and Wilfred Watson were Research Associates at the Centre for Culture and Technology in 1968–9. (See CALGARY, EDMONTON, Alta; NANAIMO, B.C.)

Other distinguished literary graduates of St Michael's include novelist **Morley Callaghan**, who received his B.A. here in 1925 (see 4. TORONTO: THE ANNEX); his son **Barry Callaghan** (B.A. 1960, M.A. 1962), a poet, short-story writer, publisher, and professor at York University (see 7. TORONTO: WEST); and the novelist **Hugh Hood**, who studied here in the late 1940s and early 1950s, receiving a Ph.D. in English literature in 1955 (see 5. TORONTO: ROSEDALE). The University of Toronto is the setting of Morley Callaghan's *The Varsity Story* (1948).

Victoria College. The author and legendary teacher **Pelham Edgar** joined Victoria as professor of French in 1897 and became also professor of English in 1902; he taught at Victoria until his retirement in 1938. Edgar's books include a study of Henry James and *The Art of the Novel* (1933); his reminiscences, *Across My Path* (1952), were edited after his death in 1948 by Northrop Frye. Edgar was born in 1871 of a distinguished Toronto family. His father, Sir James Edgar, who was speaker of the House of Commons in 1896–9, wrote a volume of poems, *This Canada of Ours* (1893), and a descriptive work, *Canada and Its Capital* (1898); his mother, Lady Matilda Edgar, was the author of *Ten Years of Upper Canada in Peace and War* (1895) and other historical works.

Edgar was a mentor of **E.J. Pratt** who came from Newfoundland to Toronto in 1907 and received his B.A. in philosophy from Victoria in 1911 (M.A. 1912). As a student he lived in several boarding houses on Charles St. In 1913 he was ordained a Methodist minister and for the next seven years followed a demanding schedule as assistant-minister at a church in Streetsville, as a doctoral candidate (Ph.D. 1917), and as a demonstrator and lecturer in the Department of Psychology. His first book of poetry, *Rachel*, was printed privately in 1917. With the help of Pelham Edgar, Pratt was appointed to the Department of English at Victoria in 1920 and remained there until his retirement in 1953. In 1946 the E.J. Pratt Room of Contemporary Poetry was opened in Victoria's library; in 1968 this library, which holds an extensive collection of his manuscripts and papers, was named the E.J. Pratt Library in the poet's honour. In the 1920s and early 1930s Pratt lived at 25 Tullis Dr (just east of Yonge St, five blocks north of Mt Pleasant Cemetery), from 1932 to 1953 at 21 Cortleigh Blvd (just west of Yonge, nine blocks north of Eglinton Ave), and until 1960 at 47 Glencairn Ave, not far west of the Cortleigh Blvd address. All of these houses are still standing and privately owned. From 1960 until his death in 1964, Pratt—with his wife Viola Whitney Pratt and his daughter Claire—lived in the apartment building at 5 Elm Ave in Rosedale. Pratt began his literary career at the age of forty. His *Newfoundland Verse* was published in 1923 by the Ryerson Press, but he took his next book, *The Witches' Brew* (1925), to another publisher when the Ryerson editors objected to the poem's language and subject. Among Pratt's many other books—which placed him as the foremost Canadian narrative poet—are *The Roosevelt and the Antinoë* (1930), *The Titantic* (1935), *Brébeuf and His Brethren* (1940), and *Towards the Last Spike* (1952). The last two works won Governor General's Awards. Pratt is buried in Mount Pleasant Cemetery. (See also ST JOHN'S, WESTERN BAY, Nfld.)

Humorist **John D. Robins** attended Victoria College (B.A. 1913, M.A. 1922), taught German and later English there, and headed the English department from 1938 until his death in 1952. He wrote *The Incomplete Angler* (1943), which won a Governor General's Award; *Cottage Cheese* (1951); and edited the popular anthology *A Pocketful of Canada* (1946).

Earle Birney, E.J. Pratt, Irving Layton and Leonard Cohen on Bloor St W. in the 1950s

Literary critic and scholar **Northrop Frye** began his long association with Victoria in 1929, when he enrolled in the honours course of Philosophy and English. He stood first in the course when he graduated in 1933, and then moved to Emmanuel College to study theology; he was ordained in 1936 in the United Church Ministry. After a brief period as a preacher in Saskatchewan, Frye went to England to study at Oxford, where he received his M.A. in 1940. He had begun lecturing the year before at Victoria, where he was appointed professor in 1947. Frye was named Chairman of the English department in 1952 and Principal of the College in 1959. After retiring from these posts he became the University of Toronto's first University Professor of English. In 1978 he was appointed Chancellor of Victoria University.

In addition to his teaching and administrative work, Frye was editor of the *Canadian Forum* from 1948 to 1952, and from 1950 to 1960 he wrote an influential critique of publications in Canadian poetry for the annual 'Letters in Canada' feature of the *University of Toronto Quarterly*. Beginning with *Fearful Symmetry: A Study of William Blake* (1947), Frye has contributed a long series of important critical works on both Canadian and English literature. Among them are *Anatomy of Criticism* (1957), *Fables of Identity: Studies in Poetic Mythology* (1963), *The Bush Garden: Essays on the Canadian Imagination* (1971), and *The Great Code* (1982), the first volume in his project, Literature and the Bible. Frye's long-time Toronto home is on Clifton Rd, just south of Mount Pleasant Cemetery. Northrop Frye Hall on Victoria's campus is a modern administrative and classroom building adjacent to the E.J. Pratt Library.

Northrop Frye, *c.*1967

Kathleen Coburn (b. 1905) also attended Victoria College (B.A. 1928, M.A. 1930) and returned from Oxford in 1932 to teach there, becoming a full professor in 1953; she is now Professor Emeritus. In 1949 she published a work of fiction, *The Grandmothers*, about a Canadian (based on her paternal grandmother) and a Czech woman. She was at the same time teaching and continuing her research on Coleridge, on whom she became a renowned authority—the editor of the Coleridge Notebooks and general editor of the Collected Works. She writes about her scholarly activities in a memoir, *In Pursuit of Coleridge* (1977).

Another member of the English department at Victoria who was also a student there is **David Knight** (b. 1926), whose books include the novel *Farquarson's Physique and What It Did to His Mind* (1971), based on his experience of teaching in Nigeria, and *The Army Does Not Go Away* (1969), a book of poetry.

Poets **Francis Sparshott** and Jay Macpherson joined the staff of Victoria College in the 1950s. Sparshott, a native of England, came to the University of Toronto in 1950 as a lecturer in philosophy. Appointed to Victoria in 1955, he is now a University Professor and the author of several criticial works in his philosophical specialty, aesthetics. Sparshott has also published four books of poems: *A Divided Voice* (1965), *A Cardboard Garage* (1969), *The Naming of the Beasts* (1979), and *The Rainy Hills* (1979). In a humorous vein he has written (under the pen-name 'Cromwell Kent') a satire of the Canadian novel, *A Book* (1970), and an irreverent look at his academic discipline, *Looking for Philosophy* (1972). Sparshott lives on Crescentwood Rd in Scarborough. **Jay Macpherson** came to Canada with her family in 1940 at the age of nine and settled in OTTAWA in 1944. She studed at Carleton, McGill, and the University of Toronto (M.A. 1955, Ph.D. 1964) and since the 1950s has been teaching at Victoria, where she is now a professor of English. Macpherson won a Governor General's Award for *The Boatman* (1957), which included the poems published in 1954 by Emblem Books as *O Earth Return*. Emblem Books was Macpherson's own imprint, which published between 1954 and 1962 a small group of early collections by poets who have since become well known. All but two were mimeographed and then hand-assembled by Macpherson; she also designed the 'emblems' that appeared on the covers of the first two booklets: her own and Daryl Hine's *Five Poems* (1955).

Jay Macpherson, *c.*1973

Macpherson's *Poems Twice Told* (1981) includes an expanded version of *The Boatman*, which had appeared in 1968, and *Welcoming Disaster*, first published privately in 1974. Her *Four Ages of Man: The Classical Myths* (1962) is a re-telling for children. Since 1959 Macpherson has lived in the Yorkville district north of the University.

Poet **Marjorie Pickthall**, born in England in 1883, came to Toronto with her family in 1889. Educated at St Mildred's Girls' School and Bishop Strachan, she lived at several different addresses as a child, including 92 Vanauley St and 169 Markham St. Pickthall became assistant-librarian at Victoria College (1910–12), and lived at 537 Euclid Ave, 102 Charles St, and 45 Breadalbane St, before leaving for a stay with relatives in England. Her first book of poems, *The Drifts of Pinions*, appeared in 1913. Her writing in England included short stories, novels, and verse dramas, as well as poetry. She returned briefly in 1920 to Toronto, where her literary publication had begun with the story 'Two Ears' in the *Globe* in 1898. Pickthall then moved to VICTORIA, B.C.; she died in 1922 in VANCOUVER and is buried in Toronto in St James Cemetery. The posthumous *Complete Poems of Marjorie Pickthall* was prepared by her father in 1925.

Lorne Pierce, the influential editor of Ryerson Press (see 2. DOWNTOWN TORONTO SINCE 1900), received a B.D. from Victoria in 1917. **R.G. Everson** (*Three Dozen Poems*, 1957) attended Victoria in the 1920s and then studied law at Osgoode Hall, receiving his degree in 1930. At Victoria, Everson edited *Acta Victoriana*, the college literary magazine, which was founded in 1878 and is likely the oldest continuously published literary periodical in Canada. Everson paid his law-school tuition fees by writing pulp mysteries and westerns; for six years after finishing law school he lived and wrote in isolation in the Muskoka region northeast of Toronto. In 1936 he moved to MONTREAL (4), Que., where he still lives and where he has written most of his many books of poems. Literary historian **Desmond Pacey** (*Frederick Philip Grove*, 1970)—who received his B.A. in English and Philosophy from Victoria in 1938—from 1944 until his death in 1975 was associated with the University of New Brunswick, FREDERICTON (see also BRANDON, Man.). Poet **Roy Daniells** (*Deeper Into the Forest*, 1948; *The Chequered Shade*, 1963) received his Ph.D. from the University of Toronto in 1936 and taught at Victoria in 1936–8. He then became chairman of the English Department of the University of British Columbia (1948–74). (See also VANCOUVER, B.C.)

Poet **Margaret Avison** graduated from Victoria in 1940, studying under Pratt and Robins. In the 1950s she met American poets Denise Levertov and Cid Corman through readings organized by Raymond Souster (see 7. TORONTO: WEST) at the YMHA at 750 Spadina Ave. As a result many of her early poems were published in U.S. periodicals such as Corman's *Origin* (1951–71). In the 1950s Avison lived about a block from the YMHA in an apartment on Washington Ave, where she wrote some of the poems in her first book, *Winter Sun* (1960). In the early 1960s she worked with Professor Kathleen Coburn, Victoria's eminent Coleridgean, in editing the Coleridge papers held by the University of Toronto (many are housed in the E.J. Pratt Library). Avison has told how Coburn 'sent me down to the women's washroom in Emmanuel College to correct proofs . . . I was sitting there, smoking, and correcting these proofs when this woman walked in and said, "Do you know the joy of knowing the Lord Jesus?" I looked up with a pen in one hand and a cigarette in the other and said: "I know the theory, but as you can see, I'm busy." ' (*Poetry Canada Review*, Sept. 1985.) This was the beginning of a chain of events that led to Avison's conversion to Christianity, which she dates to 4 Jan. 1963; her religious belief is the central subject of her later books, *The Dumbfounding* (1966) and *Sunblue* (1978). In 1964–6 Avison did graduate studies in English at Victoria. She has worked for many years as a social worker for church missions in Toronto, most recently the Mustard Seed Mission, 2279 Yonge St; her long-time home is an apartment on Lascelles Blvd, near Yonge St and St Clair Ave.

Poet and novelist **Margaret Atwood** published her first book of poems, *Double Persephone*, in 1961, the year she graduated from Victoria College. (See 4. TORONTO: THE ANNEX, 6. TORONTO: EAST, ALLISTON, OTTAWA.)

Poet, critic, editor, and television writer **Dennis Lee** was born on 31 Aug. 1939 in the Toronto suburb of Etobicoke. After graduating from Victoria (B.A. 1962, M.A. 1963), he began lecturing there and continued to do so until 1967, when his first book of poetry, *Kingdom of Absence*, was published. In that year Lee was a founder of the experimental Rochdale College, whose converted high-rise building still stands on the southwest corner of Bloor and Huron Sts; he wrote an essay, 'Getting to Rochdale', outlining the ideals of the 'open-university' program designed for the college. Also in that year Lee was co-founder, with his friend Dave Godfrey (see Trinity College above) of the House of Anansi Press—named for an African spider god—which began in Godfrey's basement on Spadina Ave and later moved to Jarvis St. (Today it is located at 35 Britain St and is now owned by Ann Wall; its chief editor is **James Polk**, who wrote the widely acclaimed novel *The Passion of Lureen Bright Water*, 1981.) In 1968 Lee published his second book of poems, *Civil Elegies*; the revised text, *Civil Elegies and Other Poems* (1972), won a Governor General's Award. He has also written *The Death of Harold Ladoo* (1976) and *The Gods* (1978); these two long poems, with the earlier *Not Abstract Harmonies* (1974), were revised and published in *The Gods* (1979). (Lee's elegy

Dennis Lee

The Death of Harold Ladoo commemorates a young novelist from Trinidad who came to Toronto in 1968 and graduated in English from the University of Toronto's Erindale College. Although Lee, and novelist Peter Such, supported Ladoo's writing, it found little acceptance before the young writer's death during a visit to Trinidad in 1973; he is believed to have been murdered. Two of Ladoo's novels were published posthumously: *No Pain Like This Body* (1972) and *Yesterdays* (1974). The setting for Lee's poem on Ladoo is the back deck of Lee's former house on Summerhill Ave.)

Lee's critical work *Savage Fields: An Essay on Literature and Cosmology* was published in 1977. In his books, and in the highly successful collections of poetry he wrote for children—including *Alligator Pie* (1974), *Nicholas Knock and Other People* (1974), *Garbage Delight* (1977), and *The Ordinary Bath* (1979) he makes extensive use of Toronto landmarks: 'And we sit down/in Nathan Phillips Square, among the sun,/as if our lives were real' (*Civil Elegeis*). In 1983 Lee became a song lyricist for the children's television program 'Fraggle Rock', produced by the creator of the Muppets, Jim Henson.

The humorist, playwright, and actor **Don Harron** received his B.A. from Victoria in 1946. He has written several books, including *Charlie Farquharson's History of Canada* (1972), in the persona of his familiar stage and television character Charlie Farquharson, the half-shrewd and half-naïve Ontario farmer given to outrageous malapropisms.

Massey College. Located at the northwest corner of Hoskin Ave and Devonshire Pl., Massey College was built in 1960–3 as a residential institution for senior scholars and graduate students. The first Master of Massey College was **Robertson Davies,** who first came to Toronto in 1929 as a student at Upper Canada College (Colborne College in his novel *What's Bred in the Bone*, 1985). An editor of the *College Times*, like Stephen Leacock and B.K. Sandwell before him, Davies graduated in 1932 and went back to his family home in KINGSTON to study at Queen's University; he then went on to Oxford. Davies returned to Toronto as literary editor of *Saturday Night* (1940–2); in 1942 he lived at 25 Aylmer Ave. During the 1950s, when Davies was editor of the PETERBOROUGH *Examiner*, many of his plays were presented in Toronto. He wrote two masques, *A Masque of Aesop* (1952) and *A Masque for Mr Punch* (1963), for the students at Upper Canada College. His play *A Jig for the Gypsy* (1954) premièred at the Crest Theatre 551 Mount Pleasant Rd, on 14 Sept. 1954; it was the first of three plays he wrote for the Crest. A dramatization of Davies' novel *Leaven of Malice* (1954)— entitled *Love and Libel*—was premièred at the Royal Alexandra Theatre, Toronto, on 2 Nov. 1959, directed by Tyrone Guthrie.

The Bell Tower, Massey College

When Davies became Master in 1963 he and his wife Brenda Mathews lived in an apartment in Massey College. Until his retirement in 1981 Davies taught classes in the English department and the Drama Centre of the University. He then bought an apartment in midtown Toronto; he also owns a cottage in the Caledon Hills northeast of Toronto, where he does much of his writing. Massey College still provides Davies with a second-floor room that houses part of his library, and where secretarial and editorial work is done on his books. Massey's 'Lower Library', which has been named the Robertson Davies Library, possesses a large bust of the author by sculptor Almuth Lutkenhaus. Davies' Deptford trilogy—*Fifth Business* (1970), *The Manticore*, (1972, Governor-General's Award) and *World of Wonders* (1975)—was written in Toronto and contains many local scenes; the model of Deptford is Davies' birthplace, THAMESVILLE. Davies took his setting for *The Rebel Angels* (1981) from the University of Toronto; the novel's Ploughwright College is based on Massey, and its College of St John and the Holy Ghost is based on Trinity College. In *What's Bred in the Bone* Trinity appears as Spook College, and the novel's Blairlogie is modelled on the city of Renfrew, Ont., where Davies lived between the ages of five and twelve.

Robertson Davies, *c.*1981

At Davies' invitation, **Robert Finch** (see University College above) moved to Massey College as a resident scholar, taking up quarters here even before construction was finished in 1963; he lives in an apartment on the third floor. Not only a teacher and scholar but a painter and harpsichordist (he studied under Wanda Landowska), Finch is also a poet who won a Governor General's Award for *Poems* (1946). He has published several books of poems while living at Massey College, including *Silverthorn Bush* (1966), *Variations and Themes* (1980); *Has and Is and Other Poems* (1981); *Twelve for Christmas* (1982; and *The Grand Duke of Moscow's Favourite Solo* (1983). A masque, 'A Century Has Roots', was written for the centenary of University College in 1953. Finch retired in 1968 and is now Professor Emeritus of French; his principal work as a scholar and critic of French literature is *The Sixth Sense: Individualism in French Poetry 1686–1760* (1966).

In the 1960s and early 1970s poet **Douglas Lochhead** was librarian of Massey College and professor of English in University College. His home in Toronto is evoked in his book *Millwood Road: Poems* (1970); Millwood Rd runs east from Yonge St, below Eglinton Ave. While living in Toronto, Lochhead became general editor of the University of Toronto Press series, *Literature of Canada: Poetry and Prose in Reprint*. This period of his writing is represented in the section entitled 'Poems Roughly Divided, 1961–74' in *The Full Furnace: Collected Poems* (1975). Since the mid-1970s Lochhead has taught at Mount Allison University, SACKVILLE, N.B. Novelist and poet **Douglas LePan** was named Senior Fellow of Massey in 1970 (see University College, above). Writers-in-residence at the University of Toronto are provided offices at Massey; among them have been Margaret Laurence, W.O. Mitchell, Adele Wiseman, Dennis Lee, Brian Moore, Mavis Gallant, John Newlove, Mary di Michele, and Al Purdy.

Other writers associated with the University of Toronto. Author, scholar, and painter **Barker Fairley** (1887–1986) joined the faculty of the University of Toronto in 1915 as associate professor of German and taught here—except for 1932–6, which he spent at Manchester University—until he retired in 1957. He participated in a radical undergraduate newspaper, *The Rebel*, which at Fairley's suggestion in 1920 became the *Canadian Forum*. A distinguished Goethe scholar, Fairley published *A Study of Goethe* (1947) and a collection of his own poetry, *Poems of 1922, or Soon After*, in 1972. The Barker Fairley Lounge of the University's Faculty Club is on Willcocks St just east of Spadina Ave. Near Fairley's address at 90 Willcocks St is Margaret Fairley Park, at the southwest corner of Brunswick Ave and Ulster St, named in honour of his first wife Margaret Keeling, who died in 1968. In 1978 Fairley married Nan Purdy, the subject of some of his late painting.

The Toronto-born **Donald Creighton** taught in the Department of History from 1927; he became University Professor in 1968 and was a Fellow of Massey College when he died in 1979. His dramatic writing style and mythic presentation of Canadian history were evident in his first book, *The Commercial Empire of the St. Lawrence: 1760–1850* (1937; rpr. 1956), and both volumes of his biography of John A. Macdonald, *The Young Politician* (1952) and *The Old Chieftain* (1959), won Governor General's Awards. From the late 1930s until 1945 he lived at 63 Alvin Ave; his last home was in Brooklin, Ont. Creighton also wrote *Harold Adams Innis: Portrait of a Scholar* (1956; rev. edn 1978), a study of his former teacher, the University of Toronto economist **Harold Adams Innis** (*The Fur Trade in Canada*, 1930; *Empire and Communications*, 1946), for whom Innis College, 2 Sussex Ave, is named.

Many other authors—a great number of them discussed in detail elsewhere in this book—have studied or taught at the University of Toronto. **Josef Skvorecky**, the Czech-language novelist (*The Engineer of Human Souls*, 1984; trans. Paul Wilson, 1985), teaches at Erindale College; French-language poet **Cécile Cloutier** (*Chaleuils*, 1978; trans. by A. Amprimoz as *Springtime of Spoken Words*, 1979) is a member of the French department; **Phyllis Grosskurth**, who is cross-appointed from the English department to New College, is the author of several distinguished biographies, including *John Addington Symonds* (1964), which won a Governor General's Award, and *Havelock Ellis* (1980); novelist and poet **David Helwig** (*It is Always Summer*, 1982) was born in Toronto in 1938 and graduated from the university in 1960, but has lived since 1962 in KINGSTON. Among other writers who have studied here are A.G. Bailey, Elizabeth Brewster, Ernest Buckler, Norman Duncan, Selwyn Dewdney, Gary Geddes, Percy Janes, George Johnson, Raymond Knister, Dorothy Livesay, Eli Mandel, Farley Mowat, Michael Ondaatje, Janis Rapoport, Arthur Stringer, Peter Such, Miriam Waddington, and Jack Winter.

Hart House Theatre. This 800-seat theatre —part of Hart House on the University of Toronto campus—opened in 1919 under the direction of Roy Mitchell. As the first Hart House director, Mitchell encouraged contributions from many student playwrights. **Merrill Denison**, who had enrolled in 1915 as a student of architecture but whose studies were interrupted by the First World War, returned to the city in 1921 to serve as stage designer and art director for Hart House Theatre. In that year Mitchell staged Denison's *Brothers in Arms*. *The Unheroic North: Four Canadian Plays* (1923) contains *Brothers in Arms*, *The Weather Breeder*, *From Their Own Place*, and *Marsh Hay*. In 1932 Denison moved to New York, and on his return to Canada in 1954 lived in Montreal and at his summer home at BON ECHO, Ont.

The University's Robarts Library, at the corner of St George and Harbord Sts, is Canada's largest library; attached to its southeast wing is the Thomas Fisher Rare Book Library. The two libraries house papers of many writers, both foreign and Canadian, including collections relating to Margaret Atwood, Earle Birney, Ernest Buckler, Leonard Cohen, William Arthur Deacon, Mavis Gallant, Archibald Lampman, Susanna Moodie, John Newlove, Josef Skvorecky, and Raymond Souster. The offices of the University of Toronto Press—one of North America's most active academic publishers—are at the northwest corner of King's College Circle. The Press publishes many scholarly and literary books, and periodicals including the *University of Toronto Quarterly*.

4. THE ANNEX

The Annex is the traditional name for an old residential neighbourhood that lies northwest of Bloor and Avenue Rd and is bounded on the west by Bathurst St and on the north by the CPR tracks; for the purposes of this article it also includes the residential areas interspersed with, and immediately west of, the University of Toronto campus. Named for its annexation to the City of Toronto in 1887, the Annex is a neighbourhood that includes many large houses that once belonged to wealthy families, including the Masseys and the Eatons. During and after the Depression of the 1930s, most of the original residents moved away and the Annex became home to Jewish, Hungarian, German, and Italian immigrants—and to students, academics, artists, and writers. Today many of the largest houses have been divided into rental units, and the smaller houses are owned by upper-income families.

Poet **Dorothy Livesay**, who was born in WINNIPEG, came to the Annex in 1920 and attended Glen Mawr School on Spadina Rd, which was housed in a building now used as a residence of Innis College (University of Toronto). Livesay walked to school from Walmer Rd (first at number 77 and later at 132). During the 1920s and early 1930s she also spent much time at the family cottage in MISSISSAUGA, where she met family friend Mazo de la Roche. Encouraged both by teachers and by her family's rich intellectual life, Livesay published her first book of poems, *Green Pitcher*, in 1928, while still a student at the University of Toronto. She received her B.A. in 1931 and graduated from the School of Social Work in 1934; her second book of poetry, *Signpost*, had appeared in 1932. During the 1930s Livesay did social work here and also became politically active as a member of the Communist Party. She moved to VANCOUVER in 1936.

Morley Callaghan lived in the Annex for three decades, during which he established his writing career and wrote much of his best-known fiction. Callaghan was born and brought up in neighbourhoods east and northeast of the downtown section, at 13 Belshaw Pl. and 35 Wolfrey Ave (see 6. TORONTO: EAST). As a University of Toronto student (B.A. 1925), and a law student at Osgoode Hall, he lived at the Wolfrey Ave address, and then spent the summer of 1928 in Paris, having met Ernest Hemingway while working summers as a trainee reporter for the Toronto *Star* (see 2. DOWNTOWN TORONTO SINCE 1900). Although he sympathized with Hemingway's distaste for Toronto as an environment not conducive to writing, Callaghan returned permanently to the city after that one summer. During the 1930s he lived at 46 Avenue Rd, 456 Brunswick Ave, and 32 Wells St, and during the 1940s and 1950s he lived at 123 Walmer Rd; all are Annex addresses.

Callaghan's first novel, *Strange Fugitive*, appeared in 1928, before his visit to Paris, and when he returned to the city he produced several more novels in quick succession: *It's Never Over* (1930), *A Broken Journey* (1932), *Such Is My Beloved* (1934), *They Shall Inherit the Earth* (1935), and *More Joy in Heaven* (1937). In 1939 Callaghan turned to writing for the stage and radio. Disappointed in the response to his plays—*Turn Home Again*, *Just Ask for George*, and *To Tell the Truth*—he established a continuing relationship with CBC radio. His later novels include *The Loved and the Lost* (1951), which won a Governor General's Award, *The Many Colored Coat* (1960), *A Fine and Private Place* (1975), and *A Time for Judas* (1983). Callaghan has lived for many years in Rosedale (see below).

Wilfrid Eggleston (*The High Plain*, 1927) lived at 39 Harbord St in 1926, when he worked as a reporter for the Toronto *Star*. He later lived for a few years at 78 St Albans Rd (see 7. TORONTO: WEST), but in 1929 Eggleston moved to OTTAWA, where he eventually headed the Parliamentary press corps.

Poet **Gwendolyn MacEwen** has lived in the Annex since the 1970s; her career is also associated with several other parts of the city. Born in Toronto in 1940, she lived at 38 Keele St (house no longer standing) until 1949, when her family moved to Winnipeg. She returned in 1952 and attended Keele Street Public School and Western Technical Commercial School. In 1962–4 she lived at 10 Second St on the Toronto Islands (see 2. DOWNTOWN TORONTO SINCE 1900); this was the period of her marriage to Milton Acorn (1962–3). She was living there when she published her book of poems *The Rising Fire* (1963) and her first novel, *Julian the Magician* (1963). From 1964 until 1969 she lived at 1512 King St W, where she wrote *King of Egypt. King of Dreams* (1971), a novel, and the poems in *The Shadow-Maker* (1969), winner of a Governor General's Award. Another book of poems, *A Breakfast for Barbarians*, appeared in 1966. MacEwen's short-story collection *Noman* (1972) and the poetry collection *The Armies of the Moon* (1972) both date from her five years at 13 Browning Ave in Toronto's east end. During 1972–3 MacEwen operated the Trojan Horse Coffee House at 179 Danforth Ave with Greek singer Nikos Tsingos, to whom she was then married. A collection of travel essays on Greece, *Mermaids and Ikons: A Greek Summer* (1978), was published while MacEwen was living at 149 St George St; translations from the Greek writer Yannos Ritsos and a version of Euripides' *The Trojan Women*, collected in *Trojan Women* (1981), appeared while she lived at 23 Albany Ave. More recent works include *The T.E. Lawrence Poems* (1982) and a volume of selected poems, *Earthlight* (1982). MacEwen now lives on Roberts St.

Gwendolyn MacEwen, 1970

The poet **bp Nichol**, born Barrie Philip Nichol in 1944 in VANCOUVER, came to Toronto in 1962 and has lived since that time in the Annex. He now lives on Admiral Rd, a street that has numbered among its literary residents **Peter Newman**, longtime editor of *Maclean's* and author of many non-fiction works, including *Home Country* (1973) and *The Canadian Establishment* (1975), and is now home to Margaret Atwood (see below). Earlier, Nichol lived at several addresses in the Annex, one of which, a house on Brunswick St, is the model of the house in his early novel *For Jesus Lunatick*. First known solely for his concrete poetry, Nichol began to publish somewhat more traditional verse with *Journeying and the Returns* (1967) and *Monotones* (1971), works that led to his most characteristic and best-known writing, the long poem-in-progress *The Martyrology* (*Books I and II*, 1972; *Books III and IV*, 1976; *Book V*, 1982; *Book IV: Continental Trance*, 1983). *Book V* evokes the Annex. Nichol received a Governor General's Award in 1970 for four small books published that year: *Still Water*, *The True Eventual Story of Billy the Kid*, *Beach Head*, and *The Cosmic Chef*. Nichol and his work of the 1960s, including his early experiments with sound poetry, are the subject of Michael Ondaatje's film *Sons of Captain Poetry* (1970); in 1972 Nichol published *The Captain Poetry Poems*. In 1970 Nichol and three other poets—Steven McCaffery, Rafael Barreto-Rivera, and Paul Dutton—formed the sound poetry performance group The Four Horsemen, which still performs and records.

Kildare Dobbs immigrated to Canada in 1952 and after a year of teaching in the small Ontario town of FLORENCE moved to Toronto. Among his many addresses in the city was 126 Lawton Blvd. Dobbs worked as an editor for Macmillan and during the 1960s as book editor of Toronto *Star*. In 1962 he won a Governor General's Award for the essay collection *Running to Paradise*. Other books include *Reading the Time* (1968) and *The Great Fur Opera* (1970). Dobbs continues to make his home in Toronto, where he works as a freelance writer, particularly of travel articles. He now lives on Prince Arthur St.

Doug Fetherling has worked since the mid-1960s as a reviewer of books and films for the Toronto *Star*, the *Canadian Forum* and other publications, and has often lived in the Annex. He lived for several years through the mid-1980s at 247 Albany Ave, and here produced a selected poems, *Variorum* (1985), and a collection of essays, *The Blue Notebook: Reports on Canadian Culture* (1985). Hungarian poet **George Faludy** lives in an apartment building near the University of Toronto, just south of the Annex proper. He settled in Toronto in 1967 after a long and distinguished career as a writer and editor in his native country and in London, Eng. His works produced in Toronto include *Erasmus of Rotterdam* (1970), a biography, and *Selected Poems, 1933–1980* (1985), translated chiefly by poet Robin Skelton (see VANCOUVER, B.C.). Playwright **David French** lives on Brunswick Ave (see 2. DOWNTOWN TORONTO SINCE 1900).

After the war **Max Braithwaite** (*Why Shoot the Teacher*, 1965) was discharged from military service in Toronto; soon after, he settled in ORANGEVILLE, north of the city. From 1969 to 1973 he lived at 170 St George St before moving to his present home, PORT CARLING, Ont. Braithwaite's novel *A Privilege and a Pleasure* (1973) is set in a metropolitan area similar to Toronto.

Mystery novelist **Howard Engel** has lived for several years on Major St. He began his popular series of Benny Cooperman detective stories in 1980 with *The Suicide Murders*. The town of Grantham in the Cooperman books is based on ST CATHARINES, where Engel was brought up. From 1956 until 1980, when he began his career as a novelist, Engel was associated with the CBC in Toronto, serving as executive producer of CBC literary programs in 1976–80. His other

Cooperman novels are *The Ransom Game* (1981), *Murder on Location* (1982), and *Murder in Algonquin Park* (1983). In 1964 he married novelist Marian Engel. Before their divorce, Marian and Howard Engel lived at two downtown locations: 16 Clarence Sq. (1964–7; the building has since been converted to a townhouse) and 114 Pembroke St (see 2. DOWNTOWN TORONTO SINCE 1900).

Chilean poet and artist **Ludwig Zeller** (b. 1927) immigrated to Canada and settled in Toronto in 1971. He has published (with his wife Susana Wald in his Oasis Editions at a house on Huron St, just north of the University of Toronto's Robarts Library) over forty books by Canadian and foreign writers, usually presenting each text in its original language and in two or three others. Many of Zeller's poems from the 1970s—such as 'Captain Cook's Last Port' and 'The Sphinx in Toronto'—evoke Toronto and Canada; these and many other poems are collected in *In the Country of the Antipodes: Poems 1964–1979* (1979), translated by John Robert Colombo, A.F. Moritz, and Susana Wald.

Poet and novelist **Joy Kogawa**, who is a native of VANCOUVER, lives on Montrose Ave, slightly west of the Annex. She came to Toronto in the late 1970s from OTTAWA, where she had worked for the Prime Minister's office and served as writer-in-residence at the University of Ottawa (1978). Her books of poetry up to that time were *The Splintered Moon* (1968), *A Choice of Dreams* (1974), and *Jericho Road* (1978). In Toronto she published her highly praised novel *Obasan* (1981), based on her experience of the wartime evacuation of Japanese Canadians from the West Coast, and her children's book, *Naomi's Road* (1985), based on *Obasan*.

Novelist and poet **Margaret Atwood** now lives on Admiral Rd, having moved here from 73 Sullivan St (see 2. DOWNTOWN TORONTO SINCE 1900) where she lived in the early 1980s. Atwood's career is also associated with several other parts of the city; in her youth she lived for a time in East York (see 6. TORONTO: EAST), and received her B.A. from Victoria University (see 3. TORONTO: UNIVERSITY OF TORONTO). After studies at Radcliffe College, Harvard University (M.A. 1962), Atwood returned to Toronto in 1963–4. From 1964 to 1971 she lived away from the city, teaching in Vancouver, Montreal, and Edmonton. She then spent two years on the faculty of Toronto's York University, and 1972–3 as writer-in-residence at the University of Toronto. After seven years in ALLISTON, Ont., north of Toronto, she returned to the city in 1980.

Margaret Atwood

Since *The Circle Game* (1966; winner of a Governor General's Award), Atwood has published many books, including nine poetry collections, six novels, two story collections, children's books, and several works of criticism. From the 1971–3 period in Toronto come *Power Politics* (1971), poetry; *Surfacing* (1972), a novel; and her influential book of literary criticism, *Survival: A Thematic Guide to Canadian Literature* (1972). Since 1980 Atwood has written, among others, *True Stories* (1981), poems; *Bodily Harm* (1981) and *The Handmaid's Tale* (1985), novels; *Murder in the Dark* (1983), stories; and *Anna's Pet* (1980), a children's story.

The main setting of Atwood's novel *Life Before Man* (1979) is the Royal Ontario Museum, at the southwest corner of Bloor St and Avenue Rd. **Selwyn Dewdney** came from LONDON, Ont. to join the staff of the Royal Ontario Museum in 1966, the year of publication of his *Indian Rock Paintings of the Great Lakes*, which told the story of his discovery of Indian art at AGAWA BAY, Ont. For him it was a return to Toronto; Dewdney studied at the University of Toronto, where he received his B.A. in 1931. In 1932 he attended the Ontario College of Education and in 1936 the Ontario College of Art. His son **Christopher Dewdney** (*Predators of the Adoration*, 1983), who was born and educated in London, worked with his father at the Museum for several years; he now teaches at York University (see 7. TORONTO WEST).

Immediately across Bloor St from the Museum is the Park Plaza Hotel, whose rooftop bar has long been a well-known meeting place for writers. **Hugh Garner**'s novel, set in the Annex, *Silence on the Shore* (1962; rpr. 1971), portrays the Park Plaza as the Parklawn Hotel, and mentions many streets in the area under slightly altered names; for example, Bedford Rd appears as Adford Rd.

Coach House Press is located at 401 Huron St (rear), just north of the University of Toronto's Robarts Library and across Huron St from Ludwig Zeller's home. Coach House was founded in 1965 by Stan Bevington with editor Wayne Clifford. Clifford's successor in 1966 was **Victor Coleman** (see 2. DOWNTOWN TORONTO SINCE 1900), who spent nearly a decade with the publisher; during that time Coach House became a leading publisher of literary books. Since 1974 Coach House has been edited by a collective that has included many prominent Toronto writers, such as York University professors **Frank Davey** (see 7. TORONTO: WEST) and **Michael Ondaatje** (see 6. TORONTO: EAST), and bp Nichol. Until 1987 Ondaatje was an Annex resident, living at 268 Major St; he now lives in East Toronto on Woody Crest Ave. Ondaatje has twice won Governor General's Awards, for his book-length narrative poem *The Collected Works of Billy the Kid* (1970) and for *There a Trick with a Knife I'm Learning To Do: Poems 1973–1978* (1979). Among his other works are the novels *Coming Through Slaughter* (1976) and *In the Skin of a Lion* (1987), and an autobiographical work, *Running in the Family* (1982).

Czech-language novelist **Josef Skvorecky** (see 6. TORONTO: EAST) operates Sixty-Eight Publishers Inc., dedicated to publishing works in Czech, from offices in a converted house at 164 Davenport Rd; it was previously located at 112 Avenue Rd, also in the Annex.

David Donnell, who won a Governor General's Award for his collection of poems, *Settlements* (1983), lived at Apt 508, 149 St George St, during the 1970s and early 1980s when the book was written. Born in 1939 in St Marys, Ont., Donnell came to Toronto in 1958 and in 1961 managed Thursday evening poetry readings at the Bohemian Embassy; in the same year his first book, *Poems*, was published, but there was a 16-year hiatus before his second, *The Blue Sky* (1977), appeared. Donnell is the author of *Hemingway in Toronto* (1982), a consideration of the American novelist's experience in the city. He now lives on Spadina Rd. (See also 2. DOWNTOWN TORONTO SINCE 1900; 7. TORONTO: WEST.)

Born in 1949 in Arezzo, Italy, **Pier Giorgio Di Cicco** went with his family to Montreal. He later moved to Baltimore but returned to Canada in the mid-1960s, completing high school in Toronto and attending the University of Toronto. He has lived in various parts of the city, including two addresses in the Annex. Many of the poems in his first major collection, *A Tough Romance* (1979), were written at Apt 1209, 35 Walmer Rd, where he lived in the mid-1970s; a decade later he produced his third major collection, *Virgin Science* (1986), largely at 25 Bedford Rd, and at 41 Boon Ave (on the west side near Dufferin St and St Clair Ave). *Flying Deeper into the Century* (1982) contains poems Di Cicco wrote in part at 322 Eglinton Ave E (near Mt Pleasant Rd) in the late 1970s; at this address many writers gathered, including Roo Borson, Mary Di Michele, Kim Maltman (*Softened Violence*, 1985), Barry Dempster, and Caroline Smart. These same writers—often joined by Greg Gatenby (*Growing Still*, 1981), Robert Priest (*Sadness of Spacemen*, 1982), and David Donnell—had been meeting since about 1974 at the Harbourfront poetry readings, at the Selby Hotel (see 2. DOWNTOWN TORONTO SINCE 1900), and at the home of Joe Rosenblatt (see 7. TORONTO: WEST).

Born in 1932, **Austin Clarke** came to Toronto in 1955 from his native Barbados and for two years studied economics at Trinity College, University of Toronto, but left without graduating. After five years at various jobs, he took over the household duties of his home on Asquith Ave and devoted himself to writing while his wife worked as a nurse. Clarke's first two novels, *Survivors of the Crossing* (1964) and *Amongst Thistles and Thorns* (1965), were about life in Barbados and won him international acclaim. His later fiction has dealt extensively with the experience of Barbadians in many parts of Toronto: the Annex, Forest Hill, Rosedale, and Chinatown, among others. Asquith Ave is just south of Rosedale; in the early 1970s Clarke established a long-time home at 432 Brunswick Ave in the Annex. His portraits of Barbadian life in Toronto include the novel *The Meeting Point* (1967) and the story collections *When He was Free and Young and He Used to Wear Silks* (1971) and *When Women Rule* (1985). Clarke was a member of the Ontario Film Review Board in 1984–6.

During the 1970s and early 1980s **Mary Di Michele** and Roo Borson were also Annex residents. Di Michele lived at 396 Brunswick Ave in 1981–6 and there wrote the poems collected in *Immune to Gravity* (1986). Her collection *Necessary Sugar* (1983) was written largely in apartments on Walmer Rd and on Spadina Rd near Bernard Ave. Di Michele—who, like Di Cicco, has written poems about the experience of Italian immigrants to Canada—was brought up in a house on Vaughan Rd near Eglinton Ave and attended Vaughan Road Collegiate; she graduated from the University of Toronto, Scarborough College, in 1972 and was the university's writer-in-residence in 1985–86. During much of the 1970s **Roo Borson** lived in an apartment on Spadina Rd near St George St, and in the early 1980s moved to Spadina Rd near Dupont St; at these addresses she wrote many of the poems in *A Sad Device* (1981) and *The Whole Night, Coming Home* (1984).

5. ROSEDALE

Rosedale is a neighbourhood of winding tree-lined streets and large houses east of Yonge St and west of Bayview Ave, bounded approximately by Bloor St on the south and Summerhill Ave on the north. There have been private homes here since the 1820s, when the area was four miles north of York (Toronto). The district takes its name from 'Rosedale', the home of William Botsford Jarvis, sheriff of York from 1827, who commanded a militia regiment during the Upper Canada Rebellion of Dec. 1837. In the late nineteenth century it developed as a residential enclave of leading families. Palatial houses and meandering wooded streets give Rosedale its dominant character, although the area also includes more modest neighbourhoods.

Anne Wilkinson, who was born in Toronto in 1910, grew up in London, Ont., and was educated abroad, lived at 4 Cluny Dr. in Rosedale until her death in 1961. One of the founding editors of *The Tamarack Review*, Wilkinson published two books of poetry, *Counterpoint to Sleep* (1951) and *The Hangman Ties the Holly* (1955). In 1956 she published her family history of the Oslers, *Lions in the Way*, which provides a lively social history of Upper Canada. Wilkinson also wrote a children's story, *Swann & Daphne* (1960). In 1968 A.J.M. Smith edited *The Collected Poems of Anne Wilkinson*, which also included 'Four Corners of My World', an autobiographical essay that had first appeared in *The Tamarack Review* (20, Summer 1961).

Anne Wilkinson, 1956

Born on 18 Jan. 1913 in Toronto, novelist **Gwethalyn Graham** was brought up in Rosedale and educated at Rosedale Public School (on Crescent Rd) and Havergal College before attending Smith College in Massachusetts. She was a daughter of Frank Erichsen-Brown, a legal insurance expert, a director of Crown Life, and a painter, who was a close associate of members of the Group of Seven. After her university education Graham settled in MONTREAL (6), where she died in 1965. Her novels, *Swiss Sonata* (1938) and *Earth and High Heaven* (1944), both won Governor General's Awards.

Hugh Hood was born in Toronto in 1928. His earliest home, 430 Summerhill Ave, is the setting for *The Swing in the Garden* (1975), the first in his *New Age* series of novels. The family moved in 1937 to 29 Cornish Rd, just north of Rosedale; this house too is a basis for the picture of a Toronto childhood given in *The Swing in the Garden*. Hood attended Our Lady of Perpetual Help School, 1 Garfield Ave, and graduated in 1945 from De La Salle College, 131 Farnham Ave. The school experiences of the *New Age* narrator, Matthew Goderich, reflect in some measure Hood's years at the University of Toronto. After undergraduate studies at St Michael's College, Hood was awarded his Ph.D. from the university in 1955. Since 1961 he has lived in MONTREAL (6). Several of the *New Age* novels, including *A New Athens* (1977) and *Reservoir Ravine* (1979), are set in Toronto. Hood re-created social and business life in 1920s Toronto in the second of these novels, which features as a principal event a dance at the Toronto Island Aquatic Club (the Royal Canadian Yacht Club). Toronto is also featured in many of Hood's most popular stories, including 'Flying a Red Kite', 'Recollections of the Works Department' and 'Silver Bugles, Cymbals, Golden Silks'. Hwy 401 as a symbolic link between Hood's two cities, Toronto and Montreal, appears in many novels and stories as well. The title essay in *The Governor's Bridge Is Closed* (1973) contains a description of the Rosedale Ravine.

Novelist **Timothy Findley** began writing full-time in 1962 while living at 85 Centre St W. in Richmond Hill, north of Toronto, but he was brought up in Rosedale, which has left a clear mark on his fiction. Born on 30 Oct. 1930, Findley spent his first two years at 91 Glenrose Ave. Because

Timothy Findley

of financial reverses during the Depression, the family then moved to a smaller house on Delisle Ave, north of St Clair, but moved back to Rosedale in 1937, to 27 Crescent Rd. This was where Findley lived while he attended Rosedale Public School and Jarvis Collegiate. Findley left school after grade 11 because of poor academic performance and frequent bouts of ill health. In 1948 he worked at the Massey-Ferguson foundry, King St and Strachan Ave, and in the 1950s at the old Toronto Stock Exchange on Bay St. Findley then became an actor (he was in the first season's cast of the STRATFORD Shakespeare Festival) and was away from Toronto until 1962. During 1962–4, when he was writing his first novel, *The Last of the Crazy People* (1967), he was also working at Radio Station CFGM. Although he has lived in CANNINGTON since 1964, Toronto remains an important place for Findley. Especially in *The Wars* (1977), which won a Governor General's Award, he places events in the settings of his youth, including St Paul's Anglican Church on Bloor St E., where he sang in the choir; the graveyard of St James-the-Less on Parliament St; and, more generally, the Rosedale district. Findley's other novels include *Famous Last Words* (1981) and *Not Wanted on the Voyage* (1985). He is also the author of short stories, collected in *Dinner Along the Amazon* (1984), and the play, *Can You See Me Yet?* (1977). (See also CANNINGTON.)

Place d'Armes: A Personal Narrative, published in 1967, was the first novel of **Scott Symons**, born in Toronto on 13 July 1933. His father, Harry L. Symons, was author of *Ojibway Melody*, winner of the first Stephen Leacock Medal for humour in 1947. Throughout the 1930s the Symons family lived at 39 Rosedale Rd, and in the 1940s at 45 Rosedale Rd; about 1950 they moved to 45 South Dr., also in Rosedale. Scott Symons was educated at Trinity College, whose library holds a collection of his papers. He worked first as a journalist, both in Quebec and in Toronto, where in 1957–8 he was a reporter for the *Telegram*. From 1962 to 1965 he was curator of the Canadiana collection at the Royal Ontario Museum's Sigmund Samuel Building and a teacher at the University of Toronto. In 1965 he left the city for MONTREAL (6). *Place d'Armes*—which, like his other fiction, has a strong homosexual content—is a record of his experiences there. *Civic Square* (1969) is a publishing curiosity: its scathing attack on Toronto's politics and social forms comes delivered in a hand-decorated box rather than a bound volume, because Symons would not shape his manuscript to fit a conventional publishing format. Symons also wrote *Heritage: A Romantic Look at Early Canadian Furniture* (1971) and the novel *Helmet of Flesh* (1986).

Since about 1960 the novelist **Morley Callaghan** has lived on Dale Ave in Rosedale. This address is associated with the two latest periods in Callaghan's long and productive career. In 1960 and 1961 respectively he published the novels *The Many Coloured Coat* and *A Passion in Rome*. After a long period of near silence, he then produced three more novels in close succession: *A Fine and Private Place* (1975), *Close to the Sun Again* (1977), and *A Time for Judas* (1983). Callaghan's son **Barry Callaghan** was born in 1937 and spent his childhood and youth in the Annex, where his father was then living (see above), and in Rosedale. Like his father, Barry Callaghan attended St Michael's College (B.A. 1960, M.A. 1962). He achieved literary prominence in his own right with the publication of his book of poetry and art, *The Hogg Poems and Drawings* (1978). His other volumes include *The Black Queen Stories* (1982), *Seven Last Words* (1983; poetry), and three translations of books by French-born poet Robert Marteau, now living in Montreal: *Atlante* (1979), *Treatise on White and Tincture* (1979), and *Interlude* (1982). Marteau has translated *The Hogg Poems* into French. A literature professor at York University since 1965, Callaghan founded the literary magazine *Exile* in 1972 and its book-publishing arm, Exile Editions, in 1975; Exile Editions' address during the late 1970s and early 1980s was the Callaghan home on Dale Ave.

The young Morley Callaghan

Across Dale Ave is an apartment building where the popular novelist **Richard Rohmer** (*Ultimatum*, 1973; *Exxoneration*, 1974) lives. The publisher and biographer **Lovat Dickson** also lived here for many years until his death in 1987. Dickson came to Toronto in 1967, when he retired from his position as director of the Macmillan Company in London, Eng. Associated with Canadian writers, including Mazo de la Roche and Grey Owl, through his editorial work, Dickson grew up in Alberta and graduated from the University of Alberta, EDMONTON, before moving to London as editor of the *Fortnightly Review*. Well known as a biographer as well as an editor, Dickson had written studies of Grey Owl and Richard Hillary before moving to Toronto. Subsequently he wrote *H.G. Wells: His Turbulent Life and Times* (1969); *Radclyffe Hall and the Well of Loneliness: A Sapphic Chronicle* (1975); a definitive biography of Grey Owl, *Wilderness Man: The Strange Story of Grey Owl* (1973); and two volumes of memoirs, *The Ante Room* (1959) and *The House of Words* (1963).

Norman Levine, the OTTAWA-born novelist and short-story writer, has lived in Toronto since 1980 and now makes his home on Summerhill Ave. His books include an account of a trip through Canada in the 1950s, *Canada Made Me* (1958), *From a Seaside Town* (1970, novel), *Selected Stories* (1975), and *I Walk by the Harbour* (1976, poetry). Another prominent literary resi-

Alexander Muir's Laing St house and its maple

dent of Summerhill Ave in the 1970s was the poet and children's writer **Dennis Lee**, (see 3. TORONTO: UNIVERSITY OF TORONTO).

6. TORONTO: EAST

This section of the Toronto entry includes Metropolitan Toronto east of Sherbourne St downtown, east of Rosedale, and east of Yonge St north of Rosedale.

An early literary resident of the east end was the Toronto teacher **Alexander Muir**, who in 1867 wrote the words and music of 'The Maple Leaf Forever' while living at 62 Laing St, south of Queen St E. The silver maple tree in the property's front yard inspired him to write the song, which he published at his own expense. Born in 1830 in Scotland, Muir was brought to Canada in 1833 and received his B.A. from Queen's University, Kingston. He taught for many years in schools in Toronto and in the nearby towns of Scarborough, Newmarket, and Beaverton. From 1889 until his death in 1906 Muir was principal of Gladstone Avenue School, West Toronto, and his later addresses were in that district, including 9 McKenzie Cr. (1891–1903) and 60 Churchill Ave (1903–6). Muir is buried in Mount Pleasant Cemetery and is commemorated by Muir Park, on the east side of Yonge St south of Lawrence Ave.

Morley Callaghan, who was born in 1903, grew up in East Toronto. His childhood home was at 13 Belshaw Pl. (south from Dundas St E between Parliament and River Sts). His family later moved to 35 Wolfrey Ave, east of the Don River and south of Danforth Ave; Callaghan lived here while he was a student (see 3. TORONTO: UNIVERSITY OF TORONTO) and during the writing of his first novel *Strange Fugitive* (1928). In the summers he had worked as a trainee reporter on the Toronto *Star* and had there met Ernest Hemingway (see 2. TORONTO DOWNTOWN SINCE 1900). In 1928, after receiving his law degree, Callaghan spent several months in Paris, but returned to Toronto where he has lived ever since (see 5. TORONTO: ROSEDALE).

Born in 1913 in England, **Hugh Garner** was brought to Toronto as a child and throughout his life lived in east-end neighbourhoods. The Garners settled first, in 1919–20, at 11 Ontario St in Cabbagetown. This neighbourhood—named for the cabbages grown in front yards by some of the English and Irish immigrants who settled in the district beginning in the 1860s—is between Sherbourne St and the Don River, south of Carlton St and north of Queen. Garner's father deserted his family and the novelist was raised by his mother; during his childhood he lived in or near Cabbagetown, on Wascana Ave, Sumach St, Berkeley St, and at 42 Lewis St (south of Queen, just east of the Don River). Garner left school at sixteen and worked as a copy boy for the Toronto *Star*. In 1933 he left the city to look for work and only returned after military service in the Spanish Civil War and the Second World War; he lived at first in a trailer on an empty lot outside the city. Garner supported his family by operating a punch press at Massey-Harris but hoped to succeed as a writer. His first novel was *Cabbagetown*, which appeared in a heavily edited edition in 1950 and did not attract critical attention until the complete text appeared in 1968. The novel was begun just after the Second World War and was partly written in rooms in the building at 6 St Joseph St. During the late 1940s and early 1950s Garner lived briefly at several downtown addresses.

Highly regarded as one of Canada's major social novels, *Cabbagetown* is set in the worst years of the Depression and follows in sad detail the ruined lives of the district's young people, including the protagonist Ken Tilling, whose experiences in many ways resemble Garner's own in his early years. His first published novel, *Storm Below* (1949), is a sea story set during the Second World War. His other Toronto novels include *The Intruders* (1976), describing life in Cabbagetown when it was being transformed by well-to-do new residents, and *The Silence on the Shore* (1962), set in a rooming house in the Annex district north of the University of Toronto campus. During the 1950s Garner became friendly with Jack Kent Cooke, then owner of several publications, among them *Saturday Night*, of which the novelist became an editor. In 1955 he moved to Apt 305, 474 Kingston Rd, where he lived until 1962. In 1962–6 Garner lived in Don Mills, and in 1963 published a collection, *Hugh Garner's Best Stories*, which won a Governor General's Award. Don Mills is portrayed in his mystery novel *Death in Don Mills* (1975), one in a series of books about the fictional police inspector Walter McDumont that also included *The Sin Sniper* (1970) and *Murder Has Your Number* (1979). In 1966–7 Garner lived at Apt 705, 66 Broadway Ave, and from 1968 until his death in 1979 at Apt 1006, 33 Erskine Ave; both these buildings are just east of Yonge St north of Eglinton Ave. It was here that he wrote his late books, including an autobiography, *One Damn Thing After Another* (1974). Garner died in Sunnybrook Medical Centre, 2075 Bayview Ave. His name was given to the Hugh Garner Housing Co-operative Inc, 550 Ontario St, not far from the site of his first home in the city; it was founded in 1982. A current resident of the co-operative is poet **David McFadden** (*My Body Was Eaten By Dogs*, 1981).

Hugh Garner in the early 1970s

Novelist and nature writer **Fred Bodsworth** came to the city in 1943 from St Thomas, Ont., to work on the Toronto *Star* (then located at 80 King St W.). Bodsworth's first home in the city was a flat at 71 Blantyre Ave, Scarborough. After four years as a reporter and editor at the *Star*, Bodsworth went to *Maclean*'s as a staff writer. He worked there until 1955. Bodsworth now lives on Beech Ave in the Beaches district, where he has written all his novels. These include *The Last of the Curlews* (1954), *The Strange One* (1959), *The Atonement of Ashley Morden* (1964), and *The Sparrow's Fall* (1967). Since the 1940s Bodsworth has continued writing non-fiction for periodicals, particularly on nature and his special interest, birds. He is the author of a history of British Columbia, *Pacific Coast* (1970).

John Newlove (*The Fat Man: Selected*

Poems, 1962–1972, 1977) worked for several years during the 1960s as an editor at McClelland & Stewart, Toronto. Writer-in-residence at Massey College in 1977–8, Newlove lived for many years at 666 Kingston Rd. (See also REGINA, VERIGIN, Sask; NELSON, VANCOUVER, B.C.). In 1969–75 poet **Gwendolyn MacEwen** lived at 13 Browning Ave, north of Danforth Ave and there wrote *Noman* (1972), a collection of stories, and *The Armies of the Moon* (1972), poems. In 1972–3 she and her former husband, Greek singer Nikos Tsingos, operated the Trojan Horse Coffee House at 179 Danforth Ave (see also 4. TORONTO: THE ANNEX).

The Czech novelist **Josef Skvorecky** lives on Sackville St, south of Wellesley. He came to Toronto in 1969, having left his native country in 1968 following the Soviet invasion. Here he became a professor at the University of Toronto's Erindale College in Mississauga. Many of his books from before 1968 have appeared in English translation; they include *The Cowards* (1970), *The Mournful Demeanor of Lieutenant Boruvka* (1974), *Miss Silver's Past* (1975), and the novellas *The Bass Saxophone* and *Emoke*, published together in 1977. Recent works by Skvorecky are set in the Toronto area; of his new books, the first to be translated into English is *The Story of an Engineer of Human Souls* (1983). The model for the story's Mourek Inn is the Benes Inn, which was at 392 Eglinton Ave W.; the fictional Edenvale College is based on Erindale. In 1971 the Czech-language publishing house Sixty Eight Publishers Inc. was founded by Skvorecky's wife, Zdena Salivarova, with assistance from the novelist and capital saved from his teaching salary. Its first publication was Skvorecky's *Tank Corps*, a novel written in 1954 that was rejected by Czechoslovakian censors, was finally scheduled for publication during the 'Prague spring' of 1968, and was again blocked by the Soviets. Since then Sixty Eight has become the world's leading publisher of Czech literature; originally located in the Skvorecky home, it now has offices at 164 Davenport Rd (see 4. TORONTO: THE ANNEX).

Three of Toronto's most prominent early journalists—**William Lyon Mackenzie**, **George Brown**, and **John Ross Robertson** (see 1. TORONTO BEFORE 1900)—are interred at the Toronto Necropolis, located at Rawling Ave and Winchester St. Three blocks north is St James Cemetery, where **Marjorie Pickthall** and Stephen Leacock's wife, Beatrix Leacock, are buried (see 3. TORONTO: UNIVERSITY OF TORONTO for Marjorie Pickthall; ORILLIA, Ont., for the Leacocks).

Marshall Saunders in her garden, 1936

East Toronto north of Bloor St includes the borough of East York, and many distinctive districts or neighbourhoods that bear the names of former settlements or of prominent local features; among them are Leaside, the Mount Pleasant district (around Mount Pleasant Cemetery), Moore Park, and Lawrence Park.

Margaret Marshall Saunders (*Beautiful Joe*, 1893) moved to Toronto in 1914 and in 1916 built her long-time home, the house at 62 Glengowan Rd in the Lawrence Park district. Saunders' garden contained a 'toad castle' and an aviary, and she also ran a shelter for lost pets. Many of the books she wrote in Toronto were animal stories, including *Golden Dicky: the Story of a Canary and His Friends* (1919); but she also wrote *The Girl from Vermont, the Story of a Vacation School Teacher* (1919), an attack on social conditions harmful to children. Saunders' last novel, *Esther de Warren: the Story of a Mid-Victorian Maiden*, was published in 1927. She died in Toronto in 1947.

Critic and humorist **William Arthur Deacon** lived at east-end addresses for more than half a century. He came to Toronto in 1922 as literary editor of *Saturday Night*. A native of PEMBROKE, Ont., Deacon had been a student in 1907–9 at Victoria College, University of Toronto. Some of his poems were published in *Acta Victoriana*, but financial difficulties forced him to leave school in his second year. Deacon was *Saturday Night's* literary editor until 1928, when he joined the staff of the *Mail and Empire*. When that newspaper was purchased by the *Globe*, he was hired by the new *Globe and Mail* as literary editor, a post he held until the end of 1960. In 1922 Deacon and his wife lived first on Ontario St and later on Aberdeen St: he settled in 1924 at 36 Dilworth Cr. During his years at *Saturday Night* Deacon published four books: two collections of essays, *Pens and Pirates* (1923) and *Poteen* (1926); *Peter McArthur* (1924), a biography of the humorist for the Makers of Canadian Literature series; and *The Four Jameses* (1927), his charming examination of four Canadian poetasters. Although he did much writing apart from his newspaper duties, Deacon wrote no other book to rival the success of the *Jameses*. In 1937–45 he lived at 66 Parkhurst Blvd (east from Bayview Ave south of Eglinton Ave) and in 1945 moved eight blocks north to 48 Kildeer Cr., his last home. Deacon was active in many Toronto writers' organizations, including the Arts and Letters Club, the Toronto Writers' Club, and the Toronto branch of the Canadian Writers' Association, of which he became national president in 1946. He was associated with the establishment of the Governor General's Awards and the Stephen Leacock Medal for humour and maintained a busy correspondence with his many friends among Canadian writers; over 18,000 pieces of his private papers are housed at the Thomas Fisher Rare Book Library of the University of Toronto. After retiring in 1960 Deacon continued his column 'The Fly Leaf' until 1963. He died in 1977.

The novelist and journalist **Ralph Allen** lived in the Moore Park district from the early 1940s until his death in 1966. Allen came to Toronto in Dec. 1938 from WINNIPEG, where he had worked as a sports reporter for the *Free Press* since graduating from high school at sixteen. Allen was also a sports reporter for the *Globe and Mail* until 1941, when he enlisted for military service. He returned briefly to the *Globe* after the war and then joined *Maclean's*. Allen's relationship with *Maclean's* varied over the years—he spent one year off the staff as a sports reporter on the Toronto *Telegram*; he was promoted from assistant to managing editor (1950–60), and then cut back his schedule (1960–4) to allow himself six months of each year for independent writing. He was seeking financial security and enough freedom to write his novels, which began in 1946 with the war story *Homemade Banners*. Allen's novels include the autobiographical *Peace River Country* (1958), *Ask the Name of the Lion* (1962), and *The High White Forest* (1964). From 1964 until his death in 1966 he was managing editor of the Toronto *Star*. Allen lived at 253 Glenrose Ave in 1946, when his first novel was published, and later at 353 Glenrose. (See also OXBOW, Sask.)

Margaret Atwood spent much of her childhood and youth in the Leaside district. Born in Ottawa in 1939, Atwood came here with her family in 1946; her father, Carl Atwood, was an entomologist and professor at the University of Toronto. The Atwoods' first home in the city was at 111 Haddington Ave, North York, but in 1948 they established their long-time home on Garden Circle, East York—just south of the eastern extremity of Mount Pleasant Cemetery. (Mount Pleasant Cemetery is the burial place of many writers, among them Alexander Muir, Egerton Ryerson, E.J. Pratt, John Coulter, and Robert Zend.) Although Atwood has lived for various periods in ALLISTON, Ont., the United States, and Europe, she has been associated with Toronto throughout her writing career: see 2. DOWNTOWN TORONTO SINCE 1900, 3. TORONTO: UNIVERSITY OF TORONTO, 4. TORONTO: THE ANNEX.

Other writers associated with the UNIVERSITY OF TORONTO who have lived in the vicinity of Mount Pleasant Cemetery include **E.J. Pratt**, who lived from 1922 to 1932 at 25 Tullis Dr., north of the cemetery and just east of Yonge St, and **Northrop Frye**, who has lived for many years on Clifton Rd, south of the cemetery and west of Mount Pleasant Rd. **Earle Birney** taught at the university and lived for a time during the late 1930s at 90 Millwood Rd. After the Second World War he lived away from the city for 20 years, primarily in VANCOUVER, but returned to Toronto in 1965. His long-time home is an apartment at 200 Balliol St, just north of the cemetery and west of Mount Pleasant Rd. His books written in Toronto include *Rag and Bone Shop* (1971), *What's So Big About Green* (1973), *The Rugging and Moving Times* (1976), *Alphbeings and Other Seasyours* (1976), and *Fall by Fury* (1978). In addition to poetry, he has published a book of stories, *Big Bird in the Bush* (1978), and two memoirs, *The Cow Jumped Over the Moon* (1972) and *Spreading Time: Book I, 1940–1949* (1980).

The poet and novelist **Michael Ondaatje** has taught since 1971 in the English department at York University's Glendon College, which has its own campus at Bayview Ave and Lawrence Ave E. Ondaatje came to Canada in 1962 from his native Sri Lanka and completed his B.A. at the University of Toronto in 1966 after studying for two years at Bishop's University, LENNOXVILLE, Que. From the University of Toronto, Ondaatje went to Queen's University, Kingston, for

Michael Ondaatje

his M.A. (1967). After teaching at the University of Western Ontario for three years, he returned to Toronto to teach at Glendon College. Before settling here Ondaatje had published three books: *The Dainty Monsters* (1967), *The Man with Seven Toes* (1969), and *The Collected Works of Billy the Kid* (1970), which won a Governor General's Award. In Toronto he has written several more books of poetry, including *Rat Jelly* (1973), *There's a Trick with a Knife I'm Learning to Do: Poems 1973–1978* (1979), which won a Governor General's Award, *Elimination Dance* (1980), and *Tin Roof* (1982). Ondaatje has also published the novels *Coming through Slaughter* (1976) and *In the Skin of a Lion* (1987); a history of his family, *Running in the Family* (1982); and a critical study of *Leonard Cohen* (1970). Ondaatje is also an editorial board member of Coach House Press; until 1987 he lived in the Annex (see 4. TORONTO: THE ANNEX).

Miriam Waddington, 1981

The Crest Theatre, 551 Mount Pleasant Rd, English Canada's first full-time professional theatre, was founded in 1953 by Donald and Murray Davis. The company presented the première performance of many Canadian plays, including three 1950s works by Robertson Davies: *A Jig for the Gypsy*, *Hunting Stuart*, and *General Confession*. J.B. Priestley's *The Glass Cage*, set in Toronto in 1906, opened on 5 Mar. 1957.

Several authors mentioned earlier in this section and elsewhere in the Toronto entry have also lived in Scarborough or northeastern districts, such as Don Mills. Novelist **Richard Wright** (see 2. DOWNTOWN TORONTO SINCE 1900) worked during the 1960s at Oxford University Press, on Wynford Dr. in Don Mills, before leaving to write his first novel, *The Weekend Man* (1973). Poet **Cécile Cloutier** lives on Farm Greenaway in Don Mills; she is a professor of French at the University of Toronto (see 3. TORONTO: UNIVERSITY OF TORONTO). A long-time literary resident of Don Mills is the poet **Miriam Waddington**, whose home is on Yewfield Cr. Born in WINNIPEG in 1917, Waddington received her B.A. from the University of Toronto. She settled in MONTREAL (5) in 1945 and became associated with the poets and writers surrounding John Sutherland's literary review, *First Statement*. Waddington settled permanently in Toronto in 1960, and from 1964 to 1983 was a professor of English at York University. Among her many volumes of poetry are *Driving Home* (1972) and *Collected Poems* (1986). She has been the editor of the writings of John Sutherland and the poems of A.M. Klein, and has written a study of Klein.

Novelist **Mazo de la Roche** lived in 1939–46 in the 17-room fieldstone and stucco mansion at the southeast corner of Bayview and Steeles Aves; modelled on an English Tudor manor, it is commonly known as 'Tudor Hill' but was called 'Windrush' by de la Roche. During her years here she produced several novels, among them *Whiteoak Heritage* (1940), *The Building of Jalna* (1944), and *Return to Jalna* (1946). (See also MISSISSAUGA, NEWMARKET, 2. DOWNTOWN TORONTO SINCE 1900, 7. TORONTO: WEST.) De la Roche had lived abroad after publishing her most celebrated novel, *Jalna*, in 1927; her York Mills home was her first on returning to Toronto; she moved to the Forest Hill district in 1946.

L.M. Montgomery in front of 'Journey's End', her house in Toronto

7. TORONTO: WEST

This section of the Toronto entry includes Metropolitan Toronto west of Spadina Ave, west of the Annex, and west of Yonge St north of the Annex.

In 1928–9 **Raymond Knister** moved from the Toronto Islands (see 2. DOWNTOWN TORONTO SINCE 1900) to 78 St Alban's Rd, Apt 3, in the Islington district; here he found that his apartment was immediately above that of **Wilfrid Eggleston**, who was then working for the Toronto *Star* (see OTTAWA). In 1929 the Knisters moved to PORT DOVER. The playwright **Len Peterson** has lived on Islington Ave since 1955 (see 2. DOWNTOWN TORONTO SINCE 1900). **Lucy Maud Montgomery** moved to 210A Riverside Dr. near the Humber River in 1936 after her husband retired from parish work in the fall of 1935. Since the publication of her first novel, *Anne of Green Gables* (1908), Montgomery had kept up a steady production of books, both in the 'Anne' series and in the semi-autobiographical 'Emily' series. In Toronto she published only one novel, *Jane of Lantern Hill* (1937). Burdened for many years by the failing health of her husband, Montgomery fell ill in Toronto. She died in Apr. 1942 and is buried in CAVENDISH, P.E.I. (See also LEASKDALE, NORVAL, Ont.)

Raymond Souster was born in 1921 and spent his earliest childhood at 22 Fermanagh Ave, east of High Park; in the 1930s the Souster family moved to 194 Colbeck St, northeast of the park in the Humberside district, where Souster's home has been ever since. He has lived for many years on Baby Point Rd. Educated at the University of Toronto Schools and Humberside Collegiate, he gained prominence during his teens as a softball pitcher; softball, baseball, and the Toronto lots and parks in which they are played, especially on the west side, are recurring subjects of his poems. Souster joined the Bank of Commerce in 1939; after the Second World War he remained with the bank until his retirement in the mid-1980s. Souster's poetry first appeared in 1942—while he was in the Royal Canadian Air Force stationed in Nova Scotia and Newfoundland—in John Sutherland's *First Statement* (see MONTREAL: 5); First Statement Press published his first book of poems, *When We Are Young* (1946), and included his work in the anthology *Other Canadians* (1947). On his return to Toronto, Souster lived at 28 Mayfield Ave, between High Park and the Humber Marshes, where he founded *Contact: An International Magazine of Poetry*, which he edited with Jack Hersh from 1952 to 1954. In 1954 he joined Louis Dudek and Irving Layton in founding Contact Press, which was also edited from his home. Between 1952 and 1967 Contact published more than fifty books, the first being *Cerberus*, which contained works by the three founders. Souster's poetry—filled with depictions of the people and places of Toronto—has been published in numerous collections, including *A Dream That Is Dying* (1954), *The Colour of the Times* (1964, winner of a Governor General's Award), and *As Is* (1967). With *Lost & found: Uncollected Poems 1945–1960* (1968) he began the long project of publishing or re-publishing all of his poetry as a coherent whole; the centrepiece of this effort has been the four volumes of his *Collected Poems* (1981–4).

Raymond Souster

Another literary resident of Baby Point Road was the humorist **Greg Clark**, whose columns and stories for the Toronto *Star* and other publications were collected in many books (see 2. DOWNTOWN TORONTO SINCE 1900). Clark lived at 90 Woodside Ave when he was beginning his columns in the *Star*, and at 3 Baby Point Rd and later at 47 Baby Point Rd in the 1930s. Clark was a resident of the district around High Park for most of his life. Born in 1892, his first home was at 52 McKenzie Cr. Clark's father, Joseph T. Clark, was a prominent journalist who at various times was an editor for the Toronto *World*, *Saturday Night*, and the Toronto *Star*. Greg Clark's youth was spent at 66 Howland Ave, where his family moved in 1903. After service in the First World War, he lived on Indian Rd; at the Woodside Ave and the two Baby Point Rd addresses; and after 1938 at 19 Indian Grove. In 1947 he went to Montreal to write for the *Herald*, but by the mid-1950s he had returned to Toronto and was living at 119 Crescent Rd until 1966; he then lived in the King Edward Hotel. Clark died in 1977.

Best known as a writer of juvenile fiction (*Tikta' liktak: an Eskimo Legend*, 1965; *Black Diamonds: a Search for Arctic Treasure*, 1982), **James Houston** is also the world's leading authority on Inuit culture. He was born on 12 June 1921 in Toronto and spent his early childhood at 209 Grenadier Rd in the High Park district; his family later moved to North Toronto, and he attended John Wanless Public School. Houston studied art with Arthur Lismer of the Group of Seven. During the Second World War he left the Ontario College of Art to enlist in the Toronto Scottish Regiment. After the war Houston studied art abroad; after returning to Canada he went to the Arctic in 1948, and in 1953 became the first civil administrator of West Baffin Island, a position he held until 1961 (see CAPE DORSET, N.W.T.). His writings, almost all of which feature Inuit and Indian subjects, include the adult novels *The White Dawn: An Eskimo Saga* (1971), *Ghost Fox* (1977), and *Spirit Wrestler* (1980).

The poet **Nora Holland** (*When Half-Gods Go*, 1924), a cousin of William Butler Yeats, was born in Collingwood but lived most of her life in the Parkdale district of Toronto's west end. She attended Parkdale Collegiate, worked as an editor for Macmillan, and lived at 26 Alhambra Ave, where she died in 1925. Poet **Gwendolyn MacEwen** was born in 1940 and lived for her first nine years at 38 Keele St in a house that stood on the present site of the Keele subway station. In 1964–9 she lived at 1512

King St, W. (see also 4. TORONTO: THE ANNEX).

The poet **W.W.E. Ross**, who was born in 1894 in PETERBOROUGH, studied at the University of Toronto before serving overseas in the First World War. In 1924 he joined the staff of the Dominion Magnetic Observatory, where he served as director of the magnetic division until his retirement in 1954; by the late 1920s Ross had established his home at 62 Delaware Ave, where he lived for almost four decades. Ross first began publishing his Imagist poems in magazines during the late 1920s; two books appeared in the 1930s, *Laconics* (1930) and *Sonnets* (1932). Recognition of his work grew following publication of *Experiment 1932–9* (1956), a volume edited by Raymond Souster. Ross died in 1966; *Shapes and Sounds* (1968) is a selection of his work edited by Souster and John Robert Colombo that contains a memoir of the poet by Barry Callaghan.

John Robert Colombo has lived for many years on Dell Park Ave near Bathurst St, south of Lawrence Ave W. The author of many volumes of poetry (*Selected Poems*, 1982), he is also well known for his many reference books and works of Canadiana, such as *Colombo's Canadian References* (1976) and *Canadian Literary Landmarks* (1984). Colombo was one of the organizers of poetry readings at the Bohemian Embassy and was managing editor of *The Tamarack Review* (see 2. DOWNTOWN TORONTO SINCE 1900). Among the many anthologies Colombo has edited are *Poetry 64 / Poesie 64* (1963), co-edited with Jacques Godbout (see MONTREAL:18) and *Poems of the Inuit* (1981).

Poet **Joe Rosenblatt** lived and wrote for many years at 15 Greensides Ave. Born in Toronto on 26 Dec. 1933, he was educated at Central Technical School and George Brown College, and began publishing in 1963 with *The Voyage of the Mood*. *Top Soil* (1976), a collection of four books that had appeared in the 1960s and 1970s, won a Governor General's Award. Rosenblatt has also published *Virgins and Vampires* (1975) and *Poetry Hotel* (1985); in the early 1980s he moved to Qualicum Beach, B.C. The novelist and journalist **David Lewis Stein** (*Scratch One Dreamer*, 1967) has lived since the 1970s on Howland Ave.

Novelist **Marian Engel** returned to Toronto, the city of her birth, in 1964 and here wrote, in whole or in part, all of her works of fiction. From 1964 to 1967 she lived at 16 Clarence Sq. and from 1967 to 1970 at 114 Pembroke St (see 2. DOWNTOWN TORONTO SINCE 1900); from 1970 to 1973 her address was 338 Brunswick Ave (see 4. TORONTO: THE ANNEX). Her main address here, however, was 70 Marchmount Rd, where she lived from 1973 until her death in 1985. Two of Engel's works, *The Honeyman Festival* (1970) and *Lunatic Villas* (1981), are set in Toronto. Engel has written, 'I'm always accused of having described my own neighbourhood or house in my Toronto novels. In fact, the house in *The Honeyman Festival* is a composite of houses I canvassed for the NDP in downtown Toronto and I always meant it to be like Mazo de la Roche's house on John St [113 John St: see 2. DOWNTOWN TORONTO SINCE 1900], which I couldn't get in; but Canadian houses fall into patterns. Most of my locations have been composites; *Lunatic Villas* is not Marchmount Rd, it's a composite of Clarence Sq. . . . and failed west-end developments.' Among her other books are the novels *Monodromos* (1973), *Joanne* (1975), *Bear* (1976), and *The Glassy Sea* (1978), and the story collection *Inside the Easter Egg* (1975). *Bear*, which won a Governor General's Award, was set on an island based on ST JOSEPH'S ISLAND, Lake Huron, where Engel summered in 1969 and where she heard a story that she altered to create the novel's plot. The Prince Edward Island settings in *The Glassy Sea* were based on a period when Engel was living and writing at a house in CAPE TRAVERSE, P.E.I.

Marian Engel

The novelist **Philip Child** (*God's Sparrows*, 1937; NCL 1978), who was a professor at Trinity College in the University of Toronto, lived at 40 Heathdale Rd, south of the Cedarvale ravine. This address is in the Bathurst St-St Clair district, where **Marshall McLuhan** (for both writers see 3. TORONTO: UNIVERSITY OF TORONTO) lived for many years; McLuhan's addresses here were 29 Wells Hill Ave and 3 Wychwood Park. Wychwood Park, where McLuhan lived until his death in 1980, is a neighbourhood southwest of the Bathurst-St Clair intersection; it was established in the 1870s as a residential area for well-to-do artists, and is designed around a private road that encircles a pond. The Park was home in the 1940s and 1950s to the English-born novelist **Margaret Bullard** and her husband, who was a visiting professor at the University of Toronto. Her *Wedlocks the Devil* (1951) is a satirical and patronizing novel based on her Canadian experience. Also in the Bathurst-St Clair district were the two addresses where **Ernest Hemingway** lived in Toronto: a cottage on the grounds of the mansion at 153 Lyndhurst Ave, where he lived briefly in the 1920s; and—from the fall of 1923 through Jan. 1924—in the apartment building at 1599 Bathurst St (see 2. DOWNTOWN TORONTO SINCE 1900).

The Nova Scotia-born poet and novelist **Charles Bruce** (see PORT SHOREHAM, N.S.) came to Toronto in 1933 to work for the Canadian Press and, except for a period overseas during the Second World War, the city remained his home until his death in 1971. He lived at 146 Hilton Ave in 1937, 107 Manor Rd E. in 1941, and after the war at 40 Farnham Ave; Hilton and Farnham Aves are south of St Clair Ave, west of Yonge. Bruce had published two books of poetry before moving to Toronto. In 1941 he wrote *Personal Note*, which, like *Grey Ship Moving* (1945), departed from his usual poetic themes of Nova Scotia life to consider the Second World War. His work after the war included

Charles Bruce

The Flowing Summer (1947) and *The Mulgrave Road* (1951), winner of a Governor General's Award. Bruce also wrote prose fiction and non-fiction devoted to his childhood home, *The Channel Shore* (1954) and *The Township of Time* (1959). Bruce was general superintendent of the Canadian Press from 1945 to 1963; he died in Toronto on 19 Dec. 1971.

John Herbert was working as artistic director of his theatre company, the Garret Theatre, 714 Yonge St, when he wrote his best-known play, *Fortune and Men's Eyes*. Written during 1964–5, the play was presented in a workshop production at the Stratford Festival in 1965 and opened off-Broadway at the Actors' Playhouse in Feb. 1967. A powerful portrayal of homosexuality in a modern prison, *Fortune and Men's Eyes* was based, in part, on Herbert's experience as a teenager of serving a six-months term in the Guelph Reformatory, which resulted from an accusation of homosexuality by a gang of toughs at a time when it was illegal. Herbert was born in Toronto in 1926 at 31 Briar Hill Ave; from 1930 to 1939 the family lived at 3 Birch Ave. Herbert attended Bala Avenue Public School and York Memorial Collegiate Institute but left school at seventeen to work in the advertising department of Eaton's. He travelled extensively and worked in many Canadian towns; these experiences are reflected in his play *Omphale and the Hero* (1974). In 1955 he settled in Toronto to study theatre, and during the 1960s was artistic director for three theatre companies, including the Garret, which he founded. Herbert, who changed his name from John Herbert Brundage, has also published a collection of four short plays in *Some Angry Summer Songs* (1976): *Peace Divers*, *Beer Room*, *Close Friends*, and *The Dinosaurs*.

The novelist and editor **Thomas B. Costain**, born in 1885 in BRANTFORD, came to Toronto as editor of the Maclean-Hunter trade magazine *Hardware and Metal*, and a few years later became editor of *Maclean's*. Until 1915 he lived at 16 Lytton Blvd; in 1916–18 he lived slightly north of there at 156 Glencairn Ave; and in 1919–20 he returned to Lytton Blvd at number 22. In 1920 Costain left Toronto to become editor of the *Saturday Evening Post*. He did not begin to publish his own popular historical fiction and histories until 1942; his books include *The Black Rose* (1945), a novel, and *The White and the Gold: The French Regime in Canada* (1954). **E.J. Pratt** (see 3. TORONTO: UNIVERSITY OF TORONTO) lived from 1932 to 1953 at 21 Cortleigh Blvd, north of Eglinton Park, and from 1953 to 1960 at 45 Glencairn Ave, south of Lawrence. Poet **Margaret Avison** (*Winter Sun*, 1960; winner of a Governor General's Award), a graduate of Victoria College, University of Toronto, lived for many years west of Yonge St, in an apartment building on Lascelles Blvd. (See also 3. TORONTO: UNIVERSITY OF TORONTO.)

Margaret Avison, 1970

Born in 1928 in WINNIPEG, novelist **Adele Wiseman** has lived in and around Toronto since 1969, when she came here as writer-in-residence at the University of Toronto. Wiseman lived first on Palomino Cr. in Willowdale and afterwards on Monalova Rd in Downsview. During 1972–5 she lived in KLEINBURG; in this period she wrote her novel *Crackpot* (1974), set in an urban Jewish neighbourhood recognizable as the north end of her native Winnipeg. After ten months in Maple, Ont., Wiseman returned to Toronto and has lived since 1977 on Rushton Rd just north of St Clair Ave. Her recent work includes, *Old Woman at Play* (1978) about her mother, who made dolls; two plays, *Testimonial Dinner* (1978) and *The Lovebound*, a portion of which was published in 1981 in the *Journal of Canadian Fiction*; and a collection of essays, *Memoirs of a Book-Molesting Childhood* (1987). Wiseman's best-known novel is *The Sacrifice* (1956; rpr. 1968), which won a Governor General's Award (see also MONTREAL: 7).

Several authors mentioned elsewhere in the Toronto entry have lived in neighbourhoods north of Dupont St and Dundas St W. In 1946 **Mazo de la Roche** moved from her house 'Tudor Hill' (see 6. TORONTO: EAST), to Forest Hill, a district centering on Spadina Rd between St Clair and Eglinton Aves. In 1946–52 she lived at 307 Russell Hill Rd. Her last home, which she occupied from 1952 until her death in 1961, was at 3 Ava Cr., where she wrote *Centenary at Jalna* (1958) and an autobiography, *Ringing the Changes* (1957). (See also 2. DOWNTOWN TORONTO SINCE 1900, MISSISSAUGA, NEWMARKET.)

The novelist and poet **Phyllis Gotlieb** was born in Toronto on 25 Oct. 1926. Her childhood homes were near movie theatres managed by her father. The Academy Theatre at Bloor St and Lansdowne Ave was built in 1913 by her grandmother, Sarah Bloom, and was the beginning of a family theatre chain, B&F Theatres, which later was amalgamated with Famous Players. Gotlieb attended Kew Beach and Withrow Public Schools in the Beaches district and graduated from Forest Hill Collegiate in 1944. She lived for many years on Chaplin Cr. Educated at the University of Toronto's Victoria and University Colleges, Gotlieb began publishing science-fiction stories in magazines in 1959. Her first novel, *Sunburst* (1964), is set in the twenty-first century when North America has been devastated by nuclear war. Gotlieb examines the human community that has grown up from the survivors, many of whom are scarred by genetic mutations. Gotlieb's novels include *Why Should I Have All the Grief?* (1969), *O Master Caliban!* (1976), *A Judgment of Dragons* (1980), and *Emperor, Swords, Pentacles* (1982).

Mazo de la Roche in the late 1920s

Phyllis Gotlieb, *c.*1973

Gotlieb's first poetry pamphlet, *Who Knows One* (1961), was followed by *Within the Zodiac* (1964) and *Ordinary, Moving* (1969). Her many verse-dramas commissioned by the CBC are included in *Doctor Umlaut's Earthly Kingdom* (1974) and *The Works* (1978), which also contains a selection of shorter poems. Gotlieb lives on Ridgevale Dr.

Irish-born playwright **John Coulter** first came to Toronto in 1936 and, except during 1938–41 when he worked for CBS radio in New York, spent the rest of his life in the city. In the 1940s he lived at 69 Gormley Ave and 9 Montclair Ave. He lived at the Montclair address through the 1970s. There he completed three plays based on the life of Louis Riel. Coulter's *Riel*, first published in 1962, followed the Métis leader's life from the Red River Rebellion of 1870 to his execution after the North West Rebellion of 1885. *The Trial of Louis Riel* (1968) was closely based on transcripts of Riel's courtroom appearance in 1885; the play has become an annual summer event in REGINA, Sask. The third, *The Crime of Louis Riel* (1975), won the Dominion Drama Festival's regional prize in 1967. Soon after arriving in Toronto, Coulter won the Dominion Drama prize for 1937 with *The House in the Quiet Glen*, which—like *The Family Portriat* (1937) and *The Drums Are Out* (1971)—was set in Ireland. Irish themes also appear in Coulter's opera librettos. Coulter worked with composer Healey Willan on three operas, two of them commissioned by the CBC. One of them, *Deirdre of the Sorrows* (1944), retells an Irish legend about an orphan girl whose lovers are fated to die. A revised text, *Deirdre* (1966), was the first Canadian opera to be produced by the Canadian Opera Company, which staged the work at Toronto's O'Keefe Centre in 1967. Coulter worked many years for the CBC; although most of the scripts remain unpublished, Coulter revised a 1970 broadcast text for *François Bigot: A Rediscovery in Dramatic Form of the Fall of Quebec* (1978). Other Coulter books include: *The Blossoming Thorn* (1946), a collection of poetry; *Turf Smoke: A Fable of Two Countries* (1945), a novel about an Irish immigrant's unhappy life in New York; and *In My Day* (1980), a memoir of Coulter's long career in the Canadian theatre. In the last few years of his life Coulter lived in the apartment building at 484 Avenue Rd, just north of St Clair Ave; he died in 1980 in Toronto.

John Coulter

Upper Canada College. Upper Canada College was founded in 1829 and until 1891 was housed in buildings downtown, on the south side of King between Simcoe and John Sts. In 1891 the college moved to its present location at 200 Lonsdale Rd; the campus is two blocks north of St Clair Ave W. and looks down Avenue Rd. Students at the King St location who later became distinguished writers included **George Taylor Denison** (see 1. TORONTO BEFORE 1900; WINNIPEG, Man.), who graduated in the 1850s, and **Stephen Leacock**, who enrolled in January 1882. Except for the 1883–4 academic year, when he stayed with his mother in rooms on John St, he lived as a boarding student at the college. Leacock, who excelled in most subjects and was editor of the *College Times*, graduated as head boy in June 1887. In the fall of 1889 he returned to Upper Canada College as a junior master and was on staff when the college moved to the Lonsdale Rd campus. During his early years of teaching here he lived in city boarding houses—sixteen by his own count—that provided the inspiration for his essay 'Boarding House Geometry', which appeared in *Literary Lapses* (1910). After graduating from the University of Toronto in 1891 with a degree in modern languages, he received a promotion at Upper Canada College that provided him with rooms at the school. (See also 3. TORONTO: UNIVERSITY OF TORONTO: EGYPT, ORILLIA, SUTTON; MONTREAL: 3, Que.)

One of Leacock's fellow teachers was **Pelham Edgar**, later a professor of English at Victoria College (see 3. TORONTO: UNIVERSITY OF TORONTO). Another of Leacock's teaching colleagues was poet **George Washington Johnson**, who joined the Upper Canada College faculty in 1891. He lived in the city until 1906 and was, for a time, a professor of languages at the University of Toronto, but returned to Upper Canada College. Johnson, author of *Maple Leaves* (1864)—in which his most famous poem, 'When You and I Were Young, Maggie', first appeared—lived at several different addresses in Toronto, including 90 Alexander St, 572 Jarvis St, and 632 Church St. In 1906 he returned to HAMILTON Ont., where he had taught before moving to Toronto. (See also BINBROOK, GLANFORD TOWNSHIP.)

A student of Leacock's from 1889 to 1893 was **Bernard K. Sandwell**; the teacher-student relationship became a friendship that lasted until Leacock's death in 1944. Like Leacock before him, Sandwell was an editor of the *College Times* (see 2. DOWNTOWN TORONTO SINCE 1900; MONTREAL: 3, Que). A later editor of the *College Times* was novelist **Robertson Davies**, who attended Upper Canada College in 1926–31; he has written a critical study, *Stephen Leacock* (1970), and edited two anthologies of Leacock's writings: *Feast of Stephen* (1970) and *The Penguin Stephen Leacock* (1981). (See 3. TORONTO: UNIVERSITY OF TORONTO, KINGSTON, THAMESVILLE.) Novelist **Edward McCourt** (*Music at the Close*, 1947) taught at Upper Canada College in 1936–8 (see SASKATOON, Sask.).

York University. York was founded in 1959 and was affiliated with the University of Toronto; it became an independent university in 1964. Its main campus is in Downsview, 4700 Keele St (at Steeles Ave). From its founding it has employed a large number of writers to teach literature, humanities, and creative writing. Former faculty members include Miriam Waddington and Irving Layton; among the current ones are Frank Davey, Barry Callaghan, Peter Such, Eli Mandel, Don Coles, Christopher Dewdney, and folklorist Edith Fowke. **Irving Layton**, the subject of a 1969 monograph by Mandel, was appointed that year as professor of English at York, a post he held until 1978. During his years in Toronto Layton lived at 200 Glen Rd. He published

Irving Layton reading his poetry, with Earle Birney

several books while teaching here, including *Nail Polish* (1971), *Lovers and Lesser Men* (1973), *The Pole Vaulter* (1974), *For My Brother Jesus* (1976), *The Covenant* (1977), and *The Tightrope Dancer* (1978). (See also MONTREAL: 5, Que.)

Eli Mandel has taught since 1967 at York, where he is professor of English and humanities. He studied at the University of Toronto after the Second World War and spent the 1963–4 academic year at Glendon College before returning to teach at the University of Alberta, Edmonton. His first book, *Fuseli Poems*, appeared in 1960. Since 1967 he has published *An Idiot Joy* (1967), winner of a Governor General's Award; *Stony Plain* (1973); *Crusoe* (1973); *Out of Place* (1977); *Life Sentence* (1981); and *Dreaming Backwards: Selected Poems* (1981). Mandel has had an important influence on Canadian poetry through the many anthologies he has edited, including *Poets of Contemporary Canada: 1960–1970* (1972). (See also ESTEVAN, Sask.)

Novelist **Peter Such** came to Toronto from England in 1953. He received his B.A. from the University of Toronto in 1960 and was later awarded an M.A. in English. Since 1972 he has taught at York University's Atkinson College, where he is a professor of humanities and co-ordinator of Canadian Studies. Before joining the York faculty Such had taught at the Ryerson Polytechnical Institute. In 1971 he founded the magazine *Impulse*, while he was writer-in-residence at Erindale College, University of Toronto, and from 1975 to 1977 was managing editor of *Books in Canada*, 366 Adelaide St E. *Fallout* (1969), based on the author's experiences as a summer worker in a northern-Ontario uranium mining town, was his first novel. *Riverrun* was published in 1973 and *Dolphin's Wake* in 1979. Poet **Miriam Waddington** (see 6. TORONTO EAST) was a professor of English at York from 1964–83; poet and novelist **Michael Ondaatje** has taught English since 1971 at York's Glendon College, which occupies its own campus at Lawrence and Bayview Aves (see 6. TORONTO: EAST). **Barry Callaghan** has taught English at Atkinson College since 1965; here he founded his literary journal *Exile* in 1972 (see 5. TORONTO: ROSEDALE).

Eli Mandel

The VANCOUVER-born poet **Frank Davey**, a co-founder of the influential British Columbia literary magazine *Tish*, came to Toronto in 1970 from Montreal, where he had taught for two years at Sir George Williams (now Concordia) University. Here he joined the writing and Canadian-literature faculty of York University, where he is now chairman of the English Department; he lives on Lyndhurst Ave. In 1972 Davey published a selection of his early poetry, *L'an Trentiesme: Selected Poems 1961–1970*. Major volumes from his years in Toronto include *Griffon* (1972), *Arcana* (1973), *The Clallam* (1974), and *Selected Poems: The Arches* (1980). In 1975 Davey edited a one-volume collection of the first nineteen issues of *Tish*. When he came to Toronto he brought with him his magazine of literary theory and criticism, *Open Letter*, which he had founded in 1965 in British Columbia; it still publishes.

In 1971 the folklorist **Edith Fowke**, a native of LUMSDEN, Sask., came to York University's English Department to teach folklore courses; she was made a full professor in 1977 and is now retired. Her many books since joining York include *The Penguin Book of Canadian Folk Songs* (1973), *Folklore of Canada* (1976), *Folktales of French Canada* (1979), and *Sea Songs and Ballads from Nineteenth-Century Nova Scotia* (1982). She lives at Notley Pl.

Poet **Don Coles** (*Landslides: Selected Poems 1975–1985*, 1986) teaches humanities at York; both he and **Eli Mandel** live on Glenview Ave, east of Yonge St south of Lawrence Ave. Poet **Christopher Dewdney** has taught creative writing at York since the mid-1980s (see LONDON).

The novelist **Katherine Govier**, born in 1948 in Edmonton, received her M.A. from York in 1971 and in the early 1980s taught creative writing here. Her works include the novels *Random Descent* (1979) and *Going Through the Motions* (1982), and the story collection *Fables of Brunswick Avenue* (1985), which evokes the Annex and the students, artists, writers, academics, and recent immigrants who live there.

Several authors have been associated with districts such as Downsview, Willowdale, and others in the northwestern and northern sector of Metropolitan Toronto. A literary resident of Willowdale was the minor romantic poet **Wilson MacDonald**. Born in 1880 in CHEAPSIDE, he came to Toronto in 1899 to attend McMaster University, which at that time was located in the building at 273 Bloor St W. that now houses the Royal Conservatory of Music. MacDonald was forced by financial difficulties to leave before completing his second year. During the next few years he published several poems in Toronto publications, including the *Globe*, but in 1903 moved to the United States to look for work. Five years later he returned to Canada, but found little interest in his work in Montreal, where he settled. MacDonald continued to write, and his first book, *The Song of the Prairie Land*, appeared in 1918. During the 1920s he reached the height of his popularity and travelled widely to give readings; his books included *A Flagon of Beauty* (1931), *Caw Caw Ballads* (1930), and *The Lyric Year* (1952). The first of these contains a lengthy poem set in Toronto's High Park, then called Howard Park (for

Wilson MacDonald

the man who donated the property to the city). In the 1920s he lived at 197 Wellesley St, the same apartment building where Charles G.D. Roberts long resided. MacDonald lived for many years at Apt 6, 34 Oakburn Place, in Willowdale, north of Toronto. He died here in 1967 and is buried in VIENNA, Ont.

Edna Jaques, the Saskatchewan 'scrapbook' poet, lived in Toronto from 1939 until her death in 1978. Jaques spent three years, 1942–5, working in the civil service in Ottawa, but for seventeen years she wrote two poems a week for the Toronto *Star*. She lived for many years at the end of her life in Willowdale at 17 Honeywell Pl. (See BRIERCREST, Sask.)

TRENTON

The poet **Alfred Purdy** considers this city southwest of Belleville his childhood home. He was born in nearby WOOLER, but his family moved to Trenton in his first year. (The Purdy family home was an apartment over a dry-goods store, still standing, at 134 Front St.) There his interest in the 'country north of Belleville' was kindled by the tales of his grandfather, Ridley Neville Purdy, a pioneer Ontario backwoodsman. Al Purdy, who was educated at Dufferin Public School and then—after a brief period at Alberta Collegiate Institute in BELLEVILLE—at Trenton Collegiate, began writing poetry at the age of thirteen. In about 1935 Wilson MacDonald came to Trenton Collegiate to read his poems, and the young Purdy was formally introduced to him as the school's poet. In the late 1930s Purdy travelled to VANCOUVER, where he worked in factories and, during the Second World War, joined the Royal Canadian Air Force. In the late 1940s he lived again in Trenton for several years and operated the Diamond Taxi Co. in Belleville. Following a period during which he lived in Montreal and elsewhere, Purdy returned to his native region to stay in 1957, taking up residence on Roblin Lake near AMELIASBURG. Purdy writes of his childhood in Trenton in his long poem *In Search of Owen Roblin* (1974).

The young Al Purdy, Trenton

UXBRIDGE

Stephen Leacock held his first job as a language teacher at the Uxbridge High School, beginning in Jan. 1889, after spending the previous four months at STRATHROY in western Ontario studying for his high-school teaching certificate. Almost immediately he found work at Uxbridge—18 miles from his family's farm at EGYPT, near SUTTON on Lake Simcoe—through the help of his former home tutor Harry Park, who was principal of the town's new school. However, soon after the school term began in the fall, Leacock was offered a position at Upper Canada College in TORONTO (7) and found a substitute to take his job at Uxbridge.

In his uncompleted autobiography *The Boy I Left Behind Me* (1946), Leacock described the town as 'a clean bright orderly little place, dull as ditchwater but quite unaware of the fact'. (See also MONTREAL: 3, Que.)

VANKLEEK HILL

The novelist and poet **Hubert Evans** was born on 9 May 1892 in Vankleek Hill, near Hawkesbury in eastern Ontario. He grew up in Galt (now part of CAMBRIDGE), which is the setting for his autobiographical novel *O Time in Your Flight!* (1979). Evans made his home in British Columbia after returning from service in the First World War; most of that time was spent in ROBERTS CREEK. (See also TERRACE, B.C.)

VERONA

Matt Cohen, a native of KINGSTON, has divided his time since the early 1970s between TORONTO (3) and a farm near Verona. The 170-acre tract north of Kingston is the inspiration for the southeastern-Ontario farm district portrayed in his four 'Salem' novels—*The Disinherited* (1974), *The Colours of War* (1977), *The Sweet Second Summer of Kitty Malone* (1979), and *Flowers of Darkness* (1981). It is a region he first wrote about in the stories collected in *Columbus and the Fat Lady* (1972). (See also HAMILTON, OTTAWA.)

VIENNA

The minor romantic poet **Wilson MacDonald** (*Caw Caw Ballads*, 1930, *A Flagon of Beauty*, 1931) is buried in St Luke's Cemetery in this village in Elgin County. A native of CHEAPSIDE, MacDonald spent most of his life in and near TORONTO (7), where he died on 1 May 1967.

WATERLOO

The University of Waterloo, founded in 1959, invited the poet **Earle Birney** to be writer-in-residence for the 1967–8 academic year—one of the first such appointments ever made by a Canadian university. While at Waterloo, Birney received the Canada Council Medal; published a volume of selected poems, *Memory No Servant* (1968); and edited (with Margerie Lowry) and published Malcolm Lowry's *Lunar Caustic* (1968). A poem about life at Waterloo, '1984 Minus 17 and Counting at U. of Waterloo Ontario', satirizes students for showing signs of conforming to a mechanized contemporary culture.

The University of Waterloo Library houses the Lady Aberdeen Collection of books by women authors and on women's issues. The wife of Canada's seventh Governor General, Lady Aberdeen was instrumental in founding the National Council of Women and several women's service and educational organizations at the turn of the century.

WAWA

While studying at McGill University, **Norman Levine** spent the summer of 1947 working in the sinter plant of the Algoma Ore Company's Helen Mine at Wawa, on the Trans-Canada Highway just north of Lake Superior Provincial Park. Here Levine received a copy of his first publication, the Ryerson poetry chapbook *Myssium* (1947). He revisited the town and the mine in 1956 on a trip that formed the basis of an autobiographical book of travel, observation, and social comment, *Canada Made Me* (1958; rpr. 1979). Wawa and the Helen Mine are

Wilfred Campbell and D.C. Scott

also portrayed in his first novel, *The Angled Road* (1952; see ST-PAUL-DE-L'ÎLE-AUX-NOIX, Que.) and provide the setting for the story 'A Small Piece of Blue', which appears in his collections *One Way Ticket* (1960) and *I Don't Want to Know Anyone Too Well* (1971). (See also OTTAWA, TORONTO: 5.)

WIARTON

Except for four years spent in MEAFORD, the poet **Wilfred Campbell** lived here from 1858—when his father, an Anglican minister, came to serve in the town—until 1880. The Campbell house still stands at 266 Mary St at the corner of Gould St. Campbell attended Owen Sound High School, and after graduating taught for one year in a country school at Zion, a nearby village. He entered the University of Toronto in the fall of 1880. Theological studies and his first parishes took him out of Ontario, but in 1891 he returned briefly to the Wiarton area as rector of the Anglican church in Southampton. After one year there Campbell resigned both his charge and the ministry; he entered the civil service in OTTAWA in 1882 and lived there until his death in 1918. The countryside around Wiarton, on the narrow peninsula that separates Georgian Bay from Lake Huron, is described in Campbell's early poetry, especially in *Lake Lyrics and Other Poems*, published in 1889 while he was pastor of Trinity Anglican Church in ST STEPHEN, N.B. Campbell is honoured with a cairn in Blue Water Park in Wiarton. (See also KITCHENER, TORONTO: 3.)

WINDSOR

The subject of nineteenth-century border struggles with the United States links the careers of three authors who lived in Windsor, Canada's busiest entry-point to the United States. Major **John Richardson** (*Wacousta; or, The Prophecy, A Tale of the Canadas*, 1832), who grew up in nearby AMHERSTBURG, lived briefly in the community of Sandwich (now part of Windsor) in 1839, soon after his return from many years in Europe. Here he wrote *The Canadian Brothers; or, The Prophecy Fulfilled* (1840), set during the War of 1812 and based largely on his own military experiences during the fighting. Richardson moved in 1840 to BROCKVILLE, where he tried without success to publish a newspaper. In 1847, before leaving Canada permanently for the United States, he returned to the Windsor area briefly. His account of the journey, 'A Trip to Walpole Island and Port Sarnia', was published in 1849 in the *Literary Garland*. Richardson—who was present at the Battle of Moraviantown when Tecumseh was killed and knew the great Shawnee ally of the British from his days at Fort Malden near Amherstburg—began his literary career with his narrative poem *Tecumseh; or, The Warrior of the West* (1828), which he wrote in London. Later Richardson often returned for material to the story of the War, both in stories and history. (See also NIAGARA-ON-THE-LAKE, QUEENSTON, ST CATHARINES.

Another account of Tecumseh's role in the War of 1812 came from **Charles Mair**, who lived in Windsor while he researched and wrote his *Tecumseh: A Drama* (1886). In 1882 Mair moved his family to a house on Victoria St here from PRINCE ALBERT, Sask., where he feared an outbreak of unrest like that he had seen in 1896 during the Red River Rebellion. Mair's years in Windsor were devoted to studies of Tecumseh, which included many excavations yielding Indian artefacts but no clear evidence on his main interest, the location of Tecumseh's grave. When the North West Rebellion broke out in 1885, Mair volunteered for military service with his friend George Taylor Denison, but both men were stationed well away from the fighting; in 1886 Mair and his family returned to Prince Albert. Despite Denison's avid support and wide critical praise, *Tecumseh* was not a financial success for Mair, who wrote Denison soon after that he had determined to abandon his efforts at a career in poetry. (See also KINGSTON, LANARK, OTTAWA, TORONTO: 1; PORTAGE-LA-PRAIRIE, WINNIPEG, Man.; HUMBOLDT, Sask.; CALGARY, Alta.; FORT STEELE, VICTORIA, B.C.)

The house in Windsor where Charles Mair wrote *Tecumseh*

Shortly before Mair's arrival in Windsor, the novelist **Robert Barr** (1850–1912) left his home in Windsor to work in the United States, at the *Detroit Free Press*. He spent much of his childhood in Windsor, where his family settled after living briefly in other Ontario towns. He attended local schools and taught here on a temporary teaching certificate until 1873, when he entered the Toronto Normal School (see TORONTO 1); his experiences there form the basis of his most successful novel, *The Measure of the Rule* (1907; rpr. 1973). Barr returned to Windsor for one year in 1875 as principal of the Central School but in 1876 moved to Detroit. There he advanced quickly to an editorship with the *Free Press* and moved to London, Eng., in 1881, where he achieved considerable success as an editor and short-story writer, and wrote twenty novels. The first of these, *In the Midst of Alarm* (1894), was set on Ontario's Niagara frontier in 1866 and centred on the Battle of Ridgeway in which a Fenian invasion from the United States was halted.

The poet **R.A.D. Ford** was director of passports at Windsor in 1940–1. He learned Russian here and since 1968 has been Canadian ambassador to the Soviet Union. Ford's first book, *A Window on the North* (1956), won a Governor General's award. (See also GODERICH, LONDON, OTTAWA.)

Assumption College was founded here in 1857 by the Basilian Fathers and was granted university status in 1953. Ten years later Assumption University became a federated member of the newly formed non-denominational University of Windsor. The communications theorist **Marshall McLuhan** taught in 1944–6 at Assumption College before joining the faculty of St Michael's College, University of Toronto. (See also TORONTO: 3; WINNIPEG, Man.; EDMONTON, Alta.) McLuhan was teaching in St Louis, Mo., when in July 1943 he visited the English writer and painter **Wyndham Lewis**, who was teaching at Assumption College (1943–4). They struck up a friendship and Lewis assisted McLuhan to obtain an appointment at Assumption in 1944. In Wyndham Lewis's novel *Self-Condemned* (1954)—which is mainly set in TORONTO (2), where he lived from 1940 to 1943, and which he hated—Assumption is depicted as the College of the Sacred Heart. Several of Lewis's commissioned portraits of former President Superiors of Assumption hang in the present building of Assumption University on Huron Church Rd. While in Windsor, Lewis lived in an apartment building, still standing, at the corner of Ouellette Ave and Ellis St, and in another, now gone, at 1805 Sandwich St (this street is now Riverside Dr. W.)

Another writer associated with Assumption College is the lawyer and novelist **Richard Rohmer**, who received his B.A. in 1948. Rohmer (*Ultimatum*, 1973) then attended Osgoode Hall Law School in Toronto and since then has lived in or near TORONTO (5).

The poet **Eugene McNamara** joined the English faculty of Assumption University in 1959 and since 1967 has been director of the University of Windsor's Creative Writing Program, which he helped found. Since 1965 he has edited the *University of Windsor Review*, with John Ditsky, who is also a poet and member of the university's English department. McNamara was co-founder in 1973 of Sesame Press and has been connected with other Windsor magazines, including *Mainline* and *Connexion*. In the 1960s he lived at 382 Sunset Ave and since 1970 has lived on Randolph Pl. A movie reviewer for the *Windsor Star* and author of two books of short stories, McNamara is best known for his poetry. Among his collections are *For the Mean Time* (1965), *Outerings* (1970), and *Love Scenes* (1970), *Passages* (1972), *Diving for the Body* (1974), and *Forcing the Field* (1981). Another faculty member is short-story writer **Alistair MacLeod** (*The Lost Salt Gift of Blood*, 1976; rpr. 1981). During the 1970s the English department included the prolific American novelist **Joyce Carol Oates**, who founded *The Ontario Review* here, and the poet **Tom Wayman**, (*Money and Rain*, 1975; *Free Time: Industrial Poems*, 1977). **W.O. Mitchell** (*Who Has Seen the Wind*, 1947) was writer-in-residence at the University of Windsor from 1980 to 1983.

WINGHAM

The short-story writer **Alice Munro** (née Laidlaw) was born in this small southwestern Ontario community on 10 July 1931 and began writing in her late teens. She left Wingham to attend university in 1949 and moved to the west coast after her marriage to James Munro in 1951. In the late 1970s she returned to southwestern Ontario to live in CLINTON. Wingham is the inspiration and model for the fictional community 'Jubilee' in many of her stories. From *Dance of the Happy Shades* (1968), her first published volume and winner of a Governor General's Award, to *The Moons of Jupiter* (1982), stories set in the Wingham region appear throughout her books. Her fictional towns of Jubilee (*Dance of the Happy Shades*, *Lives of Girls and Women*), West Hanratty (*Who Do You Think You Are?*), and Dalgleish (*The Moons of Jupiter*) are modelled on elements of Wingham and nearby towns. (See also LONDON; VANCOUVER, VICTORIA, B.C.)

WOOLER

The poet **Alfred Purdy** was born in this tiny Northumberland County community on 30 Dec. 1918, though he says, 'I never lived there.' He lived throughout his childhood in nearby TRENTON, which he considers his home town. Little more than a crossroads—a sign on Hwy 401 at exit 87 indicates the Wooler Road—Wooler is on the western edge of 'The country north of Belleville', which Purdy claimed as one of his poetic territories in the poem of that name in his book *The Cariboo Horses* (1965):

A country of quiescence and still distance
a lean land
not fat
with inches of black soil on
earth's round belly—

Purdy now lives on the shore of Roblin Lake, near AMELIASBURG, Ont.

Manitoba

ALTAMONT

Gabrielle Roy took the name for one of her three novels of Manitoba life from the town of Altamont, near Somerset, where she spent summer vacations as a teenager on her uncle's farm. *La Route d'Altamont* (1966; trans. by Joyce Marshall, *The Road Past Altamont* 1966) returns to the same family group described by Roy in *Rue Deschambault* (1955; trans. by Harry Binsse, *Street of Riches*, 1957). In the chapter entitled 'The Road Past Altamont' the heroine, Christine, and her ageing mother become lost on a drive across the Prairies and find themselves in a mysterious place called 'Altamont', which Christine later cannot find on any map. (See also CARDINAL, MEADOW PORTAGE, ST BONIFACE, ST VITAL, WINNIPEG; FORT CHIMO, MONTREAL: 16, PETITE-RIVIÈRE-ST-FRANÇOIS, QUEBEC CITY, Que.)

ALTONA

In 1908 the humorist **Paul Hiebert** came with his family to Altona from PILOT MOUND. He attended high school here and, with his brother, began composing the parodic poems that were the genesis of the fictional poetess Sarah Binks, whose 'biography' Hiebert published in 1947 (see also CARMAN, WINNIPEG; LEADER, Sask.)

Each July Altona is the site of the Sunflower Festival, which presents dramas in the Low German dialect that was spoken by the Mennonites who settled the district.

ASHFIELD

See EDEN.

BRANDON

Nellie McClung took the examination for her second-class teaching certificate in the old Brandon school (gone) on 10th St in July 1889; the next fall she entered normal school in WINNIPEG. (See also MANITOU, LA RIVIÈRE, WAWANESA; CHATSWORTH, Ont.; CALGARY, EDMONTON, Alta.; VICTORIA, B.C.)

Martha Ostenso came to Brandon in 1915 from the United States; in Brandon she lived at 716 10th St. She was then fifteen and attended Brandon Collegiate Institute, Louise Ave at 5th St, before transferring to Kelvin Technical High School in WINNIPEG and then enrolling in the University of Manitoba. Her first novel, which won a $13,500 prize from *The Pictorial Review*, the Famous Players-Lasky Corporation, and Dodd, Mead & Company—was based on a year she had spent teaching in a small town northwest of Winnipeg. In the novel it is called 'Oeland'. Ostenso left Canada in 1921 or 1922 to join another Manitoba writer, **Douglas Leader Durkin**, who was teaching at the time in New York. Durkin, whose family had come from Ontario and homesteaded near SWAN RIVER, taught at Brandon College (now Brandon University) for four years (1911–15) after earning his B.A. at the University of Manitoba, Winnipeg, in 1908. Durkin lived at 222 20th St; Brandon College was then at 270 18th St. Before coming to Brandon he was principal of the high school at CARMAN. In 1915 he joined the faculty of the University of Manitoba, where he met Ostenso. Durkin is best known for his novel of the Winnipeg strike, *The Magpie* (1923). Ostenso and Durkin were married in 1945 and eventually settled in Seattle.

In 1941–5 **Desmond Pacey** was professor of English at Brandon College; it was his first professorship in Canada after he received his doctorate from Cambridge University. His home here was 545 11th St. Pacey's influential works of criticism and his two volumes of short stories date from after he left Brandon (see FREDERICTON, N.B.) It was during his Manitoba years, however, that he grew interested in the work of Frederick Philip Grove (see RAPID CITY, FALMOUTH), which became the subject of four of his books.

CARBERRY

The writer and naturalist **Ernest Thompson Seton** lived in Manitoba for only a short time, but he is well remembered in the Carberry district, especially in Spruce Woods Provincial Park, for his dedicated study of the region, which he made the subject of numerous wildlife adventure stories and scientific treatises. Born in England in 1860, Seton left his home in TORONTO (1) (see also LINDSAY, Ont.) for Carberry in Mar. 1882 to stay with his brother Arthur, who had a farm about 2 miles east of Carberry near the old deWinton Station. Until his appointment as Manitoba's first Provincial Naturalist in 1892, Seton observed and sketched the animals and birds of the region, particularly from 1882 to 1886, though he spent most of the period illustrating and writing books in New York and studying art in Paris. Two of his favourite places were the Carberry Sandhills, now part of Spruce Woods Provincial Park, and Boggy Creek, 15 miles north of Carberry.

Carberry figures prominently in Seton's many books of stories and scientific studies, beginning with *The Birds of Manitoba* (1891). Along with Charles G.D. Roberts, Seton is regarded as the inventor of the realistic animal story, told from the perspective of the animals themselves, who are often endowed with human traits and emotions. The animal stories in Seton's *Wild Animals I Have Known*, published in 1898 with 200 of his own illustrations, were drawn primarily from his Manitoba days in the Carberry Sandhills. His novel *The Trail of the Sandhill Stag* (1899) is set here. Several of his important surveys of wild animals, notably *The Lives of Game Animals* (4 vols., 1925–7), rely heavily on his Manitoba studies. Seton's last long trip to Carberry was in 1892, when he found that development was already pushing the wilderness animals and plants farther to the north and west.

Many nature trails in Spruce Woods Provincial Park follow routes first marked by Seton. A bridge over the Assiniboine River in the park is named after him. In 1960 a tract of woodland east of Carberry was dedicated as Seton Wayside Park; a plaque honouring Seton marks its entrance from the Trans-Canada Hwy.

CARDINAL

Gabrielle Roy taught at the public school in Cardinal, near Somerset, during the 1929–30 school year. As a teenager she had spent her summer vacations on her uncle's farm in the region. In 1930 she returned to her home town, ST BONIFACE, where she taught for the next seven years. A story about the year at Cardinal, 'To Earn My Living . . .', is included in Roy's *Rue Deschambault* (1955; trans. by Harry Binsse, *Street of Riches*, 1957; winner of a Governor General's Award). (See also ALTAMONT, MEADOW PORTAGE, ST VITAL, WINNIPEG; FORT CHIMO, MONTREAL,

PETITE-RIVIÈRE-ST-FRANÇOIS, QUEBEC CITY, Que.)

CARMAN

Paul Hiebert and his wife, a native of Carman, have lived for many years in a house near the Boyne River, on a 1-acre site that Hiebert bought for $25 during the Depression. While he was a professor of chemistry at the University of Manitoba, Hiebert wrote his famous *Sarah Binks* (1947; rpr. 1964), a masterpiece of parody in the form of a biography of a mythical Saskatchewan versifier. Sarah Binks, whom Hiebert dubbed 'The Sweet Songstress of Saskatchewan', is based in part on a real Saskatchewan versifier, the prolific Edna Jaques (see BRIERCREST, Sask.) After his retirement in 1953 he continued at Carman to chronicle the literary world of Sarah Binks in *Willows Revisited* (1967) and *For the Birds* (1980). He died here on 5 Sept. 1987. See also ALTONA, PILOT MOUND, WINNIPEG.

After receiving his B.A. from the University of Manitoba, the novelist **Douglas Leader Durkin** was principal of the Carman high school from 1908 until 1911, when he left for BRANDON to teach at Brandon College. (See also SWAN RIVER, WINNIPEG; LEADER, Sask.)

Fort Prince of Wales—an engraving from Hearne's 1795 publication

CARTWRIGHT

Robert J.C. Stead, a native of MIDDLEVILLE, Ont., based several novels and books of poetry on his experience of prairie farm life, which he knew best in the Cartwright area. Reared on a farm near Cartwright, Stead returned to the community after attending WINNIPEG Business College, and from 1898 to 1909 published and edited a local weekly newspaper that underwent various name changes: the *Rock Lake Review*, the *Rock Lake Review and Cartwright Enterprise*, and the *Southern Manitoba Review*. In 1908, while in Cartwright, he published *The Empire Builders*, the first of his five volumes of patriotic verse celebrating the opening of the Prairies. After newspaper and public-relations work in CALGARY, Stead moved to OTTAWA in 1919 to begin a long career in the civil service. He began writing adventure and local-colour novels of the Prairies with *The Bail Jumpers* (1914), but only two of these books are still read. *The Homesteaders* (1916) expresses a heroic view of prairie settlement. A very different theme, modern man's alienation from the land, emerges in *Grain* (1926), Stead's best novel, which places him among such realistic western novelists as Frederick Philip Grove, Martha Ostenso, and Sinclair Ross. For both *The Homesteaders* and *Grain*, Stead drew upon his Cartwright experience. The first describes a homestead family from its arrival in southern Manitoba in 1882 until the pre-First World War period; the second portrays the troubled life of a pacifist, Gander Stake, between 1896 and 1918 on a Manitoba farm.

CHURCHILL

Fort Prince of Wales, the most northerly fortress on the continent, was built by the Hudson's Bay Company at the mouth of the Churchill River from 1731 to 1771. The explorer **Samuel Hearne** was stationed at the fort as a seaman in 1766. Assigned to find the Coppermine River, Hearne failed in two attempts, but during 1771–2 he explored not only the Coppermine but also Great Slave Lake and became the first white man to reach the Arctic Ocean overland. In 1774 Hearne founded the company's first inland trading post, CUMBERLAND HOUSE (Sask.), and the following year was appointed governor of Fort Prince of Wales. Hearne was in command in 1782 when a French fleet made a surprise attack; the fort was surrendered without a shot's being fired—though the French later burned the buildings. After resigning from the company in 1787 Hearne spent his last years in England preparing the manuscript of his famous story of exploration, *A Journey from Prince of Wales's Fort, in Hudson's Bay, to the Northern Ocean, Undertaken by Order of the Hudson's Bay Company, for the Discovery of Copper Mines, a North West Passage, &c. in the Years 1769, 1770, 1771 & 1772* (1795; rpr. 1958).

Today the restored Fort Prince of Wales—lying opposite Churchill across the river mouth—is the centre of a 66-acre national historic park. Near the site, mingled with other names long forgotten, is the legend 'Sl. Hearne, July ye 1, 1767', which the explorer carved on a rock.

EDEN

In the fall of 1919 **Frederick Philip Grove** moved to Eden, in the foothills of Riding Mountain between Dauphin and Neepawa, to take up the position of principal at the consolidated school. His young daughter, Phyllis May, lived with him while his wife Catherine studied at the Normal School in WINNIPEG. During the long evenings alone Grove wrote *Over Prairie Trails* (1922), about his experiences of travelling between GLADSTONE and FALMOUTH to spend weekends with his family, while he and his wife were teaching in different towns during the 1917–18 school year. The family was reunited on completion of Catherine's course and moved to Ashfield, north of Winnipeg, so that Catherine could teach. When *Over Prairie Trails* was accepted by McClelland and Stewart, Grove quit teaching in order to write. At Ashfield he worked on three books, all with prairie settings: *Settlers of the Marsh* (1925), *Our Daily Bread* (1928), and *The Yoke of Life* (1930). By the summer it was clear that Grove would have to return to teaching to augment the family income; both he and Catherine were hired to teach at the school in Eden, which had received high-school status. His contract was not renewed at the end of the year, however, and in the summer of 1921 the Groves moved to RAPID

CITY, where they remained until 1929. (See also WINKLER; BOBCAYGEON, OTTAWA, SIMCOE, Ont.; RUSH LAKE, Sask.)

FALMOUTH

The Big Grassy Marsh district around Falmouth provided the setting for four books by **Frederick Philip Grove**, who first saw the region in the summer of 1917. He was then looking for a rural school where his wife Catherine would be able to teach while he continued as principal of the high school in GLADSTONE. During the summer Catherine and their daughter Phyllis May lived in the small teacherage next door to the Falmouth elementary school, while Grove went to his summer job in Leifur, 26 miles from Falmouth. His later writing recalls these small marsh communities, the first as 'Hnafur' and the second as 'Plymouth'. The trips from Leifur to Falmouth that Grove took every weekend in the summer of 1917 were the subject of his second book, *The Turn of the Year* (1923). In late August he returned to his position as school principal in Gladstone.

Although Catherine was respected for her efforts on behalf of the twenty-eight pupils in her care, she was terrified of being alone at Falmouth, where wolves often approached the houses at night, looking for food. During the 1917–18 school year Grove made the trip from Gladstone to Falmouth, a distance of 34 miles, every weekend, and based his first book, *Over Prairie Trails* (1922), on these journeys. In March 1918 he moved into the Falmouth teacherage while teaching at the Ferguson school, a few miles away from the Falmouth school. Three of Grove's novels are set in this region: *Settlers of the Marsh* (1925), was inspired by a lone white house Grove passed on his weekly trips between Gladstone and Falmouth; *The Yoke of Life* (1930), a tragic story of a promising farm child's struggle to escape the rigours of pioneer life evokes the Leifur area; *Fruits of the Earth* (1933) is a chronicle of Manitoba from 1900 through the First World War. In the early summer of 1919 the family left Falmouth for WINNIPEG, where Catherine planned to study at the Normal School; in the fall Grove went to work as principal of

The school and house at Falmouth

Frederick Philip Grove

the EDEN Consolidated School. (See also RAPID CITY, WINKLER; BOBCAYGEON, OTTAWA, SIMCOE, Ont.; RUSH LAKE, Sask.)

FLIN FLON

This mining town on the Manitoba-Saskatchewan border, north of The Pas on Hwy 10, took its unusual name from the hero of a pulp science-fiction novel, *The Sunless City* (1905), by J.E. Preston-Muddoch. In the book, Josiah Flintabbatey Flonatin (Flin Flon) explores a bottomless lake by submarine and discovers a city of gold ruled by women. He escapes back to the earth's surface but leaves the treasure behind. A prospector who had found a copy of *The Sunless City* on a northern trail suggested Flin Flon in 1914 as a suitable name for the site of his gold claim, saying that he and his companions had come across Flin Flon's treasure city. A 20-foot fibreglass statue of Flin Flon, based on a design by the cartoonist Al Capp, was unveiled in 1962 and stands on a hill overlooking the town.

GIMLI

The largest Icelandic community outside Iceland, Gimli is host each summer to the Islendingadagurinn, or Icelandic Festival, which features readings of modern and traditional Icelandic poetry; the event occurs on the first weekend in August.

The novelist **Laura Goodman Salverson**, born in WINNIPEG of Icelandic immigrant parents, stayed with relatives here in about 1911 while recuperating from an illness. She returned ten years later to collect stories from the town's settlers as part of the preparation for her first novel, *The Viking Heart* (1923). This epic account of the arrival in 1876 and settlement of the first 1,400 Icelandic immigrants in the Gimli area traces the history of Gimli and the other Icelandic communities west of Lake Winnipeg until after the First World War. (See also BIGGAR, PRINCE ALBERT, REGINA, SASKATOON, Sask.; CALGARY, EDMONTON, Alta.)

Two other writers who were born in WINNIPEG, **W.D. Valgardson** and Miriam Waddington, are also associated with Gimli. Valgardson, who spent most of his childhood here, draws on his knowledge of local Icelandic communities in all of his books, including the novel *Gentle Sinners* (1980) and the story collections *Bloodflowers* (1973) and *Red Dust* (1978). Since 1976 he has lived in VICTORIA, B.C., where he teaches at the University of Victoria. **Miriam Waddington**'s family often summered at Gimli; she recalls her experience of the region in the title story of her book *Summers at Lonely Beach and Other Stories* (1982). One of her early poems (in *Green World*, 1945) is called 'Gimli'. (See also TORONTO: 7.)

GLADSTONE

In the summer of 1916 **Frederick Philip Grove** moved with his wife Catherine and their infant daughter from Virden to Gladstone, where he had been hired as principal of the high school—a job he disliked increasingly, until he finally resigned in Mar. 1918. During the summer of 1917 Catherine taught at a tiny rural school in FALMOUTH, while Grove stayed in the village of Leifur. In the fall Grove returned to Gladstone and Catherine remained with Phyllis May at the teacherage on the grounds of the Falmouth school. Every weekend during the school year Grove drove his buggy from Gladstone to Falmouth, a distance of 34 miles. These journeys were the subject of the essays in his first published book in English, *Over Prairie Trails* (1922). (See also EDEN, WINKLER, RAPID CITY, WINNIPEG; BOBCAYGEON, OTTAWA, SIMCOE, Ont.; RUSH LAKE, Sask.)

HASKETT

See WINKLER.

LA RIVIÈRE

The Archibald Historical Museum near La Rivière preserves a log cabin in which the novelist **Nellie McClung** boarded while working in the district as a teacher (see also MANITOU, WAWANESA). Built in 1878, the cabin has been furnished according to a description of its contents given in one of McClung's books, *Clearing in the West* (1936), her first volume of autobiography. Also at the museum is the two-storey house in which McClung lived in Manitou after her marriage there to Wes McClung. The museum is 2 miles east of La Rivière on Hwy 3. (See also WINNIPEG; CHATSWORTH, OTTAWA, Ont.; CALGARY, EDMONTON, Alta; VICTORIA, B.C.)

LEIFUR

See FALMOUTH.

MANITOU

Nellie McClung Elementary School here honours this small town's most famous former resident, the novelist and political activist **Nellie McClung**. Raised in WAWANESA, she lived here sporadically between 1890 and 1911. Before her marriage Nellie Mooney came to Manitou in 1890 to attend the Methodist Church while she lived in Hazel, 3 miles away, and taught in Somerset, 18 miles from Manitou. She spent the next school year at Hazel and then in 1892 was appointed to the larger four-room school at Manitou. After a year of study in WINNIPEG she moved to another town in the area, Treherne, to teach during the 1894–5 school year. The Methodist church in Manitou and the minister's family were constants in Nellie Mooney's life at this time. An active church worker, she joined the local chapter of the Women's Christian Temperance Union with the minister's wife, of whom she was so fond that she sought out her friend's son—and married him in 1896. She recalled her first encounter with Wes McClung in 1891, at the counter of his Manitou pharmacy, in *Clearing in the West* (1935), and described her married life in Manitou in *The Stream Runs Fast* (1945). The couple first lived in a four-room apartment above the drugstore and later bought a house to accommodate their growing family. The house still exists; it has been moved to the Archibald Historical Museum, west of here on Hwy 3. For several years McClung was busy with household duties and her children, but in about 1905 she acceded to her mother-in-law's urgings and began to write *Sowing Seeds in Danny* (1908), a story of the Souris River country. After Wes sold his drugstore in 1911 the family moved to WINNIPEG, where Nellie McClung became active in politics. (See also LA RIVIÈRE; CHATSWORTH, OTTAWA, Ont.; CALGARY, EDMONTON, Alta.; VICTORIA, B.C.)

Nellie McClung in 1908

MEADOW PORTAGE

This tiny (sometimes uninhabited) village is the nearest settlement to Petite-Poule-d'Eau island in Lake Winnipegosis, where the novelist **Gabrielle Roy** taught in July and Aug. 1937. This experience eventually formed the basis of *La Petite Poule d'eau* (1950; trans. by Harry Binsse, *Where Nests the Water Hen*, 1950). North of Riding Mountain National Park, Meadow Portage is opposite Winnipegosis, on the southeastern shore of the lake. In June 1937 Roy had completed her last year of teaching at the Institut Collégial Provencher in ST BONIFACE and was planning to study drama in England in the fall. To earn additional money for her trip she joined a Manitoba provincial program to teach summer school in this remote area; her salary was $5 a day for the two months. Arriving at isolated Meadow Portage, after a difficult trip, she was at first taken aback to find that 'this was not my post: this was the *village*, this was a *big* place; my appointment was to the island, eighteen miles farther away.' Although it was her first experience of the wilderness and of life untouched by city influences, it remained dormant within her for ten years, when the landscape—'a place intact, as if only just emerged from the Creator's dream'—suddenly returned to her mind and gave rise to the novel. Roy also evokes her experience at Petite-Poule-d'Eau island in an essay, 'Memory and Creation', included in her *Fragiles lumières de la terre* (1978; trans. by Alan Brown, *The Fragile Lights of Earth*, 1982). (See also ALTAMONT, CARDINAL, ST VITAL, WINNIPEG; FORT CHIMO, MONTREAL: 16, PETITE-RIVIÈRE-ST-FRANÇOIS, QUEBEC CITY, Que.)

NEEPAWA

Neepawa, in hill country about 125 miles west and north of Winnipeg, was the birthplace of **Margaret Laurence** who was born Jean Margaret Wemyss on 18 July 1926. Laurence's mother died when she was four; her mother's sister came to live with the family and eventually married Laurence's father. The relationship between Laurence and her stepmother was a close one; her stepmother was Neepawa's first librarian and encouraged the child's love of books and first efforts at writing. Laurence attended the inaugural service at Knox Presbyterian Church (now the Neepawa United Church) when she was eight. The family lived in a house on the northeast corner of Mountain and Vivian Sts and had a cottage at Riding Mountain on Clear Lake. (See also RIDING MOUNTAIN NATIONAL PARK.) In 1936 Laurence's father died and (with her stepmother and her adopted brother Robert) she moved into the house (at 312 First Ave) of her Grandfather Simpson, the town undertaker, who was a powerful force in her life and later a model for important characters in her fictional portrayal of the town. Laurence attended Neepawa Central School (a cairn marks the place where it stood) and Neepawa Collegiate Institute (now Viscount School), where she was editor of the school paper for three years. She was also active in drama, in the school orchestra, and on sports teams. Her first published story, 'The Case of the Blonde Butcher', appeared when she was twelve on the Young Writers' Page of the *Winnipeg Free Press*. In her teens Laurence filled 5¢ scribblers with stories and poems, many of them set in a town she called 'Manawaka'. Her fictional town shared many of the features of Neepawa: the river, the cemetery on the hill, her grandfather's brick house. A scholarship to United College in WINNIPEG marked her permanent departure from Neepawa. She visited it, however, in 1967 while in Manitoba to receive the title of honorary fellow at United College, Winnipeg. Her grandfather was Neepawa's oldest citizen when he died in 1953 at the age of ninety-seven.

Margaret Laurence immortalized her home town in her five-book 'Manawaka' Cycle: *The Stone Angel* (1961), *A Jest of God* (1966), *The Fire-Dwellers* (1969), *A Bird in the House* (1970), and *The Diviners* (1974). Although, like many of her heroines, Laurence left the small town behind, Neepawa remained with her: 'Because that settlement and that land were my first and for many years my only real knowledge of this planet, in some profound way, they remain my world, my way of viewing. My eyes were formed there.' Laurence named her cottage on the Otonabee River, near LAKEFIELD, Ont., for her fictional town. (See also PETERBOROUGH, Ont.; VANCOUVER, B.C.)

The poet **Dale Zieroth** was born in Neepawa in 1946 and also attended Neepawa Collegiate. After a brief time at the University of Manitoba he went to Toronto; since 1973 he has lived in British Columbia, with which his work is primarily associated. He is the author of *Clearings: Poems from a Journey* (1973) and *Mid-river* (1981). (See also VANCOUVER, B.C.)

NORWAY HOUSE

The Methodist missionary **James Evans**, who invented an alphabet for the Cree language that is still in use today, came to Norway House in 1840 as general superintendent of the northwest missions. When Evans arrived Norway House had assumed its final form, after a fire in 1824 had made rebuilding necessary; some of the buildings Evans knew are still standing. Located north of Lake Winnipeg at the mouth of the Jack River, it was a trading post of the Hudson's Bay Company, which first built in the area in 1796 to counter a Northwest Company post founded the year before. Wishing to separate his work from the Hudson's Bay Company, Evans built a church and school in a nearby settlement called Rossville. (In Evans's time Rossville—named for Dan Ross, the Hudson's Bay Company factor and a friend of Evans—was a residential community that had sprung up adjacent to the Company's Norway House post. Today the sites of both Norway House and Rossville are within the Norway House Indian Reserve.) At Rossville, Evans devised an alphabet, using nine basic symbols, that provided letters corresponding to the thirty-six basic sounds in the Cree language. His Indian pupils, children and adults alike, mastered it easily. In 1841 Evans printed his *Cree Syllabic Hymn Book*, the first book to use the new alphabet. (Evans had fashioned type from melted bullets poured into hand-carved moulds.) Its sixteen birchbark pages—containing the text of Bible passages and hymns —were bound with deerskin. Evans had become interested in translating Scripture into Indian languages before coming to Norway House. A native of England, he arrived in Canada in 1823 and taught in the Methodist missions near KEENE, Ont., at Rice Lake, in 1828. Ordained in 1833, he published a grammar of the Ojibwa language in 1837. Evans had reduced the language to eight consonants and four vowels and used this experimental alphabet in his teaching. Lack of support for his desire to publish translations of Ojibawa prevented him from making the attempt in Ontario. Evans' career at Norway House came to an end when he was accused of immorality by another clergyman. Although he was cleared of the charges, he returned to England, where he was widely accepted as a preacher and lecturer. At his death in 1846 he was buried in Kingston-on-Hull, England, but in 1955 his ashes were brought to Rossville Cemetery for burial. His church was destroyed by fire in the 1930s and replaced in the 1940s with the James Evans Memorial United Church in Rossville.

During the same period the Scottish novelist **R.M. Ballantyne** was at Norway House as a young employee of the Hudson's Bay Company. The author of *Hudson Bay: or, Every-day Life in the Wilds of North America, during Six Years' Residence in the Territories of the Honourable Hudson Bay Company* (1848) was stationed here from 1841, when he was sixteen, to 1843, when he went to York Factory. He returned briefly in 1845 on a journey east to Sept-Îles, Que., where he completed service for the Company and wrote the story of his western years, in 1847. After returning to Scotland, Ballantyne established himself as an author of boys' adventure stories; among those with Canadian settings is *Snowflakes and Sunbeams; or, The Young Fur Traders. A Tale of the Far North* (1856). (See also WINNIPEG; FORT CHIMO, Que.) **Egerton Ryerson Young**, a Methodist missionary to the Crees who was at Norway House for twenty years (1868–88), also made literary use of his experience here in his book *Stories from Indian Wigwams and Northern Camp-Fires* (1893).

PILOT MOUND

The humorist **Paul Hiebert** was born here on 17 July 1892; his father owned a general store, and Paul sometimes tended the counter. In 1908 the family moved to ALTONA, 60 miles east, where he attended high school before beginning his studies at the University of Manitoba in WINNIPEG. He went on to become a professor of chemistry there and to write his famous *Sarah Binks* (1947; rpr. 1964), a parodic biography of a fictional Saskatchewan versifier. He retired to CARMAN in 1953.

POPLAR POINT

Poplar Point, on Hwy 26 northwest of Winnipeg, is the model for the Manitoba town vividly described in **Bertram Brooker**'s psychological novel *Think of the Earth* (1936). Although Brooker, who was born in England in 1888, spent most of his life in TORONTO ( ), where he was an illustrator as well as a writer, he came to Canada as a youth, worked on railway construction in Manitoba, and lived for several years in Poplar Point. *Think of the Earth*, which tells of a mystic who visits a prairie community and experiences visions that convey the author's philosophy of universal purpose in nature and human affairs, received the first Governor General's Award for fiction. Brooker's other novels are *The Tangled Miracle* (1922) and *The Robber* (1949). (See also TORONTO (2), Ont.

PORTAGE-LA-PRAIRIE

Charles Mair (*Dreamland and Other Poems*, 1868) moved his family here from WINNIPEG in 1871, following the Red River Rebellion. In 1873 he donated a three-acre lot for a church, but in 1877 he moved west to PRINCE ALBERT, Sask., in search of a more promising settlement. (See also LANARK, Ont.; VICTORIA, B.C.)

RAPID CITY

A provincial plaque at the Rapid City Museum and Cultural Centre honours the prairie novelist **Frederick Philip Grove**, who lived here from 1921 to 1929 and is buried in the city's cemetery. His house still

The school in Rapid City where Mrs Grove taught

stands on 3rd Ave W.; it can be pointed out by local residents. Of his homes in Manitoba, Rapid City was Grove's last and longest, but like the others it was marked by career troubles and personal trials. In the summer of 1921, after the high school in EDEN failed to rehire him, Grove came to Rapid City to be principal of *its* high school; his wife Catherine was hired as teacher of senior public-school grades. The school was a large brick building one block south of Main St. Now the city museum, it bears a historical plaque in Grove's memory and houses displays pertaining to the Groves. Grove resigned in a discipline dispute in Nov. 1923 but was rehired in January to finish the school year. This was his last teaching position; Catherine became principal of the high school in the fall of 1924, while Grove devoted himself to writing and, beginning in 1926, lecturing. He had received his B.A. from the University of Manitoba in 1922, majoring in German and French. In the same year his first book, *Over Prairie Trails*, was published. Five other books followed in quick succession: *The Turn of the Year* (1923); *Settlers of the Marsh* (1925), the setting of which is based on Rapid City; *A Search for America* (1927); *Our Daily Bread* (1928); and *It Needs to Be Said* (1929). In the fall of 1929 the Groves decided to leave Rapid City, partly because of a promise of editorial work with Macmillan in Toronto, but also because this town held the bitter memory of the death of their daughter, Phyllis May, in the summer of 1927. She was buried in the hillside cemetery where twenty years later her father's body was brought after he died in SIMCOE, Ont., in 1948; for her gravestone Grove adapted a line from Shelley's 'Adonais': 'She is a portion of the loveliness/ Which once she made more lovely.' In a poem written soon after May's death, Grove wrote, 'My roots are growing down into a grave.' The author's burial place is marked by a granite tombstone; the two graves are in the southwest corner of the Rapid City Burial Ground. (See also FALMOUTH, GLADSTONE, WINKLER, WINNIPEG; BOBCAYGEON, OTTAWA, Ont.; RUSH LAKE, Sask.)

The Grove house in Rapid City

RIDING MOUNTAIN NATIONAL PARK

Riding Mountain (altitude 2,480 feet) is the centre of this 1,150-square-mile conservation area, which was established in 1930. The park, 150 miles northwest of Winnipeg, provides camping and sports facilities. **Grey Owl** (Archibald Stansfeld Belaney), the nature writer who spent the last six years of his life in Saskatchewan's PRINCE ALBERT NATIONAL PARK, was instrumental in establishing a beaver-conservation area here. A cabin used by Grey Owl in 1930 still stands at Beaver Lodge Lake, northwest of Wasagaming. (See also CABANO,Que.; COBALT, TEMAGAMI, Ont.)

The family of the novelist **Margaret Laurence**, who was born in NEEPAWA, had a cottage on Clear Lake, near Riding Mountain. The site appears in Laurence's fiction as Diamond Lake in the Galloping Mountains. Following their marriage in 1944, Margaret and her husband Jack Laurence spent their honeymoon at Clear Lake. (See also WINNIPEG; LAKEFIELD, PETERBOROUGH, Ont.; VANCOUVER, B.C.)

ST BONIFACE

The novelist **Gabrielle Roy** was born on 22 Mar. 1909 at 375 rue Deschambault in St Boniface, east of the Red River across from WINNIPEG and now part of that city's metropolitan area. Roy's father, Léon Roy, was a Dominion-government colonizing agent who helped settle Doukhobors and Ruthenians, among other groups, in the Prairie Provinces. Gabrielle was the youngest of eleven children living in the three-storey frame house built by her father in 1905 and still standing. She has made the house famous with her novel, *Rue Deschambault* (1955; trans. by Harry Binsse, *Street of Riches*, 1957; winner of a Governor General's Award). Her mother disapproved of Gabrielle's early efforts to write. Hesitating for many years before attempting to pursue writing as a career, Roy was educated in Winnipeg as a schoolteacher. She first taught for one month during the summer of 1929 at Marchand—about which she wrote a story published in *Cet été qui chantait* (1972; trans. by Joyce Marshall, *Enchanted Summer*, 1976)—and then for a year at CARDINAL. She returned to St Boniface in 1930 to begin seven years at the Provencher Institute, a bilingual school where she taught a class of six- and seven-year-old boys. During her teaching years Roy participated in theatre groups in St Boniface and Winnipeg. Twice she was a member of the 'Le Cercle Molière' troupe when it won the Bessborough Trophy for the best French production in the Dominion Drama Festival. She saved money for travel in Europe and left St Boniface in 1937 in order to study acting. In 1939, on the eve of the Second World War, she returned to Canada, but to MONTREAL (16) rather than to her native city; there she became a journalist and published her first novel, *Bonheur d'occasion* (1945; trans. by Hanna Josephson, *The Tin Flute*, 1947; retrans. by Alan Brown, 1980), which won a Governor General's Award in 1947. A visit home in 1947 led to her marriage that year to Dr Marcel Carbotte in ST VITAL, near St Boniface.

Roy's Manitoba youth and teaching years figure prominently in her writing, although all of her books and stories about Manitoba date from the time when she had taken up permanent residence in Quebec. Her novel *Rue Deschambault*, a series of episodes tracing the experiences and development of a young girl named Christine, grew out of her childhood in St Boniface. Other Manitoba novels by Roy are *La Route d'Altamont* (1966; trans. by Joyce Marshall, *The Road Past Altamont*, 1966) and *La Petite Poule d'eau* (1950; trans. by Harry Binsse, *Where Nests the Water Hen*, 1950; rpr. 1966), which is based on a summer Roy spent teaching near MEADOW PORTAGE. (See also ALTAMONT; PETITE-RIVIÈRE-ST-FRANÇOIS, QUEBEC CITY, Que.)

On 22 Oct. 1844 **Louis Riel** was born at St Boniface. His father, Louis Riel, Sr., a miller and leader in the Métis community, built a flour mill on the Seine River in St Vital parish, just south of St Boniface, which is now part of metropolitan Winnipeg. (The Riel family's log cabin in St Vital stands at 330 River Rd and is now a public museum commemorating the Riels and Lagimodières—Riel's mother's family.

Riel's writings can be found in *The Collected Writings of Louis Riel/Les Écrits complets de Louis Riel* (5 vols, 1985), which includes three volumes of political writings

The Cathedral of St Boniface; Riel's grave is to the left

and letters and a volume of poems, a few of which are in English. Riel's first poetry dates from his student days in MONTREAL (9), where he lived in 1858–65. He was chosen to study in Montreal by Bishop Alexandre Taché, who had noted Riel's academic achievement under the Grey Nuns and the Christian Brothers in their schools in St Boniface. The Grey Nuns' building, where Riel began his education in 1853, is now a museum; it is located on Taché Ave just south of the St Boniface Cathedral. Built in 1848, it is the oldest building in Winnipeg.

After leaving the Collège de Montréal, Riel spent 1866–8 in Chicago and Minnesota; in Chicago he is supposed to have stayed with the Quebec poet Louis Fréchette and written poetry under Fréchette's tutelage, but none of this work survives. He returned to St Boniface on 26 July 1868 and soon after assumed leadership of the Métis cause: he directed the Red River Rebellion and the Métis provisional government of 1869–70 (See WINNIPEG). Several of his writings date from this period, including ballads in the style of Pierre Falcon, the 'troubadour of the North West', who had celebrated the Battle of Seven Oaks and the Métis cause fifty years earlier (see SWAN RIVER, WINNIPEG, ST FRANÇOIS XAVIER).

The rest of Riel's writings come from the periods he spent in North Dakota, Quebec, and the northeastern United States (1870–8), in Minnesota, North Dakota, and Montana (1878–84), and in REGINA, Sask. (from May to Nov. 1885), where he wrote prolifically while imprisoned for leading the Northwest Rebellion of 1885. After Riel was hanged at Regina on 16 Nov. his body was brought to St Vital and lay in state in the Riel family home there. He was buried on 12 Dec. in the St Boniface Cathedral churchyard, where his monument can be seen. Also on display outside the Cathedral are grindstones from the St Vital mill of Louis Riel Sr. (See also ST VITAL; BATOCHE, REGINA, Sask.)

ST CLAUDE

From 1903 to 1914 the French man-of-letters **Maurice Constantin-Weyer** was a cattle rancher and jack-of-all trades at St Claude. Born in France in 1888, he immigrated to Canada when he could no longer afford to study at the Sorbonne. Here he married a Métis woman from whom he later separated, then returned to France to fight in the First World War. After the war, in which he was seriously wounded, he became a prominent author and editor, earning the French Legion of Honour in 1932. Of Constantin-Weyer's many books about Canada, the best known are the novels *Vers l'ouest* (1921; trans. *Toward the West*, 1931), *La Bourrasque* (1926; trans. *A Martyr's Folly*, 1930), and *Un Homme se penche sur son passé* (1928, winner of the Prix Goncourt; trans. *A Man Scans His Past*, 1929), and two essays on Manitoba: *Manitoba* (1924) and *Clarière: récits du Canada* (1929; trans. *Forest Wild*, 1932). *Vers l'ouest* is a romance set in the time of the father of Louis Riel (see ST BONIFACE and ST VITAL), in which the elder Riel plays a minor part. *La Bourrasque* is a highly fictionalized and coloured account

Maurice Constantin-Weyer

of Louis Riel himself, for which Constantin-Weyer was accused of satirizing the Métis; he was challenged on these grounds by Donatien Frémont's *Sur le ranch de Constantin-Weyer* (1932).

ST FRANÇOIS XAVIER

Cuthbert Grant, leader of the Métis at the Battle of Seven Oaks (1816) and later 'Warden of the Plains' for the Hudson's Bay Company (1828–49), founded Grantown in 1824 as a settlement of Métis farmers and buffalo hunters; its name later became St François Xavier. It was the home of **Pierre Falcon**, the 'troubadour of the North West', from 1825, when he retired from the Hudson's Bay Company to a life of farming, until his death here on 26 Oct. 1876. Falcon published nothing during his lifetime; his songs were sung throughout the Northwest long before they were written down. Today only five still exist, and another is known in an English translation; Falcon is believed to have written many other songs and ballads. His works all seem to have been written spontaneously to commemorate and interpret important events, and to have been set to his own melodies. His best-known song is 'La Chanson de la Grenouillère', an interpretation of the Battle of Seven Oaks, at which Falcon was present. St François Xavier, now a hamlet of about 100 persons, lies west of Winnipeg on Hwy 26 just north of the Trans-Canada Hwy. (See also WINNIPEG.)

ST VITAL

Gabrielle Roy was married here in 1947 to Dr Marcel Carbotte. She had been living in MONTREAL (16) since 1939 and was on an extended visit with her family in nearby ST BONIFACE when she met her future husband through the theatrical company Le Cercle Molière, with which he had been associated for many years. Soon after, the couple moved to France. Roy did not return to Canada until 1950, when she and her husband settled permanently in QUEBEC CITY. (See also ALTAMONT, CARDINAL, MEADOW PORTAGE, WINNIPEG; FORT CHIMO, PETITE-RIVIÈRE-ST-FRANÇOIS, Que.)

Louis Riel was born and baptized in St Boniface in 1844, but in 1847 Louis Riel, Sr, moved his family to St Vital and established a mill here on the Seine River. The venture failed, but the elder Riel opened a second mill here in 1854–5. A house of post-on-sill construction that the Riel family built in 1880–1, and occupied until 1968, has been converted to a museum commemorating Riel and the families from which he descended, the Riels and the Lagimodières. It is at 330 River Rd. Louis Riel never lived here, but his body lay in state in the house between his execution at REGINA, Sask. on 16 Nov. 1885 and his burial in St Boniface on 12 Dec. Riel's children and his wife, Marguerite, lived in the house from June 1885 until Marguerite's death on 24 Apr. 1886. Riel's essays, poems, speeches, diaries, and letters are available in *The Collected Writings of Louis Riel/Les Écrits complets de Louis Riel* (5 vols, 1985). (See also ST BONIFACE, WINNIPEG; MONTREAL: 9, Que.; BATOCHE, REGINA, Sask.)

SHILO

The Royal Canadian Artillery Museum, located in Building 2 of the Canadian Armed Forces Base at Shilo, contains several exhibits related to the career of Col. **John McCrae**, author of 'In Flanders Fields', who served as an artillery brigade surgeon in the First World War. Sketches by McCrae are on display, along with the plate from which the poem was first printed in *Punch* on 8 Dec. 1915. Shilo is on Hwy 340, 10 miles south of the Trans-Canada Hwy. (See also MONTREAL: 3, Que.; GUELPH, Ont.)

SWAN RIVER

At the turn of the century **Douglas Leader Durkin** (who had been born in Ontario) homesteaded with his parents in the Swan River district. The family travelled by 'prairie schooner' beyond the railhead. Durkin, who attended the University of Manitoba in WINNIPEG, taught high school in CARMAN, Man., and then taught for four years at BRANDON College. He wrote several novels set in rural Manitoba, including *The Heart of Cherry McBain* (1919), a romance set in Swan River, and *The Lobstick Trail: A Romance of Northern Manitoba* (1921), set north of Swan River in The Pas. In 1921 Durkin left Brandon for New York. In 1945 he married another Manitoba novelist, Martha Ostenso, author of *Wild Geese* (1925). Many of the novels published under Ostenso's name are now thought to be, in part, the work of Durkin.

Emily Murphy and her husband, Arthur Murphy, homesteaded at Swan River in 1904–7. Her second book, *Janey Canuck in the West* (1910), which appeared when she was living in EDMONTON, contained sketches about her life here. Murphy became a prominent author and champion of humanitarian causes, and in 1916 was named the first female magistrate in Canada. **Pierre Falcon** was born at Elbow Fort, Swan River, in 1783, but was baptized and educated in Quebec. His songs record the confrontation between the Métis people of the Red River Settlement area and both immigrants and the Dominion government, from the Battle of Seven Oaks (1816) to the Red River Rebellion (1869–70). (See also ST FRANÇOIS XAVIER, WINNIPEG.)

VIRDEN

See WINKLER.

WAWANESA

This small town on the Souris River, near its junction with the Assiniboine, is the closest modern settlement to the homestead where **Nellie McClung** grew up. Born Helene Letitia Mooney in 1873 on a farm in southern Ontario, she came here with her family in 1880. The nearest town in those days was Millford, now abandoned; Northfield School, which Nellie attended from the age of ten and where she later taught, was on the road to Wawanesa. McClung enjoyed farm life, but by the age of sixteen she had determined to become a schoolteacher. After studying at the WINNIPEG Normal School, she began teaching in 1890 in several small towns in southern Manitoba (see MANITOU, LA RIVIÈRE), but returned home for vacations. She taught at Northfield School for six months in the winter of 1895–6 before her marriage in 1896 at the Millford Presbyterian Church to Wes McClung, a Manitou druggist. At Manitou she wrote her first novel, *Sowing Seeds in Danny* (1908), which was set in the Souris River region of her childhood. Her teaching experiences at Northfield School were described in another novel, *The Second Chance* (1910). The Mooney farmhouse was built in 1882, and after the death of Nellie's father the farm was run as a family business for several more years.

> WAWANESA
>
> *I am glad I can think of the farmyard with a ring of horses' heads gathered around the sunken tub below the pump or in a row across the pasture bars; when the brood mares roamed the pasture hills, later to be followed by frisking colts on their too-long legs. I am glad I knew the farm when there were cows grazing along the creek in deep contentment or lying in some shady place out of the wind in the crisp October morning when I went to get them and where many a time I was glad to warm my bare feet in the place where they had been lying.*
>
> —Nellie McClung, *Clearing in the West* (1936; rpr. 1976)

WINKLER

The novelist **Frederick Philip Grove** came to the Winkler district in Jan. 1913 to teach at Kronsfeld School in the Mennonite village of Haskett, near Winkler on the Manitoba-U.S. border. This was Grove's first known job in Canada, although he may have been in the West between 1909 and 1912—the 'lost' period between his departure from Europe as the desperate and penniless Felix Paul Greve and his first appearance in WINNIPEG late in 1912, when he began to seek a teaching position. According to Grove's autobiography, *In Search of Myself* (1946), he came to Canada at the suggestion of a Roman Catholic priest whom he met in the railway station in Fargo, North Dakota. Grove, who was working as a farmhand near Fargo, attracted the priest's attention because he was reading Baudelaire's *Les Fleurs du mal*. After the pair had conversed in French, the priest urged Grove, who was fluent in German, to seek teaching work in Manitoba, where the influx of immigrants had created a need for bilingual teachers. Grove went to Winnipeg and, with the help of Robert Fletcher, the provincial deputy minister of education, obtained the post at Haskett, where he taught twenty children in grades one to six in a one-room schoolhouse. In the evening he tutored young men who could not leave their farms during the day to attend classes. Eventually the plight of such young men provided the plot of *The Yoke of Life* (1930), although the novel's setting is more closely identified with the Big Grassy Marsh region around FALMOUTH, where Grove lived from 1918 to 1919. After studying in the summer of 1913, Grove moved to Winkler proper as principal of the intermediate school, a two-storey, four-room building with 160 pupils. The school went only up to grade eight, and two of the four teachers were not properly qualified to give instruction at their grade level, so Grove taught them at night and also provided high-school-level courses for qualified students. He bought laboratory equipment for science classes at his own expense, almost bankrupting himself until provincial inspectors authorized a reimbursement in appreciation of his special efforts. In Aug. 1914 Grove married Catherine Wiens, one of the Winkler teachers, at Swift Current, Sask., near her family's RUSH LAKE home. The couple returned to Winkler, but Grove found himself increasingly at odds with the community, partly because of his pro-German sentiments during the First World War. In July 1915 the Groves moved to Virden, where he taught mathematics at the Collegiate Institute and began writing articles on education. The job brought a pay raise and a possibility of advancement to principal, and the couple's daughter Phyllis May was born; but another dispute between Grove and school officials caused him to move in 1916 to GLADSTONE. (See also EDEN, RAPID CITY; BOBCAYGEON, OTTAWA, SIMCOE, Ont.)

WINNIPEG

Settlement at the junction of the Red and Assiniboine Rivers grew through more than fifty years of conflict before Winnipeg was named the capital of the new province of Manitoba in 1870. The story of the battle for control of the region was told first by **Pierre Falcon**, a Métis balladeer whose songs record the struggle, as he witnessed it, from the Red River Settlement in 1812 to the Red River Rebellion of 1869–70. Born at Elbow Fort, SWAN RIVER, in 1783, Falcon was educated in Quebec. He returned to Red River in 1806 to work for the North West Company's trading post, Fort Gibraltar. The Company was opposed to permanent settlement in the West because of the impact farming colonists would have on the fur trade. Company officials at Fort Gibraltar were troubled by the appearance in 1812 of the first colonists for Lord Selkirk's Red River Settlement—planned on a 116,000-acre site, at the rivers' junction, granted to Selkirk by the Hudson's Bay Company in 1811. Falcon was present at the Battle of Seven Oaks in 1816, when his brother-in-law Cuthbert Grant, a clerk of the North West Company, led an attack on a group of Red River settlers, in which twenty of them and their governor, Robert Semple, were killed. Seven Oaks was also known as Frog Plain (La Grenouillère); Seven Oaks House, 127 Rupertsland Ave. E., stands near the site of the battle and is believed to be the oldest habitable house in Manitoba. It dates from 1851 and was built by a merchant, John Inkster, whose store and post office stand beside the house. The site of the battle, Frog Plain, was later part of the Kildonan settlement; it is now the area around the intersection of Main St and Rupertsland Ave. Falcon celebrated the Métis victory with 'La Chanson de la Grenouillère' ('Chant de Vérité'), whose last stanza identifies the composer as 'Pierre Falcon, poète du canton'. Another song, 'Le Lord Selkirk au Fort William', or 'La danse des Bois-Brûlés', satirized a ball held at the North West Company's Fort William (Thunder Bay, Ont.) by Lord Selkirk after he captured the post in retaliation for the killings at Seven Oaks. Armed conflict ended in 1817, and after Selkirk died in 1820 the growth of the Red River community was administered by the Hudson's Bay Company from Fort Garry, built in 1817–18. After 1821, when the North West Company merged with its trading rival, Falcon worked for four years with the Hudson's Bay Company. He then joined other Métis under Cuthbert Grant to found Grantown (ST FRANÇOIS XAVIER), where he lived until his death in 1876. Although Falcon is believed to have written and circulated many songs, only six survive. In addition to the two ballads relating to the Red River Settlement, he also is known to have written 'The Buffalo Hunter's Song', which exists only in English translation; 'Le Général Dickson', about an American adventurer visiting Grantown in 1837; and two songs from his old age about events relating to the Red River Rebellion, 'Les Tribulations d'un roi malheureux' and 'Le Dieu du Libéral'.

Pierre Falcon

The Red River Settlement is described by **R.M. Ballantyne**—who worked in the Northwest Territories for the Hudson's Bay Company from 1841, when he was sixteen, to 1847 (see NORWAY HOUSE)—in chapter 6 of *Hudson Bay: or, Every-day Life in the Wilds of North America, during Six Years' Residence in the Territories of the Honourable Hudson Bay Company* (1848), which was based on his journals and letters home to his mother. After returning to Scotland in 1847 he became a successful writer of adventure stories for boys. Among them were two set in the Red River district: *The Red Man's Revenge: A Tale of the Red River Flood* (1880) and *The Buffalo Runners: A Tale of the Red River* (1891). The latter follows events between 1814 and 1816, when the Red River Settlement became a focus of conflict between the North West Company and the Hudson's Bay Company. (See also FORT CHIMO, Que.) *Mine Inheritance* (1940) by **Frederick Niven** follows the story of the settlement's growth from 1811 to 1827; it is the first part of a trilogy of western expansion, which also includes *The Flying Years* (1935), set in CALGARY, Alta., and *The Transplanted* (1944), set in British Columbia. (See also NELSON, VANCOUVER, B.C.)

To support its claims in the region, the Hudson's Bay Company built a series of forts near the forks of the Red and Assiniboine Rivers. The original Fort Garry, built in 1817–18, was subject to flooding, and in 1831 a replacement for it, Lower Fort Garry, was built 20 miles north on the Red River. Lower Fort Garry, on Hwy 9 north of the city, is preserved as a national historic site and is open daily from mid-May to mid-October. In 1835 Upper Fort Garry was built near the original fort site and replaced Lower Fort Garry as the Hudson's Bay Company's administrative centre in the district. To the south of the intersection of Main and Portage Sts lies a small park containing a stone gateway, the only portion of Upper Fort Garry still standing.

The Red River Rebellion of 1869–70 resulted from a plan by the Dominon government to purchase the Hudson's Bay Company's western land holdings, and from fear among the region's Métis people that this would destroy their way of life. There were three important literary witnesses to the rebellion besides Pierre Falcon: the Métis leader Louis Riel, Alexander Begg, and the poet Charles Mair, who in fact helped to precipitate the crisis.

Charles Mair (*Dreamland and Other Poems*, 1868) arrived at Fort Garry in the fall of 1868 as paymaster to a surveying party allowed into the region by the Dominion government in anticipation of its purchase of the Hudson's Bay Company's western land holdings. Mair heightened the tensions in the community by writing several articles for the Toronto *Globe* that criticized the Red River Métis and urged eastern Canadians to settle in the region. Mair was away from the fort in the fall of 1869 for his wedding to Elizabeth Louise McKinney when the first confrontations occurred between Louis Riel and William McDougall, Lieutenant Governor of the North West Territories. When the newlyweds returned, Mair allied himself with McDougall, longtime friend John Christian Schultz, and others in opposing Riel. On 7 Dec. 1869 he was one of an armed party arrested by Riel, who had taken control of the Red River Settlement and declared a provisional Métis government. With Schultz he escaped and travelled to TORONTO (I) to seek military help. By the time Mair arrived on 6 Apr. 1870 news of Riel's execution of one of his prisoners, Thomas Scott, had reached Ontario and the Red River Expedition was organized under the command of Colonel Garnet Wolseley. Wolseley's troops arrived at Fort Garry on 24 Aug. to find Riel and his forces already gone.

Mair's house, Clover Cottage, stood at what is now the corner of Portage and Main Sts. On 2 July 1870 his wife gave birth there to Maude Louise Mair, the first child of British parentage born in Winnipeg after the passage of the Manitoba Act. In 1871 Mair moved his family to PORTAGE-LA-PRAIRIE to open a store. He always believed that Riel had destroyed several poetry manuscripts that he had been forced to leave behind at John Schultz's store when he was arrested; one of them was a long narrative poem based on events from the life of Zoroaster that was never reworked. In July 1898 Mair returned briefly to Winnipeg to join the federal Department of Immigration, which he served for many years in western Canada. See also KINGSTON, LANARK, OTTAWA, WINDSOR, Ont.; MAIR, HUMBOLDT, PRINCE ALBERT, Sask.; CALGARY, Alta.; FORT STEELE, VICTORIA, B.C.)

The businessman and journalist **Alexander Begg** lived in the Red River district from 1867 to 1884. Founder and editor of several periodicals, including the *Manitoba Trade Review* (1872) and the *Gazette and Trade Review*, Begg kept a detailed journal of events in the settlement during his years there. In the 1870s Begg held various government positions, including Provincial Auditor, Deputy Provincial Treasurer, and Queen's Printer. His house was on George Ave at the bank of the Red River, and he had offices on Rupert Ave and in the post office on Main St. He drew on his diary for historical accounts of the period, including *The Creation of Manitoba: or, A History of the Red River Troubles* (1871), and for a satirical novel *'Dot it Down': A Story of Life in the North-West* (1871). Begg was a sympathetic chronicler of all sides in the Red River Rebellion with one exception: the party surrounding John Schultz that included Charles Mair. Mair is the model for Begg's satirical character, 'Dot it Down'.

After leaving Fort Garry to Wolseley's Red River Expedition, **Louis Riel** lived briefly in the United States, but he was back in Manitoba by the end of the year. Elected to the House of Commons in 1873, he was denied his seat and forced again to flee the country. In 1885, fifteen years after the Red River Rebellion, he again directed armed Métis opposition to western settlement, this time in the Saskatchewan River valley; Riel surrendered on 15 May 1885 and was executed at REGINA, Sask., on 16 Nov. 1885. His brothers prepared a collection of his verse from his writings, *Poésies religieuses et politiques*, which was published in 1886. His complete writings, including ballads in the style of Pierre Falcon and other works occasioned by the Red River Rebellion, are available in *The Complete Writings of Louis Riel/ Les Écrits Complets de Louis Riel* (5 vols, 1985). Several sites associated with Riel can be visited on the east side of the Red River in ST BONIFACE, his birthplace, and ST VITAL, where his family lived during most of his life. (See also MONTREAL, Que.; BATOCHE, Sask.)

Riel and his council, 1869–70

Born on 11 Feb. 1871 in Stanley, Ont., **Agnes Christina Laut** came to Winnipeg in her youth and was educated at the University of Manitoba. She later worked here as a reporter for the *Manitoba Free Press* before moving to the United States, where she lived most of her life. Of the 24 books she wrote most are vivid histories of Canada and of western settlement in Canada and the United States, but two are highly interesting early novels of the West: *Lords of the North* (1900) and *Heralds of Empire: Being the Story of One, Ramsay Stanhope, Lieutenant to Pierre Radisson in the Northern Fur Trade* (1902). *Lords of the North*, set in 1816, tells the story of the conflict between the two great fur-trading companies and of the Battle of Seven Oaks.

After the Red River Rebellion, Winnipeg quickly developed as the gateway to the West. Consequently it soon became the birthplace and home of various writers concerned with the experiences of settlers and immigrants in the new land.

The children's author **Muriel Denison** (*Susannah, a Little Girl with the Mounties*, 1936) was born here in 1885. She is best known for her series of books about a girl befriended by a North West Mounted Police troop near REGINA, Sask. (See also BON ECHO, Ont.)

Laura Goodman Salverson was born in a brick house on Bushnell St on 9 Dec. 1890. The family lived at 422 Ness St from 1897–9 and then moved to Selkirk, 25 miles away on the old Red River Rd. After returning briefly to the city, the family moved to the United States when Salverson was ten. She later came back to Winnipeg to work and in 1911–13 lived at 719 William Ave. In 1913 she married George Salverson at the Old Lutheran Manse; her marriage was followed by many moves throughout western Canada because George Salverson worked as a telegraph operator for the CPR. The child of Icelandic immigrants, Salverson wrote several novels based on her personal recollections and careful research into the experiences of Canadian settlers. As a child she often visited the immigration reception buildings at the junction of the Red and Assiniboine Rivers with her father (who wrote about immigrant problems for foreign-language newspapers in Canada and in Europe). Her novels include *The Viking Heart* (1923), an account of Icelandic settlement in the area of GIMLI; and *The Dark Weaver* (1937, winner of a Governor General's

Award), a story of Nordic immigrants in western Canada in the First World War era. Salverson also won a Governor General's Award for her autobiography, *Confessions of an Immigrant's Daughter* (1939), which contains an account of her early years in Winnipeg. (See also BIGGAR, PRINCE ALBERT, REGINA, SASKATOON, Sask.; CALGARY, EDMONTON, Alta.)

Nellie McClung's family passed through Winnipeg in 1880 on the way to a homestead near WAWANESA, where McClung grew up. She returned to the city in 1889 to study at the Normal School and again in 1893 to obtain her first-class certificate from Winnipeg Collegiate Institute. McClung taught in several southern Manitoba towns, including MANITOU, where she married a pharmacist, Wes McClung, in 1896. In Manitou McClung achieved her first commercial writing success with *Sowing Seeds in Danny* (1908) and pursued her long-time interest in temperance and women's suffrage. In 1911 her husband went to work for an insurance firm, which transferred him to Winnipeg. The family lived in a three-storey stucco house at 97 Chestnut St, and McClung expanded her political activities, becoming President of the Winnipeg Women's Press Club and a prominent member of the city's Political Equality League. In 1914 she staged 'The Women's Parliament' at the Walker Theatre (Market and Main Sts) as part of the league's campaign against the premier of the province, Rodmond Roblin. (A fictional treatment of the event appears in McClung's novel *Purple Springs*, 1921.) While living in Winnipeg, she published her first book of short stories, *The Black Creek Stopping-House and Other Stories* (1912). Her husband's transfer to EDMONTON, Alta., in 1914 meant that McClung was no longer a resident of Manitoba when, in 1916, it became the first province to grant women the right to vote. (See also LA RIVIÈRE, Man; CHATSWORTH, OTTAWA, Ont; CALGARY, EDMONTON, Alta; VICTORIA, B.C.)

Charles Gordon, who wrote under the pen-name of **Ralph Connor**, came to Winnipeg in the 1890s and spent over forty years here. Gordon, who was a Presbyterian minister, was invited in August 1894 to become pastor of St Stephen's Church, then a mission on the outskirts of the city at the corner of Spence St and Portage Ave; he remained there for the rest of his life. Gordon's house, built in 1914 at 54 West Gate, is now the University Women's Club. All of Gordon's books were written in Winnipeg, although his subjects were drawn primarily from his childhood in Glengarry County, Ont. (see ST ELMO, Ont.), and from

Charles Gordon ('Ralph Connor'), *c.*1910

his missionary years near BANFF, Alta. *The Foreigner* (1909), however, vividly portrays the difficult boarding-house existence of Slavic immigrants on the outskirts of Winnipeg.

A popular lecturer, Gordon began his career when he was invited by the editor of the Presbyterian magazine, the *Westminster*, to submit stories of his missionary days. The first series of sketches, collected in *Black Rock: A Tale of the Selkirks* (1898), was an immediate success in Canada and the United States. *The Sky Pilot: A Tale of the Foothills* (1899) followed, and in 1901 Gordon wrote the first of his many books set in his home county, *The Man from Glengarry: A Tale of the Ottawa*. He wrote nearly thirty works of fiction, along with several books on religious themes, and his autobiography, *Postscript to Adventure* (1938). Gordon was active in the temperance movement before the First World War and served as president of the Social Service Council of Manitoba. After the war he was chairman of the Manitoba Council of Industry, which successfully mediated labour disputes after the Winnipeg General Strike of 1919. As moderator of the Presbyterian Church in 1921–2 he promoted union with the Methodist Church, a campaign that culminated in the creation of the United Church of Canada in 1924. During the First World War Gordon went overseas as chaplain of the 43rd Highlanders and rose to the rank of senior Protestant chaplain to the Canadian forces. His campaigning for social issues and his war experiences both figure in his later novels. *To Him That Hath: A Novel of the West Today* (1921) examines both sides of a contemporary strike. *The Sky Pilot in No Man's Land* (1919) follows the career of a Canadian army chaplain. Gordon died in Winnipeg in 1937. (See also HARRINGTON WEST, TORONTO: 1, Ont.; CANMORE, Alta.)

> WINNIPEG
>
> *. . . at the time of my coming the city was on the eve of a new development. The western boundary was practically Colony Street, now a thoroughly downtown section, and my little new mission was out on the brown prairie where the streets were black trails radiating in every direction over the prairie, fine for driving in dry weather, but the rain made them long black lines of impassable bog. By 'impassable' I mean that foot passengers were forced to stick to the wooden sidewalks if they could and all horse traffic was a matter of speculation. You might, with luck, get through. I have frequently seen a light unloaded delivery wgon bogged to the axles so that the horse after being unhitched could with difficulty get himself out of the viscous mud.*
>
> —Ralph Connor, *Postscript to Adventure* (1938)

Winnipeg before 1900 was a boom town that caught the interest of many writers, some of whom lived here briefly, while others merely visited, or gathered impressions from afar. The most important of the latter was the humorist **Stephen Leacock** (see MONTREAL: 3, Que.; ORILLIA, TORONTO: 3, 7, Ont.). Although Leacock himself did not visit Winnipeg in the nineteenth century (he passed through during a 1936 lecture tour), he provided a vivid picture of the city in the land-boom days of the 1880s in his story about his uncle, E.P., the title story of *My Remarkable Uncle and Other Sketches* (1942). E.P. and Leacock's father, Peter, arrived in the city in 1880 or 1881; the crash in land prices occurred in 1882. In 'My Remarkable Uncle' Leacock followed E.P.'s rocky fortunes after the collapse and portrayed admiringly the indomitable speculating spirit that somehow kept his uncle afloat while many others, including Leacock's father, were ruined financially. In the 1880s and 1890s E.P. Leacock lived on Taché Ave in St Boniface; he briefly held a seat in the Manitoba Legislative Assembly in 1885. Other Leacock family members—the humorist's brothers Jim, Dick, and Teddy—lived in Winnipeg at various times. **Mark Twain** visited Winnipeg in 1895 and announced, 'I have never seen real mud since I left Missouri until today.' After visiting the city in 1907, **Rudyard Kipling** wrote that 'Winnipeg has Things in abundance, but has learned to put them beneath her feet, not on top of her mind, and so is older than many cities.' (*Letters to the Family: Notes on a Recent Trip to Canada*, 1908). Canadian writers briefly associated with early Winnipeg include **Robert J.C. Stead** and **Pauline Johnson**. Stead (*The Homesteaders*, 1916; *Grain*, 1926) attended the Winnipeg Business College, then at 482 Main St, in the 1890s. (See also MIDDLEVILLE, OTTAWA, Ont.; CALGARY, CARTWRIGHT, Alta.) The Ontario-born poet and performer **Pauline Johnson** used the Manitoba Hotel, at the intersection of Main and Water Sts, from 1896 to 1899. In 1895 she published her first book, *The White Wampum*, and enjoyed considerable success giving readings in western Canada with her partner Owen Smiley. After breaking with Smiley in 1897, she became engaged that year to a Winnipeg man and seemed on the point of retiring. When her engagement was broken, Johnson began touring again, first in a series of Boer War benefits and then commercially with a new partner, Walter McRaye, with whom she first appeared in 1901. (See also BRANTFORD, MIDDLEPORT, Ont.; VANCOUVER, B.C.)

In the years before the First World War Winnipeg was the birthplace and home of many future writers. Journalist **James H. Gray**, who was born in 1906, grew up here; the Depression forced him to change employment from the Winnipeg Stock Exchange to the *Winnipeg Free Press*, where he started as a reporter in 1935. In the late 1930s he lived at 105½ Talbot St, and in 1940 at 278 Glenwood Cr.; thereafter various jobs required him to spend long periods outside Winnipeg. Gray took up the writing of social history in 1963. Some of his books are autobiographical, including *The Boy from Winnipeg* (1970) about his childhood in the city, and *Troublemaker!* (1978) about his years as a reporter. In addition Gray has written several popular studies of specific issues in prairie history. They include *Red Light on the Prairies* (1971), which follows the development of segregated red-light districts (including Annabella and Colony Sts in Winnipeg) in western Canada before the Depression.

The poet **Dorothy Livesay** was born on 12 Oct. 1909 at 116½ Lansdowne Ave. The family also lived at 166 Lipton St; Livesay attended Laura Secord Public School until she was ten, when she moved to TORONTO (4). She has written about these early years in *Beginnings: A Winnipeg Childhood* (1973). Livesay now divides her year between summers in Winnipeg and winters on GALIANO ISLAND, B.C.

Marshall McLuhan was born in EDMONTON but grew up in Winnipeg. He received a B.A. from the University of Manitoba in 1933, and an M.A. in 1934, and then enrolled at Trinity College, Cambridge University, where he received his Cambridge B.A. in 1936 (and a Ph.D. in 1943). In 1919 the McLuhan family lived at 314 Rosedale Ave and in 1920 at 105 Scotia St. From 1921 until 1934, when he left to attend Cambridge, McLuhan lived with his family at 507 Gertrude Ave. From 1946 until shortly before his death in 1980, McLuhan taught at St Michael's College, University of TORONTO (3), where in 1951 he began publishing his influential studies of the role of media and technology in communication and society.

Marshall McLuhan, brother Maurice, and friend Ed Robeneck, Winnipeg, 1928

Born in Hungary in 1912, the novelist **John Marlyn** was brought to Canada as an infant and grew up in the north end of Winnipeg at 450 Henry St. He attended high school here and began studies at the University of Manitoba but dropped out to look for work. During the thirties Marlyn went to England, where he wrote movie scripts. When he returned to Canada on the eve of the Second World War, he settled in OTTAWA, where he has worked as a writer in the civil service. Both his novels are set in Winnipeg. The first, *Under the Ribs of Death* (1957), follows the struggles for success of a Hungarian immigrant whose hopes of escaping his background are crushed by the Depression. The Salter Street Bridge is a principal locale in the story. In *Putzi, I Love You, You Little Square* (1981), which is set in Winnipeg during the 1970s, the narrator is an unborn child who comments satirically on the world from his mother's womb.

The literary critic, social historian, and poet **George Woodcock** was born on 8 May 1912 in Grace Hospital and lived in an apartment building on Portage Ave for five months. His family then moved to England, and Woodcock did not return to Canada until 1949, when he settled in British Columbia, first at SOOKE on Vancouver Island, and in the 1950s in VANCOUVER. Woodcock's early years are described in the first volume of his autobiography, *Letters to the Past* (1982). Woodcock is also a popular travel writer. He has written many books based on his world travels and presents varied impressions of his own country in *Canada and the Canadians* (1970) and *The Canadians* (1979).

The playwright **Ann Henry** was born in Winnipeg on 7 Aug. 1914. She describes her career as a journalist in the city in her autobiography, *Laugh, Baby, Laugh* (1970). Her play *Lulu Street* (1976) is set on that street during the Winnipeg Strike of 1919; it was produced at the Manitoba Theatre Centre in 1967.

The prairie novelist **Frederick Philip Grove** came to the city in the fall of 1912 looking for work as a teacher. He came from South Dakota, where by chance he had met a Manitoba priest who told him that the province needed German-speaking teachers. Grove roomed on Main St while arranging with Robert Fletcher, Deputy Minister of Education, for a first teaching assignment. Beginning in 1913 at the village of Haskett near Winkler, he taught in rural Manitoba schools for ten years. He took correspondence courses from the University of Manitoba and received his B.A. in 1922. In 1924 Grove retired from teaching and attempted to earn a living as a free-lance lecturer and writer from his home in RAPID CITY. After the publication of Grove's first two books, *Over Prairie Trails* (1922) and *The Turn of the Year* (1923), Professor Arthur Phelps of Wesley College (now part of the University of Winnipeg) helped him to publish his first novel, *Settlers of the Marsh* (1925). In 1924, during a meeting of the Canadian Authors' Association in the city, Phelps arranged for Lorne Pierce of Ryerson Press to read the novel, which Pierce immediately accepted. A series of Grove's stories appeared in the Winnipeg *Tribune* in 1926; they were collected as *Tales from the Margin* (1971). (See also EDEN, FALMOUTH, GLADSTONE, WINKLER, Man.; BOBCAYGEON, OTTAWA, SIMCOE, Ont; RUSH LAKE, Sask.)

Douglas Durkin, who grew up on a homestead near SWAN RIVER, was a member of the English department of the University of Manitoba from 1915 to 1922, although for the last two years he was on leave of absence. He received his B.A. from that university in 1908 and returned to Winnipeg seven years later after serving as a high-school principal in CARMAN and teaching at

Martha Ostenso

BRANDON College. Durkin lived at several addresses in Winnipeg: 280 River Ave (1916), 198 Langside St (1917–18), 957 McMillan Ave (1919), and 198 Langside St again (1920–1). His rural experiences were the inspiration for many of his novels, including *The Heart of Cherry McBain* (1919) and *Mr. Gumble Sits Up* (1930), but his best-known work, *The Magpie* (1923), is set in Winnipeg during the General Strike of 1919 and examines events in the city from the perspective of a returned First World War veteran. **Martha Ostenso**, who married Durkin in 1945, grew up in BRANDON, where her parents first settled in Canada after having immigrated to the United States from Norway in 1902. When the family moved to Winnipeg, Ostenso attended Kelvin Technical High School and the University of Manitoba; in about 1917 the family lived at 716 10th St and in 1918 moved to 87 Sherbrook St. A year of teaching north of Winnipeg inspired Ostenso's prize-winning novel, *Wild Geese* (1925), which was honoured as the best first novel in a contest sponsored by Dodd, Mead and Co. In 1919–21 she lived at 377 Agnes St. Ostenso moved to New York about 1921 to join Durkin, who was teaching at Columbia University.

Another graduate of the University of Manitoba was the literary critic **William Arthur Deacon** (*The Four Jameses*, 1927), who received an LL.B. degree in 1918, at which time he lived at 650 McDermot Ave. In addition to working for a Winnipeg law firm, Deacon began writing book reviews for the *Manitoba Free Press*, where he was appointed assistant literary editor in 1921. Determining to pursue a career in literary journalism, Deacon left Winnipeg in 1922 for TORONTO (2, 6), where he worked first for *Saturday Night* and then for the *Mail and Empire* and the *Globe and Mail*. **Paul Hiebert**, best known for his satirical essays on 'Saskatchewan songstress' Sarah Binks, received his B.A. from the University of Manitoba in 1916; during his student years he lived at 261 Furby St. After studying at the University of Toronto (M.A., 1917) and McGill University (M.Sc., 1922; Ph.D. Chemistry, 1924), Hiebert returned to teach for twenty-eight years in the chemistry Department of the University of Manitoba. In the 1920s he lived at 229 Young St, in the early 1930s at 330 Oak St., and for several years after 1934 at 393 River Ave. He continued the story he began in *Sarah Binks* (1947) in *Willows Revisited* (1967) and *For the Birds* (1980). In 1940–52 Hiebert lived at 399 Stradbrook Ave; this was the house in which he worked on *Sarah Binks*. A native of PILOT MOUND, Hiebert lived at CARMAN after retiring from the university in 1953.

The poet **Miriam Waddington** was born here in 1917 and grew up at 372 St John's Ave in a house designed by her father. (It was built in 1922–3 and is still standing.) Waddington attended Machray School, 320 Mountain Ave. When she was fourteen her family moved to OTTAWA, where she attended high school. She has lived in TORONTO (7) since 1960; from 1964 to 1983 she taught English at York University. *Green World* (1945), her first book, was published by First Statement Press in MONTREAL (5), where Waddington was an active member of the literary community during the 1940s and 1950s. She has attributed her work in both social service and poetry to the influence of her parents, who created in their Winnipeg home a strong intellectual environment fuelled by contacts with political activists and writers visiting the city, who were often invited by her father to stay with the family.

The novelist **Jack Ludwig** was born here on 30 Aug. 1922 and educated at the University of Manitoba, where he received his B.A. in 1944. After doctoral studies at the University of California at Los Angeles (Ph.D., 1953), he settled in Toronto, his present home. Since 1962 he has taught at the State University of New York (Stony Brook). Ludwig's novels are *Confusions* (1967), *Above Ground* (1968), and *A Woman of Her Age* (1973). In recent years he has concentrated on sports journalism: *Games of Fear and Winning* (1976) is a collection of essays previously published in *Maclean's* and the *Canadian*.

Adele Wiseman was born here to Ukrainian immigrant parents on 21 May 1928; her family was living at 600 Manitoba Ave. She grew up in an apartment over the family tailor shop at 490 Burrows Ave in North Winnipeg; the family had moved there in 1934. Wiseman worked her way through university, graduating with an Honours B.A. in literature from the University of Manitoba in 1949. She began writing as a university student and remained attached to the university as a reader and tutor from 1948 to 1955, with the exception of 1950–2, when she worked in Europe. *The Sacrifice* (1956), which won a Governor General's Award, was completed in 1952. In the early 1950s Wiseman worked as a lab technician and as executive secretary of the Royal Winnipeg Ballet. She left Winnipeg in 1956 for London; when she returned to Canada, she settled first in MONTREAL (7) in 1964 and later in TORONTO (7). *The Sacrifice* is set in a Canadian prairie Jewish community; in her second novel, *Crackpot* (1974), Wiseman draws specifically on the Jewish neighbourhood of her childhood, the north end of Winnipeg during the Depression.

Born in Winnipeg in 1929, the playwright **Tom Hendry** was a primary figure in the creation of the city's well-known Manitoba Theatre Centre. Hendry was trained as an accountant and opened his office here in 1955, but he was also writing plays and acting. At that time he lived at 1172 Fleet Ave. His first play, *Do You Remember?*, was produced by CBC Winnipeg in 1954; this TV script was revised and produced in 1957 at Winnipeg's Rainbow Stage, directed by John Hirsch. In the same year Hendry and Hirsch were co-founders of Theatre 77, later the Manitoba Theatre Centre, where Hendry's plays, *Trapped* (1961) and *All About Us* (1964), were produced. Associated for several years with the Rainbow Stage as a producer, Hendry has worked recently in Ontario, both at STRATFORD and in Toronto, where he is associated with Toronto Free Theatre.

Many other writers were associated with the city in the years between the wars. The poet **P.K. Page**, born in England in 1916, attended River Heights School in the 1920s. She lived at Fort Osborne Barracks; her story 'The Neighbours' is set here. Page's early years in Canada were spent in CALGARY, and RED DEER, Alta, as well as Winnipeg. (See also NEW RIVER BEACH, ROTHESAY, SAINT JOHN, N.B.; KINGSMERE, MONTREAL (5), Que; OTTAWA, Ont; VICTORIA, B.C.) The novelist **Gabrielle Roy** (*Rue Deschambault*, 1955; *Street of Riches*, 1957) grew up across the river in ST BONIFACE, where she taught for many years after attending the Winnipeg Normal School in 1927. Roy was active in the theatre groups in St Boniface and Winnipeg during the 1930s. (See also ALTAMONT, CARDINAL, MEADOW PORTAGE, ST VITAL; FORT CHIMO, MONTREAL: 16, PETITE-RIVIÈRE-ST-FRANÇOIS, QUEBEC CITY, Que.) The editor and novelist **Ralph Allen** came to Winnipeg in 1929 at the age of sixteen to work as a sports reporter for the Winnipeg *Tribune*. In the early 1930s he lived at 184 Walnut St, in 1935–6 at 601 Broadway Ave, and from 1938 until shortly before the Second World War at 55 Donald St. He then moved to TORONTO (6). Allen wrote two novels set during the war: *Home-made Banners* (1946) and *The High White Forest* (1964), which also draws on his experiences as a newspaperman in Winnipeg in the 1930s. (See also OXBOW, Sask.) **W.O. Mitchell**, a native of WEYBURN, Sask., entered the University of Manitoba in 1931 to take pre-med courses and study philosophy but was forced by illness to withdraw in 1934. He received a B.A. from the University of Alberta, EDMONTON, in 1942. Author of *Who Has Seen the Wind* (1947), Mitchell has made his home in Alberta since the 1940s, apart from 1948–51 when he was fiction editor of *Maclean's* in Toronto. (See also CALGARY, HIGH RIVER, Alta.)

Watson Kirkconnell, who met the novelist Frederick Philip Grove through his colleague Arthur Phelps, taught at Wesley College (now the University of Winnipeg) from 1922 to 1940. His home throughout the 1930s was 972 Grosvenor St. Until 1930 he was a professor of English; he then joined the Classics department. Kirkconnell wrote several books of poetry; while in Winnipeg he published *The Tide of Life* (1930), *The Eternal Quest* (1934), *Manitoba Symphony* (1937), *Lyra Sacra: Four Occasional Hymns* (1939), *Western Idyll* (1940), and *The Flying Bull and Other Tales* (1940), which is a group of western 'tall tales' in verse. Kirkconnell is best known for his translations, which are intended particularly as a means of introducing English-speaking Canadians to the literatures of immigrant settlers. His first book of translation was *European Elegies: One Hundred Poems Chosen and Translated from European Literature in Fifty Languages* (1927). In addition to representative anthologies from the literatures of Hungary, Iceland, and the Ukraine, Kirkconnell translated work written by new Canadians in their native languages, as in *Canadian Overtones: An Anthology of Canadian Poetry Written Originally in Icelandic, Swedish, Hungarian, Italian, Greek, and Ukrainian* (1935). In *Rest, Perturbed Spirit* (1974), Kirkconnell wrote a memoir of a Winnipeg friend, the poet **Cecil Francis Lloyd**, who lived at 493 Victor St from 1922 until his death in 1938. Lloyd, a native of England, published four books of poems, including *Landfall, Collected Poems* (1935), and two volumes of prose (*Sunlight and Shadow*, 1928; *Malvern Essays*, 1930). After his wife's death in 1926 Lloyd had increasing difficulty in his personal life. He looked in vain for work for six years until, in 1938, he was threatened with eviction from his home, where he kept his wife's place set at table. After killing his two cats to save them from starving, Lloyd shot himself on 13 July 1938. Excerpts from Lloyd's letters and poems were included in Kirkconnell's memoir. (See also WOLFVILLE, N.S.; KINGSTON, PORT HOPE, Ont.)

The novelist **Sinclair Ross** was transferred from ARCOLA, Sask., to Winnipeg by the Royal Bank of Canada in 1933. He worked at the Portage Ave branch (gone) until 1942, when he entered military service. After the war Ross returned briefly to Winnipeg but in 1946 was transferred by the bank to MONTREAL (6). During the years in Winnipeg Ross published several short stories, most of them in the *Queen's Quarterly*, Kingston; they are collected in *The Lamp at Noon and Other Stories* (1968). He also published his first novel, *As for Me and My House* (1941), during his years here. Ross, who claims that he is not a Manitoba but a Saskatchewan author, says: 'I couldn't write three hundred words on the influence of Manitoba on my work, much less three thousand, for the simple reason that it had no influence whatsoever. If I have any claim to be considered a "writer" it must be based on the stories in *The Lamp at Noon* and *As for Me and My House*, and they are, as you know, one hundred per cent Saskatchewan.' (See also ABBEY, HORIZON, LANCER, PRINCE ALBERT, Sask.)

The poet and critic **Douglas Barbour** was born in Winnipeg in 1940, and after attending university in eastern Canada he moved to EDMONTON in 1969; since then he has taught at the University of Alberta. His books include *White* (1973) and *Shoreline* (1979). **Carol Bolt** was born in Winnipeg in 1941 and grew up in British Columbia, where she graduated from the University of British Columbia, VANCOUVER, in 1961. She moved to TORONTO (2) in the late sixties from Montreal, where she had helped to found a small theatre and had written children's plays. Her Toronto plays include *Buffalo Jump* (1972), *Red Emma* (1974), and *One Night Stand* (1977).

Born in NEEPAWA, **Margaret Laurence** won a scholarship to United College (now the University of Winnipeg), which persuaded her to leave home in 1944 for Winnipeg. One of her teachers was Malcolm Ross, who later published her first story in the *Queen's Quarterly*. Laurence graduated in Honours English in 1947 and went to work for North America's first co-operative newspaper, the Winnipeg *Citizen*. In the same year she married an engineer, Jack Laurence. They lived in the north end of the city on Burroughs Ave until 1949, when they moved to England. Laurence's home town, Neepawa, is the model for the town of 'Manawaka', which appears in many of her stories and novels. Winnipeg appears less often as a setting, but in *The Diviners* (1974) the principal character, Morag Gunn, attends college in Winnipeg and meets her future husband in the city. (See also RIDING MOUNTAIN NATIONAL PARK; LAKEFIELD, PETERBOROUGH, Ont.; VANCOUVER, B.C.)

The poet **Gwendolyn MacEwen** (*The T.E. Lawrence Poems*, 1982) lived at 509½ Dominion St from 1949 to 1952. She attended Laura Secord Public School until the age of eleven, when she returned to her native city, TORONTO (4).

James Reaney also came to Winnipeg from TORONTO (3), where in 1949 he had received an M.A. from the University of Toronto. Reaney taught at the University of Manitoba from 1949 to 1960, when he joined the faculty of the University of Western Ontario, LONDON. While in Winnipeg, he lived at 299 Balfour Ave and, later, at 288 Broadway St. His first book of poems, *The Red Heart* (1949), was published the year he began teaching here. The book won a Governor General's Award, the first of three Reaney has received. (See also LUCAN, STRATFORD, Ont.)

The poet **Kenneth McRobbie** (*First Ghost to Canada*, 1979) is a member of the faculty at the University of Manitoba. He is the leading English-language translator of modern Hungarian poetry; his books in this field include *The Boy Changed Into a Stag: Selected Poems of Ferenc Juhász* (1970), with Ilona Duczynska, and *Love of the Scorching Wind: Selected Poems of Lazlo Navy* (1973).

Robert Kroetsch, a native of HEISLER, Alta, has taught at the University of Manitoba since 1978. Since coming to Winnipeg he has written the novels *What the Crow Said* (1978) and *Alibi* (1983), and the poetry collection, *Field Notes* (1981). (See also DINOSAUR PROVINCIAL PARK, EDMONTON, RED DEER, Alta; MACKENZIE RIVER, N.W.T.)

Two recent novels concern a Winnipeg girlhood. The Ukrainian novelist **Maara Hass**, born in 1920, wrote *The Street Where I Live* (1976). The street of the title is Selkirk Ave on the north side of the city. **Sondra Gottlieb**'s *True Confections* (1978) is also based on her childhood in Winnipeg.

Saskatchewan

ABBEY

A banking career that lasted some forty years began for **Sinclair Ross** (b. 1908) in 1924 at the Abbey branch of the Union Bank of Canada. He remained at this branch (which later became a branch of the Royal Bank of Canada) until 7 Apr. 1928, when he was transferred to the Royal Bank office in nearby LANCER. (See also ARCOLA, HORIZON, INDIAN HEAD, PRINCE ALBERT; WINNIPEG, Man.)

ABERDEEN

Max Braithwaite taught school in this town northeast of Saskatoon from 1935 until 1937. Aberdeen and nearby VONDA, where Braithwaite went to teach in 1937, served as models for his fictional 'Wannego' in *The Night We Stole the Mountie's Car* (1971), winner of the 1972 Stephen Leacock Medal for humour. Mentioned in the book, and still standing, are Aberdeen's Hotel, where Braithwaite and his wife had their first apartment next to the bar, and the four-room school where he taught; the school is now Aberdeen's senior-citizens' centre. (See also EYRE, NOKOMIS, PRINCE ALBERT, SASKATOON.)

ARCOLA

A job with the Union Bank of Canada, and later one with the Royal Bank of Canada, took **Sinclair Ross** to several towns in his native Saskatchewan, including Arcola, 50 miles east of Weyburn, where he worked from June 1929 to Apr. 1933. Ross published his first story in 1934 after being transferred to Winnipeg in 1933, but his life in Saskatchewan was the primary influence on his work. He says: 'If I have any claim to be considered a "writer" it must be based on the stories in *The Lamp at Noon* and *As For Me and My House*, and they are . . . one hundred per cent Saskatchewan. True, I wrote them while in Winnipeg, but I was looking back, and drew on Manitoba not at all.' (See also ABBEY, LANCER, HORIZON, PRINCE ALBERT; MONTREAL: 6, Que.)

BIGGAR

The WINNIPEG-born novelist **Laura Goodman Salverson** (1890–1970) lived here and in many other towns throughout the western provinces from the time of her marriage in 1913 to George Salverson, a railway employee. The Salversons came to Biggar, 60 miles west of Saskatoon, from PRINCE ALBERT in 1918. Although they stayed only one year before moving to Regina, Biggar was important in the development of Laura Salverson's career. It was here that she began the study of English literature and creative writing, working independently as well as through correspondence courses, that in five years led to her first and most highly regarded novel, *The Viking Heart* (1923). (See also PRINCE ALBERT, SASKATOON; GIMLI, Man.; CALGARY, EDMONTON, Alta.)

BRIERCREST

The Briercrest Community Centre and Library in this small village on Hwy 339, 12 miles south of Hwy 1, was the home from 1920 to 1924 of the sentimental poet **Edna Jaques** (pronounced 'Jakes'), whose selected work, *The Best of Edna Jaques*, was published in 1966. Jaques and her husband William Ernest Jamieson lived in one-half of the building; in the other half Jamieson operated a harness-repair shop.

Jaques was born in 1890 in COLLINGWOOD, Ont., and was brought to Saskatchewan by her family who homesteaded here in 1902. (Jaques' father was the first pioneer of Briercrest—the town was named after his farm—and her brothers Bruce and Clyde became wheat farmers in the district.) At the age of fourteen she sold her first poem to a newspaper in Calgary and thereafter produced a steady stream of verses in the tradition of Edgar Guest and Ella Wheeler Wilcox. When she was in her twenties Jaques left Briercrest, but returned for the four years of her marriage. She then left Jamieson and took up her career as a writer and speaker, travelling widely but occasionally staying with her family here. She first became prominent in 1919–20, when her poem 'In Flanders Now' (a response to John McCrae's 'In Flanders Fields') and another set of verses, said to be the first ever written in an airplane, were widely publicized. She published many volumes of verse and for seventeen years contributed two poems a week to the Toronto *Star*. Jaques is one of the models for the Manitoba satirist Paul Hiebert's character Sarah Binks, 'the Sweet Songstress of Saskatchewan'. She died in Toronto in Sept. 1978. (See also OTTAWA, Ont.; PRINCE ALBERT, Sask.; VICTORIA, B.C.)

CUMBERLAND HOUSE

A national historic site on Cumberland Lake in northeastern Saskatchewan, Cumberland House is closely associated with two of the most noteworthy books in Canada's literature of exploration. Founded in 1774 by **Samuel Hearne**, it was the Hudson's Bay Company's first inland post. Hearne, who spent only one winter at the site, laid the groundwork for what became a highly successful fur-trading centre for the Company, and an important base for Arctic explorers. After retiring from service with the Hudson's Bay Company in 1787, he wrote *A Journey from Prince of Wales's Fort, in Hudson's Bay, to the Northern Ocean . . . in the Years 1769, 1770, 1771, & 1772* (1795).

The first expedition of (Sir) **John Franklin** spent most of the winter of 1820 at Cumberland House, as did members of the first search party that went looking for Franklin's remains thirty years later. In Franklin's third polar expedition of 1845 in search of the Northwest Passage, all hands were lost. Franklin wrote the account of his first epic journey of exploration in his *Narrative of a Journey to the Shores of the Polar Sea in the Years 1819, 20, 21, and 22* (1823), as well as a *Narrative* of his second expedition (1825–7) into the Canadian North. Franklin was a friend of Alfred, Lord Tennyson, and an uncle of Tennyson's wife Emily Selwood. Tennyson's famous tribute to Franklin is engraved on the explorer's cenotaph in Westminster Abbey:

Not here! the white North has thy bones; and thou,
Heroic sailor-soul,
Art passing on thine happier voyage now
Toward no earthly pole.

DUCK LAKE

Historical events that happened in this small community southwest of Prince Albert have become important themes for several modern Canadian writers. Gabriel Dumont and Louis Riel were leading figures in the North

West Rebellion, which began in Duck Lake on 26 Mar. 1885. **Rudy Wiebe**'s epic novel *The Scorched-Wood People* (1977), a chronicle of the prairie Métis spanning the years 1869–85, portrays these events at Duck Lake. The Duck Lake Historical Museum has on its grounds a restored North West Mounted Police jail from which, on 29 Oct. 1895, the Cree brave Almighty Voice escaped. The escape set off a nineteen-month manhunt that ended in a gunfight near Batoche; Almighty Voice was killed, along with two of his Indian companions, some members of the pursuing Mountie force, and the Duck Lake postmaster. The significance of Almighty Voice's death is examined by Wiebe in his story 'Where Is the Voice Coming From?' and by **Len Peterson** in his play *Almighty Voice*. The Saskatchewan novelist **W.O. Mitchell** wrote the screenplay for a film about Almighty Voice, *Alien Thunder*, which was shot in Duck Lake; buildings constructed for the film are on the museum grounds. The museum's exhibits include Gabriel Dumont's watch and a letter in Louis Riel's handwriting—an exhibit from his trial (see REGINA)—among many other objects relating to the North West Rebellion.

EASTEND

The American novelist **Wallace Stegner**, who was born in 1909 in Iowa, lived on a homestead at Eastend from 1914 to 1921. He recalls the town and its region, at the eastern edge of the Cypress Hills, in his memoir *Wolf Willow* (1963), in which Eastend is called Whitemud. Two of Stegner's novels, *On a Darkling Plain* (1940) and *The Big Rock Candy Mountain* (1943), have Saskatchewan settings.

> EASTEND
>
> *We sat boldly on the plain, something the earth refused to swallow, right in the middle of everything and with the prairie as empty as nightmare clear to the crawl and shimmer where hot earth met hot sky. I saw the sun flash off brass, a heliograph winking off a message into space, calling attention to us, saying, 'Look, look!'*
>
> —Wallace Stegner, *Wolf Willow: A History, A Story, and a Memory of the Last Plains Frontier* (1962)

In his travel book *Saskatchewan* (1968), the novelist **Edward McCourt** tells of his summers teaching creative writing at Fort Qu'Appelle and of his most memorable student, the balladeer **Billy Bock**. One of the best of Bock's songs—which were inspired by day-to-day events in provincial life—recounts the controversy over a proposal to install sewers in the town of Eastend in southwestern Saskatchewan. McCourt quotes these lines from it:

Eastend was once a happy town where harmony and love
Were busting out at all the seams, and in the trees above.
The doves of peace were nesting, there were no signs of strife,
For each man loved his neighbour (and sometimes his neighbour's wife).

ESTERHAZY

Esterhazy was the birthplace in 1951 of **Guy Vanderhaeghe**, who lived here until he entered the University of Saskatchewan in 1968. Although Vanderhaeghe has since lived mainly in SASKATOON, his short stories draw largely on his experience of Esterhazy and eastern Saskatchewan. They are collected in *Man Descending* (1982), which won a Governor General's Award, and *The Trouble with Heroes* (1983). Esterhazy is on Hwy 22, about 120 miles east of Regina.

ESTEVAN

The poet **Eli Mandel** was born in 1922 in this mining and manufacturing centre on Hwy 39 near the U.S. border. Mandel left Estevan to attend the University of Saskatchewan. After service in the Second World War and an academic career that took him to several cities, he settled permanently in TORONTO (7) in 1967, where he is a professor of English at York University. Mandel's books of poems, many of which refer to Estevan and to the Saskatchewan landscape, include *An Idiot Joy* (1967), which won a Governor General's Award, *Stony Plain* (1973), *Life Sentence* (1981) and *Dreaming Backwards: Selected Poems* (1981).

EYRE

Why Shoot the Teacher (1965), **Max Braithwaite**'s memoir of his first years of teaching in a Saskatchewan one-room schoolhouse, is based on his experiences at Trosley School near Eyre, west of Saskatoon at the Saskatchewan-Alberta border. Braithwaite came to the school in 1933 immediately after graduating from SASKATOON Normal School. He also taught at Neepawa School near Fielding, and at ABERDEEN and VONDA, the only two towns where the schools Braithwaite taught in (from 1935 to 1940) still stand. (See also NOKOMIS, PRINCE ALBERT.)

FAIRHOLME

Near this town on Hwy 3 north of Battleford, in a log cabin on his immigrant family's farm, **Rudy Wiebe** was born on 4 Oct. 1934. He lived here until the age of twelve, when the family moved to COALDALE, Alta. Wiebe's parents were Russian Mennonites, and at Fairholme the future novelist took part in Mennonite community life, which became a central theme of his fiction. His first three novels—*Peace Shall Destroy Many* (1962), *First and Vital Candle* (1966), and *The Blue Mountains of China* (1970)—form a trilogy about Mennonite life both in Canada and other countries. The Mennonite community depicted in *Peace Shall Destroy Many*, called Wapiti, may be identified with the Mennonite settlement near Fairholme where Wiebe lived during the Second World War. When he discovered that dramatic historic events connected with the North West Rebellion (1885) of prairie Métis and Indians had occurred nearby, his indignation over never having been taught about them led to his creative use of history in *The Temptations of Big Bear* (1973) and *The Scorched-Wood People* (1979). (See also EDMONTON, Alta.)

FORT PITT

Inspector Francis Dickens (1844–86) of the North West Mounted Police, third son of novelist **Charles Dickens**, led the defence of Fort Pitt during the early days of the North West Rebellion in April 1885, when this busy Hudson's Bay Company post 40 miles northeast of Lloydminster was besieged by a Cree band led by Big Bear. After two days Dickens ordered his force of twenty-five Mounties to withdraw from the fort; they retreated to Battleford, and the attackers then ransacked the fort, taking some civilian residents prisoner.

It was also at Fort Pitt that, in 1876, Big Bear refused to sign a treaty (requiring Indians to settle on reserves) with the Canadian government. **Rudy Wiebe**'s novel, *The Temptations of Big Bear* (1973), winner of a Governor General's Award, begins with the rejection of the treaty and follows Big Bear to his death in 1888, after the chief's imprisonment for his role in the North West Rebellion. (See also FAIRHOLME; COALDALE, EDMONTON, Alta.)

Today Fort Pitt is a historic park, with plaques relating the story of the siege.

HORIZON

Sinclair Ross identifies the setting of his classic novel of prairie life, *As For Me and My House* (1941), as Horizon, Sask., a town

Sinclair Ross

at the southeastern corner of the province. In nearby ARCOLA the novelist worked in the Royal Bank from 1929 to 1933. Ross's novel tells the story of a year in the lives of United Church minister Philip Bentley and his wife, whose diary entries form the narrative. (See also ABBEY, INDIAN HEAD, PRINCE ALBERT; WINNIPEG, Man.; MONTREAL: 6, Que.)

HUMBOLDT

The poet **Charles Mair**—accompanying troops commanded by his friend Col. George Denison, who had been sent from Ontario to oppose the Métis led by Louis Riel—spent three months of military service at Humboldt, 50 miles south of Batoche, with a detachment protecting a telegraph installation. In June 1885 he returned to Ontario without having seen any fighting. (See also PRINCE ALBERT; LANARK, WINDSOR, Ont.; WINNIPEG, Man.; VICTORIA, B.C.)

ÎLE À LA CROSSE

This far-northern settlement on Lac Île-à-la-Crosse was the jumping-off point in 1924 for an abortive journey into the wilderness by the American novelist **Sinclair Lewis** (1885–1951). Lewis and his brother Claude, who was a doctor at Sauk Centre, Minn., travelled down the Churchill River on the Department of Indian Affairs' annual expedition to distribute treaty money. Lewis visited Winnipeg, Regina, Saskatoon, Prince Albert, and many other cities on his way north, speaking to local groups about his recent successful novels, including *Main Street* and *Babbitt*, and about his enthusiasm for a trip in which he intended to pack his own kit and portage his own canoe. For Lewis, however, the journey lasted only two weeks beyond Île à la Crosse: he turned back and, with a single guide, made his way quickly to civilization. In his novel *Mantrap* (1926), a fictional account of the experience, he portrayed himself as a successful member of a wilderness expedition.

INDIAN HEAD

The Saskatchewan-born novelist **Sinclair Ross** completed his formal schooling in 1924 with grade 11 at the high school in Indian Head, in the Qu'Appelle River Valley. Soon afterwards he went to work at the Union Bank of Canada in the small town of ABBEY in southwestern Saskatchewan. (See also ARCOLA, HORIZON, PRINCE ALBERT; WINNIPEG, Man.)

LANCER

Sinclair Ross worked at the Royal Bank of Canada branch in Lancer, near the Alberta border, from 7 Apr. 1928 to 6 June 1929, when he was transferred to the bank's offices in ARCOLA. (See also ABBEY, HORIZON, INDIAN HEAD, PRINCE ALBERT; WINNIPEG, Man.)

LEADER

Leader is perhaps the closest model for **Paul Hiebert**'s imaginary North Willows, although there are many towns in southern Saskatchewan with the word Willow in their names—Willow Creek, Willow Bunch, even a Willows on Hwy 13, equidistant between Moose Jaw and the American border. More famous than these, of course, is North Willows, the North East Quarter of Section 37, Township 21, Range 9, West, half-way between Oak Bluff and Quagmire, neighbour to the towns of Pelvis, Detour, Eraser, Scandal, Jitters—in short, the home of Sarah Binks, 'sweet songstress of Saskatchewan', whose life and literary influence, both fictional, have been set forth memorably by Hiebert in *Sarah Binks* (1947), *Willows Revisited* (1967), and *For the Birds* (1980). Before joining the chemistry department at the University of Manitoba in 1924, Hiebert taught briefly at a country school about 12 miles south of Leader, in the Great Sand Hills region of the province. Leader was then called Prussia; the rural post office at which Hiebert received his mail was called Happyland. Hiebert has said that his experience here was crucial in the creation of Sarah Binks and her world. He placed her in Saskatchewan because, unlike his native Manitoba, it was purely prairie: 'I always loved the prairies. I loved Saskatchewan—I love it to this day. I think it's the greatest province in Canada.' Hiebert and his brother wrote parodic verse—in the manner of Sarah Binks—during their childhood at PILOT MOUND, Man., but Hiebert began developing the character of Sarah with his student Tommy Tweed (later well known as a playwright with CBC) at the University of Manitoba. In *Sarah Binks* he celebrates the unique bond between Sarah and the Saskatchewan landscape: 'Sarah Binks has raised her home province of Saskatchewan to its highest prairie level. Unschooled, yet unspoiled, this simple country girl has captured in her net of poesy the flatness of that great province. Like a sylph she wanders through its bluffs and coulees, across its haylands, its alkali flats, its gumbo stretches, its gopher meadows.' Leader lies at the junction of Hwys 21 and 32 near the Alberta border. (See also CARMAN, WINNIPEG, Man.)

LEBRET

At Lebret, on Hwy 10 in southeastern Saskatchewan's fertile Qu'Appelle River Valley, a provincial marker records the legend of how the region was named. The poet **Pauline Johnson** (see MIDDLEPORT, BRANTFORD, Ont.) gives the most famous version of the story in 'The Legend of the Qu'Appelle Valley'. The poem tells of an Indian who hears his name pronounced by a mysterious voice while he is travelling through the valley to visit his bride-to-be. He answers 'Qu'appelle? Qu'appelle?' but receives no answer; later he learns that his future wife pronounced his name as she died, at the precise moment that he heard it spoken. The marker records the legend and quotes Johnson's poem.

LUMSDEN

The folklorist **Edith** (Fulton) **Fowke** was born in Lumsden on 30 Apr. 1913 and attended school here until the end of Grade 11, when she went to Regina College. In Fowke's childhood Lumsden was a village; it is now an exurban community north of Regina. (The house she lived in is still standing.) Fowke has edited collections of songs and tales from many provinces and on many themes. Her books include *Sally Go Round the Sun* (1969), *The Penguin Book of Canadian Folk Songs* (1974), *Folklore of Canada* (1976), and *Tales Told in Canada* (1986). (See also TORONTO: 7, Ont.)

MAIR

Mair is named for the Canada First poet **Charles Mair** (1838–1927), who lived in PRINCE ALBERT from 1877 to 1891. In the years 1898–1921 he worked for the Department of Immigration at postings throughout western Canada, contributing to the settlement of many immigrant groups, including the Doukhobors of Saskatchewan.

MOOSE JAW

The novelist, playwright, and film-maker **Ken Mitchell** was born in Moose Jaw in 1940 and raised here. He was educated at the University of Saskatchewan, where he began writing while still a student, and has lived in REGINA since 1967, when he became a professor of literature at the University of Regina. Mitchell's best-known works include the novel *Wandering Rafferty* (1972), the short-story collection *Everybody Gets Something Here* (1977), and *Cruel Tears* (1976), a musical play about truck drivers, written in country-and-western style. Poet **Robert Currie** is a longtime resident of Moose Jaw and a teacher of English at Central Collegiate Institute. His collections evoking childhood and youth in the Saskatchewan countryside include *Diving into Fire* (1977) and *Yarrow* (1980).

NOKOMIS

The humorist **Max Braithwaite** was born in this small town between Saskatoon and Regina on 7 Dec. 1911 and lived here until 1919, when his family moved to PRINCE ALBERT. His birthplace, a house on the edge of town, is still standing. Braithwaite's childhood remembrances from Nokomis play a prominent part in *Never Sleep Three in a Bed* (1970). (See also ABERDEEN, EYRE, PRINCE ALBERT, SASKATOON, VONDA; ORANGEVILLE, TORONTO: 4, Ont.)

Nokomis and Nokomis Lake are named for a character in Henry Wadsworth Longfellow's *The Song of Hiawatha* (1855). It is Nokomis who teaches Hiawatha wisdom on 'the shore of Gitchee Gumee, / By the shining Big-Sea-Water'. A moon-goddess tricked into falling from heaven by a jealous rival, Nokomis is the mother of Hiawatha's mother, Wenonah.

OXBOW

Ralph Allen—novelist, journalist, and newspaper editor—was known as 'the man from Oxbow', although he was born (in 1913) in WINNIPEG and lived in many other small western railway towns before his father, William Glen Allen, was appointed the CPR station agent here. Ralph played the cornet in the Oxbow Citizens' Band and took part in school athletics; he graduated from the town's high school in 1930. Soon afterwards he won his first newspaper position at the sports desk of the Winnipeg *Tribune*. Allen wrote little that directly refers to his childhood, but his novel *Peace River Country* (1958) relates the story of a wandering western-Canadian family much like his own. His essay, 'The Land of Eternal Change' (1955), portrays Oxbow as little changed from when he left it at sixteen, though more attractive than he remembered it. The former CPR station of Oxbow has been converted into the Ralph Allen Memorial Museum, featuring Allen papers and memorabilia, along with historic CPR artefacts and oil-drilling equipment. (See also TORONTO: 6, Ont.)

> THE SMALL TOWN IN SASKATCHEWAN
>
> *There were no other significant variations between this town and the other; brown wooded false fronts on the stores, canned soups, boys' sweaters, calico dresses, Lowney's Nut-Milk Bars, and Fels Naphtha Soap lurking beneath the green partly-drawn blinds; the yellow steeple of the United Church poking skyward at the top of the street; further on, the high board fence guarding the fair grounds and after that the prairie, clean shining snow and winterblackened poplar bluffs. It was the small town of Saskatchewan, a town much idealized by those who have never lived there, much moved-away-from by those who have, and much mourned by people of both kinds. Before she was half-way up the street Mrs. Sondern felt the town settling around her plump person as easily and familiarly as an old girdle. "My, what a lovely place!" she said.*
>
> —Ralph Allen, *Peace River Country* (1958)

PRINCE ALBERT

The poet **Charles Mair** (*Dreamland and Other Poems*, 1868) settled his family here in 1877 after several years in PORTAGE-LA-PRAIRIE, Man. Fearing that the settlement, founded in 1866, would be a centre of unrest in the event of a territorial uprising, Mair moved to WINDSOR, Ont., in 1882. He spent his summers here until 1886, when the family returned permanently to their Prince Albert home, 'Holmwood'. Mair ran a grocery store, worked as postmaster, and maintained a large farm. In 1886 he published *Tecumseh: A Drama*, a heroic portrayal of the great Indian ally to the British during the War of 1812. Although Mair worked vigorously for Prince Albert development, his businesses proved unprofitable and he moved west to FORT STEELE, B.C., to open a bookstore. His family remained in Prince Albert, where his wife was appointed postmistress. The Mair's house was sold at the turn of the century and burned down in 1960. (See also MAIR; KINGSTON, LANARK, OTTAWA, TORONTO: 1, Ont.; WINNIPEG, Man.; CALGARY, Alta; VICTORIA, B.C.)

When she was sixteen, **Lucy Maud Montgomery** (*Anne of Green Gables*, 1908) spent one year in Prince Albert, from the summer of 1890 to the summer of 1891. She came from CAVENDISH, P.E.I., where she had lived since infancy with her grandparents, to stay with her father and stepmother. They lived at Eglintowne Villa, at 1st and Church Sts. Montgomery attended St Paul's Presbyterian Church and Prince Albert High School. She first achieved publication while she was here: a poem written in Prince Albert appeared in a Prince Edward Island newspaper. Her father died here in 1900 and is buried in the Presbyterian Cemetery.

Sinclair Ross (*As for Me and My House*, 1941) was born on 22 Jan. 1908 on a homestead 25 miles from Prince Albert and 12 miles from Shellbrooke. His parents separated when he was three, and he moved often during his childhood because his mother worked as a housekeeper on farms in many parts of the province. After graduating from high school at INDIAN HEAD in 1924, Ross went to work for the Union Bank at ABBEY. (See also ARCOLA, HORIZON; WINNIPEG, Man.; MONTREAL: 6, Que.)

In 1909 the anthropologist and novelist **Selwyn Dewdney** (*Wind Without Rain*, 1946), was born in Prince Albert; the Dewdney home was at 151 20th St. W. He lived here until 1921, when the family moved to Kenora, Ont., after his father was appointed Anglican bishop of the Keewatin Mission Diocese. (See also AGAWA BAY, LONDON, OWEN SOUND, Ont.)

Edna Jaques, Saskatchewan's 'Scrapbook Poet', moved to a homestead near Prince Albert following her marriage to William Ernest Jamieson. By 1919 she had returned with her child to BRIERCREST and begun an independent life as a writer.

Laura Goodman Salverson homesteaded near Prince Albert in 1918, while her husband travelled in his work as an office manager for the Grand Trunk Railway. Salverson soon moved to Prince Albert to run a nine-room boarding house, but later in 1918 she moved to BIGGAR, where her husband had been assigned. (See also REGINA, SASKATOON; GIMLI, WINNIPEG, Man.; CALGARY, EDMONTON, Alta.) **Max Braithwaite** lived here at 161 21st St W. from 1919 to 1923. The house has since been torn down. In 1923 the family left Prince Albert for SASKATOON. The years in Prince Albert figure prominently in Braithwaite's *Never Sleep Three in a Bed* (1970). (See also ABERDEEN, EYRE, NOKOMIS, VONDA; ORANGEVILLE, TORONTO: 4, Ont.)

In recent years Prince Albert named a long-time city resident, **John V. Hicks**, municipal poet. Hicks was organist and choirmaster of the Anglican cathedral and had been publishing poetry in periodicals since the 1920s. His first book, *Winter Your Sleep*, appeared in 1980. The post carries an annual stipend and an office at city hall, 1521 6th Ave W.

PRINCE ALBERT NATIONAL PARK

On the shore of Lake Ajawaan, deep within this 1,496-square-mile park at the geographical centre of Saskatchewan, is the grave of the conservationist and nature writer **Archibald Stansfeld Belaney**, known by his adopted name, **Grey Owl**. Situated beside the lakeside cabin in which he lived for the last seven years of his life, the grave is marked by a simple stone bearing the name 'Grey Owl' and the dates of his birth and death.

Grey Owl came to Lake Ajawaan as a result of a change in his life that led both to his work on beaver conservation and to his career as a world-renowned nature writer. In 1926 he met an Indian woman, Anahareo, who persuaded him to give up trapping and hunting and encouraged him to raise two beavers that the couple had found in the wild. Grey Owl and Anahareo went to CABANO in northern Quebec to find a safe place for their beavers; it was there that he began writing, and there that the Canadian government found him and decided to support his beaver-conservation ideas. In 1930 he was moved to RIDING MOUNTAIN NATIONAL PARK in Manitoba and shortly afterwards to Lake Ajawaan. Appointed an honorary park warden, he made two successful international lecture tours while living here and published *Men of the Last Frontier* (1931), *Pilgrims of the Wild* (1934), *The Adventures of Sajo and Her Beaver People* (1935), and *Tales of an Empty Cabin* (1936). Anahareo, who left Grey Owl in 1937, wrote two memoirs covering the years at Lake Ajawaan, *My Life with Grey Owl* (1940) and *Devil in Deerskins* (1972).

The two beavers rescued by Grey Owl and Anahareo lived here with the couple in the cabin. They would push the door open and carry in mud and sticks to repair their lodge, which was built against an inside wall but was connected to the lake by an underground tunnel. Grey Owl died at Lake Ajawaan on 13 Apr. 1938. Only after his death did it become known that he was not an Indian, as he had pretended to be, but an Englishman, Archie Belaney. His life story has been told by his London publisher, the Canadian writer Lovat Dickson, in *Wilderness Man* (1973). (See also BISCOTASING, COBALT, TEMAGAMI, Ont.)

Inside Grey Owl's cabin, 1932

REGINA

Regina, capital of the province of Saskatchewan, was the site in 1885 of the trial and execution of **Louis Riel**. Exiled to the United States after the Red River Rebellion of 1869–70, Riel returned to Canada in July

Grey Owl's cabin on Lake Ajawaan, 1932

1884 at the request of Métis in the Saskatchewan Valley. Riel's campaign to secure their land rights led to armed rebellion the following year (see DUCK LAKE); he surrendered at Batoche on 15 May 1885. His trial in Regina ended with an order for his death by hanging; after a delay of several months, the sentence was carried out on 16 Nov. 1885. The following year, a volume of Riel's writings, selected by his brothers, was published in MONTREAL: 9; *Poésies religieuses et politiques* contains a long complaint against Prime Minister John A. Macdonald, whose government made the final decision that Riel should be executed. Parts of this poem are translated in *The Poetry of French Canada in Translation* (1970), edited by John Glassco. During his six-month imprisonment Riel wrote voluminously, producing his last essay, 'The Métis of the North West', declarations, poems, diaries, and letters. This material is collected in *The Complete Writings of Louis Riel/Les Écrits complets de Louis Riel* (5 vols, 1985). (See also ST BONIFACE, ST VITAL, WINNIPEG, Man.)

Rudy Wiebe's novel, *The Scorched-Wood People* (1977), tells the story of the two rebellions led by Riel. TORONTO (7) playwright **John Coulter** wrote three plays based on the life of the controversial Métis leader. The first, *Riel* (1962; 1972; rev. 1976), was completed in 1949 and staged at the National Arts Centre in 1975; of the three, this play presents the fullest account of Riel's life. *The Crime of Louis Riel* (1975) won the Dominion Drama Festival's regional prize for the best play of 1967. *The Trial of Louis Riel* (1968) is a courtroom drama based largely on transcripts from the original trial. Since its first staging in Regina, *The Trial of Louis Riel* has become an annual event. It is presented at Saskatchewan House, Dewdney Ave W., at 8:15 p.m. every Tuesday, Wednesday, and Friday from mid-June through August.

The author of the first literary work published in the Northwest Territories (originally, the name given to all lands transferred in 1870 to the Canadian government by the Hudson's Bay Company) was **Nicholas Flood Davin**, an Irish-born lawyer and writer who came to Canada in 1872 and became a newspaper journalist in Toronto. He moved to Regina in 1883 and here founded Assiniboia's first newspaper, the Regina *Leader*. In 1889 Davin published in Regina a volume of poetry, *Eos, an epic of the Dawn*, containing revised poems from his earlier book, *Eos, A Prairie Dream* (1884), which had been published in Ottawa. Davin represented West Assiniboia in the House of Commons from 1887 to 1900; he committed suicide in Winnipeg in 1901.

Riel addressing the jury in the courthouse, Regina, July 1885

The Royal Canadian Mounted Police training centre is located in Regina on Dewdney Ave. Its museum includes exhibits related to famous Mountie cases, including the snowshoes worn by the 'Mad Trapper', Albert Johnson, during his flight from FORT MCPHERSON, N.W.T., in 1931. Johnson wore the shoes backward in an effort to elude his pursuers. His story is told in *The Mad Trapper* (1980) by Rudy Wiebe. Among the many memoirs of service with the mounted police, the best known is Samuel Steele's *Forty Years in Canada: Reminiscences of the Great North-West, with Some Account of His Services in South Africa* (1915). Boys' adventure books about the Mounties were written by several authors, including Steele's son Harwood, author of the history *Policing the Arctic* (1936) and of the novels *Spirit-of-Iron (Manitou-Pewabic): an Authentic Novel of the North West Mounted Police* (1923), *The Ninth Circle* (1927), and *Ghosts Returning* (1950), and a fictionalized biography of his father, *The Marching Call* (1955). The WINNIPEG author **Muriel Denison** wrote a series of children's stories about a young girl befriended by a Mountie troop stationed near Regina in the 1880s. The series began with the well-known *Susannah, a Little Girl with the Mounties* (1936). (See also BON ECHO, Ont.)

Regina was twice home to the novelist **Laura Goodman Salverson**. She first moved here in 1913 after her marriage to an office manager for the Grand Trunk Telegraph. Shortly after, she moved to SASKATOON but returned here in 1919 from her home in BIGGAR. During the following years she began writing stories and poems. Her first story, 'Hidden Fires', won the Canadian Club Prize. In the early 1920s she moved to EDMONTON, Alta. (See also PRINCE ALBERT; GIMLI, WINNIPEG, Man.; CALGARY, EDMONTON, Alta.)

During his student years at the University of TORONTO, the poet **E.J. Pratt** regularly visited Regina in the summers. At this time—the early 1900s—Pratt was often engaged in money-making projects to support his studies. He ran a refreshment stand at the Regina Exhibition, sold encyclopedias, and bought a quarter-section of land as an investment. He also spent time in the area working for the Methodist missions. Another famous literary visitor to Regina was the fictional Sarah Binks, **Paul Hiebert**'s 'Saskatchewan Songstress', whose life story is told in *Sarah Binks* (1947). Regina, which Hiebert explains was 'at that time the Athens of Saskatchewan', figures prominently in Sarah's life as the scene of her one romance. 'Henry Welkin was eager that his young protegé should drink life to the full. He took her to the aquarium and to the public library, and together they studied what fish and what manuscripts were available at these places.' (See also LEADER.) Playwright **David French** spent the years 1968–70 in Regina. While working at the post office, he wrote short stories and plays. On returning to Toronto he wrote *Leaving Home* (1977), the play that established his career following its successful 1972 production at Toronto's Tarragon Theatre. (See also COLEY'S POINT, Nfld; TORONTO: 2, Ont.)

Born in 1940 in MOOSE JAW, the novelist and playwright **Ken Mitchell** has taught Canadian literature and creative writing at the University of Regina since 1967. His play *Davin: The Politician* (1979) tells the story of Nicholas Flood Davin, and of his

Ken Mitchell, 1977

lover Kate Simpson-Hayes, an early feminist. Mitchell's many works include the novels *Wandering Rafferty* (1972) and *The Con Man* (1979), and the musical play *Cruel Tears* (1976).

Writers born in Regina include the playwright **Len Peterson**, who has lived in TORONTO (2, 7) for many years. Born in 1917, Peterson became well known as a radio dramatist in the 1940s; he has also written documentary films, novels, and stage plays for both adults and children, including *The Great Hunger* (1967) and *Almighty Voice* (1974). The poet **John Newlove** was born here on 13 June 1938. In 1938 the Newloves lived at 1918 Robinson St and in 1939 at 2270 Argyle St. Newlove's parents separated in his early childhood, and he was raised by his mother, a teacher, in Saskatchewan farm communities, including VERIGIN. His books include *Moving in Alone* (1965, 1977), *Lies* (1972; winner of a Governor General's Award), and *The Green Plain* (1981). (See also TORONTO: 6, Ont.; NELSON, VANCOUVER, B.C.)

The three-room pioneer farmhouse of **John Diefenbaker**, prime minister of Canada from 1957 to 1963, stands in Wascana Park on Lakeview Dr. at the corner of Broad St. Diefenbaker, born in 1895 in Grey County, Ont., was brought here by his parents when he was a child. In 1905–10 the Diefenbakers homesteaded at Borden (about 25 miles northwest of Saskatoon), where they built this house. Diefenbaker described his upbringing and his life in politics in *One Canada: Memoirs of the Right Honourable John G. Diefenbaker* (3 vols, 1975–7). (See also SASKATOON.)

RUSH LAKE

The novelist **Frederick Philip Grove** visited the farm home of his future wife, Catherine Wiens, at Rush Lake for two weeks during the summer of 1914. He spent most of his time getting to know her father Johan, builder of the first large flour mill at Emerson. Wiens and his family provided material for two of Grove's novels: the hero of *Our Daily Bread* (1928), set in a town called Sedgeby—in the same grassy-plains region where Rush Lake is located—resembles Catherine's father; Johan Wiens was also the inspiration for the heroic patriarch of *The Master of the Mill* (1944). Grove married Catherine on 2 Aug. 1914 at the Anglican church in Swift Current, west of Rush Lake on the Trans-Canada Hwy. (See also FALMOUTH, GLADSTONE, RAPID CITY, WINKLER, Man.; OTTAWA, SIMCOE, Ont.)

SASKATOON

Max Braithwaite and Farley Mowat spent part of their childhood in Saskatoon and both have written humorous accounts of growing up in the city. Braithwaite lived here from 1923 to 1933; the family occupied several different houses, including the one at 705 Temperance St, where Braithwaite and his brother brought pigeons home—an episode recounted in *Never Sleep Three in a Bed* (1969). He attended Albert School (still standing at Clarence Ave and 12th St, but no longer used as a school), where Braithwaite and his sixth-grade classmates held the Christmas dinner described in *Never Sleep Three in a Bed*. Braithwaite graduated from Nutana Collegiate Institute, at 12th St and Victoria Ave, in 1930. He was active in baseball and hockey and wrote for the school paper, the *Saltshaker*. After one year at normal school Braithwaite entered the University of Saskatchewan but left in 1933 to begin teaching. He married Aileen Treleaven at Westminster United Church, Eastlane Ave and 12th St, in 1935. Braithwaite spent his Second World War service in Saskatoon on a Royal Navy training ship; the adventures of the *Unicorn*, moored at First Ave and 24th St, are told in *The Commodore's Barge is Waiting* (1975). (See also ABERDEEN, EYRE, NOKOMIS, VONDA; ORANGEVILLE, TORONTO: 4, Ont.)

Farley Mowat's family moved from WINDSOR, Ont., to Saskatoon in the mid-1930s. Mowat's father, Angus Mowat (*Carrying Place*, 1944), was chief librarian of the Saskatoon Public Library on 23rd St E., opposite City Hall. In 1933–4 the Mowats lived at 908 Saskatchewan Cr. E., in 1935 at 714 Fifth Ave N., and in 1936 at 1102 Spadina Cr. E. Mowat attended Victoria Public School and Nutana Collegiate Institute but left before graduating when his family moved to Toronto. *Mutt, the Dog Who Wouldn't Be* (1957) and *Owls in the Family* (1961) draw on Mowat's years in Saskatoon. After the Second World War he came back to Saskatchewan for several months but returned east in the fall of 1946 to enter the University of Toronto. (See also BURGEO, Nfld., BELLEVILLE, PALGRAVE, PORT HOPE, Ont.; KEEWATIN BARRENS, RANKIN INLET, SPENCE BAY, N.W.T.)

Other writers who have lived in the Saskatoon area include the novelist **Laura Goodman Salverson**, who moved here in 1913 from REGINA. She ran a successful dressmaking shop but gave it up in 1918 to move to a homestead near PRINCE ALBERT. Through 1917 Salverson lived at 508 25th St E., and in 1918 at 1116 7th St. (See also BIGGAR, GIMLI, WINNIPEG, Man.; CALGARY, EDMONTON, Alta.) During the 1930s the poet **Anne Marriott** lived on a farm outside the city for several months. On this experience she based her most famous work, 'The Wind, Our Enemy', published as the title poem in a 1939 Ryerson Poetry Chapbook. Marriott's *Calling Adventurers* (1941) won a Governor General's Award. (See also VANCOUVER, VICTORIA, B.C.)

The poet **Ann Szumigalski** came to Canada from her native England in 1951. She lives in Saskatoon and taught at the Saskatchewan Summer School of Arts from 1966 to 1979 and in 1978 was co-founder and first chairman of the Saskatchewan Writers' Colony. Szumigalski has published *Woman Reading in Bath* (1974), *A Game of Angels* (1980), *Doctrine of Signatures* (1983), and *Risks* (1983).

The University of Saskatchewan, founded in 1907, has brought many writers to Saskatoon as students. Among them are Eli Mandel, Sheila Fischman, and John Newlove, who all studied at the university. The folklorist Edith Fowke received her B.A. here in 1933 and an M.A. in English in 1937. **Edward McCourt** taught English here from 1944 until his death in 1972. McCourt's novels, all written after his appointment to the university, draw on his prairie childhood in KISCOTY, Alta, but academic life in Saskatoon is described in two of his novels: *The Wooden Sword* (1956) and *Fasting Friar* (1963). McCourt wrote travel books, literary criticism, and children's adventures, as well as the novels *Music at the Close* (1947), *Home Is the Stranger* (1950), and *Walk Through the Valley* (1956). In 1945 and for several years thereafter McCourt lived at 705 Temperance St; from about 1950 until 1953 he lived at 211 6th St E. His home from 1954 until his death was at 1310 Melrose Ave. (See also FREDERICTON, N.B.; KINGSTON, ST CATHERINES, TORONTO: 7, Ont., EDMONTON, Alta.) **Guy Vanderhaege** (*Man Descending*, 1982; Governor General's Award), who was born in ESTERHAZY in 1951, studied history here (B.A. 1972; M.A. 1975); he now lives in Saskatoon. The university library contains a collection of McCourt's papers, along with those of the poets, Ralph Gustafson, Al Purdy, and Irving Layton, among others. The library holds Paul Hiebert's typescripts of his *Sarah Binks* (1947) and *Willows Revisited* (1967).

The poet **Elizabeth Brewster** has taught at the University of Saskatchewan since 1972; her office is in the Arts Building, where formerly McCourt had his office. Saskatchewan settings are featured in Brewster's poetry collections *Sometimes I Think of Moving* (1977) and *The Way Home* (1982). The hero of **Stephen Vizinczey**'s novel *In Praise of Older Women* (1965) recalls his early days as a student in Toronto from the vantage point of his professor's chair at the University of Saskatchewan. **John Diefenbaker**, prime minister of Canada from 1957 to 1963, spent part of his childhood in Borden, about 25 miles northwest of here and attended the University of Saskatchewan, which awarded him his law degree. On his death in 1979 Diefenbaker left his papers to the university, which houses them on campus in the John Diefenbaker Centre; the Centre also contains replicas of the prime minister's office and the cabinet chamber as they were during Diefenbaker's incumbency. Diefenbaker described his Saskatchewan upbringing and his life in politics in *One Canada: Memoirs of the Right Honourable John G. Diefenbaker* (3 vols, 1975–7). (See also REGINA.)

TURTLEFORD

The short-story writer **Edna Alford** was born in 1947 at Turtleford, where her family has a farm; she now lives at Livelong, east of here and just south of Turtle Lake. Alford's collections are *A Sleep Full of Dreams* (1981) and *The Garden of Eloise Loon* (1986). Turtleford is northwest of North Battleford on Hwy 26.

VERIGIN

The REGINA-born **John Newlove** grew up in several eastern-Saskatchewan farming communities, where his mother worked as a teacher, and while in grade four lived in Verigin, named for the Doukhobor leader Peter Verigin (1859–1924), who lived here. Newlove draws a complex picture of his childhood experience of the town in 'Verigin, Moving in Alone' (*Moving in Alone*, 1965). He mentions the '2-building / 3-room 12-grade school' where his mother was principal, and recalls especially the meeting-house built by Peter Verigin in 1917: ' . . . leaping into snowbanks from /Peter the Lordly Verigin's / palace on the edge of town . . .' The house, in ruinous condition during the late 1940s when Newlove lived in Verigin, has been restored and is now a national historic site. (See also TORONTO: 6, Ont.; NELSON, VANCOUVER, B.C.) **J.F.C. Wright**'s *Slava Bohu* (1940), which won a Governor General's Award, is a vivid non-fiction account of Doukhobor immigration to Canada and Peter Verigin's prominent part in it.

VONDA

Max Braithwaite taught school here from 1937 to 1940, after having taught in nearby ABERDEEN. These two communities provided the elements of the fictional prairie town 'Wannego', the setting of Braithwaite's *The Night We Stole the Mountie's Car* (1971). Many of the Vonda buildings mentioned specifically in this book are still standing, including the Town Hall and Braithwaite's school (which has been converted to other uses). (See also EYRE, NOKOMIS, PRINCE ALBERT, SASKATOON.)

WEYBURN

W.O. Mitchell was born on 13 Mar. 1914 in this town 50 miles north of the Saskatchewan–North Dakota border. He began school here and played in the open prairie—just down the street from his home at 121 6th St—until the age of eleven, when a tubercular wrist requiring special medical attention forced his mother to take him to live first in California and then in St Petersburg, Florida. He returned to Canada in the 1930s to study at the Universities of Manitoba and Alberta, and though he has lived in Alberta since 1951, southern Saskatchewan has provided the setting for much of his fiction. Weyburn and HIGH RIVER, Alta., are generally supposed to have been the models for Crocus, Sask., the setting of Mitchell's weekly 'Jake and the Kid' series of CBC radio dramas that ran from 1949 to 1957; a selection of these scripts, collected in *Jake and the Kid* (1962), won the Stephen Leacock Medal for humour. The setting of Mitchell's classic novel of a prairie childhood, *Who Has Seen the Wind* (1947), may also be identified with the author's childhood home. (See also WINNIPEG, Man.; CALGARY, EDMONTON, Alta.)

WEYBURN

Here was the least common denominator of nature, the skeleton requirements simply, of land and sky—Saskatchewan prairie. It lay wide around the town, stretching on to the far line of sky, . . . shimmering under the late June sun and waiting for the unfailing visitation of wind, gentle at first, barely stroking the long grasses and giving them life; later, a long, hot gushing that would lift the black top-soil and pile it in barrow pits along the roads or in deep banks against the fences.

—W.O. Mitchell, *Who Has Seen the Wind* (1947)

WOOD MOUNTAIN

The poet **Andrew Suknaski** was born in 1942 on a homestead near Wood Mountain, which is located on Hwy 18 near the U.S. border. Its people, landscape, and history are featured in Suknaski's books *Wood Mountain Poems* (1976), *The Ghosts Call You Poor* (1978), and *In the Name of Narid* (1981). The child of a Polish mother and a Ukrainian father, Suknaski lived here until he attended Simon Fraser University and the University of British Columbia; he has since lived and taught throughout western Canada but has frequently returned to Wood Mountain.

One of Suknaski's subjects is the Sioux warrior Sitting Bull's historical association with Wood Mountain. After defeating the U.S. Army in 1876 at the Battle of the Little Big Horn in Montana, Sitting Bull and 3,000 Sioux under his command crossed into Saskatchewan and took refuge in the Cypress Hills. In nearby Wood Mountain Historic Park are reconstructions of the barracks and mess hall of the few RCMP officers who administered the territory and kept order among the restless warriors until they returned to Montana in 1881.

YORKTON

Born in Pittsburgh, Pennsylvania in 1907, the biographer and critic **Leon Edel** was brought to Yorkton in childhood and grew up here. He was educated at McGill University, where in the 1920s he was a member of the Montreal group of writers that included F.R. Scott, A.J.M. Smith, Leo Kennedy, and others. His literary career is associated with New York—he taught at New York University from 1953 to 1971—where he edited and wrote many books of literary scholarship, notably his five-volume biography of Henry James. He now lives and writes in Hawaii.

Alberta

BANFF

In 1890 **Charles Gordon**, who wrote under the pseudonym, '**Ralph Connor**', came as a newly ordained Presbyterian minister to Banff, the centre of Rocky Mountain Park, which had been established in 1887. For three years he served a mission field that extended from Swift Current, Sask., to Nelson, B.C., in what was then the Northwest Territories. Gordon founded a church in nearby CANMORE. Some of his experiences from this period are recounted in his novels *Black Rock* (1898) and *The Sky Pilot* (1899), both written after he had moved to WINNIPEG. (See also HARRINGTON WEST, ST ELMO, TORONTO: 1, Ont.)

In 1911, at the age of seven, the poet **Earle Birney** moved to Banff from his first home near MORNINGSIDE and lived here until 1916, when his father, returning injured from the First World War, bought a farm near CRESTON, B.C.; in this period the Birneys lived in a small house (still standing) at 308 Squirrel St. Birney returned here to work during summers while he was a student at the University of British Columbia; in 1922–3 he worked on a mosquito-control project at Vermilion Lake, near Banff. Banff National Park, the modern park that has grown from the original Rocky Mountain Park to an area of 2,564 square miles, encompasses the mountain setting of Birney's famous poem 'David', published in his first collection *David and Other Poems* (1942), which won a Governor General's Award. The poem tells the story of two youths who attempt to climb 'the Finger on Sawback' in the Rockies; one of the climbers falls, is paralysed, and asks to be killed, a request that his friend honours. There is an account of the poem's composition in Birney's book, *The Cow Jumped Over the Moon* (1972). Real geographical features named in the poem include the Sawback Range, Inglis Maldie mountain, Assiniboine mountain, and the Spray River, on which the Banff Springs Hotel is located. (See also CALGARY; TORONTO: 3, 6, Ont.; VANCOUVER, B.C.)

John Murray Gibbon, longtime chief publicity agent for the CPR and a prolific writer, is buried in the Banff Cemetery. Gibbon co-founded the Canadian Authors' Association and produced five novels, a collection of folk songs, and several historical works. There is a plaque in his memory at the administration building of the Banff School of Fine Arts. (See also MONTREAL, Que.)

Sid Marty came to Banff National Park as a park warden in 1973, the year he published his first collection of poems, *Headwaters*. Born in 1944 in England and raised in Medicine Hat and Calgary, Marty had worked summers in the mountain national parks. He became a warden in 1966, and before coming to Banff he had served in Yoho National Park in British Columbia and in Jasper National Park. His poems and non-fiction books are primarily about the people and landscapes of these 'contiguous mountain parks', as they are termed. In *Men for the Mountains* (1978; rpr. 1981) Marty recreates the legends and lore, the way of life and the distinctive speech of the park wardens. In 1978 he retired to devote his full time to writing; he now lives on a ranch near LUNDBRECK. Marty has also written a book of poems, *Nobody Danced with Miss Rodeo* (1981), and *A Grand and Fabulous Notion* (1984), a history of Banff National Park, which celebrated its centennial in 1985.

The Banff School of Fine Arts celebrated its fifteenth anniversary in 1983. Many writers, including **W.O. Mitchell** and **Robert Kroetsch**, have taught creative writing here. (In Kroetsch's novel *Alibi*, 1983, the central character begins and ends his search for a perfect spa in the Rocky Mountains near Banff.) The dramatist **Gwen Pharis Ringwood** was the school registrar in 1935–6 and taught drama and acting in 1939 (see also EDSON, EDMONTON, MAGRATH; CHIMNEY LAKE, WILLIAMS LAKE, B.C.). **Eli Mandel**'s journal, kept while he was a faculty member, forms part of his poetry collection *Life Sentences* (1981).

CALGARY

Fort Calgary was established in 1875 as a North West Mounted Police outpost to combat the liquor traffic from the United States to the Plains Indians in Canada. The story of Calgary's growth from those early days through the First World War is told in **Frederick Niven**'s novel *The Flying Years* (1935), which portrays the life of a fictional Scottish immigrant, Angus Munro. This is the second (though first-published) part of Niven's trilogy on the growth of the West, from Manitoba to British Columbia—the province where Niven, himself a Scottish immigrant, settled (see also NELSON, VANCOUVER, B.C.). The other two novels are *Mine Inheritance* (1940) and *The Transplanted* (1944), which describe the development of the Selkirk Settlement, near present-day Winnipeg, and of British Columbia.

Banff Springs Hotel in Banff National Park

Bob Edwards

Charles Gordon, whose pen-name was **Ralph Connor**, was ordained to the Presbyterian ministry in Calgary in 1890 and for the next three years worked as a missionary in the district surrounding BANFF. His experience of the Calgary-Banff region is reflected particularly in *The Sky Pilot: A Tale of the Foothills* (1899). (See also CANMORE; HARRINGTON WEST, ST ELMO, TORONTO: 1, Ont.; WINNIPEG, Man.).

Bob Edwards came to Canada from his native Scotland in 1895; he worked as a journalist in several small Alberta towns and in Calgary, where he settled permanently in 1911. From 1902 to 1922 he published, irregularly, his satirical newspaper the *Eye-Opener*, which became well known across the country for its humorous portrayal of Calgary life; for many years a supplement, *Bob Edwards' Annual*, was also published.

Edwards was elected to the Alberta legislature in 1921, but died the following year. For most of Edwards' time in Calgary he published the *Eye-Opener* and lived in a large commercial building. In 1908 he had offices in the Cameron Block at 717 1st St E., third floor, no. 5. When he returned to Calgary permanently in 1911 he took quarters in the same building. Until 1921 the *Eye-Opener* was in the Cameron Block at 715-A 1st St E., no. 15; Edwards sometimes also occupied no. 14, using one of the suites as his office and one as his home. In 1922, when he died, he was living at 112 4th Ave E. Calgary's Glenbow-Alberta Institute on 9th Ave SW at 1st St SE contains, in its extensive collection of documents and historical materials, many unique copies of the *Eye-Opener*, articles from which have been collected in *The Best of Bob Edwards* (1975).

The poet **Earle Birney** was born here on 13 May 1904 because the death of an earlier baby had convinced his parents that his mother needed hospital care at the birth. The family then returned to its bush farm near MORNINGSIDE, where Birney spent his first seven years. In 1911 he attended school in Calgary before his family moved to BANFF. (See also TORONTO: 3, 6, Ont.; CRESTON, VANCOUVER, B.C.)

The novelist **Robert J.C. Stead** came to Calgary in 1912 to join the *Albertan* after several years of newspaper work near his childhood home of CARTWRIGHT, Man. In 1913 he became a publicist here for the CPR. He had begun publishing poetry in Manitoba and continued to do so in Calgary with the volumes *Kitchener and Other Poems* (1916) and *Why Don't They Cheer* (1918). Here he also wrote several prairie adventure novels, including *The Bail Jumper* (1914), *The Homesteaders* (1916), and *The Cowpuncher* (1918). During his six years in Calgary, Stead lived at 1308 14th Ave W. In 1919 he moved to OTTAWA to work as publicity director for the Department of Immigration and Colonization. *The Homesteaders*, reprinted in 1973, is one of Stead's finest books; like his masterpiece, *Grain* (1926), it is set in the Manitoba of his youth.

About 1914 the novelist **Arthur Stringer** made an unsuccessful attempt to establish a grain farm in southern Alberta about 20 miles southwest of Calgary. He returned to his home in CEDAR SPRINGS, Ont., but the Alberta adventure provided the material for his three enduring novels: *The Prairie Wife* (1915), *The Prairie Mother* (1920), and *The Prairie Child* (1921).

In 1919 the 'scrapbook poet' **Edna Jaques** was commissioned to write a poem about Calgary while flying over the Calgary Stampede. It was, according to Jaques, the first poem ever written in an airplane.

From 1921 to 1924 the poet **Charles Mair** lived in Calgary with his daughter Fanny; he had retired from his long service in the West with the federal Department of Immigration and Colonization. Later he moved to a nursing home in VICTORIA, B.C. During these last years of his life Mair was working on the text of the final, collected edition of his poems, at the urging of Toronto editor John Garvin; the book finally appeared just before Mair's death in 1926. (See also KINGSTON, LANARK, OTTAWA, TORONTO, WINDSOR, Ont.; PORTAGE-LA-PRAIRIE, WINNIPEG, Man.; PRINCE ALBERT, Sask.; FORT STEELE, B.C.)

A native of England, the poet **P.K. Page** lived in the 1920s at 1411 7th St W, which she recalls as the subject of 'almost my first memories; the first address I ever memorized and so, the last I will probably forget.' Page attended St Hilda's School for Girls (no longer standing) during the 1920s and 1930s. Poems by Page with an Alberta setting include 'The Glass Air' and 'The First Part'. She won a Governor General's Award for *The Metal and the Flower* (1954); other important volumes are *Cry Ararat* (1967) and *The Glass Air: Selected Poems* (1985). (See also RED DEER; NEW RIVER BEACH, ROTHESAY, SAINT JOHN, N.B.; KINGSMERE, MONTREAL: 5, Que.; OTTAWA, Ont.; WINNIPEG, Man.; VICTORIA, B.C.)

Laura Goodman Salverson was living in Calgary in 1923 when her first novel, *The Viking Heart*, was published; she had moved here from EDMONTON, where she wrote the book. Her autobiography *Confessions of an Immigrant's Daughter* (1939), which won a Governor General's Award, concludes with this move to Calgary. (See also GIMLI, WINNIPEG, Man.; BIGGAR, PRINCE ALBERT, REGINA, SASKATOON, Sask.)

Like Salverson, **Nellie McClung** moved from EDMONTON to Calgary in 1923; in that year her husband was transferred here by the insurance company he worked for. The house in Calgary in which she lived, at 803 15th St SW, is a provincial historic site. Nellie McClung commuted between Calgary and Edmonton in order to serve in the Alberta Legislature until she was defeated in the 1925 election. In Calgary she wrote her last novel, *Painted Fire* (1925); a book of short stories, *When Christmas Crossed the Peace* (1923); and two popular collections of her newspaper sketches and stories: *Be Good to Yourself* (1930) and *Flowers for the Living* (1931). After her husband retired the family moved in 1935 to Gordonhead, near VICTO-

Laura Goodman Salverson

Nellie McLung, Calgary, 1923

RIA, B.C. (See also CHATSWORTH, OTTAWA, Ont.; LA RIVIÈRE, MANITOU, WAWANESA, WINNIPEG, Man.)

Sheila Watson wrote her first novel, *The Double Hook* (1959), in 1952–3 while living in Calgary. Her husband, the poet **Wilfred Watson**, was teaching at the time at the Calgary campus of the University of Alberta (now the University of Calgary). In 1952–3 the Watsons lived at 1429 8th St NW and then at 1434 8th St NW. (See also EDMONTON; TORONTO: 3, Ont.; DOG CREEK, DUNCAN, NANAIMO, NEW WESTMINSTER, VANCOUVER, B.C.)

W.O. Mitchell has been associated with Calgary for many years. He worked as an advertising salesman for the Calgary *Herald* in 1936 and did some freelance writing before entering the University of Alberta, EDMONTON, where he received his B.A. in 1942. He returned to Calgary in 1968 as writer-in-residence at the University of Calgary, a post he held until 1971. In 1970 Mitchell established his home at 3031 Roxboro Glen Rd SW. Since then, apart from frequent absences to teach at other universities, he has lived in Calgary. *The Vanishing Point* (1973) is the story of the Stony Indians of the 'Paradise Valley Reserve', located near an unnamed city resembling Calgary. Mitchell studied life at the Eden Valley Indian Reserve, 85 miles southwest of Calgary, for the book, which is about the rivalry for the leadership of an Indian band between a well-intentioned Indian agent and a revivalist preacher. (See also CASTOR, HIGH RIVER; WEYBURN, Sask.; WINNIPEG, Man.)

W.P. Kinsella taught at the University of Calgary in 1978–83. His books published during his years here include *Scars* (1978), *Born Indian* (1981), and *Shoeless Joe* (1982), which won the Houghton Mifflin Literary Fellowship in 1982 and the *Books in Canada* Award for First Novels in 1983. The success of *Shoeless Joe* allowed Kinsella to devote his full time to writing; since 1983 he has lived at WHITE ROCK, B.C. (See also EDMONTON; VICTORIA, B.C.)

Robert Kroetsch, who has also been writer-in-residence at the University of Calgary, draws on the city as a setting in his novel *Alibi* (1983), about a search for the perfect spa. The poet **Christopher Wiseman** (*The Upper Hand*, 1979) is a professor of English literature and creative writing at the university and editor of its literary journal *Ariel*. The university library has one of the country's largest holdings of the papers of Canadian authors, including those of Earle Birney, George Bowering, Michael Cook, Harold Horwood, Robert Kroetsch, André Langevin, Hugh MacLennan, W.O. Mitchell, Brian Moore, Alice Munro, Alden Nowlan, Mordecai Richler, Sinclair Ross, Rudy Wiebe, and many others.

CANMORE

Located on the Trans-Canada Hwy just outside Banff National Park, Canmore was part of the mission territory of the Rev. **Charles Gordon**, **'Ralph Connor'**, who served here in 1890–3 and in 1890–1 built one of the first Presbyterian missions in southern Alberta. Named Ralph Connor Church, it still stands on the main street, south of the RCMP barracks, and contains signs that give information about the novelist's career. (See also BANFF; HARRINGTON WEST, ST ELMO, TORONTO: 1, Ont., WINNIPEG, Man.)

CASTOR

The novelist **W.O. Mitchell** was principal of the composite school in Castor in 1944. He had married in 1942 and had spent 1943 gaining teacher's certification at the University of Alberta Faculty of Education. At Castor he began writing his first and best-known novel, *Who Has Seen the Wind* (1947), walking the five blocks from his lodgings to the school each evening after dinner to work in his office. After his year here Mitchell decided to devote full time to writing and moved to HIGH RIVER, where he completed the novel in 1945–7.

COALDALE

The novelist **Rudy Wiebe** moved to this town near Lethbridge on Hwy 3 at the age of twelve and attended the Mennonite high school here. (See also EDMONTON; FAIRHOLME, Sask.)

DEEP CREEK

Born here in 1932, the playwright **George Ryga** (*The Ecstasy of Rita Joe and Other Plays*, 1971) grew up in this Ukrainian farming community. He attended the town's one-room schoolhouse through the seventh grade but then left school and went to work. This marked the end of his formal education, except for a brief period at the University of Texas. Ryga dealt with the experiences of Ukrainian immigrants in *A Letter to My Son* (1982); an earlier version of this story of farmer Ivan Lepa was broadcast in the CBC 'Newcomers' series in 1978. (See also SUMMERLAND, VANCOUVER, B.C.)

DINOSAUR PROVINCIAL PARK

Badlands (1975), by the Alberta novelist **Robert Kroetsch**, takes the reader along the Red Deer River into the region of southeastern Alberta that has yielded some of the world's best dinosaur remains. The novel tells the story of a 1916 dinosaur hunt by William Dawe, a paleontologist working in the area. It is told through the eyes of his daughter Anna, who reconstitutes the event more than fifty years later, using Dawe's notes and photographs. Much of the region in which the novel is set has been designated Dinosaur Provincial Park, north of Patricia on Hwy 554. (See also EDMONTON, HEISLER, RED DEER; WINNIPEG, Man.; MACKENZIE RIVER, N.W.T.)

EDMONTON

Edmonton was the site of trading posts established by both the Northwest Company and the Hudson's Bay Company in the late eighteenth century. After the two companies merged in 1821 Fort Edmonton became the most important settlement in the Canadian West. **Paul Kane** visited here in the fall of 1847 during his three-year sketching trip, which took him from TORONTO (1) to Vancouver Island and Oregon. He wintered at Fort Edmonton before returning east and described the settlement in *Wanderings of an Artist among the Indians of North America from Canada to Vancouver's Island and Oregon through the Hudson's Bay Company's Territory and Back Again* (1859). A lavishly illustrated

Emily Murphy, *c.*1910–18

volume, *Paul Kane's frontier: including 'Wanderings of an artist among the Indians of North America' by Paul Kane* (1971) edited by Russell Harper, contains a definitive biography. Late in the century, after Calgary was chosen for the Canadian Pacific Railway route, Edmonton gained importance again as the starting-point for the overland Canadian trail to the Klondike gold fields.

The media analyst and critic **Marshall McLuhan** was born in Edmonton on 21 July 1911 but grew up in WINNIPEG. At the time of McLuhan's birth his family lived at 582 Highlands St. They were living at 11342 64th St in 1915, when McLuhan's father enlisted and his mother took her two sons to Winnipeg to live with her mother. (See also TORONTO: 3.)

Emily Murphy and her husband, a retired travelling missionary, settled in Edmonton in 1907, after three years on a homestead near SWAN RIVER, Man. She published her writings under her maiden name (Emily Ferguson) or under the pen-name 'Janey Canuck'. Before coming to Edmonton, Murphy had already published *The Impressions of Janey Canuck Abroad* (1901), her first book. In Edmonton she collected a series of sketches about Swan River for *Janey Canuck in the West* (1910). Two similar books with Alberta material followed: *Open Trails* (1912) and *Seeds of Pine* (1914). Murphy became Canada's first woman magistrate with her appointment to the juvenile court at Calgary in 1916. Challenges to her right to hold the post led to the famous 'Persons Case', which was settled in 1929 with the judgement by the British Privy Council that the word 'persons' in the British North America Act must be interpreted to include women as well as men. Murphy resigned her post in 1931 and died in Edmonton in 1933. Her writings also included non-fiction treatments of social issues, including drug addiction, which she became familiar with through her court work. During most of her first seven years in Edmonton, Murphy lived at 514 12th St; in 1915–16 she lived at 10325 132nd St, and in 1917 at 8702 112th St. Her long-time home was at 11011 88th Ave, where she lived from 1919 until her death.

One of Murphy's allies in the 'Persons Case', **Nellie McClung**, moved to Edmonton from WINNIPEG in 1914. She continued her work for women's suffrage here and wrote *In Times Like These* (1915), a defence of women's rights. McClung was elected to the Alberta legislature in 1921 as a liberal and served four years—commuting for the last two from CALGARY, where she moved in 1923 when her husband was transferred there. McClung's books written in Edmonton included *Purple Springs* (1925), a continuation of her first novel *Sowing Seeds in Danny* (1908); *The Next of Kin* (1917); and a novel about a First World War escaped prisoner-of-war, *Three Times and Out* (1918). In 1914–18 McClung lived at 11229 Victoria Ave; in 1917 this address became 11229 100th Ave. During her last five years in Edmonton her home was at 10303 123rd St. (See also CHATSWORTH, OTTAWA, Ont.; LA RIVIÈRE, MANITOU, WAWANESA, Man., VICTORIA, B.C.)

Laura Goodman Salverson, a native of WINNIPEG, wrote her first novel, *The Viking Heart*, while living here; it was published in 1923 after she had moved to CALGARY. (See also GIMLI, WINNIPEG, Man.; BIGGAR, PRINCE ALBERT, REGINA, SASKATOON, Sask.)

Born here on 25 May 1935, novelist and short story writer **W.P. Kinsella** spent his first ten years on a bush farm near Darwell, 60 miles northwest of Edmonton; his family then moved to Edmonton, where Kinsella received his high school education. For many years he worked in business before going to VICTORIA, B.C., where he earned a B.A. from the University of Victoria in 1974. He first gained recognition for the Indian stories published in *Dance Me Outside* (1977), his first book, and in *Scars* (1978), *Born Indian* (1981), and *The Moccasin Telegraph* (1981). These stories of Cree reservation life are largely set on the Ermeniskin Reserve near Hobbema, south of Edmonton on Highway 2A. However, Kinsella has stated that he has never visited the reserve and that much of the experience upon which his characters are based was gained while he was working as a taxi driver in Victoria. Kinsella later studied in the United States and taught at the University of Calgary; in CALGARY he wrote his novel about baseball, *Shoeless Joe* (1982). Since 1983 Kinsella has lived in WHITE ROCK, B.C.

Many writers have come to Edmonton to study or to teach at the University of Alberta, which was founded in 1906. **Lovat Dickson** entered the university in 1923 after several years of operating a weekly newspaper at the Blue Diamond Mine, Alberta. He graduated in 1927 and taught until 1929, when he moved to London, England, where he edited the *Fortnightly Review*. Dickson evokes his student years in his first volume of autobiography, *The Ante Room* (1959; rpr. 1975). His second autobiographical book, *The House of Words* (1963; rpr. 1976), recounts his experience as a publisher in Britain, where he founded his own publishing company and later became chief editor and a director of the Macmillan Company. Dickson introduced the nature-writer **Grey Owl, Archibald Stansfeld Belaney** (see CABANO, Que; TEMAGAMI, Ont; RIDING MOUNTAIN NATIONAL PARK, Man; PRINCE ALBERT NATIONAL PARK, Sask.), to Great Britain. Dickson had been a student of **E.K. Broadus**, a legendary teacher who was head of the English department of the University of Alberta from its formation in 1908 until his death in 1936. Broadus writes of Edmonton and the university during his first years there in *Saturday and Sunday* (1935). Dickson returned to Canada in 1967, making his home in TORONTO (6), where he died on 2 Jan. 1987.

The historical novelist **W.G. Hardy** (1895–1975) taught classics at the university for many years. Based largely on Roman and Biblical history, his books include *Father Abraham* (1935), *All the Trumpets Sound* (1942), *Turn Back the River* (1938), and *The City of Libertines* (1957). One novel with a Canadian setting is *The Unfulfilled* (1951). His long-time home, established in the early 1920s, was at 10828 79th Ave. (See also LINDSAY, Ont.)

Raised on a homestead near KISCOTY, the novelist **Edward A. McCourt** (*Music at the Close*, 1947) received a B.A. from the University of Alberta and went on as a Rhodes Scholar to receive an M.A. from Oxford University in 1937. (See also ST CATHARINES, TORONTO: 7, Ont.; SASKATOON, Sask.)

The playwright **Gwen Pharis Ringwood** studied for her B.A. at the University of Alberta from 1929 to 1934. She was secretary to the director of drama in the Extension Department. While working at the BANFF School of Fine Arts in 1935–6 she wrote ten radio plays for CKUA Radio, University of Alberta, to be used on the program 'New Lamps for Old'. Ringwood studied in the United States from 1937 to 1939, and spent her summers teaching at the University of Alberta summer school. She was director of drama at the Extension Department for the 1939–40 academic year, and in 1940 wrote and staged a historical pageant based on the life of Methodist missionary John MacDougall for the seventieth anniversary of the Methodist Church. Ringwood had married in 1939; her husband's medical practice took them to Goldfields, Sask., and Lamont, Alta. She returned to Edmonton in 1943, where she received a grant to write plays on Alberta themes. For the next ten years, with the exception of 1946–8, the family was settled in Edmonton, but in 1953 they moved to WILLIAMS LAKE, B.C. Between 1943 and 1953 Ringwood wrote plays (*Still Stands the House, The Jack and the Joker, The Rainmaker, Stampede, The Drowning of Wasyl Nemitchuk or A Fine Colored Easter Egg*, and others); radio plays ('The Fight Against the Invisible', 'Right on Our Doorstep', 'Frontier to Farmland', and others); and short stories ('The Little Ghost' and 'The Truth About the Ten Gallon Hat'). (See also EDSON, MAGRATH; CHIMNEY LAKE, B.C.)

W.O. Mitchell received his B.A. from the University of Alberta in 1942 and studied the next year at the Faculty of Education. In the fall of 1943 he moved to CASTOR, where he taught and began writing his novel *Who Has Seen the Wind* (1947); it was completed in HIGH RIVER, where he moved in 1945. He was writer-in-residence at the university in 1971–2. (See also CALGARY, WINNIPEG, Man.; WEYBURN, Sask.) **Robert Kroetsch** (*Alibi*, 1983) graduated from the university with a B.A. in 1948. **Rudy Wiebe** (*Peace Shall Destroy Many*, 1962), who graduated with a B.A. in 1956, has taught here since 1967. In 1967–70 Wiebe lived at 11438 75th Ave; since the early 1970s he has lived on 143rd St. Wiebe also owns rural property at Strawberry Creek about 50 miles from the city. Novels dating from his Edmonton teaching years include *The Blue Mountains of China* (1970), *The Temptations of Big Bear* (1974), and *The Scorched Wood People* (1977). The university library holds a collection of his papers. The poet **Elizabeth Brewster** taught in the English department from 1968 to 1972; poems with Alberta settings are included in *Sunrise North* (1972).

Robert Kroetsch

Rudy Wiebe, *c.*1981

For many years the poet **Wilfred Watson** and novelist **Sheila Watson**, his wife, were associated with the University of Alberta. Wilfred transferred here from the University of Alberta, CALGARY (now the University of Calgary), and Sheila Watson began teaching here in 1961. Best known for *The Double Hook* (1959), Sheila retired in 1975; Wilfred retired in 1976. They started the little magazine *white pelican* here in 1971, and continued it until 1978 in NANAIMO, B.C., where they settled after leaving Edmonton. Wilfred Watson's first collection of poetry, *Friday's Child* (1955), won a Governor General's Award; a second, *The Sorrowful Canadian*, was published in 1972. *Poems*, a collected edition, appeared in 1986. Several of Watson's plays premièred at the Studio Theatre of the University, including the anti-war, *Oh Holy Ghost, Dip Your Finger in the Blood of Canada and Write, I Love You*, and *Let's Murder Clytemnestra, According to the Principles of Marshall McLuhan*. (See also DOG CREEK, DUNCAN, NEW WESTMINSTER, B.C.)

The poet **Stephen Scobie**, who won a Governor General's Award for *McAlmon's Chinese Opera* (1980), taught at the University of Alberta in 1969–79, and while here co-founded Longspoon Press, a literary publishing house. (See also VICTORIA, B.C.) His collaborator in the venture was the poet **Douglas Barbour**, who has taught literature and creative writing here since 1969. His collections of poems include *White* (1973) and *Shorelines* (1979). Another current faculty member is the novelist **Henry Kreisel**, who began teaching here in 1947 and was named a University Professor in 1975; he has also served as chairman of the English department (1961–7) and vice-president-academic of the university (1970–5). His works of fiction are *The Rich Man* (1948), *The Betrayal* (1964; rpr. 1971) and *The Almost Meeting and Other Stories* (1981).

Wilfred Watson, 1987

HEISLER

The novelist and poet **Robert Kroetsch** was born on 26 June 1927 and raised in this town on Hwy 855 southeast of Edmonton. The family farm—its buildings are still standing—was 1 1/2 miles west and 3 miles south of Heisler. Kroetsch lived here from 1927 to 1948; he attended Heisler High

School but completed his secondary schooling at Red Deer High School in 1944–5. Kroetsch uses small-town Alberta for three novels, set respectively in the 1930s, 1940s, and 1970s: *The Words of My Roaring* (1966), *The Studhorse Man* (1969), and *Gone Indian* (1973). Their setting is the region of the Battle River (called the Cree River in the books) as it flows from Dried Meat Lake, south of Camrose, to Alliance. (See also DINOSAUR PROVINCIAL PARK, EDMONTON; WINNIPEG, Man.; MACKENZIE RIVER, N.W.T.)

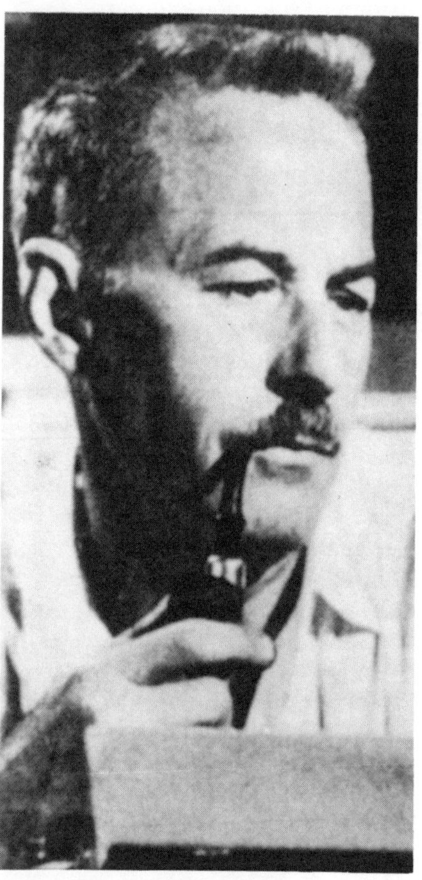

W.O. Mitchell, 1962

HIGH RIVER

This small ranching town thirty miles south of Calgary was the home of **W.O. Mitchell** from 1945 to 1969. After a year at the University of Alberta Faculty of Education in 1943, Mitchell taught at CASTOR before deciding in 1945 to strike out as a freelance writer. Mitchell and his wife and infant son moved to High River and lived in a hotel for almost a year before finding a house. The novelist completed his first and best-known novel, *Who Has Seen the Wind* (1947)—which he had begun at Castor—during his first two years here; the $5,000 advance offered for the manuscript by the Curtis Publishing Co. of Philadelphia rescued the family from poverty. Except for the years 1948–51, which he spent in TORONTO working as an editor for *Maclean's*, Mitchell lived in High River until he moved to CALGARY in 1969. His longtime home stands at 514 8 St.W.; it is privately owned. Here he wrote many of his 'Jake and the Kid' stories and scripts; along with WEYBURN, Sask., High River is a primary model for Crocus, Saskatchewan, the fictional setting of these stories, thirteen of which are collected in *Jake and the Kid* (1962), winner of a Leacock Medal for Humour. Mitchell's novel *The Kite* (1962) was also written here; it is set in the fictional town of Shelby, Alberta, described as being near Calgary. The action of *The Vanishing Point* (1973) occurs in a thinly disguised Calgary and in the fictional Paradise Valley Indian Reserve, which is described as being sixty miles south of the city; for this book Mitchell drew on his acquaintance with the Stony Indians, gained at High River and at the real Eden Valley reserve.

JASPER

Howard O'Hagan grew up in the Yellowhead Lake region of the Rocky Mountains, near Jasper, and returned to work as a tour guide in Jasper National Park after graduating from McGill University in 1928. After time spent overseas and in eastern Canada, O'Hagan again worked briefly in Jasper as a publicist for the CNR. From the late 1930s he lived in British Columbia when in Canada, (see VICTORIA, B.C.) but he based his principal novels and stories of the wilderness on his experience of the Alberta Rockies. (See also LETHBRIDGE; MONTREAL: 3, Que.)

O'Hagan's *Tay John* (1939) draws together Indian legend and the modern West in a complex work based on tales of the mythical hero of the Shushwap Indians of the Yellowhead region. Settings in the novel include Yellowhead Lake and buildings that clearly resemble those at the entrance to Jasper National Park. In his stories, the best of which are collected in *The Woman Who Got on at Jasper Station and Other Stories* (1963), O'Hagan repeatedly places the action at sites now nearby and in the Park; the Athabasca and Smoky Rivers, Brule Lake, Miette Hot Springs, Mt Robson, and Yellowhead Pass.

> JASPER
>
> *It is physically exhausting to look on unnamed country. A name is the magic to keep it within the horizons. Put a name to it, put it on a map, and you've got it.*
>
> —Howard O'Hagan, *Tay John* (1939)

KISCOTY

A native of Ireland, the novelist and literary critic **Edward McCourt** was brought to Canada at the age of two in 1909 and grew up on a farm outside Kiscoty. He was educated at home through correspondence high-school courses and then attended the University of Alberta, EDMONTON. After studying abroad and working in eastern Canada, he joined the faculty of the University of Saskatchewan, SASKATOON, in 1944. (See also FREDERICTON, N.B.; KINGSTON, ST CATHARINES, TORONTO: 7, Ont.) Three of McCourt's novels draw on his childhood experiences at Kiscoty for their depiction of prairie farm life in the era of the First World War: *Music at the Close* (1947), *Home Is the Stranger* (1950), and *Walk Through the Valley* (1958).

LETHBRIDGE

The wilderness novelist **Howard O'Hagan** was born in Lethbridge in 1902 but grew up in the Yellowhead Pass region of the Rocky Mountains, near JASPER. He studied law at McGill University, MONTREAL (3), but returned in the 1930s to work in the Jasper area as tour guide and publicist for the CNR; much of his fiction and non-fiction is set in the Yellowhead region, including his most famous novel, *Tay John* (1939). (See also VICTORIA, B.C.)

The journalist and novelist **Wilfrid Eggleston** joined the staff of the *Lethbridge Herald* about 1920; he wrote a column about the Manyberries district, where he had worked before becoming a reporter. The editor of the *Herald*, W.A. Buchanan, encour-

Howard O'Hagan

aged him in his writing, and Eggleston left Lethbridge to attend Queen's University in KINGSTON, Ont. He began his journalism career in eastern Canada in 1926 on the Toronto *Globe*. (See also MEDICINE HAT; OTTAWA, TORONTO: 4, Ont.)

LUNDBRECK

After 12 years as a park warden in Alberta and British Columbia, **Sid Marty** retired in 1978 to devote himself to writing; he now lives on a ranch 15 miles from Lundbreck near the Crow's Nest Pass. Three contiguous mountain parks—Yoho National Park in British Columbia, and Banff and Jasper National Parks in Alberta—are featured in all of Marty's works, which include *Men for the Mountains* (1978); two poetry collections, *Headwaters* (1973) and *Nobody Danced with Miss Rodeo* (1981); and a history of Banff National Park, *A Grand and Fabulous Notion* (1984). (See also BANFF.)

MAGRATH

In 1917 the family of the playwright **Gwen Pharis Ringwood** moved to Magrath, on Hwy 5 south of Lethbridge. They had been living at Barons, their first home in Canada, for three years before the move. Ringwood was seven when she came to Magrath; she attended high school here, as well as in Crescent Heights and CALGARY. She left Magrath in 1929 to attend the University of Alberta at EDMONTON but returned here in 1939 to marry Dr John Brian Ringwood of Magrath. The couple took up residence in Edmonton. (See also BANFF; CHIMNEY LAKE, WILLIAMS LAKE, B.C.)

MARKERVILLE

Stephan Gudmundsson Stephansson, born in Iceland in 1853, immigrated to the United States in 1873 and moved to Canada in 1889. He farmed at the village of Markerville, near Innisfail, 20 miles south of Red Deer on Hwy 2A. Beginning in 1898 Stephansson, who wrote in Icelandic, published several volumes of verse in his native Iceland. He has been called a poet 'unsurpassed by any other Icelandic poet since the Middle Ages'. A collection of his verse was translated by Watson Kirkconnell in 'Canada's Leading Poet: Stephan G. Stephansson', *University of Toronto Quarterly* (1936). His poetry is also featured in *The North American Book of Icelandic Verse* (1930). Translations by Kirkconnell and others have been collected in *Stephan G. Stephansson: Selected Translations* (1982). Stephansson died in Markerville in 1927; his house has been preserved as a provincial historic site and is open to the public during the summer months. The poet is buried near his home in the Christiansson Cemetery.

MEDICINE HAT

The journalist and prairie novelist **Wilfrid Eggleston** lived for five years on a quarter-section of land 50 miles south of Medicine Hat, where his father had filed blind in Feb. 1910. He attended the country school in the adjoining Hudson's Bay section and left home at fifteen to work as a store clerk and bank junior in three villages along the Manyberries railway line. During this period he published a volume of poems, *Prairie Moonlight and Other Lyrics* (1927). Eggleston began his journalism career as a sports writer for the *Medicine Hat News*; later he joined the staff of the LETHBRIDGE *Herald*. In 1938 he published *The High Plains*, an autobiographical novel of homesteading in Alberta; another novel, *Prairie Symphony*, written in the 1940s, was published for the first time in 1978. Eggleston also wrote a literary study, *The Frontier in Canadian Letters* (1957) and a memoir, *While I Remember* (1968). (See also KINGSTON, OTTAWA, TORONTO: 4, Ont.)

MORNINGSIDE

Born in CALGARY on 13 May 1904, the poet **Earle Birney** spent the first seven years of his life on a small farm called Bonnydoone Ranch, 1 mile from Morningside, which was little more than a flag station on the railway line. The closest sizeable town was Ponoka, 10 miles north. The house on the quarter section of land homesteaded by his father is now gone. Birney's reminiscences about his childhood years here appear in his book *Spreading Time* (1980). The family moved to BANFF in 1911. (See also MORNINGSIDE; TORONTO: 3, 6, Ont.; CRESTON, VANCOUVER, B.C.)

RED DEER

The family of **P.K. Page** came to the Red Deer district in 1919 from England, where Page was born in 1916. They moved to CALGARY in the 1920s and Page attended St Hilda's School. (See also ROTHESAY, NEW RIVER BEACH, SAINT JOHN, N.B.; KINGSMERE, MONTREAL: 5, Que.; OTTAWA, Ont.; WINNIPEG, Man.; VICTORIA, B.C.)

Robert Kroetsch, born in HEISLER, attended Red Deer High School in 1944–5 and entered the University of Alberta, EDMONTON, the next fall. His novel *Badlands* (1975) follows an expedition that begins in Red Deer, through the Alberta Badlands in search of dinosaur fossils. (See also DINOSAUR PROVINCIAL PARK, Alta; WINNIPEG, Man.; MACKENZIE RIVER, N.W.T.)

RICH VALLEY

The French-born novelist **Georges Bugnet** came to Canada in 1905, at the age of twenty-six, and settled at Rich Valley, a hamlet near Jasper, where he farmed for fifty years. Bugnet wrote in his spare time in an effort to supplement the small income from his farm. His best-known novel is *La Fôret* (1935; English trans. by David Carpenter, *The Forest*, 1976), a tragic story of French immigrants in the Canadian West whose failure to live in harmony with nature dooms their homestead. Bugnet's first novel, *Le Lys de sang* (1923), has an African setting; his second, *Nipsya* (1924), is based on his life in Rich Valley. Both of these early novels were written under the pseudonym 'Henry Doutremont'. Although they received little attention when first published, Bugnet's work gained popularity with the 1929 English translation of *Nipsya*. He died in 1981.

ST ALBERT

The missionary and writer Père **Albert Lacombe**, renowned for his work among the Cree and Blackfoot Indians and the Métis, founded St Albert in 1861 and organized the Métis settlement here between 1861 and 1872. He was vicar-general at St Albert from 1896 to 1912. Among Lacombe's linguistic works was a Cree dictionary and grammar based on unpublished work by Père Georges-Antoine Belcourt (see RUSTICO, P.E.I.), under whom Lacombe first served in the West in 1849 at Pembina in what is now North Dakota. Lacombe wrote journals, a book on the colonization of the West, several additional linguistic works, and his *Memoirs of the Half-Breeds of Manitoba and the Canadian North West* (1901). He travelled widely in the West, serving at WINNIPEG and EDMONTON, and acting as a peacemaker in the North West Rebellion of 1885. Lacombe, Alberta, is named for him. He died in 1916.

British Columbia

BURNABY

Daryl Hine (*Selected Poems*, 1980) was born here in 1936 and at the age of fifteen contributed poems to the final issues of the VICTORIA magazine, *Contemporary Verse*, edited by Alan Crawley. His first book, *Five Poems* (1954), appeared three years later. Since 1958, when Hine travelled to Europe on a Canada Council grant, he has lived in the United States. After studying at the University of Chicago, he joined the faculty there in 1967 as a professor of creative writing and comparative literature. From 1968 to 1978 he edited the Chicago magazine *Poetry*. His *Selected Poems* was published in Toronto in 1980.

George Woodcock lived in Burnaby in 1953–4 and again in 1956–7. During his first stay he lived in a cabin that stood on the top of Capitol Hill near the home of the painter Jack Shadbolt on Harbourview Rd; in 1956–7 the Woodcocks occupied Shadbolt's house while the painter was in Europe. (See also SOOKE, VANCOUVER; WINNIPEG, Man.) Capitol Hill provided a setting for **Ethel Wilson**'s novel *Swamp Angel* (1954).

Simon Fraser University opened its Burnaby Mountain campus in 1965; the following year the *West Coast Review* began publication here; this journal is edited by poet Frederick Candelaria. The poet and novelist **George Bowering** (*Burning Water*, 1980) has taught here since 1973, although he lives in nearby VANCOUVER, where he attended the University of British Columbia from 1957 to 1963. (See also PENTICTON; MONTREAL: 7, Que; LONDON, Ont.) The poet **J. Michael Yates** (*The Great Bear Lake Meditations*, 1970), who taught in the Creative Writing Department of the University of British Columbia in the late 1960s, is a recent Burnaby resident. (See also VANCOUVER.) The poets **Lionel Kearns** and **Robin Blaser** also teach here. The university library has excellent holdings of contemporary and avant-garde poetry, including materials from Vancouver's *Tish* movement, and the Beat, Black Mountain, and New York groups in the United States.

Roderick Haig-Brown's library

CAMPBELL RIVER

This world-famous sports-fishing centre on Vancouver Island, at the north end of the Strait of Georgia, was the home of the naturalist and distinguished nature writer **Roderick Haig-Brown** from 1934 until his death in 1976. His house is at 2250 Campbell River Rd. Born in England, Haig-Brown first came to British Columbia in 1927; he did various work, including fishing and cougar hunting, until 1929, when he returned to England. Homesick for British Columbia, he came back to settle in 1931, and after his marriage in 1934 bought the 20-acre farm, 'Above Tide', on the Campbell River, that he described in his works about the region. Haig-Brown was appointed magistrate in the village of Campbell River in 1942 and served as a provincial-court judge there for thirty-three years. Most of his twenty-five books were written at 'Above Tide', which was bought in 1975 by the province of British Columbia as a residence for conservationists and writers. Among Haig-Brown's best-known works are the tetralogy on fishing: *Fisherman's Spring* (1951), *Fisherman's Winter* (1954), *Fisherman's Summer* (1959), and *Fisherman's Fall* (1964); an adventure book for children, *Starbuck Valley Winter* (1946), set in the British Columbia bush; *A River Never Sleeps* (1946); *Panther* (1934); and his first book, *Silver: the Life of an Atlantic Salmon* (1931). The farm at 'Above Tide', often described in his work, was portrayed most fully in *Measure of the Year* (1959), which explores the cycle of the year and Haig-Brown's varied life at Campbell River.

The river at 'Above Tide' was the scene of one of Haig-Brown's most memorable

WHY I FISH

I still don't know why I fish or why other men fish, except that we like it and it makes us think and feel. But I do know that if it were not for the strong quick life of rivers, for their sparkle in the sunshine, for the cold greyness of them under rain and the feel of them about my legs as I set my feet hard down on rocks or sand or gravel, I should fish less often. A river is never quite silent; it can never, of its very nature, be quite still; it is never quite the same from one day to the next. It has its own life and its own beauty and the creatures it nourishes are alive and beautiful also. Perhaps fishing is for me only an excuse to be near rivers. If so, I'm glad I thought of it.

—Roderick Haig-Brown, *A River Never Sleeps* (1946)

experiences recorded in *Fisherman's Fall*. After a lifetime of hunting and fishing, Haig-Brown discovered that a new sport—scuba-diving in the familiar waters near his home—had permanently changed his attitude towards catching fish: 'I find that I have practically no desire to go out and catch the fish I have seen while diving; I would rather go back and have another look at them. By the time I have watched the same fish twice, he is an old friend and I wouldn't dream of going out to kill him; I would even hesitate to disturb him by catching him and putting him back.'

CHILKOOT PASS

Although **Robert Service** did not enter the Yukon through Chilkoot Pass, he immortalized this treacherous mountain passage in his novel of Gold Rush days, *The Trail of Ninety-Eight* (1910). Rising to a height of 3,485 feet through the Coast Mountains north of Skagway, Alaska, the Chilkoot Pass straddles the British Columbia border. In the winter of 1897–8 it was the only mountain pass available to would-be prospectors heading for the Yukon from the Pacific Coast (the treacherous WHITE PASS, used the year before, had been closed). Chilkoot is so steep that at some points its angle of elevation reaches 35 degrees. Despite this and the bitter winter cold, 22,000 people entered the Klondike through the pass in the winter of 1897–8; moreover, each made the climb several times in order to transport the 1,000-pound kit of food and equipment—enough supplies for one year—that the North West Mounted Police insisted every newcomer bring into the gold fields.

The American writer **Jack London**, author of many books and stories depicting the Klondike Gold Rush and its region (*God of Their Fathers: Tales of the Klondike and the Yukon*, 1902; *The Call of the Wild*, 1903; *White Fang*, 1906; *Smoke Bellow*, 1912), arrived at Chilkoot in Aug. 1897. Unable to afford the cost of Indian porters, he carried his prospecting equipment—in bundles weighing 100 to 200 pounds—through the pass, sometimes racing and beating the Indian porters in the climb. A poet of the western United States, **Joaquin Miller**, also crossed into the Yukon Territory through Chilkoot Pass in 1897 while working as a correspondent for the Hearst newspaper syndicate. In *Klondike: the Life and Death of the Last Great Gold Rush* (1958; rev. edn, 1972), **Pierre Berton** used Chilkoot as a symbol of the incredible feats the prospectors were willing to undertake in the search for gold: 'In the years that followed, they tended to run their lives as if they were scaling a perpetual Chilkoot, secure in the knowledge that any obstacle, real or imagined, can be conquered by a determined man.' (See also VANCOUVER; KLEINBURG, TORONTO: 2, Ont.; DAWSON CITY, WHITEHORSE, Y.T.)

Today there are hiking tours through Chilkoot Pass, originating in nearby Lake Bennett from the station of the White Pass & Yukon Railway, a historic narrow-gauge line that was built in 1900 to conquer the White Pass and that still operates between WHITEHORSE and Skagway. Robert Service took the White Pass & Yukon on his way to Whitehorse when he first entered the Yukon Territory.

CHIMNEY LAKE

The playwright **Gwen Pharis Ringwood** has lived at Chimney Lake since 1968, when her husband retired from his medical practice. Her plays written here include *The Lodge*, *The Magic Carpet of Antonio Angelini*, *Mirage*, and *The Garage Sale*. *The Collected Plays of Gwen Pharis Ringwood* was published in 1982. (see also WILLIAMS LAKE; BANFF, CALGARY, EDMONTON, EDSON, MAGRATH, Alta.)

CRAIGELLACHIE

The last spike of the Canadian Pacific Railway was driven on 7 Nov. 1885 in Eagle Pass, between Sicamous and Revelstoke, in the Monashee Mountains of southeastern British Columbia; the site was named Craigellachie in honour of the clan meeting-place, in Scotland, of the railway's president, George Stephen. **E.J. Pratt**'s narrative poem, *Towards the Last Spike* (1952), recreates the struggle to complete the cross-country railway. In *The Last Spike: The Great Railway, 1881–1885* (1971) **Pierre Berton** details the efforts of construction and financing that led to Craigellachie. (See also VANCOUVER; KLEINBURG, TORONTO: 2, 3, Ont.; DAWSON CITY, WHITEHORSE, Y.T.)

A plaque today marks Craigellachie as the place where 'a plain iron spike welded East to West'; it is beside the CPR tracks in Eagle Pass, 16 miles east of Sicamous, and may be reached from the Trans-Canada Hwy, which follows the CPR route through the region.

CRESTON

Earle Birney's family moved from BANFF, Alta, in 1916, when the poet was twelve, to a fruit ranch near Creston, 10 miles north of the Idaho border. Birney attended the small high school here and left the town in 1922 to study chemistry at the University of British Columbia, VANCOUVER. (See also TORONTO: 3, 6, Ont.; BANFF, CALGARY, MORNINGSIDE, Alta.)

DOG CREEK

This remote settlement in the Cariboo country, about 100 miles northwest of Kamloops, was one of several small towns in the province where **Sheila Watson** taught elementary school during the 1930s. Watson

The Chilkoot Pass, *c.*1898

modelled the community in her novel *The Double Hook* (1959) on these small towns, especially Dog Creek, where she worked from 1935 to 1937. The novel describes in poetic prose a revelation of hope to the troubled residents of an isolated community that is under the protection of a mysterious character, called Coyote, drawn from West Coast Indian legend. (See also NANAIMO, NEW WESTMINSTER; CALGARY, EDMONTON, Alta.)

A.J.M. Smith, Margerie and Malcolm Lowry

DOLLARTON

The novelist **Malcolm Lowry** came to Canada in July 1939 from California, where he had been working as a screen-writer. Born in England, Lowry was travelling on a British passport and intended to renew his visa by re-entering the United States from Canada. But he was prevented from doing so by the outbreak of the Second World War, and for the next fifteen years a beach shack at Dollarton was his home. Dollarton lies on the north shore of Burrard Inlet on the Dollarton Hwy from North Vancouver and is now part of the municipality of North Vancouver. Lowry and his second wife, Margerie Bonner, whom he married here in 1940, lived in a community of beach shacks built in the district that is now Cates Park; in his fiction he referred to this community as 'Eridanus'. The shacks stood on piles above the water line and were targeted for destruction by the town so that a park could be built at Roche Point; Lowry lived under this threat during his years at Dollarton, and some years after his death his shack was destroyed as part of preparations for the park. His shack stood 300–400 feet west of the present boaters' dock in Cates Park.

Lowry had published his first novel, *Ultramarine* (1933), before coming to Canada. He loved Dollarton but disliked Vancouver, although the city provided much of the intellectual companionship he enjoyed during his years here. He studied the cabbala with Charles Stansfeld-Jones in VANCOUVER, and his friends **Earle Birney** and **Dorothy Livesay** both lived there. In 1954, he was sought out on his Dollarton beach by **Al Purdy**, who was working in Vancouver. During the early 1940s Lowry was busy with many writing projects, chief among them being a revision of the manuscript of *Under the Volcano* (1947).

In June 1944 the Lowry shack burned to the ground. The Lowrys escaped without injury, along with the manuscript of *Under the Volcano*, but another novel, *In Ballast to the White Sea*, was destroyed except for a few charred pages that are now housed, along with many other Lowry manuscripts, at the Special Collections of the University of British Columbia Library, Vancouver. Lowry never reconstructed the novel. After the fire the couple went to stay with friends at NIAGARA-ON-THE-LAKE, Ont., where Lowry finished the final draft of *Under the Volcano* (revised to include a description of the fire). In 1945 the Lowrys returned to Dollarton and rebuilt their shack, but until 1949 they spent most of their time travelling in Mexico and Europe. In 1947 and 1948 Dorothy Livesay and Earle Birney used the Lowry shack at different times; here Livesay wrote *Call My People Home* (1950).

From 1949 until 1954 Lowry was again at Dollarton. He worked extensively on a planned series of novels that drew on British Columbia settings, to be called *The Voyage That Never Ends*, but none of the books was completed during his lifetime. Two books intended for the group— *Dark as the Grave Wherein My Friend Is Laid* (1968) and *October Ferry to Gabriola* (1970)—were prepared for publication after his death by editors, including Margerie Lowry, who worked from Lowry's manuscripts. *October Ferry to Gabriola* is based in part on the struggle between the beach dwellers and the town officials seeking to build a park. Lowry left Canada in 1954 and died three years later in England. When his shack at Dollarton was destroyed his friends collected many books and manuscripts from the site, most of them now available at the University of British Columbia Library. Malcolm Lowry Walk runs along the cliff in the eastern end of Cates Park between a picnic area and playground.

In addition to the two posthumous novels, many other works by Lowry have been published since his death in 1957. They include *Lunar Caustic* (1963), a novella; *Selected Poems* (1962), edited by Earle Birney; and *Hear Us O Lord from Heaven Thy Dwelling Place* (1961), a collection of stories that, along with many of his poems, draw on Lowry's intimate knowledge of the Dollarton landscape.

> *I can see your shack now. It's between the forest and the sea and you've got a pier going down to the water over rough stones, you know, covered with barnacles and sea anemones and starfish. You'll have to go through the woods to the store. . . . The woods will be wet. And occasionally a tree will come crashing down. And sometimes there will be a fog and that fog will freeze. Then your whole forest will become a crystal forest. The ice crystals on the twigs will grow like leaves. Then pretty soon you'll be seeing the jack-in-the-pulpits and then it will be spring.*
> —Malcolm Lowry, 'The Most Terrific Place in the World'

DUNCAN

Robert Service left Glasgow, Scot., in Mar. 1896 to look for adventure in Canada, travelling from Montreal to Vancouver Island before settling near Duncan, in the Lake Cowichan district, to work as a farm hand. From the summer of 1896 until 1903 he lived in or near Duncan, working on local farms and ranches in the summer, and during the winters travelling into the bush, or to warmer weather in California. In 1896 Service worked on a local farm owned by a family named Shetland. He spent the winter in a cabin in the woods, worked the following season for the Shetlands, and in the winter of 1897–8 travelled in the southwestern United States and Mexico. On his return to Duncan he worked as a farmhand on a large cattle ranch not far from Lake Cowichan and the village of the same name, about 20 miles west of here. Service found the Duncan and Lake Cowichan area most notable for glorifying 'the Old School Tie', but his lowly status as a farm worker separated him from the round of teas, dances, and sports that occupied the more affluent members of the community. From 1899 to 1903 he worked as the ranch's storekeeper, a job that improved his social standing and gave him more leisure for writing; he submitted a poem, 'The Old Log Cabin', to the Whitehorse *Star* and it was published on 10 May 1902. This poem was postmarked from Lake Cowichan. Increasingly discontented with his life in Duncan, Service began university studies in VICTORIA in 1903, but soon gave them up. This failure led, however, to future success, for soon afterwards he took a job with the Canadian Bank of Commerce, which sent him in Nov. 1904 to WHITEHORSE, Y.T. Although the land is still in use, the ranch where Service worked no longer exists; a provincial plaque marks its site and its association with the poet. (See also CHILKOOT PASS, KAMLOOPS, WHITE PASS; EDMONTON, Alta; DAWSON CITY, LAKE LABERGE, Y.T., FORT MCPHERSON, MACKENZIE RIVER, N.W.T.

Wilfred Watson's family brought him from England to Duncan in 1926, when he was fifteen. Watson attended Duncan High School for one year before beginning thirteen years as a worker in a tidewater sawmill. He received a Governor General's Award for his first volume of poems, *Friday's Child* (1955). He has taught at the University of Alberta in both CALGARY and EDMONTON, Alta. Since 1976 he has lived in NANAIMO.

FORT STEELE

The poet **Charles Mair** tried briefly to capitalize on the East Kootenay mineral mining boom of the 1890s by opening a bookstore in 1898 at Fort Steele, on the Kootenay River in southeastern British Columbia. The business soon failed and he left to begin a long period of travelling in the West as an agent of the federal Department of Immigration. He returned to Fort Steele in the final posting of his civil-service career; he retired from the department in 1921. In 1915, while serving at Fort Steele, Mair was approached by the Toronto editor John Garvin with an offer to publish his poems in a new series of poetry volumes. Garvin's promises, which for a time revived the disillusioned Mair's interest in poetry, were not fulfilled until a few days before Mair's death in VICTORIA in 1927, when Garvin sent him a copy of the book that had grown out of their twelve years of negotiations: *Tecumseh: A Drama, and Other Poems*. (See also VICTORIA; KINGSTON, LANARK, OTTAWA, TORONTO: I, WINDSOR, Ont.; PORTAGE LA PRAIRIE, WINNIPEG, Man.; HUMBOLDT, PRINCE ALBERT, Sask.; CALGARY, Alta.)

Today Fort Steele Historic Park, built in the 1960s, contains buildings that have been reconstructed and restored in the style of the 1890–1905 period, when Fort Steele (named for the legendary NWMP officer Sam Steele) was enjoying its second boom.

GALIANO ISLAND

Galiano Island, one of a string of islands along the eastern coast of Vancouver Island from Nanaimo to Victoria, has been a popular vacation site for British Columbia writers for many years. The playwright **Margaret Hollingsworth**, who has lived in VANCOUVER since 1968, spends the summer here. The island setting of her play *Mother Country* (1980) is based on Galiano. In recent years the poet **Dorothy Livesay** has divided her time between summers near WINNIPEG and winters on Galiano Island. Her recent books include *Ice Age* (1975) and *The Woman I Am* (1977).

Two American-born women writers have chosen permanent homes here. **Audrey Thomas**, who came to Canada in 1959, first saw her cabin on Galiano Island in 1969 and moved in after separating from her husband in 1972. Her linked novellas, *Munchmeyer* and *Prospero on the Island* (1971, published together), tell the story of a woman writer living alone on an island and writing a novel about a male writer. The woman writer, Miranda, keeps a diary, as does her fictional subject, whose diary is the text of *Prospero on the Island*; *Munchmeyer* is the text of the novel Miranda is writing. Thomas's other books include the novels *Blown Figures* (1974) and *Latakia* (1979), and two story collections, *Ladies and Escorts* (1977) and *Real Mothers* (1981). (See also VANCOUVER, B.C.)

Jane Rule has lived at The Fork on Galiano Island since 1975. She moved here from her first British Columbia home, VANCOUVER, where she had lived since 1956. On Galiano she has written the novel *Contract with the World* (1980) and *Outlander* (1981), a book of short stories, among other books. Her novel *The Young in One Another's Arms* (1977)—about a group of boarding-house residents from the city who band together when their home is destroyed and move to Galiano Island to start a restaurant—is set both in Vancouver and on the island.

Audrey Thomas, 1977

Jane Rule, 1987

KAMLOOPS

Robert Service, who joined the Canadian Bank of Commerce in VICTORIA, B.C., on 10 Oct. 1903 as an assistant teller, was transferred to this town in the British Columbia interior on 9 July 1904. Service's bank work gave him the opportunity to enjoy the pleasant social life of Kamloops, including rides into the nearby mountains, on which he travelled 'over rolling ridges, or into spectral gulches that rose to ghostlier mountains'. In November he was soon promoted to the bank's office in WHITEHORSE. Although Service loved life in the Yukon, he recalled in his autobiography, *Ploughman of the Moon* (1945), the misgivings he felt when he was first notified of his transfer, because 'many bankers went to the devil there.' (See also CHILKOOT PASS, DUNCAN, WHITE PASS; TORONTO: 2, Ont.; EDMONTON, Alta; DAWSON CITY, LAKE LABERGE, Y.T.; FORT MCPHERSON, MACKENZIE RIVER, N.W.T.)

Three Loon Lake near here, along with LYTTON and Capitol Hill in BURNABY, provided a setting for **Ethel Wilson**'s *Swamp Angel* (1954). Wilson had a summer home at Kamloops. (See also VANCOUVER.)

LYTTON

Lytton, which lies at the confluence of the Fraser and Thompson Rivers, is a principal locale in **Ethel Wilson**'s novel *Hetty Dorval* (1947). The novel opens in Lytton, where Frankie Burnaby meets the mysterious woman-of-the-world, Hetty Dorval; the action moves to VANCOUVER, Wilson's home town, and to Great Britain on the eve of the Second World War. Lytton is near KAMLOOPS, where Wilson had a summer home. (See also BURNABY.)

MERVILLE

The novelist and short-story writer **Jack Hodgins** was born in the small Vancouver Island community of Merville, between Campbell River and Courtenay, on 3 Oct. 1938. He grew up in this lumber district on his parents' farm near Merville and graduated from Courtenay High School. After receiving a B.Ed. degree in 1961 from the University of British Columbia, VANCOUVER, Hodgins returned to Vancouver Island to teach high school at NANAIMO, 60 miles south of his home town. Hodgins' first book, *Spit Delaney's Island* (1976), is a collection of stories set largely in his childhood home. He has used other island locations, including Nanaimo and the far-northern town of Port Alice, for settings in his other three books: *The Invention of the World* (1977); *The Resurrection of Joseph Bourne* (1980), which won a Governor General's award; and *The Barclay Family Theatre* (1981).

Jack Hodgins, 1981

NANAIMO

The novelist **Jack Hodgins** personally built his house in Nanaimo, where he has lived for many years and written some of his best-known novels and stories. A native of MERVILLE, north of Nanaimo on the east coast of Vancouver Island, Hodgins came here to teach high school in 1961 after studying creative writing under Earle Birney at the University of British Columbia. Northern Vancouver Island—especially the Comox Valley, where he was raised—provided Hodgins with settings for the stories in *Spit Delaney's Island* (1976) and for his two highly regarded novels, *The Invention of the World* (1977) and *The Resurrection of Joseph Bourne* (1980), which won a Governor General's Award. But Nanaimo and the surrounding region, including Lantzville and Qualicum Beach, are equally important in the makeup of his fictional places, such as the Rutherford Heights of many of his stories and the unnamed city in which *The Invention of the World* is set. A central feature of that novel, the Revelations Colony of Truth founded by the half-legendary Donal Keneally, was probably suggested in part by the Aquarian Foundation, a religious sect established in 1927 by Edward Wilson on Gabriola Island, which lies just opposite Nanaimo in the Strait of Georgia.

The novelist **Sheila Watson** and her husband, the poet **Wilfred Watson**, moved to Nanaimo from EDMONTON after retiring, in 1975 and 1976 respectively, from their professorships in the University of Alberta. They live on Place Rd. From 1971 to 1978 they co-published and edited (with three other writers) the literary magazine *white pelican*. A native of NEW WESTMINSTER, Sheila Watson is known for her experimental novel *The Double Hook* (1959; see also DOG CREEK). Wilfred Watson won a Governor General's Award for his first volume of poetry, *Friday's Child* (1955). Born in England, he was reared in DUNCAN.

The poet **Audrey Alexandra Brown** was born in Nanaimo on 29 Oct. 1904, was educated at St Ann's Convent School and public schools here, and lived in the city much of her life. Her first book of poems, *A Dryad in Nanaimo* (1931; enlarged and republished in 1934), is considered to contain her best work. In 1922 rheumatic fever made her an invalid. *The Log of a Lame Duck* (1938) is her prose record of ten months' treatment at the Queen Alexandra Solarium in Malahat Beach, Vancouver Island.

NELSON

The novelist **Frederick Niven** is remembered in the Nelson cemetery with a monument provided by the city of Glasgow, Scot., where he was educated—though as a teenager he spent a year or two in the Okanagan and elsewhere in Canada. From 1920 until his death in 1944 Niven lived in British Columbia, primarily in the Nelson region. His long-time home was in the small community of Willow Point, about 6 miles north of Nelson on Hwy 3A. The author of more than thirty books, ranging from popular adventure yarns to serious novels of the Canadian West, he is most admired for his trilogy of novels on Scottish settlement in western Canada: *The Flying Years* (1935; rpr. 1974), *Mine Inheritance* (1940), and *The Transplanted* (1944), which describes a set-

Frederick Niven and Bliss Carman

Patrick Lane, 1979

tlement like Nelson in the logging and mining region of British Columbia. (See also VANCOUVER; WINNIPEG, Man.; CALGARY, Alta.)

The poet **Pat Lane**, winner of a Governor General's Award for his *Poems New and Selected* (1979), was born in Nelson on 26 Mar. 1939. He grew up here and in Vernon, 100 miles northwest, on Lake Okanagan. Much of his poetry—especially in such early books as *Mountain Oysters* (1972) and *The Sun Has Begun to Eat the Mountains* (1972)—describes the many jobs and communities he had known, both in British Columbia and the Prairie Provinces. Lane has devoted himself to editing and publishing the poetry of his older brother, Richard Stanley **'Red' Lane**, who was born in Nelson in 1936 and died of a brain haemorrhage in Vancouver in 1962. Red Lane, like his brother, gained an intimate knowledge of much of western Canada from his youthful wanderings. During his life his poetry appeared in small magazines; since then, Pat Lane and Seymour Mayne have published *Collected Poems of Red Lane* (1968) and Pat Lane has brought out the anti-war poem *War-Cry* (1973), which he edited from his brother's manuscript.

The poet **Fred Wah** grew up in the Nelson area, and after years of study in VANCOUVER and the United States returned here. In 1979 he founded the School of Creative Writing at David Thompson University Centre, which was located at 820 10th St. The Centre was closed by the British Columbia government in 1984, but Wah continued the program at the Kootenay School of Writing, 1114 McQuarrie Ave—an independent organization that Wah still administers and that continues to attract many prominent Canadian writers to serve as teachers. Wah was also one of the founders of *Tish* magazine at the University of British Columbia. For much of the natural imagery in his writing he draws on his childhood experiences, and many of the poems in his nine books make extensive use of Kootenay scenery, particularly *Pictograms from the British Interior* (1974) and *Selected Poems: Loki is Buried at Smoky Creek* (1980). During his years at the Creative Writing Program, when many writers—Tom Wayman, Sean Virgo, David McFadden, Michael Hollingsworth, and Fraser Sutherland, among others—came to teach with him, Wah lived at nearby South Slocan.

In 1982 the poet **John Newlove** came to Nelson to teach at David Thompson University Centre, 820 10th St, for a single academic year; he now lives in Nelson. A native of REGINA, Sask., Newlove won a Governor General's Award for his collection *Lies* (1972); his selected poems, *The Fat Man*, appeared in 1977 and *The Night the Dog Smiled* in 1986. (See also VANCOUVER; TORONTO: 6, Ont.; VERIGIN, Sask.)

John Newlove, 1973

NEW WESTMINSTER

This former capital of British Columbia was the birthplace in 1909, and the childhood home, of the novelist **Sheila Watson**, author of the well-known poetic novel *The Double Hook* (1959). Her grandfather, with a business partner, built the Phoenix Cannery (one of the first fully mechanized fish canneries) on the Fraser River near New Westminster, and her father, Dr Charles Edward Doherty, was superintendent of the Provincial Mental Hospital. In an interview, Watson has said: 'I was born in British Columbia, spent the first eleven years of my life in a mental hospital because my father was a doctor there. We lived right in the institution at New Westminster. We had our private apartment but it was connected to the rest of the place. I lived there till my father died. It was, I suppose, a strange world. My father came there when everyone was in box beds and straitjackets and he got rid of all that and took the guards away from the gates. That was my world.' She attended primary and secondary school at the convent of the Sisters of Sainte Anne at 77 Albert Cres. and then studied at the University of British Columbia in Vancouver. After receiving her M.A. in 1933, Watson taught elementary school at several provincial cities and towns, including New Westminster, until her marriage in 1941 to the poet Wilfred Watson. She spent years studying and writing abroad and in other parts of Canada, and teaching at the University of Alberta, from which she retired in 1975. She then returned with her husband to British Columbia and settled in NANAIMO on Vancouver Island. (See also DOG CREEK; CALGARY, EDMONTON, Alta.)

Sheila Watson, 1987

Born in 1867 in DRESDEN, Ont., the poet **Tom MacInnes** came here with his family in 1874. His father, Thomas Robert McInnes, was a prominent New Westminster physician, a Member of Parliament (1878–81), a Senator (called to the Senate in 1881), and Lieutenant-Governor of British Columbia (1897–1900). Tom MacInnes, who introduced the changed spelling as a pen-name, was educated at the University of Toronto and afterwards travelled widely; he made his home in VANCOUVER. His books include *The Complete Poems of Tom MacInnes* (1923).

Elizabeth Smart, 1949

PENDER HARBOUR

In 1941 the OTTAWA-born **Elizabeth Smart** travelled alone to Pender Harbour to await the birth of her first child. Here she finished her first novel, *By Grand Central Station I Sat Down and Wept* (1945). Set in North America during the Second World War, it is an anguished and sometimes poetic monologue about a young woman's failed love for a married man. (The narrator, like the author, travels to the Pacific coast to have her child.) Smart dedicated the novel to Maximiliana ('Maxie') von Upani Southwell, a Viennese woman who befriended her here. She moved in with Maxie, and under her care completed the novel immediately before her daughter Georgina was born in August. During the summer Smart had been visited briefly by her child's father, English poet George Barker; after giving birth she went to live in Washington, D.C. in order to be with him. She moved to England in 1943.

PENTICTON

The novelist and poet **George Bowering** was born in this South Okanagan Valley city in 1935 and grew up here. He served as an RCAF aerial photographer after high school and was stationed at RCAF Macdonald, Man., where he began writing. Associated for many years as a student and teacher with the VANCOUVER area (see also BURNABY), Bowering has written of his childhood home in many of his stories ('Time and Again') and poems, and of the general region of the Okanagan Valley, including Oliver, south of Penticton. Bowering has published almost forty books, including two volumes of poetry, *Rocky Mountain Foot* (1968) and *The Gangs of Kosmos* (1969), which won Governor General's awards; and the novel, *Burning Water* (1980), another Governor General's award winner. (See also MONTREAL: 7, Que.; LONDON, Ont.)

PORT ALBERNI

George Clutesi, Nootka artist and storyteller, lives in the Sheshaht tribal reserve near Port Alberni, Vancouver Island. Clutesi, who worked for twenty years as a pile-driver operator before turning to painting, was encouraged to paint by Emily Carr, who first visited here in 1929. Clutesi's first book was *Son of Raven, Son of Deer: Fables of the Tse-Shaht People* (1967), a collection of stories that he illustrated and that were derived from tales of his tribe that had been preserved through more than 400 years of oral transmission by storytellers, including Clutesi's father. In 1969 he published *Potlatch*, a description and a defence of the ceremonial gift-giving celebrations of the west-coast Indians (these rituals were prohibited in Canada from 1884 to 1951). Clutesi, who was born in 1908, contributed a mural to the Indian pavilion at Expo '67 and has illustrated his own books. Clutesi's *Son of Raven, Son of Deer* was probably the first book by a native person to collect Canadian-Indian tales. Many anthropologists and ethnologists have collected and translated Indian literature from British Columbia; one of them was **Edward Sapir**, who worked in the Port Alberni region in the 1910s. The results of his collecting have been published in *Songs of the Nootka Indians* (1955).

PRINCE GEORGE

The novelist **Robert Harlow** was born in PRINCE RUPERT in 1923 and, at the age of three, moved with his family to Prince George, where his father worked as a road-master with the CNR. Harlow graduated from Baron Byng High School here in 1941 and joined the Royal Canadian Air Force the following year. His first three novels—*Royal Murdoch* (1962), *A Gift of Echoes* (1965), and *Scann* (1972)—were set in the fictional town of Linden, B.C., modelled on Prince George. (See also VANCOUVER.)

The poet **Anne Marriott** was women's editor of the Prince George *Citizen* in 1950–3. (See also VANCOUVER, VICTORIA; SASKATOON, Sask.)

PRINCE RUPERT

The novelist **Robert Harlow** was born on 19 Nov. 1923 in this busy port and fishing town 30 miles south of the Alaska panhandle. His father, a CPR stationmaster, moved the family to PRINCE GEORGE when Robert was three. The author of five novels—including *Royal Murdoch* (1962), *Scann* (1972), and *Paul Nolan* (1983)—Harlow is now a professor of English in the University of British Columbia, VANCOUVER. The poet **Tom Wayman**, born in 1945 in HAWKESBURY, Ont., was brought up in Prince Rupert. (See also VANCOUVER; WINDSOR, Ont.)

George Bowering and Fred Wah

QUEEN CHARLOTTE ISLANDS

The Queen Charlotte Islands, located just south of the Alaska boundary off the British Columbia coast, are famous for their Haida Indian traditions and wild beauty. (The old Haida village of Ninstints, on Skungwai Island, is a UNESCO World Heritage site.) In 1987 a large area in the Charlottes was designated South Moresby National Park. **Emily Carr** frequently visited the Charlottes and the Skeena River country (see TERRACE) between 1912 and 1930. Two of her friends from Skidegate, Clare and William Russ, were the models for characters named Louisa and Jimmie in *Klee Wyck* (1941), which won a Governor General's Award. (See also UCLUELET, VANCOUVER, VICTORIA.)

In the early 1970s two poets settled on the islands. **J. Michael Yates** (*INSEL: The Queen Charlotte Islands Meditations*, 1983), after teaching creative writing at the University of British Columbia, VANCOUVER, from 1968 to 1971, spent the next three years at Port Clements, located on Masset Inlet on Graham Island. (See also BURNABY; GREAT BEAR LAKE, N.W.T.) From 1971 to 1975 **Sean Virgo** was also living on the islands. In the title poem of *Deathwatch on Skidegate Narrows* (1979), Virgo contrasts the destruction of the islands' resources under white control with the Indian life of the past. (See also VANCOUVER, B.C.)

Matt Cohen set his novel *Wooden Hunters* (1975) on the Queen Charlotte Islands. This contemporary love story examines the status of the cultural conflict between the Islands' Indian and white populations. Cohen lived for a short time in the area but divides his time now between VERONA, Ont., near KINGSTON, and TORONTO: 3.

ROBERTS CREEK

In this village of 700 on the British Columbia coast near Hower Sound stands the long-time residence of the novelist **Hubert Evans**—a seaside house that he built for himself and his wife in the late 1920s. A native of Ontario, Evans lived in British Columbia from the end of the First World War and supported himself as a journalist in Nelson and New Westminster, as a freelance writer, and as a fisherman, logger, and fisheries officer. His books include a short-story collection. *The Silent Call* (1930), and the novels *Mist on the River* (1954), and *O Time in Your Flight* (1979).

Evans moved here in 1927 after seven years in the Skeena River district (see TERRACE) and at Cultus Lake, and built his house with money earned from the internationally popular books for young readers that he had begun to write, including *Forest Friends* (1926) and *Derry of Totem Creek* (1930). In 1943 Evans wrote a short novel, *No More Islands*, which was the first fiction to detail and criticize the internment of Japanese Canadians from the West Coast during the Second World War. *Mist on the River*, about the situation of British Columbia's Indians, draws on his knowledge of the Skeena River area and his experiences when he and his wife taught at Indian schools in Kitimat and Hazelton after 1945. In 1974 Evans was made a lifetime honorary member (one of only three) of the Writers' Union of Canada; in 1984 the president and chancellor of Simon Fraser University and the novelist Margaret Laurence came to Evans' home here for a special convocation ceremony to bestow an honorary degree on the ailing writer. In 1985 he moved to a rest-home in nearby Sechelt, where he died in April 1986 at the age of 94. (See also CAMBRIDGE, VANKLEEK HILL, Ont.)

SALTSPRING ISLAND

Born in 1927 in VICTORIA, poet **Phyllis Webb** settled on Saltspring Island in 1969, after having lived for 19 years in Montreal, Europe, the United States, and TORONTO (2). Webb's books published during her years here include *The Vision Tree: Selected Poems* (1982), winner of a Governor General's Award. Saltspring Island is off the southern tip of Galiano Island.

SLOCAN

Born in Vancouver in 1935, the poet and novelist **Joy Kogawa** was sent with her family to Slocan in the evacuation of Japanese-Canadians from coastal areas during the Second World War. Her childhood and youth here are reflected in poems from *A Choice of Dreams* (1974) and especially in her novel based on the evacuation, *Obasan* (1981), and in her children's book *Naomi's Road* (1986), which is based on *Obasan*. Since the 1940s Kogawa has lived in Saskatoon and OTTAWA; she now lives in TORONTO (4). Slocan is northwest of Nelson on Hwy 6.

Phyllis Webb, c.1981

Joy Kogawa, 1986

SOOKE

Born in WINNIPEG, **George Woodcock** lived in England from the age of five months to thirty-seven when he moved back to Canada. In 1949 he settled at Sooke, on the west coast of Vancouver Island. On Church Rd he and his wife built a house, which they sold in 1950; it is still standing. The next year, on their return from Europe, they built another house in Sooke, this one on a cliff near Whiffen Spit. It was sold in 1953 and, in a much altered condition, still stands. In 1953 the Woodcocks moved to VANCOUVER, where they still live. George Woodcock's publications during the Sooke years reflect emerging interests in biography and travel writing that became prominent in his subsequent work. Books from this period include *The Anarchist Prince: A Biographical Study of Peter Kropotkin* (1950), written in collaboration with Ivan Avakumovic; *The Paradox of Oscar Wilde* (1950); and *Ravens and Prophets: An Account of Journeys in British Columbia Alberta and Southern Alaska* (1952).

SUMMERLAND

Since 1961 the playwright **George Ryga** has lived here in a thirteen-room house set in a fruit orchard on the brow of Giant's Head Mountain, overlooking Lake Okanagan. Born in DEEP CREEK, Alberta, in 1932, he has devoted himself to writing since 1962, producing works on social justice in forms ranging from plays and film scripts to poems and fiction. All three of Ryga's short novels—*Hungry Hills* (1963), *Ballad of a Stonepicker* (1966), and *Night Desk* (1976)—were written in Summerland. In 1977 Ryga published two plays set in the Okanagan region. *Seven Hours to Sundown* presents the successful struggle of Summerland residents, including Ryga, to save one of the town's oldest buildings, Century House, from developers who want to raze it; Century House is now a cultural centre in Summerland. *Ploughmen of the Glacier* explores Okanagan history through the person of Volcanic Brown, an old prospector in the region who was the discoverer of Copper Mountain. Ryga's most famous work is *The Ecstasy of Rita Joe* (1971), a play about a woman who can neither live a traditional tribal life nor adapt to the contemporary world. Commissioned for the Canadian Centennial by the Vancouver Playhouse, it was the first English-language play presented at the National Arts Centre, Ottawa, in 1969.

TERRACE

The novelist **Hubert Evans** spent 1920 to 1925 at Lakelse Lake, near Terrace on the Skeena River, after serving in the First World War. Then, following a brief period at Cultus Lake near Vancouver, he and his family settled at ROBERTS CREEK, his home since 1927. Pursuing work as a commercial fisherman, Evans periodically returned to the Skeena River area, especially during the 1940s. For two years he and his wife taught school in nearby Kitimat, at the invitation of Indian friends from their earlier years in Terrace; for six years Evans made his home in Hazelton, so that his son could attend high school. His intimate knowledge of the region is seen in his novel *Mist on the River* (1954), in which he sympathetically portrays the cultural upheaval experienced by the river's Indians. The story of Cy Pitt, torn between reverence for family traditions and the possibility of financial success in white society, it is set along the Skeena River from Prince Rupert to remote Indian villages hundreds of miles inland. (See also CAMBRIDGE, VANKLEEK HILL, Ont.)

Between 1910 and the 1920s **Emily Carr** travelled regularly along the west coast of British Columbia, both on the QUEEN CHARLOTTE ISLANDS and through the river valleys of the mainland. In 1912 and again in 1928 she visited the Indian communities of the Skeena River in search of subjects for her paintings. Stories of these visits are included in her book *Klee Wyck* (1941), which won a Governor General's Award. (See also UCLUELET, VANCOUVER, VICTORIA.)

Marius Barbeau based *The Downfall of Temlahan* (1928), one of his two novels, on events that occurred among the Indians of the Upper Skeena River in 1886–7. As an anthropologist, Barbeau was familiar with British Columbia and its native peoples, among whom he had worked. His novel portrays tribal customs and dramatizes the Indians' ambivalence towards white civilization. (See also STE-ANNE-DE-LA-POCATIÈRE, STE-MARIE-DE-LA-BEAUCE, Que.; OTTAWA, Ont.)

UCLUELET

The Victoria-born painter and author **Emily Carr** visited this Indian village on the west coast of Vancouver Island, near Barkley Sound, in the summer of 1898. The visit, which was arranged through a church worker planning a stay at the mission house that served the Indians of the area, provided Carr with her first opportunity to observe the remarkable forest landscapes and the traditional Indian ways of life on the Canadian west coast that were to inspire her painting and writing during her professional maturity. Here Carr came to know the members of a band of Nootka Indians numbering about 200, who lived on a reserve about a mile away in the villages of Etedsu and Quaimata. With her was her sister Lizzy, then studying to be a missionary. Though the living conditions on the reserve were unpleasant because of poverty and disease, Carr easily made friends with the natives, who named her 'Klee Wyck' (the one who tends to laugh). She left Ucluelet with a portfolio of drawings and watercolours of the Indians, their houses, and the surrounding landscape, which appears as an impenetrable mass; she was overwhelmed, she said (in a letter to Ruth Humphrey, 22 Aug. 1937), by the forest, which was 'one continual shove of growing'. Beginning in 1913, Carr regularly left her home in southern British Columbia to travel north along the Pacific coast in search of material for her paintings. She concentrated primarily on the QUEEN CHARLOTTE ISLANDS and the Skeena River territory, opposite the islands on the mainland, avoiding even the small settlements in the region in order to camp alone or to live among the Indians. Carr drew on her years of visits for the autobiographical stories in *Klee Wyck* (1941), which won a Governor General's Award. Ucluelet is reached by Hwy 4 from Port Alberni. (See also TERRACE, VANCOUVER, VICTORIA.)

Emily Carr in 1898. Her monkey Woo chewed the photograph.

VANCOUVER

The first description in English of Canada's northwest coast was written by one of its great discoverers, Capt. **James Cook**, who recounted his 1778 voyage here in the posthumously published *A Voyage to the Pacific Ocean* (1784). Cook, however, did not enter the Strait of Georgia; his major landfall was at Nootka Sound on the northwest coast of Vancouver Island. **George Vancouver**, a midshipman on that voyage, returned to the Pacific northwest in 1791 in command of his own expedition. On 12 June 1792 he sailed into Burrard Inlet, passed what is now Stanley Park and the 200-foot bluff of Prospect Point, and anchored in First Narrows, where he was greeted by about 50 Indians. Vancouver wrote, 'These good people finding we were inclined to make some return for their hospitality, showed much understanding in preferring iron to copper'. He named the inlet Burrard Canal after a naval friend, and—in co-operation with two Spanish captains he encountered off Point Grey on 21 June—he mapped the western and northern portions of the site of present-day Vancouver, although he never entered Second Narrows, the principal harbour. His accounts are found in *A Voyage of Discovery to the North Pacific Ocean and Round the World* (1798).

The first European to see the south side of the peninsula on which Vancouver stands was the fur trader and explorer **Simon Fraser**. In May 1808 he left Fort George (now Prince George) to follow the river he took to be the Columbia in search of an easier route to the Pacific. At the end of his arduous journey he discovered that the river—later named for Fraser by the explorer David Thompson—was not the Columbia. On 2 July he reached the Musqueam village on the south shore of the peninsula, but the inhabitants fled, only to emerge and threaten him as he was leaving. There is a monument to Fraser's landing on South West Marine Dr., 1½ miles west of Camosun St. Fraser's writings were published in *The Letters and Journals of Simon Fraser: 1806–1808* (1960). The original inhabitants of the Vancouver area were the Musqueam, who lived in the southwest portion of the town site, and the Squamish, who lived along Burrard Inlet and Howe Sound. It was not until 1862 that settlers began to arrive, and by 1870 the village of Granville had grown up around Coal Harbour. Granville received its first great impetus towards growth in 1884, when Sir William Van Horne, vice-president of the CPR, determined to create a railway terminus here and changed the settlement's name to Vancouver. The city was incorporated in 1886, and its literary tradition began to take shape shortly after the turn of the century.

Novelist **Ethel Wilson** came to Vancouver as a child of ten in 1898 to live with her aunt and great-aunt following the death of her parents. Born in South Africa in 1888, she attended boarding school in Vancouver and in England. She returned here to study at Vancouver Normal School, where she received a second-class teacher's certificate in 1907. For the next thirteen years she taught in city public schools: Kitsilano Elementary (1907–9), the Model School (1909–12), Lord Roberts School (1914–18), and Dawson Elementary (1918–20). On 4 Jan. 1921 she married Dr Wallace Wilson; the couple lived in Vancouver but travelled extensively. Their home for over forty years was Apt 42, 1386 Nicola St: the Kensington Place Building, which overlooks False Creek. In the 1930s Wilson began publishing stories and wrote much of her novel *The Innocent Traveller* (1949), but her career was interrupted by the Second World War. While her husband served overseas, Ethel Wilson edited the Red Cross magazine in Vancouver. Her first novel, *Hetty Dorval*, appeared in 1947 and was followed by *The Innocent Traveller*, *The Equations of Love* (1952), *Swamp Angel* (1954) *Love and Salt Water* (1956), and a book of stories, *Mrs. Golightly and Other Stories* (1961). About 1965 the Wilsons moved to Apt 308, 2890 Point Grey Rd. After her husband died in 1966 Wilson wrote only brief autobiographical sketches. She lived in the Point Grey Rd apartment until 1972 when, having suffered a stroke, she moved to the Arbutus Nursing Home, where she died on 22 Dec. 1980.

Ethel Wilson

Wilson's life in the city spanned more than eighty of Vancouver's 100 years since incorporation. Many of her novels and stories are set in Vancouver. In *Hetty Dorval*, Frankie Burnaby is educated here and again meets the mysterious, worldly title character, whom Frankie first saw in LYTTON. The *Swamp Angel* begins in Vancouver but moves to the lake country around KAMLOOPS, where the Wilsons spent their summers on Lac Le Jeune. *The Innocent Traveller* draws on Wilson's own family history for the life of heroine Topaz Edgeworth, who was born in England and after an eventful career spent her last years in Vancouver.

VANCOUVER

In my childhood we had stood, in Vancouver, on a sort of subsoil of a culture which, as the forests came down, had been vaguely prepared by our forebears in the haste of building and earning. They had arrived at the water's edge with their violins and pianos, some books, some pictures, ideas, undoubtedly aspirations, opinions,—or nothing whatever.

—Ethel Wilson, 'A Cat Among the Falcons', *Canadian Literature*, Autumn 1959

Martin Allerdale Grainger, who was born in 1874 in London, came to British Columbia in the late 1890s, and after service in the Boer War settled permanently in the province. His only book, *Woodsmen of the West* (1908), is a fictionalized reminiscence of his experiences in logging camps in the Knight Inlet region; it mentions several Vancouver locales popular with loggers early in the century, including the Columbia Hotel, still standing at 303 Columbia St. Grainger spent his life in the logging industry; he wrote the B.C. Forest Act of 1912 and became the province's Chief Forester in 1917. From 1920 he worked in private business; his M.A. Grainger Co. Ltd was based in Vancouver. Grainger died in Vancouver on 15 Oct. 1941.

Frederick Niven, born to Scottish parents in Valparaiso, Chile, on 31 Mar. 1878, came in 1899 to stay with family friends in the Kootenay Valley at New Denver because of a lung ailment. In 1900 he ran a small store in Vancouver and worked in the Hastings Sawmill, on the Burrard Inlet at the foot of Dunlevy Ave. His first novel, *The Lost Cabin Mine* (1908), was set in Canada but published in Scotland. In 1912–13 Niven came back to Canada as a freelance writer, but he returned to Europe during the First World War. He settled in Canada in 1920, living first in NELSON and then in Vancouver, where he died in 1944. Niven wrote two autobiographical works, *Wild Honey* (1927) and *Coloured Spectacles* (1938) but is best known for a trilogy of novels that trace the course of western development: *The Flying Years* (1935), *Mine Inheritance* (1940), and *The Transplanted* (1944).

Emily Carr, born in VICTORIA in 1871, left her home in 1899 to study in Europe. When she returned from England in 1904 she stayed briefly in Vancouver and in 1906 began teaching at the Vancouver Ladies' Art Club. Before long she was dismissed, whereupon she opened a studio at 570 Granville St and soon had seventy-five pupils. Carr, who boarded at 541 Burrard St, also gave classes at Miss Gordon's School in North Vancouver. In 1912 she opened a new studio at 1465 Broadway Street West but in 1913 moved back to Victoria. Many of her trips to paint Indian villages and forest scenery along British Columbia's northern coast were made from Vancouver, including the 1912 trip to the QUEEN CHARLOTTE ISLANDS. Carr told the story of her visits in her first book, *Klee Wyck* (1941), which won a Governor General's Award. Paintings by Carr are on display at the Vancouver Art Gallery, 1145 West Georgia Street. (See also TERRACE, B.C.)

Robert Service often visited Vancouver between 1904 and 1912, when he worked in the Yukon cities of WHITEHORSE and DAWSON CITY. Service had joined the staff of the Bank of Commerce in VICTORIA in the fall of 1903 and was transferred first to KAMLOOPS and then to the Yukon. He spent the winter of 1907 in Vancouver at a resort hotel after the publication of his first book,

Songs of a Sourdough (1907), but he disliked the vacation and was eager to return north. Service passed through the city on other occasions when travelling from the Yukon, and during the summer of 1912 he spent his last months in Canada before carrying his new book, *Rhymes of a Rolling Stone* (1912), to his American publisher.

Pauline Johnson lived in Vancouver for only four years, but after retiring from the stage in 1909 she adopted the city as her final home because she had grown to love it during many previous visits here as a performer. Her home was an apartment at 1117 Howe St. She was fond of the wilderness parks in the city, especially the area around Siwash Rock in Stanley Park. Her second book of poems, *Flint and Feather*, was published in 1912. Johnson also wrote a group of prose tales and legends based on stories told to her by one of her best friends in the city, Chief Joe Capilano of the Squamish Indians. The stories were collected in *Legends of Vancouver* (1911). Johnson died after a long illness on 7 Mar. 1913 in the Bute Street Private Hospital, 786 Bute St. Her ashes were buried, as she had requested, near Siwash Rock in Stanley Park; a monument was erected to her memory at Ferguson Point. The Indian costume Johnson wore in her stage appearances, a gift from the naturalist and author Ernest Thompson Seton, is on display at the Vancouver Museum, 1100 Chestnut St. (See also BRANTFORD, MIDDLEPORT, Ont.; WINNIPEG, Man.)

One of the executors of Pauline Johnson's will was Vancouver poet and novelist **Isabel Ecclestone Mackay**, who championed the cause of many Canadian writers in her work with the Canadian Authors' Association. A native of Ontario, Mackay moved to Vancouver in 1909. Her first book of poems, *Between the Lights*, had appeared in 1904. During the 1910s she lived at 1656 Pendrell St and at 1034 Denman St and published her first novel, *The House of Windows* (1912), which featured Vancouver settings. She lived at 967 W. 10th Ave in the 1920s; her later works include *Blencarrow* (1926), a novel set in her Ontario childhood home, and *Fires of Driftwood* (1922), a book of poems. She died in 1928.

Irene Baird, aged eighteen, came to British Columbia with her parents in 1919 from England. She worked as a reporter for the Vancouver *Sun* and the *Daily Province* before leaving the city in the 1940s to work for the federal civil service in OTTAWA. Baird published three novels while working in Vancouver, all of them set on Vancouver Island and in Victoria. *Waste Heritage* (1939), her principal work, follows the course of a march on the provincial legislature in Victoria after the forceful expulsion of demonstrators from the Vancouver Post Office in 1938.

Tom MacInnes

The Toronto poet **Marjorie Pickthall** returned from several years in England in 1919 and moved to the west coast. She lived chiefly in VICTORIA, where she wrote her only novel, *The Bridge* (1921). Pickthall died in Vancouver in 1922 of the heart condition that had troubled her since childhood, and is buried in TORONTO (3).

The poet **Tom MacInnes**, born in DRESDEN, Ont., lived most of his life in British Columbia. He came as a child to NEW WESTMINSTER, where his father was mayor, Member of Parliament, and later, Lieutenant-Governor of the province. MacInnes served as his father's private secretary and was a member of several government commissions, as well as a practising lawyer in Vancouver. Involved for many years with business interests in China, MacInnes settled in Vancouver in 1922, where he died in 1951. Several books of his poetry were published during his years in the city, including *Roundabout Rhymes* (1923), *Complete Poems of Tom MacInnes* (1923), *High Low Along: A Didactic Poem* (1934), and *In the Old of My Age* (1947). His autobiography, *Chinook Days*, was published in 1926. In the 1920s MacInnes lived in the Abbotsford Hotel, 921 W. Pender St.

Bliss Carman in Vancouver, 1926

Earle Birney, founder of the University of British Columbia's Creative Writing Department, was associated as student and teacher with the university for over forty years, from 1922 to 1965. He contributed to the literary life of the city both through his own writings, many of which make use of its history and sights, and through his many students who have achieved prominence as poets and prose writers. The University of British Columbia gained independent university status in 1915, just seven years before Birney arrived from CRESTON to begin his study of chemistry. In 1922 he lived in an attic at Columbia St and 11th Ave. Birney transferred to English in his second year and was appointed associate editor of the campus newspaper, the *Ubyssey*, whose editor-in-chief he became in 1925. He graduated in Honours English in 1926. When the poet **Bliss Carman** visited the university on a reading tour in 1926 Birney was chosen to be Carman's guide; he remembers that the poet got lost on one of the school's nature trails. After graduating, Birney enrolled at the University of Toronto but returned to teach in the University of British Columbia's summer session in 1927 and eight other times before the Second World War. In the 1930s he became a party organizer for the Trotskyist branch of the Communist Party and published socialist tracts in Vancouver, using pseudonyms. Birney settled in Vancouver in 1946 as professor of medieval literature at the University of British Columbia. In 1963 he established the Creative Writing Department, the first such department in Canada, and was its head until 1965, when he left the university. From Sept. 1946 to June 1948 he was editor of *Canadian Poetry Magazine* and in 1964–5 editor of *Prism International*. Among Birney's pupils, many of whom studied with him before the formation of the writing department, are George Bowering, Lionel Kearns, Robert Harlow, Phyllis Webb, Jack Hodgins, Rona Murray, and Mavor Moore. Before coming to Vancouver in 1946 Birney had won a Governor General's Award for his first book of poems, *David* (1942). During the years here he published several books of poems, including *Strait of Anian* (1948), *Trial of a City and Other Poems* (1952), *Ice Cod Bell and Stone* (1962), and *November Walk Near False Creek Mouth* (1964). Birney's satirical war novel, *Turvey*, appeared in 1949, followed in 1955 by *Down the Long Table*, a fictionalized account of his experiences in the political movements of the 1930s. In the late forties and in 1950 Birney lived at 5606 President's Row, Union Hill. In 1951–8 his home was at 4590 W. 3rd Ave and in 1960–1 at 4584 W. 1st Ave. During his last five years in Vancouver he lived at 1938 Comox St. For many years Birney was a close friend of novelist **Malcolm Lowry**, who lived between 1939 and 1954 at DOLLARTON (on the north shore of the Burrard Inlet and now a part of the District of North Vancouver). Lowry also stayed briefly at several addresses in Vancouver: Apt 33, 1075 Gilford St (Feb.–Mar. 1952); the Bayview Apartment Hotel, 1359 Davie St (Nov. 1952–Jan. 1953); and 1058 Nelson St (Jan.–Feb. 1954). Birney has edited two books from manuscripts left unpublished at the time of Lowry's death in 1957: *Selected Poems of Malcolm Lowry* (1962) and *Lunar Caustic* (1968). (Another friend was the poet Dylan Thomas, who frequently stayed with Birney when visiting here.) Many of Birney's works draw on the life of the city, including 'Strait of Anian' and 'November Walk Near False Creek Mouth'. He published his play *The Damnation of Vancouver* in 1977, after settling in TORONTO (3, 6), his current home. (See also CALGARY, MORNINGSIDE, Alta.)

Birney and Lowry were frequent visitors on Bowen Island in the Queen Charlotte Channel, at the home of Einar Neilson, who often played host to Vancouver writers. Bowen Island was also the home for one summer during the late 1930s of **Howard O'Hagan**, who worked there on his best-known book, the novel *Tay John* (1939). (See also VICTORIA; JASPER, Alta; MONTREAL: 3, Que.) Today Bowen Island is home to poet **Robert Bringhurst** (*The Beauty of the Weapons*, 1982). Bringhurst has taught at the University of British Columbia in the Creative Writing Department.

Poet **Roy Daniells** had been a friend of Earle Birney's since the late 1920s, when both were students at the University of Toronto (see TORONTO:3). After teaching at Toronto and the University of Manitoba, Daniells came to the University of British Columbia, where he was chairman of the English department from 1948 until his retirement in 1974; he was professor emeritus from 1977 until his death two years later. His books of poetry are *Deeper into the Forest* (1948) and *The Chequered Shade* (1963).

Humorist **Stanley Burke** (*Frog Fables and Beaver Tales*, 1973) was born in Vancouver in 1924 and began writing when he was sixteen. After military service during the Second World War, he worked as a journalist for the CBC overseas, and from 1953 to 1957 he was the Vancouver *Sun*'s correspondent in Ottawa.

The novelist **Sheila Watson** was raised in NEW WESTMINSTER and came to Vancouver to study in 1927 at the Convent of the Sacred Heart, where she completed her first two years of university. The University of British Columbia awarded her a B.A. in Honours English in 1931, an academic teaching certificate in 1932, and an M.A. in 1933. Watson taught school in British Columbia from 1933 until 1951, and was for two years (1948–50) a sessional lecturer at the University of British Columbia. She was living in CALGARY when she wrote her best-known work, *The Double Hook* (1959); before moving to her present home at NANAIMO on Vancouver Island, she taught for many years at the University of Alberta, EDMONTON. Her husband, the poet and playwright **Wilfred Watson**, graduated from the University of British Columbia in 1943. He taught English briefly here before joining the faculty of the University of Alberta in Calgary in the 1950s.

Other writers associated with the University of British Columbia between the world wars are **Charles G.D. Roberts**, E.J. Pratt, Eric Nicol, and Pierre Berton. In 1927 Roberts—who had published his first book, *Orion and Other Poems*, in 1880—was the first person to be named to the chair of Canadian literature. At the time of his appointment he was busy with many writing and editorial projects, including a new book of poems, *The Vagrant of Time* (1927). The University of British Columbia was one of several universities where poet **E.J. Pratt** taught during the summers between 1930 and 1952.

Eric Nicol—born in KINGSTON, Ont.—grew up in Vancouver and for many years has lived on Point Grey, within a few blocks of the University of British Columbia Endowment Lands. Nicol attended Lord Byng High School, where he started writing as a staff member of the school paper the *Scarlet and Grey*. At the University of British Columbia he began writing a humour column as part of his work on the *Ubyssey*. Other student journalists at the same time were Pierre Berton and Lister Sinclair. Nicol

Eric Nicol, 1952

graduated in 1941 and, after military service from 1942 to 1945, returned to the university to begin graduate studies. He received an M.A. in 1948 and went to Paris to study at the Sorbonne. In 1951 he joined the Vancouver *Daily Province*, for which he wrote a syndicated column. He has also worked for the Vancouver *News-Herald* and before 1951 had published three books of humour: *Sez We* (1943), a collection of his columns from the *News-Herald* written under the pen-name 'Jabez' in collaboration with Jack Scott; *Sense and Nonsense by E.P. Nicol (Jabez)* (1947); and *The Roving I* (1950), winner of the Stephen Leacock Medal for humour. Since 1953 he has published several more books of humour, alone and in collaboration with Peter Whalley and Dave More. He has also won the Leacock Medal for *Shall We Join the Ladies?* (1955) and *Girdle Me a Globe* (1957). In addition to his work for newspapers, Nicol has written a history of the city, *Vancouver* (1970) and has become a successful playwright. His plays include *The Clam Made a Face* (1972), a dramatization of West Coast Indian legends for children; *The Man from Inner Space* (1976), a television play; *The Fourth Monkey* (1973); and *Like Father, Like Son* (1973). This last was a triumph in Vancouver but proved a failure on Broadway. The difficulties of attempting to tailor the Canadian play for American audiences are presented by Nicol in *A Scar is Born* (1968). Since 1957 Nicol has lived on W. 36th Ave.

Pierre Berton, Nicol's fellow journalist at the *Ubyssey*, became city editor of the Vancouver *News-Herald* in 1942 after graduating from the University of British Columbia. After his military service he became a feature writer for the Vancouver *Sun* but in 1947 moved to Toronto. Berton began his distinguished career as a popular historian with *The Mysterious North* (1956), the first of his three winners of the Governor General's Award. (See also DAWSON CITY, WHITEHORSE, Y.T.; TORONTO: 2, KLEINBURG, Ont.)

Joy Kogawa was born here on 6 June 1935 but was interned in the British Columbia interior with her family (her father was an Anglican minister) during the Second World War, an experience she used as the basis of her novel *Obasan* (1980). (See SLOCAN.) She worked as a writer in the Prime Minister's office in Ottawa from 1974 to 1976 and now lives in TORONTO (4). In 1986 she published *Naomi's Road*, a children's book based on *Obasan*.

Dorothy Livesay moved to Vancouver from TORONTO (4) in Apr. 1936 and in the following year married Duncan Macnair. The couple lived in North Vancouver, where their children were born in 1940 and 1942. Livesay divided her time between work for the provincial social services and writing. In 1944 she published *Day and Night*, winner of a Governor General's Award; *Poems for People*, another Governor General's Award winner, followed in 1947. In the late 1940s and early 1950s Livesay lived at 848 E. 6th St, North Vancouver, and in 1957–8 at 1828 Grand Blvd, North Vancouver. During the 1940s she was one of a group of British Columbia writers who helped Alan Crawley with his magazine *Contemporary Verse*, which published its first number in Sept. 1940 in Vancouver. The board of founders of this important journal included Livesay, Floris McLaren, Anne Marriott, Doris Ferne, and Crawley, a blind lawyer with a keen interest in Canadian literature, who was helped by the other members in reading submitted manuscripts. The magazine was edited from Crawley's home in Caulfield, now a part of West Vancouver; it continued until 1952, and during its last few years was edited in VICTORIA, where Crawley had moved. In 1975 Dorothy Livesay helped to found *CV/II* (its name was a memorial to *Contemporary Verse*). After three years' teaching in Zambia from 1960 to 1963 Livesay returned to Vancouver to study at the University of British Columbia, where she received an M. Ed. degree in 1964. In recent years she has divided her time between a house in WINNIPEG during the summers and a house on GALIANO ISLAND in the winters. After a long silence Livesay resumed steady publication of poetry with *The Unquiet Bed* (1967) and *Plainsongs* (1969).

Dorothy Livesay, *c.*1973

In the 1930s the poet **Al Purdy** came to Vancouver from southern Ontario to look for work. He spent several years working in a mattress factory and other similar jobs. His Second World War service was also spent on the west coast, both in Vancouver and in northern British Columbia on the Skeena River. In 1954 Purdy travelled across the Second Narrows Bridge on a literary pilgrimage to the shack of the novelist Malcolm Lowry at Dollarton. During the 1940s Purdy's poems appeared regularly on the poetry page of the Vancouver *Sun*. His first book, *The Enchanted Echo*, was published in 1944. Though Purdy has lived for many years at Roblin Lake near AMELIASBURG, Ont., he has continued to draw on his impressions of the west coast in his writing. *Cariboo Horses* (1965), for which he received a Governor General's Award, contains many poems set in British Columbia, including 'Vancouver'.

Two poets born here during the war years have settled in Ontario. **Gary Geddes** was born here in 1940 and attended the University of British Columbia. A teacher at Concordia University in MONTREAL (7), Que., Geddes lives on a farm in southeastern Ontario. His western roots are evident in the anthology *Skookum Wawa: Writings of the Canadian Northwest* (1975), which he edited, and in much of his early poetry, including the work in *Rivers Inlet* (1971). **bp Nichol** was born in Vancouver on 30 Sept. 1944. He received an elementary basic certificate from the education faculty of the University of British Columbia in 1963 and after one year of teaching in nearby Port Coquitlam moved to TORONTO (4), his present home. While at the university Nichol attended creative-writing classes with some members of the *Tish* group (see under George Bowering below). Nichol began writing during these years in Vancouver, and between 1965 and 1968 published twenty-nine books and pamphlets of his concrete poetry. He won a Governor General's Award in 1970 for a group of books and pamphlets, including *Still Water*, *The True Eventual Story of Billy the Kid*, *Beach Head*, and *The Cosmic Chef*.

A native of PRINCE RUPERT, **Robert Harlow** entered the University of British Columbia in 1945 after completing his military service in the RCAF. A member of one of Earle Birney's first creative-writing workshops, he received his B.A. in 1948. Harlow went to the Writer's Workshop at the University of Iowa to study for a Master's degree in Fine Arts (1950). Beginning in 1953 he worked for the CBC at 700 Hamilton St, rising to director of radio, British Columbia region, in 1955. In 1954–8 he lived successively at 1886 W. 11th Ave and 1684 Harwood St, both in Vancouver, and at 6421 Pitt St, West Vancouver. In 1959 he was one of a group of Vancouver writers who founded the quarterly literary magazine *Prism*, the forerunner of *Prism International*; his home in 1959 was at 2271 Bellevue Ave N. In 1965 he succeeded Earle Birney as head of the University of British Columbia Department of Creative Writing, a position he held until 1977; in the 1960s he lived for a time at 1911 Waterloo St, North Vancouver, and in the 1970s at 4715 Caulfield Dr., West Vancouver. Harlow continues to teach at the University of British Columbia. His first three novels form a trilogy about a fictional town called Linden, B.C., based on PRINCE GEORGE, where he grew up: *Royal Murdoch* (1962) was published before Harlow joined the Department of Creative Writing; the others are *A Gift of Echoes* (1965) and *Scann* (1972). His most recent novels are *Making Arrangements* (1977) and *Felice: A Travelogue* (1985).

The poet **Phyllis Webb** (*The Vision Tree: Selected Poems*, 1982), a native of VICTORIA, was educated at the University of British Columbia in the 1940s and returned to the university to teach for four years. Since 1969 she has lived on SALTSPRING ISLAND and in recent years has taught at the University of Victoria.

The short-story writer **Alice Munro** moved from LONDON, Ont., to Vancouver in 1951 with her first husband, James Munro. Her first home here was 445 Kings Road, West Vancouver, where she lived until 1955. Following short residences on Argyle St, West Vancouver, and at 1316 Arbutus St, Vancouver, the Munros settled at 2749 Lawson Ave, West Vancouver, where they

George Woodcock, *c.*1970

remained until August 1963. Although Munro did not publish her first short-story collection *Dance of the Happy Shades* (winner of a Governor General's Award) until 1968, she began writing in British Columbia with short stories for magazines and for CBC 'Anthology'. For a short time she rented an office on the north side of the 2400 block of Marine Dr., West Vancouver, and there wrote her story 'The Office'. The couple settled in 1963 in VICTORIA, where they ran a bookstore. (See also CLINTON, Ont.)

After several years on Vancouver Island at SOOKE, **George Woodcock** moved to Vancouver in 1953. His first home was a cabin (no longer standing) on Capitol Hill in Burnaby; he lived near the same site again during 1956–7 while staying in the house of the painter Jack Shadbolt on Harbourview Road. The Woodcocks lived in the city of Vancouver in 1955 6 in several different houses, including the basement of Earle Birney's house at 4590 West 3rd Avenue for three months. In 1958, after a year in Europe, they lived in an apartment on West 10th Avenue. The following year they found their present home on McCleery St in Kerrisdale. In 1956 and again from 1958 to 1963 he taught at the University of British Columbia. (His colleagues included Earle Birney and Phyllis Webb, who was his reader.) From 1959 to 1977 he edited *Canadian Literature*, which he had founded. In addition to his work as editor and teacher, Woodcock has written extensively in many areas: biography, social history, literary criticism, travel, and poetry. Years away from the city have produced *To the City of the Dead: An Account of Travels in Mexico* (1957) and *Faces of India: A Travel Narrative* (1964), along with several works of history, including *The British in the Far East* (1969). His works in Canadian studies range from *Canada and the Canadians* (1970) to *The World of Canadian Writing: Critiques and Recollections* (1980). His biographical studies include works on the authors Hugh MacLennan and Mordecai Richler and on Canadian political figures such as Amor de Cosmos and Gabriel Dumont. Woodcock's recent books also include poetry, *Notes on Visitations: 1936–75* (1975), and autobiography, *Letter to the Past* (1983), which records his life before he returned to Canada from England in 1949. (See also WINNIPEG, Man.)

The American-born novelist **Jane Rule** settled in Vancouver in 1956. For the next two years she lived at 4645 West 6th Avenue. In 1958–9 she was assistant director of International House at the University of British Columbia: she also began teaching at the university, and continued to do so periodically until 1975, when she moved to GALIANO ISLAND. Rule lived at 4510 8th Ave (where she wrote *Desert of the Heart*, 1964) from 1959 to 1964 and at 4504 W. 2nd Ave from 1964 to 1975, the period in which she published *This Is Not for You* (1970) and *Against the Season* (1971). Since moving to Galiano Island in 1979 she has used Vancouver as a principal setting for *The Young in One Another's Arms* (1977) and *Contract with the World* (1980). Another Galiano Island resident, **Audrey Thomas** (*Munchmeyer* and *Prospero on the Island*, 1971), received an M.A. from the University of British Columbia, where she studied from 1959 to 1963. Thomas returned as visiting lecturer in the Department of Creative Writing in 1975–6.

Other graduates of the University of British Columbia include the novelist **Jack Hodgins** and the playwright Carol Bolt. Hodgins, who has lived most of his life on Vancouver Island (see MERVILLE, NANAIMO), studied here from 1956 to 1961, when he received a B.Ed. degree. Although he hoped to become a writer and took writing classes with Earle Birney at the university, Hodgins worked for many years as a high-school teacher. His first book, *Spit Delaney's Island*, was published in 1976. **Carol Bolt**, a native of WINNIPEG, grew up in British Columbia and graduated from the university in 1961. The author of *One Night Stand* (1977), *Red Emma* (1974), and many other plays, she has made TORONTO (2) her home since the late sixties.

Margaret Laurence lived at 3556 W. 21st Ave in Vancouver from 1957 to 1962. She had begun publishing stories about her years in Africa during her husband's engineering work there before she returned to Canada. In 1960 her first novel, *This Side Jordan*, set in Ghana, appeared; in 1961 it won the Beta Sigma Phi First Novel Award. It was followed in 1963 by *The Prophet's Camel Bell* and *The Tomorrow-tamer*, the first a memoir of her life in Somaliland and the second a collection of her African short stories. While living on W. 21st Ave Laurence worked on the first draft of her first 'Manawaka' novel, *The Stone Angel* (1964), which was published after she moved to England in 1963. A native of NEEPAWA, Man. (the model for her fictional 'Manawaka'), Laurence used Vancouver as a contrast to the small towns described in her novels. In *The Stone Angel* the principal character, Hagar Shipley, recalls her life in Manawaka from the Vancouver nursing home where she is dying. In another of the 'Manawaka' series (*The Fire-Dwellers*, 1969), one of Hagar's daughters, a Vancouver housewife, reaches a crisis of dissatisfaction with her married life. Vancouver also figures in her famous novel *The Diviners* (1974). (See also LAKEFIELD, PETERBOROUGH, Ont.; WINNIPEG, Man.)

A native of HAWKESBURY, Ont., **Tom Wayman** grew up in PRINCE RUPERT, B.C., and in Vancouver, where he attended high school. His interest in poetry was stirred in part by meeting Earle Birney at a summer-camp enrichment program in 1960. An editor of the *Ubyssey*, Wayman graduated from the University of British Columbia with a B.A. in journalism in 1966. After studying in the United States, he returned to Vancouver, where he worked from 1969 to 1975. In the early 1980s he taught at David Thompson University Centre (now closed), NELSON, B.C. His poetry books begin with *Waiting for Wayman* (1973) and include five other titles, among them *Living on the Ground:*

Tom Wayman, 1981

Tom Wayman Country (1980). Wayman has also edited three anthologies of poetry about work, including *A Government Job at Last* (1976). He has said of Vancouver: 'I tried to write a long poem about that, about how my poems were exactly like Vancouver—kind of sprawling and anecdotal and doing what work they had to keep alive but not particularly liking to do it.'

The Czechoslovakian novelist **Jan Drabek** did graduate studies at the University of British Columbia in 1961 and taught high school in Vancouver from 1961 to 1976. He wrote an account of his teaching years in the city, *Blackboard Odyssey* (1973). His novels include *What Ever Happened to Wenceslas?* (1975), *The Lister Legacy* (1980), and *The New Salisbury Statement* (1981).

At the time of her death in Sept. 1975, the poet **Pat Lowther** held a one-year teaching position in the Department of Creative Writing at the University of British Columbia. She was born in Vancouver in 1935 and left school at sixteen to work in order to support her writing. Married at eighteen, she was divorced and in 1963 married a schoolteacher, Ray Lowther. Her first book was *The Difficult Flowering* (1968), which was followed by *The Age of the Bird* (1972) and *Milkstone* (1974). Lowther served a term as president of the League of Canadian Poets, and Oxford Canada published her collection *A Stone Diary* (1975) posthumously. During the last three years of her life she lived and wrote at 566 E. 46th Ave. Lowther's husband was convicted of her murder in 1977, two years after she died.

Pat Lowther, *c.*1976

Many other writers were associated with the lively literary scene in Vancouver during the 1960s. **bill bissett**, a native of HALIFAX, N.S., moved to the west coast in the 1950s. From 1963 to 1968, bissett published *Blew Ointment*, a political literary magazine whose contributors over the years included many of the decade's rising and established Canadian poets: Margaret Atwood, Michael Ondaatje, Earle Birney, John Newlove, and many others. In 1967 he founded Blew Ointment Press, from which many of his over forty books of poetry have appeared. The first collection was *we sleep inside each other all* (1966). There are also two volumes available of his selected work: *nobody owns th earth* (1971) and *Selected Poems: Beyond Even Faithful Legends* (1980). **Milton Acorn**, a native of CHARLOTTETOWN, P.E.I., came to Vancouver from TORONTO (2) in 1963. Associated for a time with the Trotskyites protesting the Vietnam War, Acorn left the group and co-founded and wrote for the counterculture newspaper, the *Georgia Straight*. His book *Jawbreakers* appeared in 1963. Among his friends in Vancouver were bissett and the Lane brothers, Red and Pat. **Red Lane**, the elder of the two, died at the age of twenty-eight in Vancouver, in 1964. He had been published in magazines, but his poetry was not collected until after his death. His brother Pat, and Seymour Mayne, prepared the *Collected Poems of Red Lane* (1968) for the Very Stone Press, which they founded in Vancouver. (See also NELSON.) **Seymour Mayne**, who studied at the University of British Columbia, taught there briefly before joining the faculty of the University of Ottawa in 1973. Acorn wrote 'Words Said Sitting on a Rock Sitting on a Saint', about the early death of Red Lane, and the last book in Lane's *Collected Poems* is, in turn, dedicated to Acorn: 'Death of a Poet (for Milton Acorn, Ultimately)'. **Pat Lane** studied at the University of British Columbia in the 1960s and began publishing with *Letters from a Savage Mind* (1966). In the late 1960s poet **John Newlove** worked in Vancouver for three years, including a period at the University of British Columbia bookstore. In 1969 he lived at 557 E. 13th St. His book, *Moving in Alone*, appeared in 1965, followed by *Black Night Window* (1968), *The Cave* (1970), *Lies* (1972, winner of a Governor General's Award), *The Fat Man: Selected Poems 1962–1972* (1977), *The Green Plain* (1981), and *The Night the Dog Smiled* (1986).

One of the most prominent parts of the Vancouver literary scene of the 1960s was *Tish* magazine, published from 1961 to 1969. This mimeographed journal began with five editors—George Bowering, Fred Wah, Frank Davey, David Dawson, and James Reid—and was devoted in its early numbers to poetry. After nineteen issues under the original *Tish*-group, the magazine was taken over by an editorial group, headed by David Dawson and including Daphne Marlatt, that produced five issues between Aug. 1963 and June 1964. *Tish* then was edited by Dan McLeod, later the founder of the *Georgia Straight* (along with Milton Acorn and other Vancouver writers). Under McLeod, *Tish* changed from a nationally oriented magazine to one emphasizing west-coast writers. The last four issues, edited by Karen Tallman, appeared in 1968–9, and *Tish* was then unofficially replaced by the *Georgia Straight Literary Supplement*. Another unofficial successor to *Tish* is Frank Davey's *Open Letter*, founded in Victoria in 1965 and now published in TORONTO (7). In its early days the Vancouver writers associated with *Tish* included the critic Warren Tallman; playwright Carol Bolt; and the poets David Cull, Red Lane, Robert Hogg, and Lionel Kearns. In its later years *Tish* became associated with the writers identified with west-coast publications like the *Georgia Straight*, *Blew Ointment*, *Island*, and *Talon*.

George Bowering, a native of PENTICTON, studied at the University of British Columbia from 1957 to 1963, earning a B.A. in history in 1960 and an M.A. in English in 1963. In 1962–3 he lived at 1719 Yew Street, in what was then a popular neighbourhood for writers and painters. In common with other editors of *Tish*, Bowering was influenced by the poets of the American Black Mountain School, including Charles Olson, Robert Creeley, and Robert Duncan. Duncan visited Vancouver in 1961, and Creeley was a visiting professor at the university and Bowering's thesis adviser during his master's program. Bowering is a contributing editor of Frank Davey's successor to *Tish*, *Open Letter*. After teaching and studying away from the city for several years, Bowering returned to Vancouver in 1973 and teaches at Simon Fraser University, BURNABY. His first collection of poems was *Sticks and Stones* (1963), published as a Tishbook with a preface by Robert Creeley. In his years away from Vancouver he often wrote about life in the city. The novel *Mirror on the Floor* (1967) is set in the Vancouver of the early 1960s: its hero, Bob Small, is a student at the University of British Columbia. North Bailey Stadium is a setting for many of the poems in the poetry collection

Baseball (1967). In 1970 Bowering published a book-length poem, *George Vancouver*. Many of his almost forty books have been written since his return to Vancouver; among them are *Selected Poems: Particular Accidents* (1980), *Smoking Mirror* (1982), and *The Catch* (1976), poetry; *Flycatcher & and Other Stories* (1974), *Protective Footwear: Stories and Fables* (1978), and *A Place to Die* (1983), stories; and his novel about George Vancouver's search for the Northwest Passage, *Burning Water* (1980), which won a Governor General's Award. Bowering has also published literary criticism and experimental fiction, including *A Short Sad Book* (1977).

Another *Tish* editor, **Frank Davey**, was born in Vancouver in 1940 and brought up in Abbotsford, B.C. A graduate of the University of British Columbia, he founded the critical magazine, *Open Letter* in 1965 in Victoria. (Two of his colleagues at *Tish*, George Bowering and Fred Wah, have been contributing editors for the new publication.) After receiving his Ph.D. from the University of Southern California in 1968, Davey joined the faculty of York University, TORONTO, in 1970. His early books dating from Vancouver include *D-Day and After* (1963), *City of the Gulls and Sea* (1964), *Bridge Force* (1965), and *The Scarred Hull* (1966).

Fred Wah, another *Tish* editor, was born in Swift Current, Sask., and grew up in the NELSON area, where he now teaches at the Kootenay School of Writing. Wah graduated from the University of British Columbia and studied in the United States—both in New Mexico and at the State University of New York at Buffalo—with Robert Creeley. Wah's first book was *Lardeau: Selected First Poems* (1965); he won a Governor General's Award for *Waiting for Saskatchewan* (1985).

Poet **Daphne Marlatt**, a *Tish* editor in 1963–4, was born in Australia in 1942 and moved to North Vancouver with her family in 1951. She graduated from the University of British Columbia in 1964 and, after studying in the United States, settled in Vancouver in 1970. She works as a freelance writer and researcher. Since settling here Marlatt has published several books of poetry, including *Vancouver Poems* (1972) and *Steveston* (1974), and the novel *Zocalo* (1977). Marlatt's association with the British Columbia Archives' oral-history project has led to rich studies in British Columbia cities: her book of poems about *Steveston*, a Japanese-Canadian fish-cannery town, was followed by *Steveston Recollected: A Japanese-Canadian History* (1975), and she has supplemented her *Vancouver Poems* (1972) with another reflection of the city, *Opening Doors: Vancouver's East End* (1980). In addition to editing *Tish*, Marlatt has been associated with the *Capilano Review* (1973–6) and *Periodics* (1977–81). She currently edits, with John Marshall, the Island Writing Series and the magazine *Island*.

Lionel Kearns, a native of Nelson, B.C., enrolled at the University of British Columbia in 1958. Associated with the editors of *Tish* and a frequent contributor to the magazine, he published his first collection of poems, *Songs of Circumstance* (1963), with Tishbooks. After receiving his M.A. in 1963 he joined the faculty of Simon Fraser University, BURNABY. His later books include *By the Light of the Silvery McLune* (1969), *Practising Up to Be Human* (1978), *Ignoring the Bomb* (1982), and *Convergences* (1984).

The Department of Creative Writing has brought several writers to the city since its formation. The poet playwright **J. Michael Yates** moved to Vancouver from the United States in 1967 and was a professor of creative writing at the University of British Columbia until 1971. In 1968 he founded Sono Nis Press. Yates's poetry was published in *Spiral of Mirrors* (1967), *The Great Bear Lake Meditations*, and *The Completely Collapsible Portable Man: Selected Shorter Lyrics* (1985), among other collections; his stories have appeared in *The Man in the Glass Octopus* (1968). Yates moved to the QUEEN CHARLOTTE ISLANDS in 1971; he now lives in Burnaby. **Michael Bullock**, a native of England, came to Vancouver in 1968 and is a professor in the Department of Creative Writing. Bullock had published several volumes of poetry before coming to Canada and, along with Yates and their student Andreas Schroeder, was a spokesman for the introduction of surrealism into Canadian writing. Bullock has published numerous volumes of prose-poetry—including *Sixteen Stories as They Happened* (1969), *A Savage Darkness* (1970), *Green Beginning, Black Ending* (1971), *Ralph Cranstone and the Pursuing River* (1975), *Ralph Cranstone and the Glass Thimble* (1977), and *The Man with Flowers Through His Hands* (1985)—and encouraged the founding of two magazines, *Contemporary Literature in Translation* and *Canadian Fiction Magazine* (1971), with which he has continued to be associated as a frequent contributor (see next paragraph). Bullock has also edited *Prism International*, which is associated with the Creative Writing Department. In addition to prose-poetry, Bullock has published several books of poetry: *Black Wings White Dead* (1978), *Lines in the Dark Wood* (1981), and *Quadriga for Judy* (1982). **Andreas Schroeder**, a native of Germany, received his B.A. from the University of British Columbia in 1969 and his M.A. in 1971. Founder of *Contemporary Literature in Translation* (1968–80), Schroeder also wrote a column for the Vancouver *Province* from 1968 to 1973. His first book was *The Ozone Minotaur* (1969), a collection of poetry. He has also published fiction, *The Late Man* (1972), and a journal of an eight-month jail term served for a narcotics conviction, *Shaking it Rough* (1976). Schroeder is now the administrator of the Public Lending Right program in Ottawa.

Several of these writers lived and worked during the late 1960s and early 1970s in a communal house (now gone) at 954 W. 7th Ave. One of the residents, Andreas Schroeder, remembers that it was in this house that *Canadian Fiction Magazine* was launched by **Wayne Stedingh** and Janie Kennon (it has since grown into a national journal and is now published in Toronto under Geoff Hancock's editorship); Schroeder's own *Contemporary Literature in Translation* began publishing; and Michael Yates founded Sono Nis Press. Books written here included Yates's *Great Bear Lake Meditations*, Stedingh's *From a Bell Tower* (1970), and many others. Among the many lodgers who stayed at the house at various times were poets Susan Musgrave, George McWhirter, Pat Lane, George Amabile, and Stanley Cooperman. Schroeder, Yates, Stedingh, and several others were permanent residents around the period 1968–71. **George McWhirter**, born in Northern Ireland, settled in Vancouver in 1967. He is the present chairman of the University of British Columbia's Department of Creative Writing, succeeding to the position held by Birney, Harlow, and Douglas Bankson. McWhirter lives on W. 13th Ave (4600 block). He is the author of complex, often experimental, works in poetry (*The Catalan Poems*, 1971), short fiction (*God's Eye*, 1981), and the novel *Paula Lake* (1984).

A native of England, novelist **David Watmough** has lived in Vancouver since 1959 and is a longtime resident of the Jericho Beach area. He has worked as a journalist and produced plays and commentaries for the CBC, becoming well known for his monodramas, designed for reading by a single person who acts out all the roles. These are collected in *Names for the Numbered Years* (1967) and *Ashes for Easter and other Monodramas* (1972). His books include the novels *No more into the garden* (1978) and *Unruly Skeletons* (1982), and the story collection *Fury* (1984).

D.M. Fraser, born in 1946 in Nova Scotia, came to Vancouver in the mid-1960s and lived for many of his years here in the apartment over the store at 4394 Main St. He graduated from the University of British Columbia and entered its Ph.D. program, but withdrew to devote his time to Pulp Press, which he co-founded in 1972 with Gregory Enright, Thomas Osborne, and Jon Furberg. Fraser's works are *Class Warfare* (1974; rpr. 1976), and *The Voice of Emma Sachs* (1983), collections of stories, and innovative essays. Fraser died on 4 Mar. 1985 in Vancouver.

The poet **Fred Cogswell** taught at the University of British Columbia during the 1974–5 academic year. He lived in the Richmond area of the city. A volume of his selected poems, *Light Bird of Life*, was published in 1974. (See EAST CENTREVILLE, FREDERICTON, N.B.)

In 1984 the University of British Columbia Library acquired the last significant collection of the manuscripts of novelist **Malcolm Lowry** (*Under the Volcano*, 1947). The purchase included drafts of two unpublished novels, one of them handwritten, along with two notebooks, a typed draft of a third unpublished novel, and two unpublished short stories. The library acquired most of Lowry's papers in 1959 from Margerie Lowry and has continued to add to the material through purchases. Several works by Lowry, including *October Ferry to Gabriola* (1970), have been published posthumously on the basis of the manuscripts. The library also houses the papers of the CAMPBELL RIVER author and naturalist **Roderick Haig-Brown**.

Other authors associated with Vancouver include **Bruce Hutchison**, who was editorial director of the Vancouver *Sun* from 1963 to 1979. Throughout the period Hutchison lived at his present home in VICTORIA and continues, as editor emeritus, to contribute occasional columns to the paper. A three-time winner of the Governor General's Award for non-fiction, Hutchison in 1981 published a book of sketches about a boy growing up in the British Columbia interior, *Uncle Percy's Wonderful Town*. The playwright **George Ryga**, who has lived for many years at SUMMERLAND, B.C., is associated with the city because many of his works were first staged here. *The Ecstasy of Rita Joe* (1971) was commissioned by the Vancouver Playhouse for presentation during 1967; a subsequent commission, *Captives of the Faceless Drummer* (1971), led to controversy when the board of directors of the Playhouse refused to produce the play, which was later staged at another theatre in the city, as well as in Toronto and in Lennoxville, Que.

Playwright **John Gray** has lived and worked primarily in Vancouver since the mid-1960s. Born in 1946 in Ottawa, he was raised in Truro, N.S., and came here to attend the University of British Columbia. In 1971 he founded Tamahnous Theatre here. For several years after 1975 he lived in TORONTO (2); on returning to Vancouver he produced several of his plays at the Vancouver East Cultural Centre. In collaboration with Eric Peterson, Gray wrote the musical play *Billy Bishop Goes to War* (1981), which won a Governor General's Award. His other plays include *18 Wheels* (prod. 1977), *Rock and Roll* (1981) and *Don Messer's Jubilee* (1985); his novel *Bedazzled* also appeared in 1985. Gray lives on West 37th Ave (3300 block).

A native of VICTORIA, the poet **Anne Marriott** has lived in North Vancouver since the 1970s and has given many workshops to elementary-school children at city libraries. Her most recent books are *The Circular Coast: New and Selected Poems* (1981), *A Long Way to Oregon: Selected Short Stories* (1984), and *Letters from Some Island: New Poems* (1985). Marriott, best known for the poem 'The Wind, Our Enemy', the title poem of her first book (1939), won a Governor General's Award in 1941 for *Calling Adventurers*. The poet **Dale Zieroth** (*Clearing: Poems from a Journey*, 1973) lives in North Vancouver. He based his collection *Mid-river* (1981) on his experiences in Invermere, B.C., where he lived in the mid-1970s and worked as a park ranger in the Banff-Kootenay region.

Since 1980 the novelist **Sinclair Ross** (*As for Me and My House*, 1941; rpr. 1957) has lived in Vancouver. After retiring from the Royal Bank in MONTREAL (6), Ross lived in Europe for many years. In 1982 he published *The Race and Other Stories*. (See also ARCOLA, HORIZON, PRINCE ALBERT, Sask.)

VICTORIA

The painter and writer **Emily Carr** was born in Victoria on 13 Dec. 1871, the year British Columbia entered Confederation, with Victoria as the provincial capital. Despite many absences for study and work abroad, Carr remained closely associated with Victoria throughout her life and died here in 1945. Her birthplace at 207 Government St has been restored by the city's Junior Chamber of Commerce, with aid from the federal government. The two-storey frame Emily Carr Home is decorated with reproductions of Carr's paintings; some of her letters and drawings are also on display. Carr grew up in this house, graduated in 1888 from Central Public School, and spent one year at Victoria High School before leaving to study painting. In 1889–90 she took art classes at the Roccabella mansion on Victoria Cres. and she then studied in San Francisco (1891–3), England (1894–1904), and Paris (1910–11). Carr began her life-long interest in painting west-coast scenery and the lives of coastal Indians in 1898 with a summer spent at UCLUELET on the western coast of Vancouver Island. From 1904 to 1910 and from 1911 to 1913 Carr made VANCOUVER her principal home. In 1913, however, she returned permanently to Victoria and built Hill House, an apartment house at 646 Simcoe St, near the family home on a lot that had also been owned by her father. She ended the often distasteful task of operating the apartment house in 1917 and opened

The Carr house on Carr St, later Government St, 1891

Emily Carr with her parrot, sheepdogs, and other animals in her garden, 1918

Bobtail Kennel, which she was forced to close in 1921 when she sold part of her property. Until 1936, when she traded Hill House for an apartment (gone) on Beckley St, she lived on Simcoe St but also spent much time travelling in British Columbia in search of material for her painting. In 1937 she suffered the first of many heart attacks that gradually forced her to abandon the arduous routine of travel she had maintained as a part of her art. Two years later, in 1939, she moved in with her sister Alice, who lived in a former schoolhouse at 218 St Andrews St (still standing). Carr then turned to writing, which she had pursued since 1927 through journals and diaries. In 1934 she took a writing course at Victoria College (now the University of Victoria). Her first book—an account of her visits among the coastal Indians who gave her the name, 'Klee Wyck' (the laughing one), which she used for her title—was published in 1941 and won a Governor General's Award. She continued with *The Book of Small* (1942), an account of her childhood on Government St, which in her early years had been called Carr St after her father. In 1944 she published *The House of All Sorts*, the tale of her apartment house and kennel on Simcoe St. She spent the last few weeks of her life at Saint Mary's Priory (formerly the James Bay Hotel, 606 Douglas St), where she died in 1945. Carr was buried in the family plot in Ross Bay Cemetery. In addition to the Emily Carr Home, memorials to the artist in Victoria include a stone bridge dedicated to her in Beacon Hill Park, near Government St. The province owns 141 of Carr's paintings, which are on display in the provincial museum in the Heritage Court complex, 601 Belleville St, and other works of the artist can be seen at the Emily Carr Art Gallery, 1107 Wharf St. Several collections of Carr's journals and essays have been published since her death; her autobiography *Growing Pains* (1946), which describes her experiences as an art student in Europe, was published posthumously at Carr's request.

After working on a farm near DUNCAN, **Robert Service** moved to Victoria in the spring of 1903 to study for university entrance examinations. He passed and began classes but dropped out in the fall. On 10 Oct. 1903 he joined the staff of the Victoria branch of the Bank of Commerce and worked there until July 1904, when he was transferred to KAMLOOPS. Service's next post was WHITEHORSE, Yukon Territory, where he added poetry to his banking success and published *Songs of a Sourdough*, his first book, in 1907. (See also CHILKOOT PASS, WHITE PASS; TORONTO: 2, Ont.; EDMONTON, Alta; DAWSON CITY, LAKE LABERGE, Y.T.; FORT McPHERSON, MACKENZIE RIVER, N.W.T.)

The poet **Anne Marriott** was born here on 5 Nov. 1913 and attended the Poplars and Norfolk House School for Girls. Best known for the title poem of her first book, *The Wind, Our Enemy* (1939), she won a Governor General's Award for *Calling Adventurers* (1941). Marriott has written radio scripts for the British Columbia Department of Education and in 1943–4 edited a poetry column for the Victoria *Daily Times*. From 1945 to 1949 she was a script editor for the National Film Board in OTTAWA. (See also PRINCE GEORGE, VANCOUVER; SASKATOON, Sask.)

The influential magazine *Contemporary Verse* was published during its last years from the Victoria home of its editor, Alan Crawley; it ceased publication in 1952. It had been founded in West Vancouver in Sept. 1940 (see VANCOUVER).

The editor and political commentator **Bruce Hutchison** was born in Ontario but raised in Victoria. He joined the Victoria *Times* in 1918 as a high-school reporter, and became the paper's political reporter in OTTAWA in 1925. Hutchison, who worked at intervals on other papers, including the Vancouver *Sun* and Winnipeg *Free Press*, was editor of the *Times* from 1950 to 1963. He then went to the Vancouver *Sun* as editorial director, although he retained his home in Victoria. He retired from the *Sun* in 1979 and still lives in Victoria. In addition to his editorial work, Hutchison has written many successful books on Canadian politics and history. He began with *The Unknown Country: Canada and Her People* (1943), which won a Governor General's Award. Hutchison has also published a novel, *The Hollow Man* (1944), and a series of sketches about growing up in British Columbia, *Uncle Percy's Wonderful Town* (1981). His autobiography, *The Far Side of the Street*, was published in 1976.

English-born poet **Marjorie Pickthall** settled in Victoria in 1920, coming here from TORONTO (3), where she spent her childhood and was educated. She wrote her only novel, *The Bridge* (1921), here but life-long

Marjorie Pickthall

health problems led to her early death in 1922. In 1920 and in early 1921 Pickthall lived at 1603 Jubilee Ave and in mid-1921 at 1115 Collinson St. She lived from late Nov. 1921 until at least Feb. 1922 in a boarding-house at 966 Bank St in Victoria's Oak Bay area. She died after an operation in a Vancouver hospital on 19 Apr. 1922. Pickthall's poetry was collected in *Complete Poems* (1936). During her residence in Victoria, Pickthall tried to recover her health by spending several weeks preceding 17 Nov. 1921 in the Fairfield Nursing Home, 526 Harbinger Ave. This is the same home in which **Charles Mair**, the Canada First poet born in LANARK, Ont., spent the last three years of his life and in which he died on 7 July 1927. On 26 Apr. 1927, shortly before Mair's death, his editor, John Garvin, rushed him the first copy of *Tecumseh: a Drama, and Canadian Poems; Dreamland and Poems; The American Bison; Through the Mackenzie Basin: Memoirs and Reminiscences* (1926), which Garvin had first proposed publishing in 1915. Mair was buried in Ross Bay Cemetery after a funeral service in Christ Church Cathedral. (See also: FORT STEELE; KINGSTON, OTTAWA, TORONTO: 1, WINDSOR, Ont.; PORTAGE-LA-PRAIRIE, WINNIPEG, Man.; PRINCE ALBERT, Sask.; CALGARY, Alta.)

William Hume Blake died suddenly on a Victoria golf course in 1924. Best known for his translation of Louis Hémon's *Maria Chapdelaine* (1921), he was also a popular essayist on fishing and French-Canadian rural life. His best-known book is *Brown Waters and Other Sketches* (1915). (See also LA MALBAIE, Que.; TORONTO: 2, Ont.)

The poet **Phyllis Webb** was born here in 1927 and educated at the University of British Columbia, VANCOUVER. After several years in eastern Canada she returned to British Columbia in 1969 and now lives on SALTSPRING ISLAND. Her books include *Naked Poems* (1965), *Wilson's Bowl* (1980), and *The Vision Tree: Selected Poems* (1982), which won a Governor General's Award. (See also MONTREAL, Que.; TORONTO: 2, Ont.) The Saskatchewan 'scrapbook' poet **Edna Jaques** worked as a stenographer in Victoria from 1929 to 1935, before resuming her career as a touring lecturer. (See also OTTAWA, TORONTO: 7, Ont.; BRIERCREST, PRINCE ALBERT, Sask.)

Charles Mair shortly before his death, being visited by Sir Charles G.D. Roberts

The novelist and women's rights activist **Nellie McClung** moved to Gordonhead, a suburb of Victoria, in 1935 from CALGARY after her husband retired from the insurance business. Her home at 1861 Ferndale Rd was called 'Lantern Lane', and she used the name in the titles of two collections of newspaper articles and sketches: *Leaves from Lantern Lane* (1936) and *More Leaves from Lantern Lane* (1937). McClung also wrote two volumes of autobiography, *Clearing in the West* (1936) and *The Stream Runs Fast* (1945). Her many years of political activity, on behalf of women's suffrage and as a member of the Alberta legislature in EDMONTON, brought her an appointment as delegate to the League of Nations in 1936 and a seat on the CBC's Board of Governors from 1936 through 1942. McClung died in Victoria in 1951. (See also CHATSWORTH, OTTAWA, Ont.; LA RIVIÈRE, MANITOU, WAWANESA, WINNIPEG, Man.)

The novelist **Irene Baird**, who grew up in VANCOUVER and worked for many years on newspapers there, set three of her novels in Victoria and Vancouver Island. The first, *John* (1937), is a character study of an island recluse named John Dorey. In *Waste Heritage* (1939) Baird dramatizes events surrounding a march on Victoria by 1,000 unemployed workers after a sit-in at the Vancouver Post Office in 1938 was forcibly ended. *He Rides the Sky* (1941) follows a Victoria airman in the Second World War through his letters home.

The poet **P.K. Page** lived at 1626 Wilmot Place in 1945–6, and in the 1960s returned to the city after several years abroad to her present home on Exeter Road. Much of the imagery from her story 'Unless the Eye Catch Fire . . .', published in *Evening Dance of the Grey Flies* (1981), is drawn from her garden. Poems based on her life in Victoria include 'Election Day', 'Stories of Snow', 'Vegetable Island', 'Now This Cold Man', 'Leviathan in a Pool', 'They Might Have Been Zebras', 'Domestic Poem for a Summer Afternoon', and 'Short Spring Poem for the Short-Sighted'. (See also NEW RIVER BEACH, ROTHESAY, SAINT JOHN, N.B.; KINGSMERE, MONTREAL: 5, Que.; OTTAWA, Ont.; WINNIPEG, Man.; CALGARY, RED DEER, Alta.)

P.K. Page, 1972

The short-story writer **Alice Munro**, born in WINGHAM, Ont., moved in 1951 to VANCOUVER and shortly after to Victoria, where her first husband James opened a bookstore in 1963 at 753 Yates St (it is now at 1108 Government St). Munro began writing her stories about southern Ontario here. Her first collection, *Dance of the Happy Shades* (1968), won a Governor General's Award. Other books from her years in Victoria include the novel *Lives of Girls and Women* (1971), and the short-story collection *Something I've Been Meaning To Tell You* (1974). During the early and mid-1960s, when Alice Munro was beginning her writing career, the Munros lived at 105 Cook St. In 1967 they moved to 1648 Rockland Ave, where she lived until she returned to Ontario. Divorced in 1976, Alice Munro now lives with her second husband in CLINTON, Ont.

Howard O'Hagan, born in LETHBRIDGE, Alta, wrote his novel *Tay John* (1939) on an island in Howe Sound. During the 1950s he contributed articles to Victoria newspapers. After several years in Europe, O'Hagan and his wife settled in Victoria in 1974, living until 1980 at Apt 111, 335 St James St. His novel *The School Marm Tree* (1983) was first published in *Event/A Journal of the Arts* in 1976. O'Hagan died in

Victoria in 1982; a posthumous collection of essays, *Cayote's Song*, edited by Gary Geddes, was published in 1983. His home in his last three years was at Apt 37, 74 Dallas Rd.

The English-born poet and scholar **Robin Skelton** joined the English department of the University of Victoria in 1963. His Victoria Ave home is a well-known mecca for writers and artists. In 1967 he began directing the university's creative writing program, and from 1973 to 1976 served as that department's first chairman. Skelton has published over 60 books. *The Collected Shorter Poems, 1947–77* (1981) is a representative gathering of his poetry. He has also devoted much energy to the editing of, and critical writing on, English and Irish writers, and was a co-founder in 1967 with the late John Peter of *The Malahat Review*, and was its sole editor from 1971 to 1982. Since 1976 he has been editor-in-chief of Sono Nis Press.

Many other writers are associated with the University of Victoria. **Dave Godfrey** went there in 1978 as chairman of the creative-writing department, a position he still holds. Godfrey won a Governor General's Award in 1970 for his innovative novel *The New Ancestors* (see also TORONTO: 3, Ont.) Another recipient of a Governor General's Award who teaches at the university is the poet **Stephen Scobie**, who won for *McAlmon's Chinese Opera* (1980). (See also EDMONTON, Alta.) The novelist, short-story writer, and poet **W.D. Valgardson** (*Gentle Sinners*, 1980) has taught in the creative-writing department since 1974. One of Valgardson's first and most noted students was the novelist and short-story writer **W.P. Kinsella**, a native of Alberta who came to Victoria in 1967 and received his B.A. in 1974. Valgardson had received an M.F.A. from the creative-writing program of the university of Iowa, and Kinsella went to study in the same program, graduating in 1978; he then taught at the University of CALGARY (1978–83) before moving to WHITE ROCK, B.C. and devoting his full time to writing on the strength of the success of his novel of baseball, *Shoeless Joe* (1982). Valgardson's earliest work consisted of stories of Cree Indian life, collected in such volumes as *Dance Me Outside* (1977). These are set on a reserve south of EDMONTON, but Kinsella has said that he has never visited the reserve and that he gained the experience on which his characters are based while working as a taxi driver in Victoria. The American-born novelist and short-story writer **Leon Rooke** has lived in Victoria since 1969 and has taught creative writing at the university. His wife, **Constance Rooke**, is a professor of English here and has edited the

W.P. Kinsella

Malahat Review since 1982. Leon Rooke's many books include *Shakespeare's Dog* (1983), a novel written in pseudo-Elizabethan English, and *Cry Evil* (1980), a collection of stories. **Susan Musgrave** (*Tarts and Muggers*, 1982) is associated with Victoria by virtue of having had her poems first presented by Robin Skelton in the *Malahat Review* in 1967, when she was only sixteen. She lives on Tryon Rd near Sidney, north of Victoria on Hwy 17.

WHITE PASS

Robert Service, poet of the Yukon, travelled by train through White Pass, north of Skagway on the Alaska–British Columbia border, in Nov. 1904, on his way to a teller's job in the WHITEHORSE (Y.T.) branch of the Bank of Commerce. White Pass rises to a height of 2,885 feet and was renowned as the Dead Horse Trail because some 3,000 horses being used to pack equipment into the newly opened Klondike gold fields perished there in the winter of 1896–7. In his autobiography *Ploughman of the Moon* (1945) Service describes his train trip from Skagway to Whitehorse on the narrow-gauge White Pass & Yukon Railway, which was built in 1900 and is still in operation today. He set some of his most famous poems along the route of this railway. Miles Canyon inspired the line 'I have gazed on naked grandeur where there's nothing else to gaze on' in 'The Spell of the Yukon'. According to Service, the wild scenery above White Horse Rapids inspired his poem 'The Call of the Wild'. (See also CHILKOOT PASS, DUNCAN, KAMLOOPS, VICTORIA; TORONTO: 2, Ont.; EDMONTON, Alta; DAWSON CITY, LAKE LABERGE, Y.T.; FORT MCPHERSON, MACKENZIE RIVER, N.W.T.)

WHITE ROCK

The novelist and short-story writer **W.P. Kinsella** has lived in White Rock since 1983; he is noted for his Indian stories (*Scars*, 1978; *The Moccasin Telegraph*, 1983) and for his stories and novels about baseball, *Shoeless Joe Jackson Comes to Iowa* (1980) and *Shoeless Joe* (1982). Born in 1935 in EDMONTON, Kinsella set his Indian stories on a reserve southwest of that city; his baseball stories are set in the United States. Since coming to White Rock, Kinsella has published *The Fencepost Chronicles* (1986), a collection of stories that won a Leacock Medal for humour. (See also VICTORIA.)

During the 1970s and early 1980s White Rock was home to the literary magazine *Blackfish* and to Blackfish Press, which published Vancouver poet Pat Lowther's first book, F.R. Scott's collected translations from Québécois poets, and John Glassco's translation of Leopold von Sacher-Masoch's *Venus in Furs*, among other books. The press was founded by two poets who still live in White Rock: Brian Brett (*Smoke Without Exit*, 1984) and Allan Safarik (*The Naked Machine Rides On*, 1980). White Rock is a coastal community south of Vancouver and just north of the U.S. border.

WILLIAMS LAKE

This historic city on the Fraser River and the Cariboo Hwy at the centre of the Cariboo region—site of British Columbia's largest stockyards and of its principal rodeo—was the home from 1953 to 1968 of the dramatist **Gwen Pharis Ringwood**. She lived at 368 N. 5th Ave. In 1961 she wrote a musical play with a score by Art Rosoman, *The Road Runs North*, for the Williams Lake Centennial Celebration; the work concerns the Cariboo Gold Rush (also called the Fraser River Gold Rush), which began in 1858 and in which Williams Lake played a prominent role. Here Ringwood wrote her one novel, *Younger Brother* (1959), and many of her more than 60 plays, 25 of which have been published in *The Collected Plays of Gwen Pharis Ringwood* (1982). (See also CHIMNEY LAKE; BANFF, EDMONTON, EDSON, MAGRATH, Alta.)

Northwest Territories

AKLAVIK

The initials 'A.J.' cut into a tree stump on Aklavik's main street form the grave marker of Albert Johnson, the 'mad trapper', who was killed near here in Feb. 1932 in a shoot-out with members of the Royal Canadian Mounted Police. Sought for questioning about interference with Indian traps near FORT MCPHERSON in the winter of 1931–2, Johnson drove off officers with gunfire, wounding one and killing another during the weeks-long manhunt that ensued. This famous incident has been the subject of several books, notably **Rudy Wiebe**'s novel *The Mad Trapper* (1980), and of Wiebe's short story 'The Name of Albert Johnson' in *Where Is the Voice Coming From?* (1974).

Aklavik is the main setting of *My Name Is Masak* (1977) by the Inuit writer **Alice French**. Born in 1930 on Baillie Island in the Beaufort Sea, she attended All Saint's Anglican Residential School here from 1937–44; her book recounts how deeply disturbed she was by her first experiences of town and school life, and describes her subsequent difficulty in re-acclimatizing herself to the traditional life of her family. French, who married an RCMP officer, Dominic French, later lived in Reindeer Station (on the Mackenzie River East Channel), and in Grand Rapids, Man., where she wrote her book. Aklavik is located on the West Channel.

AKLAVIK

My name is Masak. I was born in June 1930, on Baillie Island in the Northwest Territories. Baillie Island was quite a big settlement at one time, but now it has washed away into the Beaufort Sea. Not the whole island is gone—just the buildings that once stood on the sandy point: the trading post, the Roman Catholic and Anglican missions, the shack where the Royal Canadian Mounted Police were, and the Eskimos' houses.

—Alice French, *My Name Is Masak* (1976)

BAKER LAKE

Armand Tagoona—the first Inuit Anglican priest—served in Baker Lake in the 1970s and until 1986, when he moved to RANKIN INLET. At Baker Lake he wrote his account of Inuit Life, *Shadows* (1975), which he also illustrated. This hamlet, which has a population of some 900, is on the northwest shore of Baker Lake, west of Hudson Bay.

Baker Lake is the home of the Inuit artist **Ruth Annaqtuusi Tulurialik**, who portrays in colourful drawings and describes, with **David Pelly**, life before and after the coming of the white man in *Qikaaluktut: Images of Inuit Life* (1986).

BATHURST INLET

Bathurst Inlet is a long inlet from the south-eastern shore of Coronation Gulf; on the inlet's east coast is a hamlet of the same name. Beginning in Nov. 1923, the explorer **Knud Rasmussen** collected the songs, poems, tales, myths, and legends of the Copper Eskimos (the Umingmagtormiut, or Musk-ox People) on the Kent Peninsula, north of here, and afterwards in the eastern coastal region of Bathurst Inlet as the Copper Eskimos moved south to hunt. In his *Across Arctic America* (1927) Rasmussen calls the Musk-ox People the 'most poetically gifted' of the groups he visited; he vividly describes a celebration and song-fest at the large assembly igloo of a hunting village on Bathurst Inlet, and includes translations of many of the songs he transcribed on that occasion. (See also DANISH ISLAND, PELLY BAY.)

BERNARD HARBOUR

There is no longer a settlement at Bernard Harbour, but in July 1914, when members of **Vilhjalmur Stefansson**'s Canadian Arctic Expedition of 1913–18 arrived here to set up camp, the tiny outpost was the regional headquarters of the Hudson's Bay Company, the Royal Canadian Mounted Police, and the Anglican Mission. Stefansson, who described this controversy-plagued expedition in his autobiography *Discovery* (1964), was primarily interested in other aspects of his multi-faceted endeavour and spent no time at Bernard Harbour. But the party he established here included the ethnologist **Diamond Jenness**, who remained until July 1916; Jenness tells of his experiences in *The People of the Twilight* (1928), which includes his account of a period when he lived as the adopted son of an Inuit family. He collected anthropological data and Inuit literature among the Copper Eskimos (the Umingmagtormiut, or Musk-ox People), principally those of Victoria Island; a peninsula on the island's west coast is named for Jenness. He is the author of *The Copper Eskimo* (1922), based on his *The Life of the Copper Eskimo*, vols 12–14 of the 14-volume *Report of the Canadian Arctic Expedition: 1913–18*; volume 14, *Songs of the Copper Eskimo* (1925), provides much of the material that has since appeared in anthologies of Inuit poetry in translation.

Vilhjalmur Stefansson

BERNARD HARBOUR

Gloomy and barren seemed the country around Bernard Harbour when we first set foot upon its shore—a land of long twilights soon to be swallowed up in a longer night. A few vestiges of habitation there were—stone rings that marked old camping-sites, and shallow pits from which the hunters had launched their arrows at the passing caribou. But of the Eskimos themselves, of those dwellers in the twilight who even then were awaiting the dawn of the new age, we saw no sign.

—Diamond Jenness, *The People of the Twilight* (1928)

It was at the outset of the Canadian Arctic Expedition in Sept. 1913 that Stefansson's ship the *Karluk*, commanded by Captain Bob Bartlett, was trapped in ice and crushed; this incident is recounted by Bartlett in *The Last Voyage of the Karluk, Flagship of Vilh-*

jalmur Stefansson (1916): see BRIGUS, Nfld. Bernard Harbour is on the south shore of Dolphin and Union Strait opposite southwestern Victoria Island.

CAMBRIDGE BAY

Fr **Maurice Metayer**, O.M.I., the author of many works on Inuit mythology and language and a translator of Inuit literature, served in 1957 and in 1964–73 at Cambridge Bay, a hamlet on the southeastern coast of Victoria Island. Born in France in 1914, Metayer came to the Arctic in 1939 and served at Coppermine, Holman Island, Reid Island, Poulatuk, and TUKTOYAKTUK, as well as at Cambridge Bay, where he produced *Arlok l'esquimau* (1965), *I, Nuligak* (1966; trans. by Metayer from Inuktitut into both English and French), and *Tales from the Igloo* (1972). The latter book contains traditional stories and fables told by 22 elder members of the Copper Eskimos, the Inuit group that lives along the Arctic Ocean coast between approximately 103° and 123° west longitude and ranges south to Contwoyto Lake (see also BATHURST INLET). *I, Nuligak*, the first autobiography written by an Inuit, was written by **Nuligak** (1895–1966) partly in pencil and partly on an old typewriter; it was published in Inuktitut in a periodical, and translated by Metayer from Nuligak's original manuscript. Nuligak's youth was spent on Herschel Island; although Aklavik and Tuktoyaktuk feature prominently in his narrative, the autobiography is not mainly concerned with town life but with the 'old days' of the western Arctic Inuit. The early homeland of Nuligak's family, treated in the first portion of his book, was on the south coast of Victoria Island, not far west of Cambridge Bay. Fr. Metayer travelled in France and eastern Canada in 1973–4 and then returned to the Arctic; he died at Fort Smith in 1974. His *Inuit Legends* (1977) was edited after his death by Leoni Kappi.

Fr **Raymond de Coccola**, who ministered to the people of Cambridge Bay in the late 1930s, wrote with **Paul King** a notable account of Inuit life in *Ayorama* (1956).

CAPE DORSET

Cape Dorset, on the southern tip of Baffin Island's Fox Peninsula, is the home of the artist **Pitseolak Ashoona**, author of one of the most famous Inuit autobiographies, *Pitseolak: Pictures Out of My Life* (1971). Her brother **Peter Pitseolak** (1902–73), who was a tribal leader as well as a noted carver, artist, and photographer, was also an author. His narrative, *Peter Pitseolak's Escape from Death* (1977), edited by Dorothy Eber, is illustrated with his art.

Cape Dorset, home of the West Baffin Eskimo Cooperative, is one of the most prominent centres of Inuit art, thanks to a tradition originated in part by the artist and author **James Houston**, who in 1951 taught print-making to the Inuit and helped them to found the first artists' co-operative here. A native of TORONTO (7), Houston first visited the Arctic in 1948. He settled at Cape Dorset in 1951, and in 1953 became Civil Administrator of West Baffin Island, a position he retained for nine years. At the beginning of his tenure the vast territory he administered contained 343 persons living in 13 camps. Houston's writings on Inuit themes include the novel *The White Dawn: An Eskimo Saga* (1971), *Songs of the Dream People* (1972), an anthology of Inuit and Indian poetry, and several retellings of traditional Inuit myths for young readers. Houston left the Arctic in 1962 and now divides his time between homes in Rhode Island and the Queen Charlotte Islands.

DANISH ISLAND

On tiny Danish Island, just off the central east coast of Vansittart Island at the northwestern extremity of Hudson Bay, is a marker commemorating the headquarters of **Knud Rasmussen**'s Fifth Thule Expedition (1921–4). Here, in mid-Sept. 1921, Rasmussen and his party constructed their house, which they called the 'Blow-hole' (or the 'Bellows'); it was the base for wide-ranging investigations throughout the eastern Arctic and along the Arctic Ocean coast to Siberia that resulted in much of the present-day knowledge of Inuit culture. The songs, poems, tales, myths and legends that Rasmussen collected are found in the *Report of the Fifth Thule Expedition* (10 fols, 1931–42); the last eight volumes were edited by expedition-member Therkel Mathiassen after Rasmussen's death in 1933. The *Report* contains literature of the Igluk and Caribou Eskimos (vol. 7), the Netsilk Eskimos (vol. 8), the Copper Eskimos (vol. 9), and the Eskimos of the Mackenzie River (vol. 10). Rasmussen presented his own translations of many poems and songs in his informal account of the expedition, *Across Arctic America: A Narrative of the Fifth Thule Expedition* (1927). *Beyond the High Hills* (1961), edited by Guy-Marie Rousselière, is an anthology of Inuit poems drawn from the *Report*, which is also an important source for almost all subsequent books of Inuit poetry in translation. (See also BATHURST INLET, PELLY BAY.)

COPPER ESKIMO SONG

The little seamew
Hovers above us,
Staring and scolding.
Its head is white.
Its beak opens gaping,
The little round eyes
See far, see keenly.
Qutiuk, qutiuk!

The little tern
Hovers above us,
Staring and scolding.
Its head is black.
Its beak opens gaping,
The little round eyes
See far, see keenly.
Iyoq—iyoq!

The big raven
Hovers above us,
Staring and scolding.
Its head is black.
Its beak is sharp, as if it had teeth.
Qara—qara!

—Knud Rasmussen, *Across Arctic America: A Narrative of the Fifth Thule Expedition* (1927)

FORT McPHERSON

Fort McPherson, in the Mackenzie River delta, was an important stop on the historic Edmonton Trail at the turn of the century. An arduous overland route through the Canadian North into the Klondike goldfields, the trail passed from Edmonton north down the Mackenzie River and then, from Fort McPherson, followed a chain of rivers through the mountains of the northern Yukon Territory to Dawson City. **Laura Berton**, in *I Married the Klondike* (1954), recalls the terrible toll in human life claimed by the journey and tells how Isaac Stringer, Bishop of the Yukon from 1905, was once reduced on the trail to eating his boots. This extremity, based on an Indian practice of boiling beaver skins (stripped of hair) to make broth, became a legend of the North and inspired a scene in Charlie Chaplin's *The Gold Rush (1924)*—one of the most famous scenes in film.

Robert Service, planning his return to the Yukon after having travelled to New York in 1910 with the manuscript of his novel *The Trail of '98* (1910), determined to go to Dawson via the Edmonton Trail in the summer of 1911. He describes the trip down the Mackenzie to Fort McPherson and then along the northeastern Yukon's treacherous mountain rivers in his autobiography *Ploughman of the Moon* (1945). This journey, Service later said, converted him from a spokesman for the Yukon to a lover of the Arctic North. His last book of poems written in Canada, *Rhymes of a Rolling Stone* (1912), was based primarily on the scenery and events of the trip from Fort McPherson. (See also DAWSON CITY, Y.T.; TORONTO: 2, Ont.; DUNCAN, B.C.)

Fort McPherson was the starting point in late 1931 for one of Canada's most famous manhunts. A mysterious stranger calling himself Albert Johnson had bought supplies at the fort and then moved to an isolated cabin, where he shot at and wounded one of two Mounties who came to question him about a dispute he had had with a native trapper. Johnson fled and a Mountie, Spike Millen, pursued him for forty-nine days into the desolate Richardson Mountains of the Yukon Territory, where the fugitive was killed at Eagle River on 17 Feb. 1932. Johnson, whose true identity and motives remain a mystery, is buried in the delta town of AKLAVIK. **Rudy Wiebe** wrote about Johnson, known in legend as the Mad Trapper, in both 'The Naming of Albert Johnson', a story from *Where Is the Voice Coming From?* (1974), and in his novel *The Mad Trapper* (1980).

FROBISHER BAY

This town of over 2,000 inhabitants on southern Baffin Island was the point of entry for **Al Purdy**'s trip to the North in the summer of 1965, an experience described in his book of poems *North of Summer* (1967). Although most of Purdy's time was spent in PANGNIRTUNG, on Cumberland Sound to the north, and in an Eskimo village on the KIKASTAN ISLANDS, the book's opening poems deal with Frobisher Bay and its environs, including the Sylvia Grinnell River. (See also AMELIASBURG, Ont.)

In 1861 Frobisher Bay was the campsite of the American explorer C.F. Hall. His expedition, which took place long before Canada's claim to the Arctic islands had been enunciated and accepted, was described in his *Life with the Esquimaux* (1865), composed from notes and diaries written here. He named the Sylvia Grinnell River after the daughter of his financial backer, saying that he did so 'with the flag of my country in one hand, my other in the limpid stream'.

Frobisher Bay was the childhood home of **Alootook Ipellie**, a well-known Inuit poet and fiction writer whose work is included in the anthology *Paper Stays Put: A Collection of Inuit Writing* (1980).

GREAT BEAR LAKE

The poet **J. Michael Yates**, who from 1967 to 1971 was a member of the Creative Writing Department in the University of British Columbia, VANCOUVER, visited Great Bear Lake on a Canada Council grant and produced *The Great Bear Lake Meditations* (1970), a highly regarded book of prose-poems about his experience here. 'No one acclimatizes to the extreme north,' he wrote. 'Aurora never seems quite familiar nor natural. And the tortures of light and dark remain a threat.' (See also QUEEN CHARLOTTE ISLANDS, B.C.)

KEEWATIN BARRENS

In 1947–8 **Farley Mowat** spent several months for the federal government in the Keewatin Barrens, the part of the Northwest Territories and Manitoba that lies along the western shore of Hudson Bay. His first book, *People of the Deer* (1952), was an impassioned plea for understanding and support for the Inuit residents of the region. Mowat's return several years later led to *The Desperate People* (1959), a fuller analysis of the relationship of these same people, the Ihalmiut, to government structures and to white society in general. The years on the Keewatin Barrens also provided Mowat with material for *Never Cry Wolf* (1963), which tells how his government research led him into deep sympathy with the wolves he had been sent to observe. Mowat's experiences narrated in *People of the Deer* began at Windy Bay Camp, a single cabin on the north side of Nueltin Lake, and took him to the settlements and hunting territories of the Ihalmiut lying between Nueltin Lake and Dubawnt Lake, over 150 miles northwest. Established settlements that figure in his narratives include Churchill and Brochet, Man. (which is on the north shore of Reindeer Lake, near the Saskatchewan border), and Eskimo Point, N.W.T., on the Hudson Bay coast.

The Northwest Territories are featured in Mowat's many selections and retellings of northern explorers' writings in books such as *Coppermine Journey* (1958), *Ordeal by Ice* (1960), and *The Polar Passion* (1967). Many of the stories in his *Snow Walker* (1975) are set in this same region. (See SPENCE BAY, RANKIN INLET.) For Mowat, the North holds great hardship for its inhabitants but can offer in return a life of harmony and consolation. (See also BURGEO, Nfld; BELLEVILLE, PALGRAVE, PORT HOPE, Ont.)

Much of the best writing about the Barrenlands has been by or about explorers and adventurers. Just northwest of the area Mowat has written about lies the region of the Thelon and Dubawnt Rivers, where in 1927 a small party led by the nomadic John Hornby froze to death. Hornby's cousin **Edgar Christian**, the last to die, left a diary that was discovered and published as *Unflinching: A Diary of Tragic Adventure* (1937). A biography, *The Legend of John Hornby* (1962), was written by **George Whalley** (see KINGSTON, Ont.)

Farley Mowat, 1987

Much farther to the northwest is the region of the Coppermine River, discovered by **Samuel Hearne** during his 1769–72 trips to the Barrenlands in search of copper deposits. After two abortive attempts, Hearne discovered and named the river in 1771, and his expedition of 1771–2 followed it from its source in Great Slave Lake to Coronation Gulf, where it empties into the Arctic Ocean. Hearne told of his explorations in *A Journey from Prince of Wale's Fort, in Hudson's Bay, to the Northern Ocean . . .* (1795). (See CHURCHILL, Man.; CUMBERLAND HOUSE, Sask.)

Sir **John Franklin**, on his first northern expedition, travelled overland to the Coppermine River, down it to Coronation Gulf, and then eastward. Franklin recorded these travels of 1819–22 in his first *Narrative* (1823). The explorer and geologist **Joseph Burr Tyrrell** made official surveys of parts of the Barrenlands in 1893 and 1894, and published his findings in *Report on the Dubawnt, Kazan and Ferguson Rivers and the North West Coast of Hudson Bay* (1896); in *People of the Deer* Farley Mowat remembers this work as one of the few pieces of writing about the North that intrigued him and encouraged his own travels.

KIKASTAN ISLANDS

Al Purdy spent much of the summer of 1965 at a tiny Eskimo hunting settlement on the Kikastan Islands, near PANGNIRTUNG in Cumberland Sound, Baffin Island. The poet had originally intended to spend the entire summer at Pangnirtung, but after a few weeks he accompanied an Eskimo hunter, Jonesee, to the Kikastans 'to find some place where Eskimos lived the way they did before there were white men in the north'. About half the poems in Purdy's *North of Summer* (1967) were written in the Kikastans. (See also FROBISHER BAY; AMELIASBERG, Ont.)

KIKASTAN ISLANDS

There were perhaps a dozen people there, of whom Jonesee and his friend Simonie were the hunters. I cooked food, slept, wrote and went with Jonesee on hunting trips a couple of times. And the wind never stopped blowing. Sometimes it shoved icebergs onto the tidal rocks and pounded them to bits.

—Al Purdy, *North of Summer*

MACKENZIE RIVER

Alexander Mackenzie was in charge of the North West Company's trading in the Athabaska district when he travelled in June 1789 along the Slave River to Great Slave Lake and then followed an unexplored river—which he hoped would lead west to the Pacific—over one thousand miles to its mouth in the Artctic Ocean. He called it the 'River of Disappointment', but it was named the Mackenzie in his honour. From Great Slave Lake to the Beaufort Sea, the Mackenzie is 1,065 miles long. Mackenzie's journey is narrated in his *Voyages from Montreal, on the River St. Lawrence, through the Continent of North America, to the Frozen and Pacific Oceans. In the Years 1789 and 1793. With a Preliminary Account of the Rise, Progress, and Present State of the Fur Trade of That Country* (1801), edited by William Combe.

The Mackenzie River formed a vital part of the Edmonton Trail to the Yukon gold fields. In *I Married the Klondike* (1954), the veteran DAWSON CITY resident **Laura Berton** described the dangers of the journey down the river and then through the Yukon Territory's Richardson Mountains to the Yukon River and Dawson. That route, according to Berton, claimed more lives than any other trail to the gold fields (see also FORT MCPHERSON, WHITEHORSE, Y.T.). **Robert Service**, who had lived in both WHITEHORSE and DAWSON CITY, determined to return to Dawson in the spring of 1911 via the Edmonton Trail. The journey down the Mackenzie is described in his autobiography, *Ploughman of the Moon: An Adventure into Memory* (1945). By 1911 Service had published three volumes of poetry and a novel, *The Trail of '98: A Northland Romance* (1911), all developing themes based on his years in the Yukon. His next book, *Rhymes of a Rolling Stone* (1912), written in Dawson City during his last year in the North, is filled with poems about the Mackenzie River journey. (See also FORT MCPHERSON; CHILKOOT PASS, WHITE PASS, B.C.; LAKE LABERGE, YUKON RIVER, Y.T.)

John Buchan, Lord Tweedsmuir, Governor General of Canada from 1935 to 1940, visited the Northwest Territories in the summer of 1937. His 7000-mile journey stretched from Edmonton to the mouth of the Mackenzie. Buchan, who had been troubled by ill health since the First World War, returned from the demanding trip invigorated and filled with praise for the health benefits of life in the North. During the autumn of 1939 he wrote his last novel, *Sick Heart River* (1941), set in the same Mackenzie River region he had visited. (See also SOUTH NAHANNI RIVER; OTTAWA, Ont.)

Robert Kroetsch worked during the summers from 1948 to 1950 on riverboats hauling cargo along the Mackenzie. His first novel, *But We Are Exiles* (1965), gives a modern account of life along the still largely unsettled river. **Hugh MacLennan** travelled the Mackenzie in the late 1950s for his series of essays collected in *Seven Rivers of Canada* (1961; 1974). Important literary materials collected among the Inuit of the Mackenzie River region have been published by **Herbert T. Schwarz** in *Elik and Other Stories of the Mackenzie Eskimos* (1970).

PANGNIRTUNG

Al Purdy spent part of the summer of 1965 in this community on Cumberland Sound, Baffin Island. Here he wrote many of the poems in his book *North of Summer* (1967), which follows the chronology of his months in the Arctic, with poems from Pangnirtung framing a large group written at the KIKASTAN settlement in Cumberland Sound. (See also FROBISHER BAY; AMELIASBERG, Ont.)

PELLY BAY

Pelly Bay is an inlet from the western end of the Gulf of Boothia; on the inlet's southeastern shore is a hamlet of the same name. At Pelly Bay in Mar. 1923 the great explorer **Knud Rasmussen** met **Orpingalik**, the most gifted transmitter of traditional songs and the most original poet he encountered in his North American expedition of 1921–24.

Knud Rasmussen

A famed hunter and *angakoq* (wise man and priest), Orpingalik was at the time journeying south from Repulse Bay to trade fox skins for new rifles; he repeated many traditional poems and songs, and some of his own songs, to Rasmussen, who wrote: 'Orpingalik himself was a poet, with a fertile imagination and sensitive mind; he was always singing when not otherwise employed, and called his songs his "comrades in loneliness".' Orpingalik explained: 'Songs are thoughts, sung out with the breath, when people are moved by great forces and ordinary speech no longer suffices.' The material Rasmussen collected from Orpingalik was presented in full in the *Report of the Fifth Thule Expedition* (10 vols, 1931–42) and in part in Rasmussen's *Across Arctic America* (1927); selections have since appeared in several anthologies of Inuit literature in translation, including *Anerca* (1959), edited by Edmund Carpenter; *Songs of the Dream People* (1972), edited by James Houston; and *Poems of the Inuit* (1981), edited by John Robert Colombo. (See also CAPE DORSET, DANISH ISLAND, BATHURST INLET.)

RANKIN INLET

In 1958, ten years after the Arctic experience on which **Farley Mowat** based his first book, *People of the Deer* (1951), he returned to the KEEWATIN BARRENS in order to observe the changes in the life of the Ihalmiut, the Inuit band he had lived with. His visit centred on Rankin Inlet, a small community on the northwestern shore of Hudson Bay. Many members of the Ihalmiut had settled here to work in a nickel-mining operation that was intended to be the basis of a new permanent settlement for the formerly nomadic Inuit. In *People of the Deer* Mowat had favoured such settlements as a necessary part of Inuit adaptation to contact with the rest of Canada. But in *The Desperate People* (1959), his account of his 1958 visit to Rankin Inlet, he charged that the settlement had been a betrayal of the Ihalmiut; the mining operation had closed, leaving them without the means to return to their previous way of life and leading to many deaths in the band.

Today the Ihalmiut live in three communities on the west coast of Hudson Bay: Rankin Inlet, Whale Cove, and the largest settlement, Eskimo Point. A resident of Rankin Inlet, **John Ayaruaq** (1907–69), was the author of an autobiography; published in 1968, it was the first book written in the syllabic script devised for Inuktitut, the Inuit language. **Armand Tagoona** (see BAKER LAKE)—the first Inuit Anglican priest and the author of *Shadows* (1975)—serves at the Church of the Holy Comforter.

RESOLUTE

Harpoon of the Hunter (1970) by **Markoosie**, regarded as the first Inuit novel, was written at Resolute. Markoosie was born in 1943 in Port Harrison, Que., but spent his childhood in Resolute and here became a commercial airplane pilot. His autobiographical novel has been translated into a dozen languages. Resolute is on the southwestern shore of Cornwallis Island.

SOUTH NAHANNI RIVER

The South Nahanni River, near the Yukon border in the southwestern corner of the District of Mackenzie, resembles the river in **John Buchan**'s novel *Sick Heart River* (1941). Buchan—who as Lord Tweedsmuir was Governor General from 1935 to 1940—visited the Northwestern Territories during the summer of 1937. In the final year of his life he wrote this novel, set in the same Mackenzie River region where he had travelled; it tells of an Arctic quest undertaken by a dying British diplomat, Sir Edward

Pierre Berton on the Headless Valley expedition, January 1947

Leithen, who finds and leaves 'Sick Heart River'—a mysterious, inaccessible Shangri-La hidden somewhere on a tributary of the Mackenzie—in an attempt to save a group of Indians faced with extinction. 'He saw it from the top of a mountain, and it sort of laid a charm on him. He said that first of all you had snow mountains bigger than any he had ever seen, and then icefields like prairies, and then forests of tall trees, the same as you get on the coast. And then in the valley bottom, grass meadows and an elegant river. A Hare Indian that was with him gave him the name—the Sick Heart, called after an old-time chief that got homesick for the place and pined away.' (See also MACKENZIE RIVER; OTTAWA, Ont.)

The South Nahanni River flows through spectacular canyons as deep as 4,000 feet until it enters the Liard, a major tributary of the Mackenzie. Rumours of gold and the disappearance of early twentieth-century adventurers who went to seek it—decapitated bodies were found in 1908—led to the growth of legends about the river, much of which is now part of Nahanni National Park. The South Nahanni at least partially justifies the enduring myth of a semi-tropical paradise hidden somewhere in the heart of the Arctic: a hot spring at one point on its course creates pools of water with temperatures above 90°F and allows roses, flowering parsnips, chokecherries, and other southern plants to flourish nearby.

One of the writers to investigate this legend was **Pierre Berton**, who in 1946 was sent to the Headless Valley of the South Nahanni by the *Vancouver Sun*. His reports of this journey gained him his first prominence and earned him an invitation to join *Maclean's*. (See also VANCOUVER, B.C.; DAWSON CITY, WHITEHORSE, YT; TORONTO: 2, KLEINBURG, ONT.)

SPENCE BAY

The Boothia peninsula, at the northern extremity of the District of Keewatin, was the scene on 15–16 Apr. 1966 of a murder trial that formed the occasion and the basic incident of **Farley Mowat**'s 'The Dark Odyssey of Soosie' in *The Snow Walker* (1975). This narrative—the one non-fiction piece in Mowat's only collection of short stories—provides the background of the murder of Soosie E5–20 by her son Aiyaoot E5–22 and her nephew Shooyuk E5–883. Mowat contends that economic factors introduced by the white man led to Soosie's eventual insanity and thus to her murder, which became necessary for the safety of the community and was justified by Inuit tradition. The trial, vividly evoked by Mowat, was held in the largest classroom in the Spence Bay federal day school. (See also KEEWATIN BARRENS; BUREGO, Nfld.; BELLEVILLE, PALGRAVE, PORT HOPE, Ont.)

The poet **Jim Green** lived at Spence Bay in the 1960s and early 1970s, working as a federal administrator and recording his experiences of the Arctic in the poems of *North Book* (1975), which pictures not only Spence Bay but other regional settlements and sites, such as Gjoa Haven and the Boothia Isthmus. In the 1970s Green moved to Fort Smith.

TUKTOYAKTUK

Fr **Maurice Metayer**, O.M.I., a translator of Inuit literature and an expert on Inuit mythology and language, served in Tuktoyaktuk as chaplain to the DEW Line in 1955–7 and 1958–60. Metayer translated the traditional stories of the Copper Eskimos included in *Tales from the Igloo* (1972) as well as *I, Nuligak* (1966), the autobiography of the Inuit hunter **Nuligak**. Nuligak writes of Tuktoyaktuk at several points in his narrative. (See also CAMBRIDGE BAY.) During the 1970s Dr **Herbert T. Schwarz** was physician to the DEW Line and lived at Tuktoyaktuk; he is the author of poetry evoking the lives of both the Inuit and others in the North, most notably in the collection *Tuktoyaktuk 2–3* (1975). (See also MACKENZIE RIVER.) Tuktoyaktuk is located on Cambridge Bay in the Beaufort Sea.

Yukon Territory

DAWSON CITY

The Klondike Gold Rush began when George Carmack found gold in Rabbit Creek, a tributary of the Klondike River, on 17 Aug. 1896. By Apr. 1897, 1,500 prospectors were camped on the Yukon flats and the city was beginning to take shape. By 1898 Dawson's population was 25,000. Many writers visited the goldfields as correspondents for newspapers and magazines and went on to write books about their impressions of the region. **Hamlin Garland**, author of *Main-Travelled Roads* (1891), travelled the Ashcroft-Teslin route through the interior of British Columbia to Lake Teslin, a journey he described in *The Trail of the Goldseekers: A Record in Prose and Verse* (1899). Nature writer **Edwin Tappan Adney**, of WOODSTOCK, N.B., visited the Klondike as a correspondent for *Harper's Illustrated Weekly* and drew his impressions together in a vivid book about the gold-rush period, *The Klondike Stampede of 1897–8* (1900). Perhaps the most famous literary participant in the gold rush was the American novelist **Jack London**, who travelled with a small party of friends through CHILKOOT PASS to the Dawson area in Aug. 1897. London came not to write but to strike it rich and in Oct. he helped choose a claim site on Upper Island in Henderson Creek, 80 miles from Dawson. Returning to Dawson to stake his claim, London lived here for two months before going to Henderson Creek to prepare for a summer of prospecting. The long winter months in a cabin passed slowly; one visitor remembered stumbling into an argument, which he was surprised to discover was raging over the merits of socialism. By June 1898 London was forced to leave because of illness, but he carried away with him a wealth of memories, which he soon began turning into some of his most famous stories: *The Call of the Wild* (1903); *White Fang* (1906); *Lost Face* (1910), which includes the famous story 'To Build a Fire'; and *Burning Daylight* (1910), a novel based on an actual prospector known as 'Burning Daylight' whom London knew in Dawson. According to Merrill Denison (see TORONTO: 3), the source of London's character was Michael Ambrose Mahoney, a Canadian adventurer long associated with the Far North whose story Denison told in *Klondike Mike* (1943).

Dawson City, 1899

One of the best-known literary treatments of the gold rush is *The Trail of '98; A Northlands Romance* (1911) by **Robert Service.** Service himself did not enter the Yukon until 1904, when the rush was long over, and he did not live in Dawson City until 1908. When he arrived here from WHITEHORSE, where he worked as a teller in the Bank of Commerce from 1904 through 1907, Service found Dawson City much changed from the days of the gold rush. The population reached its peak here in 1900, when 30,000 people lived in Dawson. By 1920 the population had dropped to 5,000, and the decline was already very apparent in the empty houses and closed businesses that Service found in 1908. Service published a new volume of verse, *Ballads of a Chechako* (1909), and worked at the Dawson branch of the Bank of Commerce until Nov. 1909, when news of a promotion and transfer back to Whitehorse caused him to quit in order to stay in Dawson and devote himself full-time to a new project, his first novel. In Whitehorse, Service had been devoted to social life, but here he lived quietly in a cabin somewhat removed from the city. He studied old newspapers of the gold-rush years at the Carnegie Library and sought out prospectors who could give exact details of the city's early period. Laura Berton, author of *I Married the Klondike* (1954), describes Service as engaged in a constant struggle to find enough paper—in short supply during the winter—for his writing. Much of his composing was done on wallpaper, which he bought by the roll because it was less expensive than any other material. He covered the walls of his cabin with tacked-up sheets of manuscript as he worked. In the spring of 1910 he travelled to New york with the manuscript of *The Trail of '98*; after a winter in Edmonton visiting his mother, Service travelled back to Dawson via the old Edmonton Trail along the Mackenzie River. He spent one last summer season in his cabin at work on a new volume of poems, which featured material gathered on the Mackenzie River trip. This book, *Rhymes of a Rolling Stone* (1912), was the last Service wrote in the North. In the fall of 1911 he left Dawson for good. Service's cabin, with moose antlers hanging over the door, can be visited in Dawson City near the Dawson City Museum on 8th Ave; recitations of his poems are held outdoors there during the summer at 10 a.m. and 4 p.m. The bank where Service worked is still standing at the corner of First Ave and Queen St, and is still a branch

Robert Service's cabin, Dawson City

of the Bank of Commerce; it is one of Dawson City's few remaining buildings of gold-rush vintage. The bank's gold room, on the second floor, is open to tourists during the summer as the place where Service carried out his duties during the 1907–8 tenure here. (See also LAKE LABERGE, YUKON RIVER; TORONTO: 2, Ont.; CHILKOOT PASS, DUNCAN, KAMLOOPS, VANCOUVER, VICTORIA, WHITE PASS, B.C.; FORT MCPHERSON, MACKENZIE RIVER, N.W.T.)

Also on 8th Ave is the cabin of Jack London (moved here from Henderson Creek), where readings from London's works are given at 1 p.m. daily during the summer months.

Laura Berton came to Dawson in 1907 as a kindergarten teacher and, except for a brief period spent in WHITEHORSE, made her home here until 1932. Her account of her years in the north, *I Married the Klondike* (1954), presents Dawson as an endearing mixture of its glorious, raucous beginnings and its quiet years as a community of permanent settlers. By the early 1930s, however, the Depression had made life so difficult that the family was forced to move. Berton described Dawson as 'an artificial city once gay and bright as a spring flower, now faded and desolate, a great graveyard on the banks of the Klondike'. Her son, **Pierre Berton**, grew up in Dawson; he was born in WHITEHORSE, in 1920. For many years a journalist in VANCOUVER and TORONTO (2), Berton won two Governor's General Awards for books about the Klondike—*The Mysterious North* (1956) and *Klondike: The Life and Death of the Last Great Goldrush* (1958; rev. edn, 1972)—and continued his career as a writer with many other popular books, including several important histories.

In addition to accounts by literary figures, stories of the early days of Dawson City come from prospectors and their families. One of the best is **Martha Black**'s *My Seventy Years* (1938); Black came to the Yukon during the gold rush and remained to become one of the territory's Members of Parliament.

LAKE LABERGE

There are strange things done in the midnight sun
By the men who moil for gold;
The Arctic trails have their secret tales
That would make your blood run cold;
The Northern Lights have seen queer sights;
But the queerest they ever did see
Was the night on the marge of Lake Lebarge
I cremated Sam McGee.

One of the most familiar landmarks in the Yukon of **Robert Service** is Lake Laberge, the site of the cremation of the frozen Tennessee prospector recounted in 'The Cremation of Sam McGee', included in Service's first book, *Songs of a Sourdough* (1907). Service knew and had hunted with a Sam McGee, a trapper and prospector who had been in the Yukon since 1878, but he merely borrowed his name—the real 'Sam McGee' had never been to Tennessee. Lake Laberge is near WHITEHORSE, where Service lived from 1904 to 1907 and where he wrote the poem. (Service used poetic licence in changing the name to 'Lake Lebarge'.) McGee's cabin was at Lake Laberge, but after the poem became famous it was moved to the grounds of the MacBride Museum in Whitehorse, which commemorates the poem and its author. Service said he had heard the story from a Dawson miner who was in Whitehorse for a party; the local fame of Service's poems, which he recited at Whitehorse social occasions beginning in 1905, prompted the man to tell him the story, prefacing it with the remark 'Jack London never got this one.' During a visit to the Yukon in 1938 the real Sam McGee was amazed to find a curio vendor selling 'authentic' McGee ashes from the cremation. (See also DAWSON CITY; TORONTO:2, Ont.; DUNCAN, B.C.)

Jack London (*The Call of the Wild*, 1903) travelled across Lake Laberge on a raft called the Yukon Belle on his way to the Klondike gold fields in the early winter of 1897. The cold weather was closing in on London and his party, and he barely managed to cross before the freeze and to avoid having to spend the winter at the lake instead of in the gold fields. (See also WHITE PASS, B.C.)

WHITEHORSE

Robert Service arrived in Whitehorse, the capital of the Yukon Territory, in the fall of 1904 to begin work as a clerk in the city's branch of the Bank of Commerce. Service had been working for the bank for a little more than a year, first in VICTORIA and then in KAMLOOPS, B.C., before being sent north. He travelled on the White Pass & Yukon Railway, completed in 1900, which provided a safe alternative to the treacherous CHILKOOT PASS taken by the prospectors hurrying to the Klondike in 1897 and 1898. Almost immediately Service became an enthusiastic booster of the Yukon's unique beauties and society. He lived at the home of his employer, the bank manager, and became popular at winter social functions for recitations and songs he sang to the accompaniment of his banjo. Before moving from his job near DUNCAN, B.C., to Whitehorse, Service had published his work in the city's newspaper, the *Whitehorse Star*. The editor, Stroller White, himself a popular local balladeer, urged Service to start writing again. Inspired one night by the line, 'A bunch of boys were whoopin' it up', Service decided to sneak into the bank teller's cage, to which he had been promoted recently, in order to write undisturbed. He was almost killed by the bank guard, who thought he was shooting at a robber. Service escaped unharmed to write 'The Shooting of Dan McGrew'. A month later a Dawson miner offered to tell Service a story 'Jack London never got' and gave him the incident that Service used in 'The Cremation of Sam McGee'. Inspiration flowed quickly, with Service detailing the city life and the wild beauty of the Yukon River area around Whitehorse. In 1906 Service sent his manuscript, *Songs of a Sourdough*, and $50 to the Ryerson Press in Toronto for a private printing. The editor, William Briggs, wrote back that the typesetters working on the book had enjoyed it so much that he was prepared to publish the book and pay Service a royalty. Published in 1907, it was an immediate success, as was *The Spell of the Yukon* (also 1907). Soon Service was being sought out for his autograph in his Whitehorse teller's cage; in the fall of 1907, however, he was transferred to DAWSON CITY, where he moved in the spring of 1908 after a needed vacation away from the North, which he spent in VANCOUVER. Service tells the story of life in Whitehorse in *Ploughman of the Moon* (1945). (See also YUKON RIVER; TORONTO: 2, Ont.; WHITE PASS, B.C.; FORT MCPHERSON, MACKENZIE RIVER, N.W.T.)

Service's friends in Whitehorse included a prospector named Sam McGee, whose own life story resembled very little the fantastic events of Service's poem, although he did have a cabin on LAKE LABERGE (called 'Lake Lebarge' in the poem). The cabin has been moved into Whitehorse and stands on the grounds of MacBride Museum, 1st Ave and Wood St. McGee and Service hunted together, and the prospector was familiar with the poem bearing his name before he left the Yukon in 1909 for a home in southern Canada. On a visit to Whitehorse in 1938 McGee was offered an urn of ashes guaranteed to have come from the 'cremation of Sam McGee' but did not trouble the salesman by revealing his identity.

Another friend of Service in Whitehorse

Robert Service

was the Anglican minister **Hiram A. Cody**, a native of CODY'S, N.B., who was rector of Christ Church here from 1905 to 1910. Service regularly attended the church and passed the collection plate. Cody—who was educated at SAINT JOHN, N.B., and WINDSOR, N.S.—first came to the Arctic in 1904 as a travelling missionary. In 1910 he became rector of St James Church, Saint John, but remained attached to the Yukon through his many adventure novels set in the North, including *The Frontiersman: A Tale of the Yukon* (1910) and *The Long Patrol: A Tale of the Mounted Police* (1912). Cody's church was the cathedral of the Yukon from its construction in 1900 until 1959, when a new Christ Church Cathedral was built next to it. Now known as the Old Log Cabin, the building on Elliot St at Third St houses a museum, whose displays include vestry minutes written by Service.

Laura Berton, author of *I Married the Klondike* (1954), lived most of her Yukon years in DAWSON CITY but passed through Whitehorse regularly on the trip north. She was one of the autograph-seekers who hoped to meet Service at the bank. Berton missed Service here but eventually knew him well in Dawson City. After the First World War Berton lived here for a short time when her husband Frank had a government surveying job. The family lived at 507 Wood St. Her first child, Pierre, was born here on 12 July 1920 but was raised in Dawson City, where the family lived until the 1930s. A distinguished journalist and popular historian, **Pierre Berton** has written some of his most successful books about his native region: *Klondike: the Life and Death of the Last Great Goldrush* (1958), winner of a Governor General's Award; *The Mysterious North* (1956), another Governor General's Award winner; and for young readers *The Golden Trail: the Story of the Klondike Rush* (1954). (See also DAWSON CITY; KLEINBURG, TORONTO: 2, Ont.; VANCOUVER, B.C.)

Whitehorse, in the early 1900s

YUKON RIVER

Robert Service said he composed the famous ballad of the Arctic, 'When the Ice Worms Nest Again', during the spring of 1911 on a steamer travelling the Yukon River to Dawson City. This was the last leg of Service's adventurous trip along the historic Edmonton Trail from Alberta through the Mackenzie Delta and the northern Yukon to DAWSON CITY. The ballad was not published until 1933, in *Twenty Bathtub Ballads*. In the meantime it had become widely known, with many variations and additions, in the Arctic and was attributed to many writers. The folklorist Edith Fowke, in *Canada's Story in Song* (1960, studied the origins of the many versions and concluded that Service was indeed the originator of the poem; but she also maintained the value of preserving the many charming variations created by oral transmission from singer to singer. The first verse of Service's poem is:

There's a husky dusky maid in far Alaska,
On a slab of ice she sits and waits for me;
And some day I'm going back again to ask her,
If my little Polar baby she will be.

An anonymous version begins:

There's a dusky husky maiden in the Arctic,
And she waits for me but it is not in vain,
For some day I'll put my mukluks on and ask her
If she'll wed me when the ice worms nest again.

Index